THE WEST IN AMERICAN HISTORY

THE WEST IN
AMERICAN HISTORY

BY

DAN ELBERT CLARK

Professor of History
University of Oregon

THOMAS Y. CROWELL COMPANY
PUBLISHERS   :   :   NEW YORK

Printed in the United States of America

PREFACE

THIS book has been written mainly with a view to its service-ability as basic reading in college and university courses in Western American History. At the same time, it is hoped that it will prove of interest and use to the general reader who desires a narrative of the principal episodes and movements in the story of the settlement of the continental area of the United States. These two purposes have been kept constantly in mind in the selection, organization, and presentation of material in the pages which follow. The selection of material has been determined by the purpose to present the important features of the history of the West as a whole from the coming of the first European explorers to the close of the frontier era toward the end of the last century. The plan of organization and presentation which has been adopted can best be described by referring to the three parts into which the volume is divided.

Part one, entitled "The West under Spain, France, and England," begins with an outline of some of the geographical factors which conditioned the westward movement, and a brief sketch of the American Indians as the white men found them. Then follow two chapters which present a running account of Spanish and French explorations, missionary activities, and territorial claims in the West. The remainder of this part is devoted to the struggle of the French and the English for the control of America and to the advance of the frontier during the period of English rule down to the close of the American Revolution. Although the presence and activities of the Spanish and the French are a part of the background of the history of the West, their colonial policies and their governmental institutions have not been described, since they left no significant, permanent impress upon American development.

The second part deals with "The Frontier of the Middle West," or the region between the Appalachian Mountains and the western border of the first tier of States west of the Mississippi, with special emphasis on the upper Mississippi Valley, from 1783 to the close of the frontier era in that section. Here there was a high degree of homogeneity in physical background and in historical development. The treatment is topical, with chapters arranged as nearly as possible in the order in which the subjects and problems with which they deal arose in the process of western settlement. This method of presentation was chosen deliberately, as being more satisfactory than a strictly chronological account, even at the sacrifice of the advantages of constant correlation of factors which the latter plan affords.

In the third part, dealing with "The Frontier of the Far West," the treatment is frankly episodic in nature. As is stated more fully later in these pages, the author believes that the early history of the American occupation of the Far West must continue to be written largely on a regional or sectional basis. Geographic and economic influences worked toward diversity rather than uniformity.

The preparation of a volume of this nature would, obviously, have been impossible without the use of the great amount of monographic and other writing on various phases of the history of the West that has appeared in the last thirty or forty years. For several chapters, however, the author has gone to contemporary sources—journals, diaries, letters, newspapers, and government documents—and has made numerous quotations from the accounts of participants in, or witnesses of, the events or movements described, in the hope of adding vividness to the narrative. Footnote citations have not been employed, except to acknowledge permission given by the publishers to use quotations from copyrighted publications. The bibliographical notes near the end of the book will indicate the most helpful, though by no means all, the sources and secondary works which have been consulted. The works there listed will serve as a guide to readers interested in delving into subjects which have necessarily been neglected or given only brief mention in these pages.

When it comes to acknowledging personal assistance the author is conscious of a widely diffused indebtedness. The reactions of students over a long period of teaching have helped to shape and determine the scope and content of the volume. Numerous graduate students have done spade work that has been helpful. Many colleagues have given valuable counsel. The author's gratitude is especially given to Professor Henry D. Sheldon, who read the entire manuscript and made many valuable suggestions; to Professor John T. Ganoe, who has been generous in his aid and advice; and to the members of his family, who have constantly facilitated the task of writing and helped in preparing the manuscript for the printer and in reading proof.

DAN E. CLARK.

University of Oregon,
February, 1937

CONTENTS

PART III

The Frontier of the Far West

LIST OF MAPS

PART I

THE WEST UNDER SPAIN, FRANCE, AND ENGLAND

CHAPTER I

THE WAITING WILDERNESS AND ITS INHABITANTS

THE LURE OF THE WILDERNESS

REFERRING to the discovery of America, a writer in *The Edinburgh Review* in 1829 said: "The contemporaries of an event so marvelous, may well be excused, if, amidst the novelty of such excitements, their expectations were turned more towards an El Dorado, and a Fairy Land, than to any mere variety and modification of their own worn and 'work-a-day' world." From the time of Columbus until the frontier was a thing of the past, a host of writers, European, English, and American, put into glowing words their radiant vision of the wonderful possibilities and the ennobling and regenerating effect of life in the wilderness. The super-romanticism and credulity of the Spaniards led them to believe impossible tales of marvelous wealth told by the savages to lure them into the interior. Frenchmen also fell under the spell of the new world. La Mothe de Cadillac pictured the region around Detroit as a veritable paradise. As late as 1802 Baudry des Lozieres rhapsodized about Louisiana, where, he wrote, nature "is adorned with all her charms, and the breeze wafts voluptuous perfumes. What the poet tells of the Elysian Fields is not a fable; all their divine fancies are realized in these enchanting regions." ·

But it was not the mercurial Spaniards and Frenchmen alone whose imaginations were fired by thoughts of the American frontier. Blake, the English poet, wrote these lines:

> Tho' born on the cheating banks of the Thames,
> Tho' his waters bathed my infant limbs,
> The Ohio shall wash his stains from me;
> I was born a slave, but I go to be free.

3

Byron, in his idealization of Daniel Boone and his environment, declared:

> Crime came not near him—she is not the child
> Of solitude; Health shrank not from him—for
> Her home is in the rarely-trodden wild.

With Europeans responding thus to the lure of the frontier it is not to be expected that American writers would be less rapturous in their anticipations of blessings, spiritual and material, to be obtained "behind the ranges." John Filson in 1793 painted Kentucky in vivid colors—a country "like the land of promise, flowing with milk and honey"; a country, which, "favoured with the smiles of heaven, will probably be inhabited by the first people the world ever knew." A half century later, C. W. Dana stirred his readers with visions of the "Land of Promise and the Canaan of our time" which extends majestically from the slopes of the Alleghanies westward until "the ebb and flow of the Pacific tide kisses the golden shores of the El Dorado." "With a soil more fertile than human agriculture has yet tilled," he wrote, "with a climate balmy and healthful, such as no other land in other zones can claim; . . . it does indeed present to the nations a land where the wildest dreamer on the future of our race may see actualized a destiny far outreaching in splendor his most gorgeous visions."

"Imagination exercises more influence even upon minds the most uneducated, than we are ready to suppose," wrote Timothy Flint in 1832 in describing the eager homeseekers pouring into the West. "There is no person, about to place himself in a remote and untried position, but will find on examination, that the new scene, viewed in anticipation, is invested with a coloring of the imagination, that has a powerful bearing upon his thoughts and determinations. What mind ever contemplated the project of moving from the old settlements over the Alleghany mountains, and selecting a home in the West, without forming pictures of new woods and streams, new animals and vegetables, new configurations of scenery, new aspects of men and new forms of society. . . . New hopes, in a word, of chasing down in a new and a far country, that phantom of our desires, always pursued in things without us, and never found except within us, happiness."

Thus a glamor of romance and high anticipation was thrown over the land which awaited the coming of the white man. But in truth the reality was scarcely less enchanting than the dream. A marvelously rich empire lay beyond the ridges and highlands that for so long formed the farthest western horizon of the Atlantic colonists—a land, it might seem, prepared through countless ages to be a seat of civilization.

The Appalachian Barrier

Spaniards came into the southern reaches of the valley of the Mississippi, appropriated the Floridas and the southwest, and extended their outposts up the California coast. Frenchmen came from the region of the St. Lawrence, explored the Great Lakes and plied their canoes up and down most of the rivers in the upper portion of the valley. But, aside from the ventures of a few intrepid traders, it was a century and a half after the founding of Jamestown before lands on rivers flowing to the Mississippi were seen by the English colonists whose descendants and successors were ultimately to move westward in an irresistible flood. The reason lay partly in the character, purposes and occupations of these English colonists. More definitely it lay in the great Appalachian barrier which blocked the way to the west.

The Appalachian Mountain system contains no peaks of great height, but its ridges are sufficiently elevated and continuous to constitute a formidable obstacle in the path of the men of colonial days. With a width of about three hundred miles, it consists of range after range running parallel to each other or twisting back and forth, so that it is small wonder that the Indians called them the "endless mountains." Besides all this, these mountains were covered with a dense forest which stretched with scarcely a break from Maine to Alabama. So dense were these woods that even an Indian footpath was soon obliterated unless constantly traveled. Thus, before settlers could move across this barrier they must literally hew and dig themselves a road.

There are three divisions in this Appalachian system. Along the eastern side are the more rugged and elevated mountains and hills. They come down close to the coast in New England and stand out prominently in such ranges as the White Mountains, the Green Mountains, and the Berkshires. To the southward they leave a wider coastal plain and appear as the Blue Ridge in Virginia and the broad and relatively higher mass of the southern Appalachians in the Carolinas.

These mountains form the eastern rim of what is often called the inner valley. From Lake Champlain this valley follows the Hudson southward to the Catskills, and then runs in a southwestward direction through Pennsylvania, where its surface is rumpled by tortuous ranges of hills. Again to the southward the valley becomes narrower and more definitely cut into a series of smaller parallel valleys separated by sharp, rocky ridges which have resisted erosion. These small valleys were used extensively as highways by the Indians and they were to play a determining role in attracting thousands of settlers southwestward into the back country. Into this valley region and across it cut many streams, some of which, like the Watauga, the Holston, the French Broad, or the New River, send their waters to the Ohio River and thus to the Mississippi. But it happens that the water gaps between the ridges do not face each other; so it was much easier to follow the longitudinal valleys than it was to find a way across them.

The third division of the Appalachian system, and the western rim of the inner valley, consists of the Alleghany and Cumberland Mountains, which are in reality not mountains at all, but a high plateau with a sharp escarpment on the eastern side and a gradual slope to the westward. With the Adirondacks as an outlying projection on the north, this plateau is interrupted by the valley of the Mohawk and appears again in the Catskills. Thence it extends across central New York, western Pennsylvania, West Virginia, and eastern Kentucky and Tennessee. Like the rest of the Appalachian system it rises higher and becomes more inaccessible in its southern reaches. Here the effects of isolation were to be exhibited most strikingly in the lives and attitudes of the dwellers in the small and lonely valleys.

There was only one conspicuous break in the Appalachian barrier—the opening offered by the Hudson and the Mohawk. Although this opening was later to play a decisive role in establishing the commercial supremacy of New York City, it could be little used until the late years of the eighteenth century because it was controlled by the hostile, warlike Iroquois. In the south, below the extremities of the Appalachians, it was likewise physically possible to follow an almost level route to the Mississippi Valley. But here again unfriendly Indians—the Creeks and Cherokees and other tribes—blocked the way of all but the more adventurous traders.

Between these two easy avenues to the west there were several hidden passes that were not discovered and used until the ambitions of fur traders, the restlessness of frontier settlers, and the need of protection against the French and their Indian allies gave the necessary impetus. Across Pennsylvania several routes were found to be feasible, leading, partly by waterways and partly by land trails, to the forks of the Ohio River. One route followed the west fork of the Susquehanna and was linked to the westward flowing waters of the Alleghany by a lengthy trail over the divide. Another made use of the Juniata River. A third, later known as Forbes' Road and running through Shippensburg, Fort Bedford, and Fort Ligonier, depended less on the rivers, and in time became one of the principal highways across the Appalachians. From Virginia and Maryland the Potomac furnished a way into the interior, and from its headwaters the route taken by Braddock on his ill-starred expedition led to the Youghiogheny and the Monongahela. Finally, there was Cumberland Gap in the southwestern corner of Virginia, reached by threading the maze of upland valleys, and opening the way to Kentucky and Tennessee.

This, then, was the barrier that for nearly a hundred and fifty years faced the men of English speech when they looked to the west. Its conquest was fraught with toil and hardship and danger, but the rewards were commensurate with the effort. Beyond the Alleghanies lay the great Mississippi Valley with soil, resources, and climate better suited to the life and uses of civilized man than any other region of similar extent

on the face of the globe. Not again until the ranges of the
Rocky Mountains reared their rugged masses across the way
was there any real obstacle to the free movement of men going
singly or with their families and their possessions.

THE MISSISSIPPI VALLEY

Had the power been given to man to lay out a system of
waterways suited to the transportation needs of a country to
be newly settled he could scarcely have improved upon that
which he found in the Mississippi Valley. Throughout nearly
its whole extent the Appalachian barrier is touched on its western side, or even deeply penetrated, by streams which discharge
their waters ultimately into the Ohio. From within a short
distance of Lake Erie the Alleghany flows southward to unite
with the Monongahela, flowing northward an almost equal distance from West Virginia, to form the Ohio River. Further
south the Kanawha, the Cumberland, and the Tennessee and
their tributaries contribute to the volume of the same great
river after draining a large area including not merely Kentucky
and Tennessee, but also western West Virginia, Virginia and
the Carolinas, northwestern Georgia, and northern Alabama
and Mississippi. All three of these streams, together with the
Muskingum, the Scioto, the Miami and the Wabash emptying
into the Ohio from the north, are navigable for considerable
distances either by steamboats or by keelboats and flatboats
laden with produce. The Chattahoochee, the Appalachicola,
the Alabama and the Tombigbee offer a similar service of transportation to the Gulf for western Georgia and for Alabama
and Mississippi. Numerous smaller streams give access to the
main arteries by row-boat and canoe and in flood season by
larger craft.

The Ohio River itself, long known to the French as "the
beautiful river," is the most important eastern tributary of the
Mississippi. With a volume compounded of the waters of
12,000 miles of streams, it flows with gentle current between
banks picturesque in outline and mantled much of the distance
with stalwart forests. Above all, it flows toward the west and
thus it beckoned irresistibly onward to all those who followed

the mountain trails which converged on its headwaters. It was a ready-made highway amply suited to carry tens and hundreds of thousands of eager home-seekers into the west, and able to bear on its bosom the commerce of a rapidly growing population.

Through the center of the great valley the Mississippi River flows its crooked way from north to south, a course of twenty-five hundred miles, emptying into the Gulf of Mexico a volume of water second only in size to that discharged into the Atlantic by the Amazon. Flowing at nearly right angles to the Ohio highway from the Alleghanies, it seemed designed to distribute population over a vast area. From the west it is joined by other mighty affluents—the Missouri, the Arkansas, and the Red—all navigable by large craft, and the first named affording steamboat navigation from far distant Montana, more than 3500 miles from the Gulf. Besides these there are other tributaries of considerable size, such as the Illinois, Wisconsin, and Yazoo from the east, and the Minnesota, Iowa, Des Moines, and White Rivers from the West, and numerous smaller streams.

As though this generous river system were not enough, along the northern border of the Ohio Valley lie the five great freshwater lakes. These lakes opened the way for explorer and fur trader, and needed only that man should dig a ditch connecting them with the Atlantic to come alive with fleets of sailing and steam vessels serving a population that soon lined their shores with farms and villages and cities. Moreover, in numerous places it required only relatively short portages, and in times of high water none at all, to proceed by canoe from streams flowing into the lakes to others flowing into the Mississippi and the Ohio.

Thus, from the Great Lakes to the Gulf and from the Alleghanies to the present western boundary of the first tier of States west of the Mississippi there is scarcely a region of any size that does not have easy access to some usable waterway. The area of the lands on the very banks of navigable rivers and lakes was alone large enough to provide homes for hundreds of thousands of people.

Deciduous forests covered most of the upper Ohio Valley,

and were abundant throughout the entire region east of the Mississippi. Luxuriantly green in the spring and summer, they blazed with brilliant colors in the autumn. Despite the long and arduous toil required to clear land covered with hard-wood trees, the forests were hospitable to advancing white men. They sheltered countless fur-bearing and food-providing animals. Wild fruits grew plentifully. Materials for the building of blockhouses for defense and log cabins for homes were right at hand. In the shelter of the forests live-stock could run at large throughout nearly the entire year. Fuel was no problem in the forests, even without the coal underlying much of the region.

To the southward the forests became less continuous, being interspersed with open stretches of fertile pasture and agricultural land in Kentucky and Tennessee and rich black loam in Alabama and Mississippi; and west of the Mississippi in Louisiana, Arkansas, and southern Missouri the aspect was much the same. In the upper Mississippi Valley was the expanse of the prairies. Here was soil equal in fertility to that of any portion of the earth. Here it was that the glaciers had played their most beneficent role, bringing rich materials scraped from the hills of the north. Glacial streams and winds had further contributed to spreading this fine, fertile sediment far and wide.

Throughout the Mississippi basin the rainfall is sufficient in quantity and suitably distributed throughout the year to meet all the needs of agriculture. The climate, in spite of the extremes of cold and heat in the northern portion, is conducive to vigorous activity. At the same time the difference in climate from north to south permits a wide variety in productions and types of society.

THE TRANS-MISSISSIPPI WEST

Westward of what are now the States of Minnesota, Iowa, Missouri, Arkansas, and Louisiana there begins the slope of the high plains which rise gradually to the eastern foothills of the Rocky Mountains. This region was to be the last American frontier. It was not looked upon with favor by the settlers who spent weary weeks in crossing it on their way to Oregon and to California. Its soil is thinner and less fertile than that in the Mississippi Valley proper, it has almost no forests and the rainfall grows scantier the further west one goes. It was the original range of huge herds of buffalo, and the reasons that made it so were equally potent later in making it the scene of a great cattle industry. Later also this region was found to offer far greater opportunities to the farmer than was at first expected, especially after the building of the transcontinental railroads.

The high plains lead up to the elevated and impressive masses of the western cordillera. The Rocky Mountains are much higher than the Appalachians and yet they did not long obstruct the westward march of American settlement. Their fastnesses were the haunts of fur-bearing animals and a paradise for hunters and trappers who soon knew all the gaps and passes. To compensate for its general sterility this vast mountain region also held great stores in wealth in precious metals to lure men to feverish search over its entire length and breadth.

Once again, as in the east, the landseeking farmer found reward for the perils and toils of mountain crossing. Although the Pacific coastal region is narrow, it has large tracts in the Puget Sound country, in the Columbia and Willamette valleys, and in California abundantly suited to a varied agriculture. The hills and mountain ranges are covered with what for long seemed an inexhaustible coniferous forest of immense value and great beauty. Here also, although harbors are few, there is free access to the open sea and especially to the trade of the orient. Here, finally, is a climate unsurpassed.

Such in brief is the stage setting for the drama of the westward movement. It is small wonder that at least until the close of the last century the term "west" has been synonymous with "opportunity" to Americans. It is small wonder that the idealist, to quote Professor Turner, saw in the frontier "a fair blank page on which to write a new chapter in the story of man's struggle for a higher type of society"; or that the materialist exulted over the seemingly unlimited possibilities for exploitation.

THE AMERICAN INDIANS

Before proceeding, however, with the story of the coming of the white men and their civilization, it is fitting that a brief account should be given of the red men who had been living here for undetermined ages. How they came here is a question which need not be discussed in these pages, nor is it possible, amid all the conflicting estimates, to indicate their numbers with any degree of assurance. A recent estimate by Macleod gives "North America, north of Mexico, a pre-European Indian population of roughly three million." Few writers have suggested numbers as large as this, and some have claimed that the Indian population to-day is as large as it ever was. There is reason to believe that the larger figure is more likely to approximate accuracy.

This race whom we know as the American Indians was, within the limits of the United States, a people living in the stone age, when the first Europeans came. To the southward representatives of the same race had attained to stages of civilization that were in many respects remarkable, and are the subjects of admiring and intensive study to-day. But the cultures of South and Central America did not extend far to the northward: their influence is not in evidence beyond the region that is now Arizona and New Mexico. Elsewhere the inhabitants of North America had not risen out of barbarism. Their implements were of stone or bone. They knew nothing of iron and only a little of copper. They had no domestic animals except dogs and in some localities probably sheep, goats, and turkeys. Until introduced by white men, they had never seen a horse, and they knew nothing of the wheel and axle. Thus, aside from boats and canoes, their only vehicles of transportation were the backs of men and women and dogs.

The Indians were not generally a nomadic people. Their large dependence upon the products of nature for food and clothing made it necessary that they should make periodic journeys to hunt or fish or gather wild fruits, but they returned to a relatively fixed abode. Their dwellings presented striking variations, all the way from the rude brush shelters of the Digger Indians to the many-roomed and several-storied adobe

houses of the Pueblos or the large wooden structures of the
Haidas, with their huge carved beams, along the northwest
coast. The teepee, with its tripod support of poles and covering of bark or skins, has come to be associated with Indian
life in general, but it was used as a permanent shelter by only
a portion of the tribes, especially those of the Great Plains.
The wigwam of many eastern tribes was an oval, bark-covered
dwelling; and this type of architecture was expanded into the
communal "long-houses" of the Iroquois.

Agriculture was carried on by many Indian tribes where
soil and climate permitted. Maize was their principal crop.
Beans, squashes, pumpkins, melons, gourds, and sweet potatoes
were grown. Tobacco was likewise an American crop and its
use was widespread among the natives. Many Indians were
adept at basketry and pottery and found admirable self-expression in the arts of decoration. In Mexico and in the region
immediately north there was considerable weaving of cloth,
but in the main such clothing as the Indians wore was of
leather.

Political life exhibited many variations, from the relatively
elaborate and detailed organization of the Iroquois to the
almost total lack of any governmental system among some of
the tribes in California. Usually there was division between
civil and military authority. Where this occurred the former
was exercised by an officer whom many writers call the sachem,
and whose position was ordinarily hereditary; while the latter
was wielded by the chief, whose leadership depended upon his
prowess and recognized fitness. Because warfare was the normal state of affairs among most of the tribes and because the
Indians attracted the attention of the whites mainly during
time of war, the military chiefs are much better known than
the civil officers, whose influence and power, nevertheless, was
often very great among the tribesmen. Along with these two
leaders must be placed the shaman or medicine-man whose
supposed ability to communicate with the spirits gave him an
ascendancy over the superstitious savages. "Blood for blood"
was the rule in the punishment of crime: there was no systematic judicial machinery. Almost everywhere, says Wissler,
"the family group, the gens or clan, as the case may be, was

left to its own devices in meeting such situations. There were
always conventional ways of proceeding, but these were almost
entirely outside the jurisdiction of the tribal government.
Everywhere, of course, the concept of 'life for life' is enter-
tained . . . while in the regions of clans and gentes provision
is made for compensating the injured parties either by a single
execution, for which no retaliation is permitted or by the payment of an indemnity." [1]

Naturally, the concept of property among the Indians was
different from that among us. Personal effects, such as houses,
utensils, food, were regarded as the property of the woman
among a large number of tribes. The Indian's idea of the
ownership of land is a subject on which there is some difference
of opinion. Most writers agree with Wissler that "the right
to exclusive use of certain plots by the social group, gens, clan,
etc. was clearly recognized"; but that individual ownership of
land was unknown. Macleod, however, cites instances of private tenure of land involving "virtually what private ownership means among us." It seems probable that the idea of
individual or personal title was not by any means universal, in
view of the later experience of settlers.

The social systems and institutions of the Indians, their
ceremonies, their ideas of kinship, their marriage customs, their
curious taboos, their religion and their mythology are all of
interest to anyone who is a student of primitive society. The
very cursory and incomplete account of their life which has
been given here has been concerned mainly with those features
which had a bearing on the relationship between them and the
invading white race. It must be remembered, also, that by
the time settlers began to cross the Alleghanies the life of the
Indians, as here pictured, had in many respects been greatly
modified by long contact with Europeans with houses, iron
weapons and implements, fire-arms, and fire water.

It remains only to mention and locate the tribes which
played a leading part in the story of the white advance across
the continent. The Iroquois, or Six Nations, had their home
land in the region between the Hudson and Lake Erie. Here

[1] Clark Wissler, *The American Indian* (1922) p. 181. By permission of the
Oxford University Press, publishers.

they had their fortified villages of communal "long houses" and their fields of maize and beans and squashes; but their influence was felt over a much wider area extending in all directions. Their war parties struck terror to the hearts of many tribes far to the west and south, and their hunting expeditions ranged over regions remote from their fixed abodes in what is now New York. Aside from their fierce, war-like dispositions, their cruelty and their great energy, the Iroquois are most notable for their political organization, which was in many respects the highest type found among the red man of North America. Their principal achievement was the confederation which linked together the Mohawks, Oneidas, Onondagas, Cayugas, Senecas, and Tuscaroras—tribes which were independent in local matters, but acted together in affairs of great common importance in accordance with the decisions of a council made up of sachems representing the confederated tribes.

The Iroquois early became the enemies of the French and blocked their pathway up the St. Lawrence. In the main they were friendly to the English, not only during the struggles with the French but also during the Revolutionary War. It was for this reason that Americans could not use the Mohawk highway to the west with any safety until after danger of attack by the Iroquois was removed.

The Indians who imperiled the passage of traders and settlers around the southern end of the Appalachians were the Cherokees and the Creeks, who with their related tribes, the Choctaws, Chickasaws and Seminoles, were later known as the "five civilized tribes," because of their own cultural progress and their ready adoption of many features of white civilization. The Cherokees and the Creeks were perhaps the strongest single tribes in the eastern part of the continent numerically. They carried on agriculture extensively and were well organized politically, although not the equals of the Iroquois in the latter respect. At the same time they were aggressive, and their location on the borders of the southern colonies made them dreaded neighbors. The Cherokees lived in the mountains of eastern Tennessee and the adjoining region to the east and south. The Creeks dwelt to the south of the Cherokees in

western Georgia and in Alabama. Western Tennessee was the
home of the Chickasaws and below them along the Mississippi,
were the Choctaws; while in Florida lived the Seminoles who
were later to give Andrew Jackson experiences that helped to
make him a western hero.

North of the Ohio River lived numerous tribes of Indians
who, because of linguistic similarities, are classified as Algon-
quins. Many of these tribes, while less well organized and not
so far advanced in agriculture, architecture, and social life as
the Iroquois, Cherokees or Creeks, were nevertheless strong
and warlike; and they were not inclined to submit tamely to
the advancing white men. The Shawnees, the Miamis, the
Illinois, the Pottawattamies, the Chippewas, and the Sauks and
Foxes were among the most conspicuous tribes of this group.

Most of the Indians immediately west of the Mississippi,
north of Arkansas and Oklahoma and extending northward
across the Canadian line, were of another linguistic group
known as the Siouan. "Among the plains Indians, the Dakotas,
the main tribe of the Sioux family, are universally considered
to have stood highest not only physically but mentally, and
probably morally. Their bravery was never questioned, and
they conquered and drove out every rival except the Chippewa." The Dakotas, better known as the Sioux, lived in the
region of the States which bear their name and in Minnesota.
They were active and quarrelsome and were a scourge to the
frontier prairie settlements in the late fifties and early sixties.

The enumeration of outstanding Indian groups and tribes
need not be prolonged. Those already mentioned were those
whose names appear most frequently in frontier annals during
the first century following the beginning of the advance across
the Alleghanies. Single tribes like the Comanches, the Apaches
and the Navahos in the southwest; the Cheyennes and the
Arapahoes in the middle plains region; and the Crows, the
Blackfeet, the Flatheads, the Nez Percés and the Modocs of
the northwest, will appear in the story of more recent years.

Into this land and among these people came Spaniards and
Frenchmen and a few English traders during the sixteenth
and seventeenth centuries. The pages which follow will be
devoted chiefly to the movement of American settlers, which,

beginning in the latter half of the eighteenth century, settled the continent and dispossessed the Indians. But the background would be incomplete without an account of the "vanished pomps of yesterday" which constitute the story of the attempts of Spain and France and England to establish their rule in the vast empire of the American west.

CHAPTER II

SPANISH CONQUISTADORS, TREASURE HUNTERS, AND PRIESTS

THE EXPEDITION OF PANFILO DE NARVAEZ

"WE HELD it always certain that by going towards sunset we should reach the goal of our wishes. So we went on our way and traversed the whole country to the South Sea." These words are from the report of the first white men to cross the North American continent in what is now the United States. They were written by Cabeza de Vaca, who was one of the few survivors of the ill-fated expedition led by Panfilo de Narvaez.

By the year 1527, when this expedition set sail, Spaniards had well established themselves in the West Indies and Mexico and were eagerly seeking new lands to conquer. Tales had been told of rich cities to the northward, of gold and precious stones in abundance, and the Spaniards, the most credulous of all the Europeans who sought the New World, were only too glad to believe the most extravagant rumors. Ponce de Leon had come to Florida seeking fame and fortune and a fountain of perpetual youth. Gomez and Ayllon had sailed up the eastern coast looking for a northern strait which, everyone believed, must open the way to India. Then it was that Narvaez, who had already gained experience and wealth in Mexico, sought and was given a patent and the governorship of Florida, and in June, 1527, sailed from Spain with a large body of colonists and some Franciscan friars to explore and take possession of his domain. Fired with hopes of great wealth, the party landed at Tampa Bay in the spring of the following year.

Narvaez hoisted flags and took possession of the country in the name of the King of Spain, reading a proclamation prepared by learned men to be recited on such occasions. This proclamation told how the Pope had made to their Spanish

Majesties a gift of all this part of the world and called upon
the savages to give their consent. If they did this all would
be well with them. But in warning of what the Indians might
expect, the reader continued: "If you do not do this, and of
malice you be dilatory . . . I will enter with force, making
war upon you from all directions and in every manner that I
may be able . . . and I will take the persons of yourselves,
your wives and your children to make slaves, sell and dispose
of you, as their Majesties may think fit, and I will take your
goods, doing you all the evil and injury that I may be able . . .
and I declare to you that the deaths and damages that arise
therefrom, will be your fault and not that of his Majesty, nor
mine, nor of these cavaliers who came with me." Of course
the few Indians who may have heard these menacing words
could not understand them, but in the years that followed
they and their fellows living from Florida to the Pacific coast
had opportunity to learn that they would be fulfilled at the
hands of Spaniards.

The abandoned Indian village which Narvaez found on
Tampa Bay yielded no treasure except a single golden trinket
which, however, gave promise of greater riches not far distant.
The natives very soon learned that their troublesome visitors
could be speeded from the neighborhood by stories of gold
and jewels to be found by going further, and they rapidly became adept in the manufacture of romances pleasing to the
credulity of the Spaniards. "We inquired of the Indians (by
signs) whence they had obtained these things," wrote Cabeza
de Vaca, who was the treasurer and chronicler of Narvaez's
expedition, "and they gave us to understand that, very far
from there, was a province called Apalachen in which there was
much gold. They also signified to us that in that province we
would find everything we held in esteem. They said that in
Apalachen there was plenty."

Narvaez was all for going at once in search of Apalachen.
Despite the argument of Cabeza de Vaca and one of the other
officers that it would be unwise to leave their ships until a
better harbor and base of operations had been found, Narvaez
insisted upon going inland, and ordered the ships to cruise
along the coast. The story of the next few weeks is quickly

told. After wandering northward through "a country difficult to traverse and strange to look at, for it had very great forests," skirmishing frequently with the Indians, the Spaniards came at last to Apalachen. Instead of a city abounding in gold, they found only a rude village of forty straw huts tenanted by women and boys. The men had fled, but they returned to harry their invaders. The Indians reported that Apalachen was the largest town in all that region, "that further in less people were met with, who were very much poorer than those here, and that the country was thinly settled, the inhabitants greatly scattered, and also that further inland big lakes, dense forests, great deserts and wastes were met with."

Thoroughly disheartened, Narvaez and his followers turned back to the Gulf, which they reached at Apalachee Bay. No ships were in sight and so crude boats were built in which to make the journey to Panuco in Mexico, supposed to be ten or fifteen leagues distant, instead of more than one thousand miles, as was actually the case. In these the party embarked late in September and for six weeks they sailed and rowed westward. At one place, possibly Pensacola Bay, they had a severe encounter with the Indians; and later they passed the mouth of a great river, no doubt the Mississippi, where the current was so strong that it forced them out to sea. A few days later a storm arose, the boats were separated, four of them were wrecked near Matagorda Bay, and the fifth, bearing Narvaez, was later lost in another storm out in the Gulf.

The Wanderings of Cabeza de Vaca

We need not linger over the miseries of the survivors on the island of Malhado, or Misfortune, as the Spaniards called it, off the Texan Coast. Exposure and starvation soon reduced their number from eighty to fifteen and most of these ultimately disappear from the record. Cabeza de Vaca tells how he remained for six years a prisoner among the Indians, desiring always to escape and seek the Spanish settlements in Mexico, but refraining because he would not leave a companion whose timid soul shrank from the dangers of the undertaking. During these years he performed the most arduous labor for his captors and suffered intensely from hunger and cold, for he was obliged to go naked like the savages. For a time his status was somewhat improved by his success in the arts of the medicine man, which he was compelled to attempt at the command of the Indians. "The way we treated the sick," he wrote, "was to make over them the sign of the cross while breathing on them, recite a Pater Noster and Ave Maria, and pray to God, Our Lord, as best we could to give them good health and inspire them to do us some favors. Thanks to His will and the mercy He had upon us, all those for whom we prayed, as soon as we crossed them, told the others that they were cured and felt well again. For this they gave us good cheer, and would rather be without food themselves so as to give it to us, and they gave us hides and other small things." Vaca also became a trader among the tribes, taking seashells, shell-beads, and other objects from the coast into the interior and returning with hides and red ochre to be used as dyes, flint for arrow points, glue and hard canes for arrows, and "tassels made from the hair of deer." This trade suited him because it gave him greater freedom and an opportunity to learn something of the country. Among other things his account gives the first description of the buffalo.

Finally, Cabeza de Vaca decided to escape, and although deserted by Oviedo, the companion to whom he had so long remained loyal, he had the good fortune to fall in with three other survivors of Narvaez's party—Andres Dorantes, Alonzo del Castillo, and a negro, Estevanico—who were prisoners among another tribe of Indians. They, likewise, desired to escape, and plans were made only to meet with many unavoidable postponements. At last the opportunity came in the summer of 1535. "Two days after moving," reads Vaca's account, "we recommended ourselves to God, Our Lord, and fled, hoping that, although it was late in the season and the fruits of the tunas were giving out, by remaining in the field we might still get over a good portion of the land."

During the next year the four men wandered across southern Texas and northern Mexico, and Vaca's chronicle is our first light on the condition, manners, and life of the numerous Indian tribes in this region. The Spaniards were frequently reduced to the most abject slavery and to the extremes of suffering and hunger. Cabeza de Vaca's fame as a medicine man saved them and toward the end proved almost a source of embarrassment, for their march became a triumphal procession of hundreds of Indians conducting them from one tribe to another, and incidentally plundering the tribe next to be visited. "After leaving these people," reads Vaca's story, "we travelled among so many different tribes and languages that nobody's memory can recall them all, and always they robbed each other; but those who lost and those who gained were equally content. The number of our companions became so large that we could no longer control them." One day in the early summer of 1536 "Castillo saw, on the neck of an Indian, a little buckle from a sword-belt, and in it was sewed a horse-shoe nail." With thankful hearts they pressed on, soon finding unmistakable evidence of the nearness of their compatriots in ruined villages and frightened, fleeing Indians. At last they met a band of twenty Spaniards led by Diego de Alcaraz, and proceeding southward they came to Culiacan on the west coast of Mexico, and later to Compostela. On July 24th they reached Mexico City and were welcomed by Mendoza and Cortez, and soon afterward Cabeza de Vaca returned to Spain vainly seeking the governorship of Florida.

THE EXPEDITION OF HERNANDO DE SOTO

This coveted title had been bestowed on Hernando de Soto three months before Vaca's arrival, and he was preparing an expedition. De Soto, a man of gentle birth, had been with Pizarro in Peru and he looked forward to an equal conquest in his new grant. The tale which Cabeza de Vaca told, embellished no doubt with many of the stories of wealthy cities related by the Indians, added greatly to the excitement in the mother country. As a result, adventurers, including several noblemen, flocked to De Soto's standard in such numbers that not all could be taken. Early in April, 1538, the expedition of more than six hundred men sailed amid the blare of trumpets and the roar of cannon. Stopping in Cuba to secure horses and supplies, on the thirtieth day of May,

1539, he landed at Tampa Bay, and almost immediately members of his party killed two Indians in a skirmish. "At night the Governor, with a hundred men in the pinnaces, came upon a deserted town," wrote a "Gentleman of Elvas" whose report is the best account of this expedition, "for, so soon as the Christians appeared in sight of land, they were descried, and all along on the coast many smokes were seen to rise, which the Indians make to warn one another."

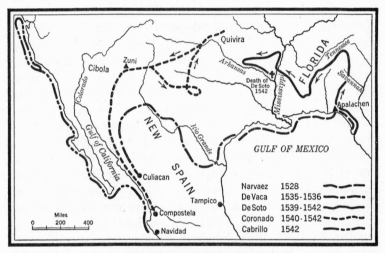

I. EARLY SPANISH EXPLORATIONS

It was more than four years later that the remnants of this gay army of invasion straggled into a Spanish settlement on the gulf coast in Mexico. During that time they traversed the region now comprised in all the American States that border on the Gulf of Mexico and in addition saw parts of Georgia, the two Carolinas, Tennessee, Arkansas, and Oklahoma. Their chroniclers give us the first European view of the Cherokee, Creek, Choctaw and Seminole Indians, as well as of other tribes. From Tampa Bay they wandered northward into the piedmont of North Carolina, southwestward across the corner of Tennessee into Alabama, and then northwestward again, leaving us a record of undaunted courage, coupled with cruelty practiced on the natives, and deception on both sides. Always

De Soto and his men were lured from place to place by promises of gold and gems to be found in distant, wealthy cities. Battles were fought with fierce savages and captives were taken and impressed into slavery. At a point north of what was probably Mobile Bay, De Soto knew that his ships were waiting him, but he refused to communicate with them and pressed on toward the northwest.

During the first week in May, 1541, De Soto and his followers came out on the bank of the Mississippi not far from the site of Memphis. While other Spaniards had doubtless seen the mouth of this great river, De Soto is rightly regarded as its real discoverer. Building boats, they crossed to the west bank. Here for another year their wanderings were continued, carrying them northward across Arkansas and probably into Missouri and westward into Oklahoma. Time after time hopes of finding rich cities of which the Indians told them were dashed by the reality of squalid and often deserted villages. Discouraged at length, De Soto descended the Arkansas to its mouth, and here, on the twenty-first of May, 1542, to use the words of the Gentleman of Elvas, "departed this life the magnanimous, the virtuous, the intrepid Captain, Don Hernando de Soto, Governor of Cuba and Adelantado of Florida." His companions, now reduced in number to about three hundred, after vainly attempting to reach Mexico by land, built boats and after many vicissitudes found their way to the Spanish settlement of Panuco in September, 1543.

Search for the Seven Cities

In Mexico the appearance of Cabeza de Vaca and his fellows and the accounts of their experiences met with a response as eager as that occasioned in Spain. For several years efforts had been made to pierce the "Northern Mystery," where was supposed to lie the Strait of Anian leading to India, and where, it was rumored, there was an island inhabited only by Amazons. By this time, also, it was fully believed that somewhere to the northward might be found the fabled Seven Cities, in which were streets on which dwelt only goldsmiths, so plentiful was the gold, and where turquoises studded the doors of the houses. On March 7, 1539, Friar Marcos de Niza, a man of wide knowledge and good reputation, set out from Culiacan with instructions to find the seven cities. He was accompanied by a lay brother, the negro Estevanico, and some Indians. Northward he went through Mexico into modern Arizona and then northeastward, learning that the name of the cities was Cibola and that beyond them were other cities even more wonderful. Estevanico went on in advance and sent back glowing reports from time to time. He might better have been less hasty, for when he and his Indians came to Cibola ahead of his leader, he was not regarded with favor by the inhabitants, who set upon him and slew him. This exploit is celebrated to the present day in a legend of the Zuni Indians. "Then and thus," runs the legend, "was killed by our ancients . . . . one of the Black Mexicans, a large man . . . and some of the Indians they killed, catching others. Then the rest ran away, chased by our grandfathers, and went back toward their country in the Land of Everlasting Summer."

The news of the death of Estevanico was a hard blow to Friar Marcos and especially to his Indian companions, but he determined that he would at least have a look at the marvelous cities which were the object of his search. At last from the edge of a high plateau he saw a Zuni pueblo village on a rounded hill. Whether the brilliant sunlight made these adobe buildings appear larger and more gorgeous than was the reality, or whether his hopes colored his vision, Friar Marcos believed that his mission had been successful. He was certain that this, the first of the Seven Cities of Cibola, was larger than the city of Mexico, and he gave credence to the tales of the Indians that the inhabitants, to quote from his report, "have Emeralds and other jewels, although they esteeme none so much as turqueses wherewith they adorne the walles of the porches of their houses, and their apparell and vessels. . . . They use vessels of gold and silver, for they have no other mettall." Making a heap of stones and raising a cross, he took possession of all the cities, and hastened back "with much more feare than victuals" to Culiacan and Compostela. There is no good reason to cast serious doubt on the good friar's sincerity. His chief fault—one which he shared with many of the Spaniards of his day—was his easy gullibility.

Coronado Seeks an El Dorado

As may be imagined, wild excitement reigned in Mexico when Friar Marcos made his report and narrated his adventures. Within a few weeks the viceroy, Mendoza, had raised a company of three hundred men, many of them of considerable rank and influence, which he placed under the command of Don Francisco Vasquez de Coronado, governor of New Galicia, with instructions to capture Cibola. By February, 1540, this army, together with about eight hundred Indians, was assembled at Compostela and reviewed by Mendoza. "Each rider held his lance erect, while his sword and other weapons hung in their proper places at his side," writes George Parker Winship, the leading authority on this expedition. "Some were arrayed in coats of mail, polished to shine like that of their general, whose gilded armor with its brilliant trappings was to bring him many hard blows a few months later. Others wore iron helmets or vizored headpieces of the tough bullhide for which the country has ever been famous. The footmen carried crossbows and harquebuses, while some of them were armed with sword and shield. Looking on at these white men with their weapons of European warfare was the crowd of native allies in their paint and holiday attire, armed with the club and the bow of an Indian warrior."

Thus in splendid array did the Spaniards once more set out to seek an El Dorado in the northern land of mystery. Neither for them nor for us were their experiences of any great interest until they came in sight of Cibola. Some idea of their discomfiture and chagrin may be gained from the words of Castañeda, the historian of the expedition, who wrote that "when they saw the first village, which was Cibola, such were the curses that some hurled at Friar Marcos that I pray God may protect him from them." The Zuni pueblo was well described as "a little, unattractive village, looking as if it had been crumpled all together." Nevertheless, the invaders had not long to give

vent to their rage and disappointment, for the people of the
village were disposed to resist capture. In the fight that ensued
before the village was taken, Coronado was knocked down
by a stone and would have been killed but for the timely
assistance of a companion.

While the expedition remained at Cibola, detachments
were sent out in various directions. One under Lopez de
Cardenas was despatched to the westward to find a large river
which flowed between deep banks. It is not difficult to
appreciate the amazement of this party when they, first of
white men, came upon the Grand Canyon of the Colorado,
which they called the Firebrand River. They spent three days
vainly attempting to get down to the river, which from the
bank looked to be not more than six feet wide. Three of
the most agile, according to Castañeda, "went down until those
who were above were unable to keep sight of them," but they
returned and reported that they had been able to go only about
one-third of the distance to the bottom. "Those who stayed
above had estimated that some huge rocks on the sides of the
cliffs seemed to be about as tall as a man, but those who went
down swore that when they reached these rocks they were
bigger than the great tower of Seville."

Late in the autumn of 1540 all the detachments, including
groups which had departed from Sonora after Coronado, were
assembled at a village called Tiguex, north of the site of
Albuquerque. Here an Indian whose appearance won him
the name of "the Turk" told them of the wonders of Quivira
far distant on the plains—a yarn inspired by the hope of luring
the Spaniards to their destruction in a further search for yellow
gold. Castañeda relates how the Turk "said that in his
country there was a river in the level country which was 2
leagues wide, in which there were fishes as big as horses, and
large numbers of very big canoes . . . and that their lords sat
on the poop under awnings, and on the prow they had a great
golden eagle. . . . He said also that everyone had their
ordinary dishes made of wrought plate, and the jugs and
bowls were of gold. . . . For the present he was believed, on
account of the ease with which he told it and because they

showed him metal ornaments and he recognized them and said they were not gold, and he knew gold and silver very well and did not care anything about other metals."

During the winter of 1540-1541 the nerves of Coronado and his followers yielded to the strain of the wilderness and its savage people, and the Indians of New Mexico learned the falsity of Spanish gestures of peace. Imprisonment, robbery, and murder of the natives leave a dark stain on the record of one of the New World's most romantic exploits. But the golden *ignis fatuus* conjured by the tales of "the Turk" floated before the vision of the intruders, and the spring of 1541 found them on the march to Quivira. Eastward and southeastward they traveled, coming upon great plains without a landmark, where even their thousand horses, five hundred cows, and thousands of rams and ewes, to say nothing of the numerous Indian allies, left no trace of their passing. Huge herds of buffalo were seen and wild tribes of plains Indians living in skin tents. On the Colorado River in central Texas they became convinced that "the Turk" had led them in the wrong direction and that Quivira lay to the north.

Here the army was divided and the greater part sent back to Tiguex in New Mexico. Coronado, with undaunted determination, and in spite of the entreaties of his men not to abandon them pressed on in the new direction with thirty horsemen and six foot soldiers and with the faithless guide in chains. In July, 1541, he reached Quivira near the big bend of the Arkansas River in Kansas. Bitter disappointment again rewarded the hopes of the explorers. Quivira was only a collection of grass-covered huts of the Wichita Indians. "Neither gold nor silver nor any trace of either was found among these people," was Castañeda's terse comment.

This culmination destroyed the hope and courage of even Coronado. The autumn of 1542 saw his thoroughly disorganized army straggling back into Mexico. "He made his report to the viceroy, Don Antonio de Mendoza, who did not receive him very graciously, although he gave him his discharge. His reputation was gone from this time on. He kept the government of New Galicia, which was entrusted to him, for only a short time. . . . And this was the end of those discoveries and of the expedition which was made to these new lands." Coronado and De Soto had both failed to find gold and their contemporaries regarded them as failures. Yet their explorations occupy a notable place in the annals of adventure and discovery, and they represent the high point of Spanish energy within the bounds of the United States.

Spaniards Explore the Pacific Coast

Meanwhile, other attempts were being made to penetrate the Northern Mystery by way of the Pacific. The elusive Strait of Anian was a source of continued anxiety to the Spanish. They wanted to find it on their own account, so that they might be the first to use it as a highway to the wealth of the East, and especially did they desire to forestall other nations who might, by its discovery, threaten Spanish possessions in America. As early as 1533, Jiménez, sent out by Cortez, discovered the peninsula of California, although it was thought to be an island, and a few years later a short-lived colony was planted near the lower end. In 1539-1540, Francisco de Ulloa rounded lower California and returned to report that it was a peninsula, a fact that was confirmed in the same year by Alarcón who, in an expedition subsidiary to that of Coronado, sailed up the Gulf of California and into the Colorado River. It was about this time that the name California, derived from a favorite Spanish romance, was first definitely used, although the region to which it was applied was as indefinite in extent as that known to the Spaniards as Florida.

Two years later, in 1542, Juan Rodriguez Cabrillo accompanied, among others, by a pilot named Bartolomé Ferrelo, was sent on another voyage of discovery up the coast in two small vessels, only one of which had a deck. San Diego Bay, the channel of Santa Barbara, Point Conception, Point Pinos, and Drake's Bay, and many other points of interest were seen by the courageous mariner as he battled his way up the coast against storms and strong head winds, but he did not see the Golden Gate or the Bay of Monterey. Early in January, 1543, Cabrillo died on San Miguel Island. The command was now taken by Ferrelo, who continued northward till he reached a point near the mouth of the Rogue River on the Oregon coast. Here he was forced to turn about and, after experiencing almost unbelievable dangers and hardships, arrived once more at the port of Navidad in Mexico. Sixty years later, when the Spanish were spurred by active English competition in the Pacific to increased apprehension lest the still-sought strait might fall into the possession of enemies, Sebastian Vizcaino sailed over much of the route of Cabrillo, and in addition discovered the Bay of Monterey. Then for more than a century and a half upper California remained in the darkness of obscurity.

THE SPANISH IN NEW MEXICO AND ARIZONA

During this period Spanish rule was pushed northward and northeastward from Mexico. Coronado's adventures had become almost legendary or were entirely forgotten before Spaniards again entered the limits of New Mexico and Arizona, although the frontier had been steadily pushing toward the Rio Grande. Interest in the northern country revived and stray copies of Cabeza de Vaca's narrative were read with new enthusiasm. One of those who seems to have read this story and to have been inspired by it with a desire to visit the Indian tribes there mentioned was a friar named Augustin Rodriguez. In 1581, accompanied by two other friars, nine soldiers and a number of Indians, and a large herd of live stock, Rodriguez set out up the Conchos River and the Rio Grande. They penetrated to the pueblo region around Albuquerque, saw the buffalo plains, the high mesa of Acoma, and the Zuni villages, and planned to establish a permanent mission. All three of the friars were killed by the Indians and their followers returned to Mexico. A rescue party, led by Antonio de Espejo, arrived too late to save the friars, but explored to the westward, visiting the Moqui and Hopi Indians in Arizona and discovered rich mines near the present site of Prescott. About ten years later, according to some accounts, a Spaniard by the name of Humaña reached the Platte River on an unlicensed gold-hunting expedition.

The real conquest of New Mexico began in 1598 when Juan de Oñate, burdened with many titles including that of Governor, and commissioned to establish a colony, led a small army of occupation out from Santa Barbara in northern Mexico. In his train were one hundred and thirty soldiers and their families, several Franciscan friars, numerous slaves, seven thousand head of stock, and more than eighty wagons and carts. At San Juan, northwest of Santa Fé, he established his colony, built the first church in New Mexico, and received the allegiance of the Indians of all the surrounding country. In the succeeding years Oñate went over much of the territory covered by Coronado, from Quivira on the Arkansas to the mouth of the Colorado and the Gulf of California. In 1608 he resigned. His successor moved the headquarters of the colony from San Juan and in 1609 founded the town of Santa Fé—a name that is written large in the annals of the West for more than two hundred and fifty years.

The history of New Mexico for nearly three-fourths of a century following the founding of Santa Fé is mainly the record of missionary activities. By 1680 there were approximately three thousand settlers living in the upper valley of the Rio Grande between Isleta and Taos, and El Paso had been established. In that year occurred the great Pueblo revolt. Spanish requirements of tribute and personal service, and their suppression of native religions, were galling to the Indians and they listened readily to incendiary admonitions of Popé, a medicine man who had his headquarters at Taos. Without warning, the Spanish settlements were attacked and more than four hundred men, women, and children, including a score of missionaries, were slaughtered. The remaining settlers abandoned their homes and fled in terror to El Paso. Uprising followed uprising and Spanish expeditions exacted a heavy toll of life and burned villages from the resisting Indians, but it was not until 1697 that Diego de Vargas succeeded in subduing the natives and reestablishing Spanish rule. Settlers returned and by the middle of the eighteenth century there were ten thousand people of Spanish and mixed blood living in El Paso, Albuquerque, Santa Fé, and Santa Cruz, in scattered villages and on haciendas and ranchos.

The Spanish advance into Arizona, like that into New Mexico, was largely the work of missionaries. The leader in this work was Father Eusebio Francisco Kino, one of the most remarkable men, both as an explorer and as a missionary, who ever served Spain in the Southwest. Accompanied part of the time by Father Salvatierra, another Jesuit of marked ability, he explored most of southern Arizona between 1691 and 1711, all the while preaching to the Indians, baptizing them, and establishing missions. Near Tucson he built the mission church of San Xavier del Bac which is still standing. He visited and wrote the earliest descriptions of the Casa Grande, the historic ruined building, four stories in height, which is to-day of such interest to achæologists and tourists. Always devoted to the success of the missions in lower California, it was one of his great concerns to find a land route to the peninsula. When he died in 1711 it was said of him that "He died as he had lived, with extreme humility and poverty. . . . He was merciful to others but cruel to himself." After Father Kino's death there were intermittent missionary ventures in Arizona, interrupted by uprisings of the Apache and Pima Indians. In 1736 there was a rush to silver mines at Arizonac, just across the border and the place from which Arizona derives its name, but the boom subsided within a few years.

Spanish Occupation of Alta California

The missions in lower California, for which Father Kino had such zeal, prospered under the administration of Father Juan Maria Salvatierra, and his associates, and later under Father Juan de Ugarte. The coasts of the peninsula were explored and charted and the interior covered with a network of trails between numerous mission establishments. Indian tribes were not only instructed in religion and useful arts, but were studied ethnologically. Fields were placed under cultivation and a system of irrigation begun. Thus by the time the Jesuits were excluded from Spanish domains in 1768 a base of operations was well established on the peninsula from which to project the conquest and occupation of upper California.

There was in New Spain at this time a man of remarkable

energy and vision—José de Gálvez, the visitor-general. He believed that a source of revenue might be developed in Alta California. Moreover, he was not content to depend upon negotiations to defend Spanish possessions from the imminent menace of Russian encroachments from the north. Accordingly, with characteristic vigor, he planned expeditions both by sea and by land to plant outposts of Spanish power at San Diego and Monterey. Two ships, the "San Antonia" and the "San Carlos," were outfitted, loaded with colonists and supplies, and sent up the coast early in 1769. Two parties were organized to proceed to San Diego by land. The first, led by Fernando de Rivera, set out in March, 1769, and about the middle of May, after suffering great hardships, reached its destination and found the two ships at anchor in the bay. The second followed two months later and was able to proceed more rapidly because the trail had been broken and weather conditions were more favorable. In this second detachment was Gaspar de Portolá, the commander of the land forces, and Father Junípero Serra, a Franciscan friar, whose name was to be woven into the history of upper California more enduringly than that of any other of his countrymen, because of the missions which he founded.

The march to Monterey began in mid-July, with Portolá in command. No serious obstacle was encountered until the party reached the Santa Lucia mountains. Thereafter the way was hard and exhausting. Coming at length to the Bay of Monterey, Portolá was disappointed not to find the excellent harbor which Vizcaino had reported, and thinking that it must lie further north, he pressed on, saw the noble redwood forest, and came to Drake's Bay, which was correctly identified. Now it was certain that the destination had been passed, and the party went into camp to rest. It was during this period that some hunters in search of food came out on the shores of San Francisco Bay lying behind the Golden Gate. Curiously enough, Portolá received the news of the discovery without enthusiasm. He had failed to find the harbor of Monterey, his men were worn and dispirited, and nothing else mattered much. He therefore returned to San Diego, where during the winter the colonists fought disease, hunger, and despair, until a relief ship brought the encouragement which made possible a permanent settlement. In 1770 another expedition went north to Monterey and this time a presidio and the San Carlos mission were established.

The foundations of San Francisco were laid six years later, in the year of American Independence, as the result of another expedition which matched and even exceeded that of Portolá in courage and endurance. Fears of Russian and English aggression still disturbed the officials of New Spain, and a settlement on San Francisco Bay was highly desirable. Furthermore, it was realized that an overland route from Sonora to California would greatly strengthen the Spanish position. Juan Bautista de Anza, commander of the fort at Tubac in Arizona, was selected to find and open such a route. In 1774, profiting by the experience and guidance of Father Francisco Garcés, who had already crossed the Colorado desert, he led a party of thirty-two men successfully to the San Gabriel mission, near Los Angeles, making the first trail of white men across the high Sierras. After visiting Monterey he returned to Tubac. Soon afterward he was ordered to conduct a colony overland to San Francisco Bay. Two hundred and forty persons, including thirty families, followed Anza out of Tubac in October, 1775. Many hundreds of horses were required for the party and a large store of supplies and equipment of all kinds. Intense cold and alternating snow and rain added to the ordinary hardships of the journey, and the crossing of the Sierras tested Anza's qualities of leadership to the utmost. Yet with almost no loss of human life the colony arrived in California, and at about the time when the Declaration of Independence was being signed in Philadelphia, a spot for the settlement on San Francisco Bay was being selected. The presidio and the mission were erected in the early autumn of that memorable year.

San Francisco marked virtually the northernmost extent of Spanish occupation of California. The life of the Californians in the years that followed has often been described as one that was full of color and romance, although the reality was doubtless less idyllic. The country was dotted with the beautifull mission churches which remain to-day, whether in ruins, in their original state, or in restoration, among the attractions of the California scene. Around them were gathered the Indians who for a time forgot their savage ways. The life of the well-to-do Castillians on their haciendas was one of ease and contentment. Probably in no other portion of Spain's new world possessions did the care-free aspects of Spanish temperament and character develop with so little hindrance. But it is one of the ironies of history that the people who of all others most desired to find rich mines of gold, should have failed to discover the Eldorado at their very door.

Spanish Expansion in Texas

Apprehensions of Russian and English encroachment were contributing emotions leading to the Spanish occupation of Alta California. Expansion into Texas was motivated by consternation occasioned by activities of the French. Sometime in 1685 word came to the authorities in Mexico and Florida of the daring attempt of La Salle to found a French colony on the Gulf at the mouth of the Mississippi. It was learned that he had missed his destination and had landed on the Texas coast. Immediately expeditions were dispatched by sea and land and in 1689 after many failures, the ruins of La Salle's ill-starred settlement were discovered on the Garcitas River by Alonzo de León. Soon afterward two missions were established on the Neches River and the province of Texas was created, although in 1693 Indian hostility led to the abandonment of the missions. Twenty years later the French menace again presented itself in a trading expedition across Texas headed by Louis Juchereau de St. Denis, who had already established a French outpost at Natchitoches on the Red River. Strong measures were necessary to meet this danger. Under the leadership of Father Espinosa and Father Antonio Margil missions were again established in eastern Texas, and in 1718 San Antonio was founded, almost simultaneously with the beginning of the French settlement at New Orleans.

The next few years were years of war between Spain and France, and of active rivalry on the frontiers, in Florida, in

Texas, and even far to the northward. Learning that the French were established on the North Platte River, the Spaniards set up a post on the same stream in Nebraska or Wyoming in 1720. During the same year a Spanish expedition under Pedro de Villazur was annihilated in northern Colorado by French-armed Indians, many of whom come from as far as Wisconsin. In the end the hold of the Spanish on Texas was made sure and firm. Thereafter, with frequent interruptions caused by Indian wars, missions were planted and settlements expanded north of the Rio Grande.

The Spanish in Louisiana

All danger of French competition in Texas or in any of Spain's American possessions was removed at the close of the Seven Years War. In 1762, in a secret treaty before the official close of the war, France gave Louisiana to Spain, as a compensation for her aid in the war and to avoid yielding it to victorious Great Britain. The Treaty of Paris in 1763 eliminated France from North America, and Florida went to England. Thus, aside from Russian pretensions in the far northwest, all North America was now divided between England and Spain, with the Mississippi as the boundary except near its mouth, where New Orleans was included in Spanish territory.

Louisiana did not at first appeal to Spain as an especially valuable acquisition. But soon its importance as a barrier to the English advance was appreciated and active measures were set on foot to extend Spanish rule over the new territory. The French had made settlements not only at New Orleans, but some distance up the Mississippi and along the Red River, with northern colonies in the Missouri country at St. Charles and Ste. Genevieve, to which St. Louis was added in 1764. The total population was probably between eight and twelve thousand, including a large number of negro slaves. These Frenchmen did not welcome Spanish control. The first governor, Juan Antonio de Ulloa, who arrived in 1766, met with unpopularity which increased within two years to the proportions of an insurrection which drove him out of the country. The Spanish authorities were now thoroughly aroused and Alexandro O'Reilly, a soldier of experience and iron will, was sent with twenty-six hundred troops, to take formal and definite possession of Louisiana. The leaders of the insurrection were executed or imprisoned, and the rigid, centralized form of Spanish colonial government was firmly established.

Spanish rule in Louisiana lasted less than thirty-five years after the coming of O'Reilly. During this period the time and thought of the governors were largely occupied with efforts to solve the problems arising out of the inevitably advancing frontier, first of England and later of the new American nation. In 1800 Napoleon coveted Louisiana and dictated its return to France. A little more than two decades later, the Mexican revolution stripped away the remaining possessions which Spain had acquired during more than three hundred colorful years of exploring, missionary work, Indian-fighting, and gold-hunting within the present limits of the United States.

REMINDERS OF SPANISH RULE

The institutions and ideas of the United States as a whole have been little affected by the fact that a portion of its area was long in the possession of Spain. In the regions, however, where Spanish control was well established, life still bears the imprint and many reminders of early Spanish occupancy. Place names all over the southwest and in California would indicate, if there were no other evidence, that Spaniards were once in those regions. The prevalence there of the Spanish type of architecture is another indication. Land titles in California and elsewhere are still frequently in litigation because of controversies over the terms and boundaries of early Spanish grants. Finally, in less tangible ways, the present-day life of the southwest and of southern California is modified by influences originating in the period before American rule was established.

CHAPTER III

FRENCH PAGEANTRY IN THE MISSISSIPPI VALLEY

"AFTER DE SOTO glimpsed the river, a fraction short of a quarter of a century elapsed, and then Shakespeare was born, lived a trifle more than half a century,—then died; and when he had been in his grave considerably more than half a century, the second white man saw the Mississippi." With this illuminative flourish Mark Twain pictures the long period of time intervening between the Spanish discovery of the Mississippi and the next undisputed view of the Father of Waters by white men—men, this time, of French nationality.

FORERUNNERS OF FRENCH RULE

It was while Cabeza de Vaca was wandering among the Indian tribes of the southwest, in 1534, that Jacques Cartier, commissioned by the king of France, sailed from St. Malo and explored the Gulf of St. Lawrence. The following year he made another voyage of discovery which took him up the St. Lawrence as far as the sites of Quebec and Montreal. He, like all Europeans who first came to the New World, was seeking a route to Far Cathay. He could not know how many thousands of miles of forests and lakes, rivers, plains and mountains stretched between him and another broad ocean which must be crossed before his goal could be reached. He could only observe the barbarism of the people among whom he found himself and experience the intense sufferings occasioned by cold, hunger, and disease during the winter he spent on the site of the future capital of New France.

Cartier had given a mighty river and valley to his king, and he had opened a gateway which gave the French easy access to the interior of North America—the only gateway which France could use for more than a century and a half.

We cannot follow the fortunes and misfortunes of the early years of attempted colonization in New France. In 1603 there appeared upon the scene Samuel de Champlain, a man of great energy and zeal, broad vision and sound judgment. It was he who in 1609 laid the permanent foundations of Quebec. It was he, more than anyone else, who established the fur trade as the great industry of the French. If he could have had his way, he would likewise have given a sound agricultural basis to the colony; but in this respect he could not communicate his vision to his fellows and the failure eventually proved fatal. Champlain explored the Ottawa River and discovered Lakes Huron and Ontario, as well as the lake which bears his name. His greatest misfortune befell when, by virtue of the white man's weapons, he turned the tide of a battle against the Iroquois in favor of a war party of northern Indians which he accompanied. The fierce Iroquois retaliated by harrying the French settlements and blocking the pathway up the St. Lawrence. This initial cause of hostility to the French might have been forgotten by the Iroquois, but they soon found it to their advantage to ally themselves with the Dutch and later the English at Albany.

Champlain not only made many explorations in person, but he also selected young men of promise and sent them into the Indian country to learn the language and ways of the natives and discover opportunities for the fur trade. One of these agents, Jean Nicolet, in 1634, pushed far westward to the western edge of Lake Michigan and became the forerunner of the French in the Mississippi Valley. The picture that we have of him as he stood on the shore of Green Bay is almost like a scene from comic opera. "He wore a grand robe of China damask, all strewn with flowers and birds of many colors," wrote Father Vimont,[1] whose relation, written eight years later, is our principal source of information concerning Nicolet's exploration. "No sooner did they perceive him than the women and children fled, at the sight of a man who carried thunder in both hands—for thus they called the two pistols

[1] Louise Phelps Kellogg (ed.) *Early Narratives of the Northwest* (1917), p. 16. By permission of Charles Scribner's Sons, publishers.

that he held." This elaborate and fanciful costume was carried by Nicolet on his long expedition and donned on this occasion because he was about to visit the "People of the Sea," of whom alluring stories had reached Champlain, causing him to think they might be Asiatics. If Nicolet still credited these stories when he reached Green Bay, he was soon disillusioned, for he found his hosts to be only Winnebago Indians, savages like those with whom he was already acquainted. Nevertheless, the Frenchman was well received. "Each of the chief men made a feast for him, and at one of these banquets they served at least six score beavers." Whether Nicolet journeyed westward beyond this point is not certain, although he may have paddled some distance up the Fox River. Contemporaneous accounts indicate that he believed himself not far from a stream which flowed into the "Great Water," then thought to be the South Sea, but he did not attempt to verify these rumors.

COUREURS DE BOIS AND VOYAGEURS

Twenty years elapsed before another Frenchman ventured as far west as Nicolet had gone. Champlain died late in 1635 and for a time there was no one at the head of New France with the vision and enthusiasm to promote western exploration. Besides, the Iroquois scourge was in action. This time it was the Huron allies of the French, dwelling in the region east of Lake Huron, who felt the might of the confederated warriors. Throughout the Huron country the Iroquois wrought death and destruction, torture and captivity, and by 1650 the surviving Hurons, as well as other tribes, were dispersed far and wide, leaving their former home land uninhabited. The relentless Iroquois pursued their quarry to the very doors of Montreal, and the French were in dire straits. Obviously this was no time for Frenchmen to be abroad in the west, even along the pathway, now familiar to them, by the Ottawa River and Lake Nipissing to Georgian Bay and Lake Huron. The only notable western exploit of the French during the two decades following Nicolet's expedition was the journey of two Jesuit priests, Fathers Charles Raymbault and Isaac Jogues, in 1641 from the Huron Mission to Sault Ste. Marie, the strait that connects Lake Superior and Lake Huron.

Gradually fear of the Iroquois diminished and the northern Indians dared once more to bring their furs to Montreal. Interest in the fur trade revived and especially among that group of intrepid and picturesque adventurers known as *coureurs de bois*. Engaging in the trade with the Indians on their own initiative and for their own profit, they connived with corrupt officials to evade governmental regulations or took their furs to Albany to trade with the Dutch and later with the English. Some of these *coureurs de bois* were thoroughly lawless, dissolute individuals who lost themselves in the wilderness and degenerated into savages worse than those among whom they lived. Others were men of a much higher type who rendered real service to the French cause. Of the latter class were two brothers-in-law, Pierre Esprit Radisson and Médart Chouart, Sieur des Groseilliers.

Some time between 1654 and 1660 these two men apparently made at least two trading expeditions to the far west, the first with government permission and the second without the knowledge or consent of the authorities. Radisson's account of these journeys was not published until late in the nineteenth century and it is so vague that it is not possible to be certain either of the dates of the expenditions or of their itineraries. It is generally agreed, however, that Radisson and Grosseilliers penetrated well into the present state of Wisconsin, that they were the first white men to explore the southern shore of Lake Superior, and that they visited the Sioux Indians in eastern Minnesota. Some historians believe that they saw the upper waters of the Mississippi, but the evidence is not indisputable, and at any rate such an important discovery was not known to their contemporaries. One extravagant interpretation credits them with making a circuit which took them far to the west of the great river, but this claim has no supporters. Whatever may have been their geographical discoveries, they gained wide experience among numerous Indian tribes and took back valuable cargoes of furs to Montreal. The later careers of the two men were featured by alternating service to the French and their great rivals of the English Hudson's

Bay Company. While they did not again return to the west, other traders were soon familiar with the land and Indians around Lakes Michigan and Superior.

Among the *voyageurs* who came into this region none is better known than Nicolas Perrot, because he was able and inclined to write and left us records of his experiences which are among the most valuable sources of information concerning the Indians of the upper Mississippi Valley when white men first saw them. He was a young man in his twenties when he first ventured into the West about 1665. For five years he was almost continually among the tribesmen, learning their languages and gaining a remarkable influence over them. On several occasions the Indians desired to pay him the homage and adoration due a god. According to a contemporary historian, Perrot "was careful not to receive all these acts of adoration, although, it is true he accepted these honors so far as the interests of religion were not concerned. He told them that he was not what they thought, but only a Frenchman," but he hastened to explain that the French were favored by the Great Spirit, who had sent them among the Indians to assist them. On another occasion, after he had been borne on the shoulders of a war chief into a village, he told the Indians of the light which the French would bring to dispel the darkness brooding over savage lands. "I am the dawn of that light, which is beginning to appear in your lands,"[2] he said. He gave the young men of the village his gun to use in hunting and in repelling attacks of enemies. To the old men he presented his kettle in which to cook their meat. Lastly, he delighted the women and children with gifts of awls and knives and bright beads.

Thus, with tact and true insight, Perrot gained an ascendancy over the affections of numerous Indian tribes. As a result, during two score years, he was well nigh indispensable to the officials of New France as an interpreter at councils and as an agent to secure the assistance of western Indians in campaigns against the Iroquois. The first instance in which he

[2] Louise Phelps Kellogg (ed.) *Early Narratives of the Northwest*, (1917), pp. 75, 86. By permission of Charles Scribner's Sons, publishers.

rendered conspicuous service was in connection with one of the most colorful episodes in the annals of the Great Lakes region.

PAGEANTRY AT SAULT STE. MARIE

Jean Talon, the energetic Intendant of New France, returned in 1670 from a visit to Paris with permission and instructions to arrange an elaborate ceremony at which formal possession should be taken of the interior of North America in the name of the king of France. Simon François Daumont, Sieur de St. Lusson, was chosen to lead the expedition and Sault Ste. Marie was selected as the place for the pageant. Nicolas Perrot was appointed interpreter and Indian agent for the occasion. His preliminary task was to visit his familiar haunts around Green Bay and to conduct as many of the tribal chieftains as possible to the scene of the ceremony. All told, fourteen Indian tribes were represented at Sault Ste. Marie by the early part of June, 1671, and soon everything was in readiness on the elevated spot overlooking the Indian village and the rushing waters of the straits. "On the morning of the fourteenth of June," to quote that painter with words, Francis Parkman, "Saint-Lusson led his followers to the top of the hill, all fully equipped and under arms. Here, too, in the vestments of their priestly office, were four Jesuits,— Claude Dablon, Superior of the Missions of the Lakes, Gabriel Druillettes, Claude Allouez, and Louis André. All around, the great throng of Indians stood, or crouched, or reclined at length, with eyes and ears intent."

A cross was blessed, raised and placed in the ground, while the Frenchmen chanted the *Vexilla*. Next a cedar post bearing a plate on which were inscribed the royal arms was erected and the *Exaudiat* was sung. Then St. Lusson, clothed in the brilliant uniform of a French officer, arose and proclaimed in a loud voice: "In the name of the Most High, Most Mighty and Most Redoubtable Monarch Louis, the Fourteenth of the Name, Most Christian King of France and Navarre, we take possession of the said place of St. Marie of the Falls as well as of Lakes Huron and Superior . . . and of all other countries, rivers, lakes and tributaries, contiguous and adjacent there-

unto, as well discovered as to be discovered, which are bounded
on the one side by the Northern and Western Seas and on the
other side by the South Sea including all its length and breath."
At the close a piece of sod was raised three times and each time
the Frenchmen shouted *"Vive le Roi!"* and discharged their
muskets, all of which was much "to the delight and astonishment of all those peoples, who had never seen anything of the
kind." Loud howls from savage throats mingled with the roar
of the musketry.

Silence was again enjoined and Father Allouez arose to
eulogize Louis the XIVth. "He lives beyond the sea," he said,
"he is the captain of the greatest captains, and has not his
equal in the world. All the captains you have ever seen, or of
whom you have ever heard, are mere children compared with
him. . . . You know about Onnontio, that famous captain of
Quebec. . . . Beyond the sea there are ten thousand Onnontios
like him, who are only the soldiers of that great captain, our
Great King, of whom I am speaking." With further comparisons and figures of speech comprehensible to the gaping red
men he told of the might and valor and wealth of the French
and their ruler. "The whole ceremony was closed with a fine
bonfire, which was lighted toward evening, and around which
the *Te Deum* was sung to thank God, on behalf of those poor
peoples, that they are now the subjects of so great and powerful a monarch." "After that," to use the words of Nicolas Perrot, "all those peoples returned to their respective abodes, and
lived many years without trouble in that quarter."[3] Surprising and childish as all this pomp and ceremony may appear to-
day, it reveals how thoroughly the French understood Indian
psychology.

FRENCH MISSIONARIES

The role of Father Allouez at Sault Ste. Marie is illustrative
of the part played by the priests, whether of the Jesuit, Recollect or Sulpitian orders, in the story of the French in New
France and in the West. The seventy-three printed volumes of

[3] The descriptions of the ceremony at Sault Ste. Marie are quoted from
Louise Phelps Kellogg (ed.) *Early Narratives of the Northwest* (1917), pp.
215-220. By permission of Charles Scribner's Sons, publishers.

Jesuit Relations and Allied Documents are alone abundant
evidence of the variegated activities of members of this most
numerous order.   Naturally, therefore, it would be futile here
to attempt any account of the services of these men of the
black and gray robes.   Not even the briefest survey of the
French régime, however, would be adequate if it failed to pay
tribute to the devotion of the men who, for the glory of their
faith, forsook ease and comfort and immersed themselves in
the misery and filth of immemorial barbarism.   For the winning of savage souls many of them endured loneliness and
unbelievable privations and suffered fiendish torture from
which death was a blessed relief.   Nearly every important exploring or trading expedition had its contingent of soldier-mis-
sionaries of the cross, seeking more distant fields for their
labors and bearing their full share of arduous toil and extreme
hardship.   Fathers Raymbault, Jogues, Allouez, Brébeuf, Dablon, Lalemont, Le Caron, Ménard, and many others left records
of heroic loyalty that illuminate the pages of French achievement.   Less pleasant to recall are some of their later brothers
who seemed more concerned with the power and glory of the
church than with the salvation of the natives, and others who
stirred the Indians to cruel raids on their enemies, whether
other red men or the pale-faced English.   In palliation, however, it must be remembered how difficult it was in those days
to distinguish the glory of king and country from the glory
of God.

One of the priests who was to win imperishable renown,
both as a man of great piety and devotion and as an explorer,
was the young Jesuit, Father Jacques Marquette. His missionary service began in 1668 at Sault Ste. Marie. The following
year he replaced Father Allouez at the mission of St. Esprit
on Chequamegon Bay near the western end of Lake Superior.
Then in 1671 he moved with his charges to the northern side
of the Strait of Michilimackinac (or Mackinac), which connects Lakes Huron and Michigan, and erected the mission of
St. Ignace.   Here he was devotedly preaching to the natives
when, in 1673, he was rewarded with the opportunity for which
he had long prayed—the opportunity to visit the tribes along
the Mississippi River, and especially the Illinois, who "had

very urgently entreated" him while at St. Esprit "to carry the word of God to their country."

THE VOYAGE OF MARQUETTE AND JOLIET

By this time the French were determined to remove all doubts concerning the existence and course of the great river to the west, about which so many rumors had been heard and the Indian name of which was now known. If Radisson and Grosseilliers, or Perrot, or any other Frenchmen had already seen this river there was no record. Accordingly Talon, the Intendant of New France, commissioned a young man named Louis Joliet to lead an expedition of discovery, and the choice was confirmed by the new and forceful Governor, Count Frontenac. Joliet was deeply interested in the fur trade and was already possessed of wide experience in the West for a man not yet thirty. He had been on Green Bay, had skirted the northern shore of Lake Erie, and had been with St. Lusson at the pageant at Sault Ste. Marie in 1671. Thus, Joliet and Marquette were both young men imbued with a sincere enthusiasm for the task assigned them. Because Joliet's journals were lost during his return voyage to Canada, we know of their memorable experiences chiefly through the journal of Father Marquette, who has perhaps been given more than his due share of credit on this account.

On May 17, 1673, Marquette and Joliet and five other Frenchmen started from St. Ignace in two bark canoes with only some Indian corn and smoked meat for food. "The joy that we felt at being selected for this expedition animated our courage," wrote Marquette, "and rendered the labor of paddling from morning to night agreeable to us. And because we were going to seek unknown countries, we took every precaution in our power, so that, if our undertaking were hazardous, it should not be foolhardy." Along the northwestern shore of Lake Michigan they went, into Green Bay and up the Fox River to the portage where the town of Portage, Wisconsin, now stands. Here two Indian guides helped them carry their canoes over the portage of twenty-seven hundred paces, "after which they returned home," says Marquette, "leaving us alone in this unknown country, in the hands of Providence." They were now on the Wisconsin River. "After proceeding 40 leagues on this same route," to quote again from the report, "we arrived at the mouth of our river; and, at 42 and a half degrees of latitude, we safely entered Mississippi on the 17th of June, with a joy that I cannot express."

Although this first report concerning the upper stretches of the mighty Mississippi is full of rare interest, we cannot follow the daily experiences of the discoverers. Trusting their canoe to the current they witnessed a constantly varying panorama, with strange fishes and new animals, among which were the buffalo which are described at considerable length. During the first eight days they saw no signs of human life. "Finally, on the 25th of June," reads Marquette's account, "we perceived on the water's edge some tracks of men, and a narrow and somewhat beaten path leading to a fine prairie." Following this path cautiously and with some trepidation, they were soon welcomed into a village of Illinois Indians on the Iowa side of the river. The speeches that were made by the Indians and their visitors at this meeting were used by Longfellow in the episode of the visit of "the black-robed priest, the prophet" in "Hiawatha."

After remaining several days in the village the voyagers continued down the stream, observing two awe-inspiring monsters painted on the rocks near the site of Alton, Illinois, and passing safely through the turmoil of the waters where the Missouri poured its muddy flood into the Mississippi. Southward they pressed, beyond the mouth of the Ohio, coming upon strange Indian tribes, some of whom showed hostility until the calumet dispelled their fears, while others endeavored to dissuade them from going further because of dangers to be encountered. At last they came to an Indian village called Akamsea, near the mouth of the Arkansas where De Soto had died more than one hundred and thirty years earlier. Here the two explorers held a council and decided to turn back. They had established the fact that the Mississippi flowed not into the Atlantic in the region of Virginia nor into the Gulf of California, but into the Gulf of Mexico. "We further considered," explains Marquette, "that we exposed ourselves to the risk of losing the results of this voyage, of which we could give no information if we proceeded to fling ourselves into the hands of the Spaniards who, without doubt, would at least have detained us as captives." [4]

Thus the glory of planting the French arms at the mouth of the great river was left to be gained nine years later by another compatriot of even more illustrious fame. Marquette and Joliet had accomplished all and more than they had been commissioned to do, and they returned to Lake Michigan. Joliet hastened on to Montreal to make his report, but unfortunately all his papers, including a carefully-made map, were lost in the La Chine rapids when almost in sight of his destination. Marquette remained in the West and after realizing his desire to preach to the Illinois Indians was granted the joy of the true Jesuit missionary—the joy of martyrdom. As result of too strenuous exertions and over-exposure, he died on May 15, 1675.

La Salle and His Dream of Empire

A few years before the fruitful expedition of Marquette and Joliet there had come into the West another young man who was destined not only to complete the exploration of these two men, but to make his name known and his ambitions felt from the St. Lawrence to the Gulf of Mexico and in the far-away court of France. Robert Cavelier, Sieur de La Salle, was born in Rouen in 1643 of a wealthy family. For several years he seems to have taught in a Jesuit school. But he was not of the temperament to be content with a life hemmed about with so many repressions and restrictions, and in his later career he exhibited a strong antipathy to the Jesuits. In 1666 he came to Canada and soon obtained from the Sulpitians a large grant of land at La Chine on the St. Lawrence a few miles above Montreal. Here his vivid imagination and his unbounded ambition found free play. Even at this time he seems to have formulated the main outlines of the plan that was to occupy the remainder of his life. He determined to discover the Mis-

---

[4] The quotations from Marquette's journal are from Louise Phelps Kellogg (ed.), *Early Narratives of the Northwest* (1917), pp. 229, 235, 236, 238, 256. By permission of Charles Scribner's Sons, publishers.

sissippi River and descend it to its mouth, hoping thereby to find the long-sought way to China. Later, when it was learned that the Mississippi flowed into the Gulf of Mexico, he altered his plan and decided to establish a colony at the mouth of the river. To this base would come the furs gathered at forts and trading posts throughout the great valley and from it they would be shipped directly to Europe. Hopes of financial profit seem to have been only a secondary motive in La Salle's plan. Dreams of personal power, of reigning supreme over a vast realm peopled by myriads of savages, were mingled with patriotic visions of extending the dominions and enhancing the glory of the French and their king. Fortunately, in Count Frontenac, Governor of New France, La Salle found a kindred spirit and a helpful ally.

Whether narrated by historians like Francis Parkman and John Carl Parish or by novelists like Gilbert Parker, the story of La Salle's activities has all the thrill of melodramatic fiction. There are heroes and villains, impending dangers and hairbreadth escapes. Something of the romantic flavor of the story can be gained from even a brief synopsis.

La Salle's first visit to the West occurred in 1669-1670. He set out from Montreal with two Sulpitian missionaries, with the discovery of the Ohio River as his objective. Near the head of Lake Ontario they chanced to meet Louis Joliet who was returning from one of his early expeditions. His accounts of the Pottawattamie and other tribes of the upper Lakes fired the zeal of the priests to preach to these Indians. La Salle, however, was of no mind to go so far out of his way and so, under pretext of illness, he let the two missionaries depart without him. His own course from this point is veiled in uncertainty. Recent writers are disinclined to credit the claims earlier advanced that he discovered the Ohio and Illinois rivers, and the even more improbable assertion that he saw the Mississippi. At least he gained some personal knowledge of the region he was to traverse many times in the prosecution of his far-reaching schemes of empire.

Several years now elapsed before La Salle was fairly launched on his western venture. In 1674, he sailed to France, was well received at court, and was granted the seigniory of

Fort Frontenac, which had just been built on the northern
shore of Lake Ontario near its eastern end, where the city of
Kingston now stands. Returning to his new post the following year, he soon found himself embarrassed and hampered
by the jealousy and opposition of the merchants of Canada,
who saw in La Salle's privileges a limitation of their own
opportunities. He was the object of complaints, plots and
intrigues in which, La Salle believed, the Jesuits were involved,
because they foresaw that his success would mean the ruin of
their alleged design to raise up an empire for themselves in
the West. Difficulties of this sort beset La Salle during the
remainder of his life. He lacked business judgment and the
ability to conciliate rivals, and he was too greedy for personal
power to secure the cooperation so essential to the accomplishment of his ambitious plan. It was characteristic of the man,
however, that he was undaunted by obstacles of any kind.

Thus it was that in the autumn of 1677 he again braved
the long and perilous sea voyage to France and presented himself at court, seeking this time even greater favors than those
hitherto granted him. In the following year he returned to the
New World, armed with a royal patent authorizing him to explore the West, build forts wherever necessary and enjoy the
trade of the interior for a period of five years. Equally important, he brought with him Henri de Tonty who was to be his
capable lieutenant and at times his almost only trusted fol-
lower. Tonty was an Italian officer, who had lost one hand
in the Italian wars. He wore an iron hand which enabled him
to strike blows that gained him great prestige among the
Indians.

Preparations were immediately begun and late in 1678
La Salle and Tonty, with a party of followers set out for their
new and larger field of activity. After numerous difficulties
and disasters a vessel, the "Griffin," was built and launched
on Lake Ontario and eventually sailed into Green Bay, where
it took on a cargo of furs. Upon the completion of the vessel,
La Salle's party proceeded in two sections toward the head of
Lake Michigan, suffering incredible hardships from storm and
cold and hunger. Reuniting in December, 1679, they made
their way to the Illinois River and to a village of the Illinois

Indians. Here in spite of Indian intrigues, the desertion of some of his men, and an attempt to poison him, La Salle erected Fort Crèvecoeur near the site of the present city of Peoria, and set about the building of another vessel with which to descend the Mississippi. Then, because nothing had been heard of the "Griffin" which should have returned to Lake Michigan long ago, the indomitable leader, with a few followers, started overland to Fort Frontenac on the first of March, 1680.

Shortly after La Salle's departure and in accordance with his instructions, Father Louis Hennepin and two other men set out to explore the upper Mississippi. They descended the Illinois River to its mouth without serious difficulty and made their way some distance up the larger stream. Then real adventure overtook them. They were captured by a band of Sioux Indians and as captives they probably saw much more of the country to the northward than they had expected to explore. The Indians conducted the Frenchmen up the Mississippi past Lake Pepin to the vicinity of the Falls of St. Anthony and the present site of St. Paul. Then the canoes were abandoned and the party struck overland to the Sioux villages on the Mille Lacs. The experiences of the white men, and especially of Hennepin, on this journey were both tragic and comic. Eventually Hennepin and his companions were rescued by Daniel Greysolon Duluth (or Dulhut), a noted *coureur de bois*, whose career in the upper Mississippi Valley constitutes a thrilling chapter in the history of the French in the West.

Meanwhile, La Salle and his men were plunging eastward through the wilderness. Thawing ground, swollen streams and extensive marshes, lack of food, and the necessity of constant watchfulness to avoid hostile Indians tried their endurance to the limit, but finally the goal was reached. Here La Salle received well-nigh crushing news. The "Griffin" had been lost on the lakes through treachery or accident. A supply ship coming from France was wrecked at the mouth of the St. Lawrence. Then, more terrible still, couriers brought word that most of his men on the Illinois had deserted, leaving Tonty with only three hired men and two Recollect friars. The deserters had not only destroyed Fort Crèvecoeur and dumped the supplies into the river, but on their way east they had plundered several other posts which La Salle had established.

"And now," to use the words of Francis Parkman, "La Salle's work must be begun afresh. He had staked all, and all had seemingly been lost. In stern, relentless effort, he had touched the limits of human endurance; and the harvest of his toil was disappointment, disaster, and impending ruin. The shattered fabric of his enterprise was prostrate in the dust. His friends desponded; his foes were blatant and exultant. Did he bend before the storm? No human eye could pierce the depths of his reserved and haughty nature; but the surface was calm, and no sign betrayed a shaken resolve or an altered purpose. Where weaker men would have abandoned all in despairing apathy, he turned anew to his work with the same vigor and the same apparent confidence as if borne on the full tide of success."

Losing no time, La Salle took the route to the West to bring aid to Tonty and repair his broken fortunes. To his horror he found in the Illinois country, instead of teeming villages, a scene of awful devastation wrought by the all-conquering Iroquois. After a long and anxious search, to his great joy, he at last found Tonty safe and sound at Michilimackinac.

Following this happy reunion there was another of La Salle's remarkable journeys back to Montreal to stave off his creditors and secure fresh resources. And then the winter of 1681-2 found him again in the Illinois country, ready to further the enterprise which he had never for a moment relinquished. Early in February, 1682, his canoes were pushed out into the current of the Mississippi, and two months later "the broad bosom of the Gulf opened on his sight, tossing its restless billows, limitless, voiceless, lonely as when born of chaos, without a sail, without a sign of life." Here on April 9th he repeated the ceremony that he and others had performed in many parts of the great valley, and took possession in the name of King Louis XIV, naming the country Louisiana.

The ascent of the Mississippi was much more difficult than the descent, and on the way a serious illness detained La Salle for forty days at the rude stockade named Fort Prudhomme, which had been erected at the Chickasaw Bluffs on the downward journey. But in September he was back in the lake regions and shortly afterward Fort St. Louis was built on "Starved Rock" on the Illinois River in the midst of a large village of Illinois Indians. Here La Salle planned to plant a colony of Frenchmen around which he would gather numerous native tribes—a plan which was carried to temporary fruition as far as the Indians were concerned. But now fate again interposed. La Salle's staunch ally, Governor Frontenac, was replaced by Le Febvre de la Barre who was anything but friendly.

Nothing daunted, leaving Tonty in charge at Fort St. Louis, La Salle retraveled the long road to Quebec and, paying scant attention to the new governor, sailed for France to seek aid in the accomplishment of the final phase of his great scheme— the establishment of a colony at the mouth of the Mississippi. This time he proposed to sail directly from France into the Gulf of Mexico and thus be wholly free of the obstacles he had so long encountered in Canada with its inhospitable winters and its hostile officials and merchants. His petitions met with favor. On July 24, 1684, he sailed from Rochelle with four ships and about three hundred colonists. Despite bitter quarrels between La Salle and the commander of the vessels, the desertion of some of the men at Santo Domingo, and severe illness, the expedition finally reached the Gulf of Mexico. Then misfortune struck its heaviest blow. The mouth of the Mississippi was missed and in January, 1685, the party gathered on the Texan shore at Matagorda Bay, without in the least knowing their location with respect to their goal. The story of the two heartbreaking years that followed cannot be related here—the building of another Fort St. Louis on Matagorda Bay, the sickness and suffering that decimated the numbers of the party, the vain expeditions in search of the Mississippi, and the rising spirit of mutiny, which the haughty, self-centered La Salle was utterly incapable of conciliating. Although he was without a superior in dealing with the Indians, he was a failure as a leader among men of his own race.

At last La Salle and a few followers set out in a final desperate effort to find their way to the Illinois country. The long strain and the growing hatreds now led rapidly to irretrievable disaster. Near the Trinity River in March, 1687, murder raised its head, claiming first some of La Salle's faithful adherents. Then the leader himself was led into an ambuscade and slain, his body stripped of all its clothing and left to the wolves and buzzards. Thus perished Robert Cavelier, Sieur de la Salle. Notwithstanding his many faults, his career constitutes one of the most thrilling chapters in the history of the American West. Few of his countrymen in America possessed his courage and dogged determination and none his sweep of vision. More than a decade elapsed before his dream of a French colony at the mouth of the Mississippi was realized. "From one end of the valley to the other the white men had traveled," to quote the words of John Carl Parish, "and yet, as the track of a canoe dies out of the water or the shadow of a flying bird passes over the plains and is gone, so now it seemed that the trail of the white men's passing had vanished out of the valley and that the dream that had led to their coming had been lost with the dreamer beneath the waving grass of the Southern plains." [5]

[5] John C. Parish, *The Man with the Iron Hand* (1913), p. 289. By permission of the Houghton Mifflin Company, publishers.

CHAPTER IV

A RIVAL ENTERS THE FIELD

THE enemies of La Salle were men of his own nationality; but if he had lived a normal span of years to prosecute his far-reaching plans his difficulties would have been immeasurably increased by the competition and hostility of the representatives of two other nations. We have already noted the consternation among the Spaniards when they learned of La Salle's projected colony at the mouth of the Mississippi, and their frantic efforts, both from Florida and the West, to find this invader of a realm which they regarded as their own. For many years the Spaniards and the French were to be active or potential contenders for the control of the Gulf coast and the lower Mississippi Valley. But a far more serious threat to French supremacy in the West lay in the activities of ambitious traders from the narrow fringe of English colonies along the Atlantic coast.

INDIAN TRADE IN THE ENGLISH COLONIES

The glamor attached to the wide-ranging operations of French traders has somewhat obscured the slower but equally determined and oftentimes equally audacious ventures of the English. From the very beginning of British colonization in America the Indian trade was a vital factor in the life and welfare of the colonists. "Evidences of the importance of this early Indian trade," says Professor McIlwain, "become more numerous as time goes on, and indicate a trade at once significant in amount and important in the eyes of contemporaries. The surprising thing in these records is the fact that, go back as far as we may, in the very earliest recorded voyages we find that the Indians had collected stores of skins in anticipation of trade with the Europeans, and that the voyagers in turn had invariably brought with them goods for this traffic . . .

more surprising still is the fact that as early as 1616 the Indians, in order to collect these stores of skins, had to penetrate the interior probably as far as the lakes. It seems remarkable that the trade had developed to such a degree and had already covered so great an area before a single permanent English settlement had been made within the present United States north of the James River."[1]

The earliest records of the Virginia colony tell of great quantities of deer skins and beaver furs accumulated by the Indians, and of the immense profits made by individuals in the trade for these commodities. No small part of the income which enabled the Pilgrims at Plymouth to maintain themselves came from the Indian trade, which began almost immediately after their landing. The eccentric Thomas Morton of Merrymount was a thorn in the flesh of his Puritan neighbors of Massachusetts Bay, perhaps less because of his pagan ways than on account of his interference with their beaver trade. Indeed, Morton testified to the economic importance of the beaver skin when he expressed his belief "that Jason's Golden Fleece was either the same, or some other Fleece not of so much value." All the New England colonies vigorously prosecuted the fur trade, and the rapid exhaustion of the fur supply, the inter-colonial rivalries, and the dangers of Dutch competition were among the causes leading to the New England Confederation of 1643.

Space will not permit an account of the development of the Indian trade within all the colonies east of the mountains. In New Jersey and in Maryland a short-lived traffic soon depleted the resources of these regions. After the founding of Pennsylvania, merchants and traders, in spite of many handicaps, reaped a lucrative harvest and in later years became real competitors for the trade of the Ohio valley. Neither can more than mere mention be made of the establishment in 1667 and the chartering in 1670 of the great Hudson's Bay Company by Englishmen, nor of the bitter rivalry of its representatives with the French in the far north.

[1] Charles H. McIlwain (ed.) *Peter Wraxall's Abridgment of the Indian Affairs* (1915), pp. xiii-xiv. By permission of the Harvard University Press, Publishers.

There were three colonies, however, in which the pursuit of furs and skins was rapidly pressed into the interior, with the result that its devotees were lured beyond the mountains and into the Mississippi basin. These colonies were Virginia, New York with its trading center at Albany, and. South Carolina. The traders of the latter two colonies soon came into conflict with the French and began the long struggle for the mastery of a continent.

VIRGINIANS DISCOVER WESTWARD-FLOWING RIVERS

While traders from Virginia did not play a conspicuous role in this struggle until it was nearing its close, there is every reason to believe that Virginians were the first Englishmen to see water that flowed through the Ohio and the Mississippi to the Gulf. As early as 1645 a line of forts was established at the fall line of the rivers flowing into the Atlantic to protect tidewater Virginia from the Indians. One of these, and in many respects the most important, was Fort Henry at the falls of the Appomattox where Petersburg now stands. The commander at this post was Abraham Wood, who made it his home for thirty years or more, and in addition to his military services became one of the colony's greatest Indian traders. Although Governor William Berkeley was greatly intrigued by the vague reports of the land beyond the Alleghanies, of the Spanish along the Gulf, and the reputed proximity of the South Sea, it is probable that it was Abraham Wood who gave the impulse or supplied the knowledge and organizing ability which led to the first English explorations in the direction of this land of mystery and allurement.

In 1650 Wood and three companions made a trip southwest over the Virginia piedmont to the falls of the Roanoke, near the present North Carolina line. In the years that followed he expanded his trading operations, although there is no sound basis for the claims, occasionally asserted, that he saw the Ohio and possibly the Mississippi in 1654. In the next decade, however, Englishmen in the mother country awakened fully to the profits to be made in the fur trade. This new interest, which was most definitely shown in the founding of the Hudson's Bay Company, was reflected in Virginia in renewed zeal for western exploration. In 1668 Governor Berkeley made preparations for a great expedition, in which two hundred men were said to have enlisted. Nothing came of this plan, but in 1669 and 1670 a German physician by the name of John Lederer made three expeditions to the summits of the Blue Mountains, apparently under Berkeley's orders.

Then the leadership in western ventures was turned over once more to Abraham Wood. In 1671, a small party led by Captain Thomas Batts and Robert Fallam took the trail westward from Fort Henry, and before they returned they had made the first recorded crossing of the Appalachian Mountains by Englishmen. They reached the New River, a tributary of the Kanawha, and thus were the first to give validity to a British claim to territory drained by waters of the Mississippi River system; although they found evidence that unknown white men had already been in the region which they traversed. Two years later in 1673 James Needham and Gabriel Arthur, also under the sponsorship of Abraham Wood, performed an even more significant exploit by journeying over the Virginia and North Carolina piedmont and across the mountains to a Cherokee Indian town on the Tennessee River or one of its tributaries in the eastern part of the present State of Tennessee. Gabriel Arthur ranged widely with the Cherokee Indians before his return, and may even have seen the Ohio River.

The fur trade was now one of the main factors in the economic and political life of Virginia. In Bacon's rebellion of 1676 it was one of the principal grievances of the frontier farmers that Governor Berkeley was slow in his measures for their defense against the Indians, because he was unwilling to risk interference with his profits in the trade with the redskins. They charged that the "traders at the head of the rivers buy and sell our blood." Before the close of the century Virginia traders had followed the trail of Batts and Fallam to the New River and had gone on to the Ohio itself. The trade with the Cherokees, opened by Needham and Arthur, became increasingly lucrative for several years until South Carolinian competition virtually put an end to the activities of Virginians in this direction. Thus the people of Virginia were early appreciative of the great stakes to be won in the Indian trade of the interior. Traders from two other colonies, New York and South Carolina, opened the contest with the French for the winning of this prize.

ALBANY TRADERS OPEN COMPETITION WITH THE FRENCH

The fur trade of New York was centered almost entirely at Albany or Fort Orange, as the Dutch called it, the frontier outpost on the Hudson. Two factors contributed to the strategic importance of Albany, both in the Indian trade and in the struggle between the English and the French for the mastery of America. One was the geographical factor. Albany controlled the open Mohawk highway to the Great Lakes region and the West. It guarded also the vulnerable route from Canada by way of Lake Champlain, Lake George, and the Hudson River, which the French would have been only too glad to seize, thus separating New England from the other English colonies. But these facts of geographical location would have been of little avail to an inadequately defended post without the other and decisive factor—the proximity of the Iroquois Indians and the continued alliance of the owners of Albany with this shrewd and powerful confederation.

The Iroquois might soon have forgotten Champlain's aid to their enemies and have sought trade relations with the French, but their own interests impelled them to ally themselves first with the Dutch and then with the English at Albany. As early as 1634 Dutch traders were in the Oneida villages. Nine years later the Iroquois made a formal and lasting treaty with the Dutch, and their friendship was transferred to the English when they gained control of New York in 1664. Two considerations led to this choice on the part of the Iroquois. From the English, at least, they received about twice as much for their furs as from the French, an advantage which even less canny natives than the Iroquois could fully appreciate. But of equal importance was the desire of the Iroquois to serve as middlemen in the trade between the Europeans and the Indian tribes further west, since the beaver and other marketable furs of their own vicinity were exhausted at an early date. They soon realized that they could not hope to serve in the capacity of middlemen for the French, whose explorers and traders eagerly pursued their own fortunes in the region of the Great Lakes and the Mississippi Valley. On the other hand, the slower and less favorably located English were glad enough to obtain an Iroquois alliance, even at the price of the accompanying limitation on their own personal activities which the intermediary services of the Iroquois implied.

Thus it was that the Iroquois served as a buffer for Albany and the colony of New York against possible attacks by other western tribes, and more especially against the French who were effectively thwarted in their desire to reach the open sea by the way of the Hudson and divide the English colonies. This alliance explains the long continued but futile efforts of the French to attract the Iroquois to their side by diplomacy or to subdue them by force, the story of which is so dramatically related by Francis Parkman. It is no exaggeration, therefore, to assign to the Iroquois Indians one of the determining roles in American history.

Albany was thus an unremovable thorn in the flesh of the French. Not only did the trade of the Iroquois and their customers further west flow to this post, but even French *coureurs de bois* were not slow to avail themselves of the advantages of trade at Albany, where prices were so much higher and where there were no troublesome regulations. It is true that the middleman status of the Iroquois was irksome to many of the Albany traders, who would have preferred to go out after furs rather than to await their arrival at their trading posts. There were some who yielded to this preference, much to the embarrassment of the officials and in spite of severe penalties. Moreover, an illicit traffic between Albany and Canada gave rise to the exchange of polite notes and attempts at repression on the part of the respective governors. Nevertheless, Albany continued to thrive on a growing trade.

As a rule the Iroquois were firm in their opposition to the desire of Albany traders to enter into direct relations with the western tribes. Occasionally, however, they either yielded or their wishes were not respected. As early as 1680 French deserters were carrying on trade for Albany with the Ottawa

Indians, and there is evidence that British were trading on Lake Erie before 1685. In that year, while La Salle was vainly wandering over the plains of Texas, Captain Johannes Roseboom led an expedition of eleven canoes to distant Mackinac in the very heart of French territory. "The usual trading season at this post had closed," says Dr. Kellogg. "The French officers had scattered to other posts . . . the English merchant made a splendid trade. . . . This first English flotilla on the upper lakes returned triumphantly to Albany, believing that the French monopoly of the Great Lakes was broken." [2] Other Albany traders repeated this exploit in 1686, but Roseboom and an associate were captured on the lakes by the French the following year when they were returning from Mackinac in two parties with canoes laden with furs.

French agents in the West were astonished and alarmed at these raids on their preserve and sent back frantic despatches to Governor Denonville at Quebec. He in turn complained to Governor Dongan of New York of the encroachments, but about the only satisfaction he received was a courteous comment that it seemed strange that all the country over which a Frenchman walked should belong to Canada. French colonial officials also sent doleful memoirs and letters to Paris, predicting the defection or annihilation of their Indian allies and the ruin of their trade, by the English and their Iroquois supporters, unless aid were speedily sent from France. Fortunately for the French the future was not to prove as dark as it seemed. The return of the vigorous and capable Count Frontenac to Quebec as governor, and his active campaigns against the Iroquois during King William's War, effectively checked the trade of Albany in the Great Lakes region.

Even during the war, however, a new direction was given to the Albany trade. A delegation of Shawnee Indians, who apparently at this time had their homes in the present State of Kentucky, appeared at Albany and offered to show the way into the Ohio Valley. The opportunity was eagerly embraced and in 1692 Arnout (or Arent) Viele, a prominent interpreter and trader, set out from Albany with a few Shawnee and

[2] Louise Phelps Kellogg, *The French Régime in Wisconsin* (1925) pp. 230–231. By permission of the State Historical Society of Wisconsin, publishers.

Delaware guides. Proceeding southward into New Jersey and then westward, he followed the Susquehanna and the Alleghany rivers and reached the Ohio. He journeyed down the Ohio as far as the Wabash, opened negotiations with the Miami Indians, thereby causing alarm to Henri de Tonty who still guarded French interests in the Illinois country, and spent nearly two years with the Shawnees. "It was not until the early part of 1694," says Miss Helen Broshar, "that news of the intrepid Dutchman, who two years before had so gallantly plunged into the unknown west, filtered to the seaboard. When rumors began to float into Albany that Viele had survived the perils of the wilderness path and was on his way east, the whole town and province were agog. . . . True to reports, in the summer of 1694 Viele headed a veritable triumphal procession into Pennsylvania. He had departed escorted by a handful of Delaware and Shawnee Indians; he returned with hundreds in his retinue. . . . Rumor is hydra-headed. In this case it whispered into hostile ears on the Mississippi as well as into friendly ears on the Hudson. Indeed, reports of Viele's audacious expedition rumbled with a five years' echo in the French west." [3]

Thus by the close of the seventeenth century French supremacy north of the Ohio River was definitely challenged by ambitious Albanians. Meanwhile, in the southermost British colony of the period an equally formidable and even more active threat was developing, and the French in defense brought to realization La Salle's dream of a colony at the mouth of the Mississippi.

THE WESTWARD PUSH OF SOUTH CAROLINA TRADERS

South Carolina, like New York and more than any other English colony, was favored by geographical conditions conducive to a rapid development of western Indian trade. It is true that no waterways were readily available, and long overland journeys by pack-train were necessitated. But the mountain barrier that discouraged trade adventures from Pennsylvania, Maryland, and Virginia was scarcely formidable

[3] Helen Broshar, "The First Push Westward of the Albany Traders," in *The Mississippi Valley Historical Review,* December, 1920.

and could be avoided entirely by South Carolinians. A comparatively level route could be followed to the Mississippi and beyond. There were powerful Indian tribes to be encountered and won to alliance or subdued, but there was none which aspired to play the role maintained by the Iroquois in the north.

Furthermore, for more than a quarter of a century after the founding of the colony the only European opponents of South Carolina were the Spaniards in Florida. Carolinians proved themselves amply able to serve as buffers for the more northern colonists against these enemies in the south. Encroachments on Spanish territory began at an early date and did not cease until most of the present State of Georgia was cleared of Spaniards. In the years that followed influences and activities emanating from Florida continued to claim the attention of the officials, agents and traders of South Carolina, but they were not effective in checking rapid commercial penetration to the westward.

By 1680 Charlestown traders had established an entrepôt for their western commerce at Savannah Town well up the Savannah River. Soon they were trading with the Cherokee Indians to the northwest on the Tennessee, with the Creeks in what is now western Georgia and Alabama, and with the Chickasaws along the Mississippi. Among the leaders in this early expansion were Henry Woodward, James Moore and Thomas Welch, whose exploits read like fiction. Much of the preliminary labor of exploration and trade was performed by men who are unrecorded. "Beyond the Appalachians," says Verner W. Crane, "in the valleys of the Tennessee and the lower Mississippi and on the broad plains of the Gulf, they were the pioneers of English enterprise, matching in audacity the Canadian *coureurs de bois*. . . . Few traces were left by the traders of their activities, save the trails which their successors followed through many decades. Only now and then did they emerge briefly into the light of history, much as when their caravans chanced to pass from the gloom of the vast southern pine forests into some sunny upland savannah." [4]

[4] Verner W. Crane, *The Southern Frontier, 1670-1732* (1928), pp. 39-40. By permission of the Duke University Press, publishers.

Deerskins took the place of beaver furs in the trade of South Carolinians, because of the scarcity of the latter in the south. The earliest profits, however, were derived from a traffic in Indian slaves, and, in spite of many protests and efforts at suppression, this infamous and cruel commerce continued well into the eighteenth century.

THE RACE FOR THE MOUTH OF THE MISSISSIPPI

Before that century opened, however, Carolina traders were confronted with rivals far more formidable than the Spanish in Florida, and the contest between France and England, already in progress in the north, was joined also on the lower Mississippi. The French were not entirely ignorant of the activities of the Carolinians. Tonty and others warned their government that English traders were on the Tennessee River and that they were endeavoring to gain control of the Mississippi—a consummation that would be fatal to French rule in the West. To forestall this danger the revival of La Salle's project for a French colony at the mouth of the Mississippi was strongly urged.

In fact the closing years of the seventeenth century witnessed the determination of three nations—France, England, and Spain—to seize this strategic location. Francis Nicholson, governor first of Maryland and then of Virginia, was awake to the necessity of preventing the French from gaining control of the Mississippi, and he carried on a correspondence with other colonial governors and with home officials urging action. Governor Joseph Blake of South Carolina was optimistic. He predicted that the success already achieved by the traders of his colony would preclude the French from gaining a foothold. The race for the mouth of the Mississippi, however, was precipitated by a project that originated in England in the brain of a man who never saw America.

This man was Daniel Coxe, a doctor of some note and for many years a court physician. He had a wide range of interests and was inclined to be visionary and over-credulous. He gained the proprietorship of large tracts of land in New Jersey. This possession whetted his appetite. Collecting maps, accounts of travel and all sorts of information and misinformation in regard to America, in 1690 he petitioned the King to grant him a vast stretch of territory west of New York, Pennsylvania, and Virginia. This petition was refused, but soon afterward he came into possession of a rather vague and much disputed title to an even larger area. This included the region between the parallels of 30 degrees and 36 degrees, running from sea to sea, which had been granted to Sir Robert Heath in 1629, under the name of Carolana. To be sure,.a portion of this tract was now owned by the Carolina proprietors. Moreover, much of the territory was claimed by Spain and by France. Even so, the grant was sufficient to stir the ambitions of the eccentric doctor, and he proposed to clinch English possession before France could reenforce her pretensions by settlement in the region discovered by La Salle.

Dr. Coxe's project was greatly furthered by the appearance in 1697 of a mendacious volume, attempting to discredit La Salle's discoveries, written by Father Louis Hennepin, now an exile from France. The writings of the disgruntled friar were professedly dedicated to the promotion of English ambitions in the West, and may even have been stimulated by an English patron of Hennepin. At any rate they stirred public interest in England in the Mississippi question and helped to create a favorable atmosphere for Coxe's schemes. Soon plans were under way for the planting of a colony of Huguenot refugees under English auspices somewhere on the Gulf coast near the Mississippi. In October, 1698, two small ships sailed from London to make a preliminary reconnaissance.

News of Coxe's proposals flew to Paris and aroused the French government to the realization that no time could be lost if disaster to their hopes in America were to be averted. Pierre le Moyne, Sieur de Iberville, who had rendered valiant service for his king against the Hudson's Bay Company in the far north, was chosen to lead an expedition to make good the claim of France to the lower Mississippi Valley. With him went his younger brother, Jean Baptiste le Moyne, Sieur de Bienville. In two vessels, with two hundred soldiers and colonists, Iberville sailed from Brest, also in October, 1698. Toward the end of the following January he attempted to enter the harbor of Pensacola, but found Spanish ships at anchor and a stockade fort in process of erection on the shore. Spain, likewise, had decided to raise her banner in the coveted region, and the Frenchmen were not permitted to land.

Undaunted by this rebuff, Iberville continued westward along the coast. In March, 1699, he entered the Mississippi and explored it for several days. All doubt concerning the identity of the stream was dispelled when Bienville obtained from an Indian a letter which Tonty had left thirteen years before for La Salle, but which, of course, had never been delivered. Iberville, deciding against a post on the Mississippi itself, built Fort Maurepas to the eastward on Biloxi Bay on a site that soon proved to be most ill-chosen, and sailed for France. The Sieur de Sauvole was left in command of a garrison of eighty or ninety men. Shortly after Iberville's departure Bienville, with five men in two canoes, was despatched up the Mississippi. As he was returning, at a bend in the river known ever afterwards as the English Turn, he encountered a British frigate, the *Carolina Galley*, bearing the advance guard of Daniel Coxe's Carolana colonists. Far from being overawed by the superior force of the unwelcome rival, Bienville politely informed Captain Bond of the English vessel that he was intruding and that the French were already in possession. The warning was effective. The ship sailed away and, in spite of the captain's threat to return the following year, its sailing ended the hope of an English colony at the mouth of the Mississippi. The French had won the race.

CHAPTER V

A HALF-CENTURY OF CONFLICT

THE Spanish governor at Pensacola looked upon the infant French colony in Louisiana with displeasure. Spain and France, however, were at peace and the king of the former was the grandson of Louis XIV. Thus, although Spain made a formal protest against the invasion of territory claimed by virtue of the famous papal bull of Alexander VI, the protest was couched in the mildest terms. Louis XIV calmly replied that Louisiana belonged to him and he would hold it; and Iberville wrote a memorial showing that it would be to the advantage of Spain to have the protection of the French against the English who were seeking to obtain possession as far west as the Mississippi. In the years that followed there were occasional acts of hostility and considerable rivalry between the French and the Spanish, but the development of Louisiana was little hindered by Spanish opposition.

SOUTH CAROLINA SEEKS TO CHECKMATE THE FRENCH

Far different was the story of Anglo-French relations. Probably the great mass of the English colonists knew little and cared less for many years about the weak and distant French post on the Gulf, but there were a few who appreciated the significance of Iberville's achievement. Governor Nicholson of Virginia and Governor Bellomont of New York were fully awake to the danger of encirclement by the French working both from Canada and from Louisiana. In South Carolina, however, there was real alarm in official and trading circles. Governor Blake's confidence in the ability of his traders to hold the western country against all comers had received a rude shock. It was clear that active measures must be taken to combat the threat to the Indian trade so audaciously and laboriously built up by the Carolinians. Patriotic ardor to save the West for the English king may have animated some minds, but fear of losing control of sources of wealth was a more general and more potent emotion.

The most spectacular move made by Blake in the effort to checkmate Iberville was in sending a party of traders to the Mississippi by way of the Tennessee River. This was a route virtually unknown to the English. It happened, however, that there was in South Carolina at this time a renegade Frenchman by the name of Jean Coutoure—a man who had seen service under Henri de Tonty. Coutoure was acquainted with the Tennessee and he acted as guide for the party. We know nothing of their journey down the Tennessee, Ohio, and Mississippi, bearing merchandise for trade with the Indians on the latter river and papers claiming the country for the English. We do know that by February, 1700, they had reached the mouth of the Arkansas and that one of them was encountered a few months later by Le Sueur. Iberville knew that English traders were well established in the Chickasaw villages, but he was not prepared for the news of these Carolinians on the river which he hoped to make an exclusively French highway. In his consternation he pictured a horde of British colonists following in the path of these traders and frustrating his ambitious designs. As a matter of fact, he need not to have worried seriously concerning English aggression by way of the Tennessee. This route, for various reasons, never became an important highway for the Carolinians or their fellow colonists. The real contenders against the French for supremacy in the south continued to be those who toiled westward over the long overland trails from Charleston and Savannah Town.

IBERVILLE'S PLANS AND ACTIVITIES

Iberville was a true brother of Frontenac and La Salle in zeal for the cause of his king and in wide-sweeping vision of the possibilities of empire in the New World. Influences and activities emanating from his post at Biloxi and from the new headquarters established in 1702 at Fort Louis on Mobile Bay, soon gave evidence that the French occupation of Louisiana was not a mere purposeless gesture. Pierre Charles Le Sueur, who had spent much time among the Sioux Indians in the 1680's was now in Louisiana, and he was sent on an expedition to his former haunts—thus being one of the first, if not the very first, to navigate the Great River throughout nearly its entire length. He built a short-lived post called Fort L'Huillier on the Blue Earth River in Minnesota and opened trade with the Sioux.

Even more indicative of Iberville's grasp of the essential strategy of extending French dominion were his schemes to combat the English. Calling Henri de Tonty down from the Illinois country, he launched a movement to gain the alliance of the powerful Choctaw tribe and to detach the Chickasaws, Creeks, and other tribes from their trading relations with the South Carolinians. The plan was temporarily successful, and the Choctaws, especially, were won to a friendship with the French which they tended to retain during the long period of rivalry which followed. Iberville also outlined a remarkable, although rather impractical, project for the re-arrangement of a large number of the tribes of the Mississippi Valley with a view to using them for a concerted attack on the English colonies. He approved of a proposal for the union of the French and the Spanish to destroy Carolina, and he looked forward to a not distant time when the French with their Indian allies could carry the conquest to Virginia, Maryland, and even to New York.

This program had too many elements of the fantastic to succeed—too many "ifs" were involved. Nevertheless, it illustrates the restless vigor and the vaulting ambition of the man who founded Louisiana, and makes it interesting to speculate as to what might have happened if he had lived to attempt its consummation. Iberville died in 1706. His younger brother, Bienville, succeeded him as governor, and, with some interruptions, furnished effective and devoted leadership to Louisiana throughout a period of forty years.

ANGLO-FRENCH RIVALRY IN THE SOUTH

The South Carolinians may not have known of all Iberville's designs, but they were well aware of his success as a negotiator among the Indians. Though thoroughly alarmed, they were of no mind to relinquish their own ascendancy over the natives living between them and the Mississippi. Consequently the struggle between the English and the French was long and bitter, with occasional attention given by both, but principally by the former, to their Spanish neighbors in Florida. The War of the Spanish Succession, known in American history as Queen Anne's War, from 1702 to 1713, gave the contestants free rein to indulge their hostility, but the peace of Utrecht was followed by little change in the activities of the rivals in the competition for the Indian trade. The details cannot be enumerated here. It is a story of forest diplomacy, of the instigation of tribe to warfare against tribe and against the white enemy, a story of Europeans playing a vast game of chess in which the red men were moved or sacrificed as readily as pawns when necessary to the winning of the game. Bienville exhibited all the Frenchman's characteristic talent in dealing with Indians, but the English offered better and cheaper goods, and they paid well for captives taken in inter-tribal warfare, although the French were not wholly guiltless of an Indian slave-trade.

Among the South Carolinians no names were better known to the French and to the Indians far to the west than Thomas Nairne and Price Hughes. These men were adepts in the politics and intrigues of the wilderness, and they had schemes, far in advance of the possibility of success in their day, for the establishment of an English colony on the Mississippi to break the connection between Louisiana and Canada. George Chicken was equally well known among the Cherokees, and the astonishing success of the eccentric Sir Alexander Cuming among these same Indians might well be made the theme of a comic opera. One notable chapter in the story centers about the Creek chieftain known to the English as the Emperor Brims, who rivalled any European in America in political sagacity, and maintained for his nation a neutrality which gave the Creeks the balance of power in the inter-colonial struggles of their white neighbors.

Expansion of French Trade in Louisiana

Through these years of rivalry the French colony of Louisiana grew slowly and experienced many vicissitudes. The venture was expensive and returned no profits to the king's coffers. Accordingly, in 1712, a monopoly of the trade of the entire lower Mississippi Valley was granted to Antoine Crozat and with it responsibility for the government and welfare of the colony. Five years later he surrendered his patent, and the colony passed under the control of "The Company of the West" or "Mississippi Company" of the notorious John Law. In 1720 this episode ended with the bursting of the Mississippi Bubble, although the company remained in control for several years. Meanwhile, New Orleans was laid out in 1718 and became the capital in 1722. Agricultural settlements spread along the lower course of the Mississippi and military posts were established further up the stream and in the Indian country to the eastward. Bloody wars with the Natchez Indians in 1716 and 1729 put the strength of the colony to a severe test. By 1731, when royal government was restored, Louisiana had a population of about five thousand whites and two thousand negro slaves.

The remarkable vigor of the little colony was shown in its determined contest with South Carolina. It was exhibited no less in a series of expeditions to the west and northwest. The French flair for exploration had by no means spent itself. Furthermore, the imaginations of Louisiana's leaders were intrigued by tales of the wealth of Spanish mines to the westward and the possibilities of profit to be gained in trade with the inland Spanish outposts.

Canadian Frenchmen already knew something of the country west of the Mississippi, and only the most credulous believed the Munchausen-like tales of the imposters Baron La Hontan, with his fabled "Riviere Longue," and Mathieu Sagean. Within a few years after the death of La Salle a Canadian is said to have reached the Rio Grande, and by the close of the seventeenth century traders from Canada were trafficking with the Missouri and Osage Indians. "In 1703," says Parkman, "twenty Canadians tried to find their way from the Illinois to

New Mexico, in hope of opening trade with the Spaniards and discovering mines. In 1704 we find it reported that more than a hundred Canadians are scattered in small parties along the Mississippi and the Missouri; and in 1705 one Laurain appeared at the Illinois, declaring that he had been high up the Missouri and had visited many tribes on its borders. A few months later, two Canadians told Bienville a similar story."

Louisiana was of course much more favorably located than Canada for reconnaissances into Spanish territory and ventures up the western affluents of the Mississippi. In 1708 an unheeded proposal was made for an expedition of one hundred men to explore the Missouri. A similar scheme projected nine years later reveals the vagueness of the geographical knowledge of its promoter and the persistence of the hope of finding a passage to the Pacific. By means of this plan, he said, "not only may we find the mines worked by the Spaniards, but also discover the great river that is said to rise in the mountains where the Missouri has its source, and is believed to flow to the Western Sea." Meanwhile less ambitious exploits were being achieved by men from Louisiana. By 1712 there were settlers around the salt wells in Missouri, and there was a period of vigorous exploration and trade in the trans-Mississippi west, from the Gulf of Mexico to Nebraska. French traders also visited the tribes of eastern and northern Texas, and even reached the Spanish settlements.

In 1713 Louis Juchereau de St. Denis established a post at Natchitoches on the Red River and in the years immediately following made the expeditions to the Rio Grande region which so alarmed the Spaniards and caused them to occupy eastern Texas permanently. Between 1719 and 1724 La Harpe, Du Tisné, and Bourgmont led parties which explored the Red, Arkansas, Missouri, Osage, and other western rivers and visited many Indian tribes well known in the history of the West— among them the Pawnees, Otos, Osages, Iowas and Missouris. Then for fifteen years there was a lull in exploration, but Louisiana traders continued to extend the area of their operations among the tribes in eastern and northern Texas. New Mexico had for French adventurers and merchants the same attraction that later made the Santa Fé Trail one of America's

highways of romance.   Only occasional traders realized this
alluring goal, however, for the Spanish policy was one of jealous exclusion, and fierce Indian tribes like the Apaches and the
Comanches barred the way through their territories.   The Mal-
let brothers made themselves famous when, in 1739, they made

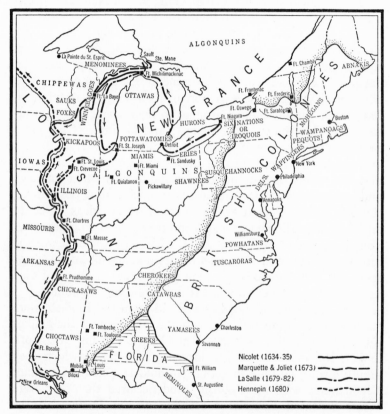

II. THE WEST UNDER FRENCH RULE, 1660-1750

a circuitous detour by way of the Missouri and Platte rivers
and thence across Nebraska, Kansas, and Colorado to Santa
Fé, where they remained for nine months.   Thus by the middle
of the eighteenth century explorers and traders from Louisiana,
together with others from Canada, made the Mississippi Valley
south of the Mandan villages on the Missouri and south of the

Ohio almost as well known to Frenchman as the region of the Great Lakes with which they had been familiar for a century.

Rivalry on the Northern Frontier

Let us now see what was happening on the New York frontier, where the English with their Iroquois allies confronted the French of Canada. As the eighteenth century opened New York was governed by the Earl of Bellomont, one of the few Englishmen of his day with sufficient vision to appreciate the dangers of encirclement by the French. He urged cooperative effort on the part of the governors of New York, Pennsylvania, Maryland, Virginia, and Carolina, to push trade and gain alliances among the western Indians; and his interest lay more in combating the French plans of empire than in trade for its own sake. He proposed that duties be removed from beaver and other skins, both in the colonies and in the mother country; and he had plans for the establishment of a trading post among the Iroquois. Unfortunately none of these ideas came to fruition. The Albany merchants and traders had no interest beyond their immediate profits and the home government was too much occupied with European affairs and too ill-informed, or indifferent, to pay much attention to America. Bellomont died in 1701 and his successors lacked his foresight and ability.

The Iroquois, lacking any real aid from the English, were much weakened by warfare with the French and their allies during King William's War. Peter Wraxall in his New York Indian Records tells of a conference in 1700 at which they stoutly professed their intention "to hold fast on the Covenant Chain made with the English," and declared that they were "from repeated Experience sensible of the Designs of the French & of their false & artful Instigations." And yet so strong was the influence of a number of Jesuit priests and other French agents among the Iroquois, and so weary were the confederated tribes of warfare with the Canadians, that within a month after this conference they made a treaty of peace with De Callières, Count Frontenac's successor. In the following year, 1701, this treaty was confirmed in the presence of representatives of numerous western tribes who were included in the peace. Another master-stroke of the French in this same year was the founding of the strategic post at Detroit by La Mothe de Cadillac.

The hold of the English on the Iroquois seemed to be slipping. And yet, strangely enough, it was in this same year 1701 that Lieutenant Governor Nanfan of New York secured from these Indians a "deed" in which, as reported by Wraxall, they agreed to "give & render up all that Land where the Bever hunting is which we won with the Sword 80-years ago & pray that He (the King) may be our Protector & Defender there."[1] This transaction involved an immense area said to extend as far west as the site of Chicago.

The peace between the Iroquois and the French had important effects during Queen Anne's War. New England was compelled to bear the brunt of the raids by the French and their savage auxiliaries, while New York, at least during the early years of the conflict, was unmolested. The French hesitated to invade New York for fear of stirring up the Iroquois. New Yorkers and particularly the Albany traders were well content to enjoy the immunity of neutrality, in spite of the sufferings of their brethren to the eastward. Trade with the French and their Indians was too profitable to be sacrificed by engaging in the war. The greed of the fur merchants not only caused them to mistreat many of the Indians who came to Albany, but deadened them to all concern for the wider issues of empire in America. Local politics also paralyzed any effective action.

It was not until 1720 that New York had another governor with Bellomont's vision and patriotic aggressiveness. In that year William Burnet assumed the duties of the office, and he immediately evinced his grasp of the relation of the Indian trade to the prospects of the French and the English for the control of America. He waged a long and determined, but in the end unsuccessful, fight to stop the trade that was being conducted between Albany and Canada. This trade exasperated the Iroquois, who regarded it as evidence of bad faith with them. But of even greater importance was the effect on the

---

[1] The quotations from Wraxall in this and the preceding paragraph are from Charles H. McIlwain (ed.) *Peter Wraxall's Abridgment of the Indian affairs* (1915), pp. 33, 40. By permission of the Harvard University Press, publishers.

fortunes of the French, for it enabled them to maintain and extend their trade and alliances with the far Indians. There were times when Albany was virtually the only source from which the French could secure supplies for their Indian trade; and the prices of these supplies were lower and the quality better than of those obtained from the mother country. Governor Burnet had substantial grounds for his prediction that, if this trade were suppressed, "Montreal will sink to nothing which now flourishes by its Trade with Albany." During the period when the suppressive acts of the New York Assembly were in force, the trade of the far Indians with Albany greatly increased. Peter Wraxall expressed his belief that "if proper methods had been taken to fix & extend this Channel of Trade . . . the French might have been drove back to their proper limits in Canada & have been ever rendered incapable of disturbing the British Settlements in N. America." [2] But powerful and influential merchants were engaged in the Canadian trade, and they eventually secured the disallowance of the New York laws by the home government. It is interesting to speculate on the extent to which American history might have been changed if Burnet's policy had been enforced.

In another of his enterprises Governor Burnet succeeded, with results that were far-reaching. This was the building, about 1726, of a fortified trading post at Oswego on the southern shore of Lake Ontario near the eastern end. Burnet was obliged to finance this project largely out of his own pocket and he was never fully repaid, although New York later spent considerable money in maintaining the post. Although the French erected Fort Niagara, near the falls, at about the same time, Oswego played a strategic role in the Indian trade and in the fortunes of the two European combatants from the time of its founding until the contest was ended in the Seven Year's War. No other outpost of the English was so much hated and feared by the French.

[2] Charles H. McIlwain (ed.) *Peter Wraxall's Abridgment of the Indian Affairs* (1915), pp. lxvii, 145. By permission of the Harvard University Press, publishers.

THE FRENCH AND THE FOX WARS

While the events which have just been sketched were transpiring in the south and in New York and vicinity, the region of the Great Lakes and the upper Mississippi remained in the possession of the French without threat from other Europeans. Other disturbances, however, checked the exploitation of this imperial domain secured for France by the earlier activities of La Salle, Tonty, Perrot, Du Luth, and the other explorers, agents, traders and *coureurs de bois*. In 1700 it seemed as though all the heroic exploits of these men had been in vain. The great quantities of furs that had poured into Montreal had glutted the market to an alarming extent. Moreover, the Jesuits and other groups opposed to western trade expansion had gained the ear of the king. The upshot was an edict issued in 1696 calling for the evacuation of the far western posts and the revocation of all licenses to trade. The only exception was Henri de Tonty who was permitted to remain on the Illinois River with greatly limited privileges. To quote the words of Dr. Kellogg: "The upper country was deserted. A few *coureurs de bois* yet lingered in the western villages; here and there a black-robe missionary was seen flitting through the woods to the cabin of some neophyte; but the enterprising Frenchmen of the seventeenth century, the men who explored the wilderness, mapped out empires, formed alliances with the tribesmen, opened routes of commerce, were gone. All was silence and stagnation in the Northwest." [3]

It was one thing to issue an edict, however, and another to enforce it, for any length of time. The lure of the Indian trade was as strong as ever, and soon an increasing number of illegal traders returned to the West and especially to the area around Green Bay. Here they encountered the hostility of the strong and warlike Fox Indians, who had already destroyed Le Sueur's Fort L' Huillier on the Blue Earth River. In time the French authorities were obliged to take cognizance of this hostility and there ensued a series of campaigns known as the First Fox War, ending in 1716 with an inconclusive truce. By

[3] Louise Phelps Kellogg, *The French Régime in Wisconsin* (1925) p. 267. By permission of the State Historical Society of Wisconsin, publishers.

this time it had become evident to the officials in Canada that
the West could not be safely abandoned to the priests and unregulated traders. This conclusion, together with various other
circumstances, caused a reversal of policy. All the important
western posts were reoccupied and many new ones were built.

A new difficulty now appeared in the jealousy which arose
between the two French colonies of Canada and Louisiana.
Traders from the two colonies met in the upper Mississippi
Valley and friction was unavoidable. The older colony resented competition in the realm where its monopoly had previously been virtually undisturbed, but the Great River was
a natural highway to Louisiana. In 1718 the Illinois country
was included in Louisiana and its trade became the possession of John Law and his Company of the West. The jurisdiction of Louisiana remained the same after the restoration
of royal government in 1731, although the boundary separating
the Illinois country from the territory belonging to Canada
was never definitely settled.

The Canadian colony's reoccupation of the West was not
achieved without another struggle with the Fox Indians
whose home was in the Wisconsin country. A fox chieftain,
apparently Kiala, whom Dr. Kellogg calls "a precursor of
Pontiac and Tecumseh," worked tirelessly and quietly to
build up a great conspiracy against the French, "stretching
all the way from the Abenaki of the East, embracing the
Iroquois on Lake Ontario, and extending to the Sioux at the
northwest and the Missouri and Oto tribes to the southwest."
He was not able to hold all the allies together, but in the
years between 1727 and 1740 all the resources of the French
were taxed to the utmost to save their western empire from
ruin at the hands of the barbarians fighting for their own
lives and independence. Battles were fought over a wide
stretch of country from the Wabash to the Des Moines River
west of the Mississippi, and many valiant Frenchman lost
their lives in this second Fox War. In the end the Indians
were completely humbled, but their fierce resistance may
well be credited with helping to determine the destiny of
America. "Because of this long series of wars," says Dr.
Kellogg, "the western trade routes were shifted to the east-

ward," and the French came into conflict with English traders. "Had the Fox Indians proved docile to French dictation, French sovereignty in the West might never have been shaken. . . . The resistance of one fierce, barbarous people, secretly dreaded yet admired by the other tribes, undermined French influence in the upper Mississippi valley, and hastened the changes which brought it to an end." [4]

Search for the River of the West

It was during the progress of the second Fox War that the far West witnessed the last notable display of that remarkable energy and endurance which distinguishes the record of French exploration and fur trade in America. Pierre Gaultier de Varennes, Sieur de le Vérendrye, was commandant at a small post on Lake Nipigon, north of Lake Superior. Here his imagination was fired by Indian tales of a water route from Lake Superior by rivers and a chain of lakes, by means of which the western ocean might be reached. Visions of forestalling the British traders from Hudson's Bay and of discovering the long-sought "river of the west," led Vérendrye to seek government aid for a project of exploration and occupation of this most desirable route. He was given encouragement by Governor Beauharnois of New France, although no more substantial official assistance was forthcoming than a monopoly of the fur trade of the region to be discovered. In 1731 Vérendrye set out on his expedition with a small party which included his three eldest sons and a nephew. Within ten years he had built a chain of six forts, known as the "Post of the Western Sea," stretching from Rainy Lake to the mouth of the Saskatchewan. In 1738 he visited the Mandan Indians on the upper Missouri. Four years later his son, Pierre, led a party westward and on New Year's Day, 1743, came in sight of the Bighorn Mountains. No lasting success crowned all this activity, but the name of Vérendrye deserves a worthy place in the list of the many Frenchmen who made courageous pageantry in the wide stretches of the West.

[4] The quotations in this paragraph are from Louise Phelps Kellogg, *The French Régime in Wisconsin* (1925). By permission of the State Historical Society of Wisconsin, publishers.

CHAPTER VI

THE FRONTIER MOVES TO THE MOUNTAINS

AFTER a century of brilliant achievement in the wide expanses in the interior of the continent it might well have seemed to Frenchmen that they had effectively confined the stay-at-home English colonists to their narrow strip of territory along the Atlantic coast. But such a belief was based on a fatal misapprehension of the character and accumulating power of their opponents. Content to let their sea-to-sea charters stand as evidence of their country's claim in the New World, the English took more than one hundred years to occupy the land between the Atlantic and the Appalachian Mountains. And yet when they were ready and desirous to go beyond the mountains there could be no serious doubt of their ability to do so. The French scattered trading posts and emblems of empire far and wide in the interior, but the English advance, though slow, was rooted deep in the soil every step of the way. It was the frontiersmen of English, or Scotch-Irish, or German stock, and not the French fur traders or missionaries, who determined the destiny of America.

As the middle of the eighteenth century approached the stage was being set for the final, decisive struggle between the French and the English for the possession of the West. In order to understand the setting, as well as the conditions which foredoomed the outcome, it is necessary to sketch the first chapter of the epic story of the westward movement.

THE FIRST AMERICAN FRONTIER

The term frontier, as used in America, is one that scarcely needs definition. It is sometimes used to indicate a line marking the fringe of white settlements that was constantly moving westward. It is more satisfactory to think of the frontier as the region where, at any given time, there was taking place the process of transforming the wilderness into a settled country. It is not sufficient, however, to regard this frontier merely as a geographical line or region. Its true significance lies mainly in the fact that life on the frontier made it necessary for the settlers to adjust themselves to a primitive environment, and gave them the opportunity to test their attitudes, customs, and institutions in a newly established society. Finally, the frontier was also significant in that it was synonymous with a state of mind, an attitude toward life, in which hope and optimism were dominant. Illustrations of these various meanings of the term frontier will appear in the later pages of this book.

The first frontier in America was found in Jamestown and Plymouth and Salem and in the other English settlements which one after another were planted on the Atlantic coast. With these we cannot stop. These colonists encountered all the perils and hardships of the wilderness. They suffered from starvation and disease and Indian attacks, but the survivors held on with remarkable vitality and reenforcements soon brought security. These settlements in reality constituted an English, rather than an American frontier, and in the course of years they lost most of their frontier characteristics. But in a short time after their founding there was a swarming from coastal towns into the interior, and it was in these inland outposts and clearings that there early appeared the unmistakable features that distinguished the American frontier from that day until the frontier was only a memory. Only a brief summary of this expansion from the seacoast to the mountains can be given here.

THE EXTENSION OF THE NEW ENGLAND FRONTIER

The first inland settlement in New England was at Concord, founded in the year 1635. Even before this time adventurous John Oldham of the Plymouth colony had been on the Connecticut River, where he established a trading post and from whence he brought back glowing accounts of the country. As a result, three groups of settlers, one led by Pastor Thomas Hooker, of Cambridge, were given permission to remove to this alluring valley. In 1635 and 1636 these pioneers, moving as organized churches and driving their cattle before them, pushed their way westward for two weeks "through swamp and forest, following Indian trails," until they reached the Connecticut, where they founded Weathersfield, Hartford, and Winsor. Springfield, still further north, was begun the latter year by a congregation from Roxbury. Within another year danger that these exposed settlements might be wiped out by hostile red men was temporarily removed by the bloody and thorough extermination of the Pequots.

At the outbreak of King Philip's War, in 1675, there was a broad belt of settlement extending well up the Connecticut valley, with Deerfield and Northfield as the extreme outposts in the northern part of Massachusetts, and Brookfield to the eastward. Settled areas fringed the coast from the Hudson to Brunswick in Maine, and widened out to include towns dotting much of Rhode Island and the eastern third of Massachusetts. "Even in so-called villages the houses were far apart," says Parkman, "because, except on the seashore, the people lived by farming. Such as were able to do so fenced their dwellings with palisades, or built them of solid timber, with loopholes, a projecting upper story like a block house, and sometimes a flanker at one or more of the corners. In the more considerable settlements the largest of the fortified houses were occupied in time of danger by armed men and served as a place of refuge for the neighbors."

Even the strongest of these fortifications in many cases proved insufficient to the defense of the settlements in the determined Indian uprising of 1675-6, led by King Philip, son of Massasoit, sachem of the Wampanoags. Scarcely a New England outpost escaped the fury of the Indians. Most of them were burned or deserted and the others were long in recovering from the blow. Then, within little more than a decade after the subjugation of Philip and his followers, there began the first of the long series of struggles between the French and the English. The New England frontier lay open to the forays of the French and their Indian allies from the north. During

King William's War (1689-1697) and during Queen Anne's War which followed with only a brief interruption, and especially in the dead of winter, the terrible Indian war whoop struck sudden terror to the settlers along the Connecticut and in other isolated sections.   Burned cabins and dead and mutilated bodies were many times left to mark the sites of thriving settlements, while the survivors were dispersed or led captives over the long trails to Canada.

No other frontier in America ever advanced in the face of such long continued peril.   Here the Indians were not merely indulging in their natural passion for warfare or expressing their hatred for the invaders of their hunting grounds, they were tools in the hands of leaders representing another nation of white men whose real object was not the scalps of a few hapless settlers, but the possession of a continent.   It speaks volumes for the hardihood, the courage, and the persistent land hunger of the New England pioneers that by 1754 the frontier had pushed its way well into Vermont, New Hampshire, and Maine.   There were settlements in most of the area south of the northern border of Massachusetts, including the valley of the Housatonic; and New Englanders had ventured into southeastern New York and into New Jersey.   No inconsiderable part of this pioneering was done by Scotch-Irish, who began to come to New England by the shipload about 1714.   Their continued arrival alarmed the authorities, who were only too glad to shunt them off to the frontier, where they would not contaminate Puritans and where they could serve as buffers against the Indians.

HINDRANCES TO FRONTIER EXPANSION IN NEW YORK

The frontier in New York remained largely a fur traders' frontier until after the French and Indian War.   The reasons for the lack of expansive power in this colony lay partly in the geographical obstacles afforded by the Catskills and the Adirondacks, partly in the jealousy of the neighboring Iroquois, and exposure to French attack, but chiefly in the unenlightened land system.   Most of the accessible land was included in large manorial estates.   Professor Turner has pointed out that it "was not simply that the grants were extensive, but that the policy of the proprietors favored the leasing rather than the sale of the lands—frequently also of the stock, and taking payment in shares. It followed that settlers preferred to go to frontiers where a more liberal land policy prevailed."

The only notable attempt to form agricultural settlements in New York during the first half of the eighteenth century was that made by Germans from the Palatinate, fleeing from the desolation of their war-ridden land, from religious persecution, and from the oppression of petty tyrants. In 1710 fully three thousand of these unhappy people landed in New York and a large number of them, with high hopes and thankful hearts, accepted the offer of Governor Hunter to settle on both sides of the Hudson near Saugerties. Soon they found that, instead of being free farmers, they were virtual serfs, bound to the impossible task of producing naval stores of tar and pitch. A few years later many of them left the Hudson and, in spite of terrible hardships, made homes for themselves along the Schoharie River. Even here conditions proved unendurably burdensome and again there was an exodus. Some of the Palatines went far up the Mohawk and settled the German Flats, while many others migrated to Pennsylvania.

Germans and Scotch-Irish on the Pennsylvania Frontier

It was in the region south of New York—in Pennsylvania, Virginia, and the Carolinas—that the colonial frontier exhibited the most virile and aggressive expansion. It was here that there appeared the characteristics that were most typical of the American frontier. It was here also that the determined westward push of pioneer farmers presented the most potent threat to the ambitions of the French. In a large way the frontier in these colonies was a unit, because of the migrations down the valleys of the Appalachian system from Pennsylvania to the Carolinas. On the other hand, each of the colonies made its own peculiar contribution to frontier development and had its own local problems.

Pennsylvania was a late addition to the English colonies, but it grew rapidly in population. It offered religious toleration and its land policy was liberal.   By 1686, five years after the granting of the charter, Pennsylvania traders were so active and so successful along the northern border as to bring an alarmed protest from the New York authorities.   Trade continued to be a prominent and profitable industry, but sturdy farmers crowded close on the heels of the fur traders and rapidly pushed the frontier toward the mountains.   Up the Delaware, the Lehigh, the Schuylkill, and the Susquehanna they went and into the intervening territory.   By 1750 the frontier line ran close to the foot of the mountains from Easton and Bethlehem, through Reading, Harrisburg, Carlisle, and Shippensburg to the Maryland border; while the more adventurous were spying out the land and marking off claims in the Juniata and other upland valleys.

This westward advance was in part the work of the Quakers and other English settlers of Pennsylvania, especially in the eastern end of the colony.   But in the task of real pioneering they were far outdistanced by the multitudes of German and Scotch-Irish immigrants who poured into the colony and constituted the cutting edge of the frontier.   Germans, responding eagerly to Penn's glowing prospectuses of his colony, began to enter Pennsylvania in small numbers as early as 1683 and settle around Philadelphia.   The movement assumed much larger proportions in the second decade of the eighteenth century and each year thousands of redemptioners from the Palatinate and southwestern Germany, with a mingling of Swiss Mennonites, came to the Quaker colony.   By this time most of the land in the eastern section was either occupied or held at prices beyond the means of impoverished immigrants.   Besides, the Quakers looked with growing displeasure upon this steady influx, which is estimated to have brought from seventy-five to eighty thousand Germans, alien in language and clannish in social life, into Pennsylvania between 1710 and 1740.   The frontier, with its cheap land, was the region for settlement best suited to the necessities of the newcomers and most agreeable to the Quakers.   Thus it was that the "Pennsylvania Dutch" settlements were founded to the northward as far as the Lehigh and to the westward around Lancaster and on beyond the Susquehanna in the modern counties of York, Adams, and Cumberland.   In the course of time many of these German pioneers were ready to participate in leading the way southward into the piedmont and mountain regions of Virginia and the Carolinas.

At least equally as hardy as the Germans and certainly more aggressive were the Scotch-Irish, a people long experienced in fighting for their liberties against political and religious oppression, and accustomed to the pinch of privation. Every English colony in America received accessions of these immigrants from Ulster, but Pennsylvania was the destination of the largest numbers. Here, as elsewhere, the Scotch-Irish found their way rapidly to the frontier. The Quakers were especially alarmed in the decade from about 1720 to 1730 when they saw themselves threatened by what seemed a veritable inundation of these "bold and indigent strangers," as Logan called them, and were highly pleased to have them move westward. The Scotch-Irish were widely scattered over the colony, but their strongest settlements were in the south along the Indian traders' trail from Lancaster to Bedford and in the region disputed with Maryland. Even on the frontier they gave cause for anxiety. They encroached on Indian lands and they paid little attention to securing legal title to their claims, saying that Pennsylvania had advertised for colonists and that "it was against the laws of God and nature that so much land should be idle while so many christians wanted it to work on and to raise their bread." They were real "squatters" of the type that was to play a leading role in the westward march across the continent. Soon we shall see them moving southward into Virginia and the Carolinas, and later pioneering the way across the mountains into Kentucky and Tennessee.

FRONTIER EXPANSION IN VIRGINIA

Frontier expansion in Virginia was the work of two streams of settlers: one which pushed westward from the tidewater region, and the other which flowed southward along the mountain troughs from Pennsylvania. By 1700 Virginia was well occupied as far west as the "fall line" of the rivers flowing into the Atlantic. This line, which was marked by falls which blocked further navigation, passed in a general way from the site of Washington through Richmond and on to Raleigh, North Carolina, and Columbia, South Carolina. As early as 1645 provision was made for the erection of forts along this frontier line and sixteen years later mounted rangers were added to the system of defense. Then, in 1701, the assembly decided to encourage settlements above the fall line, and offered liberal terms to any "warlike christian man" who would settle in "co-habitations" or societies, provided he would live permanently on his two-hundred-acre tract and equip himself for his own defense.

Glowing reports of the rich soil, varied resources, and healthful climate of the upland country reenforced the effort of official encouragement. "It was not long," wrote Professor Turner, "before cattle raisers from the older settlements, learning from the traders of the fertile plains and pea-vine pastures of this land, followed the fur-traders and erected scattered 'cow-pens' or ranches beyond the line of plantations in the Piedmont. Even at the close of the seventeenth century, herds of wild horses and cattle ranged at the outskirts of the Virginia settlements, and were hunted by the planters, driven into pens, and branded somewhat after the manner of the later ranching on the Great Plains. Now the cow-drovers and the cow-pens began to enter the uplands."

The coming of Alexander Spottswood as governor of Virginia in 1710 opened an era of active interest in the frontier and its expansion. No other English governor in America ever exhibited greater zeal than Spottswood in proposals for the defense of his colony's sea-to-sea claims against the encroachments of the French. Numerous letters testify to his concern in this matter and to his untiring efforts to gain accurate information regarding the land and the international situation beyond the mountains. To his patriotic ardor there was added a full appreciation of the opportunities for personal aggrandizement in the upland country. Thus every motive was present to incline Governor Spottswood toward any measure that would draw settlers into the Virginia hinterland.

The famous expedition of Spottswood and his "Knights of the Golden Horseshoe" across the Blue Ridge to the waters of the Shenandoah River in the late summer of 1716 was probably among the least significant of the governor's activities, but it constituted pageantry such as the English in America seldom performed. "We came to the very head spring of the James River where it runs no bigger than a man's arm, from under a large stone," reads the journal of this joyous picnic excursion. "We drank King George's health, and all the Royal Family's, at the very top of the Appalachian mountains." At the Shenandoah River it was decided to turn back. The hard stones of the region resisted all efforts to inscribe an enduring memorial of the exploit, but Spottswood "buried a bottle and a paper inclosed, on which he writ that he took possession of this place in the name and for King George the First of England." Then, before the party turned homeward, there was a dinner, the firing of salutes, and the drinking of an amazing variety of wines and other liquors to the health of the King, the royal family and the governor, and in mutual congratulation.

During the first quarter of the eighteenth century the occupation of the region between the fall line and the Blue Ridge was in full swing. As the tidewater section came more and more into the possession of large plantation owners, the small farmers moved into the interior. A law of 1723 gave each settler the right to one thousand acres of land, with liberal exemption from quit-rents. Before 1750 the same process was being repeated in the Shenandoah Valley, which was easily accessible through the low passes. Men like Robert Beverley, Benjamin Borden, and Lord Fairfax also obtained grants to hundreds of thousands of acres in the beautiful Valley of Virginia. The pioneering in this valley, however, was mainly the work of Germans and Scotch-Irish moving southward from Pennsylvania.

The first important settlement west of the Blue Ridge was made in 1732, when Joist Hite came from Pennsylvania with sixteen families and made a clearing near the site of Winchester. "The tide of Scotch-Irish immigration to the Valley commenced in 1738 and was at its height from 1740 to 1745," says C. E. Kemper. "They came chiefly from Chester, Lancaster, and adjacent counties in the southeastern part of Pennsylvania, and the country around Staunton was well settled by the year 1745. . . . They came on horse-back and their effects were brought on pack-horses.   By the year 1750, the Valley from Harper's Ferry to Roanoke was a settled pioneer country and settlers were still coming, chiefly from Pennsylvania, and it was a land of busy endeavor.   They were building houses and barns; opening roads; building mills and churches; and establishing schools to give their children at least a common school education."   By the mid-century a few adventurous backwoodsmen had built their cabins on the Cheat, the Green-brier, the Holston, and the New rivers, all westward-flowing streams.

Early Frontier Settlements in the Carolinas

The settlement of the piedmont and mountain regions in the Carolinas was accomplished in much the same manner as in Virginia, but it was longer delayed.   Even the lowlands in North Carolina long retained frontier characteristics, because they were sought by the overflow of indigent and dissatisfied farmers from Virginia.   The Tuscarora war of 1711 and the Yamassee uprising four years later were the culminations of troubles that had long made the frontier unsafe for settlers. The belt of pine barrens in the Carolinas paralleling the fall line also discouraged settlers from moving westward.   Thus, although as we have seen, South Carolinians were trading with the Indians as far west as the Mississippi by 1700, the pied-mont of the Carolinas was almost unoccupied except by the owners of scattered cow-pens as late as 1730.

As in Virginia, most of the first settlements in the up-land back country of the Carolinas were made by Scotch-Irish, Germans, and others coming from the north, and few, if any, of these hardy pioneers appeared before 1740.   The Scotch-Irish thereafter made their way into the region between the Yadkin and Catawba and by 1750 had penetrated into western South Carolina.   The vanguard of the German pio-neers came to North Carolina in 1745, but Bernheim tells us that they did not begin to come in large numbers until about 1750.   They moved in wagons in typical pioneer fashion, with their cattle and hogs and sheep driven before them.   They arrived, Bernheim says, "continuously for a number of years in succession, usually leaving home in the fall season, after all the harvesting was over and the proceeds of the year's labor could be disposed of; they arrived at their places of settlement just before the commencement of the winter season."

The Frontier Line in 1750

Thus, by 1750, the colonial frontier had pushed far into the interior in New England, there was a tongue of settlement up the Mohawk in New York, and from Pennsylvania southward clearings and cabins had appeared close up against the mountain barrier, through which the traders had for years known the passes. "A new society had been established," says Professor Turner, "differing in essentials from the colonial society of the coast. It was a democratic self-sufficing, primitive agricultural society, in which individualism was more pronounced than the community life of the lowlands. . . . It was a region of hard work and poverty, not of wealth and leisure." Especially in the upland country from Pennsylvania to Georgia did the frontier population take on the characteristics, qualities, and viewpoints that mark the true American frontiersmen. We cannot stop at this point to examine the effects of ethnic and colonial intermixture, similarity of geographical environment, and isolation. But this brief summary of frontier expansion will serve to show why it was that a decisive contest for the possession of America could not be long delayed. The westward march of the American pioneers had begun; and people who had accomplished so much and learned so much from the experience were not likely to be easily turned back when once it became their purpose to cross the mountain ranges.

CHAPTER VII

FRANCE LOSES AN EMPIRE

"THE unwarrantable Proceedings of the French in the West Indies, and North America, since the Conclusion of the Treaty of Aix-la-Chapelle, and the Usurpations and Encroachments made by them upon our Territories, and the Settlements of Our Subjects in those Parts," were the opening words of justification used by King George II of England in May, 1756, in making formal declaration of a war against France, which had in reality been in progress for two years. He went on to state more specifically that "the unjustifiable Practices of the French Governors, and of the Officers acting under their Authority, were still carried on, till, at length, in the Month of April, 1754, they broke out in open Acts of Hostility, when in Time of Profound Peace, without any Declaration of War, and without any previous Notice given, or Application made, a Body of French Forces, under the Command of an Officer bearing the French King's Commission, attacked in a hostile Manner, and possessed themselves of the English Fort on the Ohio in North America." Three weeks later Louis XV proclaimed his reasons for war. "It is notorious to all Europe," he said, "that the King of England made an attack in 1754 on the King's Possessions in North America." These assertions indicate that something had happened in the upper Ohio Valley in 1754, that served as a pretext for war between two powerful nations—a war that altered the political map of the world. We shall not follow the course or note the results of the Seven Years War in Europe, but the western phases of the French and Indian War, as the struggle in America is called, are of determining importance in our story.

The upper Ohio Valley was the scene of the rivalries which culminated in the conflict which destroyed France's dream of empire in America. While the frontier advance sketched in the preceding chapter was in progress, traders from Pennsylvania and Virginia—especially the former—were crossing the mountains and trafficking with the Indians on the upper Ohio and its confluent streams. Then, in the late forties, Virginia land companies secured large grants of land west of the Alleghanies. At this same time the French became fully aware of the significance of the Ohio country, and the necessity of making good their claim to it. Both sides soon recognized the strategic importance of the forks of the Ohio River and prepared to secure possession of the site. The French officials realized both that this region was a necessary link in the connection between Canada and Louisiana, and that it must be held by them to prevent the English from breaking through and bringing disaster to all the plans and ambitions of France in the New World. The English colonial governors and leaders, on the other hand, knew that the forks of the Ohio must be held by the English if they were either to come into enjoyment of the trans-mountain portions of their colonial claims or to defend their frontiers against inroads by the French and their Indian allies through the mountain passes.

PENNSYLVANIA TRADERS IN THE OHIO VALLEY

When Pennsylvania traders first visited western waters is uncertain. They were apparently on the Alleghany River before 1725, and by 1730 they were a subject of concern to the French at Detroit and around Lake Erie. Volwiler states that they "pushed the trader's frontier 500 miles westward in less than a half century; in 1750, this line was near the Wabash and Maumee rivers," which now constituted the chief avenue of travel for the French between the Great Lakes and the Mississippi. Nor did the Pennsylvanians stop there: they continued to push on toward the Mississippi.

The foremost figure in this aggressive advance was George Croghan, who came to Pennsylvania from Dublin in 1741, and engaged almost immediately in the fur trade. Within five years he was operating on Lake Erie and had a number of men in his employ. By 1750 he had posts and storehouses scattered all over the upper Ohio country. One of these was on the Alleghany near its junction with the Monongahela, another was located about twenty-five miles away, on the Youghiogheny. A third, and one of the most important was in the Indian village of Logstown, eighteen miles below the forks of the Ohio. He had other storehouses on the Ohio, on Lake Erie, near the forks of the Muskingum, and at Pickawillany on the Great Miami. His trade extended at least as far down the Ohio as the mouth of the Scioto, and into regions now embraced in West Virginia and eastern Kentucky. He married an Indian woman and this fact, together with his remarkable understanding of Indian character, helps to explain his success. Soon his abilities and experience were to be turned to good account in the performance of important duties as an Indian agent.

Unfortunately few of the English traders were of Croghan's stamp. Too many of them fully deserved the terms "vicious" and "abandoned wretches," which Benjamin Franklin used in describing them. Their immoral conduct and their use of rum in trade were frowned upon by Indian leaders, and only the fact that they offered more and better goods in exchange for furs than their French rivals kept the western tribesmen from expressing their resentment. In fact, colonial Indian relations became more and more strained and complicated as the frontier advanced. There was no adequate regulation of Indian trade. Each colony concerned passed its own rules, but these were poorly enforced, and there was bitter competition between the traders of rival colonies, with the Indians as the victims.

But exasperated as the natives were when cheated in trade, they had little fear of the traders who left them undisturbed in their wilderness life. They were far more seriously alarmed at the westward progress of the settlers' frontier. Settlements meant the cutting down of forests, the destruction of wild game, and the ultimate dispossession of the Indians. They meant also a line of forts and garrisons to protect the long frontier from Pennsylvania to Georgia.

Volumes could be devoted to the maze of conferences, treaties, and forest diplomacy by which the Indians were systematically pushed back to make way for the advancing settlers. The price offered by the whites may at first have seemed tempting to the natives who signed treaties ceding lands—treaties of which they only dimly understood the significance. But, as revealed in the words of an Indian quoted by Justin Winsor, they soon found that they had bartered something dear to them for things that were very ephemeral: "What little we have gained from selling the land goes soon away; but the land which you gain lasts forever!" Before the middle of the eighteenth century, Indian titles to lands east of the mountains had been largely extinguished and the Indians driven away or reduced to submission. The attention of colonial governors was now being given with considerable success to alliances with the tribes in the Ohio Valley. In 1748 George Croghan was instructed to deliver a present to a tribe living on Lake Erie, well within the French sphere of influence. In the same year the Pennsylvania officials decided to despatch an ambassador to the nations on the upper Ohio River. The man chosen to perform this delicate mission was Conrad Weiser, a German whose name is closely connected as interpreter with every important Indian transaction in Pennsylvania for thirty years from about 1730.

THE OHIO COMPANY AND ITS SEARCH FOR LAND

Pennsylvania led the way in the fur trade and in Indian negotiations in the Ohio Valley, but Virginians were the first to evince a determination to place settlements in this region. In 1749 at Lancaster, Pennsylvania, the Iroquois ceded what both they and the English knew were rather dubious rights to an indefinite extent of territory west of the Alleghanies—dubious because other Indian tribes claimed the same land. A few weeks later a group of influential Virginians, satisfied with this doubtful clearance of Indian title to land alleged to be within the charter limits of Virginia, laid plans to secure a large grant for themselves in this region. They organized the Ohio Company, which included such influential men as Thomas Lee, Lawrence and Augustine Washington, and George Fairfax, and in 1749 obtained the coveted grant. The company was given a tract of two hundred thousand acres on the upper Ohio, within limits specified in the grant, "or in such part to the Westward of the Great Mountains as the Company should think proper for making settlements and extending their trade with the Indians." The grantees were to erect a fort, establish a garrison, and bring in one hundred families within seven years, and upon meeting these conditions were to receive title to an additional three hundred thousand acres adjoining the first tract.

The Ohio Company began operations immediately. Supplies were purchased, a warehouse was built at Will's Creek on the upper Potomac where Cumberland, Maryland, now stands; and Thomas Cresap was employed to open a road westward some eighty miles from this point. To spy out a favorable location for their grant, the company, in 1750, chose Christopher Gist, a surveyor well acquainted with the frontier. "You are to go out as soon as possible to the Westward of the great Mountains," read Gist's instructions, "and carry with you such a Number of Men, as You think necessary, in Order to search out and discover the Lands upon the River Ohio, & other adjoining Branches of the Mississippi down as low as the great Falls thereof." He was to make notes concerning the mountain passes, the navigability of the rivers, the quality of the soil, and the strength and trade relations of the Indian tribes. Above all, he was to make careful observation of "large Bodies of good level Land."

On the last day of October, 1750, Gist set out from Thomas Cresap's house on the upper Potomac, and in less than three weeks he was at the forks of the Ohio. "While I was here," he wrote in his journal, "I took an Opportunity to set my Compass privately, & took the Distance across the River, for I understood it was dangerous to let a Compass be seen among these Indians." A few days later, at Logstown, he learned more emphatically the necessity of concealing the real purpose of his mission, both from the Indians and from the Pennsylvania fur traders. "The People in this Town," he wrote, "began to inquire my Business, and because I did not readily inform them, they began to suspect me, and said, I was come to settle the Indian's Lands and they knew I should never go Home again safe; I found this Discourse was like to be of ill Consequence to me, so I pretended to speak very slightingly of what they had said to me, and enquired for Croghan (who is a meer Idol among his Countrymen the Irish Traders) and Andrew Montour the Interpreter for Pennsylvania, and told them I had a Message to deliver the Indians from the King, by Order of the President of Virginia."

From Logstown Gist went overland to a Wyandot village at the forks of Muskingum near the present site of Coshocton, where he found George Croghan and the picturesque half-breed frontiersman, Andrew Montour. Shortly after leaving this place he encountered one of those strange accommodations to savage life not infrequent in wilderness villages in this troubled period—a white woman living in apparent contentment among the Indians. This woman had been taken captive in a New England raid when she was about ten years of age. "She is now upwards of fifty," wrote Gist, "and has an Indian Husband and several Children . . . she still remembers they used to be very religious in New England, and wonders how the White Men can be so wicked as she has seen them in these Woods."

Gist's course took him to Shawneetown at the mouth of the Scioto River and thence to the villages of the Miami Indians (or Twightwees as they were then called) on the upper waters of the Big Miami. Frequent and seemingly successful conferences were held with the natives, who promised to keep the road clear for their English brothers and not listen to the words of the French. Turning southward, Gist again reached the Ohio, where he was warned that if he went to the falls he would be killed or captured by Indians in the French interest. Accordingly he crossed the river into what is now Kentucky and after some exploring in that region, directed his steps eastward and reached his frontier home on the Yadkin about the middle of May, 1751, only to find his hearthstone cold and his family thirty-five miles away at Roanoke, whence they had fled because of an Indian scare. Later in the same year Gist started on another exploratory journey for the Ohio Company into the country south of the Ohio and between the Monongahela and the Kanawha.

In spite of its energy and ambition, the Ohio Company was not destined to achieve the easy success of which its members dreamed. Other land grants conflicted with their claims, the Indians were not eager to give their consent to settlements west of the mountains, and settlers were not attracted by the terms offered. Above all, the Company's activities and known purpose precipitated the conflict with the French which for a time ended all possibility of frontier expansion.

THE FRENCH ASSERT THEIR CLAIM TO THE OHIO VALLEY

The treaty of Aix-la-Chapelle in 1748, which closed King George's War, left the question of the West untouched, but it soon became evident that the peace was only a truce. The threat involved by the Ohio Company's grant was not unnoticed or unchallenged by humpbacked Governor Gallissonière of Canada. In the summer of 1749 he despatched Céleron de Blainville (or Bienville) to take possession of the Ohio country for the French and drive out the English traders. With a goodly party of soldiers, voyageurs and Indians, this emissary crossed from Lake Erie to the waters of the Alleghany, descended this stream to the forks of the Ohio, floated down the current of "la Belle Rivière," to the mouth of the Big Miami, which he ascended, portaged to the Maumee and then returned to Canada by way of Detroit. At the mouths of the important confluents of the Ohio he buried leaden plates in token, according to the words inscribed on them, "of the renewal of possession heretofore taken of the aforesaid river, Ohio, of all streams that fall into it, and all lands on both sides to the sources of the aforesaid streams, as the preceding Kings of France enjoyed it, or ought to have enjoyed it, and which they have upheld by force of arms and by treaties, notably by those of Ryswick, Utrecht, and Aix-la-Chapelle." Little did the members of this brave party know that they were performing the last act of French pageantry on American soil.

Céleron everywhere encountered English traders, and as many as he met he drove out or warned away. At Logstown he told the Indians to make the best of the year's hunting for after that year the English would not be permitted on the Ohio. But he returned to Canada much disturbed by the evidence of the widespread influence of the English among the western tribes.

There was consternation in all the colonies from New York south at the news of Céleron's expedition. Moreover, the English soon learned that this expedition was not a mere gesture. On the contrary, things happened in rapid succession to prove that the French had no intention of depending on buried leaden plates to protect their claim to the Ohio country. While he was on his expedition of 1750-51 Christopher Gist heard several times that English traders were being not merely warned out of the country but captured by the French and taken to Canada. Similar news drifted into Albany, Philadelphia, and Williamsburg. In 1752 a large force of French and Indians, led by Charles de Langlade, descended on the hated trading post at Pickawillany on the upper Big Miami, captured the traders, and burned the storehouses. Early the following year Pennsylvania and Virginia traders on the Kentucky were attacked, their goods confiscated, and most of them taken captives to Montreal. More alarming still, in the spring of 1753 the French erected Fort Presqu'Isle where Erie, Pennsylvania, now stands; Fort le Boeuf on French Creek, a tributary of the Alleghany; took possession of the English trading post at Venango further south; and were only prevented by sickness in camp from proceeding immediately to the building of a fort at the forks of the Ohio. Even the Carolina frontier was aroused by reports of a large war party of Indians under French influence proceeding against the Catawbas, who were attached to the English.

These startling movements of the French caused anxious concern and feverish activity in the English colonies most definitely effected. To keep the Iroquois in line was the main object in New York, where Governor George Clinton, hampered by factional dissensions, depended mainly on William Johnson, whose skill in dealing with the Indians was now of great service and was later to make him even more valuable and renowned. In Pennsylvania, Governor James Hamilton found the Quaker assembly willing to finance Indian negotiations in which such men as George Croghan and Conrad Weiser were busily employed, but entirely indisposed to make appropriations for frontier defense.

VIRGINIA'S RESPONSE TO THE FRENCH CHALLENGE

Virginia, however, was the colony which made the most aggressive response to the French challenge, and precipitated actual hostilities. This was due in part to the Ohio Company's vital interest in the disputed territory. But it was due mainly to the fact that Robert Dinwiddie was now governor of Virginia. Dinwiddie was somewhat irascible and not too tactful, but he was determined to protect what he regarded as the possessions of his colony and King against the aggressions of the French. Moreover, he had either the good fortune or the rare discernment to start on his public career a young surveyor twenty-one years of age, by the name of George Washington.

News of the building of the French forts south of Lake Erie convinced Dinwiddie that something decisive must be done to checkmate these operations. Late in the fall of 1753 he commissioned Washington to bear a message of warning and protest to the French commander. It was a delicate mission and one fraught with peril and with hardships due to the difficulties of winter travel in the mountains. Nevertheless, with the guiding assistance of Christopher Gist, Washington reached his destination and at Fort Le Boeuf delivered to Legardeur de St. Pierre a message from Governor Dinwiddie. "The lands upon the River Ohio, in the western parts of the Colony of Virginia," ran the laconic remonstrance, "are so notoriously known to be the property of the Crown of Great Britain that it is a matter of equal concern and surprise to me, to hear that a body of French forces are erecting fortresses and making settlements upon that river, within his Majesty's Dominions." These acts of hostility made it necessary "to complain to you of the encroachments thus made, and of the injuries done to the subjects of Great Britain, in violation of the law of nations, and the treaties now subsisting between the two Crowns."

Washington was treated with every courtesy by St. Pierre, but he was not deceived as to the determination of the French to continue their fort-building, and he carried back to Din-widdie a message which was a polite refusal to heed his warning.

Governor Dinwiddie, authorized by the home government to repel force by force, had now decided to do more than merely to protest against French aggression. Without waiting for Washington's return he had sent Captain William Trent with a small party to erect an English fort at the forks of the Ohio. Washington no sooner reached Williamsburg than he was commissioned to raise several companies of men and go to Trent's support. After delays and discouragements the expedition reached Will's Creek in April, 1754. Here startling news reached them. A superior force of French and Indians had appeared before Trent's unfinished stockade and demanded its surrender. Trent himself was absent and Ensign Edward Ward, left in command of a handful of wretchedly equipped men, had no choice but to yield to the demand. The French immediately set to work to complete the fort, which was soon named Fort Duquesne in honor of the new governor of Canada.

This was a disaster which called for prompt action. "You are to act on the Defensive," were Washington's instructions, "but in Case any Attempts are made to obstruct the works or interrupt our Settlem't by any Persons whatsoever You are to restrain all such Offenders, and in Case of resistance to make Prisoners of or kill and destroy them." Washington decided to push on to the forks without delay. He had reached a place known as the "Great Meadows," not far to the southeast of Fort Duquesne, when he learned that a party of Frenchmen was hanging on his flanks. Gaining information as to the location of this party, Washington marched a detachment of his men through the tangled thickets in the dead of night, and on the morning of May 28th encountered those whom he had every reason to believe his enemies. Washington immediately gave the order to fire, and the result, in the famous phraesology of Horace Walpole, was "the volley fired by a young Virginian in the backwoods of America, that set the world on fire." It was in reality the first shot of the French and Indian War. Washington's loss in this skirmish was slight, but the French commander, Coulon de Jumonville, was killed, together with several of his followers, and more than twenty were taken prisoners.

It was not to be expected that the French would calmly ignore this reverse. Word soon came to Washington that a large force bent on reprisal was approaching from Fort Duquesne. He retired to the Great Meadows and strained every effort to make defensible the crude entrenchments which were given the appropriate appellation of Fort Necessity. On the morning of June 3rd the attacking force of French and Indians put in its appearance and the fighting began. Toward nightfall, when Villiers, the French commander, proposed that terms of capitulation be discussed, Washington was forced to consent. He was outnumbered probably two to one, the rude fortifications were easily commanded by surrounding forest-clad hills, his men were nearly knee-deep in mud and water, and he had lost approximately one-fourth of his fighting force in killed and wounded. By the fitful light of a sputtering, windblown candle the terms of surrender were signed, and Washington was permitted to lead his men out of the sorry fort with the honors of war.

Braddock's Defeat

Actual hostilities had begun, although two years of continued conflict were to pass before there was an official declaration of war. The effect produced by Washington's defeat was immediate and far-reaching. English prestige and influence west of the Alleghanies were virtually destroyed. Most of the Indians, even a portion of the Iroquois, went over to the French, and English traders found it prudent to abandon their wide-ranging activities in the Ohio Valley. There was alarm all up and down the settlers' frontier, where raids by emboldened Indians were momentarily expected. In Massachusetts and Virginia, there was busy preparation for war, and in the other colonies the governors urged action from their legislative bodies with varying success. The English colonies, however, had not yet learned the necessity of union, as was clearly shown by the failure of Franklin's statesmanlike plan proposed at the Albany Congress of 1754.

In England anti-French fever was mounting daily, although the nation was not prepared for war and the leadership of Prime Minister Newcastle was anything but vigorous. Parliament voted to send troops to America for the protection of the colonies. As a result two regiments landed in Virginia late in February, 1855, under the command of General Edward Braddock. American writers have given this officer the name of being all that was opprobrious, conceding only that he was brave—brave to the point of recklessness. Probably the worst that be justly said of him is that he was a typical British military officer, trained in the methods of European warfare, and therefore scornful of the rustic colonial militia and wholly unacquainted with the tactics of Indian fighting in the woods. Certainly he had sufficient cause for truculence in the vexatious delays and indifference which slowed down his operations to a degree that practically foredoomed failure. It was his purpose to march at once across the mountains and re-capture Fort Duquesne, but only through the timely and patriotic assistance of Benjamin Franklin did he succeed in getting together wagons and horses essential to the expedition.

Not until the first week in June was Braddock able to mobilize his force of about two thousand men—partly regulars and partly colonials—at Fort Cumberland on Will's Creek. Then began the famous march toward Fort Duquesne, with George Washington as a member of the general's staff and the indispensable Christopher Gist as guide. "The route followed to the Great Meadows," says the English historian, A. G. Bradley, "was much the same as that used by Washington and his small force in the preceding year, but now a road twelve feet wide had to be opened over the rugged tree-encumbered ground. Its course lay neither over veldt, nor plain, nor prairie, nor sandy desert, nor Russian Steppe; but over two high ranges of mountains and several lesser ridges, clad in the gloom of mighty forests, littered with the wreckage of unnumbered years, riven this way and that by turbulent streams, and swarming with hostile Indians."

After a month of slow and laborious progress the advance detachment, consisting of about twelve hundred men, arrived within a few miles of the great objective, Fort Duquesne, confident that shortly the English flag would once more float over the fort at the junction of the Monongahela and the Alleghany. Then, on the afternoon of July 9th, the quiet of the enveloping woods was broken by the terrible war whoop and soon a murderous fire poured from all sides upon the marching column, in which the red-coated British regulars served as brilliant targets. For two hours the slaughter continued, and in spite of all that Washington and the colonials could do to fight the Indians in their own way, the disaster became irreparable. Braddock was mortally wounded. Three-fourths of his officers and two-thirds of his men were killed or wounded, and many of them were left to be victims of the scalping knife or captivity and torture. Abandoning everything—horses, wagons, ammunition and supplies—the remnants fled in the wildest confusion.

News of Braddock's overwhelming defeat brought consternation to the colonists and deep humiliation to the people of England. The French, on the other hand, were exultant and the Indians, with nothing now to restrain them, carried death and desolation all along the frontier. There was much truth, however, as later events proved, in the statement of a writer signing himself "T. W.," who expressed the belief that "it may be best, in the *end*, we have met with this loss. Shameful and mischievous as it is, it may be one of the grand links in that chain of causes, by which Heaven may intend to chastise the *French*, curb their insolence, drive them out of the encroachments they have made on us, and reduce them to a necessity of keeping within their own boundaries without disturbing us in the possession of ours." Certainly there was henceforth less scouting of the gravity of the situation, a greater respect for the abilities of the French and their red allies, and in the colonies less confidence in the protecting power of regular troops from the homeland. The lesson was severe, but it was not entirely unsalutary.

THE FRENCH AND INDIAN WAR

The story of the long struggle cannot be recited here. In 1756 war was officially declared and the conflict spread to Europe. In America, the two years following the Braddock debacle were dismal years for the English. Failure followed failure, the important post of Fort Oswego on Lake Ontario fell into the hands of the French, and only an occasional success along the northeastern border brought temporary cheer. The English colonists outnumbered the French at least twelve to one. But the latter possessed unity of purpose and aggressive leadership. For the time being their domination of the western Indians was nearly complete and their control of the interior enabled them to throw their strength at will against almost any objective. With the English it was far different. At home there was inefficiency and indecision, if not worse, under the Newcastle ministry. In the colonies there was scarcely any move toward united effort, and in many of the individual colonies—even those most endangered—bickering and politics hampered plans for defense.

Then in 1757 there came a change and the tide began to turn. In the summer of that year William Pitt became the directing force in the British ministry. Control of the sea and a vigorous campaign in America were his great policies. Decision replaced indecision, energy was substituted for lassitude. Adequate forces, well commanded and equipped, were sent to America. More consideration was given to the colonists whose feelings had been wounded by the supercilious attitude of previous commanders, and appeals were made for loyal support. The full strength of the British empire was thrown into the scale.

The results were not long in forthcoming. In 1758 Louisburg, the strongest fortress in America, succumbed to the combined naval and military attack of the English. Fort Frontenac (where Kingston now stands) was captured and thus the entire chain of French forts in the interior was rendered insecure. In the same summer General John Forbes led a well conducted expedition, in which Colonel George Washington headed the Virginia contingent, across the mountains and through the forests of Pennsylvania in the direction of Fort Duquesne. Marching slowly, seeking and heeding the advice of his American officers, he arrived at his destination to find that the fickle and impatient Indians had abandoned the weak French garrison, and that the latter had burned the fort and fled. Thus after three years the Braddock disaster was avenged. The English flag again flew over a new fort named Fort Pitt at the strategic forks of the Ohio. The French were dispossessed of the Ohio Valley, for the control of which the war had begun.

Conquest was now rapidly approaching. On September 13, 1759, on the Plains of Abraham outside the citadel of Quebec, the intrepid Wolfe defeated the flower of the defenders of New France under the gallant Montcalm. Four days later the English entered the fortress. Defying the inevitable, the French fought on with dogged courage and loyalty, but their task was hopeless. France, closely pressed in Europe, on the sea, and in India, had no aid to send to her devoted subjects in America. Montreal was surrendered in 1761, and one after another the now isolated French posts in the west were turned over to the victors.

THE ELIMINATION OF FRANCE

As far as America was concerned the war was over. In other parts of the world a late alliance with Spain gave France a temporary but vain hope that she might still avert total defeat. In November, 1762, preliminary articles of peace were signed and on the same day France, secretly relinquished to Spain all claim to territory west of the Mississippi and to the "island of Orleans" on which New Orleans was situated. By the definitive treaty signed at Paris on February 10, 1763, France yielded Canada and all her possessions east of the Mississippi (with the exception of New Orleans) to the English, to whom Spain also gave Florida in return for Cuba which the victor had captured.

Thus England and Spain faced each other across the Mississippi, and the story of France in America was brought to a close except for a few sentences to describe Napoleon's unfulfilled dream of a restored French empire in the New World forty years later. In the west a few scattered settlements and a multitude of geographical names were the only tangible reminders of a century and a half of valiant endeavor. The life and customs and institutions of the people who were soon to pour across the Alleghanies were in no appreciable manner affected by these remnants of French rule, except in Louisiana where the Civil Law remained as a reminder of early French rule. Yet it is certain that the history of America and of the West would have been far different if there had been no Champlain or Frontenac, no La Salle or Iberville or Bienville—if the French had not for so long contended with the English for the control of the interior.

The overthrow of the French in America may be explained by a number of factors. When the final struggle took place the English outnumbered them twelve to one. The English were deeply rooted in the soil, and their settlements were compact and relatively dense right up to the edge of the frontier. The French, on the other hand, had a far-flung empire of the fur trade with widely scattered trading posts and inadequate defense. Histories of colonial America reveal other comparisons which indicate why the French lost their possessions in the New World.

CHAPTER VIII

THE FRUITS OF VICTORY

IMMEDIATELY after the fall of Quebec newspaper writers and pamphleteers in England began to discuss the terms of peace which should be imposed on France, and in this discussion the disposition to be made of Canada and the region west of the Alleghanies was the chief bone of contention. As early as 1759 a writer, quoting Biblical justification for severity, and reciting the manner in which the French had launched the Indians against the frontier settlements, declared that "any argument for peace, which shall not secure us from the like injuries, that forced us into this war, ought to be exploded and treated with indignity and contempt."

About the same time "A Letter addressed to two great Men on the Prospect of Peace," demanded that Canada be wrested from France in order to protect the English colonies which were of growing importance as a market for the manufactures of the mother country. In reply it was pointed out that manufacturing was increasing in the colonies themselves, that colleges and academies were being established, and the prediction was made that the bonds of dependence upon the home country would continually weaken as the colonists pushed further away from the sea. "If the people of our colonies find no check from Canada," warned this writer with prophetic vision, "they will extend themselves almost without bounds into the inland parts. They are invited to it by the pleasantness, the fertility, and the plenty of that country; and they will increase infinitely from all causes. What the consequence will be, to have a numerous, hardy, independent people, possessed of a strong country, communicating little or not at all with England, I leave to your own reflections. . . . I shall only observe, that by eagerly grasping at extensive territory, we may run the risque, and that perhaps in no very distant period, of losing what we now possess."

Soon there appeared the suggestion that England retain the little island of Guadaloupe in the Lesser Antilles and let France remain in possession of the greater part of Canada. This plan was argued pro and con with much heat, and the rival claims of those interested in furs and in sugar became vocal. One writer argued for retention of Canada and its dependencies if for no other reason than that it would "enable Britain to supply all Europe with hats and furrs." Another retorted by asking "whether the war in America was begun for the sake of a few hats or the fur trade." Others objected to making the Mississippi the western boundary of the English possessions; and still others asserted that even if the English were left in control of all the western forts, they could not prevail against the Indians unless French influence were entirely removed. Thus the debate continued right up to the signing of the definitive treaty, and the peace commissioners were delayed with gratuitous but highly contradictory advice and warning. But in these voluminous writings is to be seen a growing appreciation of the value of the vast trans-Alleghany region, as well as uneasy forebodings of what the removal of the French menace in America might mean to the British empire.

WESTERN LAND SCHEMES

With the signing of the Treaty of Paris, English statesmen were confronted with the problem of what to do with the newly acquired territory. What happened in Canada concerns us only incidentally, but the decisions in regard to the western country and British activities in that region are full of interest.

We have already observed the plans of the Ohio Company to gain control of a large tract of land on the Ohio River. This was only one of many ambitious schemes to secure land or plant colonies west of the mountains before the French and Indian War and during its opening years. In 1749, for instance, a grant of eight hundred thousand acres lying along the northern boundary of North Carolina was made by Virginia to the

Loyal Company. At the time of the Albany congress in 1754 Franklin proposed the establishment of colonies in the West and shortly afterward he outlined more definitely his suggestions for two colonies between the Ohio River and Lake Erie. About the same time Thomas Pownall advocated a large military colony south of the Ohio and back of Virginia. The most ambitious scheme of all was one brought forward by Samuel Hazard, a Philadelphia merchant, whereby he hoped to become the proprietor of a colony with boundaries including all the Ohio and upper Mississippi valleys.

The war put an end to these and numerous lesser projects, but it only forced into temporary abeyance the increasing avidity for the possession of the rich lands west of the mountains. With the coming of peace and the exclusion of the French the speculative craze for western lands quickly revived, and the year 1763 witnessed several proposals on the part of colonial leaders, who set about securing wealthy, influential abettors in the mother country. The Ohio Company was fired with new hope for the fulfillment of its unsatisfied claims. George Washington took the lead in urging the speedy donation of western lands to Virginia soldiers in accordance with a promise which had been made by Governor Dinwiddie. Washington also joined with Richard Henry Lee and other prominent Virginians and Marylanders to form the Mississippi Company, which sought to obtain a tract of 2,500,000 acres of land along the eastern bank of the Mississippi and astride the Ohio. Even this huge area was insignificant in comparison with the colony many times its size which some New York speculators proposed to settle in the Mississippi Valley and to name New Wales, or the colony of Charlotina in the same general region suggested in a pamphlet published in Edinburgh.

THE PROCLAMATION OF 1763

No doubt hope rose high in the breasts of the proponents of these and other designs. To be sure, the granting of land in Indian territory had been taken out of the power of the colonial governors in 1761, but in America there was little anticipation of a definite restriction of western settlement after the close of the war. Bitter therefore must have been the disappointment of most of these eager land-seekers when their dreams were interrupted by news of the royal Proclamation of October 7, 1763. This famous decree embodied the decisions of England's statesmen in regard to the newly acquired territory. Three new colonies were set up on the continent: Quebec, embracing the settled portion of Canada, and East Florida and West Florida in the southern region ceded by Spain. Representative assemblies were to be established in these colonies and liberal inducements were held out to settlers.

The services of the colonial officers and soldiers in the late war were recognized. To all who made application the colonial governors were authorized to grant lands varying in quantity, according to rank, from 5,000 acres for field officers to fifty acres for privates.

It was the portion of the Proclamation which dealt with the West, however, that was of most concern to the westward-yearning colonists. It was declared to be "just and reasonable, and essential to our interest, and the security of our colonies," that the Indians "should not be molested or disturbed in the possession of such parts of our dominions and territories as, not having been ceded to, or purchased by us, are reserved to them, or any of them, as their hunting grounds." Accordingly, said the King, "we do therefore . . . declare it to be our royal will and pleasure that no governor, or commander in chief . . . do presume for the present and until our further pleasure be known, to grant warrant of survey, or pass patents for any lands beyond the heads or sources of any of the rivers which fall into the Atlantic Ocean from the west or north west . . . and we do hereby strictly forbid, on pain of our displeasure, all our loving subjects from making any purchases or settlements whatever, or taking possession of any of the lands above reserved, without our especial leave and license for that purpose first obtained." All persons who had already "wilfully or inadvertently" settled in any of the forbidden territory were ordered to remove immediately. Private purchases from the Indians were prohibited even in regions where settlements were permitted. Trade with the Indians, however, was open and free to everyone who obtained the proper license.

This proclamation dashed all hopes of immediate western grants or colonies, although there is ample evidence that it did not contemplate the permanent closure of the West. Divergent motives no doubt animated those who framed or favored the measure. Those interested in the fur trade naturally approved any restriction of the encroachment of settlements in this rich preserve. Others may have desired to curb the dangerous tendency of the colonists to spread beyond easy control. It is apparent, however, that the precipitating cause of the issuance of the proclamation was the obvious necessity of doing something to quiet the Indians. As it turned out the proclamation came too late to prevent the most determined and far reaching Indian uprising in American history.

PONTIAC'S CONSPIRACY

Pontiac's conspiracy, as this uprising has been called, was the work of a native leader whose abilities might have carried him far if he had been a member of a more fortunate race. This Ottawa chief was a thorough savage, cruel, crafty and treacherous, but these qualities were virtues in the eyes of his people. On the other hand, he possessed courage, vision, determination, and eloquence. Not only was he an Ottawa chief, but he was recognized as the leader of the Ojibwas and the Pottawattamies, with whom his own tribe was loosely confederated. "Over those around him his authority was almost despotic," says Francis Parkman, "and his power extended far beyond the limits of the three united tribes. His influence was great among all the nations of the Illinois country; while, from the sources of the Ohio to those of the Mississippi, and, indeed, to the farthest boundaries of the wide-spread Algonquin race, his name was known and respected."

The close of the French and Indian War was a time of crisis for the Indians. Before this time they might be cheated and misused by French and English traders, but their alliance was sought by the rival governments and thus they held a balance of power which protected them from deliberate exploitation or extermination. Now, however, French power was destroyed and the English remained in sole possession with no need to court the friendship of the people of the forests. All too soon the hated settlers would be pouring over the mountains and taking the land. Pontiac clearly grasped the peril of the situation. He was also sufficiently credulous to believe the false tales circulated by revengeful Frenchmen that their "great father," the King of France, was sending large expeditions up the St. Lawrence and the Mississippi, and that soon, with the help of their Indian brothers, they would drive out the English. It was with this deluded hope in his mind that Pontiac made his plans.

Far and wide, to the tribes of the Ohio Valley, the region of the Great Lakes and even the lower Mississippi, Pontiac sent his messengers bearing war belts of wampum and red-stained tomahawks. This was late in the year of 1762. On a certain day in the following May, says Parkman, "the tribes were to rise together, each destroying the English garrison in its neighborhood, and then, with a general rush, the whole were to turn against the settlements of the frontier." Everywhere the message was received with approval.

For a time it might well have seemed to the Indians that the plan would succeed. On the appointed day in May, 1763, all was in readiness. One after another the small and lonely British posts so lately won from France yielded to Indian treachery or attack, and only a few members of the inadequate garrisons escaped the brutal massacres that followed surrender. Mackinac, St. Joseph, Green Bay, Sandusky, Miami, Presqu' Isle, Le Boeuf, and Venango, all were destroyed or deserted. In all the northwest only Detroit, Fort Pitt and Fort Niagara remained intact, and of these the first two were obliged to stand a long and determined siege. Pontiac, himself, commanded the attack upon Detroit. Then, having destroyed or invested the military posts in the West, the Indians descended on the frontiers east of the mountains, burning, tomahawking, torturing, and bearing away scalps and captives.

It was amid scenes such as these that there was engendered that fierce, ineradicable hatred of Indians that filled the breasts of the American frontiersmen. Time and safety give us a perspective which enables us to see and sympathize with the viewpoint of the Indians in a way that was impossible to the backwoodsmen. Nearly seventy-five years after the events here described, Charles F. Hoffman, a discerning western traveler, noted the contrast between the attitude of later settlers "to whom the wild deeds of frontier-life are only known through the softened medium of fiction, as a tale of other days," and that of those who actually experienced the barbarity of the early conflicts. "The cause of the existing hatred of many of the borderers of the very name of Indian," said he, "must be sought for far back in the bloody annals of our frontiers. Its origin may there be found in the fierce collisions, the midnight burnings, the massacres and cruel devastations which are familiar to us in a thousand tales of our infancy. The bitter feelings, the recollection of wrongs committed or incurred—of vengeance wreaked or reaped in these desperate scenes,—have lived for generations in the families of their daring and much-enduring actors." He cited an instance of an old man killing an Indian in cold blood, for no other reason than that "not a drop of his blood ran in the veins of any living creature," because his children had been victims of Indian cruelty.

During the years 1763 and 1764 the entire frontier line was devastated. Even in the south the Indians, though not involved in Pontiac's confederacy, took occasion to harass the settlements. It was in Pennsylvania, however, that the blow fell hardest. Here Quaker scruples checked any movement of retaliation and hindered adequate measures of defense. Bitter complaints were uttered by the exposed Scotch-Irish frontiersmen. When no aid was forthcoming the so-called Paxton men gave expression to their rage and hatred of the Indians by murdering a number of inoffensive Moravian converts, some of whom were killed in the Lancaster jail where they had been taken for safety. Later a large body of backwoodsmen marched to Philadelphia with the avowed intention of destroying a more numerous group of Christian Indians who were being harbored there. This murderous purpose was not consummated, but the demonstration had a salutary effect in inducing greater concern for frontier protection on the part of the Quaker legislators.

There was much delay in organizing military expeditions to quell the Indian uprising. Sir Jeffry Amherst, commander-in-

chief in America, was not at first impressed with the seriousness of the situation and he was contemptuous toward the
Indian race in general. Most of the British regiments had
been disbanded or sent home. Even after a definite campaign
was decided upon, the colonies most affected were slow in giving needed assistance. In the end, however, two expeditions
were sent into the West. One, proceeded to the lake region and
in spite of the blunders of its commander, Colonel John Brad-
street, succeeded in overawing the Indians in that region. The
other, under the much abler leadership of Colonel Henry Bouquet, marched westward through Pennsylvania, defeated the
Indians in a sharp engagement, and penetrated into the very
heart of the Indian country northwest of the Ohio. Here the
strong Delaware and Shawnee tribes were forced to sue for
peace and return their prisoners.

Pontiac hoped to the last that he might hold at least a part
of his allies together. But when he heard from French lips the
disheartening news that no French armies were on their way to
recapture New France, he knew that the hour of doom had
come. In the spring of 1766 he made a dreary journey to Oswego on Lake Ontario, and there smoked the pipe of peace with
Sir William Johnson. Three years later the great Indian
leader was murdered in an Indian village in the Illinois country
by a member of his own race.

INDIAN AFFAIRS

Although the Proclamation of 1763 was issued too late to
avert the uprising just described, the outbreak led by Pontiac
proved conclusively that strong measures were needed to check
the increasing conflict between the frontiersmen and the Indians. At the beginning of the French and Indian War the
management of Indian affairs was taken away from the separate colonies and placed in the hands of two superintendents—
one for the northern district and one for the southern. The
superintendent in the northern district was William Johnson,
who was given a baronetcy during the war in recognition of his
military services. Johnson was vain, conceited and ambitious,
and lived in fine style at Johnson Hall on the Mohawk River.

But he was also eloquent, courageous, and remarkable in his understanding of Indian character. As a result he gained and retained a hold over the powerful Iroquois confederates that was of the utmost value in the troublous years of the French war and Pontiac's conspiracy. In the southern district the superintendent first appointed was Edmund Atkin. He died soon afterward, and the position was given to John Stuart who served with considerable ability until the Revolution.

From the close of the last French war to the outbreak of the American Revolution, problems concerned with the West received much attention on the part of the Board of Trade and the British ministry. In a general way, it may be said that the various decisions affecting the West revealed the same increasing trend toward imperial control that was shown in the stamp act, the enforcement of the navigation laws, and the "intolerable acts," which so enraged the colonists along the coast. Moreover, these western policies played a very definite part in giving rise to the grievances leading to the movement for independence. Official British interest in the West centered around four main problems: political relations with the Indians, Indian trade, the military occupation of the West, and proposals for western colonies and land grants.

Political relations with the Indians remained throughout the period under the control of the two superintendents, Sir William Johnson and John Stuart, who were released from their subordination to the commander-in-chief in 1764. This meant that it was the function and duty of the superintendents to make treaties with the Indians and to do all in their power to maintain peace and friendship. The most noteworthy achievement in this field was the establishment of the "Indian Boundary Line," for which official permission was given by the home government. In the fall of 1768 a great concourse of Iroquois and their allies gathered at Fort Stanwix in western New York. There, late in October, Sir William Johnson, by means of lavish presents judiciously displayed before their covetous eyes, induced these Indians to relinquish their claims to lands lying east and south of a line described in the treaty. Roughly, this line ran from the vicinity of Fort Stanwix southward to the Delaware River, then in a general southwestwardly direction to the Alleghany, and down that stream and the Ohio to the mouth of the Tennessee.

The southern portion of this line was fixed by a number of treaties, made mostly by John Stuart and beginning as early as 1763. The most important of these treaties were those made at Hard Labour in 1768 and at Lochaber in 1770 by which the Cherokee Indians ceded their claim to lands in the present State of West Virginia. Ultimately the line extended in a general southerly direction from the Ohio River at the mouth of the Great Kanawha to the Savannah River. Here it ran some distance westward, then turned abruptly to the southeast and paralleled the coast line around the Florida peninsula and westward to the Mississippi with a pronounced northern extension in the valleys of the Alabama and Tombigbee rivers. From the point where it crossed the mountains in west-central Pennsylvania to the southern part of North Carolina this line was well west of the Proclamation line of 1763 along the heights of the Appalachian system. The territory intervening between these two lines was especially extensive in southwestern Pennsylvania and in the region back of Virginia.

REGULATION OF THE FUR TRADE

Indian trade policies were subject to fluctuation during the years when there were frequent changes in the British ministry. In 1764 the two Indian superintendents were given a large measure of control over the trade, which was to be conducted at fixed trading posts. Prices were fixed, licenses were required, and there were numerous other regulations. After a few years under this system, the management of Indian trade was turned back to the several colonial governments, as the easiest way out of a situation that was growing increasingly expensive and unsatisfactory to the home government.

With the quelling of Pontiac's conspiracy, however, there was a rapid expansion of trade. Individual private traders, most of them thoroughly unprincipled scoundrels, swarmed into the West. Operations on a large scale were launched by trading companies. On the Ohio, for instance, Baynton, Wharton and Morgan of Philadelphia were by 1766 carrying on a business that employed six hundred packhorses on the roads from Philadelphia to Fort Pitt, and three hundred boatmen on the Ohio. It was estimated that in the same year this company shipped westward goods valued at 50,000 pounds for the Indian trade. In the south there were similar undertakings, the center of activity having now shifted to West Florida where the firms of Swanson and McGillivray and Panton, Leslie and Company were outstanding.

Nevertheless, there were many hindrances to success in the apparently unlimited field for the fur trade. The long-suffering frontier settlers did not look kindly upon the re-opening of the trade which would again supply the Indians with fire-arms

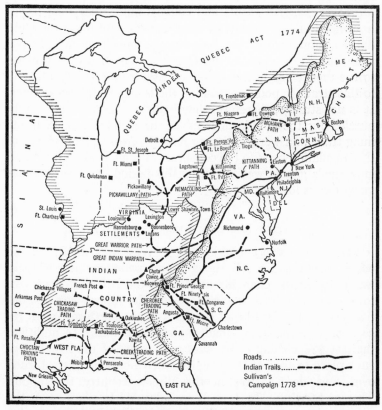

III. THE WEST UNDER BRITISH RULE, 1763-1783

and ammunition and thus equip them for recurrent raids on the settlements. In Pennsylvania the "Black Boys"—a band of frontiersmen who blackened their faces—attacked and destroyed more than one convoy of traders' goods crossing the mountains; and all along the frontier there was continued evidence of similar resentment. Out in the West, in the Illinois country, in West Florida and all along the Mississippi there was encountered the persistent and effective competition of the French traders who had removed into Spanish Louisiana. The little town of St. Louis, founded in the winter of 1763-4 by Pierre Laclede, soon gained an ascendancy in the fur trade of the upper Mississippi which it was to retain until long after the entire region had passed under the flag of the new republic. Moreover, English agents and colonial authorities soon began to complain that many of the traders who went down the Ohio did not return with their furs, but descended the Mississippi and disposed of them at New Orleans. The British had cause to rue their error in not obtaining title in the Treaty of 1763 to this strategic point controlling the traffic on the great river. It is not strange, therefore, that British ministers were sorely puzzled by the problems involved in regulating such a far flung trade and were willing to pass the expense and worry of that regulation back to the colonies. If some trading firms and individuals gained wealth during this period, it is certain that many others lost heavily.

BRITISH MILITARY RULE IN THE WEST

The military occupation of the West was another topic which occasioned much thought and policy-making wherein was reflected the changing attitude of the British government toward all American problems. After the suppression of Pontiac's revolt practically all the forts in the northwest were regarrisoned, although as inadequately as before. In addition, the last French flag to fly over a fort east of the Mississippi gave place to that of the English when Louis St. Ange turned over Fort de Chartres in the Illinois country to Captain Thomas Sterling. In 1768 it was decided to place upon the colonies the chief responsibility for defending the frontiers, and

THE FRUITS OF VICTORY 119

garrisons were withdrawn from the northwestern posts except Fort de Chartres, Mackinac, Detroit, Niagara, and Fort Pitt. The expense of maintaining more extensive military establishments was thought to be too great and out of proportion to the service to be rendered. Furthermore, by this time the British ministry was aware that they might soon have use for additional troops within the colonies themselves to overawe the mounting spirit of resistance to the stiffening measures of imperial control.

Down on the Gulf coast, as has been seen, the two new colonies—East Florida and West Florida were created by the Proclamation of 1763, with the Appalachicola River as the dividing line. There were problems of defense against the Indians in both colonies, but these problems were more acute in the western province. Here the powerful and quarrelsome Creeks, Chickasaws, and Choctaws were neighbors, and it became the policy of the authorities to play these tribes off against each other, as had been the custom in the period of Anglo-French rivalry. Of more importance was the fact that West Florida faced the Spanish on the Isle of Orleans and across the Mississippi. In 1764 the northern boundry of this province, originally placed at the thirty-first parallel, was moved north to 32 degrees 28 minutes for the purpose of including the settlements at Natchez and opening a wider field for land speculators along the east bank of the Mississippi. A fort was maintained at Natchez and at least two others further south.

West Florida was under military rule until the arrival of the first governor, George Johnstone, in October, 1764, after which a civil government was organized. Courts and English judicial procedure were established, the governor was advised by a council, and later an elective assembly was provided. The French and Spanish were given the alternatives of selling their lands and homes to Englishmen and removing with their personal effects, or of remaining and taking an oath of allegiance to the new régime. Most of them preferred the former and removed to Spanish Louisiana. Their places were more than filled by English immigrants, so that by the time of the

Revolution, British West Florida began to exhibit some features of a substantial colony.

THE PROBLEM OF GOVERNMENT FOR THE WEST

The fourth aspect of the problem which confronted the successive ministers who sought to shape British policy in regard to the West was that presented by the numerous proposals for western colonies and land grants. Consideration of these proposals was affected by many influences. For instance, there were the varying attitudes of those who favored western expansion and those who advocated the closing of the West entirely to settlements, leaving it a vast Indian reserve. In both groups there were no doubt men whose views were based on their conception of sound policy. At the same time, there was a host of influential men, both in England and America, who were personally interested in western colonial schemes; while, on the other hand, others were as definitely concerned with the success of the fur trade and opposed any disturbing action. Then there were protests from the colonies, especially Virginia, which resented any parcelling out of lands claimed by them on the basis of their sea-to-sea charters. To their support rallied all those who feared any encroachment on vested interests.

Even to give brief descriptions of all these colonial and land-grant schemes would be inappropriate in these pages, for most of them came to naught. Between 1767 and 1776 fully a dozen such schemes were broached and among them they embraced most of the territory between the Appalachians and the Mississippi and from the Great Lakes to the Floridas. One, the so-called colony of Vandalia to be located south of the Ohio and west of the Great Kanawha, seemed about to succeed, for a charter was granted in 1775 only to be nullified by the outbreak of the Revolution. Another plan, known as Transylvania and including north-central Tennessee and central Kentucky west of the Vandalia region, was based on private purchase from the Indians. It was later declared void by the Virginia assembly, but not until after a number of settlements had been made, as will be seen in a later chapter.

At length after more than a decade of vacillation and experimentation, the sorely harrassed ministry found what seemed to be a happy solution of many of the problems of western policy. On June 22, 1774, Parliament passed the famous Quebec Act, which extended the jurisdiction of the province of Quebec to the Ohio and Mississippi rivers. One very urgent reason for this action was the need for some form of civil government for the small French settlements which still existed at Detroit, at Mackinac, at Vincennes on the Wabash, and in the Illinois country at Kaskaskia, Cahokia, and neighboring places. Available evidence indicates that the Quebec Act was not passed as a coercive measure or for the purpose of closing the West forever to westward moving settlers. Nevertheless, it aroused bitter resentment in those colonies whose charters gave them claim to land in the region now attached to Quebec. It added another grievance to the list being accumulated by the colonial leaders who were by this time entering definitely on the road leading to rebellion and independence.

In the meantime, ever since 1763, in spite of royal proclamations or governors' decrees or military orders, land-hungry pioneers were crossing the mountains and staking their claims on the banks of westward-flowing rivers.

CHAPTER IX

BEHIND THE RANGES

"There's no sense in going further—it's the edge of cultivation,"
So they said, and I believed it—broke my land and sowed my crop—
Built my barns and strung my fences in the little border station
Tucked away below the foothills where the trails run out and stop.

Till a voice, as bad as Conscience, rang interminable changes
On one everlasting Whisper day and night repeated—so:
"Something hidden. Go and find it. Go and look behind the Ranges—
Something lost behind the Ranges. Lost and waiting for you. Go!"
—KIPLING.

WHILE the British authorities were struggling with the numerous problems connected with the vast empire wrested from France, the backwoods pioneers in America were giving heed to the impulse so vividly interpreted by Kipling in the lines above quoted. Hitherto only explorers, fur traders, hunters, soldiers, and other adventurers had crossed the Appalachians into the great West. Now the conquest of the mountain barrier was to be made by home-seekers. At first this movement was only a small, trickling stream of humanity, but it swelled rapidly until, after about a decade, it was checked once more by an Indian war and the outbreak of the Revolution.

THE FRONTIER CROSSES THE MOUNTAINS

In a preceding chapter there was sketched the story of the progress of settlement from the tidewater regions to the eastern foothills of the mountains. Aggressive, individualistic Scotch-Irish, more stolid but no less determined Germans, and adventurous American pioneers led this advance. A few of them had already made clearings on westward-flowing streams. The opening of hostilities in the last French war destroyed all thoughts of further penetration into the interior and even caused the frontier line to recede. It was not until after the capture of Fort Duquesne and other western posts of the French in 1758 and 1759 that settlers again dared to return to the exposed border or to follow the pathways across the mountain ranges.

Now, however, western Pennsylvania around the Forks of the Ohio offered the attractions of accessibility and apparent safety. Braddock had gone down to ignominious defeat, but he had opened a road that could be followed by settlers moving from Maryland and Virginia to the waters of the Monongahela and its tributaries. A similar service was rendered for Pennsylvanians by the wide path hewn out of the forests by Forbes on his victorious march. Fort Pitt had arisen on the ruins of old Fort Duquesne, and its garrison, together with those at Fort Ligonier, Fort Bedford, and other posts along Forbes' road seemed to offer all the protection that was needed now that the French were crushed. The cabins of settlers began to appear in the vicinity of Fort Pitt, where quite a little village had sprung up by 1760. "For two years past," wrote Colonel Henry Bouquet to Governor Fauquier of Virginia in 1762, "these Lands have been over run by a Number of Vagabonds, who under pretense of hunting, were Making Settlements in several parts of them, of which the Indians made grievous and repeated Complaints." Bouquet issued proclamations and warned the interlopers off the Indian lands, but with little effect. During this same period pioneers from Virginia were finding their way to the upper courses of the Greenbrier and New rivers; and in the Carolinas settlements were being made further and further up the streams flowing into the Atlantic.

Then came the Proclamation of 1763 and Pontiac's conspiracy. The former put a damper on large speculative schemes for a time, but it had little effect on the activities of individual backwoodsmen. The Indian uprising was caused in part by the encroachments of the settlers, and accordingly all those who had crossed the mountains were either killed, taken captive or driven precipitately eastward by the raiding bands which devastated the entire frontier. It was not until after Pontiac and his followers were subdued, therefore, that the westward movement was again resumed.

By 1764 the movement was under way once more, especially along the frontier in the Carolinas. Germans and
Scotch-Irish came directly across the Atlantic and made their
way into the interior. They were joined by larger numbers of
pioneer farmers from Pennsylvania, Maryland, and Virginia
who traveled down the valleys with their household effects and
with herds of cattle, horses and hogs. Many of them appropriated for their own use large tracts of remote pasture land,
where their stock ran at large and multiplied rapidly. These
cattle men soon came to take an attitude toward the approach
of farmers similar to that exhibited at a later day by their successors on the Great Plains.

"The frontier Inhabitants of this Colony and Maryland, are
removing fast over the Allegheny Mountains, in order to Settle
and live there." Thus reads a letter written from Winchester,
Virginia, early in 1765, indicating that fear of Indian depredations along that frontier had been quieted. It was now that
settlements in the real sense of the term first gained a foothold
in southern Pennsylvania, where fertile soil, abundant springs,
the proximity of Fort Pitt, and Braddock's road were the main
attractions. The settlers were mainly from Maryland and Virginia, and they migrated under the impression that the region
was Virginia territory. "Yet it may be assumed," says the
historian of that locality, James Veech, "that the first settlers
came, without knowing, or caring to know, whether this belief
was well founded or not. They knew that they were coming
into that vast and perilous, but fertile domain denominated the
West, where land was cheap, and liberty as exuberant as the
soil." Cabins began to appear along the banks of the Monongahela, the Youghiogheny, and other streams in this section
and on the Cheat River in what is now West Virginia.

All of these settlements were illegal. They were made in
sublime disregard or open defiance of the Proclamation of
1763, and they were made on lands to which the Indian title
had not been extinguished. News of these encroachments had
reached the King and in October, 1765, he wrote a vigorous letter of instructions to Governor John Penn of Pennsylvania,
requiring him to use his best endeavors "to suppress such unwarrantable proceedings" by compelling the intruders to aban-

don their clearings west of the proclamation line. Instructions of this nature were much easier to issue than to carry out, as several colonial governors and military officers discovered.

The veteran Indian agent and trader, George Croghan, wrote to General Gage in May, 1766, expressing his apprehension lest the aggression of the settlers should precipitate another general Indian war. About a month later the squatters in the Redstone Creek region received a warning from Gage. Alexander Mackay, with a small detachment of soldiers, posted this message. He told the intruders of the many complaints of the Indians because of their aggressions and reminded them of the King's proclamation. General Gage, he said, "out of Compassion to your Ignorance, before he proceeds to Extremity," had ordered him to call a meeting "to inform you of the lawless and Licentious manner in which you behave, and to order you all to return to your several Provinces without delay, which I am to do in the presence of some Indian Chiefs." If this warning was not obeyed troops would drive the settlers across the mountains. Governor Fauquier of Virginia and Governor Penn of Pennsylvania both issued fierce sounding proclamation after proclamation, the former telling the settlers they could expect no protection if they failed to remove at once. They would be left to the vengeance of the enraged Indians. The Pennsylvania assembly even went as far as to impose a penalty of death without benefit of clergy for failure to remove within thirty days.

All these proclamations and laws were so much paper wasted. Men of reckless dispositions or inured to the dangers and hardships of frontier life were not to be overawed by the threats of officials in far-away Philadelphia or Williamsburg, or even by soldiers who drove them temporarily out of their cabins and clearings. The Virginia executive soon realized the futility of his efforts at law enforcement, for he wrote that "no Regard is paid to Proclamations, and I can expect no great good from them." Penn admitted that even military expulsion had little effect, for the settlers came right back, and in larger numbers, as soon as the troops were out of the way. George Croghan estimated that the numbers of squatters on Redstone

Creek and the Cheat River had doubled after two years of persistent effort to warn or drive them out.

It is not surprising that illiterate, individualistic, quarrelsome backwoodsmen paid scant attention to either king's proclamation or Indians' rights, when men like George Washington were equally determined, though perhaps more respectful, in their plans to obtain land west of the mountains. In September, 1767, Washington wrote a long letter to William Crawford, who was then living on the Youghiogheny River. There had evidently been some previous correspondence between the two men. "I offered in my last to join you," wrote Washington, "in attempting to secure some of the most valuable lands in the King's part, which I think may be accomplished after a while, notwithstanding the proclamation, that restrains it at present, and prohibits the settling of them at all; for I can never look upon that proclamation in any other light (but this I say between ourselves), than as a temporary expedient to quiet the minds of the Indians. It must fall, of course, in a few years, especially when those Indians consent to our occupying their lands. Any person, therefore, who neglects the present opportunity of hunting out good lands, and in some measure marking and distinguishing them for his own, will never regain it." Washington expressed his desire "to secure a good deal of land," and he advised Crawford to keep the matter quiet and to do his land-locating under guise of hunting game.

Settlements on the Headwaters of the Ohio

In the treaty of Fort Stanwix in 1768 the Iroquois Indians gave up their claims to lands in west-central and southwestern Pennsylvania, in what is now West Virginia, and in the region south of the Ohio River. Whether the British authorities intended that the making of this treaty should remove the restrictions imposed by the Proclamation of 1763, in regard to the country concerned, is not entirely clear. In America, however, the treaty was taken as authorization of settlement in the region relinquished. The Pennsylvanian proprietors immediately put up for sale their lands lying west of the Alleghanies, and nearly three thousand applications for three-hundred-acre tracts were filed on the opening day. Preference was given to squatters already on the land, even though they had entered illegally, thus foreshadowing the practice of granting preemption rights which became such a prominent feature of public land policy.

"What number of families has settled, since the congress, to the westward of the high ridge," wrote George Croghan in 1770, "I cannot pretend to say positively; but last year, I am sure, there were between four and five thousand, and all this spring and summer the roads have been lined with waggons moving to the Ohio." In this same year George Washington in his journal of a tour of the Ohio River wrote that the "people of Virginia and elsewhere are exploring and marking all the lands that are valuable, not only on the Redstone and other waters of the Monongahela, but along the Ohio as low as the Little Kenhawa; and by next summer I suppose they will get to the Great Kenhawa at least. How difficult it may be to contend with these people afterwards is easy to be judged, from every day's experience of lands actually settled." The year 1771 was known in this region as the "starving year" because of lack of food to supply the throng of emigrants.

William Crawford was still busy locating and trying to locate land for Washington, and he was meeting with difficulties. "There will not be a possibility of taking up such a quantity as you want near Fort Pitt," he wrote in March, 1772, "as there are such numbers of people out now looking for land, and one taking another's land from him. As soon as a man's back is turned another is on his land. The man that is strong and able to make others afraid of him seems to have the best chance as times go now." Six weeks later Crawford wrote that he could not get the amount of land Washington desired, "without I could stay all summer and be on the spot; as people crowd out in such numbers the like was never seen. I believe they have settled as low as Wheeling and some lower—as far down as Grave Creek."

In fact all along the Ohio frontier there soon came angry complaints from the Indians that the squatters were exhibiting the same indifference to the Indian boundary line that they had shown toward the imaginary proclamation line. Efforts to keep the impetuous settlers within treaty limits gave Governor Dunmore of Virginia the same sense of futility that had been expressed by his predecessor. "I have learnt from experience," he wrote to Dartmouth in 1774, "that the established Authority of any government in America, and the policy of Government at home, are both insufficient to restrain the Americans; and that they do and will remove as their avidity and restlessness incite them. They acquire no attachment to Place: But wandering about Seems engrafted in their Nature; and it is a weakness incident to it, that they Should for ever imagine the Lands further off, are Still better than those upon which they are already Settled . . . they do not conceive that Government has any right to forbid their taking possession of a Vast tract of Country, either uninhabited, or which Serves only as a Shelter for a few Scattered Tribes of Indians. Nor can they be easily brought to entertain any belief of the permanent obligation of Treaties made with those People, whom they consider, as but little removed from the brute Creation." Lord Dunmore has been quoted at length because no more discerning appraisal of the spirit and attitude of the American frontiersmen has ever been written from that time to this.

THE SOUTHERN FRONTIER AND THE REGULATORS

While the region of the headwaters of the Ohio and its tributaries was thus being marked with "tomahawk claims" and dotted with settlers' cabins, a similar movement was in progress to the southward. Through Virginia and the Carolinas the frontier was steadily being edged westward through the forests and across the valleys toward the high ridges of the Alleghany and Cumberland Mountains. After the treaty of Fort Stanwix and the establishment of the southern extension of the Indian boundary line in 1768 millions of acres in what is now West Virginia were claimed by settlers. Within a few years it was reported that families were crossing the mountains with their slaves, and that it was not uncommon to meet twenty or thirty wagons a day moving toward new western homes. Smoke was now curling from numerous settlers' cabins and the ring of the axe was heard along the sources of the Dan, the

Yadkin, the Catawba and other eastward-flowing rivers. But even beyond these were the adventurous backwoodsmen who pioneered the way in Powell's Valley and on the upper waters of the Holston, the Clinch and the French Broad—all westward-flowing streams.

Unfortunately there are few diaries or journals or letters which give us realistic descriptions of the movement which peopled the southern frontier. Nevertheless, this movement, especially in southwestern Virginia and in North Carolina, was of great significance. It was to lead directly to the establishment of the first notable outposts of settlement beyond the mountains—the settlements in Kentucky and Tennessee.

As has already been said, the frontiersmen who first made their way into the western parts of the Carolinas were men of extremely individualistic and fearless dispositions. A large portion of them were Scotch-Irish and Germans who had made the long journey down the mountain valleys from Pennsylvania. Many others were discontented Virginia pioneers crowded out by the extension of the large plantations. Naturally, they were out of touch both geographically and temperamentally with the people of the tidewater regions. Thus it was that there developed here one of the best illustrations of the conflict characteristic of the relations between the frontier and the older settled sections of the colonies.

Among the many grievances harbored by the frontiersmen was the lack of provision for protection against outlaws. This was particularly exasperating in South Carolina, where cattle rustlers and horse thieves found opportunities just to their liking. Horse-stealing has always been a peculiarly heinous crime in the eyes of westerners, because of the importance of these animals to the existence of their owners. "These outlaws grew bold from impunity and numbers," says Simms in his history of South Carolina. "Burglaries and murders naturally followed horse-stealing, and there was no redress in society. There were no courts, no officers of justice to enforce the law and protect the peaceful. . . . Were the offender to be taken in the act, and carried to the seaboard for justice, he had ninety-nine chances in a hundred of being rescued from the officer before he could reach Charlestown by his comrades in iniquity."

Therefore the settlers took the law into their own hands, organized groups known as "Regulators," and meted out summary justice by inflicting whippings or more severe penalties. The outlaws banded together and civil war was threatened. Then the colonial authorities took a hand and appointed an officer to suppress the strife. He apparently took the side of the outlaws and arrested a number of the Regulators, who now found themselves arrayed against the government.

Even when western counties were organized and officers appointed there were still numerous causes for dissatisfaction among the dwellers on the frontier. Political control was entirely in the hands of the coastal sections. Officials appointed for the new counties were often corrupt and charged fees unauthorized by law. Taxes and quit-rents were a continual subject of complaint on the part of the frontiersmen who felt that they were excessive and unjust. The lack of money was another reason for discontent. The grievances accumulated and it was in North Carolina that they found most forceful expression. Here the name "Regulators" was also adopted by the angry settlers. At first there were meetings for discussion from which emanated respectful protests and petitions for redress of wrongs. When no satisfaction was given by the authorities, the hot-heads among the regulators resorted to violence and gave the whole movement the appearance of lawlessness. Lawyers and local officials were whipped, courts were interrupted, and the home of a judge was burned. Governor William Tryon now took decisive action. An army was gathered and marched to the heart of the disaffected region to meet the assembled regulators. In 1771 there was fought the so-called Battle of Alamance, in which brief contest a few men were killed and a larger number wounded. The incipient rebellion was crushed and quiet restored. Leniency on the part of Tryon's successor partially allayed the discontent and some of the most glaring malpractices were corrected.

DESCRIPTIONS OF THE FRONTIER

Thus, in Pennsylvania, Virginia, and North Carolina the Appalachian barrier had been crossed by the forerunners of the throng that was soon to follow. The eastern slopes of the mountains and the upland valleys were rapidly taking on a settled appearance, although vast stretches of forests awaited the axes of the farmers. Trails were developing into roads and rude taverns and half-way houses provided food and shelter for travelers.

Much romance has characterized the writings about the outer fringe of the frontier. Many contemporaries wearied of crowded old-world cities and the artificialities of civilization, idealized the freedom and the regenerative possibilities of life in the wilderness. For instance the Rev. Andrew Burnaby, an Englishman who traveled in America in 1759 and 1760 rhapsodized about the Shenandoah Valley. "I could not but reflect with pleasure on the situation of these people," he wrote, "and think if there is such a thing as happiness in this life, that they enjoy it. Far from the bustle of the world, they live in the most delightful climate, and richest soil imaginable; they are everywhere surrounded with beautiful prospects and sylvan scenes; lofty mountains, transparent streams, falls of water, rich valleys, and majestic woods . . . they are subject to few diseases; are generally robust; and live in perfect liberty; they are ignorant of want, and acquainted with but few vices."

An equally sympathetic but more realistic picture of the men and women who formed the cutting edge of the westward-moving frontier was presented at about the same time by Hector St. John de Crèvecoeur. He likewise traveled up and down the back country, but as the title of his well-known book indicates, he also lived for a time on an American farm. "He who would wish to see America in its proper light, and have a true idea of its feeble beginnings and barbarous rudiments," he advised, "must visit our extended line of frontiers where the last settlers dwell, and where he may see the first labours of settlement, the mode of clearing the earth, in all their different appearances; where men are wholly left dependent on their native tempers and on the spur of uncertain industry, which often fails when not sanctified by the efficacy of a few moral rules. There, remote from the power of example, and check of shame, many families exhibit the most hideous parts of our society. They are a kind of forlorn hope, preceding by ten or twelve years the most respectable army of veterans which come after them. In that space, prosperity will polish some, vice and the law will drive off the rest, who uniting again with others like themselves will recede still farther; making room for more industrious people, who will finish their improvements, convert the loghouse into a convenient habitation, and rejoicing that the first heavy labours are finished, will change in a few years that hitherto barbarous country into a fine fertile, well regulated district. Such is our progress, such is the march of the Europeans toward the interior parts of this continent."

Dunmore's War

In 1774 this frontier advance was again temporarily checked and even thrown back by Indian troubles leading to what is known as Dunmore's War. As early as 1773 men like Sir William Johnson and George Croghan were warning the authorities that the Indians were becoming sullen and threatening. Encroachments on their lands were increasing in spite of proclamations and treaties. The situation in western Pennsylvania was complicated by the fact that Virginia was now disputing Pennsylvania's jurisdiction in that area. Lord Dunmore had sent Dr. John Connolly to represent the authority of Virginia at the Forks of the Ohio. Quarrels and much bitterness ensued and a number of friendly Indians including the entire family of the noted Mingo Chief, Logan, were killed. By the spring of 1774 another general Indian uprising seemed imminent all along the frontier, for there came frequent reports of the massacre of traders and settlers. The alarm spread rapidly. Exposed settlers abandoned their farms and fled across the mountains or gathered in fortified stockades. More than one thousand were said to have crossed the Monongahela in a single day. Arthur St. Clair wrote to Governor Penn that he "did not meet less than a hundred Families, and I think two Thousand head of cattle in twenty miles riding." A similar exodus took place in southwestern Virginia, and even the frontier in South Carolina and Georgia shared in the apprehension.

Decisive measures were clearly imperative. In June Gov-

ernor Dunmore called out a portion of the Virginia militia and
prepared for an aggressive campaign in the Indian country.
On October 10th the little army of eleven hundred men re-
pelled an attack of about an equal number of Indians led by
Chief Cornstalk, at a place known as Point Pleasant at the
mouth of the Great Kanawha River. The battle was not an
overwhelming defeat, but it broke the spirit of Indian resistance and resulted in a few years of quiet on the frontier.

SETTLEMENTS IN WEST FLORIDA

While the movements which have just been sketched were
in progress settlements were being made in the isolated region
of West Florida. Here no royal proclamation sought to exclude settlers. On the contrary, every inducement was offered
to attract population to this new province. Although in 1765
it was reported that a considerable number of German and
French immigrants were expected at Mobile, danger from
Indians and the disturbed relations between the civil and military authorities in the province were deterring factors during
the first few years. In 1768, however, several Virginians arrived at Pensacola to look for land. After some exploration
they applied, according to a letter printed in the *Pennsylvania
Gazette,* for a "large Tract, obliging themselves to bring with
them ten Families, and 100 Slaves, together with a large Quantity of Cattle. There are also several Virginians settling on
the banks of the Mississippi, where the lands are as good as
any in the Universe." Another account tells of people from
western Virginia and North Carolina proceeding by land to the
Holston, where they built flatboats or barges, in which they
floated down that stream to the Tennessee and thence down
the Ohio and Mississippi to their destination in the Natchez
district.

A correspondent writing from Pensacola in 1773 waxed eloquent over the prospects of the southwestern colony. "The
Lands of the Mississippi, and the Healthfulness of the Climate," he declared, "are so perfectly inviting, that Emigrants
from the Northern Colonies are daily taking up lands there,
and improving them, so that in a few Years I hope to see in

that Part of West Florida, the most opulent Settlement of any in British America." Indeed, when he considered the great Mississippi River and the fertile lands along its borders, the writer ventured with typical western enthusiasm "to foretell that some where on its Banks, some Day or other, will be the greatest trading City of the Universe." Others apparently shared his views, for in this same year a group referred to as the Connecticut Military Adventurers laid off twenty-three townships near Natchez. Four hundred families were reported to have come from Virginia and North Carolina by way of the river, in addition to four shiploads by way of the Gulf of Mexico. Parson Sweezy also arrived with a small party from New Jersey.

Even George Washington had become interested in the possibility of obtaining lands in West Florida and had commissioned a Mr. Woods to make investigations for him. The result was not encouraging. "I have heard since Mr. Wood's departure," Washington wrote to William Crawford in September, "that all the lands on that part of the Mississippi, to which he was restricted by me, are already engaged by the emigrants, who have resorted to that country." In 1775 General Lyman and Colonel Putman both led parties from New England to sites along the lower Mississippi. These were doubtless the military adventurers to whom reference has already been made. Thus, before the beginning of the war for independence West Florida was rapidly being settled by British subjects.

CHAPTER X

THE WILDERNESS ROAD

THE SETTLEMENT ON THE WATAUGA

THE discontent reflected in the regulation controversy in North Carolina and the troubled conditions occasioned by the conflict were among the causes which contributed to a new westward movement of much consequence. About 1769 pioneers from Virginia began to settle along the Watauga River, a tributary of the Tennessee. The new settlement was in what is now the northeastern corner of Tennessee. Its founders, however, thought they were settling on lands belonging to Virginia, and only after some surveying was done was it discovered that they were within the nominal jurisdiction of North Carolina. After the Battle of Alamance many of the defeated and discouraged regulators, as well as other discontented families from North Carolina, joined the Virginians on the Watauga.

Two men soon won positions of leadership in the new community—James Robertson and John Sevier. These two men were of strikingly different backgrounds and character, but both became able leaders of men in the wilderness environment. Robertson was Scotch-Irish, illiterate until his wife taught him the rudiments of reading and writing, quiet, resourceful, and at the same time courageous and masterful. Sevier was a gentleman by birth, of Huguenot extraction, magnetic, educated, the friend of men like Franklin and Madison, but the equal of Robertson in courage and abilities as a frontier leader. Another man widely known among the settlers was Daniel Boone, descended from pioneer ancestors and thoroughly educated in wilderness lore but not in the learning of books. All three were soon to play leading parts in the next phases of the pageant of the westward movement, in the then mysterious region of Kentucky and Tennessee.

With the growth of the Watauga settlement there soon

developed the need of some form of government. Virginia could do nothing and North Carolina showed no interest. Besides, the running of the Indian boundary line showed Watauga to be in territory reserved for the Cherokee Indians. But the undaunted settlers revealed a capacity and a determination to solve their own problems that was to be repeated many times by later pioneers in similar situations. The friendly Cherokees were induced to lease the lands on the Watauga. The settlers, under the leadership of James Robertson, also proceeded to draw up "Articles of Association" establishing in the words of Dr. Archibald Henderson, "the first free and independent government, democratic in spirit, representative in form, ever organized upon the American continent." Under this "constitution" court sessions were held, wills recorded, marriage licenses issued, and other measures taken for the common welfare and protection of the scattered settlers. This was in 1772. Five years later North Carolina took cognizance of the Watauga settlement and organized it as Washington County.

DANIEL BOONE AND KENTUCKY

Before a regularly organized government was thus given to Watauga a new western community, called Transylvania by its promoters, was seeking recognition from the harassed Continental Congress and pressing its claims in the Virginia assembly. The story of Transylvania is the story of the earliest settlements in Kentucky.

What white man from the English colonies first saw Kentucky will probably never be known with certainty. Gabriel Arthur apparently wandered over the eastern section with the Cherokees about 1673. The party of South Carolinians led by Jean Coutoure in 1699 paddled down the Tennessee River into the Ohio. John Peter Salley (or Salling) and four Virginia companions saw the northern shore in 1742 when they floated down the Ohio. The first deliberate exploration of which a record remains was that conducted in 1750 by Dr. Thomas Walker as the agent of the Loyal Land Company. He traveled through the Cumberland Gap into the heart of the Kentucky country and gave to many of the rivers and moun-

tains the names which they still bear. The following year
Christopher Gist was in northeastern Kentucky prospecting
for the Ohio Company. These are a few reconnaissances
which left a record on the pages of history. It is certain, however, that numerous nameless traders and adventurers and
"long hunters" wandered over the region and brought back
tales of its beauties and resources. By 1770 Kentucky was
thus known in a vague sort of way along the frontier. By this
time it was a no-man's land, not inhabited permanently by any
Indian tribes, but used as a hunting ground by many redskins
from the south and especially from across the Ohio.

Thus it was that the man whose name is always associated
with the exploration of Kentucky cannot be rightly called its
discoverer. Nevertheless, it is true that Daniel Boone did
more than any other one man to make Kentucky known as a
land of promise for land-hungry settlers. Boone came of a
family of pioneers. His Quaker father, Squire Boone, came
to America some time in the second decade of the eighteenth
century and settled on a backwoods farm in eastern Pennsylvania. He married Sarah Morgan in 1720. The couple settled
down to hard work and the raising of children until, after a
dozen years, they had saved enough money to buy a farm of
two hundred and fifty acres in Berks County near the site of
the modern city of Reading, then a wild frontier region. Here
the sixth child, Daniel Boone, was born in 1734.

In his so-called autobiography, dictated late in life to John
Filson, the Kentucky historian, Daniel Boone said of himself:
"Many dark and sleepless nights have I been a companion for
owls, separated from the cheerful society of men, scorched by
the summer's sun and pinched by the winter's cold, an instrument ordained to settle the wilderness." This kind of life was
his by choice. Even in his boyhood he learned well the ways
of the woods and their furry creatures, as well as the habits
of the Indians; and while still in his early teens became an expert hunter. When he was sixteen his father one day announced his intention of moving to the valley of the Yadkin in
North Carolina. This must have been glad news for the
young man, for it presented visions of new adventure and a
fresh field for his prowess with the rifle. In the spring of 1750

the family set out in canvas-covered wagons for their new home.

The Yadkin country proved equal to the lad's most ardent expectations. Game of all kinds, even including the buffalo, abounded in great profusion. To be sure, there was laborious and prosaic toil to be performed, clearing the forest and preparing ground for crops; but there was always some opportunity for zestful hunting. "In imagination it is no difficult matter to see him," writes H. Addington Bruce, "his five foot ten of sinewy, buck-skinned manhood stretched at full length behind a fallen log, finger on trigger, ears alert, blue eyes gleaming, thin lips doggedly compressed, a healthy glow on his cheek. Or, it may be, cutting his way through a tangle of undergrowth, leaping silently from rock to rock across the bed of a fast-running mountain stream, and buoyantly clambering from ridge to ridge of some bristling mountain wall. Never, they say, was there such a hunter on the Yadkin, or one who so enjoyed the hunter's life." [1]

The outbreak of the last French war interrupted these pleasures and young Boone journeyed northward with the North Carolina contingent to participate in Braddock's fatal march across the Pennsylvania mountains towards Fort Duquesne. Boone was one of the wagoners who cut the traces of their horses and fled in panic from the scene of disaster, and he returned rather crestfallen to his Yadkin home, where he helped to defend the frontier against ensuing Indian raids. Yet his experiences in the campaign were not all of unpleasant memory, for he had become acquainted with John Finley, a far-ranging trapper and adventurer. Finley had been in Kentucky, which he described to Boone as a veritable hunter's paradise, as well as the scene of bloody fights between the Indian tribes who encountered each other there.

After the close of the war Daniel Boone gave himself up to his favorite occupation of hunting and exploring. He was in the Watauga region in 1760. The following year he went into western South Carolina. Another glimpse reveals him in 1764 in eastern Tennessee, where, in language which bears the stamp

[1] H. Addington Bruce, *Daniel Boone and the Wilderness Road* (1922), p. 15. By permission of The Macmillan Company, publishers.

of editing, he is said to have exclaimed: "I am richer than the man mentioned in scripture, who owned the cattle on a thousand hills—I own the wild beasts of more than a thousand valleys!"[2] The next year he extended his wanderings as far south as Florida. In 1767 he attempted to reach Kentucky—the land of John Finley's glowing stories. Winter came on, however, with deep snows. The country proved impenetrable by the route he was following, and he was forced to turn back with the products of his winter's hunting.

Curiously enough, at about this time John Finley turned up in the Yadkin settlement. His enthusiasm for the beautiful Kentucky country was unabated and now he offered to lead a party thither. Thus it was that on the first day of May, 1769, Finley, Daniel Boone, and four other men departed from the Yadkin with high anticipations and adequate equipment for a long hunt. In course of time they passed through Cumberland Gap and into Kentucky, which proved fully equal to Finley's descriptions.

John Finley soon disappears from the story, but Daniel Boone spent the succeeding two years in Kentucky, hunting and exploring, and becoming thoroughly acquainted with the country. It was during this period that he had many of the experiences which make his biography such a tale of adventure. Part of the time he had companions, but for months he was entirely alone. His accumulations of furs and his equipment were stolen by Indians. Once he and a companion were captured by the redskins but finally managed to escape. At last, in the spring of 1771, with undaunted spirits he and his brother started homeward with a goodly booty of furs. Not far from the settlements they were robbed of everything by a party of northern Indians, and obliged to return empty-handed to the Yadkin. Nevertheless, Boone was rich in knowledge of the resources and fertility of Kentucky and he was determined, in spite of everything, to return there with his family at the earliest opportunity.

Eventually this desire was to be gratified, and Daniel Boone was to lead into Kentucky not merely his own family

[2] H. Addington Bruce, *Daniel Boone and the Wilderness Road* (1922) p. 47. By permission of The Macmillan Company, publishers.

but also many other families of home-seekers. Two years elapsed before he was able even to attempt the fruition of his plans, although during this time he made more than one trip into Kentucky. His enthusiasm for the country increased with each visit and was communicated to other settlers along the frontier. In September, 1773, he and his wife and their eight children were ready to set out for their new home, and they were joined by five other families. The caravan proceeded safely until it reached Powell's Valley and was joined by other families from Virginia. Then tragedy brought an abrupt end to the undertaking. A party returning from a settlement on the Clinch River with supplies was set upon by a band of Shawnee Indians and seven men were murdered, including James Boone, the eldest child of Daniel and Rebecca Boone, now a promising lad of seventeen. Although grief-stricken, the father urged that the party proceed to its destination. But the others were unwilling to take the risk, and so they all turned back.

The decision was fortunate, as succeeding events proved. Indian resentment because of encroachments of the whites was growing apace all along the frontier. In the following year this unrest burst into the conflict of Dunmore's War, and everywhere exposed settlers were either slaughtered or forced to flee eastward for safety. Because of his extensive knowledge of the region, Daniel Boone was chosen as one of two men to carry a warning to surveying parties who were known to be in Kentucky. By this time Virginia was laying out bounty lands for soldiers south of the Ohio and private land-hunters were making surveys. George Washington had made two trips into northeastern Kentucky looking for land.

Boone and his companion succeeded in finding the surveyors and warning them of their danger. They also discovered that a settlement was already being made in Kentucky. This was the work of a group of men led by James Harrod, a man well qualified for such a task because of his character and long experience as a backwoodsman. This settlement was almost immediately abandoned because of the Indian disturbance, but it was reoccupied after the war.

THE TRANSYLVANIA COLONY

The year 1775 witnessed the launching of a new project for a western colony and in the furtherance of this scheme Daniel Boone found the long-delayed satisfaction of his wish to settle in Kentucky. The guiding genius in this new enterprise was Richard Henderson, and the nine men included in the little group finally adopted the name Transylvania Company. About the plan and activities of the company and the character and ambitions of its leader there are conflicting opinions. The fact that their operations were conducted in a region claimed by Virginia and on the eve of the American Revolution no doubt explains some of the hostile comment of contemporaries. The worst possible interpretation merely places the Transylvania Company and Richard Henderson in the same category with the numerous other western land schemes and their promoters already mentioned. The main difference was that Henderson and his associates came nearer to success and, although meeting failure in the end, nevertheless left a permanent settlement.

Richard Henderson was born in Virginia of fairly prosperous middle class parents. The family moved to North Carolina when Richard was ten years of age. The lad received better than an average education and took up the study of the law. In time he became a judge and shared with other officers in the frontier counties the distrust and hostility of the exasperated settlers during the Regulation troubles. In 1770 his court at Hillsboro was broken up by a mob, he was forced to flee for personal safety, and later his house and barn were burned.

It was apparently about this time that Henderson began evolving his plans to obtain possession of a vast body of land in the West. It is possible that Daniel Boone was spying out a favorable location for Henderson on some of his trips into Kentucky. Whatever may have been the promoter's early activities, he had his Transylvania Company organized by 1775. In March of that year a bold step was taken. At the Sycamore Shoals of the Watauga a treaty was made with the Cherokee

Indians, whereby the tribesmen ceded to the Transylvania Company approximately twenty million acres of land lying between the Cumberland and Kentucky rivers and including much of what are now Kentucky and central Tennessee. Of course such a transaction was wholly illegal. The Proclamation of 1763 was still in force, as were the prohibitions of the colonial governments against unauthorized western settlements. Private purchases from the Indians were strictly forbidden. Finally, the land thus acquired lay within the charter limits claimed by Virginia. But none of these considerations deterred the members of the Transylvania Company. The King's proclamation was no longer regarded anywhere with awe. The authority of the colonial governors was tottering. Virginia's claims might not be valid. And so the company prepared to enter at once into possession of "the dark and bloody ground" which to the associates was the land of promise.

Daniel Boone's aid was now definitely sought and secured by Richard Henderson. The explorer was asked to lead a party and cut a road to Kentucky. The result was the marking of the Wilderness Road, one of America's most famous pioneer trails. Boone gathered a party of thirty hardy and well-armed men and on March 10, 1775, the road-marking began. As directly as possible they proceeded to Cumberland Gap, beyond which they traveled northward for some distance along an Indian trail known as the Warrior's Path, and they then turned westward. Soon they came to a region where for twenty miles they were obliged to hack and burn their way through dead brush and for another thirty miles through cane-brakes. Then, at last, their labors were rewarded. "We began to discover the pleasing and rapturous appearance of the plains of Kentucky," wrote Felix Walker, a member of the party, many years later. "A new sky and strange earth seemed to be presented to our view. So rich a soil we had never seen before. . . . The woods were abounding with wild game— turkeys so numerous that it might be said they appeared but one flock, universally scattered in the woods. . . . A sight so delightful to our view and so grateful to our feelings almost inclined us in transport to kiss the soil of Kentucky—in imitation of Columbus, as he hailed and saluted the sand on his first setting foot on the shores of America." [3]

This rapturous enjoyment was soon interrupted. On the early morning of March 25th the road-makers were awakened by the horrid war-whoops of a party of wandering Indians who had quietly surrounded the camp during the preceding night. From behind trees the Indians poured a volley into the camp and then retired. One of Boone's men was killed outright, one died a few days later, and another was severely wounded. A number of the men fled immediately and although the Indians did not repeat the attack, it was only with difficulty that Boone prevailed upon the others to hold their ground. "Your company is desired greatly," Boone wrote Henderson on April 1st, "for the people are very uneasy, but are willing to stay and venture their lives with you, and now is the time to flusterate the intentions of the Indians, and keep the country, whilst we are in it." [4]

Richard Henderson at this time was on his way to Kentucky at the head of a company of prospective settlers which numbered ultimately about fifty men. The receipt of Boone's message was extremely disquieting, as was also the meeting of other settlers fleeing from the region. Some of Henderson's followers refused to go further, but the leader was undaunted. He was determined to take possession of his Kentucky domain in spite of all dangers. Pressing on, the party at last joined Boone on April 20th and were received with a joyous salute and a banquet of buffalo meat. The building of a stockaded town, fittingly named Boonesborough, was pushed with energy and a preliminary allotment of land was made.

Three other settlements in the vicinity gave Henderson much concern. James Harrod and his associates had returned and re-occupied Harrodstown, to the west of Boonesborough, and had planted another small settlement nearby at Boiling Spring. To the southwest a group of Virginians led by Captain John Floyd had established themselves. The attitude of these settlers toward the Transylvania Company was a matter of

[3] H. Addington Bruce, *Daniel Boone and the Wilderness Road* (1922) pp. 104-105. By permission of The Macmillan Company, publishers.
[4] Ibid., p. 109.

considerable importance. Happily for Henderson, they expressed a willingness to recognize the purchase from the Cherokees and take title under the company. Each of the settlements was requested to choose representatives to establish a form of government and enact the necessary laws.

On May 23, 1775, the delegates assembled at Boonesborough. Because there was no suitable building the meeting was held under a giant elm tree, where a platform had been erected. The delegates, sitting on logs, or lying on the grass, or leaning on their rifles were addressed by Richard Henderson. "You, perhaps," he said, "are fixing the palladium, or placing the first corner-stone of an edifice, the height and magnificence of whose superstructure is now in the womb of futurity, and can only become great in proportion to the excellence of its foundation. . . . We have a right to make necessary laws for the regulation of our conduct without giving offense to Great Britain, or any of the American Colonies, without disturbing the repose of any society or community under heaven."

A compact was entered into between the proprietors of the company and the representatives of the people which was to be the constitution of Transylvania. While preserving the outward form of democracy and representative government, the compact in reality left to the people little power save that of taxation. There was scarcely anything to curb the potential ability of the proprietors to fill all the important offices with men subservient to their interests. It is almost certain that friction would soon have appeared if the compact had continued long in operation.

Besides adopting this constitution or agreement the assembly proceeded to the adoption of a number of laws. Courts and a militia were established, fees were prescribed, and "profane swearing and Sabbath breaking" were prohibited. Daniel Boone drafted a measure for the protection of wild game, since it was already necessary to go fifteen or twenty miles from Boonesborough to find buffalo. He also brought in a bill "for improving the breed of horses"—thus giving an early impetus to a movement for which Kentucky later became famous.

All this law-making was desirable and important. But the Transylvania proprietors had more weighty questions on their minds. They held a questionable title from the Indians and they had established a colony; but their status was far from certain. The governor of North Carolina issued a proclamation in which he referred to them as "an infamous Company of land Pyrates." Lord Dunmore, soon to end his rule as governor of Virginia, proclaimed with even greater vehemence and more to the point, because of the encroachment on that colony's territory. The first hope of Henderson and his associates was to secure recognition as the fourteenth colony from the Continental Congress. James Hogg was for this purpose sent as an emissary to Philadelphia. The proposal elicited some interest but failed of success. The Congress was content to leave the question to Virginia's decision.

In the meantime affairs were getting out of hand in Kentucky. Many additional settlers arrived during the fall of 1775 and the spring and summer of 1776. Among the newcomers were many Virginians, including George Rogers Clark, who was soon to play a leading role in the drama of the West. These accessions to the settlements had no reason to look with favor upon the claims of a proprietary company at a time when all authority originating in the mother country was being flouted. Besides, the original settlers of Transylvania were rapidly growing discontented. Prices for land were being increased, larger fees were assessed, the proprietors had reserved for themselves much of the choicest lands, such as those at the Falls of the Ohio, and there were other grievances.

The revolt against the proprietors began in the Harrodstown and Boiling Spring settlements and soon spread throughout the entire region. While indignant because of the alleged high-handed actions of the company, the settlers were by no means disposed to try another experiment in independence. The threatening dangers of Indian hostility made them very appreciative of the desirability of coming under the protecting wing of one of the established governments. It was most natural, therefore, that they should turn to Virginia. An eloquent and skilfully worded petition was drafted and sent to Williamsburg. After stating their grievances, the petitioners declared that "as we are anxious to concur in every respect with our brethren of the United Colonies, for our just rights and privileges, as far as our infant settlement and remote situation will admit of, we humbly expect and implore to be taken under the protection of the honorable Convention of the Colony of Virginia, of which we cannot help thinking ourselves still a part, and request your kind interposition in our behalf, that we may not suffer under the rigorous demands and impositions of the gentlemen styling themselves Proprietors." [5]

Later George Rogers Clark and John Gabriel Jones were sent to Virginia with a second petition, in which the Transylvania proprietors were more severely assailed. Here again the ingenuity of the writers was revealed, for they pointed out "how impolitic it would be to suffer such a respectable Body of Prime Rifle Men to remain in a state of Neutrality." Henderson and his associates did everything in their power to bring about the failure of these petitions, but after a long struggle they were defeated.

On December 7, 1776, the newly organized legislature of Virginia passed a law of far-reaching importance establishing the county of Kentucky under its protecting jurisdiction. Transylvania was now at an end. In recognition of their services Richard Henderson and Company were granted two hundred thousand acres of land in Kentucky. Later the legislature of North Carolina gave them a similar grant in the eastern part of the present State of Tennessee. The plan for a new proprietary colony failed, but Richard Henderson deserves credit for providing the stimulus which began a movement later culminating in the first American Commonwealth west of the Alleghany Mountains.

[5] H. Addington Bruce, *Daniel Boone and the Wilderness Road* (1922), p. 148. By permission of The Macmillan Company, publishers.

CHAPTER XI

THE WEST DURING THE WAR FOR INDEPENDENCE

DURING the long struggle which began at Lexington and Concord and Bunker Hill the savage fury of the red men was unleashed in full force against the American frontier settlements. From New York to Georgia the war whoop was heard in the night and the light from burning cabins cast a glare on scenes of butchery. The hardy pioneers of Kentucky learned all too well the meaning of the name "dark and bloody ground" which had been given to their beautiful country. Vengeful campaigns of retaliation were waged. By one of the most heroic efforts of the entire war the Illinois posts were wrested from the British, and elaborate plans were made to capture the strategic stronghold of Detroit. In the South the Spanish aided the Americans and furthered their own interests by permitting financial assistance to the Americans and by capturing British posts. In the Mohawk Valley and at King's Mountain in South Carolina vital plans of the British were frustrated. These are the main features of the American Revolution in the West.

THE BRITISH WIN THE INDIANS

At the outbreak of the war both the Americans and the British sought the alliance and aid or neutrality of the Indians. At this game the latter were much more successful. Discerning leaders among the natives were not slow to see that the British in the West were either soldiers or traders, while an ever-increasing proportion of the Americans were settlers; and it was the settlers whom the Indians hated with a hatred born of fear. Besides the British were better supplied with goods with which to pay for friendship and enemies' scalps.

Thus Americans like the experienced George Morgan at Pittsburgh sought without much success to keep the chain of friendship bright with the tribes of the Ohio Valley or at least to hold them neutral. On the other hand, Henry Hamilton, Lieutenant-Governor and commandant at Detroit, had little difficulty in persuading the Indians that both their immediate interest and their hope of driving back the encroaching settlers lay in cooperation with the British. If he did not actually instruct the natives to bring back scalps, it is certain that he paid for many of these gruesome trophies, and thus earned the hateful title of "hair-buyer" given him by the frontiersmen. As a matter of fact, it was only rarely that Indians fought for the American cause during the Revolution. Practically all the combats in the West were fought between American troops, militia and settlers, on the one side, and Indians led by Englishmen and loyalists, on the other.

During the summer of 1776 John Stuart, loyalist Indian superintendent for the southern district, was busy cementing alliances with the tribes and organizing them for attacks on the frontier. The powerful and numerous Cherokees were ready to listen. In spite of the fact that their chiefs had recently made the huge cession of land to the Transylvania Company, their resentment was bitter against the on-pushing settlers. In June and July they fell upon the settlements on the Holston, at Watauga, and all along the frontier of the Carolinas and Georgia. Where the settlers fled to their stockaded forts they were able to beat off the assaults. At the Watauga fort, for instance, forty defenders led by John Sevier and James Robertson withstood an intermittent siege of three weeks. Isolated families and those who ventured outside the forts were ruthlessly slaughtered or carried into captivity. In the end, however, the Cherokees were completely humbled. From Virginia, the Carolinas and Georgia armies marched into the Indian country, defeated the various bands of the Cherokees one after the other, destroyed their villages and laid waste their fields. These campaigns had the additional effect of making the eastern portion of the Wilderness Road relatively safe for travel.

THE DEFENSE OF THE FRONTIER

Meanwhile the settlers in Kentucky were having a taste of what was to be their lot much of the time during the war. In July, 1776, Jemima Boone and two girl companions were captured by Indians while they were enjoying a boatride on the Kentucky River. As soon as they were missed a pursuing party, led by Daniel Boone and John Floyd, was organized in Boonesborough. A rescue was fortunately effected, because the girls, in true frontier fashion, had succeeded in leaving a trail marked by torn bits of clothing. This episode proved to be no isolated or accidental happening. The entire region was soon in a state of alarm with news of murders, burnings of cabins, and the theft of horses and cattle. The outlying settlers fled to the settlements and many of them took the Wilderness Trail across the mountains. In fact, if the Indians had been well organized and had conducted systematic assaults on the little forts they might well have rid Kentucky of the hated white invaders.

One of the greatest needs of the settlers was for ammunition. Fortunately George Rogers Clark and John Gabriel Jones were in Williamsburg at this time presenting the complaints of the Kentuckians against the Transylvania Company and their petition to be taken under the wing of Virginia. They succeeded in securing a supply of powder and lead. Loading it on a flatboat at Pittsburgh the two men, with seven followers, floated down the Ohio, eluded the pursuit of watchful Indians, and landed their cargo on an island near where Maysville now stands. Word was sent to the settlements and a party from Harrodstown at last brought in the precious ammuntion late in December, although not before Jones and two or three other men lost their lives in an ill-advised attack on the Indians. One of the men who played a helpful part in this affair was the famous scout and Indian fighter, Simon Kenton.

The year 1777 witnessed the launching of an organized Indian attack on the entire frontier, mainly under the direction of Henry Hamilton of Detroit, with the untiring assistance of such hated white leaders of Indian raids as Alexander McKee and Simon Girty and his two brothers. The treacherous murder of the Shawnee chief, Cornstalk, by mutinous American soldiers, made of that small but fierce tribe an inveterate scourge of all Americans who came in their way. At Pittsburgh elaborate plans were made by George Morgan, General Edward Hand, and General Lachlan McIntosh, in succession, for an attack on Detroit and for punitive forays into the Indian country. The former came to naught and the latter had scant success. The Continental Congress had little money with which to finance campaigns west of the mountains. Furthermore, frontier militia was far from dependable in any enterprise of long duration, for the men were constantly thinking of their wives and children and homes inadequately protected against Indian barbarity, and of their neglected fields. The worried officials had more than they could do to provide protection for the extended frontiers of Pennsylvania and Virginia, without carrying aggressive warfare into the enemy's country. It was left to a young Kentuckian to plan and carry out an exploit that brought him imperishable renown and checked the ambitions of Henry Hamilton and his Indian allies.

Clark's Plan for the Defense of Kentucky

During this same year, 1777, Kentucky felt the full fury of the red men. County government was established and a militia organized, with compulsory service. The latter measure was of utmost importance, for each of the palisaded settlements was called upon to withstand determined sieges. Harrodstown and Boonesborough were both closely invested and Logan's Fort was beleagured from May until September, a duration remarkable among the Indians who usually had little patience for long sieges. Only the timely arrival of reenforcements from Virginia saved the settlement from destruction.

The man who was in command of the defense measures in Kentucky was George Rogers Clark, whose previous services have already been mentioned. He was only twenty-five years of age in 1777, but he possessed qualities of leadership and knowledge of frontier life which gained him the general admiration and loyalty of the Kentucky pioneers. He was born

near Charlottesville, Virginia, not far from the birthplace of
Thomas Jefferson, and he went to school for a time with James
Madison and John Tyler; while his family was well known to
many other outstanding men of the Old Dominion during the
stirring days of the Revolution. Formal schooling, largely confined to classics, had little attraction for him, although he
developed a keen interest in history and politics and especially
in the phenomena of nature; and he was distinctly gregarious
in disposition. The wilderness appealed to him irresistibly and
he early became an adept in the ways of the woods and a close
observer of the character and habits of the Indians. The prevalent land-madness of the period also struck in him a respon-
sive chord. At nineteen he took up surveying and in the
following year, 1772, made his first trip to the Ohio region.
Like nearly all the early adventurers into Kentucky, he became
an ardent enthusiast regarding that alluring country and decided to cast his lot with its founders. Here, as has been seen,
he rapidly achieved a position of leadership.

While engaged in the strenuous task of organizing the defense of Kentucky, George Rogers Clark was constantly cogi-
tating the larger aspects of the situation. He soon saw that the
surest method of preventing or checking the British-directed
Indian raids in Kentucky would be to strike a counter blow at
the centers of British influence in the West. He seems also to
have realized the strategic importance of Kentucky. If the
British could destroy the Kentucky settlements, the way would
then be open to them to attack the entire frontier more effectively, and thus seriously embárrass the entire American cause.
His knowledge of the geography of the country north of the
Ohio was surprisingly extensive. Detroit was apparently his
main objective from the beginning, but he also knew that the
British posts in the old French settlements in the Illinois country and at Vincennes on the Wabash were important links in the
chain of British operations, as well as sources of food supplies
for Detroit. Therefore, to use his own words, "as the com-
mandants of different towns of the Illinois and Wabash, I
knew, (were) busily engaged in exciting the Indians, their
reduction became my first object, expecting that it might probably open a field for further action."

Accordingly, without divulging his purpose to anyone, in April, 1777, Clark sent Benjamin Linn and Samuel Moore to the Illinois country to ascertain the strength of the forts and garrisons and the attitude of the French inhabitants of the villages. Along the east bank of the Mississippi were the four villages of Kaskaskia, Prairie du Rocher, St. Philippe and Cahokia, the latter and most northerly being almost opposite St. Louis. The total population of the four settlements was about one thousand whites and six hundred negro slaves, with a small British garrison at Kaskaskia commanded by the Chevalier de Rocheblave. To the eastward on the east side of the Wabash one hundred and fifty miles from its mouth was Vincennes, with perhaps ninety French families, and one hundred miles north was the stockaded trading post of Ouiatenon. There were other small posts and settlements at Prairie du Chien, St. Joseph, Michilimackinac, and Green Bay. American traders had already gained wide acquaintance and considerable influence in these villages.

Clark's two emissaries returned to Kentucky after an absence of two months. They reported that although military training was maintained in the Illinois villages and every effort was made to cause the French inhabitants to fear the backwoodsmen, yet there were evidences of sympathy with the American cause. Thereupon Clark wrote a letter to Governor Patrick Henry of Virginia boldly proposing that an expedition be organized to capture Kaskaskia and the surrounding posts. Then, to follow up this letter with a personal presentation of his plans, he set out for Williamsburg on the first day of October, 1777.

Taking leave of Clark temporarily as he made this momentous journey, let us see what was transpiring on the lower Mississippi. As will be seen, the success of Clark's undertaking was largely dependent on assistance which he received from New Orleans.

Spanish Aid to Americans

The Spanish officials of Louisiana had for several years been disturbed by their inability to compete successfully with the British in the trade of the Mississippi River. At the opening of the Revolution they were further alarmed by the threatening growth of British West Florida, which became a haven for numerous loyalists from the rebelling American colonies. Governor Unzaga of Louisiana was, therefore, inclined to give such comfort and aid to the Americans as neutrality would permit, and the same policy was even more definitely followed by his successor, Don Bernardo de Gálvez. Americans were permitted to purchase at New Orleans powder which was badly needed at Fort Pitt. American ships were also protected from capture by the British. Later valuable supplies were sent to the American posts on the frontier. Much of the credit for this favorable attitude was due to the efforts of Oliver Pollock who had been in New Orleans since 1768. First as the unofficial agent of Virginia and later as the official commercial agent of the Continental Congress, he rendered invaluable service to the American cause. It must not be supposed, however, that the Spanish were inspired primarily by sympathy for the struggling Americans. They were thinking mainly of advantages which they hoped would accrue to themselves in the event of American success. In this hope they were artfully encouraged by the suggestions of such men as Patrick Henry.

Besides securing supplies from New Orleans, American officials realized the desirability of taking possession of the British posts in the Natchez district on the Mississippi in West Florida, thus keeping the river open for communication. Early in 1778 Captain Willing with a small force descended the Ohio and Mississippi, captured Natchez, and conducted destructive raids against the British plantations on the east bank of the river. Oliver Pollock, on his part, organized expeditions which captured several British boats on the river and took possession of the post of Manchac. These successes, however, were of only short duration since no force was available with which to garrison the captured settlements. The British were soon in possession again and West Florida remained in their hands until the Spanish won control after that nation entered the war.

THE AMERICAN CONQUEST OF THE OLD NORTHWEST

Returning now to George Rogers Clark, we find him in Virginia in November, 1777, presenting his daring plan in person to Patrick Henry. The governor favored the enterprise, as did also Thomas Jefferson, George Wythe, and George Mason, whose advice was sought. It was natural that Virginians should look kindly on any proposal, however rash it might seem, which had for its object the protection of that State's western settlements in Kentucky. But there was also a more deep-seated animus for their willingness to encourage aggressive measures against the British in the northwest. Virginia, because of her extensive charter claims west of the mountains, had been especially alarmed and angered by the alleged efforts of the mother country to curtail colonial limits by such measures as the Proclamation of 1763, the Indian boundary line of 1768, the grant to the Vandalia Company, and the Quebec Act of 1774. Clark's project seemed to offer a redress of these grievances.

Secrecy, however, was all-important to the success of the design. At the same time the approval of the Assembly was necessary. Consequently the members were told as little as possible of the real purpose, and legislative consent was secured for an expedition to protect Kentucky. Clark's public instructions indicated this to be the object, but he was also given private directions to attack and capture Kaskaskia. He was made lieutenant-colonel with authority to enlist seven companies of fifty men each in Virginia; he was given twelve hundred pounds in depreciated currency, and furnished with an order on General Hand at Pittsburgh for supplies, ammunition, and boats.

The success of this exploit, in spite of tremendous handicaps, has made it one of the favorite stories of American history, known in its main features to nearly every school child. It has also been celebrated in such fiction as Winston Churchill's *The Crossing* and Maurice Thompson's *Alice of Old Vincennes*.

Difficulties and disappointments sufficient to have thoroughly discouraged a less determined man attended Clark from

the very beginning. Enlistments fell far short of expectations
for the reason that Indian raids all along the frontier disinclined men to leave their threatened homes. With less than
half the contemplated quota of men he made headquarters on
Corn Island at the Falls of the Ohio. Here for the first time
the men learned the real objective of the expedition. A few
demurred and made their escape from the island, but the others
all expressed enthusiasm for the venture and their entire willingness to follow Clark. News of the French alliance coming
about this time was a distinct cause for encouragement. One
hundred and seventy-five men in four companies, captained by
Joseph Bowman, William Harrod, Leonard Helm, and John
Montgomery, now prepared to carry the war into the enemy's
country filled with thousands of Indians under British
influence.

On June 26, 1778, the expedition got under way. As the
boats shot the rapids there occurred a total eclipse of the sun,
an omen which aroused fears in the breasts of a few of the more
superstitious. At the old abandoned French post of Fort
Massac, ten miles below the mouth of the Tennessee, the boats
were secreted and the little army set out on foot on the one
hundred and twenty mile march to Kaskaskia. Fortunately
they had as guides some American traders who had recently
been in the Illinois villages and who had been encountered just
before the expedition disembarked. Marching in single file,
with necessary supplies on their backs, the borderers made
their way through a trackless forest for nearly fifty miles and
then came out on the broad prairie, which must have been an
astonishing sight to most of them. Here the trader who was
now serving as guide lost his way temporarily, causing exasper-
ation to Clark and the suspicion of treachery. "I never in my
life," wrote Clark, "felt such a flow of rage,—to be wandering
in a country where every nation of Indians could raise three or
four times our number and a certain loss of our enterprise by
the enemies getting timely notice." Soon, however, the guide
found his bearings and the march was resumed. On the evening of July 4th the Kaskaskia River was reached, a short
distance above the village.

After dark Clark led his army of backwoodsmen into the

town, captured Rocheblave, the commandant, and took possession without the firing of a shot. The dirty, unkempt appearance of the invaders seemed to bear out all the terrible tales of the "Long Knives" which the French inhabitants had heard. This impression Clark was at first careful not to destroy, in order that his leniency when he had gained full control would be all the more appreciated. "I don't suppose," he wrote, "greater silence ever reigned among the inhabitants of a place." Later a deputation came asking that the people might be permitted to gather in the church, a request which was coldly granted. Shortly afterward the priest and a few others presented themselves to Clark, begging that families might not be separated and that the women and children might be permitted to keep a portion of their clothes and some provisions. The American commander now felt that the game had gone far enough. He accordingly told the delegation of the French-American alliance and informed them that they might resume their accustomed life with perfect freedom. "They retired," says Clark, "and in a few minutes the scene was changed from an almost mortal dejection to that of joy in the extreme,—the bells ringing, the church crowded, returning thanks, in short every appearance of extravagant joy that could fill a place with utmost confusion." The allegiance of the inhabitants of Kaskaskia was thus completely won.

A small detachment under Captain Bowman had no difficulty in securing possession of Cahokia, St. Philippe, and Prairie du Rocher, and the allegiance of their people. Vincennes was won even more easily through the good offices of Pierre Gibault, a priest of Kaskaskia, who journeyed to the Wabash town with a few companions and prepared the inhabitants to welcome the Americans. Captain Leonard Helm was soon installed as commandant.

At Kaskaskia George Rogers Clark was exhibiting resourcefulness and tact no less remarkable than the qualities which had enabled him to meet the exacting tests of leadership of American frontiersmen. He gained the good will of the leading men and merchants of Kaskaskia so that they were very willing to furnish him supplies. He established cordial relations with the Spanish lieutenant-governor of St. Louis through the friendly services of Francis Vigo, a wealthy and influential trader of that town. Following instructions from Governor Henry, he drew on Oliver Pollock at New Orleans for ammunition and supplies. Indeed, to Pollock belongs much of the credit for enabling Clark to maintain himself in the Illinois country. The New Orleans agent did not hesitate to sacrifice his own personal property to provide funds when all other resources failed. Financial problems and negotiations with the surrounding Indians gave Clark constant anxiety. But he and his men were soon to face an ordeal that tried their heroism far more severely than anything they had yet experienced.

Early in August Hamilton at Detroit learned of the capture of the Illinois posts. Two months later he started with a force of whites and Indians to drive out the Americans and make good the hold of the British on the Ohio, Mississippi, and Missouri rivers. After a difficult winter expedition by lake and river and portage he arrived at Vincennes on December 17th. The French militia of that place were panic-stricken and Captain Helm had no choice but to surrender. Since it was now mid-winter Hamilton considered it both safe and prudent to postpone operations against Clark at Kaskaskia until the following spring, and accordingly he settled down in Vincennes.

Not until the closing days of January, 1779, did Clark learn this distressing news with definiteness. It was now realized that the only hope of saving the American cause in the Illinois country from irretrievable failure, as well as of protecting Kentucky against destruction, lay in the desperate expedient of a sudden, surprise attack on Hamilton. "It was at this moment," Clark later wrote, "I would have bound myself for seven years a slave to have had five hundred troops." Americans are familiar with the story of how this forlorn hope was turned into incredible victory: how Clark and his men marched the 180 miles in the dead of winter; how they waded through icy water at times up to their shoulders; how the strength of some of the men gave out and they had to be carried; how Clark performed wonders in keeping up the spirits of his men; how they at length arrived on the outskirts of Vincennes without discovery and gave the impression of much greater numbers by constantly marching and countermarching; and how, finally, against superior odds they recaptured Vincennes and made Hamilton and his soldiers prisoners of war. For its dramatic qualities and for the exhibition of sheer grit and courage this exploit has few equals in history.

Interesting as they are, we cannot follow the subsequent activities of George Rogers Clark in the West during the American Revolution. Throughout the troubled years he clung to his ambition to complete his conquest by capturing Detroit. This ambition was never realized because of circumstances beyond his control. Several times he seemed on the verge of possible achievement of his goal, but each time insuperable obstacles reared themselves in his way. He led several successful expeditions against the Indians north of the Ohio and rendered valorous service in the defense of Kentucky, giving freely not only of his strength and knowledge but also advancing his own money and pledging his credit to help defray expenses. In later pages it will be regrettably necessary to re-introduce the hero of the Illinois campaign as a participant in less glorious enterprises, at a time when he had become embittered by the failure of either Virginia or the United States government to reimburse him for his outlays and by the seeming ingratitude of the nation he had served so well.

British and Spanish at War in the West

In April, 1779, while Clark was still at Kaskaskia, Spain entered the war against England as an ally of France. Spain made no alliance with the United States and had no thought of helping to establish the independency of an American nation sufficiently powerful to endanger her own ambition to control the Mississippi Valley. Nevertheless, the Spanish in Louisiana were now freed from all trammels of neutrality, and any successes achieved by them in activities against the British were certain to benefit the American cause, at least temporarily. In the autumn of 1779 Bernardo de Gálvez, Governor of Louisiana, led expeditions which easily captured the British posts at Manchac, Baton Rouge, and Natchez on the lower Mississippi.

In May of the following year, the British launched an attack from Michilimackinac and other northern posts aimed at the recovery of the Illinois country and the capture of St. Louis and other Spanish posts. In overwhelming numbers, mostly Indians, they appeared before the little town of St. Louis, which was inadequately prepared for an onslaught. The villagers, however, put up such a stout show of defense, the expedition was so poorly managed, and the Indians were so disturbed by the discovery of the nearness of George Rogers Clark when he was supposed to be at the Falls of the Ohio, that the attackers withdrew without achieving their objectives. Another expedition was planned for 1781, but before it could be undertaken the Spanish executed a counter raid. In January, 1781, possibly with the thought of emulating Clark's midwinter march to Vincennes, a small party set out from St. Louis and later captured the British post at St. Joseph, near the site of the present town of Niles, Michigan. They destroyed stores found there, but remained in possession only one day. One important purpose of this expedition may have been revealed later during the negotiations when Spain cited this episode as entitling her to territory north of the Ohio River.

The achievements of the Spanish on the Gulf coast were of more lasting importance. Early in 1780 Gálvez captured Mobile, and one year later Pensacola, the remaining British stronghold on the Gulf, fell into his hands. Thus was laid the basis for Spanish possession of the Floridas and the controversies that troubled the early history of the United States on that border.

THE WAR ALONG THE FRONTIER

Turning now from events in the Mississippi Valley to the war along the extended frontier of settlements, we find that the outlying settlers in New York and Pennsylvania suffered terribly from raids by the Iroquois, most of whom were in the British alliance. In the summer of 1778 these Indians descended upon the town of Wyoming in the Susquehanna Valley at a time when the able-bodied men were all in the Continental army. The town and adjoining countryside were laid waste and old men, women, and children were tomahawked and scalped. Troops marched into the Iroquois country, destroyed two large villages, and then withdrew. Thereupon, the Indians wreaked their vengeance on the prosperous settlements of the German Flats in the Mohawk Valley, and in the Cherry Valley perpetrated a massacre unsurpassed for brutal barbarity.

Congress now determined to punish the Iroquois and their Tory leaders. An army under General John Sullivan marched into western New York, in 1779, burned eighteen Indian villages, and destroyed the crops. At about the same time Daniel Brodhead led another expedition up the Alleghany River from Pittsburgh and destroyed other Iroquois towns. These aggressive movements had the effect of scattering and partially subduing the Iroquois, but parties of these Indians continued to be troublesome along the frontier throughout the war. Sullivan's campaign, especially, was decisive in opening western New York to white settlement after the close of the war.

Far to the south in 1780 frontiersmen defeated the British in one of the decisive battles of the Revolution. Georgia was held by the British. Clinton had wrested South Carolina from American control, and had sailed for New York, leaving General Cornwallis in command, with instructions to move northward. Among the British officers most feared and hated by the South Carolinians was Major Patrick Ferguson, to whom was entrusted the task of crushing all further rebellion in the interior regions of the State. He sent word to the frontiersmen that if they gave him any more trouble, he would cross the mountains, burn their settlements, and hang their leaders.

This boastful challenge was accepted by the borderers. Under the leadership of Isaac Shelby, John Sevier, and Colonel William Campbell they assembled, about one thousand strong, at the Sycamore Shoals on the Watauga River. With the stirring words of a frontier preacher in their ears, they set out to find the enemy, being joined later by a body of North Carolinians under Colonel Benjamin Cleveland. Ferguson heard of their coming and decided to teach them a lesson. He established himself on flat-topped King's Mountain near the boundary between the two Carolinas. Here he might easily have beaten a much superior force of European troops, but his attackers were American frontiersmen and Indian fighters in numbers about equal to his own men. The backwoodsmen swarmed up the wooded slopes without organization or real leadership. The encounter that ensued was one of the most desperate conflicts of the war. Finally, after Ferguson had been killed and hundreds of his men were dead or disabled, the survivors surrendered. The American cause in the South was greatly heartened by this victory and the plans of the British were frustrated.

LATER PHASES OF WAR IN THE WEST

The surrender of Lord Cornwallis at Yorktown on October 19, 1781, virtually marked the end of the war east of the mountains. In the West, however, the struggle for control continued unabated. Early in 1782 a body of frontier militia committed a massacre as brutal and despicable as anything perpetrated by the redskins, when they murdered ninety defenseless Moravian Indian converts on the Tuscarawas River. Shortly afterward William Crawford, who had been Washington's land agent in the West, led an expedition from Fort Pitt against the Shawnee villages across the Ohio. The British at Detroit had learned of the plan and had despatched assistance to the Indians. Moreover, the Americans, confident of success, failed to exercise due vigilance or to follow orders strictly. The result was that the expedition was only narrowly saved from complete disaster. Crawford was captured and met a horrible death by torture which the renegade white leader of the Indians, Simon Girty, refused to mitigate.

The fury of the Indians was now turned once more against Kentucky. In the summer of 1782 Bryan's Station was fiercely besieged by a large party of Indians, with a few whites, among whom were the notorious Girty and Alexander McKee. All the strategems known to frontier warfare were used on both sides. At length the besiegers gave up hope of success and retired. A little later, however, on the Blue Licks River the pursuing Kentuckians met a crushing defeat. Fear of annihilation now spread throughout the settlements and was only allayed by a strong expedition led by George Rogers Clark which crossed the Ohio River in November and destroyed a number of Indian villages. All along the border there were continued alarms until the spring of 1783, when there came news of the signing of the preliminary treaty of peace and orders for the cessation of hostilities.

THE WEST AND THE TREATY OF 1783

The western and southern boundaries of the United States and the right of navigating the Mississippi River were among the important questions involved in the diplomacy of the American Revolution and in the negotiations which preceded the signing of the Treaty of 1783.   France sought no territory for herself in North America, but was sympathetic toward the ambitions of Spain for territory east of the Mississippi.   Spain had no love for the United States and sought not only to control the navigation of the Mississippi, but also to place the western boundary of the new nation far to the east of that river.   In the end it was the United States and England who made the agreements on those points which were embodied in the treaty.   The United States was to extend on the West to the Mississippi River, and on the south to the thirty-first parallel of latitude and a line running through the Apalachicola, Flint, and St. Mary's rivers.   The region between this line and the Gulf was given to Spain.   Article eight stated that "The navigation of the river Mississippi, from its source to the ocean, shall for ever remain free and open to the subjects of Great-Britain, and the citizens of the United States."

What influence the conquest of the Illinois country by George Rogers Clark and his other activities had in gaining the West for the United States is difficult to determine.   It is the belief of James A. James, Clark's painstaking biographer, that these achievements were an important, though unacknowledged factor in inclining Lord Shelburne to accede to the Americans' demands.   On the other hand, there can be little doubt that Shelburne's principal motives in yielding were his far-seeing purposes to limit the ambitions of Spain, cause a possible rift between France and the United States, and lay a basis for amity between the new nation and Great Britain.

Not all the people of England accepted this loss of territory gracefully.   Late in January, 1783, the *London Chronicle* reported that a committee of merchants engaged in the Canadian fur trade had just waited on Lord Shelburne. "They stated," according to the report, "that his Majesty's Ministers might as well have thrown Canada into the number of sacrifices which had been made for the purchase of peace, since they had given up all the advantages and value of Canada. Not a single fur could be brought to the British market in Quebec, after the Definitive Treaties were signed, without permission of the Governors of the American forts on the banks of the Lake, and in the Back Country, which was all ceded to the Americans." Here we find one of the motives that led to the retention of the western posts by the British after 1783, in spite of the treaty, with consequent resentment on the part of the Americans.

A little later, in the House of Lords, attention was called to the farcical character of the right of navigating the Mississippi as far as the British were concerned, since they had no territory contiguous to that river. In the light of succeeding developments, later to be described, there was uncanny foresight in the prediction of a writer in the *Morning Herald* (London), early in February, 1783. "The line of limits, drawn in the articles with America," he wrote, "curtails Canada of all the valuable territories that once belonged to it; such as the districts to the south of Lake Erie, of the Ohio, and of the Illinois. Those immense and fertile plains will now be spread over by the Americans, and when settled they will increase in them beyond all conception, and become so numerous, that all Spanish America must necessarily fall to them. The contest will soon arrive; the free navigation of the Mississippi will soon bring it on: the Americans must have a free navigation to the sea; and the Spaniards will look to it with so much jealousy that quarrels will very soon break out."

PART II

THE FRONTIER OF THE MIDDLE WEST

CHAPTER XII

AMERICANS TAKE POSSESSION

THE history of the American West is the history of the west-ward movement, of the effect of life in a frontier environment, and of the problems, local and national, arising out of the needs and demands of western settlers. In character, volume, and rate of progress the westward movement in America is not fully paralleled elsewhere in the history of the world. Conquering hordes have swept over many lands. Colonial projects, fostered by rulers and statesmen and governments have been numerous. Nowhere else has so large an area been settled in such a short period of time almost entirely through the work of individuals moving singly or in small groups and of their own volition.

We have already seen how settlements were gradually pushed back from the tidewater regions up the river valleys, into the piedmont sections and the upland valleys, and finally across the mountain barrier that had so long seemed to close the way. That process occupied a century and a half. We shall now see how the small stream of settlers through the mountain passes swelled into the proportions of a torrent that spread with amazing rapidity over the vast interior valley and, within seventy-five years from American independence, deposited outposts of settlement on the Pacific coast. Land-hungry Americans had no intention that the fertile territory beyond the Appalachians, made a part of the new nation by the Treaty of 1783, should remain the haunt of Indian tribes and the hunting-ground of fur companies.

THE FIRST THREE DECADES

Anyone who will consult the census reports for the three decades following Yorktown will discover ample evidence of the rapidity with which Americans entered into possession of this rich domain. In the first federal census in 1790 the regions soon to be known as Kentucky and Tennessee showed populations of 73,677 and 35,691, respectively; and there were small settlements across the Ohio in the Northwest Territory. Ten years later, in 1800, the population of Kentucky and Tennessee had increased three-fold, or to 220,955 and 105,602, respectively. By this time the Northwest Territory had been divided. The portion soon to become Ohio had 45,365 inhabitants and there were 5,641 in Indiana Territory. In addition there were 8,850 people living in Mississippi Territory, which then included Alabama. By 1810 Kentucky (406,511) and Tennessee (261,727) had again more than doubled in population. Ohio now had 230,760; Indiana Territory, 24,520; and Mississippi Territory, 40,352. Further spread of settlements was indicated by Illinois Territory, with 12,282 inhabitants, and Michigan Territory with 4,762; while in the Louisiana Purchase region 76,556 inhabitants were enumerated in what became the State of Louisiana and more than 20,000 in the present Missouri and Arkansas.

Figures may satisfy the statistician. By their use it would be possible to plot graphs or draw shaded maps showing the rapid growth and spread of population in the West. But at best figures and graphs and maps are cold and lifeless and purely objective. To gain a subjective view, a vivid picture of the great movement of humanity reflected in these census reports one must go to the writings of those who saw this movement when it was actually in progress. Letters, diaries, journals of travels, early histories, items in newspapers—these are the sources from which we may gain first-hand glimpses of the process and volume and rapidity of western settlement during the early years of the Republic. The selections which follow are merely illustrative of the pictures these sources reveal.

Chief Justice Robertson of Kentucky in an address quoted by Thomas Speed, the historian of the Wilderness Road, told of the "tide of emigrants, who, exchanging all the comforts of their native society and homes for settlements for themselves and their children here, came like pilgrims to a wilderness to be made secure by their arms and habitable by the toil of their lives. . . . Cast your eyes back on that long procession of missionaries in the cause of civilization; behold the men on foot with their trusty guns on their shoulders, driving stock and leading pack-horses; and the women, some walking. . . . others riding with children in their laps, and other children swung in baskets on horses. . . . see them encamped at night expecting to be massacred by Indians. . . . This is no vision of the imagination, it is but an imperfect description of the pilgrimage of my own father and mother, and of many others who settled in Kentucky in December, 1779." The same authority states that Rev. Lewis Craig's church from Virginia moved in a body to Kentucky in 1781. He quotes also a statement by Peter Cartwright who moved to Kentucky with his parents about 1783: "It was an unbroken wilderness from Virginia to Kentucky at that early day. . . . There were no roads for carriages, and though the immigrants moved by thousands, they had to move on pack-horses."

The close of the Revolution was followed by a great outpouring of people into Kentucky, especially from Virginia and North Carolina, with smaller numbers from other eastern States. Contemporary estimates indicated that as many as 12,000 men, women, and children toiled over the Wilderness Road or came by the Ohio River, in 1784, and 30,000 in 1787.

In 1796 Francis Baily, an English traveler, was on his way westward through Pennsylvania. "I have seen ten and twenty waggons at a time in one of these towns," he wrote, "on their way to Pittsburg and other parts of the Ohio, from thence to descend down that river to Kentucky. These waggons are loaded with the clothes and necessaries of a number of poor emigrants, who follow on foot with their wives and families, who are sometimes indulged with a ride when they are tired, or in bad weather."

When he reached Kentucky the following year Baily was impressed by the progress which had been made, not merely in the number but also in the character of the settlements. "Those ranks of men who form the first and second classes of society have moved off," he wrote, "and left the country for the most part to be possessed by those who have been brought up in all the refinement and civilised manners of their brethren on the eastern side of the Allegany mountains. From a few straggling settlements scattered over this vast territory, whose inhabitants were obliged to shut themselves up in block-houses, and establish their right by the point of the sword, who ranged lawless through this wilderness, every one doing that which seemed right in his own eyes—there have arisen . . . fertile fields, blushing orchards, neat and commodious houses, and trading towns, whose inhabitants have imposed upon themselves the just restraint of mild laws, and who, increasing in numbers, can lie down secure and free from all apprehensions of the tomahawk or scalping-knife. Such has been the wonderful progress of this country, to have implicit faith in which, it is first necessary to be a spectator of such events."

Across the Ohio River at the mouth of the Muskingum the Ohio Associates from New England founded the town of Marietta on May 7, 1788, thus forming the advance guard of the stream of emigrants who soon transformed that region into a land of homes and farms. "During the winter of 1787-8," wrote James H. Perkins, "their men were pressing on over the Alleghanies by the old Indian path which had been broadened into Braddock's road. . . . Through the dreary winter days they trudged on, and by April were all gathered on the Yohiogeny, where boats had been built, and started for the Muskingum." A letter written late that year described the progress of the new settlement. "We are continually erecting houses, but arrivals are faster than we can possibly provide convenient covering. Our first ball was opened about the middle of December, at which were fifteen ladies, as well accomplished in the manners of polite circles as any I have ever seen in the old States." The commandant at Fort Harmar, across the Muskingum from Marietta, reported that 4,500 persons had passed that post between February and June, 1788, and that many of them would have stopped on the lands of the Ohio Associates if provision had been made for their reception.

On account of danger of Indian attack, settlements were slow in spreading northward from the Ohio River. The ineffective campaign of General Joseph Harmar in 1790 and the disastrous defeat of Governor Arthur St. Clair in 1791 tended to check the advancing frontier. Following the decisive victory of General Anthony Wayne at the Battle of Fallen Timbers in 1794, however, there was a period of peace and settlers took full advantage of the immunity. "All the great roads of approach to the western country were crowded with adventurers directing their course towards the land of promise; and fleets of boats were continually floating them down the Ohio."

When Francis Baily witnessed the founding of Waynesville on the Little Miami in 1797 he was a spectator of scenes such as were being enacted in many other places in the Ohio Valley during this period. "After being here a few days," he wrote, "I observed this wilderness begin to assume a very different appearance; for, after having built my friend a house, the settlers set about their own plantations, and in a short time I saw quite a little town rise from the desert." He thought that in later years it would be pleasant to tell "how we raised this flourishing settlement from the howling wilderness."

Largely through the activities of Oliver Phelps and Nathaniel Gorham and later of the Holland Land Company, the lake region of western New York, so long the home of the fierce Iroquois, was now opened to settlement. A writer in 1797 told of the opening of a road from Fort Schuyler (Utica) to Geneva and Canandaigua and of the running of regular stage coaches. "This line of road having been established by law," he said, "not less than fifty families settled on it in the space of four months after it was opened. It now bids fair to be, in a few years, one continued settlement." Three years later the English traveler, John Maude, described the settlements around Bath, near the Pennsylvania line. A few years earlier this had been a region almost unexplored by white men. "Yet so rapidly," he wrote, "has the spirit of improvement gone forth in this country—so suddenly has plenty burst forth, where so late was famine— and so quick the change of scene from dark-tangled forests . . . to smiling fields, to flocks and herds, and the busy hum of men; that instead of being indebted to others for their support, they will henceforth annually supply the low country, Baltimore especially, with many hundred barrels of flour, and herds of cattle." He wrote also of a bridge near Owasco Lake "the longest in America—perhaps in the world! Yet five years ago the Indians possessed the shores of this Lake embosomed in

almost impenetrable woods." The migration of New Englanders to central and western New York that began during this
period was of great significance in the history of that State.

Observers in the southwest reported similar progress in that
section. In 1792 Gilbert Imlay declared that the settlements
in western Georgia, on the Holston, French Broad, and Cumberland, and around Natchez were already of sufficient strength
to bid defiance to the Cherokee, Creek, and Choctaw tribes.
He predicted that the Spaniards in Florida would be obliged to
watch their manners or they would be forced to retire across
the Mississippi. "To a person who observes the migration to
this country," reads a letter written from Tennessee in 1795, "it
appears as if North and South Carolina, and Georgia, were
emptying themselves into it. It is not infrequent to see from
2 to 300 people in a body coming from those southern climates,
oppressed with diseases to revive and enjoy health in this
salubrious air." F. A. Michaux estimated in 1802 that there
were five thousand whites and three thousand negro slaves in
the Natchez district which, he declared, "daily acquires a fresh
degree of prosperity."

THE GREAT MIGRATION

Pictures like these might be multiplied indefinitely to show
how in the thirty years following the Revolution wilderness
regions west of the mountains were being transformed into
lands of prosperous farms and budding cities. The movement
was somewhat checked during the War of 1812. But immediately after its close, because of hard times in the East due to
the long-continued interruption of trade, there came what has
appropriately been called the "Great Migration," when all
America seemed on the move westward. The census of 1820
revealed a startling shift of population, although of course it
did not indicate the further spread of settlements into the
western portions of New York, Pennsylvania, and all the southern states. The census figures show the following populations
in western States and Territories in 1820: Alabama, 127,901;
Arkansas, 14,273; Illinois, 55,211; Indiana, 147,178; Kentucky, 564,317; Louisiana, 153,407; Michigan, 8,896; Missis-

sippi, 75,448; Missouri, 66,586; Ohio, 581,434; and Tennessee, 422,823. By comparing these figures with those for 1810 it will be found that there were nearly 1,140,000 more people living west of the mountains in 1820 than in 1810, without counting the increase in the western sections of the older States; while the population of the entire nation had increased about 2,230,000. The comparison also shows the geographical distribution of the westward migrants during the decade. Later we shall show how this movement was reflected in the admission of new States and the creation of new Territories.

Contemporaneous accounts of the "Great Migration" are exceedingly numerous, since the phenomena attracted widespread attention. *Niles' Weekly Register* for this period is a veritable mine of information. Its editor Hezekiah Niles, was ardently interested in the West and took delight in printing all the letters and items he could gather which described western settlement and progress. Journals of travelers again furnish us with many vivid pictures. Obviously only a few selections can here be made to illustrate and enliven the story summarized by the census figures of 1820.

A correspondent from Ohio wrote to Editor Niles in January, 1815, that the emigration to that State during the preceding summer had been "beyond all example, great. The main road through the state, I am told, has been almost literally covered with waggons moving out families." The missionaries, S. J. Mills and Daniel Smith, reported from the Wabash region in Indiana that "an immense number of settlers have been crowding out on that frontier during the last season." From Auburn, New York, in April, 1815, came the statement that "during the past winter our roads have been thronged with families moving westerly. It has been remarked by our oldest settlers, that they never before witnessed so great a number of teams passing, laden with women, children, furniture, &c. to people the fertile forests of New-York, Pennsylvania, and Ohio; they are mostly from the eastern states." About the same time a "New England Emigration Society" was formed in Boston to promote westward migration.

Timothy Flint tells us that "shoals of immigrants" were seen on all the great roads leading to the West, during the years immediately following the second war with England. Towns like Oleanne, Pittsburgh, Brownsville, Wheeling, Nashville, Cincinnati, and St. Louis were overflowing with them. "Ohio and Indiana," he continued, "beheld thousands of new cabins spring up in their forests. On the borders of the solitary prairies of Illinois and Missouri, smokes were seen streaming aloft from the dwellings of recent settlers . . . Boon's-lick and Salt River, in Missouri, were the grand points of immigration, as were the Sangamon and the upper courses of the Kaskaskia, in Illinois. In the south, Alabama filled with new habitations, and the current, not arrested by the Mississippi, set over its banks, to White river, Arkansas, and Louisiana. . . . Wagons, servants, cattle, swine, horses, and dogs, were seen passing with the settlers, bound to immense distances up the long rivers." Of the moving settlers, Flint said "they drop, in noiseless quietness, into their position, and the rapidity of their progress in settling a country is only presented by the startling results of the census."

A letter from Chillicothe, Ohio, in 1816, noted that new-comers were arriving in that town more rapidly than room could be furnished for them. In a day's ride in southern Indiana, Timothy Flint was "continually coming in view of new cabins, or wagons, the inmates of which had not yet sheltered themselves in cabins." A communication from western New York this same year told of farmers exchanging their log cabins for "elegant framed or brick mansions." Auburn was now a "place of wealth and business." Waterloo, further west, had sprung into being as though obeying the "creative power of the magician's wand. Here are, at least, 50 houses, most of them of size and beauty—the work of a single summer." Even Rochester contained "above 100 houses—two years ago it did not exist." Out in Missouri it was reported that "Boon's settlement, which was a few scattered cabins the other year, in an immense forest, has now become a country containing its courts of justice and other municipal appendages." Fifty wagons passed through Zanesville in a day carrying settlers westward. Virginia, Kentucky, Tennessee, and the Carolinas seemed to be pouring their people into Illinois and Missouri. "Every ferry on the river is daily occupied in passing families, carriages, wagons, negroes, carts, &c. &c." A traveler in the south estimated that in nine days he met 3,800 people on their way to the Alabama country.

For the year 1817 similar pictures present themselves. Morris Birkbeck, whose travel notes constitute an American classic, journeyed to Illinois this year. "Old America seems to be breaking up, and moving westward," he wrote while on the road to Pittsburgh. "We are seldom out of sight, as we travel on this grand track towards the Ohio, of family groups, behind and before us."

At Pittsburgh he "heard delightful music from a piano, made in this place, where a few years ago stood a fort, from which a white man durst not pass, without a military guard." During his stay at St. Clairsville, Ohio, he saw thirteen or fourteen emigrant wagons a day passing through the town. "The wagons swarm with children," he observed. "I heard to-day of three together which contain forty-two of these young citizens." One favorite route from New England to the Ohio Valley was across New York and down the Alleghany. In nine days 260 emigrant wagons passed a house on this route, besides many persons on horseback and on foot. A New York editor met "a cavalcade of upwards of twenty waggons containing one company of 116 persons, on their way to Indiana, and all from one town in the district of Maine."

In 1818 Timothy Flint was in Missouri where he counted one hundred persons a day, for many days in succession, passing through St. Charles. He saw a train of "nine wagons harnessed with from four to six horses. We may allow a hundred cattle, besides hogs, horses, and sheep, to each wagon; and from three or four to twenty slaves. The whole appearance of the train, the cattle with their hundred bells; the negroes with delight in their countenances, for their labours are suspended and their imaginations excited; the wagons, often carrying two or three tons, so loaded that the mistress and children are strolling carelessly along . . . the whole group occupies three quarters of a mile." The aged Daniel Boone, now nearing the end of his days at his home on the Missouri River, was reported to be very restless on account of the press of population and only detained from moving again beyond the frontier by his waning strength and failing eyesight.

The southern phase of the westward movement was reflected in the setting up of Alabama as a Territory separate from Mississippi and its admission as a State in 1819. These facts indicate a large influx of population. *Niles' Weekly Register* contained many items in 1818 and 1819 revealing the exuberance and typical western optimism of the inpouring settlers. Where only a single hut had stood two years earlier a town of 2,700 inhabitants was said to have arisen by 1818; and the Black Warrior River was designated as "the Nile of the West." Within one year another site covered with a heavy forest was described as having been transformed into a "city" of eighty houses, ten large warehouses "and the largest hotel in the territory." A printing press was on the way and a newspaper was to be launched. To this town, named Blakely, one hundred brickmakers and fifty ship carpenters had recently come from New York. "The emigration is wonderful," said one writer, "and seems daily to acquire new power."

From the River Raisin near Detroit came the report that that region, so well known for the humiliating defeat of General Hull in the late war, "now presents an aspect that forbids the prospect of another such scene in its neighborhood." A new village named Monroe had appeared and "large tracts of country . . . are now so well populated that a thousand men may be called together, as it were, by the beat of a drum."

The inclination of New Englanders to migrate in groups, or to settle where others from the same section had established themselves, was noted. "They established a new Connecticut in the Ohio territory," commented Hezekiah Niles, "and that not merely in name but in fact. The inhabitants of a township in the eastern states, who may be disposed to explore the western wilds, generally understand one another, concert their measures beforehand, and if they do not depart in a body, yet they eventually come together at a preconcerted rendezvous. School-fellows and companions in infancy, reunite in a far distant spot, remote from the scenes of their early pleasures: and it often happens that the grown up man meets there and marries the playmate of his childhood." This tendency on the part of New Englanders was a continuation of the practice of pre-arranged group migration established in the early days of colonial expansion. In the south, on the other hand, people more generally moved westward as individuals or single families without concerted action either in moving or in choosing a place for settlement.

Numerous religious colonies and social experiments were established in the West during the era of settlement. There was another type of group migration which was illustrated by an account in a New York newspaper in 1819 of a caravan "consisting of eleven covered waggons, drawn by two, three, or four horses each, two coaches, a number of outriding horses, and about 120 persons, composing the expedition under Captains Blackman and Allen, for the state of Illinois." These two men, having made fortunes as ship-masters in the China trade, had now determined to form a settlement on lands which they had purchased in Illinois, and this caravan was the first of two parties organized to carry out the plan. "In the company which passed here yesterday," ran the story, "there were farmers, carpenters, blacksmiths, wheelwrights, masons, coopers, &c, &c. with their families, mostly natives of the 'northern hive.' All their equipments were in fine order, and the emigrants in fine spirits."

One more quotation will serve as a summary of the "Great Migration" in the north. In 1819 Niles reviewed the progress made in western settlement since 1812. The western parts of New York and the northern portions of Pennsylvania and Ohio "then nearly in a state of nature . . . now teem with men, and abound with large towns, villages and *ports*. . . . Buffalo and Erie, and Sackett's Harbor, remote points beyond the 'back woods,' with Rochester and other places not then upon the map, are celebrated for their shipping and commerce! Detroit and Michilimackinac, then far distant posts, and rarely heard from, now seem close to us. . . . St. Louis, now a *port* on the Mississippi, then at about the extreme point of the emigrants voyage in that direction—is turned into a *starting-place*." There was now a town called Franklin, with one thousand inhabitants, located at Boon's Lick *"somewhere* on the Missouri."

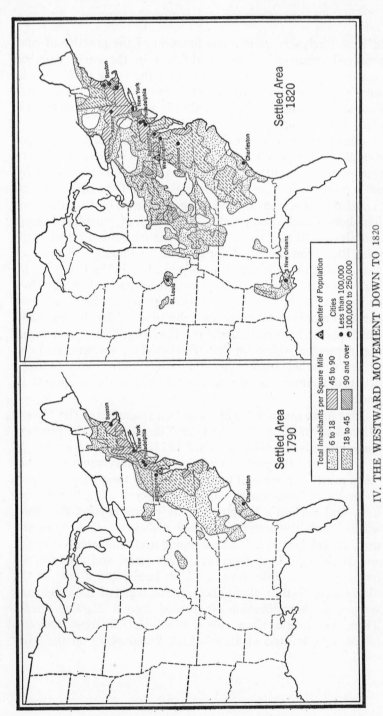

IV. THE WESTWARD MOVEMENT DOWN TO 1820

(Population density of 6 or more per square mile. Based on maps in *Report of the Eleventh Census of the United States*, 1890, Part I.)

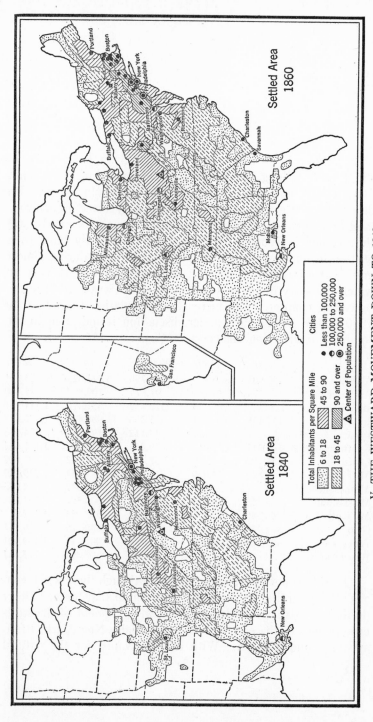

V. THE WESTWARD MOVEMENT DOWN TO 1860

(Population density of 6 or more per square mile. Based on maps in *Report of the Eleventh Census of the United States,* 1890, Part I.)

CHAPTER XIII

STILL THEY COME

"THEY come in crowds a mile long," said an Iowa editor in 1854, in describing the tide of new settlers pouring into that State, "they come with wagon-loads of household fixings, with droves of cattle and flocks of sheep—they come from every land that ever sent adventurers westward, and the cry is 'still they come.'" Words like these might truthfully have been written in many western States and Territories during almost any year of the four decades following 1820—the year to which the story of the westward movement was carried in the preceding chapter. The increase in population from 1820 to 1860 in the section now under discussion is indicated in the following figures from the census returns:

	1820	1830	1840	1850	1860
Alabama	127,901	309,527	500,756	771,623	964,201
Arkansas	14,273	30,388	97,574	209,897	435,450
Illinois	55,211	157,445	476,189	851,470	1,711,951
Indiana	147,178	348,031	685,866	988,416	1,350,428
Iowa			43,112	192,214	674,913
Kentucky	564,317	687,917	779,828	982,405	1,155,684
Louisiana	153,407	215,739	352,411	517,762	708,002
Michigan	8,896	31,639	212,267	397,654	749,113
Minnesota				6,077	172,023
Mississippi	75,448	136,621	375,651	606,526	791,305
Missouri	66,586	140,455	383,702	682,044	1,182,012
Ohio	581,434	937,903	1,519,467	1,980,329	2,339,511
Tennessee	422,823	681,904	829,210	1,002,717	1,109,801
Wisconsin			30,945	305,391	775,881

Florida is not included in this list, although there was a considerable migration to the western section of that State. Neither do these statistics reveal the continued settlement of the western portions of the eastern States, especially New York, Pennsylvania, and Virginia. With due allowance for the natural increase in population in the longer settled States of the West, these figures are worthy of study as showing the volume and direction of the westward movement. This is especially true with regard to the newer Territories and States as they appeared in the census reports from decade to decade. On the other hand, these figures fail to tell us how many people, attracted by the lure of newly opened lands, moved to the more distant frontier from many of the older States of the West. For instance, in 1821 Hezekiah Niles estimated that during the preceding decade the outflow of people from Kentucky about equalled the inflow of new settlers. The greater profits of cotton-raising in Alabama, Mississippi, and Louisiana were attracting many to that region, while the "ravages of the 'independent banks,' together with the want of employment drove off tens of thousands of the laboring classes of white people into Ohio, Indiana and Illinois."

THE WESTWARD MOVEMENT DURING THE TWENTIES

Roads thronged with movers' wagons and the sight of large numbers of Ohio River flatboats bearing emigrants to the West had largely ceased to be items of news interest in States which had five or six hundred thousand inhabitants by 1820. Nevertheless, even in such States during the ensuing decade editors and travelers frequently expressed their wonderment at the unending movement and their appreciation of the rapid transformation it was achieving. Six months after Indianapolis was laid out, on unoccupied land, to be the seat of government of Indiana, it was noted that forty dwelling houses had already been erected, besides stores, workshops, and mills. In 1822 *Niles' Register* referred to the fact that Rufus Putnam, often called the father of Ohio, was still living in that State. "He has lived to see the wilderness in which he located himself divided into three independent states," said the editor. "If the good old gentleman shall live to the year 1830, he may expect to find a population in those parts of nearly a million and a half of busy, hustling, happy beings—though the soil 50 years before, was only trodden by wild animals and untutored Indians."

Western Indiana filled rapidly with settlers during the last half of the decade. From fifty to one hundred wagons a day were said to have passed through Indianapolis all during the fall of 1826, bound for the Wabash country. Three years later emigrants were passing through the same town bound for the same region at the rate of six thousand a week. The same period witnessed a large influx into previously unoccupied sections of Tennessee. "During the present week," wrote the editor of the *Jackson Gazette* in 1825, "we have observed an increased number of moving families, passing through this place and its vicinity, for the purpose of settling on the Forked Deer, Hatchie, &c . . . no parts of the country . . . are settling faster at this time than those adjacent to the south boundary of the state."

It was in the regions where settlers' cabins were appearing for the first time that the phenomena of the westward movement naturally received the most attention. Michigan was one of these regions. In the census of 1820 this Territory showed less than nine thousand inhabitants, most of whom were of French blood or half-breeds—descendants of the fur traders and villagers who lived there in the days when Cadillac and his successors ruled at Detroit. Americans had scarcely entered Michigan, except at Detroit or as traders in the western portion. The region was away from any practicable route of travel and transportation. It was also thought to be chiefly a country of swamps and pine forests. Acquaintance gradually proved the falsity of this impression. But the chief factor in turning settlers for the first time toward Michigan was the building of the Erie Canal. As work on this epoch-making project got under way not only western New York, but also northern Ohio and even Michigan assumed an attractiveness to settlers hitherto lacking. An all-important means of communication with eastern markets would be available with the completion of the canal.

The movement to Michigan did not become voluminous until after 1830, but it began to receive notice early in the twenties. It was characteristic of the cautious temperament of New Yorkers and New Englanders, who constituted the main element in this early emigration, that they frequently sent out parties to reconnoiter before they ventured to move their families to the new country. "So numerous have been the arrivals of emigrants to this territory since the opening of navigation," declared a Detroit editor in June, 1822, "that it is difficult, at this time, to ascertain, with any degree of certainty, their actual numbers. . . . The interest which is awakened in many parts of the Union, in relation to this territory, and above all, the arrival of numerous intelligent emigrants and gentlemen who come to 'see the country,' induce a conviction that the barriers to emigration are giving way, and that a 'tide' has begun to flow which nothing will retard." Then, as for many years afterward, the principal source of incoming settlers was New York, but Vermont, Massachusetts, Pennsylvania, and Ohio were liberally represented. A colony of Quakers on the River Rouge was mentioned the following year, when many foreigners were also noted.

From this time there were numerous references in the *Detroit Gazette* to the incoming emigrants. In 1824 there was mention of "Michigan companies" being formed in various parts of New York. The following spring saw the coming of nearly five hundred settlers in two days on steamboats and schooners. "To use the words of an emigrant," said the editor, " 'the people at the east are all alive for Michigan'— hundreds of families are determined to come even if they sell their farms and property at half price." In September steamboats and schooners, as well as taverns in town and country, were reported overflowing with prospective settlers. Complaint was made that the newspapers of Cleveland and Sandusky were disparaging Michigan in the effort to dissuade settlers from going thither. "It is not to be wondered at," averred the Detroit editor, "that the people of Ohio now that our lands are surveyed and in market, should feel a little bit waspish when they see every steam-boat and other vessel which happens to touch at their ports, filled with emigrants on their way to this fertile and healthy region."

By 1829 attention was called to the fact that many people from the southern States were coming to Michigan. The *Detroit Gazette* quoted a Charleston, Virginia, paper to the effect that "during the month of Sept. it was computed that not less than 8,000 individuals have passed through that place, bound for Indiana, Illinois and Michigan. They were principally from the lower part of Virginia and South-Carolina. They jog on, careless of the varying climate, and apparently without regret for friends and the country they leave behind, seeking 'forests to fell,' and 'a new country to settle.'"

Reference to the census figures will show that Illinois received a large accession of population during the decade of the twenties. Late in 1825 an Edwardsville editor called attention to the rush of settlers to the northern counties of the State, and wrote of "astonishing" numbers of people crossing the Wabash and of roads "thronged with movers." Arkansas likewise received some notice. Hezekiah Niles was a good prophet in 1822 when he predicted that Arkansas and Michigan would come into the Union together, although that event was delayed longer than he apparently expected. Just at the close of the decade the *Arkansas Gazette* was gratified to report the greatest emigration since the organization of the Territory in 1819. Several counties, and especially the region recently acquired from the Cherokee Indians, he said, "have increased astonishingly in population, during the last twelve months, and the influx of settlers from Alabama, Tennessee, Mississippi, and the other states east of the Mississippi, and from Missouri, on the north, appears to be daily increasing." Alabama and Mississippi each more than doubled in population between 1820 and 1830.

The Westward Movement During the Thirties

During the decade of the thirties the movement to Michigan and Arkansas reached large proportions, especially in the case of the former, and bore fruit in the admission of both States into the Union. Michigan had seven times and Arkansas more than three times as many inhabitants at the end of the ten-year period as at the beginning. During these years the newspapers of New York and Michigan contained frequent news items like that in the *Buffalo Republican* in 1830, which read: "Our steam boats, and other vessels, have for several days been literally crammed with passengers, and a great part of them emigrants from the East, intending to settle in the fertile parts of Michigan and Ohio. It is said that within the past week, as many as one thousand souls passed through this place for such destination. On board one of the canal boats that arrived the other day, we saw several families that numbered together fifty-nine persons." Soon the newly opened roads also became the avenues over which the wagons of settlers poured into Michigan.

In the spring of the same year an Arkansas newspaper reported that "not only is every Steam-boat crowded with cabin and deck passengers, but the roads are also lined with wagons, conveying families to the Eden of Arkansas—as it is considered abroad—the counties of Washington and Crawford." The people of Memphis were charged with disseminating "vile and false slanders" against the soil, climate and inhabitants of Arkansas in the effort to deter settlers from crossing the Mississippi. Thus at last Arkansas, which hitherto had been too far north for those moving up the Mississippi and too far south for those coming down the Ohio, began to receive favorable attention, and in the succeeding years its population increased steadily, although never as rapidly as that of Michigan and other northern regions.

Illinois also more than trebled in population during this decade. S. A. Ferrall, who traveled the roads of that State in 1831, met several large parties of settlers moving to the Illinois River section. They were mostly "Georgians, Virginians and Kentuckians, whose comparative poverty rendered their residence in slave states unpleasant." People from south of the Mason and Dixon Line and the Ohio were conspicuous in the early settlement of southern Illinois. Many of them were poor people, but Timothy Flint saw others who were persons of some note and with property, including slaves, "whose immigration was accompanied with a certain degree of éclat." On the other hand, it was said in 1835 that "the emigration from New-York city is immense; they come in companies of hundreds, and pitch their tents in some hitherto wild and uncultivated place, and in a few days make it one of the most considerable settlements in the country. The old inhabitants are amazed and overawed by the persevering enterprise of the 'Yankees.'" The emigration to Illinois for the spring of 1839 was estimated to exceed 40,000 by a Sangamon editor.

Across the river in Missouri similar scenes were observed. A Columbia editor in 1835 denied any exaggeration when he asserted that "for several weeks past, the number of wagons, with their usual appendages, which have daily passed through Columbia, must have averaged forty! Indeed, we do not recollect ever to have seen our streets and roads so thronged. Independent of the actual movers, the number of travellers on horseback, exploring the country, is prodigious. The emigration to Missouri the present season is immense." Most of the new settlers were said to be "from Virginia and Kentucky, with a sprinkling of Tennesseans and Carolinians—substantial farmers and enterprising merchants and mechanics, with here and there a young 'limb of the law,' or a disciple of Esculapius seeking in the 'Far West' a home for themselves and a patrimony for their children."

Two new Territories appeared in the census of 1840—Wisconsin, recently set off from Michigan; and Iowa, including an extensive area west of the Mississippi and north of the State of Missouri. There had for many years been an increasing population in the lead-mining region in southwestern Wisconsin and settlements had now begun to appear along Lake Michigan and in the interior.

Lead-mining around Dubuque had likewise been the attraction that first drew people to Iowa, even when it was still Indian territory. In 1832, however, a strip of land about fifty miles wide on the west bank of the Mississippi, known as the Black Hawk Purchase, was relinquished by the Indians. When this treaty went into effect on June 1, 1833, settlers began to cross the Mississippi and stake out claims as thousands of others had done in other western regions, without waiting for the surveys to be made. Booming towns soon appeared and the process of settlement was in full swing. "The great thoroughfares of Illinois and Indiana, in the years 1836-7," wrote John B. Newhall, "would be literally lined with the long blue wagons of the emigrants slowly wending their way over the broad prairies, the cattle and hogs, men and dogs, and fre-

quently women and children, forming the rear of the van—
often ten, twenty and thirty wagons in company. Ask them,
when and where you would, their destination was the Black
Hawk Purchase." In 1839 an Iowa editor declared that "whole
neighborhoods in Illinois, Indiana and Ohio are 'organizing' for
emigration, and will soon take up their line of march for Iowa;
even the substantial yeomanry of the Keystone, the proud sons
of the old Dominion, and the enterprising 'down easters' are
turning their steps westward and looking to Iowa as their future
home."

The Westward Movement During the Forties

The movement to Wisconsin and Iowa, thus begun, continued without abatement during the "roaring forties," and led
to statehood in both cases before the decade closed. A Madison editor estimated in 1843 that two hundred new settlers for
Wisconsin were landing daily at the lake ports. "Hundreds of
emigrants," he said, "are daily and hourly pouring into the
Territory from all parts of the country, by water and by land.
The Lake and river counties and the mineral region are fast
filling up with settlers, and first rate land is rising in price."
Year after year the movement continued. In 1845 much attention was paid to the arrival of a group of more than a hundred people from Rochester, New York, sixty-two of whom
were members of the Allen family. "The patriarch of the
family," said a Rochester editor, "will be 88 years old in July.
He is one of the venerable relics of the revolution. . . . He
moved off, in his old chair, surrounded like Abraham, with his
scores of descendants, anxious to die, as he has lived, amongst
them."

In Iowa the settlements pushed rapidly westward, especially after Indian title to the New Purchase, embracing the
fertile valley of the Des Moines was relinquished in 1843.
"Emigrants rushed to the New Purchase by way of the Ohio
and the Mississippi," says Jacob Van der Zee, "or they rolled
overland in great, rumbling wagons. For weeks and months
before this wonderful country was opened to settlement alluring prospects brought hundreds of persons to the frontier

border and only military force could restrain them from building homes on the red man's soil."

The spread of settlements into Iowa and Wisconsin attracted special notice during this period because they were the cutting edge of the advancing frontier. Into all the other States between the Appalachians and the western border of the Mississippi Valley commonwealths a steady stream of people was pouring, adding to the population of the towns and filling up the farming lands. A glance at the census figures will show that this movement was quite evenly distributed, although there was greater relative gain in the States north of the Ohio as compared with those to the south. This, too, was the decade when "Manifest Destiny" became the watchword of western America. This was the decade which witnessed the romantic trek to Oregon, the march of the Mormons to their new home in the Rocky Mountains, and the gold rush to California—all of which will receive attention in later chapters.

THE WESTWARD MOVEMENT DURING THE FIFTIES

The westward movement during the fifties was not only large in volume but also of great political and economic significance when viewed in connection with the great sectional struggle which followed. During the ten years from 1850 to 1860 the total population of the eight States of Ohio, Indiana, Illinois, Michigan, Wisconsin, Minnesota, Iowa, and Missouri increased by more than 3,350,000—an increase of more than 167 per cent, due partly to natural increase, partly to foreign immigration, and mainly to the westward migration of the American people. The increase in the six States of Kentucky, Tennessee, Alabama, Mississippi, Louisiana, and Arkansas during the same period was slightly less than 1,075,000, or only 26.2 per cent. It is evident, therefore, either that emigration into these southern States had largely ceased or that the outflow practically balanced the inflow. In other words, the westward shift of population during this period definitely established the numerical and economic superiority of the North, and filled the grain-producing States with people opposed to the further spread of slavery. Because of the much greater volume and importance of the northern phase, only the movement in that section will be described.

From the standpoint of actual numbers of new settlers Illinois had a notable growth. The population of that State, already large in 1850, more than doubled during the decade. Minnesota, which achieved statehood in 1858, had an increase of 2,730 per cent in population during the ten years. In 1850 Minnesota contained only a few scattered settlements with a total of 6,077 inhabitants; but in the years that followed such a stream of emigration set in that by 1860 there were 172,023 people in the State. Iowa had an increase of over 251 per cent during the same period. The census of 1860 shows that during the decade Iowa received more than 68,000 emigrants from Ohio, over 37,000 from each of the States of New York, Pennsylvania, and Indiana, and nearly 30,000 from Illinois.

Illinois was the favorite region for settlement for emigrants from the largest numbers of States. Missouri attracted settlers from the second largest number of commonwealths, while Ohio and Iowa stood third and fourth in this respect. On the other hand, the migrations of native-born citizens of the eight States under discussion exemplified the rule that emigration tended to follow parallels of latitude or to flow into adjoining jurisdictions. Again, it is to be noted that it was during the fifties that foreign immigrants began to come into the Mississippi Valley in large numbers. The foreign-born population of these eight States was increased by 881,000, or more than doubled.

Thus it is apparent that this decade witnessed a remarkable emigration into the upper Mississippi Valley, both of native American families and of home-seekers from foreign shores. Nearly 43,000,000 acres of public land were taken up in this region during these ten years, and, to quote a contemporary, "the energies thus called into action have, in a few years, made the States of the Northwest, the granary of Europe, and that section of our Union which, within the recollections of living men, was a wilderness, is now the chief source of supply in seasons of scarcity for the suffering millions of another continent."

But a more definite picture of the great wave of humanity which swept over this region may be gained by taking a cross-sectional view of the emigration into one particular State. For this purpose no better illustration can be found than the notable rush of settlers to Iowa during the two years from 1854 to 1856. The completion of railroads to the Mississippi, and the publicity given by land companies, scores of emigrant guide-books, and hundreds of articles in eastern newspapers all helped to facilitate travel and stimulate emigration by making the name "Iowa" a household word. Farmers in the eastern States and in Ohio and Indiana were discouraged because of drouth, a fatal epidemic of cholera, or hard times. Hence the prospect of acquiring a quarter section of cheap government land in healthful, productive Iowa was very attractive to them. And so in large numbers they sold out, packed their goods in wagons or on boats or trains, and turned their faces westward toward the land beyond the Mississippi.

"The immigration into Iowa the present season is astonishing and unprecedented," ran an account in an eastern journal in June, 1854. "For miles and miles, day after day, the prairies of Illinois are lined with cattle and wagons, pushing on toward this prosperous State. At a point beyond Peoria, during a single month, seventeen hundred and forty-three wagons had passed, and all for Iowa. Allowing five persons to a wagon, which is a fair average, would give 8,715 souls to the population." This was only the emigration of one month on one road out of many.

At all the principal points along the Mississippi River an almost continuous stream of emigrants was crossing over the ferries into Iowa during the fall and early winter of 1854. Beginning at the north with the three ferries in the vicinity of Prairie du Chien and Mac Gregor, it was reported that "each of these ferries employs a horse-boat, and is crowded all the time with emigrants for Iowa. Sometimes the emigrants have to encamp near the ferry two or three days to await their chance to cross in the order of their arrival." The same situation prevailed at Dubuque where emigrants were arriving daily and almost hourly, and at Davenport where the ferry was kept busy at "all hours in passing over the large canvas-backed wagons" filled with would-be Iowans. At Burlington it was declared that "20,000 immigrants have passed through the city within the last thirty days, and they are still crossing at the rate of 600 and 700 a day." Even at Keokuk such large numbers of settlers came in by boat that a journalist was led to say that "by the side of this exodus, that of the Israelites becomes an insignificant item, and the greater migrations of later times are scarcely to be mentioned." It was said that one thousand people from Richland County, Ohio, came to Iowa that fall.

The movement was checked temporarily during the coldest winter months, but with the opening of spring in 1855 it began again with full strength, if indeed it did not assume larger proportions than during the previous year. Throughout the summer the invasion continued. "Seek whatever thoroughfare you may," wrote a traveler in central Iowa in June, "and you will find it lined with emigrant wagons. In many instances large droves of stock of a superior quality are met with. On our last days drive . . . we met 69 covered wagons seeking a home in the valley of the Des Moines." The report of the General Land Office for the year ending June 30, 1855, indicated that there had been taken up in Iowa during that year more than three million and a quarter acres of public land.

The autumn of 1855 witnessed no appreciable diminishing of the stream of land-hungry settlers pouring into the newer counties of the State. The National Road in Ohio and Indiana was again lined with wagons on their way to Iowa and Wisconsin. "The Immigration to Iowa this season is immense," wrote an Iowa editor in November, "far exceeding the unprecedented immigration of last year, and only to be appreciated by one who travels through the country as we are doing, and finds the roads everywhere lined with movers." At Rock Island, although two steam ferry-boats made one hundred trips a day they were unable to handle all the business.

Illustrations of this character might be multiplied almost indefinitely to show how the great tide of emigration spread out over the valleys and prairies of Iowa during the two years from 1854 to 1856. Furthermore, what has been said in regard to Iowa during these two years was true, though perhaps in a less noticeable way, in the neighboring States throughout the entire decade of the fifties. By 1860 the commonwealths bordering the upper Mississippi had to a large extent passed the frontier stage, and were factors to be reckoned with in national affairs during the stirring years which followed.

In this and the preceding chapter, at the risk of tediousness, the purpose has been to leave a vivid impression of the continuity and volume of the great westward movement from the winning of independence to the outbreak of the war for the preservation of the Union. Thus far we have been concerned only with the settlement of the humid, tree-covered area extending to the western border of the first tier of States west of the Mississippi. We shall now see how these people traveled to their new western homes, how they acquired land, met Indian occupants, reacted toward the presence and policies of neighboring nations on the north and south, and in general how their economic, social, and political ideas and institutions were shaped by the frontier environment. After that we shall, in a similar manner, review what happened in the semi-arid and arid plains, in the Rocky Mountains, and along the Pacific Coast.

CHAPTER XIV

ON THE WAY TO THE WEST

"THE pioneer, no matter of what date or locality, was always a traveller before he was a producer or shipper of goods, and the common experience of the people, gained on their journeys, was—save in one instance—the basis on which future permanent routes and methods of travel were planned and created. The one exception to this manner of evolution lay in the memorable demonstration that steam could be successfully used for the propulsion of travel vehicles. It was an instance wherein genius and reason overshadowed experience and precedent." So writes Seymour Dunbar in the opening pages of his admirable *History of Travel in America*.[1]

The period covered by the westward migrations described in the two preceding chapters witnessed a transformation in the means and speed of travel that was more revolutionary than that caused by the aeroplane in our own day. It was a far cry from the crude flatboat to the palatial steamboat, and from the slow-moving pack-horse on uncertain trails to the speeding railway train. The first settlers who ventured into the West made their way as best they could along Indian trails or through the roadless forests; or they used the waterways as they found them, with all their obstructions and perils. The improvements to river navigation and the building of real roads were largely the results of the needs and demands for better means of transportation and communication, after the settlers had established themselves in their new western homes. To be sure, later emigrants were immensely benefited by these improvements as long as they remained in relatively settled regions. But those who moved to the edge of the frontier always came to a "jumping off place" beyond which the conditions of the unmodified wilderness prevailed. The story of internal

[1] Quoted by permission of The Bobbs-Merrill Company, publishers.

improvements—the building of roads, the improvement of river navigation, the growth of steamboat traffic, the digging of canals in the West itself, and the construction of railroads—belongs with the narrative of economic development after settlements had been made. This chapter is concerned with the experiences and the methods of travel of the first settlers on their way to various sections of the West.

EMIGRANT TRAVEL ON THE OHIO

The only real highways which white men found ready for their use as they pushed into the interior of America were the rivers. But the system of inland waterways seemed providentially designed to lure and facilitate the movement of people westward. The great Ohio River, springing from the union of two navigable streams, flowed westward with gentle current and beckoned invitingly to all who came to its headwaters. Thus, to use the words of Archer B. Hulbert, this river "is entitled to a most prominent place among Historic Highways of America which greatly influenced the early westward extension of the borders and the people of the United States." The tributaries flowing into the Ohio from the north and the south offered access to large areas. Then, when these lands were settled or ceased to be sufficiently attractive, settlers could float down the Ohio to its junction with the Mississippi, and descend that great stream at will, breast its current hundreds of miles to the northward, or make their way up one of that river's numerous affluents. It is not surprising, therefore, that the Ohio River was a highway used by thousands and no doubt hundreds of thousands of pioneers journeying to their new western homes.

Several types of river craft preceded the coming of the steamboat. The canoe and the pirogue were mainly used by the explorer, the hunter or Indian trader, and the individual adventurer. The keelboat, the barge, and the flatboat were crafts of commerce. The flatboat, or ark as it was sometimes called, was also the well-nigh universal river vehicle of the settler moving westward with his family and his possessions. These boats were cheap and easily constructed, and they were

made of sawed lumber which the settler could use most ad-
vantageously in building his cabin upon arriving at his destination. They could be purchased at numerous "boat-yards" on
the upper Ohio in 1811 for about thirty-five dollars. The description written by Francis Baily in 1796 was equally applicable to the flatboats in use thirty or forty years later. They
were, he said, generally from thirty to forty feet in length and
twelve feet wide. Their construction consisted of "a frame-
work fastened together with wooden pins, which constitutes the
bottom of the boat, and to this is fastened a flooring, which is
well calked to prevent leaking; the sides are about breast high,
and made of thin plank; and sometimes there is a rude kind of
covering, *intended* to keep the rain out."

A covering over a portion of the boat was apparently the
rule, especially on the type called the "Kentucky flat" or
"broadhorn" because of the long oar on either side for use in
steering. The equipment of oars was employed mainly in propelling the boat to and from the bank or in avoiding obstructions in the channel. The current of the river provided the
only momentum under ordinary circumstances, and thus a flatboat journey down the Ohio was slow and of long duration.
Timothy Flint declared that the typical flatboat had much the
appearance of a New England pigstye when viewed externally.
But he hastened to add that many of the "family-boats" were
"large and roomy, and have comfortable and separate apartments, fitted up with chairs, beds, tables and stoves. It is no
uncommon spectacle to see a large family, old and young, servants, cattle, hogs, horses, sheep, fowls, and animals of all
kinds, bringing to recollection the cargo of the ancient ark, all
embarked, and floating down on the same bottom."

Two or three additional quotations from the writings of
contemporaries will furnish glimpses of these flatboats and
their occupants as they floated down the Ohio. F. A. Michaux,
writing of his western journey in 1802, told how he was traveling along the bank of the Monongahela when he saw five or six
of these strange craft on the river. "I could not," he said, "conceive what these great square boxes were, which, left to the
stream, presented alternately their ends, sides, and even their
angles. As they advanced, I heard a confused noise, but with-

out distinguishing anything, on account of their sides being so
high. However, on ascending the banks of the river, I perceived in these barges several families, carrying with them their
horses, cows, poultry, waggons, ploughs, harness, beds, instruments of agriculture, in fine, everything necessary to cultivate
the soil, and also for domestic use."

A generation later, in 1828, James Hall wrote of similar
sights and noted many variations of the typical flatboat party.
For instance, he saw a man and a woman about sixty years of
age floating and paddling down the Ohio River in a flat-bottomed boat, twelve feet long with high sides and a roof. They
were seeking a new home further west. "Why, Sir," replied
the old man when questioned as to their motives, "our boys
are all married, and gone off, and bustling about for themselves; and our neighbors, a good many of 'em's gone *out back*,
and so the old woman and me felt sort o' lonesome, and thought
we'd go too, and try our luck."

Hall also described "two large rafts lashed together, by
which simple conveyance several families from New England
were transporting themselves and their property to the land of
promise in the western woods. Each raft was eighty or ninety
feel long, with a small house erected on it; and on each was a
stack of hay, round which several horses and cows were feeding,
while the paraphernalia of a farm-yard, the ploughs, waggons,
pigs, children, and poultry, carelessly distributed, gave to the
whole more the appearance of a permanent residence, than of
a caravan of adventurers seeking a home. A respectable looking old lady, with spectacles on nose, was seated on a chair at
the door of one of the cabins, employed in knitting; another
female was at the wash-tub; the men were chewing their tobacco, with as much complacency as if they had been in 'the
land of steady habits,' and the various family avocations
seemed to go on like clock-work."

Steamboats did not by any means supplant flatboats as
carriers of emigrating families. Those with some means pat-
ronized the more comfortable and expeditious vessels, but until
the entire Ohio Valley was well settled the humbler craft
continued to be used by the impecunious and the thrifty. It appears, however, that steamboats played a large role in trans-

porting upstream emigrants to the lands along the Mississippi. This was true of those who came up from the south to settle in Arkansas and Missouri, and also of many whose destinations were the lands bordering the great river in Iowa, Illinois, and Wisconsin.

EMIGRANTS ON THE ERIE CANAL

The only other waterway in any degree comparable to the Ohio River as a highway of the westward movement was one which was partly man-made. The completion in 1825 of the Erie Canal, connecting the Hudson River with Lake Erie, was an achievement of far-reaching significance, not only in establishing the commercial supremacy of New York City, but also in facilitating the settlement and development of western New York and the lands on the shores of the Great Lakes. The greatest importance of "Clinton's Ditch" lay in its service as a link in a water highway of commerce. Nevertheless, in the early years of the canal's history it was used by many emigrants, who either settled in western New York or transferred their goods at Buffalo to schooners or steamboats and proceeded to a more distant destination in Michigan or Ohio, or later in Wisconsin. Travel by canal boat was cheap for deck passengers. For instance in 1822, before the completion of the canal, a Rochester paper noted the arrival of a boat filled with emigrants who had come a distance of 150 miles at a cost of one dollar and a half each.

The effect of the Erie Canal in accelerating the westward movement became more noticeable as it neared completion. "From some towns bordering upon the Canal, and which might therefore be expected to reap the most signal advantages from that great work," commented a New York editor in 1824, "we understand that not less than one hundred inhabitants have emigrated within the last year." The same year a Utica paper asserted that "Scarcely a boat from the east passes without a number of families on board, with their household goods and farming utensils, bound to the 'Genessee country,' 'Ohio,' or the 'Michigan Territory.' There is no method of ascertaining the number of this description of passengers on the canal, for they pay no toll, and are not reported at the collector's office;

but some estimation may be formed of the amount, when it is known that wagons with emigrants are literally swept from the roads, formerly the great thoroughfare of the west. It is not uncommon to see from thirty to forty women and children comfortably stowed away in one of the large covered canal boats, as chirp as a flock of blackbirds." More than a decade later it was remarked that "no one who does not witness it, can have any just idea of the 'immense and intermingling throng of people' who are wending their way, by the route of Lake Erie, to the West. The steam boats and schooners plying between the various ports on the Lake, are represented to be constantly crowded."

THE EVOLUTION OF ROADS

In spite of the ease and economy of travel by the Ohio River and the Erie Canal-Great Lakes route, it is safe to say that the settlement of the West was accomplished mainly by people who journeyed on land by pack-train, wagon, or on foot. The covered wagon became, and remains in retrospect, the pre-eminent visible symbol of the westward movement.

The story of the evolution of roads is full of interest and fascination. The first paths were Indian trails, many of which in turn followed buffalo traces. Some of these Indian trails were very long, especially those running north and south, like the one which followed the mountain ranges from New York and Pennsylvania to the Carolinas. They were narrow, blind paths, unblazed and only to be followed with certainty by ex-perienced woodsmen. They ran along the highlands and thus were often much more circuitous than the modern roads which utilize valleys and water-level routes. Occasionally trails be-tween Indian villages or leading to favorite hunting grounds were somewhat widened by the frequent and continued pas-sage of travails and pack-horses.

The widening of the longer trails was begun by the pack-trains of white traders and settlers. The trampling of many horses gradually broadened the pathway and the bulky loads extending on either side of the horses wore away the over-hanging branches and underbrush. With the exception of

Braddock's Road and Forbes' Road, there were few routes by which a journey across the mountains could be made before 1800 in any better manner than on horseback with accompanying pack-train.

The next step in the widening of the trails was taken when people determined to force their way through with wheeled vehicles—carts with huge wheels or wagons. Even then only the most primitive road-making was done, with results that would not be tolerated to-day in building a temporary logging road. The underbrush and trees were cut away, leaving many of the stumps; and logs were thrown down to form puncheon bridges across creeks and especially troublesome bogs. The succeeding improvements such as graded turnpikes, stone or gravel surfacing, plank roads and adequate bridges, to be described in a later chapter, came after the country was settled and there were commodities to be transported. The early settlers traveled roads that were such only in name. As Archer B. Hulbert points out, they might more properly be designated as "routes." The rock-strewn, precipitous roadway over the mountains was no worse than the rutted or muddy course through the lowlands, where the road often broadened out amazingly as each succeeding group of wagons sought a better and firmer track.

EMIGRANT HIGHWAYS TO THE WEST

Even if it were possible, it would accomplish no useful purpose to enumerate and describe all the various roads that served as highways of emigration across the Appalachians and into the Mississippi Valley. From New York to the Carolinas and Georgia, Indian trails evolved into roads and white men laid out other paths to suit their desire to reach some particular land of promise. Most romantic in its early history, because linked with the name of Daniel Boone and the exciting years of Kentucky's first settlements, was the Wilderness Road through Cumberland Gap. This highway was soon joined by a well-traveled road from Philadelphia, through Richmond, and thus it became a great thoroughfare over which hordes of emigrants traveled to settle the region south of the Ohio River.

The main roads converging on the head-waters of the Ohio, however, rivaled if they did not surpass the Wilderness Road as thoroughfares of emigration. Whether settlers were planning to "take water" on reaching the Ohio or to proceed westward overland, they were obliged to make their way over the mountains by road. Braddock's Road, the route of which was later followed in a general way by the Cumberland Road, except that its western terminus was Wheeling instead of Pittsburgh, was the favorite highway for those coming from Maryland or Virginia. Forbes' Road through the central part of Pennsylvania to Pittsburgh was heavily traveled by emigrants from that State and from the region to the east and northeast. A few excerpts from the writings of contemporaries depicting emigrant travel over these roads will serve to illustrate the methods of travel everywhere.

One of the best descriptions is that given by Morris Birkbeck who traveled across Pennsylvania in 1817, when the Great Migration was in full swing. Writing of the typical emigrant party, he said: "A small waggon (so light you might almost carry it, yet strong enough to bear a good load of bedding, utensils and provisions, and a. swarm of young citizens,—and to sustain marvellous shocks in its passage over these rocky heights), with two small horses; sometimes a cow or two, comprises their all. . . . The waggon has a tilt, or cover, made of a sheet, or perhaps a blanket. The family are seen before, behind, or within the vehicle, according to the road or weather, or perhaps the spirit of the party."

Birkbeck noted differences in the habits of people from the various eastern States. "The New Englanders," he said, "may be known by the cheerful air of the women advancing in front of the vehicle; the Jersey people by their being fixed steadily within it; whilst the Pennsylvanians creep lingeringly behind, as though regretting the homes they have left." He described also the travel methods of those not so fortunate as to own a team and wagon. "A cart and single horse frequently afford the means of transfer, sometimes a horse and pack-saddle. Often the back of the poor pilgrim bears all his effects, and his wife follows, naked-footed, bending under the hopes of the family."

A few years later James Hall journeyed through the same region and "found the roads crowded with emigrants of every description, but the majority were of the poorest class. Here I would meet a few lusty fellows, trudging it merrily along; and there a family, more embarrassed and less cheerful; now a gang of forty or fifty souls, men, women and children; and now a solitary pedestrian, with his oaken staff, his bottle, and his knapsack." Hall described one family in particular. "The senior of the party was a middle-aged man, hale, well built, and decently clad. He was guiding a pair of small, lean, active horses, harnessed to a light waggon, which contained the bedding and provisions of the party, and a few articles of household furniture; two well-grown, barefoot boys, in homespun shirts and trousers, held the tail of the waggon, laudably endeavoring to prevent an upset, by throwing their weight occasionally to that side which seemed to require ballast, while the father exerted his arms, voice, and whip, in urging forward his ponies. In the rear toiled the partner of his pilgrimage, conducting, like John Rodgers' wife, 'nine small children and one at the breast.' "

Variations from the methods of travel already mentioned were occasionally seen on western roads. Although not wholly unknown in other sections, the people of a Missouri community were surprised at the "novel method of flitting" of a man and his wife and four children, who arrived there in 1834 from Ohio. "The man and the woman walked, and the man drew a small hand wagon, in which the children and the clothing and some other articles were; this he dragged the whole distance of their journey." Several years later, near the Wabash River, Rev. James L. Scott passed a small family who "had one ox in the thills of a two wheeled cart, in which were one or two boxes, and a mat or bed. This was all we could see that they possessed. . . .This I thought, was traveling poverty indeed." And, believe it or not, a traveler passing through Tennessee in 1818, "met a travelling house, drawn by six horses, two stories high, and containing three families, or 29 persons in the whole. They reported themselves from the district of Maine, bound to Alabama."

Such a vehicle was no doubt unique, but what Timothy

Flint called the typical "southern wagon" was "strong, comfortable, commodious, containing not only a movable kitchen, but provisions and beds. Drawn by four or six horses, it subserves all the various intentions of house, shelter and transport; and is, in fact, the southern ship of the forests and prairies. The horses, that convey the wagon, are large and powerful animals, followed by servants, cattle, sheep, swine, dogs, the whole forming a primitive caravan not unworthy of ancient days. . . .The procession moves on with power in its dust, putting to shame and uncomfortable feelings of comparison the northern family with their slight wagons, jaded horses and subdued though jealous countenances."

CHAPTER XV

THE NATIONAL BOUNDARIES IN THE WEST

When exuberant American settlers poured across the Appalachian Mountains after the winning of independence they no doubt thought that now they would be entirely free from the hampering restrictions of Old World politics. In this they were greatly mistaken. For more than thirty-five years after the signing of the Treaty of 1783 westerners were keenly conscious that they were bounded and limited by territories possessed by European powers. During most of this period the West seethed with international intrigues and western problems occupied an important place in American diplomacy. Jay's treaty with England in 1794, Pinckney's treaty with Spain in the following year, the purchase of Louisiana, Burr's conspiracy, the occupation of West Florida, the War of 1812, and the acquisition of all of Florida—all these occurred or were accomplished partly or largely because of western resentments, demands, and pressures. Volumes have been written in regard to each of these episodes, but a brief survey will serve to show both their significance in western development and the part played by westerners.

The Spanish-American Frontier

The refusal of the Spaniards to allow Americans the free navigation of the Mississippi River was the first rude shock received by the buoyant settlers in the Ohio Valley It will be remembered that the Treaty of 1783 stated that the citizens of both England and the United States should have a right of freely navigating the Mississippi. It was also agreed that the thirty-first parallel should be the southern boundary of the new republic, although there was a secret understanding that the boundary should be the line running through the mouth of the Yazoo River in case England should reconquer West Florida from Spain before the final treaty was signed. Spain refused to acknowledge that England had the right to make an agreement concerning the navigation of a river over which she had no control. The Spaniards likewise declined to admit that the terms of the Treaty of 1783 regarding the southern boundary of the United States had any validity, since Spain had conquered West Florida which under England extended as far north as the Yazoo River, or 32 degrees 28 minutes.

The boundary controversy was largely conducted through diplomatic channels; although naturally Americans, and especially those living in the West, were not uninterested in the subject. In brief, during the early negotiations Spain advanced claims the most extreme of which would have left the United States very little territory south of the Ohio and west of the Appalachians. Spain's object was to interpose an Indian buffer territory between the United States and her possessions in Louisiana and the Floridas. As has been noted, the Spaniards never had ony love for the Americans. On the contrary, they hated and feared the frontiersmen, and were far-sighted enough to know that unless some barrier could be interposed it would be only a question of time until the resolute, liberty-loving borderers would be invading Spanish territory.

The navigation of the Mississippi River was far from being a mere diplomatic question to the western settlers. It was a matter of intimate personal concern to every inhabitant of the West, for the Mississippi was the highway and New Orleans was the market or shipping point for all the produce of the "men of the western waters." The lack, at that early day, of roads across the mountains made the transportation of agricultural products to Atlantic coast markets virtually prohibitive. On the other hand, shipment by flatboats floating with the current of the Tennessee or the Ohio and the Mississippi was easy and inexpensive. Even though the river traffic was actually very small in volume during the first years following the Revolution, every farmer in the West looked to the rivers and New Orleans as the outlet that would ultimately make farming profitable for him.

Imagine then the consternation of these western farmers when they learned that the Spanish had closed the Mississippi to Americans except on payment of prohibitive duties, and their resentment when they discovered that the American government was disposed to aquiesce. Don Diego de Gardoqui, Spanish chargé d' affaires, and John Jay, Secretary for Foreign Affairs under the Congress of the Confederation, carried on a series of negotiations in 1785 and 1786. In the end Jay recommended that Americans forbear to use the Mississippi within Spanish territory for twenty or thirty years in return for a commercial treaty much desired by the merchants and shippers of the northern States. Only the stout resistance of the southern states prevented Congress from adopting this policy. Even men like Washington and Jefferson expressed the opinion that it would be wise to postpone a definite showdown on the Mississippi question until the western settlement had grown sufficiently to determine the question by force of numbers.

The settlers on the Holston, on the Cumberland, and in Kentucky received this news with bitter indignation. The ties which bound them to the Union were tenuous at best. They had for some time been protesting that the federal government was negligent in providing protection against the Indians, and now this apparent willingness to permit the closure of their only highway to market was regarded as an inexcusable sacrifice of their interest.

The Spanish were quick to take advantage of this situation. There followed a period of intrigues in which nearly all of the frontier leaders—men like John Sevier, James Robertson, William Blount, George Rogers Clark, Benjamin Sebastian, and others—were involved. The arch plotter of them all was James Wilkinson of Kentucky, a man whose name will always be associated with base perfidy, even though he later held high rank in the American army. Equally colorful but less successful was the adventurer, Dr. James O'Fallon, agent for the South Carolina Yazoo Company. Talk of setting up an independent government was rife in the West. There were plots to bring the western settlements under Spanish protection and control. On the other hand the Spanish officials at New Orleans were frequently thrown into a panic by reports of expeditions of American frontiersmen being organized to descend upon Louisiana and take possession of the Mississippi by force of arms. Efforts of the Spaniards to attract American settlers to locate around Natchez and at other points along the river were matched by proposals of American land companies and speculators to establish colonies with or without Spanish consent. In 1789 the seizure of a British vessel by the Spaniards in far-away Nootka Sound brought these two nations to the verge of war in 1790. Westerners saw in the situation visions of British aid against the Spanish in Louisiana, but this hope was short-lived. The crisis passed and war was averted.

It is doubtful whether any considerable number of American frontiersmen would at this time have really placed themselves under Spanish rule with all its restrictions upon individual activity. For a time the danger of a separation from the Union was imminent, but the moment passed, and the underlying attachment of westerners to their own American government reasserted itself. After he became President under the new Constitution, George Washington showed his wisdom by conciliating the disgruntled western settlers. Overlooking their lapses, he appointed many of the favorite spokesmen of the West to civil office in the newly created Southwest Territory or to high rank in the army. The admission of Kentucky into the Union in 1792 did much to allay discontent.

All these measures, however, did not prevent the people of the West from listening eagerly to Citizen Edmond Genêt, the first representative of the French Republic, when, in 1793 and 1794, he proposed the organization of an expedition to capture the Floridas and Louisiana from Spain. One of those enlisted in this scheme was George Rogers Clark, the hero of Vincennes, who had become embittered by the seeming ingratitude of Virginia and the American government as expressed in their continued failure to reimburse him for expenses incurred in the Illinois campaign during the Revolution. To him Genêt sent a provisional commission as "Commander-in-Chief of the Independent and Revolutionary Army of the Mississippi." Genêt's plan failed largely through lack of funds, and partly because his home government disavowed his actions. Enthusiasm for his expedition in the West also cooled somewhat when it became known that the federal government was making a determined effort through diplomacy to secure the right of navigation of the Mississippi.

These negotiations were terminated at San Lorenzo on October 27, 1795, when Manuel de Godoy and Thomas Pinckney signed a treaty between Spain and the United States. By this treaty the United States gained virtually everything she had been seeking: commercial agreements pleasing to easterners and the free navigation of the Mississippi for all American subjects. The southern boundary of the United States was fixed at the thirty-first parallel. Americans were given the right to deposit their goods at New Orleans, subject only to reasonable storage charges, for a period of three years. At the end of this time the privilege of deposit at New Orleans was either to be continued or an "equivalent establishment" was to be assigned at some other point on the Mississippi. As pointed out by Arthur P. Whitaker, one of the main reasons why the Spanish acceded to these terms was the fact that, after years of experience with efforts to hold back the steady western progress of the Americans, they now "preferred a treaty with the established government of the United States to an intrigue with its irresponsible frontiersmen." There was delay in executing the boundary provisions of the treaty and within a few years the shadow of Napoleon Bonaparte fell across the American West. For the time being, however, western settlers were satisfied, for their government had secured for them the free use of the Mississippi.

Problems of the Northern Border

Another provision of the Treaty of 1783 affecting the West was one by which the British agreed to withdraw their troops from all posts in American territory with "all convenient speed." It was not until 1796 that this promise was fulfilled. At Pointe-au-Fer and Dutchman's Point in the Lake Champlain country, at Oswegatchie on the St. Lawrence, at Oswego and Niagara on Lake Ontario, at Erie on Lake Erie, at Detroit strategically located on the straits between Lakes Erie and Huron, and on the island of Michilimackinac between Lakes

Huron and Michigan, the British maintained their garrisons as though no treaty had been made. In vain did our representatives in London seek to hold England to her agreement. They were repeatedly informed that England did not propose to evacuate the western posts for the reasons that the American government had failed to carry out is promises in regard to the collection of British debts and the treatment of loyalists.

There were good grounds for this excuse, although it is an open question as to which nation first violated the provisions of the treaty. As a matter of fact, the excuse was only a convenient pretext. The real reason why the British refused to give up the frontier posts lay in the unwillingness of merchants to relinquish control of the lucrative fur trade of the Great Lakes region. Furthermore, many Englishmen confidently looked forward to the not distant time when the weak American Union would be dissolved—an expectation which seemed close to fulfillment as far as the West was concerned during the period of the Spanish intrigues just described. British officials in Canada and at the western forts, therefore, used every means to extend and strengthen their influence over the Indian tribes of the northwest. Like the Spanish, they had a project for an Indian buffer territory under British protection, and this territory was to include all the region north of the Ohio River, as well as a strip of country in what is now northern New York.

It was not difficult to convince the Indians that their interests lay with the British rather than with the Americans. The former were concerned only with trade, while the latter were seeking land for settlement. The evident weakness of the American government also served the English cause, especially after Arthur St. Clair's disastrous defeat by the Indians on November 4, 1791. Three years later, however, the situation was greatly changed and American prestige was enhanced among the Indians by the aggressive but cautious campaign under Anthony Wayne, culminating in his decisive victory at the Battle of Fallen Timbers on August 20, 1794. From the beginning of Wayne's expedition the British commanders at Detroit and at an outpost on the Maumee River were suspicious that these posts were the real objective, and they gave every possible aid to the Indians. For a time after the defeat of the redskins hostilities between Wayne's men and the British seemed inevitable, but after a few days the American commander wisely retired to Fort Defiance, which he had built the previous year further up the Maumee.

By this time the question of the western posts was in process of settlement. On November 19, 1794, John Jay and Lord Grenville signed the famous agreement known in American history as Jay's Treaty. While the provisions of this treaty with respect to commerce and the rights of the United States on the high seas were far from satisfactory to a majority of Americans, it did result in British withdrawal from the western posts by the date agreed upon—June 1, 1796. Grenville had come to the conclusion that the holding of posts within American territory was not essential to the continuance of British trade with the Indians of the northwest. Stations north of the boundary line would serve equally well. In this expectation he was entirely justified, for, as will be seen, British influence over the Indians, emanating from such points as Malden across the Canadian border, long remained a cause of complaint and indignation among the settlers in the Ohio Valley. Nevertheless, Jay's Treaty of 1794 and Pinckney's Treaty of 1795 finally led to the fulfillment of the Treaty of 1783 with respect to boundaries and the rights of Americans in the West.

THE LOUISIANA PURCHASE

The boundary line specified in Pinckney's Treaty was not run, nor did Americans come into possession of Natchez, until 1798, three years after the signing of the treaty. Westerners, however, were unhampered in their use of the Mississippi River and the right of depositing goods at New Orleans for reshipment was continued even after the three-year period mentioned in the treaty had expired. The prospect of free access to profitable markets for western produce seemed secure. Then, in the first years of the new century disturbing rumors gained currency in America—rumors that the great Corsican had looked with covetous eyes at Louisiana, the ancient possession of the French. These rumors were well-grounded, for on

October 1, 1800, at San Ildefonso, Spain had retroceded Louisiana to France in a secret treaty. With visions of a magnificent colonial empire in America, Napoleon soon made plans to take possession. Desiring a convenient naval base, he sent an army to the island of San Domingo, but disease and the resistance of the negroes led by the heroic Toussaint l'Ouverture, brought failure to this undertaking.

Meanwhile in the United States, and especially in the West, alarm was growing apace, for with France and Napoleon in control of the mouth of the Mississippi the safety and peace of America would be seriously threatened. In October, 1802, the worst fears were confirmed when the Spanish intendant at New Orleans closed the Mississippi River to Americans. Immediately the West was ablaze with excitement and with talk of an expedition to seize New Orleans and settle the Mississippi question forever by force of arms. In the words of Frederic L. Paxson, "the bad news rushed up the trail from Natchez, and reaching Washington apprised the President that either the West would act, or he; and that his action must be prompt or not at all."

President Jefferson now faced a difficult dilemma. He was an ardent friend of France and a passionate devotee of peace. On the other hand, he understood and sympathized with the westerners in their determination to use the Mississippi. He knew that unless something were done promptly a frontier army would be on the march against New Orleans and war with France would result. Even in Congress resolutions were introduced and discussed authorizing the raising of an army to seize New Orleans before Napoleon's troops could take possession. How fully Jefferson appreciated the gravity of the crisis is indicated by his statement to Robert R. Livingston. "From the moment that France takes New Orleans," he wrote, "we must marry ourselves to the British fleet and nation."

Jefferson realized that the only way to satisfy the belligerent frontiersmen and avoid war with France was, if possible, to purchase territory at the mouth of the Mississippi and thus gain a voice in the control of the river. Here again he found himself in difficulty. Being a leading exponent of the strict construction of the Constitution, he believed that he had no authority to purchase territory. Furthermore, he was opposed to an increase in the national debt, such as any substantial purchase would necessitate. Yet clearly something must be done. For what he did Thomas Jefferson well deserves the credit which history has bestowed upon him.

Early in March, 1803, Jefferson despatched James Monroe to Paris as a special envoy to join Robert R. Livingston, our minister to France. Monroe was instructed to employ every effort to purchase New Orleans, and if this concession were not obtainable then he was to seek a restoration of the right of deposit for American goods. When Monroe arrived in Paris he found Livingston already in the midst of preliminary negotiations with Barbé-Marbois. To the astonishment, not to say the consternation, of the two American commissioners, Napoleon had offered to sell the whole of Louisiana to the United States.

The offer was well-nigh overwhelming, far exceeding anything involved in Monroe's instructions. Nevertheless, the two men hastened to accept and signed a treaty bearing the date of April 30, 1803, by which the territorial area of the United States was more than doubled. They pledged their country to pay $15,000,000, agreed that French and Spanish ships should receive special privileges in Louisiana ports for a period of twelve years, and promised that the inhabitants of the ceded territory should "be incorporated in the Union of the United States, and admitted as soon as possible, according to the principles of the Federal Constitution, to the enjoyment of all the rights, advantages, and immunities, of citizens of the United States." The boundaries of Louisiana were not specified, but the ceded province was declared to have "the same extent that it now has in the hands of Spain, and that it had when France possessed it"; and the United States was to have all the rights which France had acquired from Spain under the Treaty of San Ildefonso.

Bonaparte's sudden decision to sell Louisiana was a violation of both the French constitution and of his promise to Spain. But he foresaw an approaching European struggle and he knew it would be impossible to defend Louisiana against England. His motive in selling it to the American nation is revealed in his statement that the treaty "assures forever the power of the United States, and I have given England a rival who, sooner or later, will humble her pride." The latter part of this prediction can hardly be said to have been fulfilled.

The Louisiana Purchase Treaty was ratified and the purchase money appropriated only after a bitter party wrangle in Congress, during which the Federalists reversed themselves and opposed the treaty as unwarranted by the Constitution. Westerners, however, were not troubled by constitutional scruples in such matters. To them the treaty was more than satisfactory. It opened a vast area for American expansion and it settled forever the question of the free use of the Mississippi River.

Aaron Burr's Conspiracy

What might have happened in the West without the Louisiana Purchase is suggested by the vague and enigmatic episode known as the Burr Conspiracy. The treaty quieted apprehensions and discontent and increased loyalty to the Union, but it did not destroy the ambition of restless frontier leaders or their willingness to engage in any sort of enterprise which promised personal glory or profit. To men of this type in 1805 there came Aaron Burr, disappointed because of his failure to achieve the supreme success in politics and smarting under the sting of public disapproval occasioned in the East by his killing of Alexander Hamilton in the famous duel at Weehawken in 1804. His personal charm won him ready access everywhere in the West. Here duelling was still the accepted method of settling quarrels and his killing of the great Federalist leader was regarded by many as a public service. Especially did he captivate Harmon Blennerhassett, a man of considerable wealth living on an island in the Ohio River near Marietta, who opened his home as headquarters for Burr and contributed money to his enterprise. Here in 1805 and 1806 there was organized an expedition the objective of which is not known with certainty to the present day.

It is obvious that at least a few people must have known Burr's real designs, but they left no records. To others he told whatever he thought would interest them most. Anthony

Merry, British minister to the United States, was intrigued by a proposal to bring about the separation of the West from the Union with the aid of an English fleet at New Orleans. Spanish officials in Florida and Texas were alarmed by rumors that Burr contemplated an expedition against Spanish territory. Burr talked several times with such men as Andrew Jackson and Henry Clay, but their failure to denounce him is an indication that to them he did not reveal any plan for the dismemberment of the United States. One man who almost certainly believed he knew Burr's plan and at first gave him encouragement was James Wilkinson, now western commander of the army and at the same time the continued recipient of a Spanish pension. Before the project could be carried into effect Wilkinson characteristically sought credit by turning informer. The best judgment of historians is that Burr's immediate plan was for a filibustering foray against the Spanish, with the probable hope of setting up a separate empire with himself as ruler—an enterprise which certainly would find little opposition in the West.

Every student of American history knows that Aaron Burr's dream, whatever it may have been, was short-lived. He was hailed into court in Kentucky, under Jefferson's orders, and acquitted. Once more, in 1807, he was arrested on a charge of treason and tried before John Marshall, but there was not sufficient evidence to sustain the charge and he was set free. As is well known, the political antagonism between Marshall and Jefferson had an important bearing upon the outcome of the trial.

THE WAR OF 1812 IN THE WEST

With the exception of events in West Florida and the desire of the people of the southwest to acquire entire possession of the Floridas, to be described later, the northern border became the great subject of interest on the part of westerners within less than a decade after the purchase of Louisiana. In this instance the demands and aggressive spirit of the young, western "war-hawks" plunged the nation into a war with Great Britain, from which it emerged only by good fortune with undiminished territory and without achieving most of the objects for which the struggle was ostensibly waged.

The War of 1812 has been called our "second war for independence," a description which is appropriate only in the sense that it added somewhat to our prestige in spite of its indecisive outcome, and that it contributed powerfully to the growth of the spirit of nationality. Historians long accepted the impressment of American seamen and interference with American commerce by Great Britain as the causes of this conflict; and it is true that these grievances were assigned at the time war was declared. It is now generally agreed, however, that it is in the West that we must look for the real motivation. In other words, the War of 1812 was a westerners' war.

The people of the West were noted for their aggressive, chip-on-the-shoulder dispositions. Among large numbers of them personal honor was something to be defended at all odds and by any method. The code of the West sanctioned personal encounters and even duels on slight provocation. It was natural, therefore, that they should be peculiarly sensitive on the point of national honor in the trying period of the Napoleonic wars when this nation as a neutral was subjected to the insults of both France and England. To be sure, it had not been long since westerners had been flirting with proposals for separation from a Union which seemed indifferent to their needs. But that was their quarrel. They were indignant when outsiders slighted and insulted their government. After all the West was the most nationally-minded section of the Union even at this time, for it was to the federal government that most of the people of West were indebted for their land titles, for their mail service, for defense against the Indians, and for their territorial and state governments. But there was a more immediate and potent reason for this demand for a war against England.

We have already seen that when the British withdrew their garrisons from the western posts in 1796 in accordance with Jay's Treaty, they had no intention of relinquishing their remunerative fur trade with the Indians south of the Great Lakes. They simply moved over to the Canadian side of the boundary line and continued their activities. Malden, opposite Detroit, in particular, was the center from which British influence over the Indians was exerted.

For a decade after Wayne's campaign and after British evacuation of the western posts there was little trouble with the Indians. Then depredations began to occur among the scattered settlements along the northwestern frontier. When in 1810 and 1811 news of the progress of Tecumseh's Indian confederation spread throughout the West, there was virtually a panic in the Ohio Valley which was not quieted even after the Battle of Tippecanoe. It is of little value to say that the million white people then living west of the mountains really had no cause to fear a few thousand Indians. Neither does it help to point out the incontestable fact that it was the pressure of settlements on Indian lands which was largely responsible for the depredations by the red men. From first to last, rightly or wrongly, the frontiersmen hated and feared the Indians; and every tale of outrage sent a thrill of horror along the frontier that awakened memories accumulated through generations of brutal warfare.

In this case there was an added animus to the wrath of the western settlers. Ever since Revolutionary War days there had been a settled conviction, not wholly unfounded, in the Ohio Valley that the Indians were instigated and encouraged in their raids on the settlements by the British officials and traders along the Canadian border. Charges to this effect were now revived and when English guns and ammunition were found on Indians slain at Tippecanoe the cry for revenge rang throughout the West. John Rhea of Tennessee expressed the attitude of westerners when in Congress he declared that the United States must "put it out of the power of Great Britain, or of any British agent, trader, or factor, or company of British traders to supply Indian tribes with arms or ammunition; to instigate and incite Indians to disturb and harass our frontiers, and to murder and scalp helpless women and children."

Western leaders were now convinced that the only way to accomplish this purpose was to drive the British out of Canada. They were equally sure that this desirable result could be achieved with comparative ease and in a short time. Henry

Clay of Kentucky, then Speaker of the House of Representatives, outlined plans for the invasion of Canada. "I should not wish," declared Richard Johnson of the same State, "to extend the boundary of the United States by war if Great Britain would leave us to the quiet enjoyment of independence; but considering her deadly and implacable enmity, and her continued hostilities, I shall never die contented until I see her expulsion from North America, and the territories incorporated with the United States." Other western members of Congress spoke in language equally belligerent. And so the western "war-hawks" had their war, in spite of a reluctant President and a nation unprepared. Throughout the Ohio Valley after the declaration of war on June 18, 1812, editors and state legislatures expressed their joy and approval; and at public dinners the people drank to such toasts as: "May the Twelfth Congress no longer tamely submit to British outrages, but wrest from her every foot of possession she holds in North America."

With the general aspects of the War of 1812 we are not concerned. Nor need we dwell long on the pitiable campaigns in the northwest that fell so far short of the boastful predictions and confident anticipations of western leaders and people. General Henry Dearborn in the Niagara-Lake Champlain sector was kept in a state of harmless inactivity through incompetence at Washington. William Hull, instead of penetrating deep into Canada, ingloriously surrendered Detroit on August 16, 1812, without firing a shot, and was later tried and convicted of cowardice. On the preceding day the garrison at Fort Dearborn, where Chicago now stands, was treacherously massacred by the Indian members of an attacking party who violated pledges of safe conduct made by the British commander who received the capitulation of the fort. In January, 1813, a force under James Winchester was defeated on the River Raisin. By this time all hope of the conquest of Canada was gone. The only relief in the general gloom came in September and October, 1813, with Perry's victory on Lake Erie and the campaign under William Henry Harrison which resulted in the recapture of Detroit and the defeat of a British force at the Battle of the Thames on Canadian soil. Among the slain in the latter battle was the great Indian leader,

Tecumseh, whose death hastened the disorganization and paci-
fication of his followers.

It was from the military operations in the southwest that
the people of the West gained greatest satisfaction. The Creek
Indians went on the war-path in 1813 and on August 30th
killed nearly five hundred settlers at Fort Mims at the junction
of the Tombigbee and Alabama Rivers. This massacre was
avenged in March of the following year, when the Tennessee
militia commanded by Andrew Jackson won a smashing victory
over the Indians at the Horseshoe Bend of the Tallapoosa
River. This exploit was the first of a series which established
Jackson's fame as an Indian fighter and helped to make him
the hero of the West. A little later Jackson proceeded southward into Florida and burned Pensacola, which, though neutral
territory, had been used as a base of operations by the British,
as had also other points in western Florida. The region, however, was soon restored to Spanish control.

Late in the year of 1814 it was learned that the British
were planning an attack on New Orleans. Jackson, now major-general in the regular army, gathered a nondescript force
of frontiersmen and pirates from the islands along the coast
and went to the defense of the city. There on January 8, 1815,
fifteen days after the signing of the Treaty of Ghent which
officially closed the war, he won the greatest American victory
of the entire struggle. The seasoned British troops under Sir
Edward Pakenham were completely defeated, retiring after a
loss of more than two thousand men killed or wounded. Andrew Jackson was now a man marked for high honors at the
hands of an admiring nation.

During the peace negotiations the British commissioners
again brought forward a proposal for an Indian buffer territory,
but naturally it was not considered by the Americans. The
northern boundary remained undisturbed by the events of the
war. There was some gain for the westerners, however, because after 1815 the peace of the northern border was never
again threatened. Furthermore, the Indian tribes north of the
Ohio, bereft of the hope of British aid, never again gave serious
trouble.

Trouble Along the Florida Border

The situation along the southern border was still unsettled and far from peaceful. For the beginning of the movement that culminated in 1819 in the acquisition of the Floridas by the United States we must go back to the period immediately following the purchase of Louisiana. With Spain still controlling the Floridas it required no gift of prophecy to forsee the early appearance of trouble along the boundary, scarcely less disturbing than that occasioned by the closing of the Mississippi. The settlers in the southwest were certain to demand access to the Gulf, and rivers, like the Flint, Chattahoochee, Coosa, and Tombigbee, which served as their avenues of transportation, had to cross Spanish territory before reaching the sea.

Soon after the Louisiana Purchase, through Monroe and Pinckney, Jefferson endeavored to secure the cession of the Floridas from Spain. France seemed for a time to lend encouragement to these efforts, but Napoleon finally lost interest and the project fell through. Nevertheless, within a few years the United States was in possession of the greater part of West Florida. This occupation was based upon a rather doubtful interpretation of the Louisiana Purchase Treaty in accordance with which it was contended that Louisiana as ceded by France extended as far east as the Perdido River, now a part of the eastern boundary of Alabama. Spain's objections to this interpretation were of little concern to the American frontiersmen. They moved into the western portion of West Florida, staged an insurrection, declared their independence of Spain, and appealed to the United States for annexation. In response President Madison issued a proclamation declaring that the region belonging to the United States extended to the Perdido River, and ordered the official occupation of a portion of it, asserting, however, that his government was ready to make a "fair and friendly negotiation and adjustment" with Spain. In 1812 the country as far east as the Pearl River was incorporated in the newly admitted state of Louisiana; and the region between the Pearl and the Perdido was added to Mississippi Territory.

Spanish possession of East Florida remained undisturbed, except for a short-lived "revolt" early in 1812, stimulated by United States military officers acting under instructions from President Madison. Nevertheless, the people of the southwest joined their brethren of the Ohio Valley in demanding war with Great Britain in 1812, partly at least, because they hoped for the conquest of all of Florida from Spain, then an ally of England as far as the European war was concerned. In this hope they were disappointed. We have already seen that the British made use of Florida posts during the War of 1812 and that the region was invaded by Andrew Jackson after he had defeated the Creek Indians.

After the close of the War of 1812 troubles along the Florida border speedily reached a climax. Smugglers and bandits infested Amelia Island at the mouth of St. Mary's River. Runaway slaves found a ready asylum among the Seminoles. Desparadoes of all sorts made various points below the boundary line their haunts. Indians made sorties from the same region to harass the frontier settlements in Georgia and Alabama. Little or no government was maintained by the Spanish. In view of this situation the United States decided to take a hand. The hero of New Orleans was placed in command of the expeditionary force and early in 1818 he entered East Florida. Proceeding in the belief that he had the approval of President Monroe for his proposal to pacify Florida (a point over which there was waged a vitriolic controversy), Jackson soon increased his popularity in the West by his vigorous actions. He captured and summarily executed two British traders whom he accused of instigating the Indians to attack American settlements. He also seized Spanish posts and deposed the governor. Of course such measures might easily have brought on a war with both England and Spain. Fortunately England chose to accept Secretary of State Adams' contention that the two traders deserved their fate. Spain protested, but confronted with the necessity of either maintaining order in Florida or making the cession desired by the Americans, she chose the latter alternative.

In 1819 there was signed a treaty by which Spain ceded claim to the Floridas to the United States, in consideration of the latter's agreement to assume the payment of claims for damages up to the amount of five million dollars. As will be described in more detail later, the same treaty defined the boundary between the United States and the remaining Spanish possessions in Texas and the farther west. When Florida was formally transferred to its new owner in July, 1821, the desires of the western expansionists were temporarily or at least partially satisfied. In the same year the Territory of Florida was established, with Andrew Jackson as its governor.

CHAPTER XVI

THE RECEDING RED MEN

EARLIER in these pages it was shown that the native tribes of North America were often used as pawns by the French and the Spanish and the English in their struggles for the control of the continent. The preceding chapter indicated that the controversies and conflicts of the United States with the English along the Canadian border, and with the Spanish in Louisiana and the Floridas, were aggravated by troubles with the Indians. For the frontiersmen, however, these international complications were only intensifying factors in a situation of irrepressible antagonism wherever the two races came into contact. From the landing of the first English colonists on the Atlantic coast to the passing of the frontier, nearly three centuries later, there was always some region in which the long-standing hatreds were freshly in evidence.

THE FRONTIERSMEN AND THE INDIANS

"There are moralists," said John Quincy Adams in an oration delivered in 1802, "who have questioned the right of the Europeans to intrude upon the possessions of the aboriginals in any case, and under any limitations whatsoever. But have they maturely considered the whole subject? The Indian right of possession itself stands, with regard to the greatest part of the country, upon a questionable foundation. Their cultivated fields; their constructed habitations; a space of ample sufficiency for their subsistence, and whatever they had annexed to themselves by personal labor, was undoubtedly by the law of nature theirs. But what is the right of a huntsman to the forest of a thousand miles over which he has accidentally ranged in quest of prey? Shall the liberal bounties of Providence to the race of man he monopolized by one of ten thou-

sand for whom they were created?   Shall the exuberant bosom
of the common mother, amply adequate to the nourishment of
millions, be claimed exclusively by a few hundreds of her off-
spring? . . . No, generous philanthropists! Heaven has not
been thus inconsistent in the work of its hands. Heaven has not
thus placed at irreconcilable strife, its moral laws with its
physical creation."

Such, in essence, has been the line of argument advanced
by the most moderate spokesmen of the white race in justification of its actions whereever, throughout the world, it has
taken possession of lands occupied by primitive peoples. Substantially this same attitude has been the basis of the Indian
policy of the United States government. Concerning the basic
morality of this attitude there have been relatively few protests. But there the general agreement has ended. From first
to last our treatment of the Indians has been the subject of a
wide range of views and opinions, from vigorous defense to
caustic criticism.

This much can be said: the frontiersman living in daily
contact with the Indians could scarcely be expected to view
that race with the perspective that was possible to the person
dwelling in safety in a settled community far removed from
scenes of conflict and irritation. Felix Grundy of Tennessee
in a speech in the United States Senate once expressed the attitude of the first generation of frontiersmen—those whose hatred of all Indians was based on ineradicable memories. "I can
remember," he said, "when death was in almost every bush,
and every thicket concealed an ambuscade. If I am asked to
trace my memory back, and name the first indelible impression
it received, it would be the sight of my oldest brother bleeding
and dying under wounds inflicted by the tomahawk and the
scalping knife. Another, and another, went the same way! I
have seen a widowed mother plundered of her whole property
in a single night. . . . Sir, the ancient sufferings of the West
were great." Men living through such experiences were not
qualified to give judicial consideration to the wrongs suffered
by the Indians at the hands of white men.

On the other hand it is noticeable that when once the Indians had been removed from a given region and settlements had grown and prospered for a few years in complete security, many western spokesmen were ready to defend the receding natives against governmental approval of the demands of pioneers on a further western frontier, where the conflict was now in process. Thus, for instance, in 1827 Representative Vinton of Ohio apparently ran little risk of disfavor among his constituents when he said that, no matter to what distant district the Indians might be removed, "the pioneers would be there in advance of them; men of the most abandoned and desperate character, who hang upon the Indians to defraud them. You cannot run away from these men nor shut them out from access to Indians, scattered over the wilderness; for, with the pioneers, the law is a jest, and the woods.their element."

INDIAN POLICY OF THE UNITED STATES

When the United States government took over the regulation of Indian affairs it followed the practice and adopted the policy in force during colonial days. Indian tribes were regarded as possessing at least some of the attributes of sovereignty, including the right of occupancy of their lands—a right which could be extinguished only by treaties negotiated by official representatives of the government and ratified by the United States Senate (after the adoption of the Constitution). The motives which led to the adoption of such a policy were doubtless honorable and represent a consideration for the rights of the natives not always exhibited by the white race in other parts of the world. And yet it is the judgment of history that the policy was a mistaken one and that in operation it produced results not much different from what might have been achieved by a program of frank and deliberate exploitation. Our first treaty was made with the Delaware Indians in 1778. Long before treaty-making was abandoned nearly a century later, in 1871, the veil of pretense had worn very thin, and the Indians had received treatment far different from that any nation would accord peoples whom it sincerely regarded as in any sense sovereign and independent.

There were several basic factors which made treaty-making with the Indians an unsatisfactory procedure. In the first place, with a few possible exceptions the Indians had no conception of either individual or tribal ownership of land corresponding to the ideas of white men. To the natives land was like air and water—something they needed and enjoyed but not something to be bought and sold. They only vaguely understood the meaning of a treaty ceding their right to a given region. Not until after repeated, bitter experiences did they finally learn that they could not return to hunt on land to which they had relinquished their title by making a few marks on a sheet of paper. Then again, chieftains and leaders did not have the power or authority to bind their fellow-tribesmen to an agreement such as resides in official representatives among civilized nations. Finally, numerous tribes frequently hunted over the same territory, and therefore a treaty made with one tribe did not extinguish titles held with equal validity by other tribes.

On the other hand, the United States government was virtually powerless to control the actions of its own citizens. To be sure there were stringent laws prohibiting trespassing on Indian lands, with severe penalties for offenders. Occasionally half-hearted attempts were made to drive settlers off forbidden territory, but even more determined efforts would have been fruitless. In fact, it is only fair to say that the government's good intentions with respect to the Indians were frustrated by irresponsible traders and aggressive settlers. Plans to establish the relationship between the two races on a peaceful basis were one after another brought to naught. "The story of one failure," to quote Ruth A. Gallaher's terse description of the oft-repeated cycle, "has been the story of all such attempts. A treaty was made; friendship was declared; the Indians ceded lands and received in return annuities and presents; a boundary line was marked off; and for a few years there was a peace that was only suspended hostility. Then the pioneers, driven westward by insatiable land-hunger, crossed the line and settled on the unceded lands of the Indians. There were protests, massacres, and retaliations, a campaign by the troops, and another treaty in which more land was ceded, more presents given, and another 'peace' was established." [1]

To this outline should be added the statement that there is good ground for suspicion that traders all too frequently helped to bring about situations leading to treaties, in order that they might claim the annuities in satisfaction of debts contracted by the Indians for goods and whiskey at greatly inflated prices. For instance, in 1839 an Illinois editor asserted that as much as $100,000 was thus secured by a single trading company.

It would be tedious and unprofitable to mention all the treaties made with the Indians before the principal tribes were removed to their new locations west of the Mississippi. Naturally the treaties negotiated at the close of Indian disturbances or so-called "wars" attracted the most attention and were hailed with the greatest satisfaction by the advancing settlers. A brief sketch of the most notable Indian campaigns, with the resulting land cessions, will illustrate the most spectacular phase of the process by which the tribesmen's title to large areas was extinguished and the land made available for white settlement.

EARLY INDIAN WARS AND TREATIES IN OLD NORTHWEST

In 1784 the Iroquois Indians signed a treaty at Fort Stanwix reaffirming the agreement made at the same place in 1768, relinquishing all right to the land north of the Ohio River which they had claimed on the basis of ancient conquests. The tribes occupying this region did not recognize the validity of this treaty as far as they were concerned. In 1785, however, a number of these tribes agreed at Fort McIntosh, below Pittsburgh, to remain north of a boundary line running in a general way along the watershed between the Ohio and Lake Erie. These treaties made little impression on the Miami, Wyandot, Delaware, Shawnee, Chippewa, Ottawa, and other tribes, who continued to roam at will over the region bordering on the Ohio. Thus when white settlements were planted at Marietta

---

[1] Ruth A. Gallaher, "The Indian Agent in the United States before 1850," in *The Iowa Journal of History and Politics,* January, 1916, pp. 4-5. Published by the State Historical Society of Iowa.

in 1788 and began to spread to other points on the north bank of the river, there was constant danger of attack by Indians.

At Fort Harmar on the Ohio a treaty was made in 1789 by which the tribes re-affirmed the agreements made at Fort Mc-Intosh. But even this did not result in the departure of the Indians from the region along the Ohio. In addition to their lack of understanding of the full meaning of treaties, it is evident that the Indians were encouraged in their resistance by the knowledge that the British were still in possession of the posts along the Great Lakes and by secret suggestions made by English officers and traders. Accordingly General Joseph Harmar was sent on an expedition to the northward to overawe the tribesmen. Harmar's troops were poorly equipped and without discipline. When attacked by the Indians they were not entirely routed, but retired in poor order and with severe losses to Fort Washington at Cincinnati.

Governor Arthur St. Clair of the Northwest Territory was now ordered by President Washington to lead an expedition to punish the Indians and bring peace to the settlements. The outcome was a disaster comparable to that suffered by General Braddock. In extenuation it is only fair to state that St. Clair was growing old, he was physically unfit for such an arduous campaign, and he lacked any adequate military experience. The army furnished him was of the most nondescript character, inexperienced, unruly, and poorly equipped. The plan of campaign was well conceived, namely to establish a chain of forts from Fort Washington to the Maumee River. The expedition, consisting of about two thousand fighting men, got under way early in October, 1791, and for a time proceeded according to plan. Fort Hamilton was erected about twenty-five miles above Cincinnati and Fort Jefferson near the present site of Greenville, Ohio. Then at daybreak on November 4th catastrophe befell the army encamped in the forest on the Wabash near the present Ohio-Indiana boundary line.

The sleeping troops were suddenly awakened by warwhoops and volleys of bullets and arrows from the encircling forest. A scene of the wildest confusion ensued as the halfclothed soldiers rushed to their arms and sought to return the fire of their hidden foes. Despite the fact that he was ill, St.

Clair exhibited the utmost bravery. Three horses fell beneath him and his clothing was repeatedly perforated by bullets. Nothing he could do, however, could prevent an utter rout. More than six hundred of his men were killed and nearly three hundred wounded—altogether nearly half of his entire force. The dispirited remnants straggled back to Cincinnati, leaving the Indians jubilant and confident. Over the frontier settlements hung a cloud of gloom and apprehension.

The man chosen to administer retribution to the Indians and restore the lost prestige of the United States army was "Mad Anthony" Wayne of Revolutionary War fame. In the campaign which he conducted he exhibited none of the apparent recklessness that had earned him his sobriquet. In the fall of 1792 at Pittsburgh he took command of an army of 2500 men of about the same type as had followed Harmar and St. Clair. Instead of moving at once into the Indian country he spent the winter a short distance below Pittsburgh drilling his men. Even the next year he proceeded with the greatest deliberation. Near Cincinnati he spent the summer and autumn of 1793, everlasting drilling and forging his units of infantry, cavalry, and artillery into a competent fighting machine. Still another winter was spent at Fort Greenville, where there was still more drilling. During this period a fort, significantly named Fort Recovery, was built on the site of St. Clair's debacle. All this preparation was trying to the impatient settlers, but it likewise kept the Indians in a state of nervous excitement.

Not until late in July, 1794, was the real advance into the Indian country begun. Every precaution was taken. There were scouts in advance and on the flanks and a protected line of communication with the rear was maintained. Fort Defiance was built on the Maumee River at the mouth of the Auglaize. Then as he was proceeding down the Maumee towards the head of Toledo Bay on August 20th, Wayne was confronted by the Indians under Little Turtle, arrayed behind natural breastworks of trees uprooted by a tornado at a place known as Fallen Timbers. The presence of Englishmen among the Indians was presumptively indicated by their very unusual readiness to fight a pitched battle. In the conflict which ensued the Indians were decisively defeated and their finest warriors slain. Wayne remained for a short time in the neighborhood, giving, as we have already seen, much worry to the British authorities in Detroit and vicinity. Then he proceeded westward, destroyed a number of Miami Indian towns, erected Fort Wayne near the source of the Maumee, and retired to Fort Defiance.

In the summer of 1795 Wayne gathered representatives of ten or eleven tribes at Fort Greenville. There on August 3rd, after nearly two months of feasting and speech-making, the thoroughly humbled Indians signed a treaty giving up all claim to the southern half of the present State of Ohio and the southeastern corner of Indiana. This time the treaty was observed, at least on the part of the Indians. For a period of fifteen years peace was unbroken on the northwestern frontier.

Tecumseh's Confederation

During these years, however, the resentment of Indian leaders smoldered and increased. Traders cheated the tribesmen and plied them with bad liquor until sturdy braves were degraded into slinking sneak-thieves. Social diseases spread rapidly as the baser element among the frontiersmen found easy access to Indian women, and thus the physical stamina of the natives was further weakened. During the early years of the nineteenth century various tribes were induced by prospects of annuities, or when their chiefs were under the influence of liquor, to sign treaties ceding land beyond the line established by the Treaty of Greenville. Thus the farming frontier pressed steadily into Indiana Territory. For the Indians the most disheartening feature of the situation was the fact that even the most respectable and law-abiding frontier farmers were inexorable in their demand for more and more lands for settlement. Added to all these festering grievances were the secret encouragements given by British traders and officials at Malden across the Canadian border, and the hope that some day the English would join the Indians in a war against the Americans.

The leader who became the spokesmen for the Indian tribes

north of the Ohio was the Shawnee brave, Tecumseh—a man
still in his thirties when he began the plans which made him
notable among Indian statesmen. He was not a chief, but he
possessed the qualities of leadership which won him a wide influence among the tribes equal to that earlier exerted by
Pontiac.   Scarcely less influential among the superstitious
natives, although less capable, was Tecumseh's brother, known
as The Prophet and reputed to have powers of magic and divi-
nation. As Tecumseh brooded over the desperate situation of
his race he saw only one hope. To his mind the Indians' right,
of occupancy was one which all enjoyed in common and which
no tribe or tribes could alienate without the consent of all. Of
course he could not fully realize that this view never could or
would be accepted by the whites, because it would mean a
permanent Indian barrier to further expansion. But with this
principle as the basis of his statesmanship Tecumseh set about
the task of winning the tribes over to a plan of passive resistance and of refusal to make any further land cessions. In 1808
Tecumseh and The Prophet established themselves at a place
which became known as Prophet's Town, on the Wabash near
the mouth of Tippecanoe Creek, and across from the site of the
present city of Lafayette, Indiana. Here was the region of the
densest Indian population and through it ran the great pathway traveled by the tribesmen from Malden, opposite Detroit,
to Pensacola and the other Spanish settlements on the Gulf.
From this point Tecumseh began preaching the gospel of a
great Indian confederacy that would check white aggression
and save the race from extinction.

The Governor of Indiana Territory was William Henry
Harrison. When he took office in 1800 there was scarcely any
land in the Territory to which the Indian title had been extinguished. In the succeeding years he took the lead and
secured treaty after treaty opening lands in the southern
part of the Territory, the most notable being the Treaty of
Fort Wayne in 1809 by which three million acres were secured
from the Indians. Naturally these activities made Harrison
popular among the settlers, but among the Indians they caused
growing alarm. The last named treaty, especially, was repudiated by Tecumseh and the chiefs who were not signatories.

Settlements were now approaching the Indian stronghold along the Wabash.

Harrison was particularly watchful of Tecumseh as his plans for an Indian confederacy began to develop. The two men held several conferences without any important result. It was noted that Tecumseh made frequent trips to Malden, and Harrison, like most of the frontiersmen, became convinced, and not without some justification, that the British were giving aid and encouragement to the Indian leader. Moreover, there was growing resentment along the frontier as people saw Indians returning from Malden with guns and scalping-knives which they had obtained in exchange for furs. In the early summer of 1811 the situation along the Indiana frontier became acute. Tecumseh set out on a tour of the southern Indian tribes. His young braves, who had been restrained with difficulty, now felt greater freedom. Soon there were complaints of depredations among the isolated settlements and there was widespread fear of an Indian war.

Harrison had apparently long been hoping for the time when he could make a name and win glory for himself as an Indian fighter. The opportunity seemed to present itself in the apparent need of decisive action to quiet the restless Indians. Late in the summer he gathered an army of about nine hundred men and marched up the Wabash. Fort Harrison was built on the site of Terre Haute and the army proceeded to Prophet's Town which was not destroyed in spite of the advice of some of Harrison's men. The night of November 6th found the army encamped in the rain on a ridge of ground south of Tippecanoe Creek. Before daylight the next morning the sentries gave the alarm and immediately a large number of Indians attacked the camp. Harrison and his men were able to hold their position, although with considerable loss, and at length the Indians withdrew. This was the famous Battle of Tippecanoe which was celebrated in song twenty-nine years later, when its hero was elected President of the United States. As has been indicated the struggle was virtually a draw, with neither side winning a decisive victory. Harrison retreated rapidly to Vincennes and the battle assumed more of the proportions of a great triumph with every mile traveled away from the scene of action and with every report sent to Washington.

Nevertheless, although the battle was inconclusive it did discourage the Indians. When Tecumseh returned from his southern tour he found his influence weakened and all hope for his confederacy gone. As we have seen, Indians figured on the British side in most of the western engagements during the War of 1812. But after the close of that war the frontier north of the Ohio River was not again disturbed by anything approaching a real Indian scare for nearly another generation.

THE WINNEBAGO WAR

In 1827 there was a short-lived disturbance in southwestern Wisconsin where, in the lead-mining region, miners and settlers had encroached on the lands of the Winnebago Indians. The Indians complained ineffectually and a few members of the tribe murdered and scalped several white men, women, and children. Immediately there was wild excitement in the entire region as settlers and miners, fearing an Indian war, fled to Galena and to various forts. A strong body of regular troops and volunteers was soon in the field, however, and the terrified Winnebagoes hastened to surrender.

THE BLACK HAWK WAR

Five years later in this same region of southern Wisconsin and northern Illinois there occurred the so-called Black Hawk War. In 1804 representatives of the Sauk and Fox tribes, said to have been intoxicated at the time, signed a treaty at St. Louis by which those Indians ceded all their land between the Wisconsin and Illinois rivers to the United States, retaining the right to occupy the land until such time as the government decided to make it available for settlement. This treaty was confirmed in 1816 and again in 1825. In course of time two factions appeared among the Sauk and Fox Indians. One, following the lead of Chief Keokuk, moved across the Mississippi into the present State of Iowa. The other division, which remained in the tribal village on the Rock River in Illinois, was headed by the elderly Black Hawk, a man who at an earlier period when the odds were not so heavily against him might well have won for himself a place among Indian statesmen like Pontiac and Tecumseh. He and his followers continued to make annual pilgrimages to Malden and for this reason were often called the British band of the Sauk and Fox tribes.

By 1830 settlers without any legal right began to encroach on the Sauk and Fox lands along the Rock River, occupying their cornfields and plowing up their burying grounds. Black Hawk made frequent protests to no effect. In the summer of 1831 he became more threatening and destroyed some of the fields and houses of the settlers. Thereupon there arose a great outcry and urgent demand for protection. A strong force was raised under Edmund P. Gaines. At this show of force Black Hawk and his followers sued for peace and fled across the Mississippi.

In the spring of 1832, Black Hawk and from six to eight hundred warriors, with women and children, recrossed the river into their old haunts. Apparently he had conceived some visionary scheme of an Indian confederation with British aid, which would hold the white invaders at bay. Soon a number of white settlers and an Indian agent were murdered, as wandering groups of Indians visited their old homes. Among the settlers there was widespread fear. Volunteer companies were raised and from various directions regular troops were despatched to the scene of trouble. Ultimately as many as four thousand troups were in the field, under such leaders as General Henry Atkinson, General Winfield Scott, Colonel Zachary Taylor, and Colonel Henry Dodge.

The result of such an uneven contest, of course, was never in doubt, although the first meeting of a raw, undisciplined company of volunteers with a small group of warriors ended in the ignominious flight of the former. Black Hawk and his braves were pursued into the Four Lakes region of Wisconsin, where Madison now stands, and then back again to the Mississippi. There, as they were endeavoring to escape to the west bank, they were hopelessly overwhelmed and defeated, Black Hawk himself being captured. Even numbers of Indian women and children were victims of the bullets of the exultant victors. This was the famous Black Hawk War which enabled many a resident of Illinois and Wisconsin to tell his children and grand-children how he fought the redskins. As a result of the war the Sauk and Fox Indians signed a treaty in September, 1832, by which they relinquished title to a fifty-mile strip of land along the west bank of the Mississippi in what soon became the Territory of Iowa. Soon, also, Indian claims to most of the region between Lake Michigan and the Mississippi were ceded to the United States government, and settlers poured into the upper Mississippi Valley.

JACKSON'S CAMPAIGNS IN THE OLD SOUTHWEST

In the Old Southwest the pressure of settlements on Indian lands did not begin as early as in the region north of the Ohio River. Consequently it was not until the War of 1812 that the United States government faced any Indian disturbance in the territory now included in Mississippi, Alabama, and western Georgia. In the fall of 1812 Georgia militia conducted a par-tially successful campaign against the troublesome Seminole Indians in Florida. During the following year one faction of the powerful Creek tribe took up the hatchet. Inflamed by the teachings of Tecumseh on his southern tour, and emboldened by the easy capture of Detroit by the British, these Indians seized the occasion to begin a war of extermination against the scattered settlements. On August 30, 1813, they attacked Fort Mims near the junction of the Alabama and Tombigbee, which the settlers had built as a place of refuge. Nearly five hundred settlers lost their lives in the massacre that ensued, and the entire frontier was panic-stricken.

Of several expeditions immediately organized to punish the Creeks only the one led by Andrew Jackson accomplished its purpose. Jackson's title to fame as a frontier hero rested not only on his victory over the Indians, but equally on the skill with which he handled his raw, undisciplined, mutinous Ten-nessee militia and their Choctaw and Cherokee allies. Mixing cajolery with severity, he won the obedience and confidence and even the affection of his men, and kept them in the field until his object had been achieved in spite of short-term enlist-ments. He met the Creeks in several minor engagements during the winter of 1813-1814. Then on March 27, 1814, at the Horseshoe Bend of the Tallapoosa River, he administered a crushing defeat to his foe. Fully two-thirds of the nine hundred Creek warriors participating in this battle were slain and the remainder fled for their lives.

Jackson then moved on down the Tallapoosa and erected Fort Jackson at the junction of that stream with the Coosa. Here in August, 1814, he concluded a treaty with the surviving Creeks, most of whom had been friendly to the whites, by which peace was pledged and a portion of the Creek lands were relinquished. Jackson was rewarded by being appointed Major-General in the United States Army.

Three years later, in 1817 and 1818, there occurred another so-called Seminole War. These Indians, who had their retreats in the fastnesses of the Florida everglades, were the cause of intermittent trouble for many years, and small bands, because of their inaccessibility, never were conquered. The difficulties at this time were those already described as a part of the conflicts and annoyances along the Florida border which hastened the negotiations culminating in the Florida Purchase Treaty of 1819. General Gaines led one expedition into the Seminole country and subdued a portion of the troublesome natives. It was during this disturbance that Andrew Jackson took possession of Spanish territory and hanged the two British traders, Arbuthnot and Ambrister.

THE UNPLEASANT STORY OF TREATY-MAKING

Military campaigns and "wars" constitute only the most spectacular and, on the whole, the most creditable part of the story of the dealings with the Indian tribes resulting in their dispossession of their homes and hunting grounds east of the Mississippi. The record of treaty-making with the aborigines is dreary and unpleasant reading even to one fully convinced of the inevitability of savagery giving way to civilization. North of the Ohio the process was accomplished with comparative ease, partly because of the successful campaigns of Wayne and Harrison, and partly because the tribes were relatively weak and poorly organized, except during the short period of Tecumseh's ascendancy. Even so, the methods employed in securing treaties were seldom above question.

It was in the Old Southwest and on the Georgia frontier, however, that the worst features appeared. Here were the powerful Creek, Cherokee, Chickasaw, Choctaw, and Seminole nations—the first two, especially displaying the traits which have given the whole group the appellation of the Five Civilized Tribes. For three decades these populous, intelligent tribesmen exhibited remarkable powers of resistance to every kind of pressure. The situation in Georgia was complicated by the compact made by the federal government in 1802 when that State relinquished her western land claims. At that time the United States had promised that title to Indian lands within the boundaries of Georgia should be extinguished as soon as it could be accomplished peaceably and on reasonable terms. At no time thereafter until the compact was finally fulfilled were the people of Georgia satisfied with the progress made by the federal government. Pressure of settlements on Indian lands in Alabama and Mississippi soon caused situations scarcely less troublesome. Every President from Jefferson to Jackson was forced to give much time and attention to the problems involved. Long and acrimonious debate occurred in almost every session of Congress.

Among the Indian tribes council after council was held, sometimes resulting in treaties, but as often ending in failure. In council and out of council, Andrew Jackson and a score of other equally determined agents and commissioners sought to bend the Indians to their wills by false promises, bribery, threats, and intimidation. It speaks volumes for the sturdy qualities of these southern tribes that they were able to resist so long and cling year after year to their ancient home lands. The pity of it all is revealed in the backward view, which indicates that Indians already so far along the path toward civilization as the Creeks and Cherokees might without serious difficulty have been absorbed in the citizenry of the States where they were living. But land-hungry settlers had no sympathy for such a solution, and in the end the Indians had to go.

It should not be thought that during all these years no voice was raised in behalf of the Indians. As a matter of fact numerous religious and philanthropic individuals and organizations were much concerned about the spiritual and temporal welfare of the natives. Private funds were raised for missionary and educational activities, and beginning about 1818 some aid was afforded by Congressional appropriations. Many devoted and capable men gave their lives to work among the Indians and, especially among the Cherokees, proved that noteworthy results could be achieved. In 1820 the Rev. Jedidiah Morse made an extended tour through the Indian country at the request of Secretary of War and later published an elaborate and valuable report on the condition of the various tribes, ending with the suggestion of a plan for the establishment of "education families" in various regions. During the debates in Congress numerous eastern Senators and Representatives sought earnestly to protect the Indians from the designs and practices of frontiersmen and from legislation drafted by their spokesmen.

THE INDIAN REMOVAL POLICY

Finally what seemed a happy solution for the perplexing Indian problem was formulated. Experience had shown only too clearly that the onrushing settlers would not tolerate the presence of any considerable body of red men in their vicinity. The haphazard and temporizing practice of securing land cessions and pushing the Indians further west in advance of the settlements was increasingly unsatisfactory to all concerned. A definite and practicable policy was badly needed. Such a policy, based on the suggestions of John C. Calhoun, Secretary of War, was recommended to Congress by President James Monroe in 1825 in his last annual message.

During the decade of the twenties the people of the United States as a whole were satisfied with their national boundaries and convinced that the Rocky Mountains would forever mark their western limit. Moreover, explorers and scientists had told them that the high, arid plains stretching eastward from the Rockies to the Missouri River were unsuited to white settlement. Here, then, was a region to which the Indian tribes east of the Mississippi might be removed and where they might be allowed to dwell permanently without further molestation by white men. This was the proposal which Secretary Calhoun made to President Monroe and which he in turn communicated to Congress in 1825.

The idea of removing the Indians west of the Mississippi did not originate with Calhoun. It had occurred to Thomas Jefferson and was embodied in the constitutional amendment which he drafted in 1803 but did not submit to Congress, for the purpose of satisfying his political scruples at the time of the purchase of Louisiana. Furthermore, the act establishing the Territory of Louisiana contained a clause authorizing the President to negotiate treaties with the Indians providing for the exchange of their lands east of the Mississippi for lands west of that river. In the succeeding years the plan of removal met with some favor, especially in the South. A few tribes, notably the Delawares, Kickapoos, and a portion of the Cherokees were induced to move to the western country, but no effort was made to secure a location for them there. They were left to find new homes as best they could.

The Calhoun-Monroe plan contemplated an elaborate series of treaties, first with the tribes already inhabiting the western plains securing room for the prospective newcomers, and next with the eastern tribes inviting and urging them to accept new lands in exchange for those they then occupied. Schools and other agencies of civilization were to be provided for them. The border of the Indian country was to be patrolled to protect the tribesmen from unscrupulous white traders and settlers. In short, the Indians were promised that if they would move to new western homes they could settle down secure in the assurance that they would never again be disturbed.

Congress did not immediately take action on Monroe's proposal, but treaty-making proceeded rapidly. With the accession of Andrew Jackson to the presidency in 1829 the removal policy became a party measure and in spite of strong opposition from religious and other organizations interested in the Indians, in 1830 Congress passed a law authorizing the President to exchange lands held by tribes within a State or Territory for lands beyond the Mississippi. There was no suggestion of compulsion in the law, but with a thorough-going westerner in the White House there could be little doubt of the outcome. The removal process was soon in full swing. The Cherokees and Creeks clung desperately to their southern homes and the years from 1835 to 1838 were marked by numerous disturbances. The Seminoles were even more unwilling to move, with the result that there was another "Seminole War" lasting from 1837 to 1842. The conditions under which the once-proud southern tribes were conducted to much less satisfactory lands west of Arkansas were difficult at best. These migrations attracted much attention at the time and they constitute a pathetic chapter in the story of the American Indians.

By 1840 the new Indian frontier was practically complete. In general the boundary ran west from Green Bay to the Mississippi, down that river to the lead-mining region near the mouth of the Wisconsin, in a southwestwardly direction into the Territory of Iowa, then south to the Missouri line and west on that line to the Missouri River, down that river and the western boundary of Missouri and Arkansas to the Texan line. The Commissioner of Indian Affairs in 1837 estimated that approximately 12,400 Indians remained in the States, more than 51,000 had already migrated, nearly 40,000 were under agreement to migrate, and that the tribes already resident in the western Indian country numbered nearly 232,000.

Thus was created the solid and supposedly permanent Indian frontier. It is reasonable to believe that the removal policy was conceived honestly and with the expectation that the promises made the Indians would not be broken. It can at least be said of the policy that, in view of all the factors involved, it was better than the ill-considered practices which it replaced. The policy was executed consistently and certainly without greater wrongs to the Indians themselves than they had previously suffered. The main cause for regret is that there did not exist the will and the wisdom to give some plan of assimilation a thorough and persistent trial.

In later pages we shall see that, in just a few years, the policy of a permanent Indian territory was abandoned and forgotten. The events and practices recorded in the present chapter will then appear honorable in comparison with what followed.

CHAPTER XVII

THE PUBLIC DOMAIN

MINGLED motives and varied compulsions actuated the millions of individuals who participated in the long-continued westward movement. Restlessness, yearning for new scenes, the contagious nature of the moving fever, dissatisfaction, distress, failure—all these had their effect. But land-hunger was the most potent of the impelling forces. Cheap and fertile land was the lure above all others which year after year filled the roads and waterways with emigrants to the West. Timothy Flint expressed the power of this attraction somewhat rhetorically, but none the less vividly, when in 1832 he wrote: "Sickness, solitude, mountains, the war-whoop, the merciless tomahawk, wolves, panthers, and bears, dear and distant homes, forsaken forever, will come over their waking thoughts, and revisit their dreams in vain, to prevent the young, florid and unportioned pair from scaling remote mountains, descending long rivers, and finally selecting their spot in the forests, consecrating their solitary cabin with the dear and sacred name of home."

The very earliest settlers throughout most of that portion of the West with which we are now dealing apparently were little concerned about land titles. They squatted where fancy or necessity dictated, built rude cabins, made small clearings, lived mostly by hunting, and after a few years moved on to some more distant frontiers, there to repeat the process. Those who followed them, however, were of different dispositions. They came with the intention at least of making permanent settlements. Land to them was something of great value and therefore the acquiring of valid title was of supreme importance. Out of this need and desire grew our public land policy. Because of the demand of westerners for a progressive liberalization of this policy thousands of pages were filled with Congressional debates and reports, political parties inserted planks in their platforms, and chief executives were compelled to express their views. In the history of the West and in that of the nation as a whole, therefore, the story of public land legislation and its operation constitutes a chapter of great significance.

THE CESSION OF THE WESTERN LANDS

When the thirteen Ameriacn colonies threw off the English yoke the new state governments claimed jurisdiction in accordance with the boundaries established by the colonial charters and the subsequent adjustments made by Parliamentary legislation. Thus there were seven States—Massachusetts, Connecticut, New York, Virginia, North Carolina, South Carolina, and Georgia—which maintained title to lands west of the Appalachian Mountains. The Proclamation of 1763 had been interpreted in America as not abrogating the western land claims of the various colonies, but only as deferring their settlement. The Quebec Act of 1774, placing the region north of the Ohio River under the jurisdiction of the Canadian province, was cited as one of the grievances of the colonists, and it was not regarded as binding upon them, especially after the exploits of George Rogers Clark.

Beginning at the north, Massachusetts laid claim to a broad strip of territory extending across the southern part of the modern States of Michigan and Wisconsin and the northern edge of Illinois. Next was the claim of Connecticut to a narrower belt stretching across the northern border of the present Ohio, Indiana, continuing through Illinois and including the very southern fringe of Michigan. New York's claim to land west of Pennsylvania and reaching into Kentucky was of a more shadowy nature, since it rested on that colony's alleged suzerainty over the Iroquois Indians who, in turn, had asserted their jurisdiction over a vast region.

All three of these western land claims were disputed by Virginia, whose pretensions were the largest of all the States. That colony's second charter had specified that the colony should extend "all along the sea-coast" two hundred miles north and an equal distance south of Point Comfort, and that it should reach "up into the land throughout from sea to sea, west and northwest." The last statement was extremely indefinite and ambiguous. It is not surprising that the grantees chose to interpret this provision as meaning that the boundary lines should run west from the southern point on the sea-coast and northwest from the northern point. The southern boundary of Virginia was later modified and made definite when the Carolina grant was made. Consequently Virginia claimed not only modern Kentucky but all the land north of the Ohio and west of Pennsylvania, and for a time even the southwestern corner of that State. After the division of the Carolina grant, North Carolina included what is now Tennessee. South Carolina also extended indefinitely westward, but her claim was later limited by the creation of Georgia, at the most, to a narrow strip south of the present southern boundary of Tennessee. Georgia was given the land to the west of that colony, and there was some contention that this grant entirely obliterated South Carolina's claim.

There is every evidence that these seven States were planning to use their western land as a source of revenue. The six landless States (if we include Pennsylvania which had vast unoccupied areas in its western portion) naturally looked with envy upon the vast holdings of their more fortunate neighbors. This jealousy and ill will, as well as the prospect of quarrels between the States whose western claims overlapped, threatened to block the effort to secure unified action even in the midst of the war for independence. The Articles of Confederation, weak as they proved to be, were far better than no plan of union. But in 1780, three years after these articles of government were first submitted to the legislatures, they still lacked ratification by the requisite number of States. The question of the western land claims was the main stumbling-block.

Maryland was the spokesman for the small and landless States, refusing staunchly to ratify the Articles until the western land claims had been surrendered to the general government. The Maryland legislature asserted that this western land "if wrested from the common enemy by the blood and treasure of the thirteen States, should be considered as a common property." In September, 1780, Congress issued an appeal to the land-claiming States to yield in the interest of union. New York was the first to respond, when on March 1, 1781, she ceded her somewhat doubtful claims unreservedly to the federal government. On the same day Maryland ratified the Articles of Confederation. There was considerable negotiation between Congress and Virginia before that State ceded her western lands on March 1, 1784, reserving Kentucky and such land between the Scioto and Little Miami Rivers as might be necessary to satisfy outstanding warrants.

Cessions by the remaining five States followed at intervals until 1802. Massachusetts surrendered her western lands

VI. WESTERN LAND CLAIMS OF THE STATES

without reservation in 1785. Connecticut followed in 1786, retaining until 1800 what was known as the "Western Reserve" along the southern shore of Lake Erie in Ohio. South Carolina ceded whatever claim she possessed unconditionally in 1787. Three years later North Carolina yielded jurisdiction over the present State of Tennessee, but there were so many outstanding claims that very little land in that area was left for disposal by Congress. The last cession, that by Georgia, came in 1802 after long controversies between the State and the federal government, and after a notorious public scandal had grown out of the transactions of the Yazoo Land Companies.

These self-denying cessions created a public domain that proved a strong bond of union between the discordant States during the so-called "critical period" and the early years under the Constitution. Later accessions with each territorial acquisition by the United States, ending with the purchase of Alaska in 1867, greatly enlarged the area of the public domain. But in formulating a public land policy and a plan of territorial government the otherwise ineffective Congress of the Confederation won its chief title to remembrance. Both the Land Ordinance of 1785 and the Northwest Ordinance of 1787 setting up territorial government were of vital importance in the development of the West. Only the former ordinance will be discussed in this connection, since the latter did not deal with land policy.

The Establishment of a Public Land System

Scarcely had the Articles of Confederation gone into effect when Congress was called upon to decide what was to be done with the public domain. Revolutionary soldiers, still under arms, were clamoring for the lands that had been promised them at the time of their enlistments. They and others were also suggesting that the depreciated continental currency be accepted in payment for western land. Settlers were pouring into the West and many of them were squatting on lands north of the Ohio, causing discontent among the Indians. After his return from a western journey in 1784 George Washington wrote to R. H. Lee that "The spirit of emigration is great; people have got impatient; and though you cannot stop the road, it is yet in your power to mark the way." Clearly some policy must be established and some plan devised for the disposal of the western lands.

Two lines of colonial procedure furnished precedents for the study of Congress in seeking a solution for this problem. In New England the practice had been early established of permitting new settlements only in compact bodies and after prior government survey and marking of the lands to be occupied. The entire process was under the careful supervision of the colony, which made provision for adequate records and laid down the conditions under which settlements could be made. In the South, on the other hand, there was much less colonial oversight. New settlements were largely the work of individuals, who were permitted to locate on any unappropriated land that might suit them, mark their own boundaries, and record their claims accordingly. The New England system had the advantage of greater orderliness and compactness of settlement and greater certainty of boundaries and land titles. The southern procedure appealed more to the typical pioneer, but it led to endless disputes and litigation over poorly defined boundaries and titles. The plan which Congress finally adopted was a compromise between these two systems, although the New England procedure predominated.

A committee, of which Thomas Jefferson was a prominent member, reported a plan for a land system to Congress in 1784. Government survey into rectangular units prior to settlement was an outstanding feature of this report. The unit of the survey was to be the "hundred" ten miles square, divided into one hundred "lots" one mile square. This report was not acted upon at the time, but came up for discussion again the following year. In the course of the debate and committee action the plan was modified in many respects, including the reduction of the unit of survey to a "township" at first seven miles and later six miles square. On May 20, 1785, the ordinance was finally adopted.

The Land Ordinance of 1785, which laid the foundation of our public land system, contained the following important features, as well as many other details. Indian title to the land must be extinguished before it could be opened to entry. Surveys must be made prior to settlement, the rectangular plan being adopted, with townships six miles square divided into thirty-six lots or sections, as the subdivisions were soon called. The first meridian line was established and provision made for the survey of seven ranges of townships in southeastern Ohio. One-seventh of the land, selected by lot, was set aside for the Revolutionary soldiers and the remainder was to be put up for sale by auction in the various States at a minimum price of one dollar an acre. Two plans of disposal were to be used in alternate townships. One-half of the townships were to be sold entire and the other half in units of one section. Another provision of far-reaching significance was the reservation of section sixteen in each township for the maintenance of public schools.

The Ohio Associates and the Scioto Associates

If Congress expected an immediate income from the sale of western lands it was largely disappointed. Sales were slow and small. Strong competition was offered by more favorably located land within the States. The Indian menace in the region northwest of the Ohio was not conducive to settlement. At the same time frontiersmen, especially those from Virginia and other southern States, were disinclined to abandon their habit of marking out "tomahawk claims" and making indiscriminate settlements to suit their own fancies, with little regard to the provisions of the Land Ordinance. Thus it was that in 1787 the poor old Congress of the Confederation was ready to listen to proposals for large grants to land companies, and to nullify some of the important features of the plan it had adopted two years earlier.

In 1786 a group of Revolutionary soldiers in New England, led by Rufus Putnam, the Reverend Manasseh Cutler, Benjamin Tupper, Samuel Parsons, and others, organized the Ohio Associates or Ohio Company, which is not to be confused with the earlier Virginia company by the same name. The purpose of this group was to obtain a large tract of land in Ohio primarily for the benefit of soldiers who, it was hoped, could in this way obtain some value for the virtually worthless government certificates paid them for their military service. Under the skillful management of Manasseh Cutler this proposal was presented in Congress in a manner that would do credit to the modern manipulator and lobbyist. Members of Congress were visited at their lodgings at the seat of government and even in their own homes in their respective States. The prospect of selling one million dollars worth of land, even in return for depreciated currency, was very attractive. Still more alluring and effective was the suggestion of Cutler that members of Congress and other interested individuals might indulge in promising speculation by joining in the organization of a similar company to be given similar privileges. The suggestion was followed and a group known as the Scioto Associates was formed. With this backing the request of the Ohio Company was granted in the summer of 1787.

The Ohio Associates were allowed to contract for the purchase of more than a million and a half acres of land on the Ohio River west of the seven ranges, upon making a down payment of $500,000 in continental currency worth about twelve cents on the dollar. They never were able to complete payment for the entire amount of land granted them. Nevertheless, they planted permanent and thriving settlements in Ohio, and it was their proposal that led to the adoption of the fundamental charter of territorial government in the United States—the Northwest Ordinance of 1787.

The Scioto Associates were given the right to purchase nearly five million acres. This group, however, did not affect any real organization and their only success was in duping some six hundred French artisans and peasants to come to America. By the time they arrived here the tenuous Scioto organization was virtually defunct. The unfortunate emigrés were sent to Ohio, where on lands of the Ohio Company they formed a settlement known as Gallipolis. Here they lived a miserable existance, relieved only in part by later Congressional donations of lands totalling 25,200 acres.

One other large land deal was made by the Congress of the Confederation in its last days. John Cleves Symmes of New

Jersey was permitted in 1788 to purchase one million acres of land north of the Ohio and between the Great Miami and the Little Miami rivers. He was never able to complete payment on the entire amount. Moreover, the affairs of his purchase gave much trouble to the territorial government and to Congress before they were finally adjusted.

THE LAND LAW OF 1796

This was the situation when the Constitution went into operation and the new Congress, with vastly increased powers and prestige, assumed the legislative function. As might be expected, the public land question soon demanded consideration. It was not until 1796, however, that anything in the nature of a general land law was enacted. In the meantime there were numerous reports and much debate, and it seemed for a time as though the sound and workable system outlined in the Land Ordinance of 1785 might be abandoned. Alexander Hamilton as Secretary of the Treasury made his well-known report of a uniform system for the disposition of the public lands. His object clearly was to use the lands primarily as a means of raising revenue for the federal government, although he recognized the rights of individual settlers. It is fortunate that his plan was not adopted, for it ignored many of the most beneficial features of the Ordinance of 1785. Equally fortunate was the failure of the efforts of members of Congress from the frontier section, like Thomas Scott of Pittsburgh, to return to a system of indiscriminate settlements, allowing the individual pioneer to settle virtually where he chose and on as much land as he wished. Other aspects of the land problem which were discussed were the respective merits of cash and credit sales, of sales in large or small amounts, and of a land office confined to the seat of government or branch offices situated in the regions where the land was to be offered for sale.

On May 18, 1796, a law was finally approved "providing for the sale of the lands of the United States in the territory northwest of the river Ohio, and above the mouth of the Kentucky river." Only lands to which the Indian title had been extinguished were to be surveyed. The system of survey prior to settlement and of townships six miles square was retained and established for all time. Half of the townships were left undivided to be sold in quarter-townships at Philadelphia. The other half of the townships were to be surveyed and sold in sections of 640 acres at land offices at Pittsburgh and Cincinnati. Sales were to be made at auction, with the minimum price at two dollars an acre. One-twentieth of this amount was to be deposited at the time of application, the remainder of one-half within thirty days and the balance within one year, with a discount of ten per cent for cash. Failure to make these payments caused forfeiture of both the land and any payments already made. The establishment of western land offices was a concession to the wishes and convenience of settlers. The increased minimum price was thought to serve as a discouragement to speculators.

The Harrison Land Law of 1800

The law of 1796 proved a discouragement not only to speculators but to actual settlers as well, and scarcely more than 120,000 acres were sold in the four years following its enactment. On December 2, 1799, William Henry Harrison took his seat in Congress as delegate from Northwest Territory. He was thoroughly imbued with the frontiersman's point of view and demands in connection with public land policy. Within three weeks he introduced a resolution calling for the appointment of a committee to consider necessary alterations in the land law. The result was the submission of a report, which, without material change, was adopted and incorporated in what is known as the Harrison Land Law, bearing the date of May 10, 1800.

In this law the argument of the settlers that a section was too large a tract for a poor man to buy was met by the reduction of the smallest purchasable unit to a half-section. The other contention of the westerners, that credit of one year was no credit at all for the farmer on new lands, was likewise accepted and a real credit system was provided, with installments over a period of four years. Four land offices were established at Cincinnati, Chillicothe, Marietta, and Steubenville, with a register and a receiver at each office. Land was to be offered at auction for a period of three weeks and afterwards sold at private sale, the minimum price at auction and the regular price at private sale still being two dollars an acre. Thus, to quote Frederic L. Paxson, "under the Harrison Law, the United States became the partner of every settler who wished to try his luck upon the public domain, required him to put up only fifty cents an acre in advance and took its chance with him as to the success or failure of the enterprise. In four years, if successful, the settler expected to earn his farm out of its produce. Whether it was a good system for the country, or a vicious inducement to speculation and evasion of obligations, remained to be seen as the law directed the flow of settlers into Ohio, Indiana, Illinois, Alabama, Mississippi, Louisiana, and Missouri." [1]

Mixed motives led to the passage of the Harrison Land Law. Those who looked to the western lands primarily as a source of revenue expected that their purpose would be served by the relatively high price prescribed, in combination with the credit system. The pioneers and their friends felt that they had gained a point in the adoption of the credit system and the smaller unit of sale. Both groups were certain that the two-dollar minimum price would discourage speculators from purchasing large tracts of land. The results failed to verify the accuracy of these predictions.

To be sure, much land was sold under the Harrison Law— over nineteen million acres by 1820—but it was not until after the close of the War of 1812 that the annual sales ran into the millions. The statistics of sales, however, are misleading, for nearly one-third of this land eventually reverted to the government because of the inability or unwillingness of the purchasers to complete payment, although a series of twelve relief laws had been passed in their behalf by Congress. In 1804 the smallest unit of sale was reduced to the now familiar quarter-section, and more favorable terms with respect to interest were granted. But even then to complete payment in four years on one hundred and sixty acres of land was in reality

---

[1] Frederic L. Paxson, *History of the American Frontier* (1924), p. 122. By permission of The Houghton Mifflin Company, publishers.

beyond the means of the poor men who constituted the large majority of the westward emigrants. There is no way of knowing how many thousands of wistful but prudent families were deterred from making the venture by the evident impossibility of getting together enough money to finance the migration, the eighty-dollar first payment, and sustenance until crops could be raised. There is ample evidence, however, that a great number of too optimistic families undertook the impossible.

The hope that the relatively high minimum price would discourage speculation was also vain. As the years passed and especially as the Great Migration following the War of 1812 got into full swing, Indian treaties were made and land offices were opened in rapid succession in the Old Northwest in Ohio, Indiana, Illinois, and Michigan; in the south in Alabama and Mississippi; and across the Mississippi in Louisiana and Missouri. Surveyors with line and chain were busy marking off the metes and bounds of millions of farms. Land fever was epidemic in America from 1814 to 1820, and in many regions it assumed the virulent form of wild speculation.

Town-booming was one of the favorite forms of speculation throughout the West. "When you hear about market-houses, and seminaries, and streets No. 1, 2, and 3, in the midst of a wilderness of fallen logs," wrote Timothy Flint concerning Vevay, Indiana, in 1816, "you will have some idea of the language appropriate to a kind of speculation, almost peculiar to this country, that is to say, town-making." In 1818 Hezekiah Niles wrote of "a town somewhere in the Alabama territory, to be called 'Florence'—52 lots in it were lately sold for eighty-two thousand dollars." Later reports from this new town showed that a townsite company paid from $150 to $251 per acre for a quarter-section and then sold 284 lots for $226,411. "The highest went at $3,500. The average was nearly $800 for half an acre of woods." These are illustrations of what was happening all over the West. Some of the towns grew and prospered and thus justified the great expectations of speculators and bona fide buyers alike, even at boom prices. Others never existed except on paper, while still others after promising beginnings, dwindled away and became "ghost towns," sad reminders of shattered hopes.

Speculation in agricultural land was less spectacular but nevertheless widespread. North of the Ohio it did not reveal itself in inflated prices at the auction sales. Statistics indicate that the actual receipts did not average much in excess of the minimum price of two dollars per acre, but these figures do not account for the large amount of land reverting to the government because of uncompleted payments. The original buyers, however, were not so modest in their confidence in the future of the region. Morris Birkbeck in 1817 found that fifty dollars an acre was frequently asked for improved land in Ohio. "I have," he wrote, "been asked thirty for a large tract, without improvements, on the Great Miami, fifty miles from Cincinnati, and similar prices in other quarters."

It was in Mississippi and Alabama that speculative fever was most in evidence in the bidding at the auctions. Even granting that the rich, black soil of that section justified the offering of relatively high bids by actual settlers and plantation operators planning to engage in cotton culture, many of the prices paid were clearly speculative and attracted national attention, besides inducing bona fide settlers to offer more than they could pay or the land was worth. Senator Walker of Alabama declared on the floor of the Senate that the sales were made "under a sort of delirium—the most prudent, calculating men in the country were swept away by the delusion." Newspaper reports of various land sales in that region in 1818, for instance, indicated that "very little land that was good went for less than thirty dollars an acre," that "some of the best lands sold at 73 dollars an acre," and that "the highest quarter section was bid off by a responsible planter at one hundred and seven dollars per acre." A St. Louis editor, contrasting these prices with the three-dollar average for the sales in Missouri, consoled himself by the reflection that "if the south belongs to the rich alone, the substantial yeomanry of the country will turn their attention to the Missouri."

A plan adopted by a company of speculators in Alabama may have had its counterparts in other regions. They agreed among themselves not to bid more than two dollars an acre for any land. At this price they succeeded in obtaining two valuable townships and were ready to bid for more, but the

Register of the land office had discovered the scheme and discontinued the sale. The speculators then sold their two townships at auction and netted profits amounting to $1980 for each of the forty members. "We presume," was the comment of an Alabama editor, "that the gentlemen speculators formed their plans on the commonly received principle, that the public is a goose, and that while its enchanting plumage offered so many temptations to pluck a few feathers, no other danger was to be apprehended than that of being hissed at!"

CHAPTER XVIII

THE FIGHT FOR FREE LAND

THE DEFECTS OF THE CREDIT SYSTEM

THE defects and the unfortunate results of the credit system in the disposition of the public lands were very apparent by 1820, not only among easterners but also in the West among those in whose supposed interest the Harrison Law had primarily been enacted. A writer in a Kentucky paper in 1819, signing himself "Franklin," sounded an ominous note of warning which no doubt found foreboding echoes in the minds of many thoughtful persons. "The debts which it has already produced," he said in commenting on the credit system, "will be a source of almost endless and infinite embarrassment to the general government. Year after year will indulgence be *entreated*, till our strength will enable us to *demand it*, in a voice of thunder. . . . Let numberless individuals of every description, from the most wealthy, intelligent, and influential, down to those who are the reverse, be deeply indebted to the government of the Union, and will they not be in some measure disinclined to support it? . . . No people are more patriotic and firmly attached to the government of the Union than those of the west; the idea of a separation has never been indulged; it is literally abhorred; but their patriotism and fidelity are not invincible."

"Let not, therefore," he continued, "the general government credit the people of the west to the amount of fifty or a hundred million dollars, if it would not foolishly drive them into a declaration of independence. . . . The Rubicon is not yet passed; but we now stand upon the shore, and it depends on the measures to be adopted by the next congress, whether we shall remain a peaceful, happy and united people, or advance, with a steady and certain pace, to civil war and a dissolution of the union."

Congress, indeed, found itself embarrassed by the problems arising out of the uncomfortable situation and for several years after 1820 was still engaged in passing laws for the relief of those who were in arrears in the deferred payments on their land. The extent to which land was over-bought under stimulus of the credit system was also revealed in the long lists of lands to be sold for taxes which began to appear in western newspapers. These lists indicate to what a surprising extent individuals had undertaken to pay for lands in amounts much in excess of the minimum unit of one hundred and sixty acres.

Inability to make the deferred payments was one thing. Unwillingness to make them was a natural outgrowth of the system and it spread by example. The government was in no position to take drastic measures against defaulters. Instead it was compelled to pass laws for their relief. The hard-working farmer who saw that nothing happened to his neighbor when he let installments go unpaid often decided to omit his own payments. Viewing the effects of this attitude from the perspective of time and a knowledge of later trends, Professor Paxson suggests that "the measurement of the injury done by the system to frontier standards of commercial honor would make an interesting study in group psychology." [1]

THE LAND LAW OF 1820

Altogether, the credit system was thoroughly in disfavor by 1820, and in that year Congress passed a new land law which provided for its abandonment. There was a strong and growing sentiment in the West in favor of free land, an objective partly in accord with the frontiersman's long-standing contention of right and justice and partly brought to the fore by the mental state of a debtor farming population. The time, however, was not ripe for the fulfillment of this desire. The revenue motive in land policy and the political strength of the Atlantic States, which feared and opposed any measure that would tend to further drain population from their borders, were still too strong to be overcome. The law of 1820 reduced

[1] Frederic L. Paxson, *History of the American Frontier* (1924), p. 223. By permission of The Houghton Mifflin Company, publishers.

the minimum price to $1.25 an acre to be paid in one cash payment. It also established eighty acres as the smallest unit of purchase. One hundred dollars would now secure the settler immediate title to at least a small farm, whereas under the credit system and the quarter-section unit eighty dollars would pay only one of four installments.

SPECULATION IN WESTERN LAND

A period of twenty years again elapsed before another general law affecting the basic principles of public land policy was passed. The question was far from being forgotten during this interval, however; on the contrary, it became one of the great topics of national concern. Congress enacted numerous laws dealing with various phases of the land problem, and spent much time at each session debating other proposals. The subject of the public lands became enmeshed in the sectional politics of the period and in the growing antagonism between the industrial East and the rapidly strengthening agricultural West.

The Land Law of 1820 went into operation while the effects of the Panic of 1819 were still strongly in evidence. It was probably for this reason, rather than primarily because of the cash payments required by the law, that the volume of sales of public lands fell off greatly. Not until 1829 did the total annual sales again exceed one million acres. During the early thirties the amount showed a steady increase as another great wave of migration got under way, and in 1835 and 1836 the sales reached astonishing proportions and constituted one of the causes of the severe Panic of 1837, as will be seen in a later chapter. In 1836 more than twenty million acres of public land were sold. There is ample evidence that much of this buying was speculative in nature.

Town boomers and others of what would now be called the "booster" type were inclined to regard the speculator as a useful citizen because of his loud advertising of various regions. More thoughtful and conservative people in 1836 both East and West, regarded the speculative rage as dangerous and detrimental. A Boston paper reported that "money is passing from the Atlantic to the Western States, almost as fast as steamboats and railroad cars can carry it, to be invested in lands. Are all these facts indications of real prosperity, or are they the projects of speculations, whose fruits will be as disastrous, and as much beyond parallel calamities as the present appearances are attractive and exhilarating?" A New York editor, in satirical vein, reported a recent conversation: " 'Well, how are the folks getting on in your country,' said we to a resident of the interior of this State. 'O, finely,' said he, 'Many of the people after three weeks absence, have returned from the far West—having purchased everything up to the Rocky Mountains, are now so rich, that they talk of casting every man in the poor house, who is not worth more than $100,000.' "

In western newspapers the widespread speculation also received disapproving attention. For instance a Galena, Illinois, editor stated that out of the total sales in the entire country in 1836, "eight millions of acres of public lands have this year passed into the hands of a few wealthy speculators, who will hold them up at an extravagant value. These lands, therefore, will remain unoccupied for many years, or occupied only by a dependent tenantry. The owner and cultivator of a single farm confers greater benefits upon the community than the monopolist of thousands of acres, permitted to lie waste and uncultivated." The same editor declared it was generally conceded that a number of members of Congress had joined with others in a company to speculate in public lands and had purchased millions of acres. The factual content of these statements may have been open to question, but the attitude expressed was typical of that of many western editors. A Dubuque, Iowa, editor pointed out that speculation was a "species of gambling" demoralizing to those who indulged in it. "Happy," he said, "is the man who escapes unscathed the enticing vortex." In any discussion of land speculation, however, it must be remembered that many of those who engaged in it lost heavily.

Cession, Graduation, and Distribution

During these years a large number of proposals in regard to land policy were being discussed persistently and eloquently both in and out of Congress. As will be seen later, the policy of making land grants in aid of internal improvements was firmly established during this period. Cession of unsold lands to the States in which they lay was ardently approved by westerners, and as vigorously opposed by the East. This idea was so at variance with the fundamental conception of a public domain belonging to the whole nation that it has never been adopted in full. Donation of land to actual settlers was, as has already been noted, warmly espoused on the frontier, and at this time had the general approval of the South. The industrial East, however, was violently hostile to a procedure that would greatly reduce the federal revenue received from land sales, and enhance the attractiveness of the West that was already depriving the eastern States of any excess population and thereby forcing a relatively high wage scale. Free land was not to be achieved for many years, after long-continued agitation.

Graduation was the name given to another proposal which failed of adoption during this period, but was put into operation later. In each of the land districts there was land that did not secure purchasers either at the auction sales or by private sale afterward. Sometimes this land was inferior in quality to that which was readily sold; sometimes its location away from avenues of transportation made it less desirable. Ever since the land system was established there had been supporters for a plan that would result in a progressive reduction of the price of such land according to the length of time it remained on the market. The suggestion was logical and during the thirties it was strongly advocated by such westerners as Thomas Hart Benton, who saw in it the next best thing to free land. But again the revenue argument and eastern opposition stood in the way of success. It was not until 1854 that a graduation law was passed.

The arguments in favor of using the public lands as a source of revenue were greatly weakened during the thirties by the fact that each year the income of the government exceeded the expenditures. In 1834 the national debt was entirely wiped out, and still the surplus continued to grow. Out of this situation there developed a formidable movement to distribute among all the States that portion of the surplus that was due to the sale of public lands. The sectional support of this measure was just the reverse of that given to the program already discussed. The eastern States were naturally heartily in favor of the distribution plan; while westerners were generally opposed to it, because it would give added strength to the sentiment against free land. Henry Clay was the most prominent sponsor of the distribution idea, which accorded nicely with his ambition to achieve a successful political combination of interest between the industrial East and the agricultural West.

In 1833 a distribution law passed Congress, giving one-eighth of the net receipts from the land sales to the States in which the land lay, and distributing the remainder among all the States on the basis of their representation in Congress. President Jackson vetoed the bill, on the grounds that it violated the original agreement in regard to the public domain and that it would weaken the position and dignity of the States by making them dependent on subventions from the federal government. He had another veto message all drafted in 1836, when the passage of another distribution bill seemed imminent, but was not obliged to use it. With curious inconsistency, he failed to disapprove another law passed the same year, directing that the greater part of the surplus in the treasury should be "deposited" with the States in four installments. The term "deposit" was pure camouflage, for there was no intention that the money should ever be returned by the States. Only three deposits were actually made. The Panic of 1837 prevented the payment of the fourth installment, and the law was repealed.

PREEMPTION LEGISLATION

Despite the fact that a surplus ceased to embarrass the federal government, the movement for a distribution law was too effective as political bait to be abandoned. In 1841 the advocates of this project won an empty victory by linking it in one bill with a favorite objective of westerners—namely, the right of preemption.

The right of preemption meant the right of the settler who had squatted without authority on Indian land or unsurveyed land to purchase that land after the survey at the minimum price in advance of the auction sale. Obviously such a right was directly contrary to the fundamental principles of public land policy. Nevertheless, the justice of such a privilege was firmly entrenched in frontier morality, and from the first session of Congress under the Constitution it was supported on the floor of the national legislature. In that session Thomas Scott from western Pennsylvania declared that "The emigrants who reach the Western country will not stop until they find a place where they can securely seat themselves . . . they must have a well grounded hope that the lands they cultivate may become their own." But Congress was not then or for many years in a mood to listen to such arguments. Instead, laws were enacted invoking forcible removable and dire penalties for intruders on the public domain before the date of legal entry. Year by year the futility of such laws became more and more evident.

There is no denying the fact that the advance guard of land-hungry pioneers paid little heed to Indian boundaries or to federal land laws. Hatred bred of brutal warfare had convinced the frontiersmen that the rights of the red men were no more entitled to respect than those of the wild beasts. The land laws were regarded as oppressive and out of accord with frontier needs. As the westward movement continued, and especially as it greatly increased in volume during the decade of the thirties, Indian treaties and government land surveys frequently lagged behind the pressure of land-seekers. In other cases many well-intentioned settlers found themselves illegally on lands which they had supposed to be within established land districts. Altogether, it is not difficult to understand how westerners could sincerely contend that the squatter who went ahead, even in technical or open violation of the law, and made improvements on his land had rendered a public service and merited a reward rather than punishment.

Time after time Congress was faced by the dilemma caused by the presence of large numbers of squatters on lands not open to entry. Nothing short of a determined campaign by the army could have dispossessed them, and such a drastic measure was wholly inexpedient. Eastern members of Congress might brand the western settlers as a brawling, lawless rabble. In the end they were obliged to listen to the petitions of these very intruders and to the memorials of western legislatures, and grant preemption rights. It was easier and far more comfortable to relieve the genuine or alleged distress of land law violators than it was to enforce the provisions of the law. Before 1841 sixteen special or temporary acts were passed giving preemption rights to squatters in particular regions or for limited periods.

When this right was denied or postponed the settlers frequently took matters into their own hands and provided their own means of protection. There was good ground for the warning issued by an Iowa editor in 1838. "Refuse to our hardy settlers the privileges heretofore granted and you create a necessity for combinations among them. They will combine to protect their fields and their homes." This is exactly what they did, by organizing claim clubs or claim associations. As has been stated, settlers who squatted on land, even though illegally, built cabins and put in crops, felt that they were entitled to the first right to the land and to protection against speculators or later purchasers whom they regarded as claim-jumpers. Accordingly when preemption rights were not granted they banded themselves together for mutual protection against outsiders when the land should be put up for sale. The spirit of these organizations is illustrated in the resolutions of a Wisconsin land club. They declared that "in case any person or persons shall purchase lands in this vicinity at the time occupied by claimants; that they be disregarded as neighbors, and that no dealings of any kind be had with them. That we will neither lend to them nor borrow from them, nor visit them, nor act with them in any capacity whatsoever, nor upon any occasion." Further, they resolved, significantly that if any person should undertake to deprive any claimant of his rights, "we will not fail to rebuke his conduct with such severity as has been common in the settlement of this western country."

Although found in various western States the claim club reached its greatest perfection in the Territory of Iowa, where, according to Benjamin F. Shambaugh, "over one hundred of these extra-legal organizations existed." Many of these clubs adopted rather elaborate constitutions, by-laws, and resolutions, which prescribed the basis of membership, the officers and their duties, the amount of land which could be claimed, the method of keeping records, the action to be taken against claim-jumpers, and various other details. Each member marked off his claim as best he could with reference to natural features such as streams, trees, and large boulders; and these claims were recorded in the secretary's book. When the auction sale opened the club attended in a body, often with weapons freely displayed. As the various pieces of land were put up for sale the secretary bid for them at the minimum price of $1.25 an acre in the names of the respective claimants. Outsiders who had the temerity to bid higher were usually politely advised to desist. If this warning failed to discourage them more forceful means were frequently employed. In the main, the claim clubs served the same purpose for the settlers as a preemption law. They even went further and protected claimants who, for one reason or other, were unable to purchase their land during the progress of the auction sales.

In view of the effective operation of these organizations and after ample precedents set by a series of special acts, it is not surprising that a general preemption law was passed in 1841. Even then, however, it would doubtless have failed if it had not been linked with the distribution idea in one bill. In this form, after vigorous debate, it attracted both eastern and western voters, was passed, and received President Tyler's signature. The preemption provisions of the law gave the permanent right of preemption to heads of families, to men over twenty-one years of age, and to widows, providing they were citizens of the United States or had declared their intention of becoming citizens. Another limitation excluded all who were owners of more than 320 acres of land in addition to their preemption claim. All who met the provisions of the law could settle on

160 acres of land and later purchase it at the minimum price of $1.25 an acre, without submitting to competitive bidding at the auction sales. There were numerous other clauses dealing with the amount of improvement required and the method of establishing a claim.

An Iowa editor was entirely correct when he said that the Preemption Law of 1841 "legalizes a course which, although universally in vogue, was in fact unlawful," and that the bill had passed "under the influence of the argument that it is better to legalize what is incurable and inevitable, than to keep on the statute book a provision which is a dead letter." The law was also characterized contemporaneously as merely "declaratory of the custom of the common law of the settlers." On the whole it is perhaps fair to say that at the time of its adoption the law was the most practicable solution of a difficult problem. In the succeeding years numerous minor changes were made. Fifty years after its passage the defects of the law in actual operation were so apparent that it was repealed.

The distribution features of the Preemption-Distribution Law were not destined to be actually effective. The law provided that ten per cent of the net proceeds of the sale of public lands should be given to the States in which the land was sold and the balance distributed among all the States and Territories in proportion to their population. Southern Senators, however, succeeded in inserting an amendment in the bill stipulating that distribution should cease whenever customs duties in excess of twenty per cent were imposed. By 1843 the condition of the federal treasury was such that a tariff bill was passed with rates higher than twenty per cent. The distribution of funds was therefore suspended, and although nominally not repealed, the distribution features of the law were virtually inoperative. Thus the law of 1841 is generally known simply as the Preemption Law.

The Movement for a Homestead Law

The two decades following the passage of the Preemption Law witnessed the enactment of a number of laws on the subject of the public lands, but until 1862 no important change was made in underlying policy. In 1850 Stephen A. Douglas secured a liberal land grant for the Illinois Central Railroad which served as a precedent for later subsidies of a similar character and on a large scale. A law of 1854 put into operation the long-advocated plan of graduating the price of land according to the time it had remained on the market. The reduced prices ranged from one dollar per acre for land that remained unsold for ten years down to twelve and a half cents an acre for land still on the market after thirty years or more. Since there was no limit on the amount of such land one person could buy, it has been asserted, and probably with good reason, that non-resident speculators availed themselves generously of the provisions of this law. Nevertheless, it did result in the disposition of much land that otherwise would have been long in finding purchasers. Another law which unfortunately opened the door to speculation and fraudulent practices was one framed in 1850 and later amended, ceding to the States swamp and overflowed land with the intention that they would use the proceeds in reclamation work. As it turned out, an amount of land was selected and sworn to be swampy and overflowed that was many times the amount contemplated by the law.

All this time the West had by no means forgotten its ultimate objective—free land. The decade of the forties passed without any appreciable progress toward this goal, but during the fifties the section that was gaining political and economic power by leaps and bounds was increasingly able to make its voice heard and its wishes respected, especially among the politicians. In 1848 the Free Soil party declared in favor of free lands to actual settlers "in consideration of the expenses they incur in making settlements in the wilderness . . . and of the public benefits resulting therefrom." Four years later they renewed this support, but on different grounds. Now they asserted that "all men have a natural right to a portion of the soil; and that, as the use of the soil is indispensable to life, the right of all men to the soil is as sacred as their right to life itself." Therefore, they contended, "the public lands of the United States belong to the people, and should not be sold to individuals nor granted to corporations, but should be held as a sacred trust for the benefit of the people, and should be granted in limited quantities, free of cost, to landless settlers." From first to last these two arguments—reward for public service in developing the country, and natural right—were the chief lines of justification employed by advocates of the homestead or free land program.

Before achieving final success the homestead plan, as it was now called, was forced to run the gauntlet of all the interests, motives, and prejudices that were opposed to a measure that would inevitably hasten western development. Advocates of the maintenance of the time-honored revenue policy were naturally hostile. Easterners saw in free land only a further inducement to the draining of their labor supply and a corresponding increase in the political power of the West. As the fifties progressed the South, the old and the new States alike, became convinced that slavery could not spread further westward and that accordingly the chief beneficiaries of homestead legislation would be farmers bent on establishing free commonwealths. Adherents of the Know-Nothing or Native American movement were disinclined to countenance the granting of valuable privileges to alien immigrants. Moreover, it was charged that a homestead law would make people thriftless.

A homestead bill passed the House of Representatives in 1852, but failed in the Senate. From this time until 1860 the subject was constantly before Congress, but not until the latter year did a bill command enough votes to pass both houses. Even then a price of twenty-five cents an acre was retained. President Buchanan promptly vetoed the bill, basing his action on the principal arguments that had long been advanced by opponents of the measure. The advocates of the bill in Congress were not able to override the veto.

The very sectional conflict, however, which had raised the most formidable obstacle to homestead legislation, soon led to a situation which left the road to success entirely open. The new Republican party in 1860 achieved a successful combination of interests between the manufacturing East and the farming West by espousing both a protective tariff and free land. In their platform of that year the Republicans announced that "we protest against any sale or alienation to others of the Public Lands held by actual settlers, and against any view of the Free Homestead policy which regards the settlers as paupers or suppliants for public bounty; and we demand the passage by Congress of the complete and satisfactory Homestead measure." The victory of the Republicans in November, 1860, was followed by the secession of the southern States, leaving the triumphant party free to carry out its program. On May 20, 1862, Abraham Lincoln attached his signature to the Homestead Law and free land—the goal sought by generations of westerners since the inception of the public land policy—was attained.

The Homestead Law gave to "any person who is the head of a family, or who has arrived at the age of twenty-one years, and is a citizen of the United States, or who shall have filed his declaration of intention to become such," the privilege of acquiring 160 acres of land free of any charge except a small filing fee. The only requirement was that he must live on the land for five years and meet certain conditions in regard to cultivation. The Preemption Law was retained. Provision was likewise made for the commutation of homestead entries at any time by the payment of the regular price for the land. With numerous modifications, the basic features of the law are still in force to-day.

SUMMARY OF PUBLIC LAND POLICY

The Land Ordinance of 1785; the Harrison Law of 1800, experimenting with the credit system; the Land Law of 1820, recognizing the failure of the credit plan and reducing both the price of land and the minimum area that could be purchased; the general Preemption Law of 1841; and the Homestead Law of 1862—these are the high points in the development of our public land policy. A later chapter will describe the changes and additions that were made as new problems arose when settlements spread into an environment of semi-arid plains, mountains, and coniferous forests.

We have seen how the public land question became entangled in political maneuverings and how its solution was affected by every form of personal and sectional interest and prejudice. We have seen, also, what a prominent place speculation, greed, fraud, and illegal actions have in the history of the occupation of the public lands. It must be remembered, however, that these phases of the story are those which are spectacular, the aspects which were most played up in the public prints and in Congressional debates. No records were left by the millions of law-abiding families, both native Americans and immigrants from foreign shores, for whom the public lands were synonymous with opportunity. We can obtain only occasional glimpses of the exaltation of spirit which came to hosts of individuals when they plowed the first furrow on land that was their own. Not often are we permitted to know the plans and hopes and sacrifices that centered in innumerable farms carved out of what was once wild government land. While not overlooking the mistakes or condoning the abuses, it is still possible to regard the public land policy of the United States down to the Civil War as substantially beneficent.

CHAPTER XIX

TRANSPORTATION—INLAND WATERWAYS

LAND was the first interest of the settlers as they moved west. After they had located themselves, built their cabins and begun to raise a surplus of agricultural produce their greatest need was for avenues and facilities of transportation to markets. Farmers and residents of the rapidly growing western towns were also soon clamoring for means of reducing the enormous freight costs on manufactured goods. Extension of mail service and the establishment of public conveyances for passengers were other demands which quickly followed. Private enterprise, state and local governments, and the federal government were all enlisted in the task of meeting the vital need for means of transportation and communication in the West. Out of these demands grew the great public question of internal improvements which became entangled in constitutional interpretations, caused embarrassment to Presidents, occasioned long debates in Congress, and became a leading issue between political parties. More than all other factors contributing to the improvement of transportation was the revolution caused by the application of steam power to the propulsion of water craft and land vehicles.

FLATBOATS AND KEELBOATS

Rivers were the first highways of inland commerce and, with a few exceptions, they were accepted and used in their natural state. The era of river improvement, with its "pork barrel" politics, did not dawn until after the frontier stage had passed. The importance of the Mississippi River system to all the settlers on its waters was clearly shown during the period of the Spanish intrigues from 1783 to 1795 and just preceding the purchase of Louisiana. New Orleans had no important rival for the trade of the Mississippi Valley until the building of the Erie Canal and the coming of the railroads.

The earliest and simplest craft for the transportation of agricultural products, aside from canoes, pirogues and row-boats, was the "Kentucky flat" or "broadhorn" or "ark," as it was variously called. This was a flat-bottomed craft, oblong in shape, ordinarily about fifteen feet wide and fifty feet long, although the size varied. There were high sides and at least a part of the boat was covered. Obviously such a craft was designed almost entirely for downstream use. Little or no attempt was made to propel it, the main activities of the boat-men being confined to keeping it in the current and avoiding snags and obstructions by means of long oars. A crew of three or four men was sufficient to handle the boat, but their labors were prodigious when, as often happened, they ran upon a sandbar. Great quantities of farm produce and large numbers of cattle and hogs were floated down the Ohio and Mississippi in these flatboats, but there was no thought of a return trip. At New Orleans, before the days of the steamboat, the boat-men abandoned their craft and returned either overland by the Natchez Trace or by ocean to the Atlantic Coast and then across the mountains.

A great improvement as compared with the flatboat was accomplished by the introduction of the keelboat. As its name indicates, this boat was not flat-bottomed, but was built upon a keel. It was long and narrow, pointed at both ends, and was well roofed for the protection of cargo or passengers. It pos-sessed the special advantage that by the expenditure of great labor it could be propelled upstream. Thus this type of boat made it possible to supply the settlements along the Mississippi and Ohio with manufactured goods purchased in New Orleans. The larger keelboats, sometimes called barges, were confined to the Mississippi and its principal tributaries. Smaller craft could be used on the smaller streams, such as the Alleghany and Monongahela, the Tennessee and Cumberland and the rivers flowing into the Gulf. They were even carried across portages from one stream to another. For instance, in 1821 an Alabama newspaper reported the arrival at Montgomery of a loaded keelboat which hailed from eastern Tennessee, whence it had come one thousand miles by way of the Tennessee River and its tributaries, a land carriage of ten miles, and then down the Coosa and the Alabama. Going downstream the keelboat drifted with the current or its speed was accelerated by the use of oars and poles. Various means of propulsion were employed on the upstream trip: square sails, oars, poles, and the cordelle. It was seldom that a favorable wind made it worth while to put up the sail. Oars were used in deep water and wide channels. Poling was the method most practiced. On each side of the boat was a running-board along which the members of the crew walked with their poles. Starting at the front of the boat they "set" the poles on the river bottom and with their shoulders against the upper end walked toward the stern until, at the command of "lift" from the steersmen, they raised the poles and hastened again to the front to repeat the process. The cordelle was a rope or cable by which, when shore conditions permitted, the men towed the boat. At other times the cordelle was used in "warping," which consisted of fastening one end of the rope to a tree some distance along the bank and pulling the boat up to that point and repeating the operation as long as trees were available. "Bushwhacking," or pulling on the bushes and overhanging trees along the bank, was another means of locomotion frequently employed.

Obviously the labor of propelling a loaded keelboat against the swift current of the Mississippi or lower Ohio was prodigious. Fifteen miles a day was considered good progress. Usually it took three months to make the trip from New Orleans to the Falls of the Ohio. The men who performed this labor were a rough lot and helped to give travelers their impression of the wild character of western people. When at work these boatmen were prompt, cheerful, and uncomplaining. Their periods of leisure were occupied with carousing, fighting, and boasting. They liked to refer to themselves as "half horse, half alligator." It was the favorite boast of the celebrated Mike Fink that "I can out run, out hop, out jump, throw down, drag out, and lick any man in the country. I'm a Salt River roarer, I love the wimmen, and I'm chock full of fight."

Some idea of the volume of traffic by flatboat, keelboat and barge is indicated by the fact that in 1807 a total of more than 1800 of these craft arrived in New Orleans, although only eleven set out upstream. Even after the coming of the steamboats these more primitive vessels were long used for downstream transportation. In 1818 a passenger on an up-river steamboat counted 643 flatboats descending the Mississippi and Ohio. Timothy Flint, writing in 1826, told of walking along the river bank at New Madrid, Missouri, and seeing these boats arriving in fleets. He was especially impressed, he wrote, by "the immense distances which they have already come, and those which they have still to go. . . . You can name no point from the numerous rivers of the Ohio and the Mississippi, from which some of these boats have not come. In one place there are boats loaded with planks, from the pine forests of the southwest of New York. . . . From Kentucky, pork, flour, whiskey, hemp, tobacco, bagging, and bale-rope. From Tennessee there are the same articles, together with great quantities of cotton. From Missouri and Illinois, cattle and horses . . . together with peltry and lead from Missouri. . . . They have come from regions thousands of miles apart."

Ship-Building on the Upper Ohio

Henry Clay once related an anecdote concerning a port official at Leghorn, Italy, who at first refused to accept the papers presented by the captain of a sailing vessel indicating that he had cleared from Pittsburgh. The official insisted that there was no such port. Whereupon the ship captain produced a map of the United States, "pointed out the mouth of the Mississippi, led him a thousand miles up to the mouth of the Ohio, and thence another thousand up to Pittsburg. . . . The astonished officer, before he had seen the map, would as readily have believed that this vessel had been navigated from the moon."

The background of this incident was furnished by the enterprise of Tarascon, Berthoud and Company, and others, beginning in 1792, in building sailing vessels on the upper Ohio and loading them with produce for export to ports on the Atlantic coast, in the West Indies, and in Europe. Two such ships, one of 120 tons and the other of 250 tons, were built in 1792, and sent down the river the following year, with St. Thomas and Philadelphia as their destinations. Presumably the ships were sold, for of course they did not return up the rivers. The experiment was apparently successful, for by 1800 there were ship-yards at Pittsburgh, Wheeling, Marietta, Louisville, and possibly at other points on the upper Ohio. F. A. Michaux reported that when he was in Marietta in 1802 "they were building three brigs, one of which was of two hundred and twenty tons burthen."

T. M. Harris who visited Marietta the following year witnessed the departure or passage of several vessels. "The second week after our arrival, in consequence of three or four rainy days, the water of the Ohio rose fifteen feet, and gave opportunity for several vessels, which were waiting for a flood, to set sail. Accordingly on May 4th the schooner 'Dorcas and Sally,' of 70 tons, built at Wheeling and rigged at Marietta, dropped down the river. The following day there passed down the schooner 'Amity,' of 103 tons, from Pittsburg, and the ship 'Pittsburg,' of 275 tons burden, from the same place, laden with seventeen hundred barrels of flour, with the rest of the cargo in flat-bottomed boats. In the evening the brig 'Mary Avery,' of 130 tons, built at Marietta, set sail."

There are no records to indicate how many ocean-going vessels were turned out by the Ohio River ship-yards in succeeding years. It is certain that the business disappeared with the introduction of steamboats. The industry gives a colorful touch to river transportation probably never duplicated elsewhere in the world at an equal distance from the ocean. It is not difficult to imagine that the passage of these ships down the stream gave the dwellers along the Ohio a peculiar satisfaction because of the direct contact thus afforded with the markets of the world.

STEAMBOATING ON THE OHIO AND THE MISSISSIPPI

A new and brighter era for transportation on western waterways, and especially for up-river traffic, dawned when Nicholas J. Roosevelt launched his steamboat "New Orleans" at

Pittsburgh in the autumn of 1811. "There is now on foot a
new mode of navigating our western waters, particularly the
Ohio and Mississippi rivers," exultingly wrote Zadock Cramer
in his little publication *The Navigator,* earlier that same year.
"This is with boats propelled by the power of steam. . . . A
Mr. Rosewalt, a gentleman of enterprise, and who is acting it
is said in conjunction with Messrs. Fulton and Livingston of
New York, has a boat of this kind now on the stocks at Pittsburgh, of 138 feet keel, calculated for 300 or 400 tons burden
[100 tons was nearer the truth]. . . . It will be a novel sight,
and as pleasing as novel to see a huge boat working her way
up the windings of the Ohio, without the appearance of sail,
oar, pole, or any manual labour about her—moving within
the secrets of her own wonderful mechanism, and propelled by
power undiscoverable!— This plan if it succeeds must open
to view flattering prospects to an immense country, an interior
of not less than two thousand miles."

The *New Orleans* arrived at Louisville on October 28th,
after a voyage of sixty-four hours from Pittsburgh. "Frequent experiments of her performance," it was reported, "have
been made against the current, since her arrival, in the presence
of a number of respectable gentlemen, who have ascertained
with certainty she runs thirteen miles in two hours and one
half."

If the people of Louisville and vicinity had visions of the
immediate establishment of steamboat service to and from New
Orleans they were destined to disappointment. The *New Orleans* served as a Natchez packet for two years until it struck
a snag and sank. The vicissitudes of early steamboating are
illustrated in the brief history of the *Vesuvius,* which was built
on the upper Ohio and descended to New Orleans in the spring
of 1814. During the summer of the same year she attempted
the ascent of the river, reached a point about seven miles up
the Mississippi and was grounded on a sandbar, where she remained until floated by high water early in the winter. Thereafter for a year she made trips between New Orleans and
Natchez. In 1816 she burned to the water's edge. Later her
hull was salvaged and refitted and she engaged in the Louisville service until condemned in 1819.

Apparently the first steamboat to reach Louisville from New Orleans was the *Enterprise,* which made the trip in 1815 in twenty-five days. "How do the rivers and canals of the old world dwindle to insignificance compared with this," was Hezekiah Niles' comment in connection with the exploit, "and what a prospect of commerce is held out to the immense regions of the west, by the use of these boats!" The Ohio must have been sufficiently high that summer to permit the steamboat to ascend the rapids at Louisville. Late in July a newspaper published at Brownsville on the Monongahela in Pennsylvania announced the arrival of "the steamboat Enterprise, *Shrieve,* of Bridgeport, from New Orleans, in ballast, having discharged her cargo at Pittsburg. . . . She made the voyage from New Orleans to this port in 54 days, 20 days of which were employed in loading and unloading freight at different towns on the Mississippi and Ohio, so that she was only 34 days in active service, in making her voyage, which our readers will remember must be performed against powerful currents, and is upwards of 2200 miles in length."

The number of steamboats on the Ohio and Mississippi now increased steadily. By 1817 there were twenty; two years later the number had nearly doubled; by 1825 there were 125; and thereafter the number increased until there were more than a thousand by 1860. Improvements in the design and machinery of the boats made greater speed possible. For instance, in 1822 it was reported that the steamboat *Paragon* made the round trip from New Orleans to Louisville in twenty-five days. Fares decreased with competition and the growth of traffic. In 1818 it cost $30.00 to travel first class by steamboat from New Orleans to Natchez, $90.00 from New Orleans to New Madrid, and $125.00 from New Orleans to the Falls of the Ohio. Fares downstream from the Falls were lower; $22.50 to New Madrid, $60.00 to Natchez, and $75.00 to New Orleans. By 1835 fares were much lower. "The number of passengers which these boats carry is very considerable," wrote Michael Chevalier, "they are almost always crowded, although there are some which have two hundred beds. . . . The rate of fare is low; you go from Pittsburg to New Orleans for 50 dollars, all found, and from Louisville to New Orleans for 25

dollars." Flatboat men and others who were satisfied with
scanty accommodations could return from New Orleans to
Louisville as deck passenger for a fare of five or six dollars.

In the course of years the river steamboats assumed the
appearance with which succeeding generations were long familiar. Usually there were two main decks and a "hurricane"
deck. The first deck contained the boilers, the engine, and the
wood used for fuel. On the second deck were the cabins, the
dining room, a bar and social hall for men, and a ladies' parlor.
The pilot house and the officers quarters were on the "hurricane" deck. Freight was stored in the hold and frequently on
portions of the decks.

Many of these boats were fitted out in fine style. "A
stranger to this mode of travelling," wrote Timothy Flint,
"would find it difficult to describe his impressions upon first
descending the Mississippi in one of the better steam-boats.
He contemplates the prodigious establishment, with all its
fitting of deck common, and ladies' cabin apartments. Over
head, about him and below him, all is life and movement. He
sees its splendid cabin, richly carpeted, its finishings of mahog-
any, its mirrors and fine furniture, its bar-room and sliding-
tables, to which eighty passengers can sit down with comfort.
The fare is sumptuous, and every thing in a style of splendour,
order, quiet, and regularity, far exceeding that of taverns in
general." Not all travelers were so favorably impressed. Michael Chevalier, writing in 1835, referred to the steamboats as
"floating barracks." "Excellent as these boats are," he said,
"great as is the service they render America, when the first
feeling of curiosity is once satisfied, a long confinement in one
of them has little that is attractive for a person of a cultivated
mind and refined manners."

It is of course true that all sorts of people were thrown into
close contact on a long steamboat trip. Gamblers infested
many of the boats and reaped such rich harvests from the un-
wary that passengers were warned, both by notices on the boats
and in the newspapers, to be on their guard against these suave,
quiet-mannered sharpers. Liquor of course was abundant and
intoxicated passengers troublesome. But the travelers as a
whole were just a cross-section of the population of the West,

with an admixture of easterners and foreigners apt to look askance at the numerous departures from the manners and practices of "polite" society.

Accidents to steamboats causing loss of life and property were of frequent occurrence. Part of these were due to snags or "sawyers" and floating logs in the river which crushed holes in the wooden hulls of the boats. For instance, in the spring of 1823 the *Tennessee,* with sixteen cabin passengers and 180 deck passengers, struck a log during the night in the Mississippi above Natchez and went down in five minutes. Thirty passengers lost their lives. The bursting of boilers was the cause of other disasters. "A steam boat called the Constitution (late the Oliver Evans) burst her boiler nearly opposite St. Francisville, on the Mississippi, by which every person in the cabin, 11 in number, at breakfast, were scalded to death." This newspaper items is typical of many during the succeeding years, and often the loss was much greater. Defective materials and workmanship in the boilers was sometimes responsible. It was also charged that new boats were frequently equipped with worn-out boilers taken from condemned or wrecked vessels in order to save expense.

Fires were other cause of disasters. In 1832 the *Brandywine* was burned near Memphis and all the 110 persons on board lost their lives. The following year an Arkansas newspaper reported six river accidents, three of which were the result of fires, two of snags, and one of a bursted boiler. In four cases there was loss of life, varying from one to sixty or seventy. "The Americans show a singular indifference in regard to fires," was Chevalier's comment, "they smoke without the least concern in the midst of the half open cotton-bales, with which a boat is loaded; they ship gunpowder with no more precaution than if it were so much maize or salt pork, and leave objects packed up in straw right in the torrent of sparks that issue from the chimneys." In fact he gained the impression that "the essential point is not to save some individuals or even some hundreds; but, in respect to steamers, that they should be numerous; staunch or not, well commanded or not, it matters little, if they move at a rapid rate, and are navigated at little expense."

There is no doubt that efforts to attain excessive speed were the frequent cause of fires and exploding boilers. Competition with boats of rival lines and the ambition to make records impelled the captains not only to fill the fire-boxes to the limit with wood, but to add turpentine or pitch or oil; and to cover the safety-valve in order to increase the steam pressure. Especially were all these means of increasing the speed employed during the numerous steamboat races which became a spectacular feature of the old days on the rivers. Racing so often ended in catastrophe that efforts were made to discourage it. In 1836 a Kentucky editor remarked that the practice of racing was sometimes condoned on the ground that it gave pleasure to the passengers. "That is natural," he said, "There is more than one mode of *intoxication*—and if a steamboat captain were to get his company mad with wine, and then put daggers in their hands to use upon each other, it would be just as good an excuse for him, that they were pleased with the debauch, whatever murders might flow from it, as it is for scalding them to death with hot steam, that they are childishly and irrationally desirous that he should outrun a competitor by a mile or two. Banters are made for bets of $20,000 dollars. Such bets should be punished by high fines."

Lloyd's Steamboat Directory for 1856 contained descriptions of eighty-seven "major disasters" to steamboats on western rivers up to that time, due to explosions, fire, snags, and collisions. In numerous instances the names of those losing their lives totalled more than one hundred. Then there followed accounts of 220 "minor disasters," in a majority of which there was loss of life, running in some cases as high as forty or fifty.

During the thirties the War Department superintended the work of improving the navigability of the Ohio and Mississippi by removing snags, sawyers, and other obstructions. By 1839 nearly ten thousand such hazards had been removed. Efforts were also made by riprapping to confine the stream to narrower channels at certain points to improve navigation in periods of low water. Appropriations for such enterprises ceased in 1844 and the work was not resumed until after the Civil War.

Previously the most important obstacle to steamboat traffic

on the Ohio had been overcome.   The business of portaging cargoes around the Falls of the Ohio had long given employment to considerable numbers of men at Louisville.   The coming of the steamboats, however, soon inspired a determined movement looking toward the building of a canal around the rapids.   In 1825 the Louisville and Portland Canal Company was organized.   The federal government aided the enterprise by taking more than half of the four thousand shares of stock. The canal, two and one-half miles in length, was completed late in 1830.   The following year steamboats made more than four hundred passages through the canal, to say nothing of keelboats and flatboats, and the number increased rapidly in succeeding years in spite of the high toll rates which were characterized as highway robbery.

Steamboating on Other Western Rivers

Steamboating was early extended to all the navigable tributaries of the Mississippi and the Ohio.   In 1818 the first steamboat reached Kaskaskia on the Mississippi.   In May, 1823, the *Virginia* reached Fort Snelling far to the northward. J. C. Beltrami, an Italian refugee who was a passenger on this boat, noted the astonishment of the Indians.   "I know not," he wrote, "what impression the first sight of the Phoenician vessels might make on the inhabitants of the coast of Greece, or the Triremi of the Romans on the natives of Iberia, Gaul, or Britain; but I am sure it could not be stronger than that I saw on the countenances of these savages at the arrival of our steam-boat."

Within a few years the Missouri, the Arkansas, and the Red rivers were teeming with steamboats.   The expansion of the fur trade and the transportation of supplies for distant military posts furnished the initial stimulus for the rapid extension of steamboating on the first named stream.   Supplying frontier forts also afforded business for these craft on the Arkansas and Red, which rivers witnessed the carriage by steamboat of thousands of Choctaw and Creek Indians to their new homes west of the Mississippi.   The spread of settlements provided increasing traffic with each passing year.   A peculiar obstruction to the navigation of the Red River was what was known as the Great Raft in northern Louisiana. This consisted of great masses of tangled logs, snags and tree-trunks that extended for a distance of more than 160 miles and at certain points bridged the river completely. Beginning in 1833 the federal government, through the War Department, undertook the removal of this raft. Captain Henry M. Shreve was placed in charge of the work, and with a large force of men and several snag-boats he began loosening the logs and floating them downstream. It was five years before the work was entirely completed. Even after that time it required constant activity to keep the raft from re-forming.

THE ERIE CANAL

The Mississippi River system constituted a network of navigable inland waterways admirably suited to the transportation requirements of the West during the early periods of settlement, and as long as New Orleans served the needs of all concerned as an outlet for produce and a source of supplies of merchandise. But with the growth of towns and the increasing taste and requirements of the people of the West for manufactured goods and luxuries there arose a demand for commercial connection with Atlantic coast cities. Similarly the merchants and manufacturers of New York, Philadelphia, Baltimore, and Charleston viewed with covetous eyes the expanding markets beyond the mountains and sought for means to break the virtual monopoly enjoyed by New Orleans. The building of the Cumberland Road, as will be seen in the next chapter, promised at first to solve the problem for Philadelphia and Baltimore, and it was an achievement of great significance in facilitating travel and communication between the coast and the trans-mountain region. Even on an improved roadway, however, freighting by wagon over a mountain range was laborious and exceedingly expensive. Thus it was that easterners and westerners alike centered their hopes on canals connecting eastward-flowing rivers with the waterways of the west.

Canal-building was not an innovation in America when the first projects to carry these hopes into the realm of reality were inaugurated. Several canals had been put into successful operation or begun in New Hampshire, Massachusetts, Pennsylvania, Virginia, and South Carolina between 1785 and 1812. The disappointing results achieved by the Potomac Company, in which George Washington was the prime mover, had demonstrated the futility of attempting the canalization of rivers. "Locks in Rivers are subject to many more Accidents than those in still water canals," wrote Benjamin Franklin. "Rivers are ungovernable things especially in Hilly Countries. Canals are quiet and very manageable." It had been demonstrated that it was advantageous to construct artificial waterways along the courses of rivers from which the necessary supply of water could be secured.

As early as 1788 Elkanah Watson and others in New York were preaching the desirability and practicability of making a connection between the Hudson River and Lake Ontario by the use of the Mohawk River and the streams flowing into the lake. In 1792 the Western Inland Lock Navigation Company was chartered by the New York legislature. Four years later this company had completed a canal nearly a mile long and containing five locks, around the Little Falls in the Mohawk, which had hitherto proved an effective obstacle to navigation. It was now possible for small boats to ascend the river as far as Rome, near the site of Fort Stanwix. There was enthusiastic talk of continuing the project westward, but the funds were not forthcoming. There was little to stimulate investments in an enterprise of this nature in a region still almost devoid of settlements.

Interest in the proposal did not entirely disappear and it revived after Albert Gallatin's comprehensive report on internal improvements in 1808, and especially after the authorization of the building of the Cumberland Road which would provide a trade route between Pennsylvania and Maryland and the Ohio Valley. Gouverneur Morris was continuously active in promoting the idea of a canal, but the man who was most responsible for the success of the plan was DeWitt Clinton. Lake Erie, rather than Lake Ontario, was now selected as the western terminus, and a canal extending the entire distance to the Hudson at Albany was substituted for the earlier project to use the Mohawk and other rivers. Congress refused to give financial aid and efforts to interest Ohio and Indiana were without result. The War of 1812 caused the temporary suspension of all agitation, but immediately after the close of that struggle the promoters resumed their activities. In 1817 an elaborate memorial drafted by DeWitt Clinton was presented to the New York legislature, in consequence of which an act was passed pledging the credit of the State to finance the undertaking.

The canal was to be built in three sections: from Albany to Rome, from Rome to the Seneca River, and from the Seneca River to Lake Erie. It was to be four feet in depth, forty feet in width at the surface and twenty-eight feet at the bottom. Clinton, now governor of New York, broke ground on the eastern section at Rome at a great celebration held on July 4, 1817. Soon rows of stakes stretched across the State, up hill and down, through forests and swamps, following the course of the Mohawk to Rome, then in a general westwardly direction through a region where Syracuse, Palmyra, Rochester, and Lockport soon became thriving villages, and along the Tonawanda and Niagara Rivers to Buffalo on Lake Erie. The skeptical still ridiculed the plan as visionary and impractical. But when workmen, horses, wagons, plows, scrapers, and large quantities of materials began to appear and work actually began, scoffing gave way to enthusiasm and pride in the steady progress of achievement. There were periods of despondency as during the Panic of 1819, when there seemed no more money to be spent on the canal, but the courage and determination of Governor Clinton found the necessary funds and kept the legislature and people to the task they had undertaken.

Section after section of the canal was opened and put into use as rapidly as it was completed. Then on October 26, 1825, came the day of triumph when cannon stationed along the entire length of the canal boomed the message that the work was finished. On that day the *Seneca Chief,* on which were Governor Clinton and a party of notables, led a small flotilla of boats out of Buffalo headed for Albany and New York City. At each town along the canal stops were made for processions, banquets, and other festivities. On November 4th the fleet, now greatly augmented, arrived in New York City. Well out in the harbor there was held a ceremony of wedding Lake Erie with the Atlantic, when Governor Clinton poured two kegs of lake water into the ocean. "This solemnity, at this place, on the first arrival of vessels from Lake Erie," said Clinton, "is intended to indicate and commemorate the navigable communication, which has been accomplished between our Mediterranean Seas and the Atlantic Ocean, in about eight years, . . . by the wisdom, public spirit, and energy of the people of the state of New York; and may the God of the Heavens and the Earth smile most propitiously on this work, and render it subservient to the best interests of the human race."

As the work on the Erie Canal progressed newspapers throughout the nation, and especially in New York and in the West, were filled with glowing predictions of the benefits to flow from the achievement. The reality actually exceeded the predictions. In the course of a few years New York City outdistanced all her rivals as a commercial and shipping center. Western New York, hitherto largely an unbroken forest, rapidly filled with prosperous farms, and Rochester and Buffalo became thriving cities. Thousands of settlers now poured into Michigan Territory which had previously been far removed from the stream of the westward movement. Northern Ohio, Indiana, and Illinois received large accessions of emigrants from New York and New England who laid out farms, built towns and cities, and changed the political and social complexion of these States in which people from south of Mason and Dixon's line had predominated. The great inland lakes now began to teem with an ever-increasing volume of traffic, borne in sailing vessels and steamers, after the *Walk-in-the-Water* made its first voyage on Lake Erie in 1817. It is not too much to say that no other single man-made highway of transportation in the United States ever produced such far-reaching results as did "Clinton's Ditch."

The Era of Canal-Building

As might be expected the building and the success of the Erie Canal spurred other eastern States to emulation in the hope of preventing New York from getting the lion's share of the western trade. Pennsylvania, disappointed in the effects of the

Cumberland Road, in 1826 began the building of the famous
Pennsylvania System—a transportation project that was
unique and picturesque, but remunerative chiefly to the contractors and workmen who constructed it. This consisted of a
combination of canals, tramways, and a series of inclined
planes over the mountains, with a tunnel at the summit. The
tramway ran from Philadelphia to Columbia on the Susquehanna. Here the horse-cars were at first unloaded onto canal
boats. Later cars in the form of boats were devised that could
be removed from their trucks and lowered into the canal without disturbing their cargoes. The canal extended along the
Susquehanna and the Juniata Rivers to Hollidaysburg. Here
the boats were once more placed on cars and by means of
stationary engines and cables hauled by a series of inclined
planes up the mountains nearly 1400 feet and lowered in a
similar manner down the western slope more than 1100 feet
to Johnstown on the Conemaugh River. Another canal ran
along the Conemaugh and the Alleghany to Pittsburgh. A trip
over this route was one long to be remembered, but the financial
returns were disappointing and the entire system was later
sold to the Pennsylvania Railroad Company and dismantled.

Maryland and Virginia, not to be outdone by Pennsylvania
and New York, revived the early plan of Washington's Potomac Company to connect the waters of Chesapeake Bay with
the Ohio River. The Chesapeake and Ohio Canal was the
name given to the new project, launched in 1828, which was to
extend along the Potomac to Cumberland and thence across
the mountains to the Youghiogheny River. The canal was
never completed further than Cumberland and even this point
was not reached until 1850, when more than $11,000,000
had been expended. The canal was well constructed and
serviceable, but it had the misfortune to meet bitter competition from the Baltimore and Ohio Railroad which was begun
in 1828 and built along the same route.

The canal fever now spread into the West. The completion
of the Erie Canal opened up alluring prospects to the people of
Ohio, Indiana, and Illinois if only they could establish water
connection with the Great Lakes. The numerous points at
which the headwaters of streams flowing into the lakes inter-

laced with those of rivers flowing into the Ohio suggested the feasibility of constructing canals along these routes. The middle twenties saw all three States busy with plans for artificial waterways to give them connections with the eastern markets by way of the northern lakes. Four of these canals were eventually completed, in addition to other minor undertakings.

In Ohio what was known as the Ohio Canal was begun in 1825 at a ceremony which Governor Clinton of New York honored with his presence. The year 1832 witnessed the completion of the canal from Portsmouth on the Ohio along the Scioto, Muskingum, Tuscarawas, and Cuyahoga to Cleveland on Lake Erie. DeWitt Clinton also participated in the dedicatory ceremonies of another Ohio canal in the summer of 1825. This one, known as the Miami Canal, extended along the Miami and Maumee rivers from Cincinnati to Toledo. Financial difficulties delayed the construction of this waterway and operations were suspended during the period of the Panic of 1837, so that it was not finished until 1845. In Indiana the Wabash and Erie Canal was begun in 1832, opened from Toledo to Lafayette on the Wabash in 1843, and was later extended to Evansville on the Ohio. The Illinois project was known as the Illinois and Michigan Canal and as its name indicates, connected the lake with the navigable waters of the Illinois River. It was begun in 1836 and completed in 1848, by which time interest in canal-building had largely been swallowed up in the new enthusiasm for railroads.

To finance the building of these canals the States pledged their resources, but were obliged to market the canal stocks and bonds in the East, where they found buyers to the extent of millions of dollars. The Miami, Wabash and Erie, and Illinois and Michigan canals also received federal aid in the form of land grants. Congress not only gave rights of way through the public lands for the canals, but also donated to the States alternate sections of land for five miles on either side of the canals to be used in financing construction. In support of the land grant policy it was argued that the federal government would lose nothing, since the value of the alternate sections which it retained would be greatly enhanced by the building of the canals. In adopting this practice, as we shall see, they established a precedent for the later policy of making land grants in aid of railroads.

The canals in Indiana and Illinois proved somewhat disappointing, especially since railroad-building had made artificial waterways rather old-fashioned by the time of their completion. The reckless abandon with which the people of all three States had thrown themselves into the canal projects contributed to the severity of the Panic of 1837. Nevertheless, these western canals rendered an important service in the development of the northern portions of the States through which they ran. Prosperous farming sections rapidly appeared along their routes. The growth of Cleveland and Toledo and the beginnings of Chicago date from the period of their building. These waterways also helped, along with the Cumberland Road and later the railroads, to bind the Ohio Valley to the East by ties of commerce and to loosen the connection with New Orleans and the South.

CHAPTER XX

TRANSPORTATION—FROM TRAIL TO RAIL

WATERWAYS served the transportation needs of western settlers as long as they lived along rivers and were satisfied with such commerce as could be carried on through New Orleans. As soon, however, as the settlements began to spread away from the banks of navigable streams and as soon as the need was felt for direct communication between the West and the cities of the Atlantic coast a system of roads became a vital necessity. The most conspicuous outcome of this need was the building of the Cumberland Road linking the trans-montane region with the East. But for a half-century after the launching of the national government interest in the laying out and improvement of long-distance highways was widespread. Then the building of railroads claimed public attention and roads were left largely to the uncertain care of local authorities until the day of the automobile.

EARLY WESTERN ROADS

Road improvement in America showed little progress until the last decade of the eighteenth century. Information concerning the success of Macadam and Telford in England in constructing drained highways with a surface of crushed rock suggested the use of the new process in this country. The first macadamized road in America was the Lancaster Turnpike, built by a private company and extending from Philadelphia westward a distance of about sixty-six miles to Lancaster. This road, completed in 1794, was not only such a marvel of smoothness and all-year-around usability, but the prospect of profits to be made from tolls by similar enterprises was so attractive, that a large number of turnpikes were built in eastern States during the succeeding years.

The so-called roads across the mountains were little better than trails, such as the earliest settlers had followed in making their way into Kentucky and Tennessee or into western Pennsylvania and Ohio. To be sure the Wilderness Road through Cumberland Gap and Braddock's Road and Forbes' Road to the headwaters of the Ohio were well-worn highways. But as late as 1800 even these roads were traversed with great difficulty by wheeled vehicles, and elsewhere the packtrain was the only means of transportation across the mountains. The cost of such traffic was prohibitive for all bulky commodities and extremely burdensome for even the most necessary articles. Even when wagons could be used the cost of freighting by land from Philadelphia to Pittsburgh was $125 a ton, due to tolls on the turnpikes and bad roads the rest of the distance.

West of the mountains the first roads were merely Indian trails or paths made by the successive passage of packtrains and occasional wagons. They were free from the troublesome rocks and the dangerous declivities of the mountain roads, but throughout much of the year they were virtually impassable on the account of mud. Two of these roads early became well known, because they served as important post-routes and were used on the return trip by persons who had descended the Ohio and the Mississippi on flatboats or keelboats. In 1796 Congress authorized Ebenezer Zane of Wheeling to open a road from Wheeling to Limestone, Kentucky, later named Maysville. He was granted three sections of land as compensation for his labor. Zane's Trace, which was the result, was far from being a real highway in its early years, for the road-making done by Ebenezer Zane and his assistants consisted of cutting down the small trees and opening a path that could be followed by horsemen.

Although Zane's Trace officially terminated at Limestone (Maysville), it was continued by a road at least equally good to Lexington and the interior of Kentucky. This stretch later played a noted role as the Maysville Pike in the controversy over the question of internal improvements. From Lexington there was a path to Nashville, Tennessee, where it joined another famous trail leading to Natchez on the Mississippi and known as the Natchez Trace. "Notwithstanding the fact that

it traversed for a great distance a most inhospitable region,"
says Julian P. Bretz, "the Natchez Trace was already one of
the best known routes in the old Southwest. It possesses, for
the historical student the fascination peculiar to an ancient
line of travel. As an Indian path of great antiquity it connected the Gulf and the Great Lakes and in recent times it
had been adopted by the boatmen returning overland from
Natchez and New Orleans to their homes in the Ohio Valley." [1]
The Natchez Trace became a post-route in accordance with an
act of Congress in 1800.

THE CUMBERLAND ROAD

The vital importance of roads in the West was recognized
in 1802 in the enabling act for the State of Ohio, by a provision that later bore fruit in the Cumberland Road. Five
per cent of the net proceeds of the sale of public lands within
the State were to be "applied to the laying out and making
public roads leading from the navigable waters emptying into
the Atlantic, to the Ohio, to the said state, and through the
same, such roads to be laid out under the authority of Congress,
with the consent of the several States through which the road
shall pass." Another Congressional act passed the following
year specified that three-fifths of this five per cent fund should
be devoted to roads within Ohio and the remaining two-fifths,
or two per cent, to a road connecting the Ohio with waters
flowing into the Atlantic. Similar provisions were later included in the enabling acts of Indiana, Illinois, and Missouri.

In 1805 a Congressional committee recommended the laying out of a road from Cumberland on the Potomac to some
convenient point on the Ohio between Steubenville and Wheeling. A law passed the following year authorized President
Jefferson to appoint three commissioners to select and mark
the route of the proposed road and make an estimate of the
cost of construction. The route was to be cleared of trees to
the width of four rods and in the center there was to be a raised

---

[1] Julian P. Bretz, "Early Land Communication with the Lower Mississippi
Valley," in *The Mississippi Valley Historical Review*, June, 1926, pp. 6-7. By
permission of publisher.

carriage-way of stone, earth, or gravel, with drainage ditches on either side. The President was requested to take the necessary steps to secure the consent of the States through which the road would be run.

Maryland and Virginia readily acquiesced, but Pennsylvania, largely through the influence of Albert Gallatin, made her consent conditional upon the routing of the road through Uniontown and Washington. Wheeling was finally chosen as the Ohio River terminus, partly because a connection would thereby be made with Zane's Trace, and partly because of the influence of Virginia and Kentucky—the latter represented by Henry Clay. Thus the route selected for the Cumberland Road extended from Cumberland, Maryland, to Uniontown, Pennsylvania, thence westward through Brownsville on the Monongahela and Washington to Wheeling.

The first contracts for the building of the road were let in 1811 and work began west of Cumberland. Construction was practically suspended during the War of 1812, but was resumed afterward and by 1818 the road was completed to Wheeling. Immediately a great stream of traffic flowed over the road, amply proving that it served a most useful purpose. In fact, each section of the highway had been opened to travel as rapidly as it was finished, with the result that by the time the western portion was ready for use the eastern sections were nearly worn out.

No provision for maintenance and repair had been made by Congress, and the prospect was not good for the passage of such a law. The question of internal improvements had become one of the great political issues involving views of constitutional interpretation, which in turn hinged on sectional and economic interests. Henry Clay had launched his idea of an American System to make Americans self-sufficient by means of a protective tariff, for the benefit of eastern manufacturers, and projects of internal improvement to open home markets both for manufactured goods and for the produce of western farms. The American System had strong support in the West and in the middle States on the Atlantic coast, but it made little appeal to New Englanders who saw no profit in it for themselves, and it met with opposition in the South. Here the protective tariff was opposed for economic reasons, and federal aid in internal improvements was viewed with growing dislike, because it meant the enhancement of the power of the central government and ran counter to the doctrine of states' rights which the South was more and more coming to regard as essential to the defense of its economic system.

In 1822 a bill passed Congress providing for the repair of the Cumberland Road by means of funds to be raised by a series of toll-gates to be established and operated by the federal government. President Monroe, strong in the tradition of his Republican predecessors, promptly vetoed this bill. He rejected the doctrine of implied powers recently enunciated by John Marshall, and declared the law unconstitutional on the ground that it violated the sovereignty of the States. Two years later, however, Clay's American System was obviously gaining in popular favor, not only in the West but in the eastern States as well. Monroe now found it possible to satisfy his scruples by agreeing that the power given Congress by the Constitution to maintain an army and establish military and post roads warranted federal aid in laying out and maintaining roads. An appropriation was made for the repair of the Cumberland Road and it was planned that it should then be turned over to the States through which it passed for future care and maintenance, as was later done.

The repair work was thorough-going. A macademized surface consisting of several layers of crushed rock was laid throughout the entire distance, the drainage was improved by means of spillways and permanent culverts, and massive stone bridges were built across streams. Altogether the Cumberland Road was an excellent piece of road-building. The work was so well done that some portions of the roadbed and many of the bridges and culverts are still in use.

In 1825 Congress approved of the extension of the road to Zanesville, Ohio, and authorized surveys of a route as far west as Missouri through the capitals of Ohio, Indiana, and Illinois. Successive acts provided for construction westward. Columbus, Ohio, was reached in 1833. Work was pushed in both directions from Indianapolis at the same time and the Indiana section completed by 1850. Grading was carried as far west

as Vandalia, Illinois, but here it ended. Interest in the road
had by this time been overshadowed by enthusiasm first for
canals and then for railroads. West of Wheeling the highway
was known as the National Road or National Pike, although
the names Cumberland or National have been applied inter-

VII. PRINCIPAL ROADS TO THE WEST

changeably to the entire extent. All told, Congress appropriated nearly $6,825,000 for the construction and repair of the
road.

The Cumberland or National Road was a highway the like
of which was never again built in America until the automobile worked a revolution in the character of roads. It stretched
like a ribbon from the Potomac through the forests and over

the mountains of Maryland and Pennsylvania. "Leaping the Ohio at Wheeling," to use the words of Archer B. Hulbert, it extended across Ohio and Indiana, "straight as an arrow, like an ancient elevated pathway of the gods, choping hills in twain at a blow, traversing the lowlands on high grades like a railroad bed, vaulting rivers and streams on massive bridges of unparalleled size. . . . It is doubtful if there are on this continent such monumental relics of the old stone bridge builders' art."

After the road was turned over to the States, laws were immediately passed prescribing heavy penalties for damage to the roadway, milestones, culverts, or bridges. In Ohio, for instance, a person convicted of vandalism might be fined five hundred dollars or "imprisoned in a dungeon of the jail of the county, and be fed on bread and water only, not exceeding thirty days." Each commonwealth through which the highway passed took a real pride in seeing that its portion received proper care. In order to provide funds for repair and maintenance toll-gates were established. In Pennsylvania there were six gates and in Ohio one at least every twenty miles. Detailed schedules of toll rates were posted at each gate, the charges being determined by the wear on the road. Thus, Pennsylvania charged six cents for a score of sheep or hogs, twelve cents for a score of cattle, and four cents for a horse and rider. Rates for vehicles depended on the width of the wheels.

A retrospective view of the Cumberland Road enables us to recognize it as a significant bond of unity between the Ohio Valley and the eastern States. It was a visible symbol of the power and fostering care of the national government. While, as has previously been mentioned, it did not fulfill all the anticipations of its eastern advocates as an avenue of commerce, because the transportation costs were still necessarily high, it did greatly accelerate communication between the West and the federal capital. The possibilities of increased speed of travel received much comment. Hezekiah Niles noted that Senator Richard M. Johnson of Kentucky traveled from Washington to his home, a distance of 600 miles in seven days, and intimated that if anyone had predicted such a journey twenty-five years before he would have been thought extremely vision-

ary. A Cincinnati newspaper told of a steamboat passenger
who had made the trip from Baltimore in five and one-half
days. James Veech was not exaggerating, therefore, when he
wrote that the Cumberland Road, "served to harmonize and
strengthen, if not to save, the Union."

FREIGHTING OVER THE CUMBERLAND ROAD

No doubt many of the contemporaries of the road's early
years realized some of these effects. Whether or not they were
conscious of intangible values, they were fully awake to the
practical uses of the great highway. A great freighting business sprang up immediately, using the huge six-horse Cones-
toga wagons, or "mountain ships," as they were sometimes
called on account of their boat-like bodies and their canvas
covers. In 1822, four years after the road reached Wheeling,
one of five commission houses at that place paid $90,000 for
hauling charges on freight unloaded from 1081 wagons carrying loads averaging 3500 pounds. Wagoning became a lucrative occupation, employing a large number of regular teamsters,
as well as farmers, dubbed "sharpshooters," who thus supplemented their incomes in slack seasons. The rates paid for
freighting explain why teamsters occasionally undertook to
haul prodigious loads. In 1838 one teamster hauled 3800
pounds of merchandise from Baltimore to Mt. Vernon, Ohio, a
distance of 400 miles for $4.25 a hundred, making the trip in
thirty days. He returned with a load of 7200 pounds of tobacco at $2.72 a hundred. About the same time a wagoner
was reported to have hauled a load of tobacco weighing 10,375
pounds net from St. Clairsville, Ohio, into Wheeling. A little
later a load almost equally heavy was hauled over the mountains.

As the traffic grew wagon houses were erected every few
miles along the road for the accommodation of teamsters. Here
at modest prices the wagoners could procure food or prepare
their own meals, and make their beds on the floor of a large
room before a great fireplace on winter nights, while outside
there was a yard for the horses. It is not difficult to imagine
the story-telling, the merriment, the quarreling, and fighting

that took place in these wagon houses during the years when the wagon freight business was at its height.

In addition to the regular freight lines the road was thronged during portions of the year with the wagons of western farmers hauling their produce to market and returning with needed merchandise. About the only way in which western grain could be profitably marketed in the eastern cities was in the form of livestock, which could furnish its own transportation. Large herds of hogs and cattle were frequently driven over the mountains. Timothy Flint, while traveling through Pennsylvania encountered "a drove of one thousand cattle and swine" from Ohio on their way to market in Philadelphia. Morris Birkbeck met near Zanesville "a drove of very fat oxen on their way from the banks of the Miami to Philadelphia. They might, on the average, weigh six hundred pounds, cost about thirty dollars, and sell at Philadelphia at about fifty or fifty-five dollars per head."

Stage-Coach Lines and Taverns

More interesting and glamorous than the freighters, though economically not so important, were the stage lines which began operating over the Cumberland Road as rapidly as it was completed, section by section. "The great western mail and stages, . . . from Washington City to Wheeling, on the national turnpike, arrived in Brownsville—for the first time—on Wednesday last," reported a Brownsville newspaper in August, 1818. "It will pass three times a week. A regular line of stages is, also, established, by which the passenger will be enabled to reach either extreme—a distance of 270 miles—in five days." The first stage-coaches were little better than wagons, without springs and with seats running crosswise and with the door in front, making it necessary to crawl over the front seats to get to those in the rear. Before long, however, the familiar Concord type of coach came into use. These were slung on leather straps, which served as springs to absorb the worst shocks. The doors were at the sides and there were usually three seats inside, each capable of accommodating three passengers. There was a driver's boot on top in front and a baggage boot in the rear. Many of these coaches were hand-somely painted and decorated and richly upholstered. Some of them were named, after the fashion of the modern Pullman cars.

Large stage line companies came into existence. The two greatest rivals on the Cumberland Road were the National Road Stage Company and the Good Intent Line, but there were other lesser concerns such as the Mail Pilot Line and the De-fiance Fast Line. Time tables were printed somewhat like modern railroad schedules, showing distances between towns, time of arrival, and connections with other lines. Fares appar-ently varied at different times and on different runs from as low as four cents a mile to as high as six cents. For instance, at one time the fare from Cumberland to Wheeling was about eight dollars. The coaches ran day and night. About every twelve miles there was a sudden and brief halt at a stagehouse, the steaming horses were unhooked, a fresh relay was substituted, and with a crack of the whip they were off again.

The speed of the stage-coaches varied with the season of the year, the nature and condition of the road, and the charac-ter of the service being rendered by the particular coach, whether it was a local passenger or an express mail coach. In 1837, for example, the time of the ordinary passenger coaches from Washington, D. C. was indicated by the following illus-trations: to Wheeling in 59 hours; to Columbus, Ohio, in 88 hours; to Indianapolis in 164 hours; and to St. Louis in 244 hours. The contract for the Great Western Express Mail called for the following time: to Wheeling in 30 hours; to Co-lumbus in 45½ hours; to Indianapolis in 65½ hours; and to St. Louis in 94 hours.

Just as small boys today hope, when they grow up, to be air-mail pilots or drivers of racing cars, so many of the lads of the twenties and thirties of the last century nursed ambitions to become drivers of stage-coaches and especially of the mail coaches. Names like those of Redding Bunting, Jim Reynolds, Billy Armor, David Gordon, and James Burr were widely known and each had his admirers because of his exploits or his particular style of driving. These men and others like them also enjoyed a wide acquaintance among the noted men and women of the period before the Civil War who traveled by stage-coach over the Cumberland Road: Andrew Jackson, James K. Polk, William Henry Harrison, Henry Clay, and other Presidents and statesmen, to say nothing of Jenny Lind, General Lafayette, Black Hawk, and P. T. Barnum.

Thomas B. Searight is authority for the statement that the excellence of the taverns along the Cumberland Road, even in the isolated mountain sections, was a constant surprise to travelers. "That they were equal to the best on the road is conceded," he says, "and that the old taverns of the National Road have never been surpassed for bounteous entertainment and good cheer, is likewise conceded; in fact, has never been disputed." Most of these western taverns were named for their proprietors or their geographical location, but some of them bore more colorful appellations, such as the Sign of the Indian Queen, the Temple of Juno, the Sign of the Rising Sun, or the Sign of the Red Lion. Many of the tavern-keepers were men of social grace and administered with distinction as hosts to the comfort of the travelers whose names adorned their registers. Altogether a lengthy stage-coach journey, with stops overnight at some of the better taverns, must have been an experience long to be remembered.

ROAD-BUILDING IN THE SOUTH

The Cumberland Road was the de luxe highway to the West in its day. It was the only real road built at federal expense and under federal supervision. Elsewhere the roads were only such as local funds and local initiative produced, and in the main they were rough, unimproved pathways difficult to traverse at any time and impassable on account of mud in the spring of the year. The stage-coaches were less luxurious or dependable and the inns meaner and less comfortable on these side roads, except on routes enjoying heavy traffic on account of growing centers of population.

The region south of the Ohio River never enjoyed a highway comparable to the Cumberland Road. Such road work as was done by the federal government was motivated by the need of facilitating the carrying of the mails. In 1801 and 1802 troops stationed in the southwest were employed in clearing and widening the Natchez Trace from Nashville to Natchez and in building rude bridges and causeways. Other appropriations were made for the improvement of this road, which for several years was the main post route from Washington, D. C., through Richmond, Knoxville, Nashville, and Natchez to New Orleans. For many years the mail was carried on horseback, indicating that the road was far from being a real highway.

After the close of the War of 1812 Congress made an appropriation for the opening of another road in the southwest. The result was what was known as Jackson's Military Road, extending from Florence, on the Tennessee River in northwestern Alabama, across Mississippi to a point not far from New Orleans. There was rejoicing at both ends of this road when the work, done by troops under Jackson's supervision, was completed in 1820. "The whole road was cut out, and bridges, and ferries, and houses of entertainment established, at the last advices," reported a New Orleans editor. "It is understood, this road will shorten the distance to New Orleans by land from three to four hundred miles." A Florence newspaper exulted in the prospect that "the day is not far distant when a line of stages will be established from Nashville to New Orleans, which must necessarily render the military road the most important of any other on the continent." He reported that the Postmaster General had been instructed "to run the southern mail through this route instead of sending via Natchez; and as this regulation, when put in operation will furnish New Orleans with dates several days earlier than usual, we hope that it will take effect without further delay." This hope was soon gratified.

Other appropriations resulted in some improvement of a route of travel from Georgia westward through Alabama and Mississippi and a portion of the mail from all the Atlantic coast points was eventually carried by this route. But one of the greatest ambitions of the South—for a great national highway running southward through the coast States—was destined to disappointment. Such a highway was suggested in Albert Gallatin's elaborate report on internal improvements in 1808. Hope for the project was revived in 1816 at the time of the establishment of the Second United States Bank. The law contained provision that the Bank should pay into the national treasury one and one-half million dollars. A bonus, in return for its franchise and as interest on the stock owned by the government.

In Congress the friends of internal improvements at national expense seized the opportunity to pass a bill specifying that this bonus should be expended on such projects. Among others John C. Calhoun supported the bill and urged that provision be made to facilitate communication from Maine to New Orleans. President Madison's veto of the Bonus Bill in 1817 dashed all these hopes. In 1826 a board of engineers reported on three routes from Washington through the southern States and westward to New Orleans, and in 1830 Congress debated a project for a highway connecting Buffalo, Washington and New Orleans. By this time, however, the southerners were set in their opposition to internal improvements at federal expense and proved their sincerity by discountenancing even projects designed for the benefit of their own section.

It was in 1830 that the advocates of internal improvements received their most discouraging set-back, when to their surprise and consternation President Jackson vetoed the Maysville Road Bill, authorizing a government subscription of stock in the "Maysville, Washington, Paris, and Lexington Turnpike Company." The citizens of Maysville were reported to have burned Senator Bibb of Kentucky in effigy because he voted against the bill. Southern strict constructionists, however, heartily approved the veto. "The great number of petitions which are annually urged upon the nation, calling for the aid of the general government in the construction of works, all of which are claimed to be of a national character, would," declared a Tennessee editor, "if sanctioned and adopted, in a short time exhaust the pecuniary resources of the government. . . . This cannot escape the observation of the people. They will no longer fold their arms and vainly look to the general government for the exertion of a power which does not legitimately belong to it, but with new energy and spirit put into requisition that individual enterprize, which will eventually lead to an efficient prosecution of their labours."

Aside from a considerable number of military roads laid out by the federal government, the story of road-making in the West is to be found in the histories of the various Territories and States. Legislatures enacted a large volume of road legislation, most of which, no doubt, was designed to meet a real need, but some of which was the result of log-rolling and pork-barrel politics. A number of excellent turnpike roads were built either by the States themselves or by private companies. In general, however, the tendency was toward turning the making and care of roads over to the local units of government—counties and townships. The practice of allowing people to work out their taxes on the roads produced results that varied with the industry and community pride of the workmen and the judgment and skill of the overseers.

THE FIRST RAILWAYS

The decade of the thirties witnessed the appearance of widespread enthusiasm for a new means and method of transportation which in the succeeding generation largely took the place of highways, canals, and rivers for long-distance hauling both of freight and of passengers. There had been talk about railroads almost from the beginning of the eighteenth century. The early proposals looked mainly to the providing of smooth tracks over which wagons could be drawn with greater ease and speed than over the ordinary roads. It was the thought that anyone might use these tracks who was willing to provide vehicles that would fit them. In 1808 Benjamin H. Latrobe made such a suggestion in a letter to Secretary Albert Gallatin.

Four years later John Stevens of Hoboken wrote a pamphlet in which he endeavored to prove the superiority of railroads, with carriages drawn by steam power, over canals. In the same year Oliver Evans, who had long been experimenting with "steam wagons," came to the support of Stevens, and became an outright prophet of steam railways. "When we reflect," he wrote in an article which appeared in *Niles' Register*, "upon the obstinate opposition that has been made by a great majority to every step toward improvement, . . . it is too much to expect the monstrous leap from bad roads to railways for steam carriages, at once. One step in a generation is all we can hope for. If the present shall adopt canals, the next may try the railways with horses, and the third generation use the steam carriage. . . . I do verily believe the time will come when carriages propelled by steam will be in general use, as well for the transportation of passengers as goods, traveling at the rate of fifteen miles an hour, or 300 miles per day." Evans and Stevens and others continued their propaganda in favor of railroads during the succeeding years, but the idea took hold slowly.

Naturally advocates of canals and improved highways were not likely to espouse the new movement. Besides, the conservatism of people stood in the way of the ready acceptance of an idea so revolutionary. Speed was one of the merits claimed for railroads. There were those who shook their heads and said that human beings could not stand the strain of travel at the rate of fifteen miles or more than an hour: serious nervous and mental disorders would result. Some said it would be sacrilegious to attempt to devise a method of traveling more rapidly than by the means which Providence had provided. As late as the early thirties the promoters of the Boston and Worcester Railroad were called "fools" and "idiots" and "knaves" and efforts were made to prevent them from launching their project.

Gradually, however, apathy and opposition gave way to interest in railroads, especially as news was disseminated concerning the growing success of the new method of transportation in England. There George Stephenson and others were experimenting with steam locomotives. By 1825 steam was being used as motive power on the Stockton and Darlington Railroad, and in 1829 Stephenson's *Rocket* hauled a loaded train over the Liverpool and Manchester Railroad at an average rate of fifteen miles an hour and attained nearly twice that speed at times.

The year 1827 may be said to mark the beginning of railroads in America. About that time two short railroads, using horse power, were constructed and attracted wide attention. One was a short road extending from Quincy to the Neponset River in Massachusetts and built for the purpose of hauling the granite used in constructing the Bunker Hill Monument.

The other was the Mauch Chunk Railroad, nine miles in length, running from a coal mine near Carbondale to the Lehigh River in Pennsylvania. It was in this year 1827, however, that charters were granted for the first real railroads in the United States: the Charleston and Hamburg in South Carolina, and the Baltimore and Ohio.

The Charleston and Hamburg Railroad, one hundred and thirty-six miles in length, was built to the falls of the Savannah River, in the hope that it might insure for Charleston a share in the cotton trade of the interior. It was started in 1830 and from the beginning was constructed with a view to the use of steam locomotives. It was on this road that the *Best Friend of Charleston*, the first locomotive built in America, was employed.

The Baltimore and Ohio Railroad had its origin in the desire of the citizens of Baltimore to check the growing ascendancy of New York City in the trade of the West, resulting from the opening of the Erie Canal. The plan to build a railroad over the mountains to the Ohio River was indeed a bold one for that early day. After the company had been organized and a charter secured the promoters were still so ill-informed that they appointed committees of investigation to find out what railroads really were and how they were operated. But enthusiasm ran high and stock in the road was over-subscribed. On July 4, 1828, ground was broken at a huge public celebration in Baltimore, at which time Charles Carroll, a signer of the Declaration of Independence, turned the first spadeful of earth. It was the original intention to use horse-drawn cars. Experiments were also made with vehicles propelled by sails and by horses operating a sort of tread-mill. But when in 1830 Peter Cooper ran his steam engine, the *Tom Thumb*, over the thirteen miles from Baltimore to Ellicott's Mills in one hour and fifteen minutes, the decision for steam power was finally made.

RAILROAD-BUILDING IN THE WEST

The story of how the region between the Alleghanies and the Mississippi gained its network of railways before the open-

ing of the Civil War is too long and too full of details for in-
clusion here. The Baltimore and Ohio did not reach the Ohio
River until more than twenty years after it was begun. By
1857 it was possible to make a railway journey from Baltimore
to St. Louis by changing cars five times, crossing rivers twice
on ferries, and making two short trips on steamboats. In 1854
the Pennsylvania Railroad reached Pittsburgh, after having
purchased and scrapped the famous Pennsylvania System of
canals, railways, and inclined planes upon which the people of
the State had centered such high hopes. Travel from Albany
to Buffalo was possible as early as 1842 by patronizing six
different short railway lines which were later consolidated by
the New York Central. The Erie Railroad was completed
from the Hudson River opposite New York City to Dunkirk on
Lake Erie in 1851. In the South railway construction faced
greater handicaps, especially in the comparative absence of
free capital for investment. Charleston long nursed the hope
of railway connection with Cincinnati, but without realization.
Before the Civil War, however, the Charleston and Memphis
Railroad was in operation. By means of several short lines
there was also a connection between Richmond and Chat-
tanooga.

In the region north of the Ohio River enthusiasm for railroads was widespread during the thirties and by 1837 a short
line from Toledo, Ohio, to Adrian, Michigan, was in operation,
with at least one steam locomotive in use. The Panic of 1837
put an end to actual building of railroads until the latter part
of the next decade. After this time, however, there was great
activity, and the movement continued unabated until the outbreak of the Civil War. In 1860 of the total railway mileage
in the United States (30,000 miles) nearly one-third was in the
Old Northwest. Chicago by this time was the hub of a railway
system that shortly enabled that rapidly growing city to become the metropolis of the West, displacing St. Louis which
had pinned its faith on the control of the river trade. Railroads from the east, particularly the Michigan Central and the
Michigan Southern, raced to enter Chicago. Lines reached out
to the Mississippi at several points and Chicago also had connections with St. Louis and Indianapolis. Elsewhere in the

States of the Old Northwest lines were being built, north and south and east and west, so that by 1860 there was no region south and east of Lake Michigan not fairly well served by railroads.

THE CHARACTER OF EARLY RAILROADS

As has been suggested this railway network was made up mainly of a large number of short, independent lines. This fact alone would have compelled passengers to make frequent changes of cars on long journeys and necessitated the unloading and reloading of much freight. In addition the tracks varied in width from three to six feet. Only a few lines at first adopted the now familiar standard gauge of four feet, eight and one-half inches between the rails. The rails themselves at first were of hard wood topped by a thin strip of iron. This plan soon proved unsatisfactory, especially since the iron strips showed a tendency to loosen and cause accidents, and solid iron rails were introduced. The earliest railway passenger cars closely resembled the stage-coaches, giving way after a time to the American type of car with doors at the ends and an aisle down the center. Certainly when compared with modern conditions a long railway journey over these early lines was a trying experience. There were vexatious delays at junction points or when the engine broke down; the cars were poorly heated and ventilated; burning cinders from the engine were a constant menace both to passengers and adjoining fields in the summer time; and disastrous wrecks were not infrequent. But railway trains made much greater speed than any other mode of travel or transportation, and railroads were accepted as one of the great improvements of the age.

THE FINANCING OF RAILROAD-BUILDING

The financing of railway-building in the Old Northwest taxed the resources of the region to the limit. There were huge conventions at Memphis in 1845, at Chicago in 1847, and at St. Louis in 1849, and innumerable smaller gatherings at other places throughout the West, for the purpose of arousing enthusiasm for the building of railways. Enthusiasm was aroused without difficulty, but enthusiasm would not build railroads. Money was needed and in amounts far greater than those required for any previous American enterprises. In the Old Northwest the States pledged their credit and authorized local units of government, such as counties and towns, to do likewise by issuing bonds and using the proceeds to aid in railroad building. Joint stock corporations were organized and charters were granted. Experience with such companies was very limited and laws for their control were wholly experimental and inadequate. Irresponsible groups, as well as legitimate promoters with definite plans for railroads, were allowed to print bonds and stock certificates and sell them wherever they could, with little or no restraint. As a matter of fact, most of the capital secured by the sale of stocks and bonds, whether by the state and local governments or by the joint stock companies, was obtained in the East and in Europe. Later when some of these stocks proved fraudulent or when local governments defaulted the payment of their obligations because no railways were forthcoming, the antagonism between the East and the West was decidedly increased.

The Illinois Central Land Grant

Throughout the period of railroad promotion persistent efforts were made to secure direct aid from Congress, but with very little success until 1850. Rights of way through the public lands were readily granted. In 1852 a general law was enacted providing that whenever a railroad met certain conditions as to actual construction it should receive a right of way one hundred feet wide, with additional space for stations and the privilege of cutting necessary timber. Long before this time westerners, accustomed to receive land grants for various enterprises, had been urging Congress to grant lands in aid of railroads. The Senate was willing, but the House of Representatives, in which eastern and southern influence strongly predominated, repeatedly rejected the proposal. It remained for Stephen A. Douglas to achieve success in this method of railway finance, thereby establishing a precedent that was eagerly followed later when millions of acres of public lands were granted to railroads in the Far West.

Ever since 1836 there had been a project for an Illinois Central Railroad from Galena, in the lead-mining region of northwestern Illinois, through the fertile but isolated and relatively unsettled interior of the State to Cairo, at the junction of the Ohio with the Mississippi. In spite of active support, the plan for such a railroad remained only a plan. The State had no funds with which to build the road, nor could they be secured. Congress was importuned for land grants but to no avail. And yet, through the efforts of the State's young Democratic Senator, Stephen A. Douglas, such a law passed Congress in 1850 and received the executive approval. The victory was achieved through a masterful process of log-rolling and manipulation of sectional interests. The original plan for a line entirely within Illinois was not one to attract the votes of Senators and Congressmen from other sections. Douglas now added a proposal for a railroad known as the Mobile and Ohio from Cairo to Mobile, thus transforming the plan into one of national proportions and winning southern votes. Eastern support was gained by provision for a branch connection with Chicago which indirectly offered connection with the East.

The law gave the Illinois Central and the Mobile and Ohio a generous right of way through the public domain. In addition six sections of land for each mile of railway, arranged alternately in six-mile strips on either side of the right of way, were granted to the States through which the roads should run to be used by them in aiding railroad construction. The alternate sections retained by the federal government were to be sold at a minimum of $2.50 an acre, or double the usual minimum price. In this way the national treasury would not be the loser on the account of the land grants. If any of the sections allotted for the railroads were already occupied, substitute selections might be made within a distance of fifteen miles on either side of the railroad. Curiously enough, southerners including John C. Calhoun were willing to approve this method of investing a portion of the public domain, although they were still opposed to internal improvements at federal expense.

The brief outline here presented indicates some of the main

features of railroad-building between the East and the West and in the western region itself before the Civil War. It is difficult to exaggerate the significance of this progress to the western States and especially in its bearing on the destinies of the nation. The transportation facilities enjoyed by the region north of the Ohio River, as compared with those in the South, were of immense advantage to the North in the four-year conflict between the sections. Moreover, the railroads, as they pushed west from Chicago, played a large part in facilitating and encouraging the phenomenal rush of emigration into the grain-growing regions of the upper Mississippi Valley during the decade of the fifties—a movement of population which not only helped to change the political complexion of that section but greatly increased the economic superiority of the North.

CHAPTER XXI

ECONOMIC DEVELOPMENT OF THE MIDDLE WESTERN FRONTIER

THE STAGES OF WESTERN DEVELOPMENT

No MORE graphic summary of the economic evolution of the American frontier has ever been presented than that contained in *A New Guide for Emigrants to the West,* written by J. M. Peck and published in 1837. "Generally, in all the western settlements," wrote Peck, "three classes, like the waves of the ocean, have rolled one after the other. First comes the pioneer, who depends for the subsistence of his family chiefly upon the natural growth of vegetation, called the 'range,' and the proceeds of hunting. His implements of agriculture are rude, chiefly of his own make, and his efforts directed mainly to a crop of corn and a 'truck patch'. . . . A log cabin, and, occasionally, a stable and corn-crib, and a field of a dozen acres, the timber girdled or 'deadened' and fenced, are enough for his occupancy. . . . With a horse, cow, and one or two breeders of swine, he strikes into the woods with his family, and becomes the founder of a new county, or perhaps state." He was the type of pioneer or backwoodsman of whom Kipling wrote: "His neighbors' smoke shall vex his eyes, their voices break his rest." When hunting became less productive, when neighbors of a different disposition began to appear, he generally sold his holdings and moved on to some new frontier, there to repeat the process.

"The next class of emigrants," wrote Peck, "purchase the lands, add field to field, clear out the roads, throw rough bridges over the streams, put up hewn log houses with glass windows and brick or stone chimneys, occasionally plant orchards, build mills, schoolhouses, court-houses, etc., and exhibit the picture and forms of plain, frugal, civilized life."

This class made made up of those whom we are accustomed to call settlers. They came with the intention of making real farms, and so, with prodigious labor they extended the clearings and opened up fields for grain, erected dwellings offering rude comfort, and, as Peck indicated, effected striking improvements in the habitability of the region. Frequently, the lure of lands further west was too strong to be resisted by these pioneer farmers. Many of them disposed of their farms and improvements after a few years and joined the procession of those moving to some newly opened region.

"Another wave rolls on. The men of capital and enterprise come. The settler is ready to sell out and take the advantage of the rise in property, push farther into the interior and become, himself, a man of capital and enterprise in turn. The small village rises to a spacious town or city; substantial edifices of brick, extensive fields, orchards, gardens, colleges, and churches are seen. Broadcloths, silks, leghorns, crapes, and all the refinements, luxuries, elegancies, frivolities and fashions are in vogue. . . . A portion of the two first classes remain stationary amidst the general movement, improve their habits and condition, and rise in the scale of society." When any given region had reached this third stage of progress the frontier was a thing of the past in that section. The wilderness had been transformed into a land enjoying a material civilization comparable in most respects to that of the longer settled areas further east; and each succeeding generation witnessed continued progress and increasing wealth and resources.

Practically all portions of the Ohio and upper Mississippi valleys passed through these or similar stages of development. It was not so in the plantation region of the Old Southwest. Here the backwoods pioneer came and went as in other sections of the West, and the clearings were enlarged by the small farmers. But here the similarity ended. The cotton planters appeared upon the scene. They needed large areas for cotton culture and for the employment of large numbers of slaves. Negro labor proved very inefficient when set to such tasks as clearing land. Consequently the planters found it most advantageous to purchase the cleared holdings of settlers; and as this trend became evident many enterprising individuals

took up land and cleared it with the definite expectation of
selling it for a good price to some cotton planter. When
plantations covered the area progress had reached its highest
point. For a number of years there was prosperity. Then the
soil began to show the effects of single-cropping, of raising cotton year after year. Instead of a steady advance, there was
gradual decline as debts piled up and productiveness decreased.
Whenever possible the owners sold their plantations before
diminishing returns became too evident and sought fresh land,
where the process was repeated. Thus the concentration on
cotton production, with its accompaniment of slave labor,
halted the progress of frontier development that was normal
in other sections with free labor and wide diversification of
products and activities.

The present summary of western economic history is confined mainly to the Old Northwest and the upper Mississippi
Valley. Kentucky and Tennessee, being border States, exhibited some of the characteristics of the free farming section
as well as some of those of the plantation area.

PIONEER HOMES

The first concern of the settler as he moved with his family
onto the land he had chosen was the building of a cabin. Until
this task could be completed the family lived in the open or in
the wagon, or a rude shelter was made. Senator James Harlan,
in his autobiography, told how his father constructed such a
shelter by using the trunk of a huge, fallen tree as one side.
Forked sapling poles were placed in the ground a short distance from the tree and across these a beam was laid. Other
poles extended from this beam to the tree trunk and a covering
of bark was laid on. Bed clothing and pieces of canvas formed
the other sides. While the family camped in some such way
the men and older boys cut logs from the forest, and hewed
out rafters, joist and puncheon flooring. Then when all was in
readiness the neighbors gathered for the cabin-raising. The
logs, notched at the ends, were put in place alternately on the
sides and ends. When the desired height had been reached
the roof poles were added and a covering made of bark or

"shakes," often held in place by saplings fastened at the ends with wooden pegs. All this was done to the accompaniment of jovial badinage, with frequent swigs at the whiskey jug and such feasting as resources permitted.

Later the finishing touches were added, by cutting a door and a window or two, filling in the chinks between the logs with moss or mud or clay, building a fireplace, laying the puncheon floor if there was to be any floor, building the bunks along the wall, and perhaps constructing a ladder to the loft. James Harlan wrote that their cabin was completed and ready for occupancy "in about six or eight days from the date of our arrival, with no tools other than a common chopping ax, an auger, frow and hand-saw, and without a single nail or screw, or metalic material of any description."

Inside these first cabins all was crude and lacking in what would to-day be regarded as the barest necessities. The fireplace furnished heat and most of the light in the evenings, for the making of tallow candles was costly in time and labor. Here the food was boiled in iron pots, suspended from cranes, fried in skillets, or baked in "Dutch ovens" thrust into the coals. The beds were springless bunks, with "ticks" filled with straw or corn-husks. All the furniture was home-made, unless perchance some prized chair or chest or dresser had survived the westward journey. Food was served in wooden bowls and eaten with iron knives and forks and wooden spoons. Windows were covered with blankets or oiled paper, since window glass was too expensive. Unusual was the cabin-roof which did not leak copiously in times of heavy rain.

Pioneer Life and Labor

The cabin was the realm of the pioneer wife and mother. Here she prepared the daily food, of which there was generally an abundance—wild game, meat of domestic animals but mostly pork, wild and later cultivated fruits, and vegetables in wide variety. Here she made hominy, salted and dried meat for the warm months, made woolen and linen cloth and fashioned linsey-woolsey garments for the family, raised a swarm of children, and too often went to an early grave. The annals

of pioneering have never given full justice to the heroism of
the women pioneers. Their labors were arduous and unceasing. In addition, they suffered more than the men from the
psychological hardships of frontier life—loneliness, fear of
Indian attacks, longing for loved relatives and friends left
behind, worry and anguish in times of sickness without the
possibility of even the poor medical care of the period.

If the men were less affected by these mental stresses, their
toil was no less strenuous. The clearing of land covered with
hardwood trees was a task for the strong and the persevering.
First the small trees were cut and the underbrush grubbed out,
raked into piles along with the accumulated debris of ages,
and burned, the ashes serving as excellent fertilizer. Then the
standing trees were "girdled" or "deadened" by cutting a ring
deep through the bark so the sap could not flow and the trees
would die. A garden patch was made in some open spot the
first year and a small field of corn was planted among the
deadened trees and left to mature as best it could with very
little cultivation. In succeeding years the trees were cut down,
some of the more suitable logs saved for making fence rails
and the remainder rolled into piles and burned, unless a saw-
mill had made its appearance in the neighborhood and logs for
lumber were in demand. There still remained the tenacious
stumps to be dug, chopped or burned out, or left to rot if the
energy requisite to their eradication was lacking. Needless to
say, it was usually many years before a farm of as much as
one hundred and sixty acres was completely cleared.

James Harlan pictured what was doubtless the normal situation in these frontier settlements. "Each of these settlers
was the owner of a team of horses, a few cattle, hogs, sheep
and poultry," he wrote in describing his boyhood environment.
"Their livestock lived with but little care from the owners on
the spontaneous products of the country. The women converted the fleeces from the sheep into clothing. . . . The
country was alive with game, such as deer, elk, bear, turkey,
and grouse. So that these settlers had from the first year onward an abundance of excellent food and comfortable raiment,
the fruits of their own industry, frugality and skill." In the
course of years large fields, enclosed by stake-and-rider or

worm fences, extended where once forests had covered the land. Cabins were enlarged and improved or replaced by frame dwellings, either by the original owners or newcomers. Window glass became available. Tinware, "China" dishes and numerous other articles of utility and comfort found their way into the farm homes. In short, advancing material civilization eventually brought life in each frontier region up to the standard of sections further east.

Frontier Failures

Just as every community had a few families who, because of wealth or good fortune or excess of energy, rose above the common average in their style of living and evidences of prosperity, so also it had others who failed to keep step with the march of progress. In periods when the westward movement was in full swing and easterners were alarmed by the drain of their labor supply and by the rising political power of the West, it was often alleged that the western settlers were lawless, indolent, profligate, and, to use the words of Timothy Dwight, "too shiftless to acquire either property or character." Some recent writers, in the reaction against the over-idealization of the pioneer and the influence of frontier life, have asserted that the westward migrations were largely composed of the failures, the misfits and the unfit, if not worse. Such a characterization is, of course, as unwarranted as one which assigns superior qualities and motives to all pioneers.

Nevertheless, there was a closer relationship between the frontier and thriftlessness, failure, and deterioration, even in the economic realm, than we have been willing to admit. Making due allowances for the prejudices of their writers, the journals and letters of travelers leave no ground for doubt that in every western community families were living under conditions implying either confirmed indolence and thriftlessness, malajustment to environment, or the slackening of standards formerly observed in their previous homes.

Thomas Chapman, on a journey made in 1795, found a family of eight living on the Ohio River a short distance below Pittsburgh in "a Log Cabin not bigger than a good Hog Sty in

England, nor half so comfortable in appearance." He noted
that they had "Plenty of fine rich Land, if they would but take
the Pains to cultivate it." Francis Baily was shocked at the
filthy, unkempt appearance of a doctor's cabin in Cincinnati
in 1797. "It seemed to me very strange," he wrote, "that one
who appeared to be a man of information should not take more
pains about his habitation, and endeavor to render things about
him more comfortable, particularly as it might be so easily
done; but such is the force of example, that very few of the
emigrants who come into this kind of half-savage, half-civilized
state of life, however neat and cleanly they might have been
before, can have resolution to prevent themselves from falling
into that slovenly practice which everywhere surrounds them."
Forty years later J. M. Peck gave similar testimony. "Many
persons," he said, "on moving into the *back woods,* who have
been accustomed to the decencies of life, think it little matter
how they live, because *no one sees them.*" Statements of this
nature might be quoted indefinitely.

Similarly, numerous writers described the reverse side of
the westward movement—the return eastward of people who
had failed or were dissatisfied on the frontier. For example,
Zerah Hawley, writing from Ohio in 1821, reported that families "are continually returning to the East, and many more
designed to do the same, and still greater numbers desired to
do so, but have it not in their power. There are many reasons
for these returns, viz. the indifferent society, the want of market, where they may dispose of their produce, the impossibility
of procuring many articles, which by habit have become necessaries of life, and the very great want of many other articles
which are indispensably necessary to comfortable existence."
The editor of the *Detroit Gazette* wrote of "instances in which
the disappointment of too sanguine expectations and the parti-
ality for home, has turned back with disgust a portion of the
emigrants from situations possessing every advantage which
could be reasonably looked for." A year or two later the same
paper cited the case of a family from Connecticut who had
moved to Illinois and purchased land costing five hundred dollars. After living for five years on this land the man became
dissatisfied and homesick, wrote to friends in Connecticut for

money, sold his land *"for an old horse and cart,* crammed his wife and children into his cart, and started for 'the land of steady habits.'"

AGRICULTURAL PROGRESS

Agricultural progress is the central theme in the story of the transformation of the middle western frontier into a land of great productivity in the period before the Civil War. Diversity of crops, together with an increasing output of live-stock, early enabled the region to supply its own needs and to produce a surplus. While there was a tendency for settlers to take more land than they could afford or farm, especially under the Harrison Land Law of 1800, there were several influences which helped to keep down the size of the farms. The difficulty of meeting deferred payments under this law convinced the more prudent of the undesirability of taking too much public land. The land taxes imposed by western States operated in the same direction. The rising price of lands adjacent to growing towns and transportation routes limited the purchases of the later emigrants. Finally, the absence of slaves or other adequate labor supply compelled the settlers to depend largely upon themselves in clearing the land and in planting and harvesting their crops; and this fact had an important bearing on the size of the farms.

New Orleans was the natural outlet for the products of the western country. We have already noted the urgent demand of the westerners for the opening of the Mississippi preceding Pinckney's Treaty with Spain in 1795. This demand was stimulated more by the prospective need for the Mississippi as a free highway of commerce than by current use. During this period Ohio Valley farmers found markets for their surplus in supplying the needs of the newly arriving settlers and of the army in the Indian campaigns. By the opening of the nine-teenth century, however, traffic on the Ohio and Mississippi began to assume a volume that steadily increased in the suc-ceeding years. A few figures will reveal this growth as well as the variety of products exported from the region.

An estimate in *Niles' Register* for the seven months from October 5, 1810, to May 5, 1811, said to represent only about three-fourths of the total, indicated that 743 flatboats and keel-boats had passed the Falls of the Ohio. Their total cargoes included, among a long list of enumerated items, 129,483 barrels of flour, 604,810 pounds of bacon, 9,477 barrels of whiskey, 47,795 barrels of corn, 24,691 pounds of butter, 465,-402 pounds of lard, 630,562 pounds of hemp, 113,015 pounds of yard and cordage, 2,311 hogsheads of tobacco, and 1,207,338 fowls. A similar estimate for the entire year 1820 offers a basis for comparison in regard to a number of commodities, "The whole number of boats which passed the Falls of the Ohio last year," according to this statement, "is estimated to be 2,400, wafting the rich produce of the western world to the markets on the seaboard; the principal part of which consisted of 1,804,810 lbs. of bacon, 200,000 bbls. of flour, 20,000 bbls. pork, 62,000 bushels oats, 100,000 bushels corn, 10,000 bbls. cheese, 160,000 lbs. butter, 11,207,333 fowls and 466,412 lbs. of lard." Lumber from western Pennsylvania and New York also became an important part of the cargoes which came down from the Alleghany and Monongahela. By 1830 a considerable amount of fruit, principally apples, was shipped from the Old Northwest.

After the opening of the Erie Canal and especially after the building of the canals in Ohio and Indiana, the Great Lakes-Erie Canal route carried much of the produce directly to the markets on the eastern seaboard. An excellent illustration is found in the export of flour and wheat by this route. In 1835 it was reported to be the equivalent of 543,815 bushels of wheat, in 1840 of 3,300,000 bushels, and in 1851 of 12,193,-202 bushels.

Even after the building of the Cumberland Road the hauling of grain over the mountains by wagons was prohibitive. Such traffic was limited to the less bulky and more condensed products, such as maple sugar, whiskey, cured tobacco, potash, linen, and hemp. For many years cattle and hogs were also driven over the mountains from Kentucky, Ohio, and Indiana to Philadelphia and Baltimore, but the profits were uncertain because of the competition of livestock raised in the western sections of the eastern States. With the coming of the railroads direct access to the markets on the Atlantic seaboard was gained for all the products of western farms and the traffic down the rivers to New Orleans rapidly diminished. As Robert R. Russel has pointed out, the railroads not only "caused self-sufficing rural economy to give way to commercial agriculture with distant markets," and thus "brought prosperity to countless rural communities, but they caused countless others, sometimes century old, to die out, unable to withstand the new competition with more naturally favored districts far away." [1]

MERCHANDISE AND SUPPLIES FOR THE WEST

Another chapter in the story of the economic transformation of the frontier is concerned with the manner in which westerners were supplied with merchandise and manufactured articles. While cheap and fertile land was the West's primary attraction, it must be borne in mind that with the development of the country more and more people moved westward to take advantage of the constantly increasing opportunities in trade, commerce, and transportation. Zadock Cramer, in *The Navigator* for 1811, held out alluring prospects. He described how the ambitious merchant secured "a small square ark boat, which he loads at the head waters with various wares, liquors, fruits, dry goods and small groceries, and starts his bark for the river traffic, stopping at every town and village to accommodate the inhabitants with the best of his cargo—This voyage performed, which generally occupies three months, and the ark sold for half its first cost, the trader returns doubly invigorated, and enabled to enlarge his vessel and cargo." After several trips of this kind he might set himself up as a merchant or in some other occupation and live "amidst wealth and comforts the remainder of his days."

On account of the scarcity of specie in the West most of the trade in the early years was conducted by means of barter. For instance, when Thomas Ashe traveled west of the mountains in 1806 he decided to sell his horse at the headwaters of the Ohio. "I was offered in exchange for him," he wrote,

[1] Robert R. Russel, "A Revaluation of the Period before the Civil War: Railroads," in *The Mississippi Valley Historical Review*, December, 1928, p. 343. By permission of the publishers.

"salt, flour, hogs, land, cast iron salt pans, Indian corn, whiskey—in short, every thing but what I wanted, which was money. The highest offer made was cast iron salt pans to the amount of a hundred and thirty dollars. I asked the proprietor of this heavy commodity, how much cash he would allow me instead of such an encumbrance; his answer was, without any shame or hesitation, *forty dollars* at most. I preferred the pans; although they are to be exchanged again for glass bottles at Pittsburg, tobacco or hemp in Kentucky, and dollars in New Orleans."

Before the coming of steamboats on the western rivers practically all the merchandise had to be hauled over the mountains, and prices were accordingly high. A good illustration of the way in which business was conducted under these circumstances is to be seen in the case of Pittsburgh, which became a center for the trade not only of the surrounding country but also for the whole Ohio Valley. "The merchants here, as well as those of the western country," wrote T. M. Harris in 1803, "receive their goods from Philadelphia and Baltimore. . . . The terms of credit are generally nine to twelve months. The produce which they receive of the farmers is sent to New Orleans, the proceeds of which are remitted to the Atlantic States, to meet their payments." Payment at New Orleans was made either in credit on eastern firms or in Spanish dollars, which were especially prized throughout the West. Similar procedures were followed by the merchants of Steubenville, Wheeling, Louisville, Cincinnati, and other towns along the Ohio.

In a surprisingly short time, in spite of all the handicaps, local merchants in the larger frontier towns were able to supply their customers with a wide variety of merchandise. Thus, before the settlements in Ohio had advanced into the second decade the newspapers were advertising not only the common necessities of life but some of the luxuries. Tea, coffee and chocolate were on sale, as were also figs, raisins, almonds, pickled fish and oysters from the Atlantic coast, and choice wines from abroad. Ladies might purchase perfumery, madras handkerchiefs, kid shoes, silk umbrellas, hair powder, shawls, and many other articles. Queensware for the table, glass for windows, scythes, and various iron implements were listed.

Supplies of merchandise were more limited in the small villages and in isolated farming regions. Even there the cross-roads store soon brought the necessities within reach, and itinerant peddlers, tinkers, and shoemakers were welcome visitors. Floating shops and stores conducted a brisk trade in the settlements along the Ohio and Mississippi. "While I was at New Madrid," wrote Timothy Flint, "a large tinner's establishment floated there in a boat. In it all the different articles of tin-ware were manufactured and sold by wholesale and retail. . . . A still more extraordinary manufactory, we were told, was floating down the Ohio, and shortly expected at New Madrid. Aboard this were manufactured axes, scythes, and all other iron tools of this description, and in it horses were shod. . . . I have frequently seen in this region a dry goods shop in a boat, with its articles very handsomely arranged on shelves."

Early Manufacturing in the West

The middle western frontier was not long dependent entirely upon the East for its manufactured goods. The presence of raw materials and the high freight charges stimulated the early establishment of local manufacturing along various lines. Grist-mills and saw-mills became abundant, and not only supplied local needs but produced a surplus for shipment. Salt wells were developed in Ohio, and especially in the "Wabash Saline" in southern Illinois. Domestic manufacture of woolen and linen cloth likewise provided clothing for the immediate family or community and an increasing amount for export. Breweries, distilleries, tanneries, flour mills, and paper mills transformed the products of field and forest into commodities of commerce. Early in the nineteenth century people began to speak of Pittsburgh as the Birmingham of America, and before many years Cincinnati was noted for the smoke pouring from its factory chimneys. By 1810 it was estimated that the value of goods manufactured annually in Ohio was nearly three million dollars.

As early as 1800 Kentucky newspapers advertised locally-

manufactured leather, paper, spinning wheels, hats, and clothing. Shortly afterward several nail-cutting establishments were
set up. In 1816 Lexington received comment for its six steam
factories and other prosperous industries. Manufacturing in
the interior of Kentucky, however, seems to have been unable
to survive the competition made possible by the lower freight
rates which attended the introduction of steamboats on the
Ohio River. No doubt similar effects were produced in other
western communities, then and later, as improved transportation facilities gave increased advantages to some localities and
impaired the possibilities of others.

"If we except the cordage, bale rope, bagging, and other
articles of hempen fabric, manufactured in Kentucky, the chief
part of the western manufactures originates in west Pennsylvania and Ohio," stated Flint's *History and Geography of the
Mississippi Valley* published in 1832. "Glass is manufactured
in various places, at present, it is supposed, nearly to an amount
to supply the country. Manufactures in woolen and cotton,
and pottery, in laboratories, as white and red lead, Prussian
blue, and the colors generally, the acids and other chemical
preparations, in steam power machinery, saddlery, wheel irons,
wire drawing, buttons, knitting needles, silver plating, Morocco
leather, articles in brass and copper, hats, boots and shoes,
breweries, tin and other metals, cabinet work; in short, manufactures subservient to the arts, and to domestic subsistence,
are carried on at various places in the western country with
great spirit."

The Growth of Western Towns

Where late the savage, hid in ambush, lay,
Or roamed the uncultured valleys for his prey,
Her hardy gifts rough Industry extends,
The groves bow down, the lofty forest bends;
And see the spires of towns and cities rise,
And domes and temples swell into the skies.

These closing lines from a "poem" recited by Return J.
Meigs at Marietta on July 4, 1789, breathe the exuberant
optimism of the founders of countless towns which sprang up
in the service of expanding trade and transportation and manu-

facturing. Some of these towns grew to be proud cities like Pittsburgh, Buffalo, Cincinnati, Louisville, Chicago, St. Louis, and New Orleans, boasting of populations ranging between seventy and one hundred and seventy thousand in the census of 1860. Others, like Detroit, Cleveland, Dayton, Toledo, Columbus, Indianapolis, Milwaukee, Memphis, and Nashville, made steady progress that pointed to further growth in later years. A host of other places gained the security of comfortable county seat towns or trading centers for prosperous farming communities. There were also the "paper towns"—each one sure to be a future metropolis—many of which became only soon-forgotten names or maintained a precarious and disheartening existence because their locations were without other justification than the dreams of speculators, honest or otherwise.

Points at which there was a break in transportation routes or strategic locations on waterways were the most promising sites for towns and future cities. Pittsburgh owed its early growth to its position at the forks of the Ohio River, where the principal land route across Pennsylvania met the main water highway to the West. Morris Birkbeck noted in 1817 that the town "contains about 7000 inhabitants, and is a place of great trade, as an entrepôt for the merchandise and manufactures supplied by the eastern states to the western." The business of portaging cargoes around the Falls of the Ohio gave occupation to many of the early inhabitants of Louisville. In 1826 a New York editor described the phenomenal progress of the new town of Buffalo at the western terminus of the Erie Canal. "Where but a few years since the croaking of frogs was the only music that broke the charms of solitude," he wrote, "the bugle from the decks of a procession of canal boats, mingles its notes with the merry peal of the hotel bells—the sturdy mariner of the lakes with his 'ho, heave o' is busy loading his vessel for a voyage to Detroit, or transhipping the products of the west, to be passed on the canal to an eastern market." Seven years later a Buffalo editor found it not unusual to see as many as thirty sailing vessels on the lake at one time. "The warehouses are full—many of the docks are filled six feet high with goods, and canal boats are constantly discharging fresh cargoes upon the top of the mass," he said. "All is hurry and activity; every thing carrying a sail or a steam engine is in constant requisition; and the jaded appearance of the dock clerks bears sufficient evidence of the task they daily accomplish."

Similar scenes were witnessed in Cleveland, Toledo, and other towns which came into existence at points where traffic on Lake Erie touched transportation routes by road or canal across Ohio, or in Detroit whose dreamy French-Canadian habitants found themselves out of place in the bustle and stir that transformed their village into a thriving American town after the opening of the Erie Canal. Cincinnati gained an early start and maintained a steady growth that by 1830 made it the principal western rival of Pittsburgh as a manufacturing and distributing center. By this time St. Louis had greatly outgrown the limits of the little village founded by Laclede and his French companions in 1764. Its inhabitants still had no reason to fear that their city would lose its position as the metropolis of the upper Mississippi Valley—a position based upon its control of the fur trade and the growing traffic of two mighty rivers. Then during the fifties, where once had stood an Indian village and later an ill-starred American fort and still later a struggling settlement, Chicago became the hub of a railway system, as well as a busy lake port, and grew in population by leaps and bounds, although not until after the Civil War did it overtake and outdistance St. Louis in the race for supremacy.

So the entire roll of the rapidly growing towns and cities might be called. There is a real fascination in the story of western town-building. Life and movement, buoyancy and boastfulness were everywhere in evidence. If in many cases fondest dreams were unfulfilled, in innumerable other instances the actual achievements exceeded the hopes and predictions of the founders. The building of hundreds of houses each year was common in many towns on sites which a year or two earlier were covered by forests. Often the annual growth was limited by the dearth of building materials and the lack of a sufficient number of workmen. It is true that in most cases there was little or no planning and much that was distinctly ugly in these upstart towns. Streets and alleys and vacant lots long remained filthy for want of adequate drainage and sewage systems. Hogs and cattle ran at large. For years, also, vestiges of their frontier village days remained. Alongside of "palatial" business blocks and well-built churches and attractive frame and brick dwellings were cabins and shanties of the first comers, and tree stumps were reminders of the original forest covering.

THE LAND OF OPPORTUNITY AND EQUALITY

This middle western frontier was the land of opportunity for thousands and hundreds of thousands of people during the six or seven decades which followed the establishment of the republic. Millions of acres of cheap and fertile land held out the promise of a competency to men and women of meager means who were willing to undertake the toil and hardship of pioneering. There were good wages to be earned in helping to build roads and canals and railroads, or in the manifold occupations connected with transportation. The springing towns called for armies of carpenters, bricklayers, plasterers, blacksmiths, and mechanics of all kinds. They also offered alluring inducements to merchants, lawyers, doctors, preachers, and school teachers. It is small wonder that the manufacturers and employers in the eastern States viewed with alarm the movement of population that played such havoc with their wishes for a cheap and constant labor supply.

It is obvious also that in the early stages of its development the frontier was a region where substantial economic equality prevailed—at least a real equality of opportunity. Neither wealth nor family availed much when it came to clearing land, building cabins, and making farms. Every man was cast largely upon his own resources, and he was known for what he could do, and not for what he had been—whether a success or a failure—in the place from which he had come. Initiative, resourcefulness, perseverance, and courage were the qualities demanded and respected in the new environment. Because this was true and because the opportunities for everyone seemed so unlimited the westerners were ardent champions of individual freedom, at the same time that they insisted on the maintenance of equality. Later chapters will show how economic equality on the frontier helped to give rise to the demand for political equality, and how it was reflected in social relationships. First, however, it is necessary to sketch the story of how the western development just outlined was financed and how westerners fared in periods of economic depression.

CHAPTER XXII

FRONTIER FINANCE IN PROSPERITY AND DEPRESSION

RELATIVELY few settlers were able to migrate westward, purchase land, and maintain themselves until their new farms became productive, without borrowing money or obtaining credit, or both. Similarly the new western communities and States were obliged to seek eastern capital with which to build roads, canals, and railroads. In short, the frontier was a debtor region.

During periods of prosperity when, to use the words of an English observer, "the Progress of the Country" was the great western staple, this debtor status imposed no restraint on the spirits or activities of westerners. Unregulated banks providing easy credit and an inflated currency, were eagerly welcomed; while eastern capitalists and money-lenders were regarded with equal cordiality. But when panic and depression came these erstwhile beneficent agencies were viewed in a very different light by the people of the frontier. When loans were called in, and mortgages were foreclosed, and banks closed their doors, these institutions appeared suddenly to have assumed the role of monsters. The "money power" of the East likewise seemed a veritable ogre of greed and oppression to communities unable to pay the interest on stocks and bonds so blithely sold to finance internal improvements. The experiences gained in financing western development left the West with an ingrained antipathy to commercial banks in general and the two United States Banks in particular, and led to much bitterness in the attitude of the West and the East toward each other.

THE FINANCIAL NEEDS OF PIONEERS

There is no reliable data upon which to base an estimate of the percentage of the western migrants who were able to finance their own transfer to homes further west. Obviously a considerable number of them had lands and property to sell before they moved, and horses, wagons, and farming tools with which to make the journey and begin farming in the new environment. A smaller number, especially in the later stages of settlement, were men of relatively large means, able to migrate in fine style and even with companies of employees and tenant farmers. The migration of plantation owners with their retinues of negro slaves were notable features of the settlement of the southern cotton belt. On the other hand, such evidence as exists points to the fact that a large proportion of the early settlers were without means with which to equip themselves even for the westward journey, and that they borrowed from, or were helped by, more fortunate relatives or friends.

Upon arrival at their destination the settlers were confronted by their second basic financial need—money with which to buy land, or at least to make the initial payment if it were during the period when the Harrison Land Law was in operation. Doubtless in most cases the settlers brought this money with them. Letters, diaries, and reminiscences often tell us of the great care with which migrating families guarded the precious money-bag containing the wherewithal to purchase the land that had lured them westward. There is no way of proving in how many cases this money was borrowed, but there is reason to believe the number was not small. Down to 1820, while the credit system of land sales prevailed, the federal government became the creditor for the deferred payments. As has already been described, large numbers of settlers were unable or unwilling to make these payments and Congress was obliged to enact a series of relief measures; while much land eventually reverted to the government. By the time the Great Migration got under way after 1815 banks began to play their versatile and disastrous role in connection with land purchases, both speculative and bona fide. In any case, there is evidence that one cause of the financial difficulties of western settlers was their tendency to take up more land than they could pay for or make remunerative.

Even when payments on land had been met the financial problems of the settlers were not entirely solved. Log cabins cost little or nothing to build.   Wild game and fruits and truck-patches provided much food.   But shoes and clothing wore out and had to be replaced, and some essential groceries must be purchased.   Western merchants were generally ready to extend credit until crops were harvested.   The merchants, in turn, were carried by eastern mercantile firms and commission houses.

Banking and Currency in the West

The coming of banks of issue was hailed as the dawn of a new era in a region where debt was the general rule and where specie or any circulating medium was exceedingly scarce.   The growth of the number of independent banks during the life of the first Bank of the United States was slow.   Only twenty-six were in existence in the entire country in 1800.   There were eighty-eight in 1811 when the Bank's charter expired and several of these were west of the Alleghanies.   Many of the evils of the unregulated issuance of bank notes, with woefully inadequate reserves, appeared even during this period.   But until 1811 the Bank of the United States exercised a certain measure of control by its practice of calling for the redemption of the notes of banks which were thought to be unsound.   Even so, it could do little to protect the holders of worthless bank paper.

When this partial control was removed in 1811 the number of private banks increased with great rapidity, until there were 392 such institutions in the country by 1818.   The West had more than its share of this number, as legislature after legislature had yielded to the popular demand and granted charters, and as wildcat banks were established.   This meant an enormous expansion of credit and currency, since the banks launched large issues of bank notes with virtually no regulation.   Prices of land, farm products and commodities of all kinds rose rapidly.   Neither speculators nor settlers gave sufficient attention to the question of whether the inflated currency had a sound basis or whether credit was extended beyond all bounds of safety.   They easily dismissed any vagrant thought that eventually there must be a day of reckoning.   Doubters were silenced by calling attention to the unexampled prosperity and the great progress that would make easy the payment of all loans and the redemption of all bank paper within a few years.

It is not difficult to discern the elements of disaster that were inherent in the situation. In the first place, banking was in the experimental stage, and often developed as an adjunct of other business enterprises. The bankers were nearly all amateurs. Few of them had any knowledge of the business based on experience. It had been discovered that notes could be issued in large amounts and placed in circulation, and that most of them might remain in circulation until worn out before being presented for redemption. This made it possible for the bank to lend many times the amount of actual capital which it possessed. But even among those who were thoroughly honest there was no certainty or agreement as to what constituted an adequate reserve for the redemption of their notes. The unscrupulous made no effort to find out.

As a matter of fact even the better banks were often started with only a very small part of their capital paid up in actual coin. In other cases specie was used only for exhibition purposes to inspire confidence and was later loaned to subscribers to stock, who gave as security the stock certificates thus purchased. In spite of such unpromising beginnings many such banks were able to achieve a position of security and permanence. But there were the "wildcat" and "saddle-bag" banks, which were launched by gamblers and other unprincipled individuals or groups, without any tangible assets whatever. A well-appearing man would come into a community with a supply of bright, new bank notes, and set up an office. This attractive paper would be loaned to eager borrowers on the most liberal terms in return for promissory notes. These, in turn, were sold to gullible but greedy note-shavers for cash at large discounts; and then the perpetrator of the fraud would take his departure between dusk and dawn. Thus the West was deluged by a flood of bank notes, many of which were absolutely worthless and a very large proportion of which could not possibly have been redeemed in currency.

During the years from 1814 to 1817 there was complete suspension of specie payments. Bank notes continued to circulate and were issued in ever increasing amounts—especially in view of the fact that they could not be presented for redemption. Nevertheless, they soon depreciated in value, and year after year the situation of the currency became more and more confusing. Some effort was made to gather information upon which to base a schedule of discounts to be applied in accepting the notes of various banks, but it was next to impossible to know the value of any particular issue at any given time. Moreover, counterfeiting was easy, widely prevalent, and difficult of detection. Professor McMaster illustrates the desperate condition by citing the situation in Zanesville, Ohio, where in 1817 "more than thirty kinds of paper were passing from hand to hand. There were bills of the Canton Bank, the Owl Creek Bank, the Virginia Saline, the Granville, the Perryopolis, the Mansfield and New Philadelphia banks, and the Saddlebag Bank, as that at Parkersburg was nicknamed from the fact that all its capital had been carried in a saddlebag from Pittsburg to Parkersburg. But most plentiful of all were the 'shinplasters' issued by bridge, turnpike, and manufacturing companies, city authorities and borough authorities, merchants, tavern-keepers, barbers, and shoeblacks, and ranging in value from three cents to two dollars." [1]

The defects and inconveniences in the currency situation were readily appreciated and people not in debt welcomed the resumption of specie payments. The dangers, to banks and borrowers alike, attending the enormous extension of credit were not apparent until curtailment and liquidation began. It seemed as though the millenium had arrived when men could go to a bank and borrow money with which to buy land, giving in return mortgages at appraisals based upon optimistically anticipated, rather than actual, valuations. Furthermore, these loans were of necessity for long periods, since short time loans are of little use to farmers, especially in a new country. Thus the western banks, unlike those in commercial centers, had a great preponderance of their assets "frozen" or tied up in securities which could not be quickly converted in case of a sudden demand for redemption of the large issues of bank notes.

[1]John B. McMaster, *History of the People of the United States* (1883-1913), Vol. IV, pp. 317-318. By permission of the D. Appleton-Century Company, publishers.

THE PANIC OF 1819 IN THE WEST

Premonitions of approaching difficulties began to be felt with the chartering of the Second Bank of the United States in 1816 and were increased by the resumption of specie payments in 1817. A curtailment of loans soon became evident. To be sure the Second Bank with its numerous branches, five of which were in the West, was almost as reckless in its operations during its first two years as were the state and private banks. In 1819, however, Langdon Cheves assumed the presidency of the Bank and at once initiated measures to save the institution from ruin. The Bank now exercised all its coercive powers to compel the local banks to meet their obligations.

Even before this time the wrath of westerners had turned against the Second Bank, which they regarded as a gigantic engine of destruction designed for the purpose of annihilating the prosperity which they had been enjoying. In their constitutions of 1816 and 1818 the new States of Indiana and Illinois sought to prohibit the establishment of branches of the Bank within their borders. Ohio, Kentucky, and Tennessee joined Maryland, North Carolina, and Georgia in the attempt to tax the branches out of existence. Even after John Marshall's decision in the historic case of McCulloch *vs.* Maryland in 1818 the defiance continued, most notably in Ohio. Here the legislature reaffirmed the doctrines of the Virginia and Kentucky resolutions, and denied the protection of the laws to the branches within that State, even in cases of burglary and arson. The dispute was not settled until the decision was rendered in 1824 in the case of Osborn *vs.* United States Bank.

With the coming of the Panic of 1819 and the subsequent period of depression the rosy dreams induced by easy credit, inflation, and high prices were completely dispelled. Prices dropped to low levels. Lands, whether improved or wild, would not bring more than a fraction of their previous prices even where valuations had not been definitely exaggerated. Cotton prices tumbled rapidly because of decreasing demand from abroad. Agricultural produce would not bring prices sufficient to pay the charges for water transportation to New Orleans, much less for hauling across the mountains to eastern markets. Western newspapers were filled with long lists of lands to be sold for taxes amounting in some cases to only a few cents on a hundred acres. Bankruptcy was widespread. Worst of all, the West was deeply blanketed with debts and mortgages.

In the minds of westerners the Second Bank of the United States was the arch conspirator causing all this distress. But their resentment burned only slightly less fiercely against all banks. These institutions which so recently had seemed so kindly and generous now assumed a malevolent mien. Many of them closed their doors at the first approach of stringency. The others, in the effort to maintain solvency, brought all possible pressure to bear to collect their loans. Mortgages were foreclosed by the wholesale and banks incurred the popular odium which attaches to this process. In many instances public opinion made it difficult to sell the land on which foreclosure had been completed. Everywhere the people turned to their legislatures for protection, and stay laws, replevin acts, and other measures for the relief of debtors were enacted. Kentucky created the Bank of the Commonwealth, virtually without capital and with power to make a large issue of notes, which creditors were compelled to accept or submit to a prolonged postponement of collection of debts due them. The politics of the State were thrown into turmoil, the Supreme Court was legislated out of existence for declaring the relief laws unconstitutional, a new court was created, and two rival tribunals bade defiance to each other before sanity returned and the old court was restored to its prerogatives in 1826.

Recovery from the depression took place as the decade of the twenties advanced. Rising prices and relief measures enabled western farmers to pay off their mortgages and for a time the severity of the recent lesson was sufficient to inhibit any tendency to incur new indebtedness. The existing currency, including the circulating bank notes which had been curtailed by more than fifty per cent during the panic, was sufficient for all needs. The demand for credit likewise decreased, since hard times and the cash purchase provisions of the Land Law of 1820 diminished the volume of public land sales. Gradually open resentment toward banks died away, but throughout the West there were memories only waiting the proper occasion to be revived in full force. Especially was there a continued undercurrent of fear and distrust of the Second Bank of the United States.

THE WESTERN BACKGROUND OF THE PANIC OF 1837

Unfortunately only fifteen years elapsed before the country was headed toward another and even more destructive crash. The western setting of the new crisis exhibited all the familiar factors that had preceded the Panic of 1819: wild speculation, reckless banking, inflation, and over-extension of credit. To these were added other intensifying elements: the rage for internal improvements, Andrew Jackson's war on the Bank, and the Specie Circular.

Sales of public land, which had dropped sharply in 1820, began to mount slowly toward the end of that decade and by 1834 almost equalled the volume of the previous record year of 1819, when more than five million acres were sold. In 1835 the sales advanced surprisingly, almost trebling the amount of any previous year, but that record was far out-distanced in 1836 when more than twenty million acres were sold. The proceeds this year (nearly $25,000,000) were equal to the total of those for the thirteen years from 1820 to 1833. Most of this land was bought on borrowed money, and a large part of the purchases were speculative in character. This speculative mania has been described in a previous chapter. "The farmer, the manufacturer, the city merchant, the county merchant, bought land and paid their debts, if paid at all, not with dollars but with overvalued acres," wrote Professor McMaster. "Land bought from the government for a dollar and a quarter an acre was at once valued at ten or fifteen dollars an acre. The more a man bought, and the more he borrowed to pay for it, the richer he was." [2] Western steamboats, stage-coaches, taverns, and towns swarmed with land-buyers, and for every buyer there were several owners or speculators eager to sell at fancy

[2] John B. McMaster, *History of the People of the United States* (1883-1913), Vol. VI, p. 324. By permission of the D. Appleton-Century Company, publishers.

prices, promising certain wealth from future increases in value.

Speculation was by no means confined to agricultural land. This was heyday of the western town-boomers. New towns by the hundreds were plotted in the forests and on the prairies, and lots sold to avid purchasers at prices exceeding values in well-established eastern centers. When Harriet Martineau visited Chicago in 1835 she observed this mania of town-lot speculation in all its virulence. "I never saw a busier place than Chicago was at the time of our arrival," she wrote. "The streets were crowded with land speculators, hurrying from one sale to another. A negro, dressed up in scarlet, bearing a scarlet flag, and riding a white horse with housings of scarlet, announced the times of sale. At every street-corner where he stopped, the crowd flocked around him; and it seemed as if some prevalent mania infected the whole people." Thomas Ford also gave a vivid description of the scene. "Chicago had been for some time only one great town market. The plats of towns, for a hundred miles around, were carried there to be disposed of at auction. The eastern people had caught the mania. Every vessel coming west was loaded with them, their money and means, bound for Chicago, the great fairy land of fortunes. But as enough did not come to satisfy the insatiable greediness of the Chicago sharpers and speculators, they frequently consigned their wares to eastern markets. . . . In fact, lands and town lots were the staple of the country."

Once more the banks furnished the currency and credit with which to finance this orgy of buying and speculation. The number of private banks in the entire country in 1830 was reported to be 329; by 1834, after Jackson's veto of the bill rechartering the Second United States Bank, it had risen to 506, and by 1837 to about 800. Many of the newer banks, to use the words of a Louisville editor, had "perhaps an amount of capital in their vaults barely sufficient to pay the engraver of their notes." Bank capitalization often consisted of the promissory notes of the stockholders or of certificates of deposit in other banks. In other cases specie was loaned to new banks and exhibited for a short period and then passed on to perform a similar service for another institution. And yet all these banks put their notes into circulation with almost no limit other than the willingness of the public to accept them. From a per capita circulation of $6.69 in 1830 the issues of bank notes increased until in 1837 the per capita amount was $13.87. Both in number of banks and in the amount of circulating medium the West again had more than its share. Once more also the country was flooded with the worthless notes of defaulting banks, and the counterfeit-detector had to be kept at hand by every merchant.

Prices rose with the increase of the money supply, and as the region of diversified agriculture found growing market for its products in the expanding cotton-planting areas in the lower South. Wheat brought from two to three dollars a bushel in 1836, flour sold at fifteen dollars a barrel in Cincinnati and pork at twenty-five dollars a barrel in Chicago. Hogs running wild in the woods or in the streets of towns were worth seven dollars a hundred. Wages likewise mounted to new levels. Times were good, with prices high and money plenty.

As a consequence credit was also easy. Speculators and land-buyers found the banks ready and almost eager to lend them money with which to buy land, accepting the land itself as security, not at the purchase price but at prospective valuations. Again, as fifteen years earlier, the banks had their assets tied up in long-time loans and their resources anything but fluid. Neither banks nor borrowers saw any cause for worry, or if they did they were willing to take the risk. The country was booming, progress was on the march, and that person was foolish who did not seize the opportunity to get in line for the fortunes that were sure to come.

Then, as though not desiring to appear less enterprising and confident of the future than their citizens, the western States plunged into debt to finance roads and canals and railroads. After the opening of the Erie Canal and the beginning of projects by other eastern States designed to attract the trade of the West the commonwealths beyond the mountains caught the contagion. Not a western State escaped the rage for internal improvements at any cost. Every portion of every State demanded its share. If the southern States were less affected than those north of the Ohio River it was only because they lacked the means and the credit to undertake such ambitious progress.

Indiana, for instance, began building the Wabash Canal in 1832 and at the same time chartered several railroads. Four years later the legislature authorized the sale of bonds to the extent of ten million dollars, or an average of more than twenty dollars for every inhabitant of the State, to aid internal improvements. It was confidently expected that tolls and tariffs would soon produce an income sufficient not merely to pay the interest and principal of the debt, but even to relieve the people from taxation for the support of the government. Illinois was equally optimistic. In 1837 that State sold five million dollars worth of bonds to finance nine railroads. It was suggested that by selling these bonds abroad and taking advantage of the exchange rates, by depositing the proceeds in banks at interest until needed, and by other means, the improvements could be secured without cost to the State. No sooner had Michigan been admitted into the Union in 1836 when that State sought to rival its more populous neighbors in the mad scramble for canals and railroads. So the entire roll of the western States might be called, and each would be found pledging its credit for internal improvements to an extent far beyond the bounds of safety.

It is generally agreed that all this indulgence in reckless banking, speculation, and debt-creation was facilitated and encouraged by President Andrew Jackson's war on the Second Bank of the United States. Jackson paid little attention to the Bank in the first year of his presidency. But he was a westerner, thoroughly imbued with all his section's latent antagonism toward that institution. When his advisers convinced him that the Bank was being used in opposition to him by his political enemies he began his attack in each successive annual message. Although the charter would not expire until 1836, in 1832 the supporters of the Bank, with Henry Clay as their leader, decided to force the issue on the eve of the presidential election. A bill rechartering the Bank was introduced in Congress and passed. Jackson promptly vetoed it. Once more the Bank forces threw down the gage of battle and in the campaign of 1832 the Bank question was the main issue. Jackson emerged with a smashing victory which he interpreted, rightly or wrongly, as a vindication of his course with respect to the Bank.

The President now determined to destroy the Bank without waiting for the expiration of its charter. In 1833, after having removed two Secretaries of the Treasury, he found in Roger B. Taney a man who was willing to carry out his wishes and withdraw the government deposits from the United States Bank and place them with private banks throughout the country. To be sure, the money already deposited with the Bank was not immediately withdrawn, but no further deposits were made, and the Bank was compelled to place itself in readiness to honor drafts for funds already on hand as rapidly as they were made.

This action produced a temporary money famine. The Bank of the United States throughout all its branches was compelled to call in its loans, refuse new ones, and curtail the circulation of its notes. Somewhat the same necessity faced the state banks which were in debt to the United States Bank. Furthermore, in order to be placed on the list of "pet banks" to receive government deposits the local institutions were obliged to show that they were in a sound financial condition. The whole country experienced a period of depression, with unemployment, distress, and business stagnation.

In the West, especially, this depression was of short duration. The years from 1834 to 1837 witnessed the worst features of the speculation, currency inflation, easy credit, and rage for internal improvements which have already been described. The depression of 1833-4 caused a great outpouring of people into the West, eager to purchase land for farms and for speculative purposes. As the steadying influence of the Bank of the United States ceased to be felt, the number of private banks increased rapidly with a corresponding expansion of the issues of bank notes. Then, after deposits in the "pet banks" began, and when the sales of public lands increased by leaps and bounds, the available funds for loans multiplied indefinitely. Individuals went to banks and borrowed money with which to buy land. This money was paid into the land office, and then deposited in the nearest depository bank where it was immediately used in additional loans. Thus an endless chain or vicious circle was established.

By the summer of 1836 the federal government was greatly concerned about two problems connected with the enormous sales of public lands. One of these problems was that of the surplus piling up in the treasury, a temptation to extravagance and recklessness. The public debt had been paid in 1834 and each year there was an excess of income over expenditures of the government. As a remedy for this situation Congress passed the Distribution Law of 1836. In accordance with the terms of this law the Treasurer was to set aside five million dollars as a working capital and then, beginning on January 1, 1837, distribute the remainder among the States in four quarterly installments in proportion to the representation of the various States in Congress. To satisfy the strict constructionists this money was ostensibly to be merely deposited with the States, but there was no real expectation that it would be returned.

The other cause for worry was the growing doubt concerning the real value of the bank notes which were being received in payment for public lands. In 1835 President Jackson issued orders forbidding the reception of bank notes of small denominations. He sought also, without success, to secure a Congressional act requiring that payments to the government be made in coin. In this effort he was supported by Thomas Hart Benton, who thus gained his sobriquet of "Old Bullion." Failing to secure legislative approval, Jackson took matters into his own hands and, on July 11, 1836, issued his famous Specie Circular to all receivers of public money. "In consequence of complaints which have been made of frauds, speculations, and monopolies, in the purchase of the public lands, and the aid which is said to be given to effect these objects by excessive bank credits . . . and the general evil influence likely to result to the public interests, and especially the safety of the great amount of money in the Treasury, and the sound condition of the currency of the country, from the further exchange of the national domain in this manner," the receivers of the land offices were directed after August 15th to receive nothing but gold or silver in payment for land. Exceptions might be made until December 15th in favor of actual settlers and bona fide residents purchasing not more than 320 acres.

These two measures—the Distribution Law and the Specie Circular—had the effect of pricking the rosy-hued bubble that had been dazzling the eyes of the people of the West. The Specie Circular was the first to be felt, and many westerners were apparently dazed by it. There were various surmises as to its purpose. Some thought it was designed to fill the vaults of the "pet banks" preparatory to paying out the surplus revenue to the States. There were also rumors that the circular had been issued at the suggestion of New York speculators who had secured all the land they wanted and wished to throw obstacles in way of others doing likewise. "Whatever the object may be," declared a Lexington editor, "the western farmers may say, as the frogs in the fable said to the boys who were stoning them, 'what is fun to you is death to us.' " One marked effect of the refusal of the government to receive bank notes was a widespread destruction of confidence in the banks and their currency.

The Distribution Act brought about a sudden and almost complete curtailment of credit. Instead of making further loans, the depository banks were compelled to accumulate money with which to meet drafts from the Treasurer in order that that officer might make the quarterly distributions of surplus funds to the States.

The Panic of 1837 in the West

This then was the western background of the Panic of 1837 which ushered in a period of depression from which the country did not recover for five or six years. Banks suspended specie payments in 1837 and hundreds failed completely. Land sales for that year were less than one-third of those in 1836, and in 1838 they again fell off by more than one-half of the volume of 1837. Works of internal improvements were abandoned, leaving States heavily in debt for transportation facilities which they did not possess and the bond-holders with securities which were worthless or of little immediate value. Currency depreciated and prices and wages fell. Everywhere mortgages were being foreclosed and debts liquidated. Before the date for the fourth installment under the Distribution Act arrived, the treasury was facing a deficit rather than a surplus. The State of Mississippi entirely repudiated a debt of five million dollars.

Details of the distress throughout the West during this period need not be enumerated. Neither can space be given to the measures and circumstances which eventually brought recovery after long years of hard times. A few States apparently profited from lessons learned in the Panic of 1819 in regard to stay laws and extreme efforts at relief by legislation. This was notably true of Kentucky, where mutual aid and leniency to debtors on the part of the courts were the main reliance. A Lexington editor commented on the "property laws, stop laws, and the whole machinery of a relief system," which were being demanded in Mississippi. "It may be," he warned, "that the evils which you now suffer may be light in comparison with those to which you are hastening. Kentucky in a voice of thunder would admonish you to beware how you interfere with the obligations of contracts."

The experiences of the Panic of 1837 cannot be said to have led to any real appreciation of the evils of land-speculation or over-buying of land; nor did they long deter western States from again pledging their credit extensively for railroads and other public works. The defects of the banking system, however, made a more definite and lasting impression. Antagonism to unregulated banks of issue was vividly reflected in the constitution-making of the succeeding years, as, for instance, in Iowa and Wisconsin. A member of the Iowa constitutional convention expressed the sentiments of many of his fellows when he declared that "the whole concern of Banks, from big A down were a set of swindling machines, and now was the time for the people of Iowa to give an eternal quietus to the whole concern."

THE PANIC OF 1857 IN THE WEST

Severe and distressing as were the experiences during the period following the Panic of 1837, the lesson was not long effective after recovery took place. Settlers continued to pour into the West, including a large number of foreign immigrants after the European revolutions of 1848. By the time of the Panic of 1857 the Middle West had very largely passed out of the frontier stage. But the western background of that crisis was very much like that of the previous panics. In spite of deep-seated antagonism and efforts of regulation by general legislation, banks increased greatly in numbers and engaged in practices that showed little or no improvement over those in the past. Land speculation once more became prevalent. Railroad-building was in progress everywhere. Then there came a time when the demand for capital exceeded the supply and there was a money stringency. The close of the Crimean War brought curtailment of the European market for American grain. When the telegraph flashed the news of the failure of the Ohio Life Insurance and Trust Company in the mid-summer of 1857, the country again found itself in the throes of a panic, shared by the West together with all other sections except the South, which escaped the worst features because of the strong demand for cotton.

Thus the story of frontier finance has debt as its central theme. In part this chronic condition of debt was based upon the fundamental necessities of a developing region; in part it was due to recklessness of consequences. Periodically there came times of reckoning characterized by painful liquidation—either by the slow process of repayment or by repudiation, default, and failure.

CHAPTER XXIII

STATE-MAKING ON THE MIDDLE WESTERN FRONTIER

WESTERN DEMANDS FOR SELF-GOVERNMENT

"FINDING ourselves on the Frontiers, and being apprehensive that for want of a proper legislature, we might become a shelter for such as endeavored to defraud their creditors; considering also the necessity of recording Deeds, Wills, and doing other public business; we by consent of the people formed a court for the purposes above mentioned, taking (by desire of our constituents) the Virginia laws for our guide, so near as the situation of affairs would admit." Thus did the Watauga settlers describe and explain the organization of their "Association" when, in 1776, they petitioned the legislature of North Carolina to take them under its wing and create for them the county of Washington. They went on to express the hope that "we shall be considered as we deserve, and not as we have (no doubt) been many times represented, as a lawless mob." One year earlier, in his address to the delegates assembled to frame a government for Transylvania, Richard Henderson declared, "we have the right to make laws for the regulation of our conduct without giving offense to Great Britain or any of the American colonies."

Throughout the period of the Revolutionary War, as Professor Turner so clearly revealed, there was constant agitation for the creation of new States west of the mountains, not only on the part of land companies but on the part of the settlers as well. In a memorial to Congress in 1777 the frontiersmen of western Pennsylvania and Virginia asserted that they had "imbibed the highest and most extensive ideas of liberty" and as a consequence they would "with Difficulty Submit to being annexed to or Subjugated by (Terms Synonomous to them) any one of these Provinces, much less the being parti-

339

tioned or parcelled out among them." Three years later, in
another memorial to Congress, the settlers of this same section
called attention to their remoteness from the cis-Alleghany
region, from which fact "proceeds a different Interest & consequently a Coolness." Continuing they enunciated the doctrine
"that the people have a right to emigrate from one state to
another and form new states in different Countries, whenever
they can thereby promote their own Ease & Safety."

More than a half century later, in 1836, the demands of
settlers living west of the Mississippi River were expressed
with equal vigor in a memorial asking for the creation of the
Territory of Wisconsin. "That ten or twelve thousand freemen, Citizens of the United States, living in its territory,
should be unprotected in their lives and property, by its courts
of civil and criminal jurisdiction," declared the petitioners, "is
an anomaly unparalleled in the annals of republican legislation." The request was granted and the Territory of Wisconsin was established. Within less than two years Congress was
the recipient of an urgent petition that the jurisdiction be again
divided and the separate Territory of Iowa be set up for the
people living on the west bank of the Mississippi. The memo-
rialists had no hesitation in asserting that "no Territory of the
United States has been so much neglected by the parent Government, so illy protected in the political and individual rights
of her citizens. . . . It will appear that we have existed as a
portion of an organized Territory for sixteen months, with but
one term of court." They considered themselves entitled to
the granting of their request "by principles of moral right, by
the sacred obligation that rests upon the present government
to protect them in the free enjoyment of their rights, until such
time as they shall be permitted to provide protection for themselves."

These typical selections from frontier political literature
require no analysis to make their meaning clear. They speak
eloquently of the westerner's ardent adherence to the doctrine
of natural rights and the social compact theory, of his desire and
aptitude for self-government, of his insistence upon autonomy, and of his distrust of absentee government. In other
words, whenever a group of settlers found themselves beyond

the pale of any organized government or within the jurisdiction of a government inattentive to their needs, they either proceeded with one accord to draw up rules and regulations of their own, or they sought by every possible means to secure the prompt extension of adequate governmental services to the region where they lived.

Frontiersmen recognized the need of political organization, but they were determined to have a deciding voice in their own government. One important chapter in the story of colonial politics is concerned with the long struggle of the frontier against the tidewater regions to secure legislative representation, lower taxes, agencies of local government, and protection against the Indians. When the delays and disappointments experienced in this contest became unbearable the frontiersmen exhibited their wrath in such demonstrations as Bacon's Rebellion in Virginia, the forays of the "Paxton men" in Pennsylvania, and the Regulation movement in the Carolinas. These episodes, however, were only the more spectacular events in the unceasing conflict which imbued the individualistic, liberty-loving westerners with a deep-seated distrust of governments remote from them and unsympathetic with their interests and needs. This same attitude was shared by later settlers as they crossed the mountains and advanced westward. Autonomous self-government at the earliest possible moment was their goal in every new community. It was, therefore, fortunate that at the time when the federal Constitution was being drafted the expiring Congress of the Confederation laid the foundations of a colonial system which made possible the orderly and certain attainment of this goal.

THE ORDINANCE OF 1787

The Ordinance of 1787, providing government for the territory northwest of the Ohio River, has had a significance in the history of the United States far exceeding the dreams of those members of the Congress of the Confederation whose affirmative votes resulted in its adoption on July 13th of that momentous year. From that day to this it has served as the basic charter of the unique American system of colonial or territorial government. Only the briefest sketch of the movements leading up to the adoption of this important document or of the origins of its various provisions can here be presented.

It must be regarded as fortunate that a report drafted by Thomas Jefferson and embodied in a so-called Ordinance of 1784 never became operative in its original form. This plan contained no provision for territorial preparation for statehood, but divided the Old Northwest into ten potential States, each of which might be admitted into the Union on an equal footing with the original States when it contained a population equal to that of the smallest State already a member of the Union. The vagaries which even a capable man like Jefferson might display were revealed in the method of dividing the territory by artificial straight lines, and by the names suggested for the new States. If his proposal had prevailed we should now be speaking of Chicago, Assenisippia; Cincinnati, Pelisipia; Duluth, Sylvania; and Detroit, Metropotamia; and there would be other States with names as classical in allusion and as difficult in pronunciation. This plan, for various reasons, was abortive, and the question of government for the western country remained in abeyance.

Then, in 1787, as was described in a previous chapter, a group of New England men, known as the Ohio Associates, presented an offer to purchase a large tract of land on the Muskingum River. The members of this organization were desirous of securing land beyond the Ohio, but as a condition to the purchase they insisted that a government be provided for the region where they proposed to settle. Thus the purchase and a plan of government were inextricably bound together. It is clear that neither could have been achieved without the other. Congress was badly in need of revenue for the support of the government, and the prospect of a large sale of public land was very attractive. Individually, also, many members of Congress became interested in the proposal after the agents of the Ohio Associates, to quote from the diary of the Rev. Manasseh Cutler, broached a plan "for a private speculation in which many of the principal characters in America are concerned." No doubt other and more praiseworthy motives also actuated the members of Congress. At any rate, on July

13th "An Ordinance for the Government of the Territory of
the United States, north-west of the river Ohio" was adopted.
Shortly afterward a law was passed authorizing the sale of
1,500,000 acres of land to the Ohio Associates.

The Ordinance of 1787 contained a bill of rights, a list of
obligations and prohibitions, a plan for dividing the Territory
into smaller units as population increased and advanced westward, and a system of government, although these features
were not arranged in the order indicated. The bill of rights
included the time-honored guarantees so dear to the hearts
of English-speaking people, such as religious freedom, habeas
corpus, trial by jury, right of bail, moderate fines and punish-
ments, due process of law, and the obligation of contracts. In
addition, a section dealing with the transfer and descent of
property struck at the rules of primogeniture and entail which
Thomas Jefferson had fought in Virginia. Property of intes-
tates was to be divided equally between the children, and the
widow was to have one-third of the property during her life.
Finally, the Ordinance contained another statement that was
reflective of the New Englanders' belief in, and prophetic of
the westerners' insistence upon, public education. "Religion,
morality and knowledge, being necessary to good government
and the happiness of mankind," ran the classic words, "schools
and the means of education shall forever be encouraged."

The obligations and prohibitions imposed by the Ordinance
were equally interesting and important. With fine optimism it
asserted that good faith should be observed in all dealings with
the Indians, that their lands and property should never be
taken without their consent, and that they should never be
invaded or disturbed, "unless in just and lawful wars authorized by Congress." The States to be formed out of the Territory were to remain forever in the Union. The people of the
Territory were to pay their share of the national debts and
expenses. The legislatures of the future States were never to
interfere with the disposal of the public lands by Congress.
No tax was to be imposed on the property of the United States,
nor were non-residents to be taxed more heavily than residents.
The waterways leading to the Mississippi and the St. Lawrence
were to remain free. Of far-reaching significance was the

declaration that "There shall be neither slavery nor involuntary servitude in the said territory, otherwise than in punishment of crimes whereof the party shall have been duly convicted." Such a clause had been included in Jefferson's original report of 1784 and it was demanded by the Ohio Associates. Interestingly enough, this prohibition was included with the full acquiescence of the southern members of the Congress which adopted the Ordinance.

The section which dealt with the division of the Territory made provision for three or five States as circumstances might dictate. If only three States were to be created, then the boundaries between them were to be the lines which now separate Indiana from Ohio and Illinois from Indiana, except that these lines were to extend northward to the Canadian boundary. If five States should become desirable the two additional jurisdictions should be formed out of the northern portion of the Territory north of a line running east and west through the southern extremity of Lake Michigan. With some minor, though important, variations the present States of Ohio, Indiana, Illinois, Michigan, and Wisconsin correspond closely with the five divisions outlined in the Ordinance.

Important as were many of the provisions of the Ordinance of 1787 already described, the greatest significance of the document lies in the system of government aiming at, and culminating in, statehood which it laid down. With some modifications, this portion of the Ordinance was followed in all later acts establishing territorial governments in the United States. Moreover, the progressive system of government here provided was unique in the history of colonial government, in that it led by definite steps to statehood on an equal basis with the older States and with full participation in the government of the nation. Fortunately, whether by accident or design, it was calculated to meet the demands for autonomy on the part of frontiersmen. No matter how much they might chafe under Congressional delays or the vexations of a territorial status, they knew that ultimately they would attain their desires.

Three stages of government were prescribed, each successive stage giving the people greater participation than the one which preceded it. The first stage was simple, autocratic, and closely under federal control. A governor, a secretary, and three judges were to be appointed by Congress, (although the appointive power was soon transferred to the President, with the consent of the Senate, when the Ordinance was re-adopted by Congress after the Constitution went into operation). The governor and judges constituted the legislative body, with power to adopt such laws of the original States as appeared suited to territorial needs. When the adult, male population of the Territory numbered five thousand, the people were given the right to an elective legislature. This body was empowered to choose a Delegate to Congress, who might sit in the lower house of Congress and participate in the debates, but without the right to vote. This constituted the second stage of government. Then, when any of the divisions outlined in the Ordinance contained sixty thousand free inhabitants, the people were authorized to draw up a constitution and be admitted into the Union "on an equal footing with the original states in all respects whatsoever."

These, in brief, were the provisions of the Ordinance of 1787. In October of that year the Congress of the Confederation chose as Governor of the Northwest Territory the man who had been its presiding officer when the Ordinance was passed, Arthur St. Clair. In July of the following year he, together with the secretary and the judges, arrived in Marietta and the long history of territorial government in the West was begun. Before tracing the process by which the region north of the Ohio River was carved into self-governing commonwealths, however, it is necessary to turn our attention to events and movements to the southward of that stream, where the first States of the American Union west of the Alleghanies came into being.

THE ADMISSION OF KENTUCKY AND TENNESSEE

In earlier chapters we have followed the progress of events in Kentucky preceding, during, and immediately after the Revolution: the beginning of settlement, the short-lived Transylvania experiment, the hazardous times during the war, the great influx of settlers after the close of hostilities, and the disturbed state of the public mind during the period when the free navigation of the Mississippi River was abrogated by Spain. There is no doubt that some of the settlers were cordial to the idea of establishing an independent government in Kentucky, and even to the arranging of some form of accommodation with the Spanish in New Orleans. The general sentiment, however, seems at most times to have been inclined toward negotiations with Virginia and with Congress, looking toward statehood within the Union.

Late in the year 1784 a convention was held at Danville, at which the delegates passed resolutions favoring separation from Virginia. Two more conventions in the following year voiced the same request, and the General Assembly of Virginia yielded to the demand. But Virginia made her relinquishment conditional upon the admission of Kentucky by Congress before June 1, 1787. This condition introduced the prospect of delay and uncertainty, while the Kentucky settlers wanted immediate statehood. Within the next four years Virginia made three more offers to dissolve the ties binding Kentucky to that State, but each time circumstances prevented the Kentuckians from taking advantage of the offer. By this time, however, the Constitution of the United States had gone into operation, and States might now be admitted into the Union by simple act of Congress. In February, 1791, such an act was passed by Congress admitting Kentucky as a State on June 1, 1792.

Delegates assembled at Danville in April, 1791, for the tenth convention in the long series of gatherings connected with Kentucky's movement toward statehood. A constitution was drafted, which was patterned largely after that of Virginia, although it reflected the spirit of frontier democracy by providing for universal white manhood suffrage. By the first of June, 1792, Kentucky, with a population of perhaps one hundred thousand, had a state government installed and senators and representatives chosen and ready to give the West its first full voice in the affairs of the nation.

Meanwhile, in the valleys of the Tennessee and the Cumberland to the southward events were running a checkered course. The frontiersmen in this region were of the type of those who had migrated to the Watauga settlement after the

Battle of the Alamance, or they came from Virginia and had little love for the authorities of North Carolina within whose jurisdiction they were now living. Therefore it was apparently with some satisfaction over the prospect of ridding itself of a troublesome problem that the legislature of North Carolina, in April, 1784, ceded its western land to the federal government. Before the year ended the act of cession was repealed, in the hope of securing better terms from Congress at a later time. Before this time arrived, however, the settlers in the Tennessee region, realizing that they could hope for little or no help from North Carolina in the way of either civil government or military protection, had taken matters into their own hands.

The frontiersmen assembled at Jonesborough to consider their situation. The maintenance of a connection with the older counties of North Carolina was felt to be hostile to the interests of the western settlements. "They are the most numerous," it was declared, "and consequently will always be able to make us subservient to them; that our interest must be generally neglected, and sometimes sacrificed, to promote theirs, as was instanced in a late taxation act." Therefore, the convention drew up a constitution and named their organization the State of Franklin, hoping thereby to gain the sympathy and sponsorship of the aged Benjamin Franklin—a hope in which they were disappointed. At its first meeting in March, 1785, the legislature chose as governor John Sevier, who was by general consent recognized as the outstanding leader in the State of Franklin.

The new commonwealth maintained a turbulent and precarious existence for more than four years. Intrigues with the Spanish, troubles with the Indians, overtures to the Kentucky settlers, controversies with North Carolina, and ineffectual efforts to obtain recognition from Congress were among the episodes which marked its career. But it was internal dissension which brought an end to the State of Franklin. A political rival to Sevier arose in the person of John Tipton, who sought and obtained aid from North Carolina. For a time two sets of officials, the one representing North Carolina and the other the State of Franklin, endeavored to collect taxes and govern the harassed settlers. John Sevier was outlawed, but in 1789 he took oath of allegiance to North Carolina, was pardoned, and elected to the senate of the parent State. The State of Franklin was now only a name to be remembered, along with that of Transylvania, as that of an unsuccessful attempt to establish a self-created commonwealth in the West.

In 1789 North Carolina repeated its cession of its western lands and Congress accepted. Recognizing the claims of the settlers to some form of government, in 1790 Congress established the "Territory of the United States south of the river Ohio." The new territory, included the Tennessee region, the narrow strip of country just to the south which had been ceded by South Carolina, and in theory at least the land below the Yazoo line, still in the actual possession of Spain. The law specified that the inhabitants should enjoy "all the privileges, benefits and advantages" guaranteed in the Ordinance of 1787 and that the government should be similar, with the significant exception that the prohibition of slavery was omitted. The creation of the Southwest Territory satisfied the settlers temporarily and helped to allay the tendencies toward Spanish intrigue, especially since a number of the frontier leaders were appointed to important offices in the new government. Six years later, Tennessee drew up a constitution and was admitted into the Union on June 1, 1796, with John Sevier as governor, William Blount as one of the United States senators, and Andrew Jackson as representative.

OHIO: THE FIRST STATE IN THE OLD NORTHWEST

Neither of these first two western States can rightly be said to have been a product of the peculiar American process of state-making contemplated by the Ordinance of 1787 and followed by Congress. Kentucky had never been a Territory. Although Tennessee had passed through the territorial status, its people drew up a constitution without asking anyone's permission and Congress felt constrained to pass an act of admission without serious demur. Thereafter, however, it became the practice, followed in a majority of cases to admit no State into the Union until after Congress had passed an "enabling act" authorizing its people to draw up a constitution. This process was begun in the Old Northwest.

Although space will not permit, it would be instructive to narrate the history of the Northwest Territory during the period of its existence from 1787 to 1803. Many of the tendencies and episodes which characterized later territorial history were foreshadowed during this period. Arthur St. Clair was an able, honest, well-intentioned man, a veteran of the Revolutionary War. Yet his selection as governor of a western Territory was not a happy one. He was an autocrat and a Federalist in a region where democracy was in the air and where a constantly increasing number of the people were Jeffersonian Republicans. His defeat by the Indians in 1791 greatly weakened his prestige among the hardy frontiersmen whose heroes were successful Indian-fighters. The plan of government, also, was experimental and without precedent, so that numerous problems arose which taxed the ability of the officials to the limit and gave occasion for complaints upon the part of those who were not pleased with the solutions.

In 1798 the Northwest Territory was sufficiently populous to enter the second stage of government. A territorial legislature was elected. In the following year it assembled for its first session—and chose William Henry Harrison as Delegate to Congress. The settlers now had an agency through which to express their antipathies toward Governor St. Clair. The next few years were filled with bitter controversies over questions both trivial and serious, such as the provision of a seal for the Territory, the establishment of counties, the location of the seat of government, and the very liberal use of the veto power by the governor.

The advance to the second stage of government was only the prelude to a movement toward statehood, which was vigorously opposed by Governor St. Clair. Various motives contributed to the movement. Political partisanship was becoming a powerful force and the Jeffersonians were desirous of adding to their strength in Congress by the admission of another western State. Personal ambition to attain offices in the proposed government was clearly not lacking. Permeating the entire frontier society was the passionate desire for autonomy, the wish to escape from the leading strings of Congress and the control of officials in whose selection the people had no voice. It may be said, in passing, that these motives are discernible in most of the later movements which resulted in adding State after State to the Union.

As a preliminary to statehood for the more populous eastern section of the Territory, and in order to provide a government more closely identified with the needs of the scattered settlements in the western part, on May 7, 1800, Congress passed an act dividing the Northwest Territory. The region west of a line running roughly north from the Ohio opposite the mouth of the Kentucky became the Territory of Indiana. Then on April 30, 1802, Congress adopted an enabling act authorizing the people of Ohio to frame a constitution, at the same time restoring the western boundary to the line running through the mouth of the Great Miami River; while the northern boundary was to be an extension of the line running through the southern tip of Lake Michigan—both of which had been laid down in the Ordinance of 1787. The people proceeded at once to form a convention to draft a constitution. The resulting frame of government reflected the long opposition to Arthur St. Clair by depriving the governor of the veto and appointive powers. The justices of the supreme court were to be chosen for a term of years by a joint ballot of the two houses of the legislature. The suffrage was given to all male tax-payers over twenty-one years of age. On February 19, 1803, Ohio become a State. It need only be noted here that the Ohio constitution contained a provision regarding the northern boundary which was destined to give rise to a controversy with Michigan later.

THE ADMISSION OF INDIANA AND ILLINOIS

Indiana Territory, with William Henry Harrison as its governor, was allowed to enter upon the second stage of territorial government, whenever its inhabitants so desired, on the ground that they had already gained the requisite political experience as citizens of the Northwest Territory. In 1805 the region east of a line through the middle of Lake Michigan was cut off to form Michigan Territory. Four years later, in 1809, the area of Indiana was still further curtailed, after an exciting contest, by the creation of Illinois Territory west of a line running up the Wabash River to Vincennes and thence north to the Canadian border. The population of Indiana increased rapidly, especially after the close of the War of 1812, and a statehood movement developed as soon as the required sixty thousand had been reached. In the year 1816 Congress passed an enabling act, a constitution was adopted and on December 11th Indiana was admitted into the Union. Recognizing the justice of the complaint that a northern boundary through the southern tip of Lake Michigan, as prescribed by the Ordinance of 1787, would leave the new State with no frontage on the lake, Congress drew the line ten miles further north.

Illinois waited only nine years for statehood after becoming a Territory in 1809. Ninian Edwards of Kentucky served successfully as governor throughout the entire period. Factional controversies, Indian troubles preceding and during the War of 1812, and popular discontent because of federal regulations or inaction were among the problems which claimed his attention. In the spring of 1818 Congress passed an enabling act for Illinois, although the Territory was far short of having sixty thousand inhabitants. Despite the prohibition embodied in the Ordinance of 1787, the question of slavery was a lively topic of debate in the constitutional convention of that year; and the constitution contained a compromise on this subject, thus giving countenance to the fact that a number of slaves were actually being held in the Territory. Along the Ohio River slavery sentiment was strong, and it was not until 1824 that a persistent effort to secure a pro-slavery amendment to the Illinois constitution was decisively defeated.

Illinois became a State on December 3, 1818. The northern boundary marked an even greater departure than that of Indiana from the terms of the Ordinance of 1787. In the enabling act Congress permitted Illinois to extend northward about sixty miles along the western shore of Lake Michigan. The portion of the Illinois Territory north of this line was attached to the Territory of Michigan.

Nineteen years now elapsed before another State came into

existence in the Old Northwest. Long before the close of this period two new commonwealths had been created in the Old Southwest and the process of state-making had been begun west of the Mississippi. Therefore, the movements resulting in these achievements will next claim our attention.

CHAPTER XXIV

THE FURTHER SPREAD OF STATEHOOD

THE FIRST STATE IN THE LOUISIANA PURCHASE

SHORTLY after Ohio became a State and while Indiana and Illinois were advancing toward the same goal, the American process of state-making was put into operation west of the Mississippi River. Article three of the Louisiana Purchase Treaty contained the covenant that "The inhabitants of the ceded territory shall be incorporated in the Union of the United States, and admitted as soon as possible, according to the principles of the Federal constitution, to the enjoyment of all the rights, advantages and immunities of citizens of the United States."

Accordingly, the official transfer of the new purchase to the jurisdiction of the United States had scarcely been consummated at New Orleans on December 20, 1803, and at St. Louis on March 10, 1804, when on March 26th of the latter year Congress divided the acquired region by a line running west from the Mississippi on the thirty-third parallel. South of this line the Territory of Orleans was set up, under the governship of William C. C. Claiborne. The enormous area north of the line became known as the District of Louisiana and was attached for governmental purposes to the Territory of Indiana, although this arrangement was of short duration. The attempt to govern the people of St. Louis and other settlements in the present region of Missouri from Vincennes on the Wabash was unsatisfactory to everyone concerned. In 1805, therefore, what had been merely a district was constituted the Territory of Louisiana. Despite all his previous career in intrigue James Wilkinson seems to have stood high in the opinion of President Jefferson and he was appointed governor of the new Territory. After a stormy incumbency of less than two years in that office he was replaced by Meriwether Lewis, who had just returned from his great western exploration and was thus given recognition for his services.

Meanwhile, in the Territory of Orleans, Governor Claiborne was finding his hands more than full in governing a population composed of French, Spanish creoles, and a constantly increasing number of Americans. The Territory probably contained fifty thousand white inhabitants when it was created. Sentiment in favor of statehood soon developed, and early in 1811 Congress passed an enabling act. In the debates on this measure and in those preceding the final act of admission the next year, the Federalists in Congress ranged themselves in opposition, just as they had done in the effort to prevent the ratification of the Louisiana Purchase Treaty.

Not only party rancor, but sectional fear, and distrust of western democracy, were expressed in the tirades of New England Federalists against the admission of Louisiana. Representative Josiah Quincy was their most eloquent spokesman. Suppose, he suggested, it had been foreseen in the federal constitutional convention that "the whole population of a world beyond the Mississippi was to be brought into this and the other branch of the legislature, to form our laws, control our rights, and decide our destiny. Sir, can it be pretended that the patriots of that day would for one moment have listened to it?" He had heard of at least six new States to be created beyond the Mississippi, and it had been predicted that the mouth of the Ohio would ultimately be far east of the center of the nation. "You have no authority," he exploded, "to throw the rights and property of this people into a 'hotch-pot' with the wild men on the Missouri, or with the mixed, though more respectable, race of Anglo-Hispano-Gallo-Americans who bask on the sands, in the mouth of the Mississippi. . . . Do you suppose the people of the northern and Atlantic states will, or ought to, look on with patience and see representatives and senators from the Red river and Missouri, pouring themselves upon this and the other floor, managing the concerns of a seaboard fifteen hundred miles, at least, from their residence?"

All such fulminations were wasted. Louisiana was admitted into the Union on April 30, 1812. Its boundaries were identical with those of the Territory of Orleans, except that they extended eastward to the Pearl River. Thus Louisiana included the western portion of West Florida which had recently been seized by American frontiersmen and officially declared to belong to the United States, despite the protests of the Spanish. In order to avoid a duplication of names the Territory of Louisiana was renamed the Territory of Missouri, and the people were permitted to enjoy the second grade of government and elect a legislature. William Clark, the companion of Meriwether Lewis on the expedition to the mouth of the Columbia, was appointed governor, and served with conspicuous success throughout the entire period of the Territory's existence.

MISSISSIPPI AND ALABAMA

The beginning of the movements leading up to statehood for Mississippi and Alabama in 1817 and 1819 must be sought in a period antedating that of the events which have just been narrated. When Tennessee was admitted in 1796 the Southwest Territory passed out of existence for all practical purposes. Georgia had not ceded her western lands lying just to the south of Tennessee. Spain still kept possession of the strip between the thirty-first parallel and the line passing through the mouth of the Yazoo River, in spite of the terms of Pinckney's Treaty of 1795. In 1798, however, the Spanish could find no further excuse for delay and they surrendered this region. Congress immediately constituted it the Territory of Mississippi. When, in 1802, Georgia belatedly ceded her western lands to the federal government the jurisdiction of the new Territory was extended northward to the Tennessee line. In 1812 frontage on the Gulf was afforded by the addition of the country between the Pearl and Perdido rivers.

Mississippi Territory was somewhat off the earliest routes of travel westward and as a consequence its growth in population was slow. As we have seen, this region was the center of violent Indian disturbances just before and during the War of 1812, and it was here that Andrew Jackson gained most of his fame as an Indian fighter. By the close of the war new roads had opened the way to Mississippi and its rich, black soil attracted an ever increasing number of settlers and plantation-seekers. In 1817 the Territory was divided by a line running south to the Gulf of Mexico from the Tennessee River at the mouth of Bear Creek. The same year witnessed the admission of the western division into the Union on December 10th as the State of Mississippi. It is interesting to note that here for the first time in western constitution-making was the instrument of government submitted to the voters of the State for ratification. Hitherto the constitutions had been put into force by promulgation. Thereafter the precedent set by Mississippi was followed in most of the new western States.

The eastern division of the Territory of Mississippi became the Territory of Alabama in 1817, but its probationary period was of brief duration. The westward movement was in full swing. Population increased rapidly, in 1819 Congress passed an enabling act, and on December 14th of that year Alabama became a State.

THE STRUGGLE OVER THE ADMISSION OF MISSOURI

Scarcely had Alabama been admitted when the nation was stirred to its depths by a controversy connected with another statehood proposal. The population of Missouri Territory did not grow appreciably until the Great Migration after the War of 1812 got under way. Then the lower Missouri Valley began to receive a steady stream of settlers, a large proportion of whom were from the South. Although the inhabitants did not yet number sixty thousand, as early as 1817 Congress was asked to permit the people of Missouri to form a constitution; and in 1818 the legislature of the Territory repeated this request. A bill for an enabling act was accordingly introduced and came up for discussion in February, 1819. Shortly afterward on March 2, 1819, Missouri was divided and the Territory of Arkansas was created. The new Territory extended from the Louisiana boundary northward to the parallel 36 degrees 30 minutes, except that the parallel 36 degrees became the dividing line in the New Madrid region so that these settlements would be included in Missouri. Westwardly the Arkansas Territory extended to the one hundredth meridian, which in that latitude was the western boundary of the United States as determined by the recent treaty with Spain.

The bill for the Missouri enabling act failed to pass in that session of Congress. Representative James Tallmadge of New York introduced an amendment virtually making slavery impossible in the proposed State, and the House adopted the amendment. The Senate, however, refused to accede, and the two houses became deadlocked on the issue. During the ensuing two years the whole nation was thrown into turmoil by the first great sectional contest between the North and the South.

The main facts concerning the Missouri Compromise are so well known to every student of American history that they need not be repeated here. A brief statement will serve to show how the demands of the advancing frontier precipitated a sectional struggle on the slavery question. Southern leaders were by this time convinced that slavery was necessary to their economic and social welfare. Therefore, it was essential that they should maintain equality with the free States in Congress. The prospect of parity in the lower house was becoming poorer and poorer, since the free States were increasing in population much more rapidly than those favorable to slavery. In the Senate, however, equality would prevail as long as each section contained an equal number of States. Such a situation existed after the admission of Louisiana, and the balance had not been upset by the creation of the next four commonwealths. Indiana, a free State, admitted in 1816, was matched by Mississippi, a slave State admitted in 1817; and Illinois in 1818 by Alabama in 1819.

Now, however, the outlook was far from reassuring to southerners, as they surveyed the possibilities for additional States in the West. The treaty of February, 1819, with Spain, relinquishing the claims of the United States to Texas in return for the Floridas, seemed to close the door to the creation of new slave States in that direction. The prevailing opinion credited the Great Plains region with being inhospitable to white settlements—an opinion that was soon to be confirmed by the report of Stephen H. Long after an extensive exploration. As a consequence, Missouri, Arkansas, and Florida were the only possible States in sight which could be expected to favor slavery. On the other hand, Maine was already seeking admission, two more free States could be anticipated in the Old Northwest, and there was the region along the west bank of the Mississippi north of the proposed State of Missouri—a region clearly unsuited to slavery—out of which additional States might be carved.

It is not surprising, therefore, that southerners were thoroughly aroused to the vital necessity of securing the admission of Missouri with slavery in order to maintain the balance between the sections in the United States Senate. In this they were successful, but whether or not it was a real victory for the South is still a mooted point. Maine became a State in March, 1820; and after further delay Missouri was admitted on August 10, 1821, as a slave State, but with the express provision that in all the remaining portion of the Louisiana Purchase north of 36 degrees and 30 minutes "slavery and involuntary servitude, otherwise than in punishment of crime . . . shall be and is hereby forever prohibited."

Before leaving this subject it should be noted that, while slavery was the great moral question over which the people of the nation became aroused during the Missouri struggle, there were other issues involved. One was the question of the right of Congress to impose restrictions on an incoming State or dictate the contents of its constitution. Certain restrictions or obligations had been previously laid down by Congress in enabling acts, and this practice was frequently followed in later years. As a matter of fact the question was a rather futile one, since within limits there is nothing in the federal Constitution to prevent a State from amending its instrument of government after once having been admitted into the Union. The other issue was the right of Congress to prohibit slavery in the Territories. This point seemed to be settled by the provision forbidding slavery north of 36 degrees 30 minutes. How the frontier advance upset this decision thirty years later will appear in a subsequent chapter.

MICHIGAN AND ARKANSAS

Fifteen years now passed before another State was ready to enter the Union; and it was fortunate that at that time two Territories were seeking statehood, one as a free State and the other with slavery.

Michigan Territory, established in 1805, was enlarged and extended to the Mississippi River after the admission of Illinois in 1818. The first governor of the Territory was the ill-starred William Hull. After the War of 1812 he was succeeded by Lewis Cass, who served with great success until 1831. The population of the Territory in its early years was made up chiefly of descendants of the original French colonists, with an admixture of American fur traders. Detroit, on the eastern border, was the principal settlement, while the remaining inhabitants lived in small groups along the shores of the lakes—especially at the heads of Lake Michigan and Lake Superior, on Green Bay, and at Prairie du Chien on the Mississippi. The American settlement of the region was long delayed. The established routes of the westward movement were further south. Moreover, there was a general belief that the interior of Michigan was an uninhabitable swamp. But the completion of the Erie Canal in 1825 wrought a great change. As has already been seen, settlers now began to pour into Michigan in such numbers that the census of 1830 gave the Territory a population of about thirty-two thousand. In 1834 the jurisdiction of Michigan Territory was extended over the vast region west of the Mississippi, north of Missouri and reaching westward to the Missouri and White Earth Rivers.

Agitation for statehood for Michigan began in 1832. A vote taken that year showed an overwhelming majority in favor of the proposition. The interest of the people was temporarily distracted, however, by the Black Hawk War and by a severe epidemic of cholera which raged through the region. A census taken in 1834 revealed a population of more than eighty-seven thousand. Congress was thereupon asked to pass an enabling act. Without waiting for this action, the people of the portion of the Territory east of Lake Michigan elected delegates to a convention. This body met in May, 1835, and drafted a constitution which was ratified by the voters in October and under which state officials were elected. This was all done on the assumption that a Territory was entitled to form a state government when it had reached a population of sixty thousand, in accordance with the terms of the Ordinance of 1787. This document, together with the Congressional act establishing the Territory of Michigan, was relied upon by the constitution-makers when they fixed the southern boundary of the proposed State along the line running through the southern extremity of Lake Michigan. This action, however, precipitated a boundary dispute with Ohio, led to a complicated situation in Michigan itself, and delayed admission for fifteen months.

As we have seen, the Ohio enabling act set the line through the tip of Lake Michigan as the northern boundary of that State from the northwest corner to Lake Erie; but the constitution of Ohio contained a provision looking to a possible readjustment. There was no exact knowledge as to where this line would strike Lake Erie and there was fear that it might pass entirely to the south of it. To guard against such a contingency the Ohio constitution stipulated that in case this fear should prove to be well founded the northern boundary should, with the consent of Congress, run along a line from the southern extreme of Lake Michigan to the northern cape at the mouth of the Maumee River on Lake Erie—thus including the land where Toledo now stands. With this constitution Congress admitted Ohio without any further word about the boundary. The people of Ohio claimed that silence gave consent to the provision in their constitution, although they sought several times in subsequent years to secure confirmative action by Congress.

The statehood movement in Michigan caused the Ohio authorities to take action. Governor Robert Lucas secured from the legislature in 1835 an act extending the jurisdiction of Ohio into the disputed tract and providing for the election of local officials. The youthful Governor Stevens T. Mason and the legislature of Michigan were equally belligerent in making it a criminal offense for anyone to accept office in the area except under Michigan auspices. Soon the so-called, though fortunately bloodless, "Toledo War" was in progress.

The militia of each jurisdiction was called out, and Governor Lucas backed by about six hundred men confronted Governor Mason with about one thousand.

The situation was an embarrassing one for President Jackson. In response to his request, the Attorney General expressed the opinion that until Congress had given its consent, the Michigan contention regarding the boundary should be upheld. Yet the presidential election of 1836 was approaching and the large electoral vote of Ohio was not to be lightly placed in jeopardy. "Never in the course of my life," declared John Quincy Adams who warmly advocated the Michigan claim, "have I known a controversy of which all the right was so clear on one side, and all the power so overwhelmingly on the other; never a case where the temptation was so intense to take the strongest side, and the duty of taking the weakest was so thankless."

Commissioners were sent from Washington to make peace between the contending jurisdictions. In June, 1836, Congress passed an act authorizing the President to admit Michigan by proclamation whenever the people through a convention accepted the boundary desired by Ohio. To compensate Michigan for yielding the disputed tract the new State was given the peninsula between Lake Michigan and Lake Superior. A bill had already been enacted into law erecting the new Territory of Wisconsin out of the western part of what had previously been Michigan. In September a convention assembled at Ann Arbor and emphatically rejected the proposal made by Congress.

While the boundary dispute was raging the governmental situation in Michigan was anomalous. A full set of State officers, headed by Governor Stevens T. Mason, had been elected under the constitution adopted in 1835, and they were performing most of the duties of their positions. This government, however, was without legal status since it had not been recognized by Congress. President Jackson indicated that he still regarded Michigan as a Territory by appointing John S. Horner as acting governor. When Horner arrived in Detroit he was treated with such lack of respect that he soon betook himself to the region west of Lake Michigan. Nevertheless, the long controversy was now nearing a close. Despite their wrath because of the terms of admission which they regarded as flagrantly unfair to them, the leaders in Michigan realized that their case was hopeless. Congress held the whip hand. The addition of the northern peninsula had somewhat tempered the general resentment. Besides, the new State government was Democratic and political pressure was constantly being exerted. Accordingly, in December, 1836, a second convention, illegally constituted, met at Ann Arbor and accepted the boundary which Congress had prescribed and Ohio demanded. When President Jackson was notified, instead of issuing the proclamation authorized by Congress, he referred the matter back to that body. Here, after a protracted debate, Michigan was formally admitted as a State on January 26, 1837.

Before this date a new southern State had been added to the Union. It was for this reason that no sectional opposition had been raised to statehood for Michigan. Arkansas was without any considerable number of inhabitants when it became a Territory in 1819. Settlement progressed slowly, since the region was not easily accessible. Settlers moving down the Ohio and the Mississippi long found desirable locations before reaching Arkansas, and the same thing was true in some degree of those advancing up the Mississippi. In 1828 the western boundary of the Territory, previously at the one hundredth meridian, was fixed at the present line. The western portion became a part of what was expected to be the permanent Indian country set up in connection with the removal policy described in a previous chapter. The statehood movement in Arkansas was contemporaneous with that in Michigan, but its goal was achieved without difficulty. A constitution was drafted in the spring of 1836 and put into effect by promulgation. On June 15th of that year Congress admitted Arkansas as a State.

FLORIDA AND IOWA

Less than a decade after the admission of Arkansas and Michigan another pair of would-be States were knocking at the doors of Congress—Florida and Iowa. Once again the southern State succeeded in gaining admittance without dis-

turbance or opposition. To be sure, the people of Florida desired statehood many years before their wish was granted. In
1838 they adopted a constitution and sought admission, but
for seven years Congress turned a deaf ear to the request
because there was no northern State ready to be admitted.
Finally, a law of March 3, 1845, made Florida a State. The
same law provided for the admission of Iowa, but imposed
boundaries which the people refused to accept. Nearly two
years passed before Iowa entered the Union.

The Iowa region was included in the various territorial
jurisdictions of the Louisiana Purchase down to 1821. When
Missouri was admitted the country to the northward was left
without any territorial government—a fact that was of no
significance for more than a decade, since there were almost
no white inhabitants. In 1833, however, settlers began to
flock to the fifty-mile strip along the west bank of the Mississippi known as the Black Hawk Purchase. Soon the need for
courts and other agencies of local government became apparent.
In 1834 the jurisdiction of the Territory of Michigan was extended over the region. Two years later it became a part of
the newly created Territory of Wisconsin. Then on June 12,
1838, an act of Congress established the Territory of Iowa.
The law was not passed until after there had been considerable
debate, occasioned by the significance of the move to begin
the process of carving Territories, with statehood in the offing,
in the extensive area north of Missiouri. Several eastern and
southern members of Congress spoke rather vehemently in
opposition to the measure. Some of them bitterly assailed the
settlers of Iowa for having entered and held choice lands in
direct violation of law. It will be remembered that it was in
Iowa that the claim associations had their greatest vogue.

The first years of the new Territory were enlivened by
petty but virulent bickerings between Governor Robert Lucas
and William B. Conway, the territorial secretary, and quarrels
between the governor and the legislative assembly. Even
greater excitement was engendered by a boundary dispute with
Missouri. This story cannot be related here; but it was an
interesting coincidence that the man who had been chief executive of Ohio during the boundary controversy with Michigan

was now the leader of the Territory of Iowa in its contest with Missouri. In both instances the contention which he supported was the winning one. For a time feeling ran high. Rival officials sought to collect taxes in the disputed tract, mails were stopped, property was seized, armed men gathered on either side of the border, and lead was being melted into bullets by the farmers. The question was not settled until 1848, after Iowa had become a State, when the Supreme Court of the United States handed down a decision supporting the Iowa claim.

Sentiment in favor of statehood began to be expressed early. The proposition was twice submitted to a vote of the people, once in 1840 and again in 1842, and each time the vote was in the negative. The certainty of increased taxation was the deciding factor. Most of the settlers had come from States where, during the years following the Panic of 1837, the burden of taxation seemed unbearable. As long as they remained a Territory the expenses of their general government were paid out of the federal treasury. In 1844 the question was again submitted, and by this time the popular attitude had changed so that a favorable vote was returned. Accordingly in August a convention assembled to draft a constitution. Under the boundaries set forth in this constitution the proposed State would have extended northward to the St. Peters (Minnesota) River, while a small region in what is now the northwestern corner would have been omitted.

This constitution was submitted to Congress. Under it, and before the people of Iowa had ratified it, admission to statehood was granted by Congress in the act of March 3, 1845, which extended the same privilege to Florida. But there was this difference: the boundaries proposed in the Iowa constitution were rejected. In their place Congress substituted boundaries which would have extended the State somewhat farther north than at present, but would have cut it off by a considerable distance from the Missouri River on the west. The reason seems to have been the determination of northern members of Congress to prevent, if possible, the admission of northern States with too generous boundaries, in order to leave room for a greater number of additional States, with a correspondingly greater representation of the North in Congress. This determination was strengthened, before the passage of the bill, by the joint resolution of March 1, 1845, providing for the annexation of Texas, out of which it was confidently anticipated that five slave States would ultimately be carved.

The act of March 3, 1845, did not result in the admission of Iowa. When the constitution with the boundaries substituted by Congress was twice submitted to the people of Iowa they rejected it both times. In May, 1846, a new constitutional convention assembled and drafted a new instrument of government, modelled in general upon the rejected constitution of 1844. The northern boundary, however, was placed along the parallel 43 degrees and 30 minutes. Since this compromise line had already been suggested by the committee on territories in the federal House of Representatives, all obstacles to admission were now removed. Accordingly Iowa became a State on December 28, 1846.

The Iowa constitution reflected the deep-seated antagonism to banks of issue which had been aroused in the West during the long period of depression following the Panic of 1837. The ninth article declared that "no corporate body shall hereafter be created, renewed, or extended, with the privilege of making, issuing, or putting in circulation any bill, check, ticket, certificate, promissory note, or other paper, or the paper of any bank, to circulate as money. The General Assembly of this State shall prohibit, by law, any person or persons, association, company or corporation, from exercising the privileges of banking, or creating paper to circulate as money."

THE ADMISSION OF WISCONSIN

One more State remained to be created in the Old Northwest. The Territory of Wisconsin as established in 1836 embraced all the country north of Illinois and Missouri and between Lake Michigan and the Missouri and White Earth rivers. Two years later the portion west of the Mississippi River was given a separate status as the Territory of Iowa. Even during the incumbency of the first territorial governor, Henry Dodge, agitation for statehood began in Wisconsin. As in Iowa the movement failed to gain wide support and for the same reason—the heavier taxation which statehood would entail. When the question was submitted to the people early in 1846, however, they voted overwhelmingly in favor of drawing up a constitution and applying for admission into the Union. In the meantime Congress had passed an enabling act, in order that Wisconsin might be paired with Texas which had just been admitted.

A Wisconsin convention drafted a constitution in 1846, but it was two years before statehood was achieved. Disappointment was caused by the boundaries prescribed by Congress, cutting the proposed State off from the Mississippi above the St. Croix River, but this was by no means the main cause of the delay. Conflicting political and economic viewpoints among the different areas of settlement within the Territory were the principal complicating factors. The southwestern portion was settled first and its people were ardent Jacksonian Democrats, many of whom had come from the southern States. The eastern border along Lake Michigan was settled largely by people from the North Atlantic States, with a constantly increasing number of recent immigrants from foreign lands. The southeastern corner contained a population very much like that of northern Illinois and Indiana, somewhat more conservative in their democracy than the people of the southwestern portion.

The radical Democrats had control of the convention of 1846 and they succeeded in embodying in the constitution a number of ideas and principles that were unacceptable to the people of the eastern and southeastern sections. One of these was the absolute prohibition of banks of issue and the circulation of any bank notes of denominations less than twenty dollars. Another was the requirement of residence for one year as a qualification for the franchise. There were other provisions that met with objections as being too radical. When the constitution came to a vote in the spring of 1847 it was rejected. Late in the same year another convention assembled and drafted a new constitution which removed some of the main objections to the first document. Especially was this true of the clause dealing with banking. The legislature was author-

ized to enact a general banking law if the question of chartering banks had first been referred to the people and approved
by them.   The law itself must likewise pass the gamut of a
referendum.   This constitution was ratified by a large vote,
and Wisconsin became a State in accordance with an act of
Congress dated May 29, 1848.

THE ADMISSION OF MINNESOTA

The story of the movements resulting in the admission of
Texas, California, and Oregon in 1845, 1850, and 1859, respectively, is reserved for later chapters, where also will be found
a narrative of the establishment of Territories on the Great
Plains and in the Far West before 1860.   The present account
of western state-making will close with a brief synopsis of the
territorial history of the last Mississippi Valley commonwealth
and its admission into the Union.

The Minnesota country was without territorial government
for a short period after the admission of Iowa and Wisconsin.
In March, 1849, however, the Territory of Minnesota was
established.   At this time the population was very small, numbering only 6,077 in 1850.   Moreover, settlements were confined to the section east of the Mississippi which had been
detached from Wisconsin when that State was admitted with
the St. Croix River as a portion of the western boundary.   The
more extensive region west of the Mississippi was still Sioux
Indian country.   The situation was greatly changed after
1851, when the Sioux ceded most of their lands.   The Indians
were treated with gross unfairness by the federal government,
by the traders, and by the settlers.   Nevertheless, the entire
area was now an open field for settlement, and such a stream
of people poured into the region that the census of 1860 credited Minnesota with 172,023 inhabitants.

Before this date, as might be expected with population
increasing so rapidly, a movement for statehood was launched
and pushed to fruition.   After considerable debate, during
which many southern members of Congress opposed the bill, an
enabling act was passed on February 26, 1857.   Bitter rivalry
between Republicans and Democrats featured the election of

delegates to the constitutional convention. The result was close and both sides claimed to have won the victory. As a result two bodies, each claiming to be the duly chosen representatives of the people, held sessions and each adopted a constitution. Curiously enough the two documents were strikingly similar, so much so that it was possible to agree on a compromise which was ratified by the people. Minnesota entered the Union on May 11, 1858. The chain of five States on the western side of the Mississippi River was now complete.

POLITICS IN THE WEST

Among the motives which, in all the Territories, inspired agitation for statehood were personal ambitions to obtain the many new offices which would thereby be created, the avidity of the national political parties to increase their voting power, and the sincere desire of aggressive pioneers to enjoy a voice in shaping national affairs. A study of the early history of any frontier commonwealth reveals the lively manner in which westerners availed themselves of the opportunities along these lines which statehood afforded.

Frontiersmen took to the game of politics with great zest. From the beginning the voting population was practically co-extensive with the number of white, adult males. The numerous offices in the State government were attractive prizes to be gained, even though the salaries were usually shockingly low. Besides, there were the more numerous smaller plums to be plucked in the rapidly increasing number of counties, townships, and towns. Political campaigning, especially after the inauguration of stump-speaking and mass-meetings, was an enjoyable diversion, satisfying a social need among frontier people much in the same way as did the religious camp-meeting. The hilarious campaign of 1840 was nowhere so colorful as in the West. With a frontier hero as a presidential candidate and with the log cabin, the coonskin cap, and the barrel of hard cider the glorified emblems of the Whig party, it was inevitable that westerners should march and shout and sing and attend monster mass-meetings.

The first newspapers in the western States were established

primarily to serve as political organs or to obtain the government printing. Politics was the all-absorbing topic during
campaign periods, both in the editorials and in the news columns. The editors as a rule were vigorous and aggressive in
their espousal of candidates and parties. All too commonly
they attacked opponents with a virulence and scurrility that
make us gasp. In 1835 a Kentucky editor described a competitor of opposing political views as "one of the dirtiest villains, the most reckless liars, and ineffable paltrons, that ever
walked." In a gubernatorial campaign in Iowa in 1859 a newspaper account of a speech by one of the candidates contained
the statement that "he descended to the lowest depths of vul-
garity and blackguardism. . . . No species of low circus-act-
ing clownishness that he would not use for effect. Even his
political friends admit that he is a blackguard, and yet some
of them honor him for it." These quotations selected at ran-
dom are by no means extreme: they could be duplicated
indefinitely. They apparently did not meet with serious disapproval in frontier communities, although they frequently
involved the editors in duels and other personal encounters.

As a section the West was naturally Jeffersonian Republican in national politics down to 1820, and it shifted its support
with alacrity to Andrew Jackson when his star arose on the
political horizon. For some of the same reasons that caused
them to follow Jackson the westerners cast their votes for
another frontier hero—William Henry Harrison—in the boisterous campaign of 1840. Ohio, Indiana, and Michigan, as
might be expected, gave their electoral votes to Harrison, but
so did Kentucky, Tennessee, Mississippi, and Louisiana. Only
Alabama, Arkansas, Missouri, and Illinois returned Van
Buren's electors. Thereafter, until 1856 the West was overwhelmingly Democratic. The most interesting exceptions were
Kentucky and Tennessee which chose Whig electors down to
and including 1852.

The middle of the decade of the fifties witnessed a break
in the political alignment of the free States north of the Ohio
River. The long-standing alliance between the grain-growing
West and the cotton-planting South began to dissolve. Various
reasons explain the change of sentiment. In the first place,

the Mississippi River, so long depended upon by southerners to bind the West to the South as an avenue of transportation, had ceased to function in that capacity. Railroads were yearly identifying the West more closely with the East in economic interest. In the second place, the great outpouring of people during the fifties from the New England and Middle States and from northern Europe into the upper Mississippi Valley changed the social and political complexion of that region. Finally, the passage of the Kansas-Nebraska Bill with its repeal of the time-honored Missouri Compromise alienated many Democrats and led to the formation of the new Republican party. This party had its birth in the Old Northwest which the Ordinance of 1787 had pledged to freedom. Ohio, Michigan, Wisconsin, and Iowa gave their support to John C. Frémont and the new party in its first national campaign in 1856. Four years later all the seven free States of the West were enrolled under the Republican banner.

Economic motives no doubt in large measure explain the hearty welcome thus accorded the Republican party, which espoused free lands and opposed the further spread of slavery. But sincere idealism also played a part. There was real hatred of slavery as an institution in the region which had witnessed the manifold operations of the Underground Railroad. Even more widespread was the spirit of nationalism which pervaded the section which still bore the impress of growth and development fostered and encouraged by the federal government.

CHAPTER XXV

FRONTIER SOCIETY

"AMERICA does not belong to one age alone," wrote a distinguished English historian, A. F. Pollard, in a book published in 1925. "The East might wax old like a garment, but the frontier was always reverting to nature as it moved farther towards the West. That is why the nation is still so young. Some of its parts have reached the most finished phases of social development and are almost as *blasé* as Europe itself. But in the real America which lies beyond the Alleghanies they are—or were till the end of last century—beginning all over again and repeating in each community the experience of mankind and the progress of civilization." Continuing, he made the comment that "the frontier lay midway between the refinements of society and the savagery of the wilderness; and the pioneer was a cross between the friends he left behind and the foes he went to meet." [1]

THE FRONTIER IN ROMANCE AND REALITY

The romantic interpretation of the frontier is to be found in the writings of three main groups: those who had never seen it, or only hastily, but who looked forward to it as the land of hope for the race or the individual; those who have given expression to the ideals and dreams and aspirations of the pioneers; and those who have looked back wistfully to the vanished life of the frontier as one of color and adventure and freedom.

Quotations from writers in the first of these groups appear in the opening pages of this volume. Another typical illustration is to be found in Francis Baily's apotheosis of the frontiersmen contained in the journal of his western tour in 1796

[1] A. F. Pollard, *Factors in American History* (1925) pp. 136-137. By permission of The Macmillan Company, publishers.

and 1797. "Happy men!" he wrote, "who, ignorant of all the deceits and artifices attendant on a state of civilization, unpracticed in the vices and dissipations of degraded humanity, unconscious of artificial and unnecessary wants, secluded from all those pomps and ridiculous ostentations which serve to enslave one-half a nation for the gratification of the other; unshackled with the terrors which fanaticism and superstition inspire; enjoying equally the free blessings which nature intended for man, how much, alas! how much I envy you!"

Turning to the second group of writers dealing with the frontier in a romantic manner, it is to be noted that the pioneers themselves wrote very little about their own life. Timothy Flint was one of a very small number of early western authors who have left us contemporary accounts that approach adequacy. He was a keen and indefatigable observer of men and events, and many of his descriptions entitle him to be classed with the realists. Yet he also sensed and expressed the romantic side of the westward movement and the forward-looking spirit of the frontier. "What mind," he asked "ever contemplated the project of moving from the old settlements over the Alleghany mountains, and selecting a home in the West, without forming pictures of new woods and streams, new animals and vegetables, new configurations of scenery, new aspects of men and new forms of society." Flint himself was frequently so enraptured with the prospect that he expressed himself in poetic form. For instance, in 1820, when he viewed the potential development along the Missouri River, he wrote:

> And then anticipation, rapt away,
> Forestalls thy future glory, when thy tide
> Shall roll by towns, and villages, and farms,
> Continuous, amidst the peaceful hum
> Of happy multitudes, fed from thy soil;
> When the glad eye shall cheer at frequent view
> Of gilded spires of halls, still vocal with the task
> Of ripening youth; or churches, sounding high
> Hosannas to the living God.

J. K. Paulding, although not a resident of the West, also gave expression to the hopes and aspirations of the pioneers in a poem containing the following lines:

Hence comes it, that our meanest farmer's boy
Aspires to taste the proud and manly joy
That springs from holding, in his own dear right,
The land he ploughs, the home he seeks at night.

Other contemporary writers in this group might be quoted
to illustrate the statement made by Frederick J. Turner that
"the men and women who made the Middle West were ideal-
ists." The pioneer, in Turner's words, saw "beyond the harsh
life of the log hut and the sod house to the home of his children, where should dwell comfort and the higher things of life,
though they might not be for him."

The most romantic of all writers dealing with frontier life
are to be found among those of recent years and the present
time. The dull and prosaic and sordid sides are all forgotten
or neglected by these writers, and the glamorous features are
retained to make us believe in a time and a place where men
were free and adventure was met at every turn. "The frontier!" exclaimed Emerson Hough in his little book entitled *The
Passing of the Frontier.* "There is no word in the English language more stirring, more intimate, or more beloved. . . . It
means all that America ever meant. It means the old hope of
a real personal liberty, and yet a real human advance in character and achievement. To a genuine American it is the dear-
est word in all the world." [2] It is not necessary to give further
illustrations of this backward-looking view, which mourns for
the finished romance of the days that will never return.

On the other hand, writers of the realistic school of recent
years have sought to depict the pioneer as a figure of much less
than heroic proportions and to throw doubt upon the beneficial
effects of the frontier experience. This is especially true of
those who have attempted a description and an evaluation of
American culture. Says Louis Mumford, one of the most sympathetic of this group of critics, in his delightful little book entitled *The Golden Day:* "What happened was just the reverse
of the old barbarian invasions, which turned the Goths and
the Vandals into Romans. The movement into backwoods
America turned the European into a barbarian."

[2] Emerson Hough, *The Passing of the Frontier* (Vol. 26, *The Chronicles of
America*), p. 152. By permission of the Yale University Press, publishers.

As a matter of fact, if realism necessarily implies emphasis on the sordid and brutal and degenerative aspects of life, there were realists among numerous contemporaries of the pioneer period who saw the frontier through glasses that were not rose-tinted. Among these, of course, were English and eastern writers who could see nothing but the crudities and brutalities of the conspicuous frontiersmen, easterners who were alarmed at the exodus to the West and were quick to depict the seamy side, and preachers who were shocked at the irreligious habits of westerners. For instance, Thomas Ashe's *Travels in America*, 1806, was so critical that even *Niles' Register* gave much space to ridicule and refutation. Ten years later H. B. Fearon gave his English readers a picture scarcely less unfavorable.

William Faux, writing in 1823 of *Memorable Days in America*, added still darker colors. "The traveler," he wrote, "who must necessarily often mix with the very dregs of society, in this country, should be prepared with plain clothes, or the dress of a mechanic; a gentlemanly appearance only exciting unfriendly or curious feelings, which defeat his object, and make his superiority painful." Kentucky was bad enough, but when he crossed into Indiana he felt "quite out of society; everything and everybody, with some exceptions, looks wild, and half savage." A writer in *The Quarterly Review* in 1809 described the westerners as "a worse race than the Indians upon whose border they trespass"; and the same magazine several years later predicted that "long ages must pass away before the population, now thinly spread over the immense vale of the Mississippi, will become sufficiently dense to render any part of it a desirable habitation for civilized beings." Harriet Martineau, Mrs. Trollope, and Charles Dickens were other writers whose strictures, in the main well founded, aroused the ire of westerners.

Somewhere between the brightly colored visions of the romanticists and the deeply shaded pictures of the super-realists lies the true portraiture of frontier society. Generalizations, here as elsewhere, are likely to be misleading. It is certain that a pioneer community in which most of the people hailed from New England exhibited different characteristics from one the inhabitants of which came from the back country of Virginia or the Carolinas. Both of these types of settlement differed from those where foreign-born settlers were numerous. Moreover, the state of society in any given region depended to a considerable extent on the length of time which had elapsed since the first settlements were made.

The pages which follow will be devoted to an estimate of the personal characteristics and qualities developed or accentuated by frontier life, and of the most salient features of society in the middle western frontier. Frequent recourse will be had to the writings of contemporary observers who, because of long association or keen discrimination, were competent to express judgment.

THE BACKWOODSMEN

The first-comers in every frontier region, at least until the prairies of Illinois were reached, were of the class to whom the name "backwoodsmen" has been generally applied—a class typified by some of James Fenimore Cooper's characters. Hector St. John de Crèvecoeur described these people in the late colonial period in his classical *Letters from an American Farmer*. "By living in or near the woods," he wrote, "their actions are regulated by the wildness of the neighborhood. . . . The chase renders them ferocious, gloomy and unsociable. . . . That new mode of life brings along with it a new set of manners, which I cannot easily describe. These new manners being grafted on the old stock, produce a strange sort of lawless profligacy, the impressions of which are indelible. The manners of the Indian natives are respectable, compared with this European medley." Crèvecoeur hastened to add that there were some individual exceptions and numerous group exceptions, as in the case of the Moravians, the Quakers, and the New Englanders. But he concluded his description by saying: "Thus are our first steps trod, thus are our first trees felled, in general, by the most vicious of our people; and thus is the path opened for the arrival of a second and better class."

Later writers who came in contact with backwoodsmen in

the country north of the Ohio River described them in much the same terms as Crèvecoeur, but frequently they were less severe in their judgments. Timothy Flint testified that before he went into the West he had heard "a thousand stories of gougings, and robberies, and shooting down with the rifle," but that he had traveled unarmed thousands of miles in the wilderness without being insulted, much less being in danger from the frontiersmen. "He carries a knife, or dirk in his bosom," wrote Flint of the typical backwoodsman, "and when in the woods has a rifle on his back, and a pack of dogs at his heels. An Atlantic stranger, transferred directly from one of our cities to his door, would recoil from an encounter with him. But remember that his rifle and his dogs are among his chief means of support and profit." The kindly Morris Birkbeck admitted that the frontier was always a place of retreat for "rude and even abandoned characters, who find the regulations of society intolerable. . . . These people retire, with the wolves, from the regular colonists, keeping always to the outside of civilized settlements." At another time, however, he felt called upon to assert that "they are not savage in disposition, but honest and kind; ready to forward our wishes, and even to labour for us, though our coming will compel them to remove to the 'outside' again."

Since they depended largely upon the hunt for their subsistence, the backwoodsmen lived lonely, isolated lives, far apart from each other, and they resented the coming of the regular settlers. Henry O'Reilly cited the instance of a man named Hincher in western New York who lived twelve miles from his nearest neighbor. He looked with jealousy upon the arrival of newcomers who would disturb the tranquillity of the "neighborhood." It was not infrequent to find men of this type moving two or three times in a single year, building a rude cabin in each place and then abandoning it or selling it to some settler.

The continuous life in the woods gave these people an appearance that was often noted by travelers. Morris Birkbeck declared he could tell the extent of the clearings in which people lived by observing their color. "Buried in the depths of a boundless forest," he said, "the breeze of health never reaches these poor wanderers; the bright prospect of distant hills fading away into the semblance of clouds, never cheered their sight: they are tall and pale, like vegetables that grow in a vault, pining for light. . . . The blood, I fancy, is not supplied with its proper dose of oxygen from their gloomy atmosphere, crowded with vegetables growing almost in the dark, or decomposing; and, in either case, abstracting from the air this vital principle."

It was of this type of individual that the fiery John Randolph spoke in Congress, when he said: "I had as lief be a tythe-proctor in Ireland, and met on a dark night in a narrow road by a dozen white boys, or peep-of-day boys, or hearts of oak, or hearts of steel, as an exciseman in the Allegheny mountains, met, in a lonely road, or by-place, by a backwoodsman." It was these people, together with the river men, with their ferocious curses and boasting, and their rough and tumble fighting in which eyes were often gouged and ears and noses torn, who gave many travelers their first impression of the westerners. Easterners were all too ready to attribute similar characteristics to all the people of the West. Our chief concern, however, is not with them, but with the much larger class of real settlers who felled the trees and transformed the country into a land of homes. It was not until their coming that there was anything that can be called society on the frontier.

FRONTIER TRAITS AND QUALITIES

Contemporary observers, as well as modern writers, agree that frontier society was characterized by social democracy. This is entirely natural. In an environment where there was substantial economic equality there was no basis for social distinctions. Neither wealth nor family standing nor previous position in life meant much in the early years of settlement. All stood on an equality in facing the tasks of cutting down trees, building cabins, putting in crops, and stringing fences. Grinding labor, with little leisure, was the common lot. When a man needed help in performing some of the larger tasks his neighbors were glad to rally to his assistance. Otherwise the individual was expected to stand or fall according to his own abilities and labor. There was no occasion to give lip service to equality as a theory or ideal: equality was an inescapable fact. Thus it was that anyone was regarded with suspicion who sought to live or demean himself in ways that differed conspicuously from those of the settlers in general. This does not mean that superiority was not recognized, when that superiority displayed itself in greater ability to do the things demanded by frontier life. The notables among pioneers were those who excelled in such activities as Indian fighting, rail-splitting, corn-husking, stage-coach driving, or the maneuvering of flatboats.

"There is in the West a real equality, not merely an equality to talk about, an equality on paper," wrote the keen and impartial Michael Chevalier in 1835, "everybody that has on a decent coat is a gentleman; every gentleman is as good as any other, and does not conceive that he should incommode himself to oblige his equal . . . he expects no attention from others, and does not suspect that his neighbor can desire any from him. In this rudeness, however, there is not a grain of malice; there is on the contrary an appearance of good humour that disarms you. The man of the West is rude, but not sullen or quarrelsome." Chevalier was also deeply impressed with the fact that the law of the westward movement was the law of armies. "The mass is everything, the individual nothing."

Where self-reliance was imposed by the environment as a condition of success, the individual who met the test was likely to be imbued with a high degree of self-confidence. Inventive resourcefulness was another quality developed by life on the frontier. When people moved into the West and began life anew under the most primitive conditions they were obliged to make the best use of the slender means at hand. They knew what they wanted to do, but in the early years they lacked the equipment with which such things had been done in the older settled communities. Few tools and no nails were available for use in the building of a cabin. New methods of providing shelter had to be learned. Chairs and beds and other articles of furniture were necessarily left behind, and substitutes had to be devised. So it went, through the whole range of activities essential to existence and economic success.

When these two traits or qualities of self-confidence and resourcefulness were applied in the realm of material things they were generally beneficial. But when confidence in self, based upon economic success, was extended into other fields it was not always justified by the results. Transferred into the political sphere this attitude made it easy and natural to believe that every man of sound mind and adult years was capable of holding and administering any office of government. This same trait of the pioneer inclined him to believe that what he did not know or could not do were not worth knowing or doing; and so he was apt to ridicule and resist the activities of those who sought to introduce some of the elements and aspects of culture into the region. The success of inventive resourcefulness in solving problems in the material realm, as they arose, may also have contributed to the tendency to deal with all questions in a similar manner and on an emergency basis.

Frontiersmen were optimistic people. Hope and expectation of improving their condition were among the motives impelling them westward. They endured the labor and hardships of the early years because they knew that their labors would be rewarded and the hardships would be forgotten in the better times that were sure to come. Growth, progress, movement were everywhere in evidence in the rapidly developing frontier regions, and the spirit of optimism was the natural result. Many observers of pioneer life were impressed with this optimism and some of them became its eloquent apostles. "The West is a young empire of mind, and power, and wealth, and free institutions, rushing up to a giant manhood with a rapidity and power never before witnessed below the sun," wrote Lyman Beecher in 1835. "And if she carries with her the elements of her preservation, the experiment will be glorious."

In an address before the Historical and Philosophical Society of Ohio in 1850 William D. Gallagher expressed his conviction that "to suppose that we are here to see but a segment of the old circle traveled over again, is to give mankind a place in the scale of being lower than that which I have heretofore assigned them. . . . It is my firm belief, that out of the crude materials now collected and collecting in this mighty North-West . . . are to come arts and institutions and education, better fitted for the uses and enjoyments of man, and more promotive of those high developments that are within the capacities of his nature, than anything which the world has yet seen."

Frequently this optimism led westerners across the border line into boastfulness concerning the superiorities of their particular region or into comparisons unfavorable to the East or Europe. For instance, Timothy Flint related an anecdote which, he said, was well known in the West, of a preacher from Kentucky, who was preaching in a neighboring State on the topic of the happiness of heaven. "In short, my brethren," said the preacher when he reached his climax, "to say all in one word, heaven is a Kentuck of a place." Gilbert Imlay, writing to a friend in England in 1792, pointed out numerous respects in which Kentucky society excelled that of the old world. A European might doubt this statement, but said Imlay, "a few years residence with us teaches him that important truth, and self-conviction is always the most lasting." Another illustration of this self-complacent, boastful spirit was given by James Hall. "One would have thought," he wrote, referring to the people of Ohio and Indiana, "they were speaking in parables, who heard them describing the old thirteen states as a mere appendage of the future republic—a speck on the map of the United States—a sort of out-lot with a cotton field at one end, and a manufactory of wooden clocks at the other; yet they were in sober earnest." Of course, in reading the impressions of travelers it must always be kept in mind that westerners enjoyed "tall stories" and that they found great fun in "stuffing" strangers who seemed too inquisitive.

Pioneer farmers were scarcely less migratory than the backwoodsmen whom they succeeded. For this reason among others, frontier society did not become static. Restlessness was in the air. There seemed so much to be done, so much to be gained, and such a short time in which to accomplish it before the entire country would be settled. Reports of better lands further west were for many people too alluring to be resisted. Travelers from the eastern States or from Europe, where families were accustomed to live in one locality through successive generations, were much surprised at, and rather critical of, the nonchalant manner in which people in the West changed their abodes without any apparent necessity or reason. "Though they have generally good houses," wrote Timothy Flint, "they might almost as well, like the Tartars, dwell in tents. Everything shifts under your eye. The present occupants sell, pack up, depart. Strangers replace them. Before they have gained the confidence of their neighbors, they hear of a better place, pack up and follow their precursors." Flint lamented the absence of "those permanent and noble improvements which grow out of a love for that appropriated spot where we were born, and where we expect to die."

Other traits of westerners may be briefly mentioned. One of these was aggressiveness. "Personal resistance to personal aggression, or designed affront," remarked Morris Birkbeck, "holds a high place in the class of duties." This characteristic may have been innate with many frontiersmen, but it was also developed and accentuated by life in a region where such an attitude was often necessary to self-preservation or success. Again, the pioneers were tolerant, within limits. Differences of creed or social viewpoints, or even personal idiosyncracies were seen to be of little consequence so long as people devoted themselves to the common tasks of life on the frontier. Tolerance was apt to cease, however, when individuals or groups sought to conduct themselves in ways that were markedly different from those of typical frontier people. Finally, there was the trait of hospitality exemplified by the familiar phrase, "the latch-string is always out." Strangers traveling through the country were seldom denied such rude accommodations as pioneer cabins afforded. One important factor in producing this far-famed western hospitality was the loneliness which inclined the settlers to welcome visitors, whether acquaintances or strangers.

HEALTH AND DISEASE ON THE FRONTIER

An aspect of frontier society which deserves some consideration is that which is concerned with health and vital statistics. It was assumed by numerous writers contemplating the benefits of life in the wilderness that general good health would be one of its blessings. This assumption does not seem to have been borne out by the actual facts. Timothy Flint summarized the situation quite accurately when he wrote that "there appears to be in the great plan of Providence a scale, in which the advantages and disadvantages of human condition are balanced.—Where the lands are extremely fertile, it seems to be appended to them, as a drawback to that advantage, that they are generally sickly."

This statement is corroborated by numerous other contemporary writers. The first settlements were mainly in the forest where the sun's rays could not destroy the generally prevailing miasma, or on the low lands along streams or in the vicinity of stagnant water. The first clearings did little to improve the situation. Birkbeck noted that the settlers "ignorant of the dangers they were incurring, found good land along the course of the rivers; and there they naturally fixed their cabins, near enough to the stream to dip out of it with a bowl." Most of the towns were similarly located, their founders "prefering convenience or profit to salubrity. . . . Short-sighted and narrow economy! by which the lives of thousands are shortened, and the comfort of all sacrificed to mistaken notions of private interests." Charles F. Hoffman, writing in 1833, found conditions equally unhealthful in the newly settled prairie regions where, in the hope of securing crops the first year, newcomers arriving in June were turning over the sod with its carpet of tall grass, weeds, and wild flowers, "and allowing the accumulation of vegetable decomposition to be acted upon by a vertical sun, and steam up for months under their very nostrils."

It was generally agreed that life in environments and under conditions such as these caused the wide prevalence of ague, with its alternating chills and fever, and other types of malarial diseases. Much more fatal were the epidemics of typhoid fever which swept western communities, especially in seasons of low water. Newspapers often devoted much space to the ravages of these diseases. The year 1823, for instance, was one in which there was much sickness in the Ohio Valley. Many communities in Ohio were said to have few families that were not affected. In Kentucky numerous families had lost "two or three of their members, and in others six or eight are sick." Still more dreaded was the terrible scourge of cholera which proceeded so rapidly to a fatal termination for large numbers of its victims. "There are not enough well persons left to take care of the convalescent and later the dead," runs a newspaper report from Lexington in June, 1833, "It is useless for any one to attempt to guess how many have fallen. Three hundred would probably be a reasonable computation." A Little Rock newspaper contained several columns filled with accounts of the ravages of the cholera epidemic in the Mississippi Valley. Similar visitations in other years caused equal consternation.

There is also evidence that, because of exposure and poorly constructed dwellings, frontier settlers were particularly susceptible to respiratory diseases such as bronchitis, diphtheria, pneumonia, and tuberculosis. Among small children cholera infantum or cholera morbus in the summer and croup in the winter were widespread and greatly dreaded.

The horrors of epidemic periods on the frontier were enhanced by the great dearth or unavailability of physicians. Medical science was still in its early stages, and at their very best even the most honest and skilful practitioners could do little to check the progress of most of the diseases. On the other hand, "quack doctors" flourished in such a situation—especially the herb doctors who peddled sure-cure panaceas for all sorts of ailments. Concoctions almost as weird as that brewed by the witches in *Macbeth* had a wide currency. Many of the so-called remedies may have been harmless; others were no doubt efficacious for certain illnesses; but seldom was there any definite knowledge to serve as a guide in their use.

No dependable vital statistics give any accurate knowledge of either birth-rate or death-rate on the frontier. Travelers frequently commented on the large number of children that swarmed out of settlers' cabins, and there is no doubt that large families were the general rule. On the other hand, there is ample evidence that the rate of infant mortality was extremely high. Some writers estimate that at least one-half of the babies died before reaching the age of four. It is equally certain that early graves claimed a shockingly great proportion of the mothers who brought these large families into the world

and endured the physical and psychological hardships of frontier life.

Social Life on the Frontier

It is pleasant now to turn to an aspect of pioneer life that
is far from being doleful or somber. The backwoodsmen deliberately chose isolation and resented the coming of neighbors
because it limited their opportunities to pursue the type of
existence they enjoyed. The pioneer farmers, on the other
hand, were not ungregarious. Frontier conditions imposed
isolation and loneliness upon them, but they welcomed the
arrival of new settlers, both because of increased economic advantages and because of greater prospect for companionship.
Although for the greater part, the lives of the pioneers were
spent in perpetual toil, they seized with great avidity upon
every occasion to enjoy the society of their fellow settlers.

From miles around the settlers came to help a newcomer
build his log cabin. The women folk prepared a bountiful re-
past, visiting all the while to make up for the long periods of
solitude. Similar opportunities came at log-rolling time. After
a settler had felled the trees to make a clearing, the neighbors
gathered to assist him in rolling the heavy logs into piles.
Friendly rivalry occurred among the men to prove their
strength or among groups to see which could make the largest
heap of logs in a given time. Competition also added zest to
harvesting grain, when there were often races between cradlers
to see which could reach the end of the row first; or at corn-
husking bees to determine the championship in this line. To
be sure, there was usually an abundance of whiskey on all such
occasions and the fun at meal time and in the evenings was
likely to be rude and boisterous, sometimes ending in wrestling
and rough-and-tumble fighting in which there were no rules or
restraints. In addition to preparing hearty meals for the men
folks, the women were apt to parallel the activities in the fields
with a "quilting bee" or a "sewing bee," thus making play of
work and displaying their skill with the needle.

Later, when small towns appeared, shooting matches, horse-
racing, and other sports offered welcome diversion. Court days
in the county seat towns were sure to attract a large gathering

of settlers from the surrounding country. Some of those in attendance were interested in the cases being tried, but more of them came merely for the sake of visiting or engaging in the various contests of skill or strength that were always afoot.

Weddings, of course, were occasions of great festivity on the frontier. To travel a long distance on horseback or in a jolting wagon, and then merely listen to a brief ceremony and go home again, was far from the pioneer's thought or intention. Feasting, sometimes at the homes of the parents of both the bride and groom, was confidently expected. At night the strains of the fiddle were heard as, hour after hour, the young people danced the square dance or the Virginia reel. Later, when the newly married couple had established themselves in a home of their own, a "house warming" occasioned another social gathering.

Thus the social life of frontier people in the early years was largely a by-product of their need for assistance in performing many of the tasks necessary to their existence. Social life for its own sake came later when the country had become more thickly settled, and the most arduous labors of pioneering had been completed. The following chapter will deal with the cultural beginnings which were an accompaniment of the growth of western towns.

CHAPTER XXVI

CULTURAL BEGINNINGS

Much has been written, especially in recent years, concerning the anti-cultural aspects of life on the frontier. It is obvious that regions undergoing the processes of settlement did not furnish an environment congenial to the growth of cultural ideas or institutions. Michael Chevalier recognized this fact in 1835 when he pointed out that the pioneer "has been obliged to occupy himself much more with the cultivation of the soil than of himself." In *A Plea for the West* written the same year, Lyman Beecher remarked that: "No people ever did, in the first generation, fell the forest, and construct the roads, and rear the dwellings and public edifices, and provide the competent supply of schools and literary institutions."

It is unquestionably true that frontier society was inclined to view the possessor of intellectual attainments or cultural interests with ridicule and contempt. Persons exhibiting superior educational acquirements often found themselves at such disadvantage that they hastened to conform to the general pattern in speech and manners. As Timothy Flint expressed it, "an unwarrantable disdain keeps back the better informed and more powerful minds from displaying themselves." On the other hand, it is safe to say that few frontier communities were without some individuals who appreciated cultural activities and facilities, and were ready to co-operate in securing their introduction at the earliest opportunity. After all is said, there is less reason for surprise that the frontier experience delayed cultural development than there is that the cultural advance was so early in making its appearance.

Religion on the Frontier

Except for the few instances in which whole congregations migrated to the West, taking their ministers with them, church-

386

going was not possible during the early stages of settlement, since there were no churches. The pioneers, however, were not irreligious, as was sometimes charged by critical writers. They responded eagerly to every opportunity to hear religious teaching from ministers and itinerant preachers. Among the earliest acts passed by the House of Delegates of the short-lived Transylvania colony was one "to prevent profane swearing, and Sabbath breaking"; and the first legislative bodies of the new western States hastened to enact laws to protect and encourage religious observances. On the other hand, the forms and practices of religion underwent many changes in the process of adaptation to frontier conditions in the region west of the Alleghanies.

There were Roman Catholics among the first settlers west of the mountains, especially in Kentucky, but for many years the chief centers of Catholic influence were in the old French towns, such as Detroit, Vincennes, and St. Louis. Members of the Protestant Episcopal Church were apparently few in number in the West until long after the frontier era had come to a close. Congregationalists early gained a foothold in the New England settlements at Marietta and in the Western Reserve in Ohio. Later, as a consequence of the large migrations from New England following the opening of the Erie Canal, this denomination came to exert a strong influence throughout the upper Mississippi Valley, not only in the religious field but particularly in the promotion of education. The Congregationalists early joined with the Presbyterians in a plan for cooperation in the establishment of new churches.

The three denominations which had the largest number of adherents on the middle western frontier were the Presbyterians, the Methodists, and the Baptists. Presbyterians were apparently in the lead numerically in Kentucky and Tennessee during the later years of the eighteenth century, since Scotch-Irish predominated among the settlers who poured into that region after the American Revolution. By 1800 several presbyteries had been established west of the mountains under the jurisdiction of eastern synods; and before long western synods appeared—the first being the Synod of Kentucky organized by David Rice. The Presbyterian Church, however, clung to its insistence upon an educated clergy, and its ministers retained their fondness for doctrinal sermons—gloomily Calvinistic. For these reasons it can scarcely be said that Presbyterianism was popular on the frontier, where the demand was for a religion that was more adaptable to the everyday life of the pioneers.

This demand was admirably met by the Methodists. Under the leadership of the zealous, strongly evangelistic Bishop Francis Asbury, this denomination had a rapid growth in the West. Its preachers proclaimed a democratic gospel—one which placed great emphasis upon equality in the sight of God and upon individual responsibility, rather than upon any doctrine of predestination. The Methodist form of local organization was also well suited to frontier conditions, since it included not only ordained ministers but lay exhorters and class leaders. But the most significant contribution of Methodism to the religious life of the pioneers was the itinerant preacher or circuit-rider. Scores of the preachers of this type traveled through the western country on horseback, preaching nearly every day in the week in pioneer cabins, in outdoor places, or wherever people could assemble to hear their teaching. Some of these circuits were hundreds of miles in length. In spite of every hardship, with only a pittance for their pay, these missionaries rode their circuits year after year. Not less important than their preaching was their influence over the isolated families in whose cabins they were welcome guests and bearers of tidings from the outside world.

The Baptists, likewise, early proved their adaptability to frontier needs. By 1800 they were well organized in Kentucky and Tennessee and within another decade they had several Associations, embracing numerous churches north of the Ohio River. They depended more on local, established preachers than upon itinerants, and were less inclined to emotionalism in their preaching than were the Methodists. On the other hand, their democratic form of church organization and their evangelical aggressiveness appealed to the pioneers and led to a rapid growth in membership.

Some writers are inclined to doubt whether religion in certain of its aspects can be counted as a cultural force on the

frontier. This attitude of skepticism is based upon the crude-
ness of some of the preachers, and especially upon the extreme
emotionalism manifested in what is known as the Great Revival, which raged through the West during the opening years
of the nineteenth century. Presbyterians, Methodists, and
Baptists all joined in this widespread evangelistic activity, but
the last two were the denominations which entered into the
movement most wholeheartedly and continued its practices the
longest as a part of their regular policy. Revivals were under
way in the West as early as 1797. The device of the camp-
meeting was soon adopted, because it fitted the needs of
pioneer peoples. It served some of the same social purposes as
the wedding, the house-raising, or the log-rolling, only on a
larger scale. No single pioneer family or group of families was
able to supply food and shelter for the ever-increasing crowds
that attended the preaching services as the movement gained
momentum. As a consequence meetings were held in groves,
and people came long distances in their wagons, with bedding
and provisions, prepared and eager to spend several days. The
intense excitement evoked by the revival spirit, together with
the opportunity for human companionship, provided a welcome
relief from the loneliness of pioneer life.

It is generally agreed that the Great Revival reached its
highest point in the huge meeting at Cain Ridge in Kentucky
in August, 1801, lasting without interruption from Friday until
the night of the following Wednesday. Thousands of people—
some estimates place the number as high as 25,000—gathered
from all parts of Kentucky, from Tennessee, and even from
north of the Ohio. Preaching on the part of seven or eight
preachers was almost continuous from morning until late at
night. It was at night that the scene at this and similar meetings was most impressive: the huge, milling crowd, the hundreds of torches flaring against the dark background of the
surrounding forest, the hoarse voices of the preachers, and the
cries and wailing of those under conviction of sin. The emotional frenzy was also expressed by remarkable physical mani-
festations. Men, women, and children fell to the ground by
the hundreds and lost the power to move, so that they had to
be carried to places where they would not be trampled upon.

Others were seized with an uncontrollable jerking which became unbelievably violent. Still others "would start up suddenly in a fit of barking, rush out, roam around, and in a short time come barking and foaming back. Down on all fours they sometimes went growling, snapping their teeth, and barking just like dogs."

The Great Revival continued throughout the West at least down to 1805, when the movement seems to have abated somewhat. The camp-meeting and periodic revivals, however, became permanent institutions among such denominations as the Methodists, the Baptists, and the Cumberland Presbyterians. Catherine C. Cleveland, the most competent authority on this great religious upheaval, expresses her belief that the beneficial results outweighed the detrimental. She attributes the growth of the philanthropic spirit in the West, the beginning of the temperance movement, the awakening of many people to the evils of slavery, and other similar changes of attitude largely to the effects of this stirring revival. Among the church organizations themselves the results were seen in a phenomenal increase in membership; in the scism among the Presbyterians eventuating in 1810 in the separate establishment of the Cumberland Presbyterian Church; and in the appearance of the Campbellite or Christian Church. In general, to quote Miss Cleveland, "the forces set in motion must be reckoned with as important factors in the development of western society in the years that followed."

EDUCATIONAL BEGINNINGS

"Religion, morality and knowledge, being necessary to good government and the happiness of mankind, schools and the means of education shall for ever be encouraged." In these words did the drafters of the Ordinance of 1787 seek to inspire the people of the new commonwealths to be formed beyond the mountains. Congress gave added force to this admonition by granting the sixteenth section of each township of the public lands to the States as they were admitted for the maintenance of schools. Most of the new constitutions contained clauses dealing with education. For example the Indiana constitution of 1816 contained the stipulation that "It shall be the duty of the general assembly, as soon as circumstances will permit, to provide by law for a general system of education, ascending in regular gradations from township schools to a State university, wherein tuition shall be gratis and equally open to all."

Despite all these encouragements and expressions of pious hopes, progress in the establishment of state systems of public education was slow and beset with many reverses. In fact, with a few exceptions, the frontier period had passed before the ideal of free public schools was realized in any of the midwestern States. Those regions which received large numbers of settlers from New England, New York, and Pennsylvania were first to lay adequate foundations for a system of public education; while the sections where emigrants from the southern States predominated were the most backward in developing educational support. The people of the frontier were intent upon the problems and labors of settling a new country. They were poor and opposed to any project that would increase taxes without prospect of immediate economic benefit. Elementary education was not wholly unappreciated, but the plan of tax-supported schools, open to all, was an idea of slow growth which gained wide acceptance only after the first stages of frontier development had been achieved. Ohio and Michigan were the earliest to make notable progress in the establishment of public school systems.

It would be a mistake, however, to assume that the Middle West was without educational facilities during the pioneer period. As soon as any region received a nucleus of settlers schools of all kinds began to appear—elementary schools, academies, seminaries, and so-called colleges and universities. Although most of these institutions were exceedingly crude and rudimentary in character, they reveal an educational fermentation that modifies the picture presented by the slow development of statewide school systems at public expense. Many of these early schools were public in the sense that they were supported by local levies or rate-bills, and frequently children of indigent parents were admitted free of charge. Others were "subscription schools" maintained, at least in part, by those whose children were in attendance. The growing cities, such as Cincinnati, Lexington, Louisville, Detroit, and Chicago, made the greatest advancement, and by 1840 could boast of public school systems which cared for a majority of their children of school age in attractive, commodious buildings. In the smaller towns and throughout the rural areas in the log school houses, with their split-log seats and benches and oiled-paper windows, migratory and usually illy-prepared teachers taught the children of the pioneers the rudiments of reading, writing, and arithmetic. Terms were short, school books were woefully scarce and inadequate, and the pay of the teachers a mere pittance. Yet poor as most of these schools were, many a faithful teacher succeeded in inspiring his pupils with a thirst for knowledge, and by his presence in the frontier homes as he "boarded around" he exercised a cultural influence that extended beyond the school room.

Private grammar schools and academies were numerous. The latter were peculiarly adapted to frontier needs, and performed a valuable service. Some of them had a brief existence; others succeeded in maintaining themselves for considerable periods. The educational experiments of the period were not unknown in the West. For instance, in the newspapers and the journals of travel for the period between 1820 and 1840, one may read of Lancastrian schools of "instruction mutuelle"; of Pestalozzian establishments; of agricultural schools. In St. Louis a group of "professors" offered to teach most of the languages and all the sciences. They promised to impart proficiency in the Hebrew language in twelve lessons, and in Greek and Latin with proportionate ease.

A notable feature of the educational history of the middle western frontier is the large number of colleges and universities which were founded and given legislative charters before the Civil War. Mortality was very high among these institutions projected with high ambition and local enthusiasm. Out of forty-three colleges launched in Ohio during this period only seventeen are now in existence. In Tennessee only seven out of forty-six are still in operation; in Missouri only eight out of eighty-five. A few of these defunct colleges never actually opened their doors to students. The others struggled along for varying periods and then succumbed. Catastrophes such as fires were sufficient to bring total discouragement to some institutions. Internal dissensions and bitter rivalries wrecked others. But the most common cause of failure was lack of success in securing the necessary funds for maintenance.

While every effort was made to secure local support, most of these frontier colleges were largely dependent upon the generosity of eastern donors for funds in their early years. Strong appeals for aid were made, especially in the years of panic and depression. "What will become of the West," asked Lyman Beecher in 1835, "if her prosperity rushes up to such a majesty of power, while those great institutions linger which are necessary to form the mind, and the conscience, and the heart of that vast world? . . . We must educate! We must educate! or we must perish by our own prosperity. . . . And let no man at the East quiet himself, and dream of liberty, whatever may become of the West." He warned especially against sending misfits and failures to the West to be its teachers. "The men, who, *somehow,* do not succeed at the East, are the very men who will succeed still less at the West." So numerous were appeals of this kind and so importunate the pleas for financial aid that several groups were formed in the eastern States, similar to the influential "Society for the Promotion of Collegiate and Theological Education at the West."

State universities were established by law early in the history of each western commonwealth, but pioneer days had passed before most of them actually opened their doors. With these exceptions the colleges of the frontier period were founded by the various religious denominations. Those churches which insisted upon an educated clergy, such as the Catholics, the Presbyterians, and the Congregationalists, were earliest to establish colleges in the West. Late in the pioneer period the Methodists and the Baptists joined in the movement, and the former, especially, soon made up for their late start by establishing a large number of institutions. The Congregationalists and the Presbyterians had early adopted a policy of co-operation and non-competition in their western missionary and educational activities, and as a result numerous colleges were founded under their joint auspices. Before the Civil War about fifteen different religious denominations were instrumental in establishing colleges in the region west of the Alleghanies.

Most of the colleges of this period, while professing to be institutions of higher learning, would fall considerably short of the standards of a good modern high school. On the other hand, they did not differ greatly in quality from a majority of their contemporary eastern colleges. Many of the instructors were graduates of Harvard, Yale, Princeton, and other eastern institutions of high rank, and they labored valiantly in the face of the most discouraging handicaps. The "Yale Band" who founded Illinois College in 1829, and the equally famous "Iowa Band" who in 1847 established the institution now known as Grinnell College in Iowa, furnished notable examples of the devotion of these early educators on the frontier. Despite their meager resources, their inadequate equipment, and their restricted curricula, these pioneer colleges exercised a cultural influence which it would be difficult fully to evaluate. Many of them,—to mention only Center, Denison, De Pauw (originally Indiana Asbury), Franklin, Kenyon, Knox, Oberlin, Marietta, and Western Reserve, out of a long list—survived the long struggle for existence, steadily improved their standards, and are now among the best of the nations' institutions of higher learning.

Two colleges founded very early in the pioneer period in the West deserve special mention because of the high quality of instruction they offered and because of their widespread cultural influence. One of these was the first American institution of higher learning west of the Alleghany Mountains—Transylvania Seminary, founded in 1783. The name was changed to Transylvania University in 1798. Even during its early years the fame of this school gave to Lexington, Kentucky, the title of the "Athens of the West." In 1818 Horace Holley came to the presidency and in the succeeding decade he advanced the institution to real collegiate standing, with a student body of more than four hundred, representing fifteen States, and with instruction in liberal arts subjects, medicine, and law. The faculty contained such men as Constantine Rafinesque, the eminent scientist; Mann Butler, the Kentucky historian; Robert H. Bishop and James Blythe, both of whom were later western college presidents; and Daniel Drake and

Charles Caldwell, leaders in the medical profession. The other notable institution of the early pioneer period was Miami University at Oxford, Ohio. It was founded in 1809 and attained collegiate rank in 1824, when Robert H. Bishop became its president. One of the members of the Miami faculty whose name became widely known was William Holmes M'Guffey, author of a series of readers which were used in the elementary schools throughout the West down to comparatively recent years.

Professional education received some attention in the Middle West before 1840. It has already been noted that Transylvania University early offered instruction in law and medicine. There were several other law schools and five or six other medical schools, among which were the Medical College of Ohio at Cincinnati and the Louisville Medical College. The training of ministers was given special attention in a half-score theological schools or seminaries, a majority of which were established by the Presbyterian denomination. Although there was a growing professional interest among teachers, no colleges or schools devoted primarily to teacher-training were in existence in the region before 1840.

OTHER CULTURAL AGENCIES AND ACTIVITIES

Supplementing the schools and colleges, and in many cases exceeding them in real influence, were other cultural agencies and activities which made an early appearance in frontier society. Subscription libraries and book stores reveal a growing taste for good literature; and book-publishing concerns were established. Newspapers and gazettes devoted considerable space to literary productions. Westerners themselves began to write fiction, essays and poetry of varying degrees of merit. Dramatic productions, home-talent and professional, made a wide appeal, as did also the lyceum. Debating societies and singing schools multiplied. In short, in the growing towns an indigenous culture gradually developed and helped to create a taste for the better things of life, although music and art, as was perhaps natural, lagged far behind and had little attention during the pioneer era.

Books were extremely scarce on the frontier. A literate family was regarded as fortunate if it possessed a Bible, an almanac, and some such book as Hervey's *Evening Meditations*. An occasional family brought a more extensive library from its eastern home. That there were in many communities, however, groups of settlers who wanted books is shown by the fact that subscription libraries began to appear here and there at an early date—even before 1800. Vincennes had such a library of more than two hundred volumes by 1808, including history, geography, biography, and poetry. The library at Lexington was begun about 1795: by 1837 it contained more than six thousand volumes. Cincinnati had several subscription libraries of fair size by 1840. St. Louis, Dayton, and numerous other towns supported similar enterprises. Stores devoted exclusively to books were slow in appearing, but general stores and news-papers offices had books for sale. These included, in addition to a preponderance of religious works, many of the classics, contemporary English novels, scientific treatises, and the poetry of Milton, Byron, Pope, Burns, Addison, and others. Scott and Byron were the favorites among frontier readers. By 1840 western publishing houses were issuing a surprisingly large number of locally-printed books. Cincinnati was the greatest center of this industry. It is estimated that by 1840 the print-ing houses of that city were turning out as many as a half-million bound volumes annually. Of these a majority were school books and the remainder consisted of a variety of orig-inal works and of reprints of English novels and other books. No copyright law at that time prevented "piratical" printing.

Before the close of the pioneer era a large output of writings from the pens of midwestern authors had found its way into print. Much of this writing was devoid of any literary merit. Unfortunately, although perhaps naturally, such frontier fic-tionists as possessed real talent failed to produce stories or novels based on the normal life of the people whom they knew so well. Thus they are of little help to us in interpreting the frontier experience. Two of the most prolific western writers of fiction in the period between 1820 and 1840 were James Hall and Timothy Flint—both of whom wrote books of travel which reveal their keen observation and which are valuable as source material. Yet in his fiction Hall, while drawing his themes from his own environment, selected the picturesque and even the melodramatic, as in the *The Harpe's Head; a Legend of Kentucky*. Flint, who knew the midwest thoroughly, chose rather to write novels about the Far West which he had never seen, as in *Francis Berrian, or the Mexican Patriot* and *The Shoshonee Valley*. John M'Clung and Frederick William Thomas, two other popular western novelists, laid the scenes of their stories in the eastern states. Only Caroline M. Kirkland, in a book called *A New Home,* approached a realistic depiction of frontier life as the author observed it.

Poetry held a place not far below that of fiction, both in the interests of frontier readers and in the efforts of early western writers. One important outlet for the urge to versify was found in song-making, most often in writing new words for familiar airs. A large number of religious songs were the work of western writers, especially during the periods of revivalist fervor. Original political songs were also popular. Another group of poets adopted the satirical mood and no doubt expressed views of frontier life which were at least as nearly realistic as the imaginative poems of the more romantically inclined. Representatives of the latter group found abundant material for themes in the stirring episodes of Indian wars and other conflicts in the West.

A large part of these writings appeared in the columns of the rapidly increasing number of newspapers, gazettes, magazines, and other periodicals which constituted the most influential literary product of the frontier period. The first newspaper west of the Alleghanies was *The Kentucky Gazette,* established at Lexington in 1787 by John Bradford. Newspapers appeared in rapid succession in the towns which marked the progress of western settlement. By 1840 a total of three hundred and fifty-four western newspapers were reported in the census of that year. Many of these sheets were established to serve as political organs. In many cases the owners derived their most dependable income at first from contracts for government printing—laws, proclamations, and official notices. Advertising was meager in the early years. Subscription lists grew slowly and pay was far from certain. Nevertheless, editors wielded a powerful influence in frontier communities. In the heat of political campaigns and in the midst of other controversies they often expressed themselves so vigorously as to draw them into violent personal encounters resulting occasionally in the death of one of the parties.

A large majority of these journals were issued weekly, but during the decade of the eighteen twenties newspapers began to appear daily in some of the larger towns, such as Cincinnati and Louisville. Comparatively little local news of a personal nature was contained in these papers. Local political news and accounts of commercial and economic progress received some attention. It was not unusual for half the space to be devoted to news, often a month or more old, regarding events and movements in eastern States and foreign countries. A "Poet's Corner" or column with some other similar heading was found in nearly every paper, and frequently considerable space was given to prose literary productions of a nondescript character. After a time special periodicals, issued weekly, bi-weekly or monthly, made their appearance to serve as purveyors of entertainment or instruction along literary, religious, educational, and scientific lines.

Rivaling the editor in popularity in pioneer society was the orator and public speaker. For people whose vocabularies were extremely limited the orator who possessed a stentorian voice and a gift for florid, extravagant language seems to have had a strong fascination. This fascination no doubt helps to explain the eagerness with which frontier people flocked to listen to the interminable sermons of camp-meeting preachers, the spread-eagle Fourth of July orations, the stump-speaking of political campaigns, and the pleas of attorneys in jury trials.

Interest in the drama was manifested at a very early period in the western settlements in the presentation of amateur theatricals. Thus, in 1799 the students of Transylvania University presented two comedies, *The Busy Body* and *Love a la Mode*, and within a few years Lexington boasted a theater. In 1801 a theater was opened in Cincinnati with the performance of *The Poor Soldier* by a group of amateurs, who later presented *She Stoops to Conquer*. "Thespian societies" were formed in Louisville, St. Louis, Detroit, and numerous smaller towns in the early years of their existence, and there is evidence of a real interest both in this form of self-expression and in the drama itself. Later, beginning about 1810 professional troupes of players made their appearance in the West and soon established circuits embracing the larger towns, where their productions apparently met with a hearty welcome. Edwin Forrest, then at the beginning of his histrionic career, was seen in several western cities during the winter of 1822-3, and returned a few years later when he had attained considerable fame. Before 1840 western audiences had witnessed performances by such famous actors and actresses as Junius Brutus Booth, Mlle. Celeste, Clara Fisher, Charles Kean, James H. Hackett, Dan Marble, and Ellen Tree.

The other fine arts can scarcely be said to have gained even a foothold in the Middle West during the frontier period. Group singing, without accompaniment, was conducted in churches, and in some of the larger places singing societies were popular. Singing masters were conducting schools in Cincinnati and Marietta and other villages as early as 1802. The Harmonical Society and the Euphonical Society were names of organizations in existence in Cincinnati by the end of the next decade. This vocal music was largely a social activity and in no sense approached the status of an art. Instrumental music was even less developed. Pianos were extremely rare. The fiddle and the flute were the most common musical instruments. Their players were usually entirely self-taught and their music was heard by the public most frequently at dances and other social gatherings.

Appreciation of painting and sculpture was very rudimentary, and opportunities for instruction in either of these subjects were virtually non-existent. It is true that a painting academy was opened in Cincinnati in 1812, but its character is reflected in the advertisement of the instructor offering to paint signs and do other similar "practical" work. Some indifferent sculpturing was done in the West, especially by Hiram Powers, whose "Slave Girl" gained wide notoriety because of its nudity. Far more popular than these artistic efforts were the figures in such exhibitions as the Museum of Wax Works opened in Cincinnati in 1815. In a word, persons who devoted, or desired to devote, their time to the painting of pictures or the sculpturing of figures were quite generally regarded as effeminate and useless in frontier society.

PART III
THE FRONTIER OF THE FAR WEST

CHAPTER XXVII

AMERICAN EXPLORATION OF THE FAR WEST

COMPARATIVELY few Americans knew anything of the vast territory which came so unexpectedly into the possession of the United States by the Louisiana Purchase Treaty of 1803, or of the land that lay between the ill-defined western boundaries of that cession and the Pacific Ocean. The west bank of the Mississippi below the mouth of the Missouri was familiar to many Americans; and fur traders had pushed up the Missouri River at least as far as the Mandan villages in the present State of North Dakota.

Well informed people, with an interest in history and geography, were doubtless acquainted with the activities of the French and the Spanish in the Great Plains region, and with the explorations and settlements of the latter in the southwest and in California. They also possessed some knowledge of the general features of the Pacific coast line, even if they were ignorant of the achievements of the early Spanish explorers who had sailed northward as far as Alaska. Shortly after the close of the Revolutionary War New England ship captains began trading along the north Pacific coast. Then in 1792 Captain Robert Gray sailed into a river to which he gave the name of his ship—the *Columbia*—thus proving the actual existence of the mysterious "River of the West" which the French had sought in vain, and to which Jonathan Carver had applied the name "Oregan" in a book published in 1778. About the time of Gray's discovery an Englishman, George Vancouver, was exploring Puget Sound; and in 1793 his countryman, Alexander Mackenzie, completed his remarkable overland expedition across Canada and reached the Pacific after descending the Fraser River. Among the mass of Americans, however, these exploits were little known, and in 1803 the greater part of the region west of the Mississippi was a *terra incognita*.

Fifty years later the entire area between the Mississippi River and the Pacific Ocean not only belonged to the United States, but it was so well known that maps could be published which were so accurate that they needed only minor corrections of details. Such a notable achievement was made possible through the explorations and observations and writings of a large number of groups and individuals representing a wide variety of types and motives. From the standpoint of motives these explorations may be roughly divided into five groups. First, there were the official expeditions directed and financed by the government, for purposes of general exploration. Actually more important, but seldom yielding written reports, were the far-flung activities of traders in furs and in merchandise with the Spanish towns of the southwest. In the third place, a vast amount of detailed information was supplied by scientists who were attracted to the new fields of study. Then, there was a fourth group of men who can scarcely be called explorers, but who journeyed into the Far West in search of adventure or health, and wrote accounts that added to the available knowledge concerning the region. Finally, in the early fifties, a series of elaborate governmental surveys for a route for a railroad to the Pacific produced voluminous reports of great value.

Even a brief account of each of these many explorations would fill a large volume. Within the compass of the present chapter it will be possible to sketch only the most important official expeditions, with occasional reference to a few notable illustrations of the third and fourth groups of explorers just mentioned. The discoveries of the fur traders and the railroad surveys will more properly receive consideration in later chapters.

THE LEWIS AND CLARK EXPEDITION

Thomas Jefferson was one American for whom the unknown trans-Mississippi country long held a strong fascination. As early as 1783, twenty years before the launching of the plan that culminated in the first American overland expedition to the Pacific, he wrote to George Rogers Clark, the hero of Vincennes, proposing that he lead a party of explorers into the Far West. At this time he was troubled by fears that the British might explore and colonize this region. Clark, however, did not respond favorably to the suggestion. Three years later, in 1786, while in Paris as minister to France, Jefferson became acquainted with John Ledyard, who had accompanied Captain James Cook on his voyage to the Pacific in 1776. Ledyard was now footloose and ready for further adventures. He readily acceded to Jefferson's proposal that he proceed to Kamchatka, cross over to Nootka Sound in a Russian vessel, and make his way back to the United States overland from the Pacific. The permission of Catherine II was gained and Ledyard actually reached eastern Siberia, when the empress changed her mind and ordered the arrest and deportation of the explorer. Thus this project fell through.

During the winter of 1792-3 Jefferson encouraged the American Philosophical Society of Philadelphia to finance a scientific expedition to the Pacific to be led by André Michaux, a French botanist. Michaux's usefulness as an explorer was soon destroyed, however, when it was learned that he was involved in the intrigues of Edmond Genêt. In the meantime, in 1790, at the suggestion of Henry Knox, Secretary of War, Captain John Armstrong started up the Missouri with the hope of continuing on to the Pacific. But he had not proceeded far when he encountered some traders, who warned him of the hostility of the western Indians, and he turned back. After the failure of these projects no further proposals for American exploration of a region that was still foreign territory were made until the eve of the Louisiana Purchase. Even then the possibility that the United States might acquire this immense area had not entered men's minds.

Thomas Jefferson was now President. On January 18, 1803, he sent to Congress a secret message that was to bring to fulfilment the dream of western exploration which he had cherished so long. Neither mere curiosity regarding an unknown country nor desire for the gathering of scientific data were the mainsprings of Jefferson's proposal to Congress. "An intelligent officer, with ten or twelve chosen men," he said, "might explore the whole line, even to the Western Ocean, have conferences with the natives on the subject of commercial intercourse, get admission among them for our traders, as others are admitted, agree on convenient deposites for an interchange of articles, and return with the information acquired, in the course of two summers. . . . The interests of commerce place the principal object within the constitutional powers and care of Congress, and that it should incidentally advance the geographical knowledge of our own continent, cannot but be an additional gratification."

Since the men engaged in the exploration would receive pay from the War Department, Jefferson asked that Congress appropriate the small sum of $2500 "for the purpose of extending the external commerce of the United States." Congress responded favorably and Jefferson now proceeded to launch the expedition. For a leader he turned to his private secretary, Meriwether Lewis, a man not yet thirty years of age who had seen military service in the Old Northwest under Anthony Wayne and was thoroughly accustomed to life in the open. Lewis asked permission, which was granted, to select a companion to share his leadership, and his choice was William Clark, the younger brother of George Rogers Clark. Lewis held a commission as Captain and Clark as second lieutenant. It was the wish of Lewis, however, that the two men be regarded in all respects as of equal rank; and thus they were each generally called captain, and their names are associated impartially with the great expedition.

"The object of your mission," wrote Jefferson in his instructions to Meriwether Lewis, "is to explore the Missouri river, and such principal streams of it, as, by its course and communication with the water of the Pacific Ocean may offer the most direct and practicable water communication across this continent, for the purpose of commerce." Observations were to be made and notes kept concerning the latitude and longitude of all important places; the names and population of the Indian tribes encountered and all pertinent information in regard to the possibilities of trade with them; the animal and vegetable life of the country traversed; and any other geographical features that might be of interest or value. As a matter of fact, not only did the two leaders keep rather detailed journals, but the sergeants likewise kept diaries which are of considerable value.

Before the expedition got under way, the Louisiana Purchase had been consummated, and consequently the party would not be exploring foreign territory, as had been anticipated when the plans were first made. All during the summer and autumn of 1803 Lewis and Clark were busy enlisting men, collecting necessary materials and gathering information. Winter quarters were established at the mouth of the River Dubois on the east side of the Mississippi. On March 9 and 10, 1804, Lewis witnessed the ceremonies at St. Louis attendant upon the formal transfer of the upper Louisiana country to the United States. Then on May 14th the party, consisting of about forty-five men, one-third of whom were to go only as far as the Mandan villages, crossed the Mississippi in three boats and entered the Missouri. The great adventure had begun.

It would be interesting, if space permitted and the story had not been so often told, to recount the adventures of the Lewis and Clark party as they pushed their boats up the Missouri, combatting the shifting currents of that treacherous stream, meeting traders with fur-laden canoes from far up the river, and holding councils with Indian tribes. Late in October they reached the villages of the friendly Mandan Indians, north of the present Bismarck, North Dakota, about 1600 miles from the mouth of the Missouri. Here they built Fort Mandan and spent the winter. Here also they had the good fortune to secure the services of a French-Canadian, Toussaint Charbonneau, and his Indian wife Sacajawea, the "Bird Woman." Sacajawea was a Shoshone who had been taken as a captive from her home on the upper waters of the Missouri. She was destined to give invaluable assistance to the explorers when they reached the country with which she was familiar and the Indians to whom she belonged.

Early in April, 1805, the expedition set out from Fort Mandan. About three weeks later they passed the mouth of the Yellowstone River; and on August 12th they reached the headwaters of the Jefferson fork of the Missouri, where it was possible at some points for a man to stand astride the stream they had been following so long. The boats were left in hiding, and on foot, with packhorses secured from the Indians, the party crossed the continental divide and soon found a stream that flowed to the Pacific. The first weeks of September were spent in the difficult and perilous crossing of the Bitter Root Mountains. On October 16th they were on the Columbia; and on November 7th William Clark was able to write, with an expression of joy: "we are in view of the Ocian, the great Pacific Ocian which we have been so long anxious to see." After investigating possible sites for winter quarters Fort Clatsop was erected on Young's Bay, south of the mouth of the Columbia.

The return journey was accomplished in the period of six months, between March 23 and September 23, 1806. Early in the latter month the explorers began to meet traders ascending the Missouri. At the little village of La Charette, near which Daniel Boone was now living, the inhabitants received with astonishment a party of men who had been given up as lost and almost forgotten. Great rejoicing was shown upon their arrival at St. Louis, and a dinner and ball were given in their honor.

For various reasons it was several years before the public received an adequate account of the experiences and discoveries of the Lewis and Clark party. Furthermore, no immediate use was made of the information thus acquired. Yet the expedition is one of the most significant and remarkable achievements in the realm of geographical exploration, and it assumed great importance later when it was made one of the bases of the claim of the United States to the Oregon country.

Meriwether Lewis became governor of the Territory of Louisiana in 1807 and retained that position until October, 1809, when he either died suddenly or was murdered as he was journeying eastward across Tennessee. William Clark spent the remainder of his life, until his death in 1838, west of the Mississippi, as Indian agent, governor of Missouri Territory, and superintendent of Indian affairs.

EXPLORATION OF THE RED RIVER

Besides the Lewis and Clark expedition a number of other explorations were projected in the years immediately following the purchase of Louisiana. President Jefferson wrote to Meriwether Lewis that he desired to have explorations of all the principal streams flowing into the Mississippi and the Missouri from the west. He mentioned particularly the St. Peters (Minnesota), Des Moines, Platte, Kansas, Arkansas, and Red rivers. As it turned out, only a few of these projects were undertaken at this time, and none of them was attended with complete success. Nevertheless, considerable information was gathered regarding the lower part of the new acquisition, and in some instances American settlers profited by pushing rapidly into regions of which knowledge was thus gained.

Jefferson was embarrassed by his lack of knowledge concerning the western boundaries of the new purchase in the south. He sought geographical data from Daniel Clark of New Orleans; from Governor William C. C. Claiborne; from William Dunbar, a scientist living in what is now Mississippi; and from Dr. John Sibley, who had moved in 1803 from North Carolina to Natchitoches, on the Louisiana-Texas frontier. Sibley had done some exploring along the lower Red River and was able to furnish information of value. With such meager data as he could secure, the President made a report to Congress and sought an appropriation with which to finance exploration. The sum originally granted—$3,000—was much less than was requested, but it furnished authorization for exploration.

The result was an expedition in the winter of 1804-1805, under the leadership of William Dunbar and Dr. George Hunter. The plan was to explore the Red River, but the Spanish authorities in Chihuahua were hostile to any American expeditions in the direction of the Louisiana-Texas frontier. Furthermore, it was learned that the Osage Indians were at this time illy disposed toward any incursion into their territory. Accordingly the Dunbar-Hunter party proceeded only a short distance up the Red River, and then turned into the Ouachita, which was followed to the vicinity of Hot Springs, Arkansas. The plan to explore the Red River, however, was not abandoned. Congress made an additional appropriation, and in 1806 Thomas Freeman ascended that river at the head of a small military party. When he had reached a point about six hundred miles from the mouth of the river, he found himself face to face with an overwhelmingly superior force of Spaniards, whose commander forbade further progress. Freeman could do nothing but retire and return the way he had come.

THE EXPEDITIONS OF ZEBULON M. PIKE

Considerably greater significance attaches to two other governmental expeditions of this period, both of which were commanded by the same man—Zebulon Montgomery Pike. It was from General James Wilkinson, best known for his Spanish intrigues, that Pike received instructions in the summer of 1805 to lead an exploring party to the headwaters of the Mississippi. He was directed to discover the source of that river, hold councils with the Indian tribes, ascertain the activities of British traders on American soil, and obtain information concerning the possibilities of the fur trade. Starting up the river in August, he visited the Dubuque lead mines on the west bank of the river, stopped at Prairie du Chien, and above that point traveled through an unbroken Indian country. Arriving in the region of Cass Lake, Leech Lake, and Sandy Lake, he found the traders of the Northwest Company in undisputed possession of the field and the British flag flying over Indian villages. He sought to impress the Indians with the fact that they now owed allegiance to the United States, and he warned the English traders to give heed to the laws of the nation upon whose soil they were operating. Owing in part at least to the winter season, he erroneously decided that Leech Lake was the source of the Mississippi, and so reported upon his return to St. Louis on the last day of April, 1806. It was not until 1832 that the true source of the Mississippi, Lake Itasca, was discovered by Henry R. Schoolcraft.

Pike had scarcely compiled his report on the Mississippi expedition when he received a commission from General Wilkinson to lead a more important exploration into the southwest. On account of a well-grounded suspicion that Wilkinson was in some way connected with Aaron Burr's mysterious plans, there remains much uncertainty concerning the general's real purpose in despatching Pike on this expedition. It is reasonable, however, to credit Pike himself with innocence of knowledge of any plot hostile to his own government, although he can scarcely have been ignorant of Wilkinson's desire to obtain information regarding the Spanish in and around Santa Fé. The Spanish seem to have been aware, or at least suspicious, of such a design, for before Pike set out, a large party of Spaniards visited the Pawnee Indians and obtained from them a promise to turn back the Americans. The ostensible purposes of the expedition, as revealed in Pike's instructions, were to return to their people a number of Osage Indians who had been on a visit to Washington, to make peace between the Osage and Kansas Indians, and to explore the country drained by the Arkansas and Red rivers.

Pike set out from St. Louis the middle of July, 1806, with a party of twenty-three. The Osage Indians were restored to their people and the expedition proceeded overland. Late in September the Pawnee villages were reached and a council was held. The Pawnees, fierce and dreaded Indians of the plains country, exhibited the effects of Spanish influence and showed distinct hostility to the Americans. Pike, however, paid no heed to their warning to turn back, but rather defied them. Turning southward he came to the great bend of the Arkansas. Detaching a small party to explore this river to its mouth, he led the others up the stream and into the mountains. A fort was erected near the site of Pueblo, Colorado, and the surrounding country was explored. Pike was especially disappointed at his inability to scale the heights of a mountain that loomed on the western skyline, but nevertheless the peak has ever since borne his name.

After reaching the region of Canyon City and Leadville, Colorado, Pike crossed the Sangre de Cristo Range after suffering severe hardships, and found himself on the Conejos, a small tributary of the Rio Grande, where he built another stockade. He believed, or professed to believe, himself on the Red River. From this point Dr. John H. Robinson, a member of the party, set out for Santa Fé partly to collect a debt due a friend, but probably also to spy out the land. Shortly afterward the Spaniards sent out a captain with one hundred mounted men to take Pike and his companions into custody. Resistance was futile. The Americans were escorted to Santa Fé, where they were examined and their papers taken; and then

they were sent to Chihuahua. Here they were again examined
and held prisoners for a time. Finally, they were escorted
across Texas to the Louisiana frontier and turned over to the
American authorities at Natchitoches on July 1, 1807.

While this southwestern expedition ended disastrously, it
cannot be counted a failure. A mass of information regarding
a hitherto unknown region was gathered and made available in
Pike's report. In view of the later development of the myth
or tradition of a Great American Desert, one portion of this
report was significant. Pike wrote of great desert-like prairies
incapable of supporting any considerable white population.
"But from these immense prairies," he said, "may arise one
great advantage to the United States, viz: The restriction of
our population to some certain limits, and thereby a continuation of the Union. Our citizens being so prone to rambling and
extending themselves on the frontiers will, through necessity
be constrained to limit their extent on the west to the borders
of the Missouri and Mississippi, while they leave the prairies
incapable of cultivation to the wandering and uncivilized aborigines of the country."

EXPLORATIONS EAST OF THE ROCKIES, 1809-1821

Following Pike's return more than a decade elapsed before
the government despatched another exploring expedition into
the Far West.   In the meantime some additions to knowledge
of the region were made by individuals or parties who penetrated various sections of the country between the Mississippi
and the Rockies. In 1809 John Shaw appears to have ventured
west from Missouri as far as Colorado, and to have spent most
of the ensuing three years hunting in eastern Kansas and western Arkansas and Missouri. Two years later John Bradbury,
a naturalist, took advantage of an invitation from Wilson Price
Hunt to accompany the Astorian expedition up the Missouri
as far as the Arikara villages. He later went further up the
river to the Mandan villages, making scientific observations
that were soon made available by publication. Upon his return
journey he met his friend Henry N. Brackenridge, who had

accompanied Manuel Lisa, a St. Louis fur trader, up the river. Brackenridge likewise published an account of his travels.

Late in November, 1818, Henry R. Schoolcraft, who was later to gain considerable renown as a geologist and ethnologist, started from Potosi, Missouri, with the expressed purpose of traversing "the plains and mountain elevations west of the Mississippi, which had once echoed the tramp of the squadrons of De Soto." The headwaters of the White River was the most western point reached by Schoolcraft, but before returning to Potosi in February, 1819, he explored the upper portion of that stream and made valuable observations concerning what the title-page of his book called "the Semi-Alpine Region of the Ozark Mountains of Missouri and Arkansas."

Before Schoolcraft had terminated his expedition Thomas Nuttall, a botanist, was on his way up the Arkansas River. He was given much assistance by the military authorities at Fort Smith and by traders. Among the latter was Nathaniel Pryor, one of the sergeants of the Lewis and Clark expedition, whom he found at a trading post near the mouth of the Verdigris River. So intent was Nuttall upon gathering botanical specimens that at one time he became lost and might have fared badly, had not he encountered a lonely settler who offered him hospitality. Late in August, 1819, he reached the mouth of the Cimarron River, in the present State of Oklahoma, but upon attempting to ascend this stream the difficulties became so great that he turned back, and finally reached New Orleans in February, 1820. In the following year Nuttall published a journal of his travels that possesses so much literary charm that it deserves to rank among the classics of early western travel.

The year 1819 witnessed also the beginning of the first governmental expedition into the Far West since that led by Zebulon M. Pike. The War Department had decided to launch what was known as the "Yellowstone Expedition," the main purpose of which was to erect a fort at the Mandan villages, on the upper Missouri River. A considerable body of troops under the command of Colonel Henry Atkinson proceeded up the Missouri and went into winter quarters at old Council Bluffs, where they built Fort Atkinson. The scientific portion of this expedition commanded by Major Stephen H. Long left

Pittsburgh in April, 1819, on board a steamboat, the *Western Engineer*. This was a stern-wheel craft of very light draft; and although it carried its passengers to old Council Bluffs, it seems to have been designed as much for the purpose of frightening the Indians as of navigating western rivers. "The bow of this vessel," according to a contemporary description, "exhibits the form of a huge serpent, black and scaly, rising out of the water from under the boat, his head as high as the deck, darted forward, his mouth open, vomiting smoke, and apparently carrying the boat on his back."

Major Long left his men in winter quarters and journeyed back to Washington. When he returned in the spring of 1820 he bore new instructions. The original plans for the expedition had met with opposition in Congress and further funds were denied. As a substitute for the more elaborate undertaking Long was directed to lead a small exploring party to the Rocky Mountains, with the purpose of discovering the sources of the Platte and Red rivers, exploring the upper Arkansas, and gathering scientific data regarding the country. Accordingly, he set out up the Platte River early in June, with Dr. Edwin James, a geologist and botanist, and eighteen other men. By July 5th the party had reached the site of Denver. The peak which now bears Long's name was seen, and Dr. James with two companions succeeded in making the first recorded ascent of Pike's Peak. Turning southward, the party reached the Arkansas River near the site of Pueblo. Soon afterward Captain John R. Bell was despatched with a few men to descend the Arkansas. Long, with the remainder of the party, crossed the Purgatory and upper waters of the Cimarron, and finally reached the Canadian River near the present boundary between New Mexico and Texas. They believed this stream to be the Red River and were not fully aware of their error until they descended it to its junction with the Arkansas. The two sections of the party were reunited at Fort Smith, from whence they proceeded to Cape Girardeau, Missouri, and were disbanded in October, 1820.

The Long expedition failed in at least two of its main objectives, namely, to discover the sources of the Platte and Red rivers. The report, compiled by Dr. Edwin James and published in 1823, contained scientific data of considerable value, as well as much useful information concerning various Indian tribes. Of more importance was the contribution which the chronicles made to the tradition of a Great American Desert, corroborating the reports made by Pike and others. "In regard to this extensive section of the country," wrote Long, "I do not hesitate in giving the opinion, that it is almost wholly unfit for cultivation, and of course uninhabitable by a people depending upon agriculture for their subsistence." Even where fertile tracts were occasionally encountered the scarcity of wood and water would "prove an insuperable obstacle in the way of settling the country." The whole region seemed "peculiarly adapted as a range for buffaloes, wild goats, and other wild game." Long agreed with Pike in predicting that the region "viewed as a frontier, may prove of infinite importance to the United States, inasmuch as it is calculated to serve as a barrier to prevent too great an extension of our population westward, and secure us against the machinations or incursions of an enemy that might otherwise be disposed to annoy us in that part of our frontier."

While Long and his companions were on their expedition Captain Mathew J. Magee with several other officers, among whom was Captain Stephen W. Kearny, led a small expedition to explore a route from Council Bluffs to Camp Cold Water, at the mouth of the Minnesota River where Fort Snelling was soon to be erected. Two years later, in 1823, Stephen H. Long was in command of a well organized exploring party which ascended the Minnesota River (then known as the St. Peters) and visited the Pembina settlement on the Red River of the North, founded in 1812 by Lord Selkirk. In accordance with his instructions, Long took observations and located the forty-ninth parallel in this region, thereby proving that Pembina was located on territory belonging to the United States—a result which was apparently pleasing to the settlers. After visiting Lake Winnipeg, the party journeyed eastward to the north shore of Lake Superior and returned to the East by way of the Great Lakes. A detailed report, compiled by William H. Keating, was published in 1825.

The Explorations of John C. Frémont

Thus far all the official explorations of the Far West, with the exception of the Lewis and Clark expedition, had been confined to the region east of the Rocky Mountains. The great stretches of inter-mountain plateaus, the Great Basin, the Sierras, the Cascades, the valleys of California and the Oregon country, and the Coast Range were in time penetrated by venturous fur traders. But the geographical knowledge obtained by these men was seldom committed to paper and the general public remained in ignorance of the extensive area west of the Rockies. As a matter of fact, this region lay beyond the range of practical American politics. The Great Plains, regarded as unsuited to white habitation, had been turned over to the Indians with the expectation that there they would never be disturbed. The Rocky Mountains were looked upon as a boundary beyond which the United States would have no need or wish to expand, at least for many generations.

This confident attitude was strangely short-sighted. The decade of the forties had scarcely begun before opinion regarding the Far West showed a marked change. The Oregon country became attractive not merely to fur traders, but to American settlers whose trans-continental trek will be described in a later chapter. The government now became vitally interested in securing more detailed information concerning the land beyond the Rockies. Thus it was that there appeared in the list of American explorers the colorful figure of John Charles Frémont. The title "Pathfinder of the West," which was applied to him, was not wholly deserved, for he obtained invaluable information and guidance from such experienced mountaineers and fur traders as Christopher (Kit) Carson, Thomas Fitzpatrick, Jim Bridger, and Bill Williams. And yet Frémont's published reports, with their detailed descriptions, their maps and their scientific data were widely circulated and read in the years immediately succeeding, when Manifest Destiny and the lure of gold drew hosts of Americans across the plains, over the mountains and on to the Pacific Coast.

In 1842, when John C. Frémont started west in command of his first expedition, he was twenty-nine years of age. Despite his youth, he had served an apprenticeship in wilderness life which fitted him well for the adventures ahead of him. He had been a member of a party surveying a route for a railroad through the mountains of South Carolina and eastern Tennessee. He had assisted in a military reconnaissance of the Cherokee Indian country. Still later he had served under J. N. Nicollet in a survey of the region between the Minnesota and Missouri rivers. These experiences had taught him much wilderness lore, brought him in contact with numerous Indian tribes, and given him thorough training in the making of topographical and scientific observations. Returning to Washington after the last of these expeditions, he had come in contact with Senator Thomas Hart Benton who was now keenly interested in the Far West, had eloped with his daughter Jessie, been forgiven and welcomed into the family circle. Thus he had gained a patron through whose influence came his commission to lead a party of exploration.

Frémont wrote in his *Memoirs* that the exploration of 1842 "was intended to be 'auxiliary and in aid to the emigration to the Lower Columbia'; it was to indicate and describe the line of travel, and the best positions for military posts; and to describe, and fix in position, the South Pass in the Rocky Mountains, at which this initial expedition was to terminate." After several months spent in collecting information and preparing equipment, Frémont set out on June 10th from Cyprian Chouteau's trading post on the Kansas River with a feeling akin to that of "leaving the shore for a long voyage." The party consisted of about twenty-five men, including Charles Preuss as topographer, Kit Carson as guide, Lucien Maxwell as hunter, and a score of French-Canadian voyageurs.

Proceeding a short distance along the Kansas River, the party crossed over to the Platte the main stream and the southern fork of which were followed to St. Vrain's Fort, north of the present site of Denver. Thence the route led northward to Fort Laramie and up the Sweetwater River to the South Pass, which was reached on August 8th. The credit for discovering this famous pass, which was to be crossed by so many thousands of emigrants to Oregon and California, is usually assigned to Jedediah S. Smith and Thomas Fitzpatrick who in 1824 defi-

nitely located it while engaged in trading activities with
William H. Ashley. Although the altitude of the pass is nearly
7500 feet, the approach was so easy and gradual that Frémont
compared it to "the ascent of the Capitol Hill from the Avenue,
at Washington . . . the traveller, without being reminded of
any change by toilsome ascents, suddenly finds himself on the
waters which flow to the Pacific Ocean."

The Frémont party spent several days in the Wind River
Range, where the leader was stirred by the scenic beauties of
lakes and forests and snow-capped mountains. On August
15th he and five companions climbed the peak which now bears
his name, 13,730 feet in height, and "unfurled the national flag
to wave in the breeze where never flag waved before." The
return journey was made along the North Platte. On October
10th the mouth of the Kansas River was reached and by the
last of the month Frémont was back in Washington, D.C.

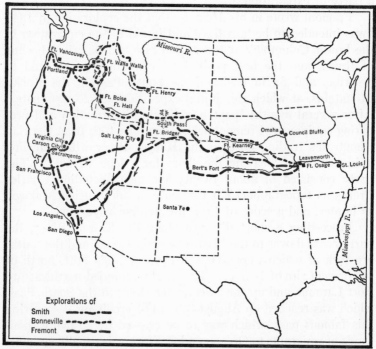

VIII. EXPLORATIONS OF SMITH, BONNEVILLE, AND FRÉMONT

Within a short time Frémont was busily preparing for a second and more extended official expedition—the enterprise of 1843-4 upon which rests his chief fame as an explorer. The purpose of this expedition, in Frémont's words, was "to examine the broad region south of the Columbia River, lying between the Rocky Mountains and the Pacific Ocean." Gathering a party which again included Charles Preuss, Thomas Fitzpatrick, Lucien Maxwell, and later Kit Carson, Frémont repaired to the mouth of the Kansas River to outfit the expedition. There, late in May, 1843, he received a mysterious letter from his wife, who was now in St. Louis, urging him to set out at once and proceed to Bent's Fort on the Arkansas. The letter gave no explanation, but Frémont knew there must be some good reason for his wife's urgent suggestion which he hastened to follow. Not until his return the following year did he learn the reason. He had added a howitzer to his equipment for possible use against hostile Indians. News of this acquisition had come to Washington and had aroused much criticism. Consequently Colonel John J. Abert, commanding the topographical corps, had written to Frémont ordering him to return to Washington and explain the presence of a howitzer in the equipment of an expedition that was scientific and not military in character. Jessie Fremont had opened this letter, and realizing that if it were obeyed the expedition would be greatly delayed and perhaps entirely abandoned, she had sent the cryptic advice to her husband.

It was on May 29th that the expedition started westward. On November 4th the party reached The Dalles of the Columbia River. To give even a sketchy description of the experiences of the intervening months would require much space. Several times the party was divided, one section being led by Thomas Fitzpatrick. Frémont and his companions made careful observations in the eastern portion of the present State of Colorado, encountered Kit Carson near Pueblo and added him to the party, proceeded northward, skirted along the base of the Medicine Bow Mountains, crossed the South Pass, and gazed upon the waters of Great Salt Lake. Concerning the last named achievement he wrote: "I am doubtful if the followers of Balboa felt more enthusiasm when, from the heights of the Andes, they saw for the first time the great Western Ocean." Although sorely tempted to explore the surrounding regions, he turned northward, reached Fort Hall where fresh oxen and supplies were obtained, passed along the Snake River to Fort Boise, traversed the beautiful Grande Ronde Valley, visited the Whitman mission in the Walla Walla country, and finally arrived at The Dalles. Leaving most of his party here, Frémont paid a visit to the Hudson's Bay headquarters at Fort Vancouver, where he was given a cordial welcome and much needed supplies by Dr. John McLoughlin.

On November 25th the party of twenty-five men set out from The Dalles on the homeward journey, with more than one hundred horses and mules, several cattle, and supplies for three months. Southward along the Deschutes River they traveled until the Klamath Marsh was reached. Thence the route led eastward and southward into a region unknown even to Fitzpatrick and Carson. Summer Lake and Lake Abert in Oregon received their names at this time, as did also Pyramid Lake in Nevada. After pushing on south past the present site of Carson City the leader changed his plans, on account of the dwindling supply of food and the wretched condition of the animals, and decided to cross the Sierras into California in the dead of winter. It was a desperate undertaking and was accomplished only after the severest labor and intense suffering from cold and hunger and exhaustion.

At Sutter's Fort on the Sacramento River the party spent two weeks from March 8 to 22, 1844, in much needed rest. New horses, mules and cattle and fresh supplies of provisions were secured, and the journey was resumed. In excellent spirits the party proceeded up the San Joaquin Valley, passed along the western edge of the Mohave Desert, and at a point not far north of Los Angeles turned east and traveled the old Spanish trail leading toward Santa Fé. In the Wasatch Mountains they left this trail, visited Utah Lake, crossed the mountains into the Colorado region, descended the Arkansas River for a distance, and then struck off across the prairies to the mouth of the Kansas River. On August 6, 1844, the expedition was disbanded at St. Louis. Thus ended Frémont's greatest expedition—one for which he and his men received much deserved credit.

Later expeditions led by John C. Frémont were not so fortunate. In 1845 he began his last official expedition which took him up the Arkansas River, to Utah Lake and Great Salt Lake, and across the Sierras to California. Here after a time he exchanged the role of explorer for that of a soldier and became involved in the revolt which resulted in the establishment of the Bear Flag Republic. When he returned from California it was as a prisoner facing court-martial for disobedience to his superior officer, Colonel Stephen W. Kearny. After his conviction by the court-martial, Frémont sought consolation in a privately-financed expedition to survey a southern route for a railroad to the Pacific coast. In spite of the warnings of experienced mountain men, he undertook to cross the southern Sierras during the severe winter of 1848-9, and met disaster. He lost one-third of his men and all of his equipment. In 1853 he returned once more to the project with better success, but without contributing anything to geographical knowledge. Neither conviction by court-martial nor the virtual failure of his later expeditions, however, were sufficient to diminish Frémont's widespread popularity. His exploits had captured the imagination of the people in a period when the Far West was a center of public attention. And so in 1856 he became the first presidential nominee of the new Republican party.

CHAPTER XXVIII

FUR TRADERS AND THE FUR TRADE

OFFICIAL explorers did much to acquaint Americans with the great trans-Mississippi West during the first half of the nineteenth century. But, with a few exceptions, these official explorers were preceded by a host of trappers and traders in furs who, to use the words of Hiram M. Chittenden, "sought out these inhospitable wilds, traced the streams to their sources, scaled the mountain passes, and explored a boundless expanse of territory where the foot of the white man had never trodden before."

It was La Salle and Tonty, Duluth, Perrot, Radisson and Groseilliers, and others of their kind, seeking furs, who carried the banners of France into the region of the Great Lakes and the Mississippi Valley. Men like William Johnson, George Croghan, Conrad Weiser, and Henry Woodward, likewise seeking furs, opened the eyes of the English to the importance of the land behind the Alleghanies. No less adventurous were the lives and no less significant were the services of Manual Lisa, William H. Ashley, the Sublette brothers, Jedediah Smith, Jim Bridger, Thomas Fitzpatrick, Kit Carson, and their fellows in the fur trade of the region from the Rockies to the Pacific during the years from 1800 to 1850.

Comparatively few of these wide-roving trappers kept diaries or journals or wrote letters which found their way into print during their own day. Yet their indirect contributions to geographical knowledge can scarcely be overestimated. They knew all the streams and mountain passes and trails so well that, without compass or other aid, they could travel with the utmost certainty from Santa Fé and Taos in the south to the northermost haunts of the fur men along the upper Missouri and in the old Oregon country. They also knew and understood the Indians better than any other white men. Thus it was that veterans of the fur trade like Kit Carson and Thomas Fitzpatrick and Jim Bridger and Bill Williams were called upon to serve as guides and scouts for official exploring parties, military expeditions, caravans of merchants, and companies of emigrants.

The story of the fur trade belongs with those other chapters in the romance of the Far West which recite the colorful history of the mining camps, the overland stage-coach and the pony express, and the days of the cowboys and the cattle kings. It is a story replete with adventures of lonely trappers, of fierce battles between parties of fur traders and Indians, of gay scenes at mountain rendezvous, of bitter, no-quarter competition between rival fur companies. It tells of a life that possessed an unappeasable attraction for its devotees, even though the fortunes that were made accrued mainly to a few safely-sheltered individuals, and the only reward of a large proportion of those who bore the brunt of the trade, aside from the zest of the game, was an early and tragic death or old age harassed by poverty.

The Fur Trade in the Upper Mississippi Valley

When American independence was won and the United States came into existence the upper Mississippi Valley and the Great Lakes region had been the theater of a great fur trade development extending over a period of nearly a century and a half, as has already been described. American traders, individually and in groups, no doubt frequented these regions in the years following the Treaty of 1783 which closed the Revolutionary War and gave the United States jurisdiction as far west as the Mississippi. But it was twenty-five years before an American fur trading company entered the field. In the meantime the trade was carried on almost entirely by two British companies. In the year which witnessed the signing of the treaty above mentioned there were organized the Northwest Company and the Mackinaw Company. The former, destined to become the most formidable rival of the century-old Hudson's Bay Company in the great Northwest, had its headquarters in Montreal, but maintained important posts at

Michilimackinac and later at Fort William on the northern shore of Lake Superior. The Mackinaw Company had its headquarters at Michilimackinac. Both companies conducted an active trade in the country now included in Michigan, Wisconsin, Minnesota, Iowa, and Illinois for many years after that region had become American territory.

In 1808, however, there was chartered the American Fur Company, which was merely the business name of the greatest figure in the American fur trade—John Jacob Astor. The career of this early capitalist fully satisfies the formula of the poor immigrant lad who came to America and rose to a position of wealth and power. Born in 1763 in the little village of Waldorf on the edge of the Black Forest in Germany, Astor went to London in 1779 and landed in the United States in January, 1784, with the equivalent of twenty-five dollars in cash and a stock of seven flutes with which to start business. Aboard the ship on which he sailed were a number of Hudson's Bay Company men and a young German who had been engaged in the fur trade. John Jacob was much fascinated by the tales which he heard from these men of the adventure and profits of the trade in furs.

Scarcely had he settled himself in New York when young Astor himself was experiencing all the thrills of active participation in this industry. Within a year after his arrival he had made two trips into the fur country. During the succeeding fifteen years he made frequent journeys into the wilds, at least once as far west as the Grand Portage on the northern shore of Lake Superior. More often he traveled to Montreal, where he made the acquaintance of many of the veterans of the Northwest Company. Thus, through personal experience and association with men of wide knowledge, he learned the fur trade in all its details. No story of individual achievement is more striking than that of the manner in which, by the turn of the century, he made himself the greatest fur merchant in the United States, with a fleet of ships engaged in the trade of the Pacific coast and of China. When, therefore, he organized the American Fur Company in 1808, John Jacob Astor secured the act of incorporation, creating what was really a holding company, merely to facilitate and give broader scope to his already extensive and successful operations.

As will presently be seen, in 1810 Astor launched a project for a trading enterprise in the Columbia River region which was the only real failure of his career. Neither anticipations of the profits to be derived from this venture nor disappointment because of failure however, deterred Astor from his intention to make the American Fur Company supreme in the trade of the upper Mississippi and around the Great Lakes. When he found his efforts hampered by the traders of the Mackinaw Company, he bought out that company just at the close of the War of 1812. Then in 1816, largely through Astor's influence, Congress passed an act excluding foreign fur trading companies from operating in the territory of the United States. Accordingly the Northwest Company was obliged to retire beyond the Canadian border. Thereafter the American Fur Company virtually controlled the trade of this region, with headquarters at Mackinac in charge of Ramsay Crooks.

During the period when these events were happening the government of the United States itself was a competitor, although on unequal terms, with the private companies and individual traders. By an act passed in 1796 Congress made provision for the establishment of trading houses, or "factories" as they were called, in the Indian country. The purposes of this measure were entirely benevolent: to assure the Indians fair dealing on a cost basis and to check the evil practices of the private traders. But the plan was not sufficiently thoroughgoing. Instead of retaining a monopoly of the trade in its own hands, the government issued licenses to private traders and thereby doomed its "factory system" to ineffectiveness. The factors at the government trading-houses were instructed not to go out among the Indians to trade. They were not allowed to extend credit to Indians, nor to issue liquor to them, and they were supplied with inferior goods. On the other hand, the private traders went directly to the Indians, extended credit to them, and, although forbidden to do so, they used liquor as an important item in their stock of trade. As a consequence they secured most of the furs.

In 1822, after weathering many persistent attacks, the

factory system was abolished. There is evidence that, in spite of its many handicaps, the system was self-sustaining and that it was not the total failure which its enemies claimed. It is at least revealing to find that the traders, large and small, were the most bitter opponents of the government trading-house system and that John Jacob Astor lobbied untiringly to secure its abolition. Ramsay Crooks wrote to Senator Thomas Hart Benton congratulating him upon his part in destroying "the pious monster" and delivering the country from "so gross and unholy an imposition."

Manuel Lisa and the Missouri Fur Company

The fur trade of the north-central area under American rule is worthy of study, but it was in the Far West that this industry attained its greatest magnitude and is characterized by the most romantic features. The Louisiana Purchase opened up an immense and attractive field for the activities of American trappers and traders. To be sure, roaming Frenchmen had pushed up the Missouri and into the Great Plains region. Spaniards had made a few attempts to trade for furs in the southwest. St. Louis was already the head-quarters of a considerable fur trade which had been growing since the founding of the village in 1764 to serve, as a trading post for the firm of Maxent, Laclede and Company. During the period of Spanish control in Louisiana numerous other traders received licenses or grants. Among those best known was Manuel Lisa who was so well established in the fur busi-ness by 1800 that he was given the exclusive right to trade with the Osage Indians on the Osage River. Two other men who not only engaged in the fur trade, but also established families which long occupied leading positions in the growing town of St. Louis were Pierre and Auguste Chouteau. And yet when the American flag was unfurled in the country west of the Mississippi the extensive fur resources of the Far West had scarcely been touched.

The transfer of Louisiana to the United States, and espe-cially the report made by Lewis and Clark upon their return from their expedition in 1806, greatly stimulated the desire of the St. Louis traders to extend their operations to the rich fur country of the upper Missouri River. No one was more prompt and energetic in translating this desire into action than Manuel Lisa. Associating himself with William Morrison, Pierre Menard, and others, he led an expedition up the Missouri and Yellowstone and established a trading post at the mouth of the Bighorn in the heart of the Crow Indian country. On the journey up the Missouri, at the mouth of the Platte River, Lisa had the good fortune to meet John Colter, a member of the Lewis and Clark party who had remained on the upper Missouri to trap. Recognizing the value of a man who was acquainted with the country into which he was venturing, Lisa induced Colter to join his party.

While Fort Manuel or Fort Lisa, as it was variously called, was being erected Lisa sent Colter out alone, with only a thirty-pound pack, a gun and some ammunition, to open negotiations with the Blackfeet and other Indians some five hundred miles to the westward. Colter's adventures on this mission and on another similar journey in the following spring constitute one of the most colorful chapters in the annals of the West. There is much uncertainty regarding his route on these trips, but some writers credit him with being the discoverer of the Teton Mountains, the South Pass, Green River, the headwaters of the Snake, Pierre's Hole, Jackson Hole, and the region now embraced in Yellowstone Park. Even if all these claims cannot be substantiated, John Colter deserves a high place as an explorer.

Manuel Lisa returned to St. Louis in 1808 and in the following spring he organized the St. Louis Missouri Fur Company, or the Missouri Fur Company as it was later known. Among the members of this company, besides Lisa were William Clark, Pierre Chouteau, Auguste Chouteau, Reuben Lewis, Pierre Menard, William Morrison, and Andrew Henry. In June of that year, 1809, an expedition of one hundred and fifty men started up the Missouri. Several posts were established on the upper river and the party reached Lisa's fort at the mouth of the Bighorn in safety. Here the fall and winter were profitably spent in trading and trapping. In the spring of 1810 a portion of the men led by Pierre Menard and Andrew Henry set out for the Three Forks of the Missouri in the country of the hostile Blackfeet in what is now southwestern Montana. Here a post was built and for a time all went well. Then suddenly the Blackfeet descended upon the trappers, killed five of them, and carried off their guns, ammunition, horses, traps, and furs. All during the summer the Indians continued to harass the traders. Menard, with some of the men, departed with such furs as had been obtained, but Andrew Henry, was determined to hold on. Finally, even he became discouraged after re- peated attacks by the Blackfeet, and in the fall of 1810 he and his men crossed the continental divide and established a temporary post on the Henry Fork of the Snake River near the site of the present town of Elgin, Idaho.

Altogether the expedition was unprofitable, barely meeting the costs. In 1812 the company was reorganized, and then the War of 1812 interfered with trading activities. During the following years several reorganizations took place and the company bore various names, although in general it seems still to have been known as the Missouri Fur Company. However, at no time was it an organization like Astor's American Fur Company. In 1820 when Manuel Lisa died he was the last of the original partners still associated with the company. Joshua Pilcher was the head of the firm when it finally passed out of existence about 1830.

THE ASTORIA ENTERPRISE

It was while Andrew Henry and his men were fighting the Blackfeet at the Missouri Fur Company's post at the Three Forks of the Missouri that John Jacob Astor perfected his au- dacious plan to establish a trading post at the mouth of the Columbia River. His purpose was to have a base of operations at which to gather furs by trapping and by trade with the Indians of the northwest, ship the pelts to China where they could be exchanged at a profit for tea and silks and other goods, which could be sold at a second profit in the home markets on the Atlantic coast. He even visioned a chain of posts up the Missouri and across the mountains to the Columbia, establish- ing a line of overland communication with St. Louis.

The prosecution of this ambitious enterprise was entrusted to the Pacific Fur Company, organized in 1810 as a subsidiary of the American Fur Company. For partners Astor desired men of long experience in the fur trade, and so he turned, unfortunately as events proved, principally to his old friends of the Northwest Company who were British subjects, rather than to Manuel Lisa and his associates who were Americans. Astor himself agreed to supply the capital, not to exceed $400,-000, and to stand all losses for the period of five years, such was his faith in the success of the venture. Of the one hundred shares of stock he retained fifty and the remaining fifty were distributed among his nine partners, who were to engage personally in the operations of the company. Two expeditions were fitted out, one to go by sea and the other overland. Thus was inaugurated the venture the story of which has been immortalized by Washington Irving in his fascinating account of *Astoria; or, Enterprise Beyond the Rocky Mountains.*

Early in September, 1810, the *Tonquin,* a ship of two hundred and ninety tons burden, sailed from New York. Her captain was Jonathan Thorn, a capable and experienced naval officer. He seems not to have realized, however, that the rigid discipline of a man-of-war could not be applied to his strongly individualistic passengers on a commercial vessel. As a result there was engendered much ill will, which at times threatened to find expression in personal violence. Otherwise the voyage was comparatively uneventful. The vessel entered the Pacific Ocean on the day before Christmas; the Hawaiian Islands were reached about the middle of February, 1811; and on March 22nd land was sighted at the mouth of the Columbia.

Captain Thorn exhibited poor seamanship in crossing the bar and entering the river. One small boat was lost, with a crew of five including the first mate; and three more men were drowned in a second attempt. At length an entrance was made and in April a site was chosen on the southern bank of the river, and the men began the erection of a post which was named Astoria. This was a task for which the men possessed little experience, since the ground must be cleared of huge trees. Accordingly much time was consumed and there was continued bickering between the partners and Captain Thorn, who wished to proceed on a trading voyage up the coast, pursuant to Astor's instructions.

Early in June the *Tonquin* sailed on a voyage that ended in a terrible tragedy. Vancouver Island was reached without mishap and trade opened with the Indians. Unfortunately an altercation arose during which a chief was struck in the face. Dissembling their resentment, the Indians were admitted on board the vessel in large numbers. At a signal they suddenly attacked the crew, killing all but five of the twenty-two men. The Indians finally withdrew, and four of the survivors of the massacre escaped to the shore where they were later hunted down and put to death by torture. Only one wounded man was now left on the ship. When the Indians again swarmed on deck in high anticipation of plunder, this lone survivor fired the powder magazine and the *Tonquin* was blown to bits.

Meanwhile Astor's overland expedition was making its way westward under the leadership of Wilson Price Hunt, one of the partners in the Pacific Fur Company. Other partners who accompanied him were Donald McKenzie, Ramsay Crooks, Joseph Miller, and Robert McLellan. The story of the journey up the Missouri during the spring of 1811, is enlivened by a keelboat race in which Manuel Lisa, with a small party, put forth prodigious efforts to overtake Hunt and his larger company before reaching the country of the hostile Sioux Indians. Hunt had expected to continue up the Missouri River to its headwaters and follow in general the route of Lewis and Clark. At the Arikara villages, however, a change of plan was made, owing to the dangers of a passage through the country of the Blackfeet. Horses were secured and the party resumed the journey on land. The route led through the Bighorn Mountains, up the Wind River, across to the headwaters of the Green River, thence to the Snake, where they found Andrew Henry's abandoned post, and down the Snake and the Columbia to Astoria, which was reached early in 1812. The latter part of the journey was characterized by terrible hardships and the loss of several men.

About the middle of July, 1811, there arrived at Astoria a small party bearing a British flag and headed by David Thompson of the Northwest Company, who had already made several exploring expeditions to the upper Columbia and had established trading posts for his company in that region. He had lost the race for the mouth of the Columbia by a little more than three months. After Thompson's departure, the Pacific Fur Company's leaders at Astoria hastened to expand the range of their trade into the interior. David Stuart led a party which established a post at the mouth of the Okanogan River in what is now northern Washington. Later Robert Stuart and a number of trappers began operations on the Willamette. Still later other posts were built in the upper Columbia region; and a party was sent back over the long overland trail to carry despatches to Astor in New York.

Despite all these activities, Astoria's days were now numbered. Late in December, 1812, two employees of the Northwest Company arrived at the Spokane trading post with news that war had been declared between the United States and Great Britain, and that a British ship of war was soon due at Astoria. This exciting information was carried with all haste to Astoria. It was now that the British citizenship and the previous connection of Astor's leading partners became a matter of vital importance. It was easy for Duncan McDougal and Donald McKenzie, now the dominating factors at Astoria, to reach the conclusion that their enterprise was hopeless, especially in competition with the great Northwest Company. Thus when a brigade of Northwesters under John Stuart and Joseph McGillivray reached Astoria, negotiations were soon begun and in October, 1813, Astoria and all the interests of the Pacific Fur Company were sold to the Northwest Company. Thus ended in failure John Jacob Astor's dream of a vast empire of trade on the Pacific—an enterprise which had cost a large sum of money and more than sixty lives.

About a month after the sale, the *Raccoon,* a British war vessel reached Astoria. The Captain took possession of the place and renamed it Fort George. Thereafter, for several years Americans were seldom seen in the old Oregon country, although a treaty of joint occupation was signed by the United States and Great Britain in 1818. The Northwest Company remained in possession of the fur trade of the region until it was absorbed by the Hudson's Bay Company in 1821.

The Rocky Mountain Fur Company

The story of the fur trade now takes us back to St. Louis and the Rocky Mountains and to the activities of a group of the most resourceful, energetic, and picturesque men who ever pursued the fur trade under the American flag. While the title of Rocky Mountain Fur Company seems not to have been definitely used until 1830, many of the men who were active in the business of this company had been closely associated under various firm names from as early at least as 1822. In general parlance, therefore, the name Rocky Mountain Fur Company is often used to designate this group of traders and trappers during the entire period of its activities.

In March, 1822, there appeared in a St. Louis newspaper an advertisement announcing that William H. Ashley wished to engage one hundred young men "to ascend the Missouri river to its source, there to be employed for one, two, or three years." With Ashley was associated the same Andrew Henry who had been one of the founders of the Missouri Fur Company and who in 1810 had been so harassed by the Blackfeet around the Three Forks of the Missouri. The requisite number of men was readily obtained and an expedition, under Andrew Henry, was sent up the Missouri. The sinking of a keelboat and supplies valued at ten thousand dollars, the loss of fifty horses to the Assiniboine Indians, and a decisive defeat by the Blackfeet Indians constituted an inauspicious record of the first year's venture. In 1823 Ashley collected a second party of one hundred men and personally led another expedition which came to complete disaster at the hands of the Arikara Indians. In the battle which took place fourteen of Ashley's men were killed and nine wounded; and he lost all of his horses and much of his other property.

About 1824, doubtless due in part to the disasters of the first years, Ashley decided to abandon the Missouri River and the practice of establishing trading posts. Instead, he struck off boldly into the mountains and inaugurated the famous *rendezvous*, or agreed meeting-place for periodical trading activities, which became one of the most picturesque features of the fur trade. In 1824 two of his men, Jedediah S. Smith and

Thomas Fitzpatrick, while on a trading expedition, discovered and crossed the South Pass—thereby making a most significant contribution to geographical knowledge. Jedediah Smith made two expeditions to southern California between 1826 and 1829, in the course of which he made several other important discoveries. On the last of these trips he traveled practically the entire length of California and across the present State of Oregon. At the mouth of the Umpqua River his party was attacked by Indians. Fifteen men were killed and all their furs were stolen. It is pleasant to record that Smith received very substantial assistance from Dr. John McLoughlin of the Hudson's Bay Company at Vancouver, where he stopped before ascending the Columbia on his return journey.

William H. Ashley fared much better in his fur trading ventures after the first two years and laid the foundations of a very comfortable fortune. He sold out in 1826 to the firm of Smith, Jackson and Sublette, made up of Jedediah S. Smith, David E. Jackson, and William L. Sublette, all of whom had served under Ashley. Four years later, in 1830, these men in turn disposed of their interests to a group of somewhat younger men—Thomas Fitzpatrick, Milton G. Sublette, Henry Fraeb, Jean Baptiste Gervais, and James Bridger—who called their firm the Rocky Mountain Fur Company. In 1834 the company was dissolved, although most of the partners continued actively in the fur trade for several years.

It is not possible to follow the operations of these fur traders of the Rocky Mountains in their wide-ranging operations under various firm names from 1822 to 1834. "The whole country around the sources of the Platte, Green, Yellowstone and Snake rivers and in the region around Great Salt Lake was opened up by them," says Hiram M. Chittenden. "Their adventures gave names to the Sweetwater river, Independence Rock, Jackson Hole, and the tributaries of Green river and Great Salt Lake. They discovered this lake and also South Pass. They were the first to descend Green river by boat, and likewise the first, after Colter, to enter the Yellowstone Wonderland. They were the first to travel from Great Salt Lake southwesterly to southern California, the first to cross the Sierras and the deserts of Utah and Nevada between California and Great Salt Lake, and the first, so far as is known, to travel by land up the Pacific coast from San Francisco to the Columbia."

The roll of the leaders in these exploits contains the names of a score or more men, each one of whose life-story is a tale of exciting adventure. Many of these men likewise rendered services of great importance, aside from their participation in the fur trade. After his retirement William H. Ashley was elected to Congress from Missouri. In Washington, D. C., he was consulted constantly for information regarding the Far West. Jedediah S. Smith, the "knight in buckskin" whose Bible was as much a part of his equipment as his rifle, made contributions to geographical knowledge that were used by the map-makers of his day, although he was not thirty years of age when a Comanche Indian arrow ended his career in 1831. Thomas Fitzpatrick, known to the Indians as "Broken Hand," later served as guide to emigrants and explorers, including John C. Frémont, and as Indian agent on the upper Platte and Arkansas rivers. Kit Carson performed similar services, especially in the southwest, where his old home at Taos is still pointed out to tourists. Jim Bridger, the "Old Man of the Mountains," continued for years in the fur trade, until in 1843 he built Fort Bridger on Black's Fork of Green River, where his aid was sought by countless travelers and emigrants. So the list might be extended to include mention of other members of the group, whose knowledge of the Indians and the wild mountain regions was placed at the disposal of later comers.

The American Fur Company in the Far West

The Rocky Mountain Fur Company and its predecessors did not have undisputed possession of the field at any time. The competition of two powerful rivals was encountered—the American Fur Company on the upper Missouri and the Hudson's Bay Company in the far northwest. It was in 1822, the same year in which Ashley began operations, that John Jacob Astor's American Fur Company established western headquarters at St. Louis, with active management in the hands of David Stone and Company, or Stone, Bostwick and Company as it was sometimes called. Three years later the firm of Bernard Pratte and Company became Astor's western representatives. In that same year, 1827, the American Fur Company absorbed the Columbia Fur Company, which had been getting a large share of the trade among the Sioux and Omaha Indians.

The American Fur Company proceeded slowly and cautiously, but with great determination and skill, to gain supremacy in the northern country. A department called the Upper Missouri Outfit and generally known simply as the U.M.O., was organized and placed under the command of the capable and experienced Kenneth McKenzie. In 1828 a trading post, which was shortly afterward named Fort Union, was erected at the mouth of the Yellowstone. Then, two years later, McKenzie achieved what both the Missouri Fur Company and Ashley and Henry had failed to accomplish. He succeeded in establishing trading relations with the Blackfeet Indians and built Fort Piegan in their country at the mouth of the Marias River, later replacing it by Fort McKenzie a few miles further up the Missouri.

The vision and superior resources of the American Fur Company were revealed in 1830, when, after some reluctance, it was decided to try the experiment of replacing the slow and laboriously-moving keelboats with steamboats on the upper Missouri. In 1831 the *Yellowstone* was put into service and made its way up the river as far as Fort Tecumseh, opposite the site of Pierre, South Dakota. On a second voyage in the following year the steamboat reached Fort Union. The experiment proved convincingly successful, and the hold of the American Fur Company on the trade of the upper Missouri was assured. Thereafter steamboats played an important part in the company's operations, pushing further and further up the river until, in 1859, they reached the head of navigation at Fort Benton.

During the two years from 1832 to 1834 the American Fur Company and the Rocky Mountain Fur Company engaged in bitter rivalry, and the fur trade exhibited all of its worst features in aggravated form. The Indians were everywhere debauched with liquor, in defiance of rigid prohibition by the federal government, and were instigated to attack parties of the rival's traders. The American Fur Company, in particular, has not been excelled by any more recent business concerns in the ruthlessness with which it crushed small traders in a region where there was no law except the law of cut-throat competition. In 1834, as has been stated, the Rocky Mountain Fur Company was dissolved, and many of its strongest men entered the service of the American Fur Company. The western successors of this firm, after the retirement of Astor in 1834, continued to be known as "The Company," and for a decade or more possessed virtually monopolistic control of the trade of the Rocky Mountains. But by the middle of the century the great days of the fur trade were rapidly drawing to a close.

The Hudson's Bay Company

Out in the Pacific Northwest during these years the Hudson's Bay Company reigned supreme, after the absorption of the Northwest Company in 1821. Three years later Dr. John McLoughlin came to begin his long and remarkable rule as chief factor. Fort George, on the old site of Astoria, was retained largely as a lookout station. The headquarters of the company were established at a new post, Fort Vancouver, on the north bank of the Columbia, nearly opposite the mouth of the Willamette. Here, in course of time, were to be found comfortable and well-furnished quarters, large storehouses, extensive fields, orchards, and herds of cattle, hogs and horses. And here, like a king, Dr. McLoughlin, the "White-headed Eagle," ruled over a vast area, for the wishes of the Hudson's Bay Company were always law in the region where it held sway, and the chief factor was the spokesman of the company.

Absolute as was the rule of the "Great Company," it was benevolent as far as the natives were concerned. The contrast is great between the treatment of the Indians under the monopolistic control of this company and that accorded them in the vicious competition of the American companies. It was the policy of the Hudson's Bay Company, as exemplified by Dr. McLoughlin, to deal firmly with the Indians, to allow no disobedience, but to treat them fairly in all the relations of trade, and to conserve the fur-bearing animals upon which they depended for a livelihood. The giving of liquor to the Indians was strictly forbidden, although unfortunately this rule was later relaxed when it seemed necessary to fight American traders with their own methods.

Toward rivals the company naturally maintained vigorous opposition. When competing traders arrived at Hudson's Bay Company posts they were treated with every courtesy and politeness. If they were in personal distress, as in the case of Jedediah Smith, they were given every consideration the dictates of humanity required. But there benevolence ended. Opponents could expect no aid that would equip them to continue their rivalry in the fur trade.

The Hudson's Bay Company's realm, of which Fort Vancouver was the center, extended from the Fraser River on the north to northern California on the south, and from the Rocky Mountains to the Pacific. Well established posts were maintained in the upper Columbia region at Fort Walla Walla, Fort Colville, and Fort Okonagan; and in the Idaho country at Fort Boise and Fort Hall. The latter post, which was destined to be an important stopping-place on the Oregon Trail, was purchased from Nathaniel J. Wyeth in 1837. Other trading houses were located on Puget Sound and in what is now British Columbia, and one at the mouth of the Umpqua River in Oregon; while posts of a more temporary nature were scattered far and wide. From these distant points fur brigades carried the pelts down to Fort Vancouver. Regular supply ships came up the Columbia and sailed away loaded with furs.

James Douglas, Francis Ermatinger, Thomas McKay, Archibald McDonald, Alexander Ross, Pierre C. Pambrun, and other subordinates of Dr. McLoughlin became well known to Americans, but none better than Peter Skene Ogden. This vigorous leader of fur trading parties had a fondness for exploration. His numerous expeditions made him familiar with central and eastern Oregon, with northern California, with the Snake River country, and in general with the entire region north and west of Great Salt Lake. On several occasions he came into direct contact with American traders during the period of bitterest rivalry.

For twenty-five years the Hudson's Bay Company ruled

supreme in the old Oregon country, gathering in to Fort Vancouver great quantities of furs, which in good years brought
sums equal to hundreds of thousands of dollars in European
markets. Then, in 1846, the United States gained possession
of the region of the company's activities below the forty-ninth
parallel. During the succeeding years the company gradually
withdrew from its posts on the American side of the boundary
line. On the Canadian side the brigades continued to bring
furs to trading posts, and even to-day, in the far north the
Hudson's Bay Company still carries on—the oldest commercial
enterprise on the North American continent, dating back more
than two and one-half centuries to its chartering in 1670.

Small Firms and Independent Fur Traders

The organization and achievements and rivalries of the
great fur trading companies no doubt rightly claim major
emphasis in the history of the fur trade of the Far West. But
they by no means constitute the whole story. There were
many smaller companies and firms whose names have not even
been mentioned in these pages. Moreover, there were numerous individuals who operated on their own account for periods
of varying length, without connection with any of the companies. Some of these men, like Ceran St. Vrain, and Charles
and William Bent, erected forts or trading houses which bore
their names and were noted landmarks in the vast stretches of
the western country. Others headed parties of hunters and
trappers who made extensive expeditions into the mountains.

For instance, there was Captain Benjamin L. E. Bonneville
of the United States army. In 1832 he secured a leave of
absence for the ostensible purpose of exploring the northern
Rockies and acquiring information concerning the Indians.
Actually, it was his plan to satisfy a long-felt desire to try his
hand at the fur trade. For three years he was at the head of
a party of more than one hundred men in the country between
Green River and Fort Walla Walla; and to him belongs the
credit of having been the first to take wagons over the South
Pass. The story of Bonneville's adventures, as related by

Washington Irving, is one of the classics of western historical
literature.

Contemporaneously with Bonneville's exploits was the venture of Nathaniel J. Wyeth, an ice-dealer of Cambridge, Massachusetts. The scope of Wyeth's plan to establish himself in
trade along the Columbia River was indefinite, but it included
traffic in furs among its principal features. In the spring of
1832 he set out from Boston with a small party. They went
by ship to Baltimore, thence for sixty miles over the newly-
built Baltimore and Ohio Railroad, and on foot to the Monongahela River. Steamboats took them to Pittsburgh and St.
Louis and up the Missouri. They had the good fortune to
reach Independence, Missouri, in time to secure permission to
accompany a Rocky Mountain Fur Company supply party
under William L. Sublette on the long overland trip to the
mountains. After a comparatively uneventful journey, during
which he gained much valuable experience, Wyeth arrived at
Fort Vancouver late in October, 1832. Here for various reasons the party was disbanded.

Two years later Wyeth started from Independence on a
second expedition. In the party were two scientists, Thomas
Nuttall and J. K. Townsend, and a party of missionaries led
by Jason Lee, whose experiences in the Oregon country will
receive attention later. Before ill health and lack of success
compelled him to abandon his enterprise in 1835, Wyeth had
built Fort Hall on the Snake River, and trapped extensively on
the Willamette and Deschutes rivers. Fort Hall, as has been
mentioned, was sold to the Hudson's Bay Company.

Among the numerous other men who led fur trading expeditions in the region further south were Jacob Fowler, whose
wanderings during the years 1821 and 1822 took him through
the country now included in Oklahoma, Kansas, Colorado, and
New Mexico; Sylvester and James Ohio Pattie, whose indis-
creet fur trading activities in southern California between 1824
and 1828 brought them a year's sojourn in a Mexico prison at
San Diego; and Ewing Young, under whom Kit Carson served
his apprenticeship as a trapper in the southwest between New
Mexico and the Pacific in 1829 and 1830.

The Fur Traders and Their Services

Those who have been mentioned in this narrative are notable representatives of the group of leaders in the great industry of the fur trade—the proprietors, partners, factors, partisans, or clerks—whose names have found their places in the pages of history. Under them were the thousands of unknown men who performed the actual work of trapping, tending camp, rowing canoes and poling keelboats, skinning animals, preparing the furs for shipment to headquarters, and making the long and dangerous expeditions to and from the distant trading posts. Most picturesque of all were the *voyageurs,* as the boatmen were called long after the flag of France had disappeared from America, and the trappers. The former were mainly French-Canadians or creoles, a happy-go-lucky lot, patient, long-enduring, and fond of their joyous boat songs; but lacking resourcefulness in an emergency.

In the Rocky Mountains the trappers, on the other hand, were mainly Americans, self-reliant, independent, and courageous. Their days were spent in lonely camps in mountain fastnesses, watching their traps. In dress, in habits, and in knowledge of wilderness ways they came to differ little from the Indians whom they so often fought. Many of them were no doubt fugitives from justice to whom the mountains offered a safe asylum. But there were many more who were attracted to the life because of its freedom from the restraints of society and the fierce excitement and adventure which it offered. "They will undergo the most incredible privation, and leave their friends for years for the sake of adventure or gain," said a contemporary. "On the wilderness of the prairie, or in the recesses of the Rocky Mountains they breathe freely, though it may be in the midst of danger, for they know they are as swift of foot, have as quick an eye, are as expert in stratagem or with the rifle, as their wily enemies."

The passing of the great days of the fur trade brought to a close one of the most fascinating phases of the history of the Far West. The fur traders, with all their faults and shortcomings, were the pathfinders of civilization. They marked the trails that were followed by settlers. They built trading posts where later appeared thriving towns and cities. They knew the Indians better than any other class of white men who came among them. Whether for good or for evil, the Indians whom the settlers encountered were a race whose life and habits had been greatly modified by their contacts with the traders.

CHAPTER XXIX

MANIFEST DESTINY

"GENTLEMEN are talking of natural boundaries. Sir, our nattural boundary is the Pacific ocean. The swelling tide of our population must roll on until that mighty ocean interposes its waters, and limits our territorial empire." Thus orated Francis Baylies of Massachusetts in the lower house of Congress, during the debate in the winter of 1822-23 on Floyd's bill to occupy the mouth of the Columbia River. Although George Tucker of Virginia was opposed to the bill, he admitted that "we cannot arrest the progress of our population to the West. In vain may the government attempt to set limits to its course. It marches on, with the increasing rapidity of a fire, and nothing will stop it until it reaches the shores of the Pacific." In 1825 Timothy Flint, describing his personal observations of the westward movement, wrote: "Alas! for the moving generation of the day, when the tide of advancing backwoodsmen shall have met the surge of the Pacific. They may then set themselves down and weep for other worlds."

All these words were prophetic, but they did not represent any widespread demand or expectation on the part of the American people at the time they were uttered or written. Indeed, while Flint was inditing his recollections plans were being proposed which soon eventuated in removing the eastern Indians to the Great Plains. Here, it was expected, or at least asserted, the tribesmen would never again be disturbed; for the region was believed to be ill-suited to the uses of white men. Zebulon M. Pike and Stephen H. Long had both regarded the plains as a barrier providentially setting a limit to the westward march of settlements. And so, for years, maps bore the legend "Great American Desert" and people in general were contented to assume that one tier of States west of the Mississippi would round out the settled portion of the nation. All beyond could be left to the Indians and as a profitable field for the operations of the fur traders.

Except for continuing demand for the acquisition of Texas and occasional reminders of our joint occupation with Great Britain of the Oregon Country, the Far West beyond the boundary of the Louisiana Purchase remained outside the range of practical politics or general public interest until the decade of the forties.

Then came the "fabulous forties" when American buoyancy reached one of its highest points. Now it was that, for the first time since the days of the "war hawks" of 1812, the desire for territorial expansion came out into the open, unashamed and aggressive. Before the decade ended the delusion of a great American desert in the plains region was rapidly being dissipated, and with it went all thoughts of a permanent Indian territory stretched along the western border of the settled area. Such a limit or obstruction to expansion could no longer be accepted or tolerated. Our national boundaries had, within a period of three years been enlarged to include Texas, the great southwest, California, and the Oregon country.

This immense territorial expansion cannot be explained by the citing of any single or simple cause. In part it was due to the fact that the Far West had come definitely within the field of American politics. The leaders of the South were desirous of additional territory out of which could be carved States favorable to slavery, thus enabling them to maintain a parity with the North in the Senate. A more general and more realistic cause can be found in the activities of typical Americans who, in search of fertile farms or opportunities for trade, passed beyond the bounds of the United States and into Texas, California, and Oregon. And then there was the emotional doctrine of "Manifest Destiny" which, though not new in spirit, was apparently first definitely put into words during this exuberant decade of the forties.

Manifest destiny is the chosen-people, beacon-to-mankind interpretation of America's mission and duty. At this particular period it included belief in a pre-ordination or inevitability governing the westward progress of the "star of empire." For some it was divine command and the superintending guidance of Providence that furnished the irresistible impulse. Others based their prophecies on the ceaseless inward urge which had for so long been impelling Anglo-Saxon peoples westward. As used in the forties the doctrine meant a "new revelation of right" based upon a divine purpose and command that we should extend far and wide the blessings of liberty and self-government. It would be too much to expect that any great number of those Americans who went to Oregon or California before 1846 were inspired solely or mainly by the thought of helping to fulfill America's manifest destiny. It is not difficult, however, to imagine that the doctrine was eagerly appropriated by some of those advocates of expansion who may have been troubled by secret misgivings that national aggrandizement was not an entirely altruistic ambition.

The facts regarding the diplomacy, the military campaigns, and the political maneuverings that culminated in, or accompanied, this expansion need receive but little attention in these pages. A brief sketch of the western aspects of the movements leading up to the successive territorial acquisitions will serve to lay a basis for the story of later events, when Americans rushed in to take possession of the Far West.

THE SANTA FÉ TRADE

Before the close of the eighteenth century Yankee sea captains entered Spanish ports on the coast of California and began a brisk and lucrative trade, which was continued in succeeding years in spite of stringent regulations. With this exception, the earliest efforts of Americans to establish trading relations with the Spanish in the southwest were directed toward Santa Fé, the capital of New Mexico. It was Zebulon M. Pike who first described the attractiveness of the Santa Fé trade in the report of his southwestern expedition of 1806-7.

The information supplied by Pike aroused much interest in Missouri, but it was not until 1812 that there is any record of an attempt to test the possibilities of trade with Santa Fé. In that year Robert McKnight, James Baird, and Samuel Chambers, with a small party from St. Louis, set out across the plains. They reached Santa Fé in safety. But instead of finding the free market they had expected at this particular time, they were clapped into prison, where they remained for more than nine years. The disastrous outcome of this adventure discouraged further attempts for several years. It appears that in 1815-17 A. P. Chouteau and Julius De Munn of St. Louis made another effort which ended only in a short imprisonment and the confiscation of all their goods.

When in 1821 Mexico threw off the Spanish yoke, the prospects of trade with Santa Fé were much brighter, for the restrictions on commercial transactions with Americans were relaxed. The residents of Santa Fé had plenty of Spanish coin, their warehouses were well stocked with furs from the surrounding region, and they raised mules which would bring a ready sale in the American settlements. But on account of their isolation there was a dearth of manufactured goods and prices were exorbitant. Thus on both sides the opportunity to open trade between the American settlements and Santa Fé was eagerly welcomed.

Numerous Americans took immediate advantage of the changed situation. Among those who pioneered the way in this profitable activity chief credit is usually given to William Becknell, although John McKnight, Hugh Glenn, Jacob Fowler, Braxton Cooper, and others were not far behind him. Becknell started late in the autumn of 1821, reached Santa Fé safely, and returned to Missouri the following spring laden with the profits of his successful trading operations. He immediately organized a larger party and not only repeated the success of his first venture, but also demonstrated the practicability of hauling wagons over the long trail.

The Santa Fé market was now open to American trade. Thereafter annual caravans scarred a trail across the plains that became one of the historic highways of the Far West. "The fall company of Traders to Santa Fé have all arrived at their several homes in this state," reads an item in the *Missouri Republican* in November, 1834. "The Company brought in, as near as can be ascertained, $40,000 in gold, $140,000 in specie, $15,000 worth of Beaver, 50 packs Buffalo Robes, 12,000 pounds of Wool, and 300 head of mules, valued at

$10,000. It was composed of 140 men, and numbered 40 wagons." This was probably one of the good years in the Santa Fé trade; but Mexican specie was much appreciated in the West, especially in years that followed the Panic of 1837. Of greater significance than the actual volume of the traffic were the experiences of the men who annually crossed the plains to Santa Fé and helped to discredit the tradition of a great American desert.

The Santa Fé trade had little direct effect in hastening American territorial expansion. But a considerable number of men became familiar with the trails to the southwest. The contacts which they made helped to prepare the way for the acceptance of American rule when it came. Meanwhile, in Texas a movement was in progress that eventually led to expansion on a grand scale.

AMERICAN EXPANSION IN TEXAS

It will be recalled that when Florida was acquired from Spain in the treaty negotiated in 1819, the Sabine River was accepted as the boundary between Texas and Louisiana. The entire line delimiting the possessions of Spain ran up the west bank of the Sabine to its intersection with the thirty-second parallel of north latitude, thence north to the south bank of the Red River, which it followed to the one hundredth meridian of west longitude, then up this meridian to the Arkansas River, up this stream to its source, thence north to the forty-second parallel, and along this parallel to the Pacific Ocean.

It is almost certain that the American negotiators of the treaty of 1819 would not have agreed to the Sabine River as a boundary if they had known that Napoleon, before he sold Louisiana to the United States, had regarded the Rio Grande as the southwestern boundary of his possessions. But they did not know this, and the boundaries of the Louisiana Purchase had never been definitely determined. Texas was relatively unknown to Americans, it lay beyond any immediate pressure of population and, as Monroe indicated, there was opposition in the East to "aggrandizement to the West and South." On the other hand, the acquisition of Florida was an urgent necessity, and so the advice of Monroe, that "we ought to be content with Florida for the present," was followed and the Sabine boundary was accepted.

The treaty was not ratified without vigorous protest. Henry Clay, Thomas Hart Benton, and others denounced the surrender of Texas on the floors of Congress. Western editors also expressed their disapproval. In 1820 a St. Louis editor voiced objections to "the cession of this province" and pointed to "the shame of dismembering the valley of the Mississippi by giving up two of its noblest rivers to the enemies of our country." As late as January, 1821 the *Louisiana Advertiser* (New Orleans) complained that "Territory belonging to the U. S. is ceded away to a despot, a country that would give to the great cause of liberty, millions of freemen, is transferred to slaves. . . . The province of Texas is worth ten Floridas; it is larger, and more fertile, and more healthful than any state of the Union. . . . Our present politicians are as short-sighted as those who a few years ago were prepared to abandon the navigation of the Mississippi." A more belligerent response to the news of the treaty was exhibited by about three hundred borderers from Natchez and Louisiana who invaded Texas in 1819, under leadership of Dr. James Long, with the avowed purpose of establishing the independence of that province. Though this expedition achieved some temporary success, it was soon overwhelmed by Spanish troops. The treaty was finally ratified, and American expansion to the southwest seemed to be definitely checked.

There was one man, however, who was not daunted by the retention of Texas by the Spaniards. This man was Moses Austin, then nearly sixty years of age. Born in Connecticut, Austin had moved to Philadelphia in early manhood and from there to Virginia. There he heard of the rich lead mines in what is now Missouri, but which then was Spanish territory. In 1798 he migrated with his family, became a Spanish subject, and obtained a valuable grant in the lead region. The purchase of Louisiana made him once more an American citizen and he continued to work his lead mines. But fortune did not favor him. In 1819 the family, in poor financial condition, moved to the newly established Territory of Arkansas. Austin's thoughts now turned to Texas as a region where his losses might be recouped. That Texas was a Spanish possession did not trouble him, for he had previously received substantial favors from the Spanish government.

In November, 1820, Moses Austin set out from Little Rock, with a horse, a mule, a negro servant, and fifty dollars which he had borrowed from his son Stephen. Late in December he arrived in San Antonio and filed an application to be allowed to lead a colony of three hundred Catholic families into Texas from the United States. His own remuneration would be received in the form of fees to be collected from the settlers. After some delay, the local official approved the petition and forwarded it to his superior. Austin immediately started for home to organize his colony, but shortly after his arrival, early in 1821, he died from pneumonia—not, however, before receiving word of the granting of his petition.

The grant made to Moses Austin now devolved upon his son, Stephen F. Austin, not yet thirty years of age, a man well qualified by experience and personality to lead the enterprise to success. He advertised for colonists and received many more responses than he could accept. The effects of the Panic of 1819 were still being felt and times were hard in the West. The land law of 1820, abolishing the credit system, temporarily discouraged land purchases. Thus the prospects of obtaining title to large tracts of land in Texas at very nominal rates were most attractive. From Louisiana, Mississippi, Tennessee, Arkansas Territory, and Missouri came most of the three hundred families who made up Stephen F. Austin's first colony. The achievement of Mexican independence in 1821 caused some delay and revision of the plan of colonization, but for nearly a decade Mexican policy was hospitable to emigrants to Texas.

Austin was later given further grants and similar privileges were extended to other "impressarios," as these contractors were called. By 1830 there were probably twenty thousand Americans in Texas—more settlers than had come into the province during all the years of Spanish possession. In the meantime efforts were made by the government of the United States to purchase Texas. Early in the administration of John

Quincy Adams negotiations were begun by Joel R. Poinsett, our minister to Mexico, but he made no headway. As Poinsett's successor, President Jackson sent Anthony Butler, with instructions which ultimately directed him not only to attempt to buy Texas, but California as well. Butler was a blunderer and he only succeeded in antagonizing the Mexicans and arousing their suspicions.

The Mexican authorities now began to feel that they had been too liberal in their welcome to American settlers. A series of restrictive laws and decrees was initiated, culminating in a law of 1830 which forbade further immigration from the United States. Mexican troops were stationed in various settlements. Soon custom-houses were opened and duties imposed which the settlers considered oppressive. Discontent spread rapidly. The settlers were Americans with the westerners' dislike of governmental interference. Above all, they wanted home rule. If Texas could have been made an autonomous province under Mexican control they might have been satisfied, but this repeated request was denied. For a time after Santa Anna, a professed constitutionalist, came into power in Mexico early in 1833 there was hope of a satisfactory adjustment. But Santa Anna adopted a policy of centralization and set up an autocratic government.

Events now moved rapidly toward open revolt. Even Stephen F. Austin, who long remained patiently and hopefully loyal to Mexico, finally became convinced that there could be no peace or prosperity in the settlements without independence. In November, 1835, a convention set up a provisional government, although still voting to remain a part of the Republic of Mexico if the provisions of the constitution of 1824 were restored. The movement for independence, however, grew apace. On March 2, 1836, in a second convention, the Texans adopted a declaration of independence and a constitution for the new republic was drafted. The gage of battle had now been thrown down. Mexican troops had already marched into Texas and for a time carried all before them. At San Antonio the Texan defenders barricaded themselves in the Alamo, and there on March 6th the Mexicans overwhelmed them, killing the garrison to the last man.

This savage massacre, far from intimidating the Texans, aroused them to a fury of hatred. Rallying under General Sam Houston, with "Remember the Alamo" as their battle-cry, they met the Mexicans under Santa Anna on the San Jacinto River on April 21st and administered a crushing defeat. More than six hundred Mexicans were killed, two hundred wounded, and nearly all of the remaining half of the army were captured, including Santa Anna himself. The defeated leader's life was spared in return for his recognition of the independence of Texas with territory extending to the Rio Grande. Although the Mexican congress repudiated this pledge, the war was over and Texas was an independent republic.

Among the early acts of the Texans was to vote, by a majority of more than three thousand to ninety-two, in favor of annexation to the United States. Emissaries were sent to Washington in the confident expectation that this much desired connection would be speedily accomplished. But in this they were disappointed. With the election of 1836 approaching, President Jackson was not willing to risk advocacy of a measure that was violently opposed in the northern States. President Van Buren was lukewarm on the subject and, besides, he and the people of the United States had many other problems to occupy their attention after the Panic of 1837. The utmost that could be achieved was the formal recognition of Texas and the exchange of diplomatic representatives. The annexation question was inextricably involved in the sectional antipathies of North and South. Southerners saw in Texas an area large enough to be carved into as many as five States cordial to slavery, and thus offering them a comfortable reserve upon which to draw in maintaining their control of the United States Senate. Anti-slavery northerners saw the same thing and were determined that the South should not gain this new territory. As a consequence Texas remained outside the American Union for nearly a decade after achieving her independence.

THE ACQUISITION OF OREGON

While this series of events was occurring in Texas, American interest in, and desire for, the Pacific Northwest were increasing—slowly and uncertainly at first and later with a determination that would not accept defeat.

When the old Oregon country first entered the realm of American diplomacy and the United States asserted its right to the region after the War of 1812, four nations had claims of possession. After Vizcaino sailed as far north as the southern border of Oregon in 1603 nearly a century and three-quarters elapsed before there is another record of Spanish explorers in north Pacific waters. Then in 1774 Juan Perez entered Nootka Sound. During the following year Bruno

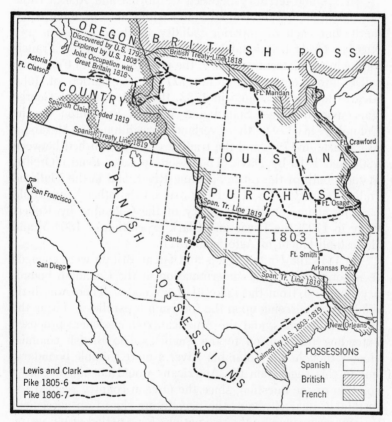

IX. CONTROVERSIES AND TREATIES AFFECTING THE FAR
WEST, 1803-1819
(Showing Expeditions of Lewis and Clark and Zebulon M. Pike)

Heceta sighted the mouth of the Columbia, and later landed at Point Grenville north of Gray's Harbor, while Juan Francisco de Bodega y Quadra sailed north as far as the fifty-eighth parallel and landed on the coast of Alaska. These ventures were inspired by Spanish fear of Russian aggression, after the daring voyage of Vitus Behring in 1741. In subsequent years the Russians pushed their trade down the coast as far as northern California. Thus Spain laid claim to territory extending indefinitely northward from California, and the Russians held Alaska with claims extending indefinitely southward.

In the mid-territory between California and Alaska came Great Britain and the United States with claims of about equal merit, but each of superior validity to those of Spain and Russia. Great Britain could point to the voyage of Sir Francis Drake in the sixteenth century, the voyage of James Cook who sailed into Nootka Sound in 1777, the expedition of John Meares to Nootka Sound in 1788, the explorations of George Vancouver in Puget Sound and William Broughton on the Columbia in 1792, the overland expedition of Alexander Mackenzie in 1793, and the trading posts established between 1808 and 1810 by David Thompson on Lake Pend d'Oreille, at the mouth of the Little Spokane River, and in the Flathead Indian country. The United States, on the other hand, could base its claims on the discovery of the Columbia by Robert Gray in 1792, the Lewis and Clark expedition of 1804-6, and the establishment of Astoria in 1811.

In 1818 the United States and Great Britain were engaged in negotiations for the determination of the Canadian boundary line west from the Lake of the Woods. There was little difficulty in agreeing upon the forty-ninth parallel as far as the Rocky Mountains, and the American commissioners proposed extending this line on to the Pacific. The British commissioners thought the Columbia River a more suitable boundary, but to this suggestion the Americans would not agree. As a solution of the question, since the Oregon country seemed too distant to quarrel about, the negotiators signed an agreement of joint occupancy by the two nations for a period of ten years.

Soon after the adoption of this treaty, the claimants to the Oregon country were reduced to two—Great Britain and the

United States. Spain was eliminated by the Florida Purchase Treaty of 1819 which, as has been noted, fixed the forty-second parallel as the northern limit of Spanish possessions on the Pacific. In 1821 Czar Alexander of Russia issued an *Ukase* asserting the exclusive right of his country to all territory north of the fifty-first parallel. This brought a protest from the American government, whose spokesman, John Quincy Adams, maintained that Russia had no valid claim to territory south of the fifty-fifth parallel. As is well known, the announcement of the Monroe Doctrine was partially inspired by the aggressive attitude of the Russians at this time. In April, 1824, however, Russia signed a treaty with the United States in which the parallel 54 degrees 40 minutes was established as a line beyond which neither nation would establish settlements. Thereafter the Oregon country, in the joint possession of Great Britain and the United States, extended from 42 degrees on the south to 54 degrees 40 minutes on the north, and from the Pacific to the Rocky Mountains.

During this decade John Floyd of Virginia made persistent efforts to induce Congress to pass an act providing for the American occupation of the Columbia River region. In the Senate valiant assistance was given by Thomas Hart Benton of Missouri. Between 1821 and 1827 Floyd introduced four such bills, but in spite of extended debate, especially during the session of 1822-3, none of them was adopted. On the other hand, after absorbing the Northwest Company in 1821, the Hudson's Bay Company established its headquarters at Vancouver on the Columbia and began to push its trading activities throughout the entire Oregon country. In 1827 commissioners of the two claiming nations agreed to extend the arrangement of joint occupancy indefinitely, with the proviso that either nation might terminate the agreement by giving notice one year in advance. The Oregon question now dropped into the background and received but little attention in Congress until 1838.

In the meantime the writings and lectures of Hall J. Kelley, sometimes called the "Prophet of Oregon," and the expeditions of Nathaniel J. Wyeth, already described, kept the advantages of the Oregon country before the public. Then in 1834 there began a series of missionary enterprises, which paved the way for American emigration and gave the United States the advantage of settlements, agricultural as well as missionary in nature, in the disputed region.   In the spring of 1834 Jason and Daniel Lee and three other missionaries, representing the Methodist Board of Missions, set out for Oregon with Nathaniel Wyeth on his second expedition.   By September they were at Fort Vancouver, where they were hospitably received by Dr. John McLoughlin; and before the end of the year they had established a mission in the beautiful valley of the Willamette about sixty miles from the mouth of the river.   Two years later, in 1836, Dr. Marcus Whitman, Henry H. Spalding, and W. H. Gray set up mission stations in the Walla Walla region, under the jurisdiction of the American Board representing the Presbyterian, Congregationalist, and Dutch Reformed churches.   In the following years these missionary enterprises were expanded and many new recruits were added.

There was no doubt now about American interest in the Oregon country.   The glowing letters and reports of the missionaries, published in eastern newspapers, together with information furnished by fur traders, made the far northwest very attractive.   During the early forties there occurred the migrations, described in the following chapter, which made the Oregon Trail one of the famous highways of the Far West. In 1842 one hundred and thirty persons with eighteen wagons made the journey under the leadership of Dr. Elijah White. The following year witnessed the so-called "great migration" to Oregon, when about one thousand persons made the long trek.   Thereafter migrations of considerable size were annual occurrences.

Beginning in 1838 with the introduction of a bill to establish the Territory of Oregon, Senator Lewis F. Linn of Missouri kept the subject of American rights in the Oregon country constantly before Congress.   His efforts and those of other advocates of American occupation were supplemented by numerous reports and maps, and the publication of Greenhow's *History of Oregon and California* as a government document in 1840. During the negotiations that preceded the signing of the Webster-Ashburton Treaty of 1842, the Oregon boundary line was discussed, but no agreement could be reached.   American settlers in Oregon, however, were making their wishes known in no uncertain terms, especially after they set up a provisional government at Champoeg in the Willamette Valley in 1843.

Then came the presidential campaign of 1844 when the expansionist, James K. Polk, was the Democratic standard-bearer. Texas was now ardently desired by the pro-slavery leaders who controlled the Democratic party. In order to gain northern votes they coupled their demand for the "re-annexation of Texas" with one even more belligerent in tone for the occupation of the whole of the Oregon country. "Fifty-four forty or fight!" became their stirring slogan during the campaign. Well might people have wondered whether the United States was to be plunged into war with both Mexico and England when Polk was triumphantly victorious at the polls. While, as will be seen, the inauguration of the new President was soon followed by the annexation of Texas and war with Mexico, American possession of the Oregon country was fortunately attained through the peaceful method of diplomacy. In his first annual message President Polk recommended that Congress give England the required year's notice of termination of the agreement of joint occupancy; and Congress responded with a joint resolution. The situation was tense in the Oregon country, where talk of war was rife.

Great Britain sent Richard Pakenham as plenipotentiary to negotiate a boundary agreement and on June 15, 1846, he and James Buchanan negotiated a treaty. In spite of some opposition in Congress the United States abandoned the line of 54 degrees 40 minutes, up to which, in the ironic words of Thomas Hart Benton "all true patriots were to march! and marching, fight! and fighting, die! if need be! singing all the while with Horace—'*Dulce et decorum est pro patria mori.*'" On her part, England retreated from her long-continued insistence on the Columbia River as the boundary. Instead, both nations agreed on the forty-ninth parallel from the Rocky Mountains to the coast and a line along the mid-channel between the southern side of Vancouver Island and the mainland to the Pacific Ocean. Thus there was added to the undisputed jurisdiction of the United States an area of more than 280,000 square miles, without the firing of a gun or the payment of a dollar of purchase money.

AMERICAN PENETRATION OF CALIFORNIA

On the day preceding the signing of the Oregon Treaty a small group of Americans in the Sacramento Valley raised a flag on which were painted a five-pointed star, the figure of a grizzly bear, and the words "California Republic." The episode occurred suddenly and without pre-arrangement, but toward some such culmination American interest in, and penetration of, California had been moving for half a century. The fascinating story of the manner in which California came within the range of Manifest Destiny can be sketched only very briefly in these pages.

The earliest contacts of Americans with California were those made by the captains and crews of New England sailing vessels engaged in the oriental trade, beginning shortly after the close of the Revolutionary War. Furs, gathered along the Pacific coast, especially sea otter furs, came to be among the most profitable staples of the Chinese trade. The Boston ships were stocked with cotton and silk cloth, shoes, hardware, crockery, and many other manufactured goods which, despite stringent regulations, found a ready market among the Spanish missions and settlements in California. Before the decline of the fur trade, whaling vessels also plied up and down the coast, put into San Diego, Monterey, and San Francisco for repairs and fresh provisions, in return for which the ship captains traded articles which the isolated Californians greatly desired. Then, after the winning of Mexican independence and the relaxing of commercial restrictions, New England merchants developed a lucrative trade in hides and tallow with the California missions and ranches. There is no better account of this traffic than that contained in Richard Henry Dana's classic sea story, *Two Years Before the Mast*. All these commercial ventures had an importance in themselves from an economic standpoint; but they had a wider significance in the knowledge which they gave Americans of the resources and attractions of California.

Even more stimulating to American interest in California was the overland advance that began in 1826. In that year the fur trader, Jedediah S. Smith, led the first party of Americans into California from the east. He had some difficulty with the Mexican authorities, but was finally allowed to depart. The next year he was back again. This time he was obliged to spend several days in jail, and only avoided being sent to Mexico as a prisoner by promising to leave the province immediately. It was on his return trip that he explored a route northward into the Oregon country and narrowly escaped death at the hands of Indians, who massacred his companions and confiscated his furs at the mouth of the Umpqua River.

Contemporaneous with the exploits of Jedediah Smith were the adventures of another party led by Sylvester Pattie and his son James Ohio Pattie. These two men had been engaged for several years in the fur trade and in mining in the region around Santa Fé. In September, 1827, they started westward and after terrible hardships reached Santa Catalina. They were taken under guard to San Diego and there thrown into prison. Sylvester Pattie died soon afterward and it was some time before his son and the other members of the party were liberated. James Ohio Pattie soon left California, but most of his companions remained permanently.

Following Jedediah Smith and the Patties came other parties of American traders and trappers, including such well known leaders as Ewing Young, Joseph Walker, David E. Jackson, and William Wolfskill. During the decade of the thirties these men became thoroughly acquainted with the routes into California and with the resources of the Pacific slope. Many of them settled down in the country they found so pleasant, thus adding year by year to the foreign population of the province. The reports and stories which were brought back by those who returned to the States were printed in local newspapers and spread rapidly in the frontier settlements of the Middle West. This publicity was supplemented by the writings of Richard Henry Dana, Thomas J. Farnham, and Hall J. Kelley which gained a wide popularity.

The result was the growth of great interest throughout the United States in California as a region for American settlement.

In the spring of 1841 the first organized emigrant party, led by John Bidwell, left the Missouri River and after many vicissitudes reached California. The succeeding years witnessed the migration of increasing numbers of Americans, until, by 1846, it was predicted that the influx would total several thousands. Emigrant guide-books were being published. Newspapers and periodicals throughout the United States were devoting much space to articles and letters about California, including the frequent letters of Thomas O. Larkin, United States consul in California. This widespread interest and the steady penetration of California, together with the very loose hold of Mexico on her Pacific coast province, foretold the rapid approach of the day when Mexican rule would be overthrown.

Meanwhile, the authorities at Washington were becoming increasingly determined that California must come into the possession of the United States. President Jackson's instructions to Anthony Butler urging efforts to purchase California as well as Texas, have already been mentioned. Martin Van Buren had little time or inclination to give attention to territorial expansion. But after John Tyler came to the presidency, following the death of William Henry Harrison, both Daniel Webster, Secretary of State, and Waddy Thompson, minister to Mexico, were enthusiastic in their endeavors to negotiate the purchase of California. Then the election of 1844 placed James K. Polk, an avowed advocate of expansion, in the White House. Polk's undisguised purpose to acquire California was inspired not only by his desire to open a new and inviting area to American settlement and commerce, but also by his fears, not wholly groundless, that England had designs on the same region.

Polk's first act was to direct the opening of negotiations for the purchase of California and New Mexico. But before the outcome of this mission, entrusted to John Slidell, was learned, Lieutenant Archibald H. Gillespie was sent with a communication to Thomas O. Larkin at Monterey. It was known by the government that the Californians were growing increasingly restless under Mexican rule. Larkin was told, therefore, that while the United States would do nothing to foment a revolution, he was authorized to promise the Californians protection in case they should decide to separate from Mexico. Larkin was given wide discretion as Polk's confidential agent, and warned to prevent any move that might result in any European power gaining a foothold in California. There is reason to believe that Larkin's maneuverings among the Californians might have produced the desired result, but before he could bring his plans to fruition a group of Americans took affairs into their own hands.

It will be recalled that at this time John C. Frémont was in California on his third expedition. He had been warned out of the province and had retired to the Klamath Lake region. There Lieutenant Gillespie sought him out, and delivered to him private letters from Senator Thomas H. Benton and other confidential information, the exact nature of which is still in doubt. At any rate Frémont considered it his duty to return to California. Thus he was on hand with his company of sixty well disciplined men, when on June 14, 1846, a small group of Americans led by William B. Ide, fearing an attack by the Californians, took possession of Sonoma, raised the Bear Flag of revolt, and proclaimed the Republic of California. Whether this local revolutionary movement might have eventuated in the independence of California and annexation to the United States can never be known. News of the beginning of war with Mexico soon drew California into the scope of a larger conquest. For the events leading up to the Mexican War we must turn our attention once more to Texas.

THE ANNEXATION OF TEXAS

As has already been stated, the Texans were eager for annexation to the United States after winning their independence in 1836. But Jackson was not willing to risk approval of the proposal and Van Buren was both disinclined and too busy with other matters to give it favorable attention. The most that Texas could secure at this time was recognition and the exchange of diplomatic representatives. In 1838 the Texans withdrew their request for annexation and for several years the subject remained in abeyance. The sectional struggle between the North and the South made it virtually certain that

any treaty of annexation would be rejected in the Senate, especially in view of the fact that no northern State was ready for
admission at this time. Early in 1844 such a treaty was negotiated, but it failed to pass the Senate.

Then came the presidential campaign of 1844, during which
James K. Polk and the Democratic party declared boldly for
the "re-annexation of Texas," while Clay, the candidate of
the Whigs, left his attitude in doubt. The triumph of Polk
promised the early achievement of annexation. In addition to
the expansionist views of the President-elect and the desire of
the South for additional slave territory, there were other influences which helped to gain public support for the movement.
There were fears in Washington circles that England had designs on Texas. As a matter of fact, England had manifested
an interest in establishing friendly commercial relations with
the Texans in order to gain a source of cotton supply. Her
agents had also worked against annexation and in favor of the
abolition of slavery in Texas. There is no valid evidence that
England desired actual possession of the young republic.
Nevertheless, the activities of Englishmen aroused suspicions
in the United States. Another factor inclining certain people,
even in the northeastern States, toward annexation was the
fact that they held Texan land scrip and especially bonds of
the republic which were rapidly depreciating in value. It was
anticipated that annexation would immediately increase the
worth of these securities.

President Tyler decided that conditions were now ripe for
the incorporation of Texas into the Union, and accordingly he
proposed to Congress that annexation be accomplished by joint
resolution, a procedure which required only a simple majority
in both houses, instead of a two-thirds vote in the Senate as in
the ratification of a treaty. In spite of vigorous opposition,
Congress followed this suggestion. On March 1, 1845, as one
of his last official acts, Tyler signed a joint resolution annexing
Texas as a State. The new Commonwealth was to retain its
public lands, pay its own debts, and might be divided into as
many as five States, with its consent. The provision regarding
the debts must have been a bitter disappointment to the speculators in Texan securities, who were obliged to wait until after

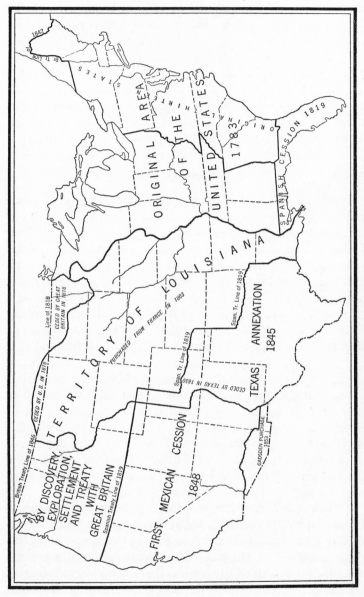

X. TERRITORIAL EXPANSION OF THE UNITED STATES

the passage of the Compromise of 1850 to obtain even partial realization of their hopes. The South had to be satisfied with one additional slave State, for Texas refused to be divided.

News of the resolution of annexation was carried post-haste to Texas. The legislature approved the measure in June. On July 4, 1845, a convention at Austin accepted the terms of annexation and proceeded to draft a constitution which was ratified in October. On December 29, 1845, Texas was admitted into the Union by act of Congress.

THE MEXICAN WAR

President Polk was well aware that the annexation of Texas would in all probability lead to war with Mexico, and he was far from being dismayed at the prospect. He desired that New Mexico and upper California as well as Texas should be added to his country's possessions; and while he prepared to secure them peaceably, he was so impressed with our long-standing grievances against Mexico that he was not averse to war as a last resort. Late in 1845 he sent John Slidell on a fruitless mission to Mexico with the proposal, that the Rio Grande be accepted as the boundary between Texas and Mexico and that New Mexico and upper California be ceded to the United States. In return the United States would assume the claims of Americans against the Mexican government, amounting to more than six million dollars and pay an additional sum of money. Zachary Taylor was also ordered to move with his troops to the western boundary of Texas, to prevent any Mexican invasion. By April, 1846, Taylor was on the Rio Grande, near the present town of Brownsville, where he received an indignant protest from the Mexican authorities.

This was the situation on May 9th when Polk discussed with his cabinet the advisability of declaring war against Mexico, in order to collect the debts owed Americans and to redress wrongs done to our citizens. That same evening there came news which provided all the justification the President required. Mexican forces had crossed the Rio Grande late in April into territory which they regarded as their own, and on May 8th and May 9th there had been fought the battles of Palo Alto and Resaca de la Palma, in which the American troops were victorious. President Polk now sent a message to Congress in which he stated that war already existed. He referred to the "grievous wrongs perpetrated by Mexico upon our citizens throughout a long period of years," and declared that "now, after reiterated menaces, Mexico has passed the boundary of the United States, has invaded our territory and shed American blood upon the American soil." Congress voted by large majorities in both houses in favor of the declaration of war, which was signed on May 16, 1846.

The only feature of the inglorious war which followed that need concern us is the conquest of New Mexico and upper California. While Winfield Scott and Zachary Taylor were preparing their forces for the campaigns into Mexico which were to bring the war speedily to a close, Colonel Stephen W. Kearny was leading his Army of the West along the Santa Fé Trail, with California as his goal. Although there were reports of Mexican armies forming to block his way, Kearny entered Santa Fé without encountering opposition. He declared New Mexico a part of the United States, made arrangements for territorial government, despatched a large part of his army under Colonel A. W. Doniphan to join General J. E. Wool in Chihuahua, and set out with the remainder of his expedition toward California.

A few days after leaving Santa Fé he met Kit Carson, who was on his way to Washington with despatches. Carson brought the news that California was already in the possession of the Americans. Kearny thereupon ordered three companies of dragoons to return to Santa Fé. Arrangements were made to have Thomas Fitzpatrick carry the despatches to Washington, while Kit Carson turned back to guide Kearny and his small army, now reduced to one hundred men, into California. After a hard march of about a month the little force reached the mouth of the Gila River, where they received disquieting information of a successful counter-revolution in California.

. After the Bear Flag revolt and the receipt of news of the beginning of hostilities between the United States and Mexico, Commodore John D. Sloat entered Monterey in July, 1846, and soon the American flag was floating over that port and over San Francisco, Sonoma, and Sutter's Fort. Shortly afterward Sloat was superseded by Commodore Robert F. Stockton, an aggressive officer who assumed command of military, as well as naval, operations in California. With the aid of John C. Frémont, who was commissioned a major, Stockton, was soon in possession of San Diego and Los Angeles. Leaving A. H. Gillespie, now a captain, in charge at the latter place, with a force of fifty men, Stockton and Frémont returned to Monterey satisfied that the conquest of California was complete. Scarcely more than a month passed, however, until Gillespie was faced with a revolt of the Californians, which finally forced his surrender and retirement to San Pedro. The uprising spread rapidly and soon San Diego and Santa Barbara were in the hands of their former owners. Before surrendering Los Angeles, Gillespie sent a messenger to Stockton for assistance. After a heroic ride of five days the messenger reached Monterey. Stockton immediately sent a ship with 350 men to San Pedro, prepared to follow with more troops and ordered Frémont to proceed southward by land.

This was the situation when Kearny's little command, described as "the most tattered and ill-fed detachment of men that ever the United States mustered under her colors," after a terrible march across the desert, reached Warner's ranch near San Diego on December 2nd. Four days later these weary dragoons, aided by thirty-five soldiers sent by Stockton, fought a battle near the Indian village of San Pasqual, in which Kearny claimed the victory although he lost a fourth of his men in killed and wounded.

Despite their courage the Californians were soon obliged to capitulate. On January 10th, 1847, the American forces again entered Los Angeles and raised the flag of the United States. Three days later at Cahuenga the Californians laid down their arms and signed articles of peace. The war of conquest in California was at an end. The relations of Commodore Stockton and Colonel Kearny were marred by an unseemly controversy concerning the question of which was in command in California. John C. Frémont, who had been taking orders from Stockton, chose to continue to do so, with the result that he was charged with disobedience by Kearny and sent to Washinton to face court-martial.

In Mexico the armies of the United States had been proceeding from victory to victory. On September 14, 1847, Winfield Scott entered Mexico City. Although peace did not come immediately, negotiations, conducted by Nicholas Trist, were consummated by the signing of the Treaty of Guadalupe Hidalgo on February 2, 1848. The boundary followed the Rio Grande to the southern line of New Mexico, and continued along that line to the Gila River, down that stream to the Colorado, and along the line between upper and lower California to the Pacific Ocean. The United States paid Mexico $15,000,000, and assumed the claims of American citizens against the Mexican government. The treaty was displeasing to those who contended that we should not have demanded any territory at all. It was equally disappointing to others, including Polk, who wanted a larger cession, and to a smaller number who saw an opportunity to acquire all of Mexico. The Senate, however, ratified the treaty by a narrow margin. Thus there was added to the national domain of the United States an area of more than half a million square miles. If the acquisition of this territory settled some of the points in dispute with Mexico, it gave rise to far graver problems connected with the growing sectional bitterness between the North and the South, and precipitated a crisis that was only averted by the Compromise of 1850.

THE GADSDEN PURCHASE

The phraseology of the Treaty of Guadalupe Hidalgo which fixed a portion of the boundary along the southern border of New Mexico gave rise to further dispute. The southern boundary of New Mexico had never been definitely located, and the provisions of the treaty were contradictory. This uncertainty was used to good advantage in the early fifties when the United States was desirous of securing additional territory in order to lay out a route for a railroad to the Pacific along the thirty-second parallel. James Gadsden was sent to Mexico in 1853 to conduct negotiations. Exceeding his instructions, he sought a cession that would have included a large part of northern Mexico. He failed in this effort, but he did succeed in purchasing about thirty thousand square miles of land along the border between the Rio Grande and the Colorado, for which the United States paid Mexico ten million dollars.

The continental area of the United States, with the exception of Alaska, was now complete. Manifest Destiny, for the time being, had been fulfilled, although private filibustering expeditions such as those of William Walker did not cease. The acquisitions of the years from 1845 to 1853 not only increased the territory of the nation by approximately fifty per cent, but they led to marked changes in national attitudes, problems, and policies. The succeeding chapters will be devoted to some of the principal features of American occupation of the Great Plains and of the newly acquired domain.

CHAPTER XXX

GREAT TRAILS TO THE FAR WEST

DURING the decade of the eighteen forties several trails to the Pacific coast and to the inter-mountain region were worn deep by the passage of thousands of migrating Americans. First came the movements to the Oregon country which played a determining part in achieving American possession of that territory, and made the Oregon Trail one of the great highways to the Far West. The year in which the Oregon Treaty was signed witnessed the beginning of the organized trek of the Mormons to their new home in Utah. Then two years later, came news from California that aroused the entire country to a high pitch of excitement and lured an unnumbered host of eager men across plains and mountains and deserts, and by ship to the Pacific coast in search of gold.

The story of these early migrations to the Far West constitutes a chapter in the history of the westward movement that is markedly unlike those which precede it. Hitherto the great majority of those who moved westward traveled to a region fifty, one hundred or, at most, a few hundred miles west of the place where they previously lived. Much of their journey, especially after 1820, was through a country partially settled. They could secure supplies and assistance along the route, and they were seldom in danger from Indians or other causes. Far different were the conditions faced by those who, in the early years, made the long overland trip to Oregon and California. From the settlements along the Missouri to the Pacific stretched more than two thousand miles of wilderness unpeopled by white men, except at widely separated trading posts and later in the Mormon colony in Utah. Such a journey, occupying at best a period of three or four months, required courage, careful preparation, organization, obedience to leaders, and dogged determination. One who would appre-

ciate fully the fortitude and despair, the dangers and hardships, the pleasures and high ambitions of those who traveled
the transcontinental trails must peruse their diaries, journals,
letters and memoirs, many of which have fortunately been
preserved and published. The generalizations which follow
can only serve to illustrate the early migrations to Oregon,
the hegira of the Mormons, and the mad rush of gold-seekers
to California.

THE MIGRATIONS TO OREGON

In the preceding chapter mention was made of the journeys
of Jason Lee and Marcus Whitman in 1834 and 1836 to
establish missions in the Willamette Valley and in the Walla
Walla country, and of the migration of one hundred settlers to
Oregon in 1842 under the leadership of Elijah White. Space
forbids any description of the adventures of these early
pioneers on the long pilgrimage or of their activities and
services in the Oregon country. It was the migration of 1843,
when one thousand people crossed the plains, that made a
well-marked trail to Oregon—the "Great Medicine Road of
the Whites," as the Indians called it. The caravans of this
year and those immediately following may well be selected
to illustrate and typify the early movements to the Oregon
country.

The early months of the year 1843 were marked by a widespread interest throughout the Middle West in the Oregon
country, and especially in the Willamette Valley. Government reports, bills in Congress to organize Oregon Territory,
and letters from missionaries, early settlers, and other enthusiasts—all served to spread information regarding the advantages of the lower Columbia Valley as a region for American
settlement. The beauty and fertility of the Willamette Valley,
its varied resources, and its easy access, by river and ocean,
to the markets of the world were described in a manner that
was very enticing. Harassed by hard times, many midwestern
farmers were strongly attracted by these alluring reports. In
the border States, there were many families who were becoming increasingly displeased by the continual spread of slavery.
Love of adventure—the prospect of seeing a strange country of

vast plains, immense herds of buffalo, wild Indian tribes, and towering mountain ranges—must have inspired descendants of generations of frontiersmen. Finally, there is evidence that a few, at least, were animated by a patriotic desire to help settle the Oregon country, and thus establish forever the claims of the United States to that rich and resourceful region.

Whatever may have been their motives, people in Missouri, Iowa, Illinois, Ohio, and other States of the Middle West were discussing in small groups or in public meetings the question of migrating to Oregon. For instance, on March 3, 1843, the citizens of Clear Creek precinct in Johnson County, Iowa, met "for the purpose of taking into consideration the propriety of organizing a company to emigrate to Oregon, and devise rules by which said company shall be governed." A few weeks later an elaborate constitution for an "Oregon Emigration Society" was adopted. On March 30th a public meeting was held at Bloomington (now Muscatine), Iowa. A committee previously appointed, reported that "from the information they have obtained from various sources, they believe the Oregon Territory to be far superior in many respects, to any other portion of the United States—they believe it to be superior in climate, in health, in water privileges, in timber, in convenience to market and in many other respects; they believe it to be well adapted to agriculture and stock raising, also holding out great inducements to mechanics of the various branches. They would therefore recommend to every person possessing the enterprise and patriotic spirit of the true American citizen to emigrate to Oregon Territory at as early a day as possible, and thereby secure to themselves a permanent and happy home, and to their country, one of the fairest portions of her domains."

Abundant advice was furnished prospective emigrants by speakers at public meetings, by communications in newspapers, and by guidebooks. The route was described in general, with information concerning camping places, Indians likely to be hostile, and difficulties to be encountered along the way. Possibly a small portion of the emigrants followed the detailed admonition of some experienced writers regarding all phases of desirable equipment, from light sturdy wagons to articles of personal apparel. In view of the fact, however, that the Oregon Trail soon became strewn with wreckage of broken-down wagons and cast-off furniture and supplies, it is evident that many families chose to ignore much of this advice.

Although other points along the Missouri River, such as St. Joseph and Council Bluffs, became well known "jumping-off places" for the journey across the plains, Independence, Missouri, near the site of Kansas City, was the favorite gathering and outfitting place for early emigrants to Oregon. To Independence they made their way in the spring from all directions, traveling mostly in small parties with their wagons and loose horses and cattle. By the middle of May, 1843, the little frontier town was a scene of bustle and activity, as hundreds of men, women, and children made ready for what has been called the Great Migration, because of its significance in determining the ownership of the Oregon country.

On May 22nd the emigrants left Independence, headed for Elm Grove, which was the first rendezvous. For several days their numbers were augmented by late arrivals, until there were nearly one thousand persons in the company, with about five thousand head of livestock. For about forty miles they followed the Santa Fé Trail, and then came to a place where a sign-board announced the "Road to Oregon" as nonchalantly as any modern road marker directs the traveler to the next town. By the time the Kansas River was reached the party had effected a permanent organization for the journey. Peter H. Burnett was first elected captain and James W. Nesmith orderly sergeant. Later the party was divided into two companies of about sixty wagons each. One known as the "light column" chose William Martin as its leader; while the other, called the "cow column" because it was made up of the emigrants who had herds of cattle, elected Jesse Applegate as its captain. John Gantt was the official guide as far as Fort Hall, but the entire party profited greatly by the presence with them of the famous missionary, Marcus Whitman, whose knowledge, cheerfulness, and untiring services were invaluable, especially beyond Fort Hall.

The trail from Independence ran in a northwestwardly direction from the crossing of the Kansas River to the Platte, and up that stream and its northern fork to Fort Laramie, 667 miles from the point of departure. Continuing up the North Platte and the Sweetwater, the road led past Independence Rock (which the emigrant party of 1843 reached on July 26th), through Devil's Gate, over the famous South Pass, and along the tributaries and the main stream of Green River to Fort Bridger, 1,070 miles from Independence and a little

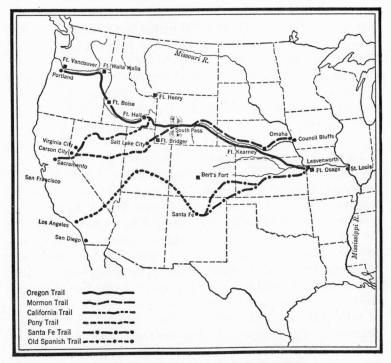

XI. GREAT TRAILS TO THE FAR WEST

more than half way to the mouth of the Willamette. From Fort Bridger the route ran northwest 218 miles to Fort Hall, then a post of the Hudson's Bay Company, which was reached on August 27th. Less than eight hundred miles now lay between the emigrants and their destination, but it was by far the most arduous part of the journey. It was the end of November before the weary emigrants arrived in the

Willamette Valley, after traveling along the Snake River, past Fort Boise, into the Grand Ronde valley, over the Blue Mountains to Whitman's mission at Waiilatpu, down the Columbia, either on rafts or by land, to The Dalles, and thence in the same manner to the Willamette.

Although the emigration of 1843 was of vital importance in establishing American rule in the Oregon country, its numbers were exceeded by those of parties arriving in several succeeding years. The best estimates indicate that 1400 new settlers arrived in Oregon in 1844; 3000 in 1845; 1350 in 1846; and between 4000 and 5000 in 1847. The census of 1850 gave Oregon a population of 13,294; while the enumeration of 1860 credited the new State with 52,465 people.

No better description of the routine followed by a well-organized emigrant company on the Oregon Trail, at least in the journey across the plains, has been written than Jesse Applegate's account of "A Day with the Cow Column." "It is four o'clock A.M.," he wrote, "the sentinels on duty have discharged their rifles—the signal that the hours of sleep are over—and every wagon and tent is pouring forth its night tenants, and slow-kindling smokes begin largely to rise and float away in the morning air." Sixty men set out to drive in the cattle, oxen and horses. Breakfast is prepared and eaten, tents are struck, wagons loaded, and teams yoked or harnessed. "All know when, at 7 o'clock, the signal to march sounds, that those not ready to take their proper places in the line of march must fall into the dusty rear for the day." Each wagon has its turn in the coveted position at the head of the line. "The clear notes of a trumpet sound in the front; the pilot and his guards mount their horses; the leading divisions of the wagons move out of the encampment, and take up the line of march; the rest fall into their places with the precision of clock work, until the spot so lately full of life sinks back into that solitude that seems to reign over the broad plain and rushing river as the caravan draws its lazy length towards the distant El Dorado."

After about five hours of steady travel the caravan halts for the noon meal at a spot selected by the pilot. At one o'clock the bugle sounds and the westward march is resumed.

Now, however, "drowsiness has fallen apparently on man and beast; teamsters drop asleep on their perches, and even when walking by their teams; and the words of command are now addressed to the slowly creeping oxen in the soft tenor of women or the piping treble of children."

Toward evening the pilot indicates the camping-place for the night, the wagons are drawn in a circle and fastened securely together, tents are pitched, fires kindled, and supper prepared. "It is not yet 8 o'clock when the first watch is to be set; the evening meal is just over, and the corral now free from the intrusion of cattle or horses, groups of children are scattered over it. Before a tent near the river a violin makes lively music, and some youths and maidens have improvised a dance upon the green; in another quarter a flute gives its mellow and melancholy notes to the still night air, which, as they float away over the quiet river, seem a lament for the past rather than a hope for the future. . . . But time passes; the watch is set for the night; the council of old men has been broken up, and each has returned to his own quarter; the flute has whispered its last lament to the deepening night; the violin is silent, and the dancers have dispersed. . . . All is hushed and repose from the fatigues of the day, save the vigilant guard and the wakeful leader, who still has cares upon his mind that forbid sleep," until "the last care of the day being removed, and the last duty performed, he too seeks the rest that will enable him to go through the same routine tomorrow."

In other diaries and reminiscences we get glimpses of many aspects of the trip over the long trail. We read of terrific storms, when, to quote the words of Francis Parkman in his classic, *The Oregon Trail*, "lightning flashed all night," thunder "roared over the boundless waste of prairie, seeming to roll around the whole circle of the firmament with a peculiar and awful reverberation," and the belongings of the more careless were drenched with rain or strewn over the prairie by the wind. Occasionally stampedes of huge herds of buffalo caused the terror-stricken flight of emigrant parties in their pathway. Indian scares were numerous, but fortunately they seldom were more than scares. Comparatively little loss of life was due to Indian hostility. The greatest damage done by the redskins was in stampeding and stealing livestock.

Flour and bacon were the main food staples carried by the emigrants. But we also read of dried fruits and vegetables, of cereals, beans, root vegetables, and of canned fruits, packed in the barrels of flour, to say nothing of coffee, sugar, salt and lard. Milk was abundant as long as there was sufficient grass and water for the cows. Butter could be churned without effort by the simple expedient of putting milk in a can and letting the continual jolting of the wagon do the work. Fresh buffalo meat was a most welcome addition to the diet while crossing the plains; and "jerked" meat, while far less appetizing, helped to maintain the strength of many emigrants on the further western stages of the trip. There is ample evidence that migrating women became exceedingly proficient in camp-fire cookery and in baking even raised bread in "Dutch ovens" and by means of "reflectors." It was a fortunate party, however, whose supply of food was not exhausted or its variety severely limited before the Oregon country was reached. Great privation, amounting to near-starvation, was the lot of large numbers.

The major events of life occurred with about normal frequency among those who traveled the Oregon Trail. Rare was the emigrant party of any size which did not contain several expectant mothers when it left the Missouri River, or celebrate the arrival of "covered-wagon babies" before the destination was reached. The marvel is that so many mothers survived the ordeal, and that so many of the babies born on the trail lived through the early months when proper care was well nigh impossible. Weddings took place between young men and women who had either known each other before setting out on the journey or became acquainted while on the road. The number of deaths was large in the aggregate, especially in the terrible years of cholera epidemic. But, with the exception of these periods and the instances when attempts were made to break new trails, the death rate was not abnormally high, when all the hardships and perils of the undertaking are taken into consideration. Each death, however, was attended by special pathos and by anguish to

relatives and friends, because of the necessity of pressing forward with a minimum of delay, leaving behind, in most cases,
unmarked graves.

Altogether, a journey over the Oregon Trail was an experience never to be forgotten. For the young and strong it was,
in the main, a long picnic excursion. The older men found
the adventure of the trip and the hope of prosperity to be
attained in the new home sufficient to counterbalance the toil
and hardship they endured on the way. The most heroic
aspect of the entire story is the record of the patience and
fortitude with which the wives and mothers bore the discomforts and privations and dangers of the long trek.

The Mormon Migrations

In 1846, while the migrations to Oregon were still in full
tide, a large group of people were driven from their homes on
the eastern bank of the Mississippi and inspired by their leader
to begin a march to an unknown destination in the Far West.
The hegira of the Mormons to new homes on the shores of the
Great Salt Lake is one of the most unique and remarkable
episodes in the entire history of the westward movement.

Mormonism was one of the many sects that had their
origin in the period of ferment and upheaval which we usually
call the Jacksonian era. In 1827 Joseph Smith, Jr., a young
man of shiftless habits and visionary proclivities whose home
was in Palmyra, New York, announced that there had been
revealed to him some golden plates on which were inscribed
a number of previously unknown books of the Bible. In 1830
the *Book of Mormon,* which was a translation of these sacred
tablets, was published and the Mormon Church was formally
organized, with Joseph Smith as its prophet and divine intermediary. Converts came slowly at first. The New York
environment was uncongenial to the new faith, partly because
its leader was too well known. Consequently a temporary
domicile for the church was selected at Kirtland, Ohio, a short
distance east of Cleveland.

A revelation received by Smith this same year designated
Independence, Missouri, as the permanent location of the zion

of the church. Before the year 1831 was over it is said that fully one thousand converts had flocked to the new headquarters of the sect. Friction soon developed between the Mormons and the Missourians, who looked with growing disfavor upon these strange newcomers. Haystacks of the Mormons were burned, their houses were stoned and windows broken, members of the church were tarred and feathered, their printing press was destroyed, and armed encounters took place. The upshot was that late in 1833 the Mormons were forced to abandon Independence. They went to the north of the Missouri River and established a new temple city which they named Far West. Here for about three years they enjoyed prosperity and comparative peace, and their numbers grew steadily.

Then, however, the dislike of their neighbors began to manifest itself in much the same way as at Independence. The "Gentiles" were particularly incensed by the calm assertion of many of the Mormons that they were a chosen people destined to inherit the earth, by their opposition to slavery and their missionary zeal. In 1838 Joseph Smith and Sidney Rigdon, who had remained in Kirtland, arrived at Far West and began to exhort their followers to defiance of their persecutors. On July 4th Rigdon delivered a sermon in which he spoke of a "war of extermination" if the Mormons should be attacked. The situation soon reached such a pass that the Missouri militia was called out, and Governor L. W. Boggs issued an order that the Mormons "must be exterminated or driven from the State if necessary for the public peace." The days of Far West were now numbered. In 1839 the Mormons once more abandoned their settlements, and this time they turned to the east to find a new location.

The place selected was on the east bank of the Mississippi River in Illinois a short distance north of the mouth of the Des Moines. Here they purchased the land and the deserted buildings of an abandoned experimental colony named Commerce, as well as some land on the Iowa side. Nauvoo alleged to mean "beautiful place" in ancient Hebrew language, was the name given to the new zion of the church. By 1846 the Mormon population of the settlement was fifteen thousand.

Before that time, however, the people of Illinois were as determined to get rid of the Mormons as the Missourians had been. The religious tenets and practices of Smith's followers, their political strength, their assumption of superiority, the avowed candidacy of their leader for the presidency of the United States, and especially persistent rumors of an announced approval of polygamy were among the causes for aversion on the part of the neighboring citizens of Illinois. In 1844 Joseph Smith and his brother Hyrum were arrested and while in jail at Carthage were murdered by a mob. It was now clear that the Mormon Church must move once more.

After the death of the prophet, Joseph Smith, the mantle of leadership fell upon Brigham Young, who for some time had been one of the "Twelve Apostles" of the church. The new leader was not only fully as zealous in the faith as his predecessor, but he possessed greater practical abilities as an organizer and director of his followers. When he and his fellow apostles decided that an asylum should be sought beyond the Rocky Mountains, in a region then belonging to Mexico, nearly all of the Mormons at Nauvoo were ready to accept the decision without question.

After very careful preparations the first unit of the Mormon migration crossed the Mississippi River into the Territory of Iowa in February, 1846, and by September of that year Nauvoo was evacuated by its former occupants. All during the spring and summer the trail across southern Iowa was alive with the moving companies, with their wagons, horses, cattle, and sheep. There were hardships and privation, but no confusion. Little settlements were made by the first party, as rest stations for the accommodation of later comers. Crops were planted for later parties to reap. Planning and organization were at all times in evidence. When the Missouri River was reached a portion of the Mormons remained on the Iowa side at Kanesville (now Council Bluffs), but the main encampment was at Winter Quarters on the west bank of the river.

In April, 1847, Brigham Young at the head of a "pioneer band" of about one hundred and forty men and three women, with seventy-three wagons, started across the plains to seek a home for the church beyond the mountains. The Mormon

Trail, thus begun, followed the north bank of the Platte River, rather than the main track of the Oregon Trail along the south bank, to Fort Laramie. From this point the route was almost identical with that of the Oregon Trail to Fort Bridger, and then it struck off into the mountains to the southwest. Late in July the party reached the southeastern shore of the Great Salt Lake. Here, whether guided by the voice of revelation, as he claimed, or influenced by more mundane considerations, Brigham Young determined to locate the Mormon Headquarters.

Even on the day of arrival plows were put to breaking up the soil preparatory to the planting of vegetables and grain. Ditches were soon dug and a beginning made of the extensive system of irrigation which became a notable feature of the colony. Within a month a city two miles square had been laid out, with wide streets and spacious lots, to say nothing of a stout fort and dwelling houses. Later in the year a party of nearly 1600 emigrants arrived from Winter Quarters, to be followed by others in succeeding years—each one marked by the orderly, disciplined procedure characteristic of all enterprises directed by Brigham Young. Thus Salt Lake City was established as the temple city and center of one of our most remarkable religious and social groups.

Thus was founded a community which was destined long to prove a disturbing factor in the life of the Far West and of the nation, as later chapters will indicate. Fate decreed that the people who had so courageously sought a sanctuary outside our national boundaries should be brought once more within the jurisdiction of the United States by the Treaty of Guadalupe Hidalgo, and thus subject once more to many of the antipathies which had driven them from their previous homes.

THE CALIFORNIA GOLD RUSH

While the migrations to Oregon were in progress and while the Mormons were on the march westward from Nauvoo, California was the destination of a smaller number of emigrants. It has been estimated that out of about two thousand people who set out on the Oregon Trail in 1846 one-fourth went to California. Most of these parties reached their goal in safety, but one of them—the famous Donner party—suffered a disaster that is one of the most tragic episodes in the annals of the westward movement. Separating from a larger company at Fort Bridger, a group of eighty-seven men, women, and children commanded by George Donner determined, against advice, to attempt to reach California by the so-called Hasting's cut-off around the southern end of Great Salt Lake. Time was lost in finding the trail and the party was forced to winter in the Sierras. Scarcely more than half of the members of the party survived the terrible suffering, which reduced some of them to the direst extremity that civilized men can experience—the eating of human flesh to maintain life.

The first place toward which most of the emigrants to California by the northern and central trails directed their steps was Sutter's Fort, or "New Helvetia" as it was called, on the Sacramento River near the mouth of the American River. Here lived and ruled John A. Sutter, a native of Baden who had come to the United States in the early eighteen thirties. By successive stages he drifted westward to St. Louis, to Santa Fé and the Rocky Mountains, and finally to California. In 1840 he secured permission from the Mexican authorities to establish a colony on the Sacramento River. The project was remarkably successful. Within a few years Sutter had not only a well defended and efficiently garrisoned fort, but extensive fields of grain and large herds of cattle and horses. He operated a grist mill, engaged in the fur trade, and carried on various other activities. He was always courteous and generous to Americans, among whom Sutter's Fort became known as a place of succor and recuperation after the hardships and exhaustion of the long overland journey.

It was within the limits of Sutter's grant that, on January 24, 1848, a discovery was made that brought ruin to the proprietor, but produced an excitement throughout the nation and, indeed, throughout the civilized word, that of its kind has probably never been exceeded. On that day James W. Marshall, one of Sutter's employees, saw some glistening, yellow particles in the tail-race of a saw mill which he was constructing about forty-five miles northeast of the fort. He gathered them up and hastened to Sutter. Tests were made and they proved to be gold. Instead of being elated, Sutter was troubled by premonitions of disaster to his prosperous enterprises if a gold rush should occur. Consequently the two men agreed to keep the discovery secret. In this effort, of course, they failed. The news inevitably leaked out, and other finds were made in the vicinity. In San Francisco, Sonoma, Monterey, and other coast settlements what at first were only rumors became certainties by early spring, and the great California gold rush was begun.

"Our town was startled out of its quiet dreams today, by the announcement that gold had been discovered on the American Fork," wrote Walter Colton, the American *alcalde* at Monterey, in his diary on May 29th. "The men wondered and talked, and the women too; but neither believed." Colton sent a messenger to the American River to investigate. On June 20th this emissary returned and "dismounted in a sea of upturned faces. As he drew forth the yellow hunks from his pockets, and passed them around among the eager crowd, the doubts, which had lingered till now, fled. . . . The excitement produced was intense; and many were soon busy in their hasty preparations for a departure to the mines. The family who had kept house for me caught the moving infection. Husband and wife were both packing up; the blacksmith dropped his hammer, the carpenter his plane, the mason his trowel, the farmer his sickle, the baker his loaf, and the tapster his bottle. . . . I have only a community of women left, and a gang of prisoners, with here and there a soldier, who will give his captain the slip at the first chance."

In the succeeding entries in his diary Colton continued to describe the effects of gold fever upon the town of Monterey. The holding of servants to their engagements, he said, "is like attempting to drive fish into a net with the ocean before them." When another bag of gold arrived about the middle of July, carpenters who were building a school house, "threw down their saws and planes, shouldered their picks, and are off for the Yuba. Three seamen ran from the Warren, forfeiting their four years' pay; and a whole platoon of soldiers from the fort left only their colors behind."

In San Francisco and other towns there was similar excitement. Thomas O. Larkin wrote to James Buchanan on June 28th that three-fourths of the houses in San Francisco were deserted; that almost all forms of business, trade, industry and professional life were at a standstill; and that ships were losing their crews and military posts their garrisons. Governor Richard B. Mason wrote a similar report after a mid-summer tour of the mining region. He saw idle mills, wheat fields open to horses and cattle, farms entirely neglected, and houses vacant.

There was reason for all this abandonment of ordinary pursuits. The California gold fields constituted an El Dorado rich beyond even the wildest dreams of the Spaniards who, by a strange twist of fate, had failed to discover it when it was in their possession. Governor Mason saw a ditch not more than one hundred yards long where two men had secured $17,000 worth of gold in seven days. Walter Colton told of seven men who, with the assistance of thirty Indians, worked for about fifty days and at the end divided gold worth nearly $77,000; of a man who had more than $5,300 as the result of two months work; of a fourteen-year-old boy who made $3,467 in fifty-four days; and of a woman who worked forty-six days in the dry diggings and had $2,125 as the result of her efforts. "Is not this enough," asked Colton, "to make a man throw down his ledger and shoulder a pick?" These were not rare exceptions, for gold was so abundant and accessible that the average person who had any luck or any industry at all might expect to make from ten to fifty dollars a day.

During the year 1848 the population of the gold region was made up of residents of California, Mexicans from Sonora and adjacent provinces, the crews and passengers from vessels coming into California harbors, and a considerable number of the settlers of Oregon to whom the prospect of finding gold was suddenly more attractive than the cultivation of their newly-located farms. Despite the feverish excitement, life and labor in the diggings was notably different during this

brief period than in the years which followed. General honesty
and good will prevailed. Gold was so abundant and was so
easily found that stealing seemed scarcely worth while. There
was room for all and little temptation or inclination to enter
into quarrels or fights with fellow miners. Gold was found at
the roots of bushes, pried out of crevices in rocks, and
"panned" and "cradled" from rich "pay-dirt" and neither
experience nor expensive machinery was necessary to success.

It was late in the year 1848 before authoritative news of
the gold discovery reached the eastern part of the United
States. There had been rumors before this time, but they
received little attention. A Baltimore newspaper printed
an item in September. A little later the *Journal of Commerce*
published a letter from a correspondent in California. "Talk
to a laborer about hiring him for fifty dollars a month,"
declared the writer, "and he will turn up his nose at you.
Offer him ten dollars a day, and he will tell you he is bound to
Feather river. One man who resides next door to me, gathered
five hundred dollars worth in six days. . . . It beats all the
dreams of romance and all the marvels of the golden wand of
Midas." Then, late in November, the federal authorities
received Governor Mason's report in which he expressed his
belief that "There is more gold in the country drained by the
Sacramento and San Joaquin rivers than would pay the cost
of the late war with Mexico a hundred times over." In his
annual message on December 5th President Polk gave official
recognition to accounts which were "of such an extraordinary
character as would scarcely command belief were they not
corroborated by the authentic reports of officers in the public
services." By this time all doubts and indifference had disappeared, and the entire nation was seized with gold fever.

"The excitement seems to grow by what it feeds on, and
there is no prospect of abatement," declared a Milwaukee
editor late in December. Newspapers were soon filled with
letters and reports from California, information concerning the
gold region, descriptions of the routes to the Pacific coast,
and advice to those planning to make the trip. There were
announcements, especially in eastern newspapers, of ships
about to sail, either around the Horn or to Chagres or some

other point on the eastern coast of Central America or Mexico. Advertisements proclaimed the virtues of a large variety of mechanical devices for the discovery, extraction, or washing of gold. Articles declared necessary to the health, comfort or safety of those making the journey, whether by land or sea, were offered for sale; as were also the businesses, professional practices, and personal property of many men who were affected by the irresistible attraction of the gold fields. There were notices of associations being formed, either to make the journey as a group or to finance the trip of one or more representatives. California and gold were, for several months, the all-absorbing topics of interest and conversation throughout the nation. It may safely be said that there were few communities in the United States unrepresented in the multitude that responded to the magic lure of the El Dorado.

In Europe the news of the discovery of gold produced widespread interest. Before the year 1849 was more than one month old there were accounts of ships sailing for California from ports in Great Britain, Germany, Holland, France, and Spain. Numerous California mining companies were formed in London; and in France, it is said, lotteries were established in which the winners received expense-money for the voyage to the gold fields. Later, even China and Australia felt the restlessness of gold mania.

There were two main sea-routes to California. The one around Cape Horn was too long and too expensive to be adopted by more than a small portion of the gold-seekers. The other consisted of a voyage from ports on the Atlantic or Gulf coast to Chagres on the Caribbean side of the Isthmus of Panama, from whence the passengers made their way as best they could overland to the town of Panama on the Pacific side, where they waited, with such patience as they could command, for a place in a vessel that would carry them to San Francisco. It was estimated that by the middle of March, 1849, fully 17,000 persons had sailed from American ports bound for the diggings, and by the close of that year at least 230 American ships had reached California harbors. Among these were the three steamships, the *California,* the *Oregon,* and the *Panama,* of the newly established Pacific Mail Steamship Company. The first of these reached San Francisco on February 28th, and was almost immediately deserted by her entire crew except the captain. A letter from San Francisco printed in the *New York Herald* in November stated that "There are about two hundred and fifty vessels in the harbor, many of them large ships, and mostly abandoned and going to ruin."

A greater number of forty-niners, especially those from the western States, reached California by the various overland trails. Typical of innumerable items in western newspapers was the following which appeared in the *Wisconsin Argus* (Madison) early in March. "Small companies belonging to several counties in this state numbering from half a dozen to twenty, are already on the road to California. The 'caravans' that will cross the plains this year will beat anything ever before witnessed on the continent." This prediction was amply fulfilled. The most conservative estimates indicate that nearly 35,000 Americans reached California by the overland routes in 1849. How many more started, and turned back discouraged or died on the way can never be known.

The Santa Fé Trail was followed by numerous gold-seekers to Santa Fé, and thence they made their way by various routes to the Sacramento. People from the southern States crossed Texas and pressed on, either to Santa Fé or by a more southern route, eventually following the Gila to the Colorado and into California. Others outfitted at Fort Smith and proceeded by the newly-opened Cherokee Trail which led into Colorado and to Fort Bridger. Many of those who followed the southern trails experienced terrible suffering or met their deaths in the deserts or in Death Valley, where the temperature reached 140 degrees and no water was to be found. By far the greatest number of those who crossed the plain traveled the well-worn Oregon Trail and Mormon Trail. Beyond the South Pass there were several variations of route. Many preferred to continue on to Soda Springs or Fort Hall, where they turned southwest to the Humboldt River and across the Sierras to the Sacramento Valley. Others followed the somewhat shorter route from Fort Bridger around the southern end of Great Salt Lake.

The account of the experiences of the forty-niners on the overland journey would in many respects be a repetition of the story of the migrations to Oregon. There was the same custom on the part of the wise and well informed to organize themselves into fairly large parties, to select competent leaders and guides, and to submit to rather rigid discipline while on the road. In general, those who adopted this procedure reached their destination without unbearable hardship, if they escaped the dread scourge of cholera which pursued them across the plains. Those who neglected these precautions, those who were inadequately prepared for the journey, and those who chose to disregard sound advice were all too likely to be human wrecks when they reached California, if they arrived at all. Even under the best circumstances the passage of the alkali-covered stretches of the Humboldt Sink and the crossing of the high Sierras taxed the strength of the strongest.

On the other hand, the personnel of the gold rush differed from that of the Oregon and Mormons migrations. Instead of mid-western farmers or followers of a religious faith, the forty-niners were a cross-section of the people of the United States impelled across plains and mountains by a frenzied desire for gold. While there were many women and children in the parties, there was a great predominance of men; and while there were many accustomed to frontier life, there were many others wholly inexperienced in an undertaking of this nature. It was doubtless partly because of this heterogeneous character of the emigrant parties, as well as because of the great impatience of all to reach the gold fields, that relationships often became unusually strained, and that people sometimes gave way to such senseless acts as the destruction of cast-off property and supplies in order that others might not be able to use them. Fortunately the entire picture is not so dark. Diaries and journals tell us of singing and dancing, of amateur theatricals, of religious meetings, and of pleasant conversations around the nightly campfires. Generosity, good-will, and heroism were by no means lacking.

The heterogeneous character of the population that poured into California in the years of the gold rush is reflected in the names of the mining camps. "The race of the earliest inhabitants," says Owen C. Coy, "may have given names to Irish Creek, Italian Bar, French Corral, German Bar, Dutch Flat, Kanaka Bar, Malay Camp, Chinese Camp and Nigger Hill. One can almost picture the various groups of men that moved westward and gave such names to their new location as the following: Missouri Bar, Iowa Hill, Wisconsin Hill, Illinoistown, Michigan Bluffs, Tennessee Creek, Kentucky Flat, Minnesota Flat, Cape Cod Bar, Vermont Bar, Georgia Slide, Alabama Bar, Dixie Valley and Mississippi Bar." Other camps and towns were given names, either by the inhabitants or by others, which may indicate the general characteristics and background of the various groups. For instance there were such names as Whisky Slide, Poker Flat, Lazy Hollow, Poverty Hill, Ragtown, Gouge Eye, Murderers' Bar, Hangtown, Helltown, Fair Play, Industry Bar, Piety Hill, Methodist Creek, Gospel Gulch, Alpha, Omega, Rubicon Creek, Damascus, Auburn, and Charity Valley.

Because of the intense excitement aroused by the news of the gold discovery, there is a glamor attached to the story of the rush of the forty-niners that does not appear in the accounts of the migrations of 1850 and succeeding years. As a matter of fact, the trails to the gold region were equally crowded during these years. The census of 1850, probably with only approximate accuracy, credited California with 92,597 inhabitants. Ten years later the number had increased to 379,994. From the beginning there were those who made the long journey with the intention of settling permanently, and engaging in occupations and professions other than mining. This number increased yearly as the gold excitement waned. At the same time, the experience in the California diggings produced a considerable group of men who became habitual prospectors, chronically affected with gold fever and participating in the mining stampedes of succeeding years in various portions of the Far West.

Effects of Western Expansion

The territorial acquisitions of the forties and the migrations to Oregon, Utah, and California had profound effects upon the politics, policies, attitudes, and prospects of the people of the United States. As will be seen in the following chapter, the problems of setting up governments in the newly acquired regions and in the Great Plains greatly accentuated the sectional bitterness between the North and South, and led to a series of events and controversies that ended in the Civil War. The migrations across the plains and the extension of our national boundaries to the Pacific terminated all thought of a permanent Indian territory in the region of the Great Plains, and opened the most ignoble chapter in the story of our dealings with the American Indians. The rapid growth of population on the Pacific coast created a demand for overland transportation and communication that was met by the development of stage-coach and freight-wagon companies on a grand scale, by the pony express and the telegraph line, and later by the railroads. By 1850 the entire nation was well informed concerning a vast area of rich and varied resources which lay open for occupation and exploitation.

CHAPTER XXXI

PROBLEMS OF GOVERNMENTAL ORGANIZATION
1848-1861

THE Compromise of 1850, the Kansas-Nebraska Bill, and the resulting struggle in Kansas loom large in the history of the United States between the close of the Mexican War and the beginning of the Civil War. As every student of our history knows, the year 1850 found Congress faced by a series of problems, the seriousness of which as national issues was due to the fact that each question was affected by the bitterness of the sectional struggle between the North and the South. Northern demands for the abolition of slavery and the slave trade in the District of Columbia, and southern complaints concerning the ineffectiveness of the fugitive slave law and its enforcement were alone sufficient to arouse intense feeling. To these were added the controversial demand of California for admission into the Union, the question of the status of slavery in the remaining territory acquired from Mexico, and the problem of determining the boundaries of Texas. A solution was found in the great compromise measures of which Henry Clay was the chief proponent. The entire nation breathed a sigh of relief, for a grave crisis had been averted. Then, four years later, the passage of the Kansas-Nebraska Bill, with its repeal of the time-honored Missouri Compromise, rudely shattered the hope of peace between the sections.

The story of these great Congressional measures, in their national aspects, need not be repeated in these pages. It is necessary, however, to describe the establishment of territorial and state governments in the Far West before the Civil War, and to indicate the problems, both local and national, which affected that process.

GOVERNMENT FOR THE OREGON COUNTRY

The first portion of the newly acquired domain to receive territorial government was the Oregon country. Even before the region had been given into the possession of the United States by the treaty of 1846, the settlers in the Willamette Valley had, true to American pioneer custom, entered into various agreements and finally adopted a provisional government to administer their local affairs. As early as 1838 they elected a justice of the peace and a constable. In 1841 they chose a larger number of officials. Then in 1843, in the so-called "wolf meetings" held ostensibly to adopt measures for the protection of livestock against wild animals, steps were taken that led, a few months later, to the adoption at Champoeg of a written constitution and a definite provisional government. Executive power was vested in a committee of three, financial support was to be by voluntary subscription, there was provision for legislative and judicial officers, and the statute laws of the Territory of Iowa, enacted in 1838-39, were adopted as far as they were applicable. In 1844 and again in 1845 revisions and improvements were made in the constitution. Even the former employees of the Hudson's Bay Company living in the Oregon country now threw in their lots without reservation with the much larger body of American settlers.

During all this time, petition after petition had been sent to Congress praying for the establishment of territorial government. An early response to these entreaties was confidently expected in 1846 when the United States gained undisputed possession of the Oregon country as far north as the forty-ninth parallel. But the Mexican War, now in progress, claimed much of the attention of federal authorities and legislators. Even more important as a cause of delay was the sectional controversy over the status of slavery in the newly acquired territory. The Oregon settlers had twice voted against slavery. As a consequence pro-slavery members of Congress did not look with favor upon the establishment of territorial government in the northwest, at least until they were assured of a compensating Territory where slavery might exist. Additional memorials were therefore sent to Congress by the impatient settlers. It was only after the tragedy of the Whitman massacre had dramatized the need for efficient government that these prayers were answered.

The missions established in 1836 by Dr. Marcus Whitman and his associates at Waiilatpu, Lapwai, and near the Spokane River in the upper Columbia region, had met with eager response from the Indians during the first few years. Then some of the novelty wore off, a number of hostile and troublesome Indians came into the country, and interest began to slacken. Late in 1842 Whitman received word that the American Board had decided to close the missions at Waiilatpu and Lapwai. He immediately set out for the East on a heroic winter journey by way of Fort Hall, Taos, Bent's Fort, and St. Louis. Arriving in Boston, he succeeded in inducing the board to rescind its resolution. On his return trip in 1843 he rendered valuable assistance, as we have seen, to the large emigrant party of that year. But the missions did not thrive, although Waiilatpu was a haven of rest and succor to the weary travelers over the Oregon Trail. By 1847 affairs had reached a crisis and the missionaries delayed too long in leaving their station. The Cayuses had become increasingly insolent, and now they determined that Whitman must die, because of their suspicions that he was responsible for a fatal epidemic of the measles. The blow fell on November 29th. Dr. and Mrs. Whitman and seven others were brutally killed. Five other victims met a like fate a few days later; and more than fifty men, women and children, mostly emigrants, were held as captives.

There was alarm throughout the settlements when news of this massacre reached the Willamette Valley, for there was fear of a general Indian uprising. A regiment of volunteers was quickly recruited and despatched up the Columbia. In the meantime Peter Skene Ogden of the Hudson's Bay Company had succeeded in rescuing the prisoners. The Cayuses were severely punished in the ensuing campaign, but the war taxed the slender resources of the settlers to the utmost.

Joseph Meek (always known as Joe Meek) was sent to Washington with a report of the massacre and the Indian war, and a memorial calling upon Congress in no wavering manner to give Oregon a government capable of coping with the problems facing the people. Action was now secured. On August 13, 1848, Congress passed a law creating the Territory of Oregon, embracing all the country from the Rocky Mountains to the Pacific and between the forty-second and the forty-ninth parallels. Joseph Lane and Joe Meek, whom President Polk appointed as governor and United States marshal, respectively, arrived in Oregon City on May 2, 1849, and on the following day the new territorial government was declared in operation.

The development of the Oregon country during the succeeding years was rapid, in view of the remoteness of the region. Troops stationed at Vancouver and Oregon City and at Nisqually on Puget Sound brought money into the country, and gave a feeling of security to the settlers in the Willamette Valley, although Indian uprisings in other parts of the Territory devastated outlying settlements and kept the soldiers almost constantly in the field. The discovery of gold in California at first caused a great stampede from Oregon. But in the end it proved a boon to the new Territory. Not only did Oregonians return to their homes with bags of gold, but California furnished a ready and lucrative market for the produce of Oregon farms and forests. A generous donation land law enacted by Congress, giving free land to actual settlers before December 1, 1855, added to the attractiveness of the northwest. It is said that fully 15,000 people migrated to Oregon in 1852, and it is estimated that the population numbered more than 35,000 by the close of the following year.

The Willamette Valley continued to attract the largest number of the emigrants to the Oregon country. As early as 1845, however, a few settlers ventured into the region north of the Columbia. In the Cowlitz valley and northward to the shores of Puget Sound, scattered cabins began to appear. As population increased there grew a demand for separate territorial government. There were no roads, with the result that communication with the capital of the Territory was exceedingly slow and difficult. The trade and business connections of the northern settlements were almost entirely with California. Early in 1853 Congress acceded to the requests of the settlers and created the Territory of Washington, consisting of the portion of the original Oregon Territory lying north of the Columbia River and the forty-sixth parallel.

In the meantime a movement for statehood was in progress in Oregon. Finally, in the late summer of 1857, a constitutional convention assembled at Salem and drew up a constitution, which was ratified by the people at an election held in November. Without waiting for Congressional action, state government was organized in 1858. On February 14, 1859, Oregon was admitted into the Union with its present boundaries. The region between the eastern boundary and the Rocky Mountains was added to the Territory of Washington, in which jurisdiction it remained until 1863, when the Territory of Idaho was created.

The Territory of New Mexico

The slavery controversy, which was a cause of delay in the establishment of territorial government in Oregon, brought on a grave national crisis when government for the vast area acquired at the close of the Mexican War was under consideration. Even before the Treaty of Guadalupe Hidalgo was signed David Wilmot's famous proviso that slavery should never exist in territory obtained from Mexico was twice adopted by the federal House of Representatives. Although the proposal failed to pass the Senate, it definitely raised the issue of the status of slavery in the territories that was permanently settled only by the Civil War.

When Colonel Stephen W. Kearny was in Santa Fé in 1846 on his way to California, he set up a temporary civil government for the people of New Mexico which received the approval of federal authorities. He exceeded his powers, however, when he drafted an organic law for a territorial government and set a date for the election of a Delegate to Congress, and his actions were repudiated. President Polk repeatedly urged Congress to provide a regular government for New Mexico. In October, 1848, the inhabitants of the region held a convention and petitioned Congress for territorial status; but at the same time they expressed opposition to the introduction of slavery. About a year later they went further, when they drew up a code and chose a delegate to Congress. In 1850 they even drafted and adopted a state constitution. In Congress no action could be obtained, because the House, controlled by northerners, would not adopt any measure that did not exclude slavery from the proposed territory; while the southerners in the Senate were able to defeat any plan that did not permit slavery.

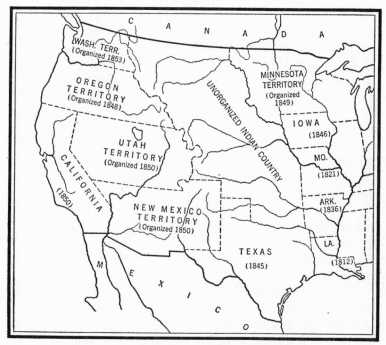

XII. THE ORGANIZATION OF THE FAR WEST, 1848-1854

The problem of providing territorial government for New Mexico was made more difficult by the claim of Texas to all the region east of the Rio Grande River, including Santa Fé itself. The legislature of Texas twice established counties in the disputed area and sent officers to organize local government. In each instance the commissioners were coldly received by the people of Santa Fé; and they were given no encouragement by the military authorities, who maintained that the civil government set up by Colonel Kearny would remain in force until other orders were received from Washington. The people of Texas were angered by this treatment, and the situation was quite tense in 1850. In some parts of Texas there was talk of withdrawal from the Union, while the legislature discussed a measure providing for the raising of troops with which to enforce the authority of the State as far west as the Rio Grande. In Congress the boundary question caused much debate. Proslavery members supported Texas in her claims, anti-slavery members opposed because of the enlargement of slave territory, and there was another deadlock.

As is well known, the creation of the Territory of New Mexico and the settlement of the Texan boundary dispute were two of the group of measures which constituted the Compromise of 1850. In return for the sum of ten million dollars Texas gave up to the federal government not only the region in dispute with New Mexico, but a wide strip of country along the southern bank of the Arkansas River, west of the one hundredth meridian, and a long pan-handle stretching northward to the forty-second parallel in the present State of Wyoming. Texas thus received her present boundaries on the north and west, and her people were reasonably satisfied with the bargain, for the money received from the federal government was more than sufficient to pay their public debt incurred during the period of the independent republic.

The Territory of New Mexico, after the addition of the region acquired from Mexico by the Gadsen Purchase in 1853, included the present States of New Mexico and Arizona, together with a small area in southeastern Colorado and a triangular region in southern Nevada. This large area was reduced, first in 1861 when the Territory of Colorado was established with the thirty-seventh parallel as its southern boundary, and again in 1863 when the Territory of Arizona was created with boundaries which included the southern tip of Nevada until 1866. In New Mexico, as in the Territory of Utah, the status of slavery was left by the organic acts of September 9, 1850, to be determined by the people when they should draw up constitutions and be admitted into the Union. Long before statehood was achieved by either Territory the question of slavery had been settled by the Civil War.

Government for the Mormons in Utah

As has already been noted, when the Mormons left Nauvoo on their hegira to a new home in the mountains they thought they were removing beyond the boundaries of the United States. But while they were on the march, the Mexican War was begun, and before their settlement on the Great Salt Lake was completed they found themselves again within the jurisdiction of the nation they had sought to leave. The first year was one of great hardship and it was not until the crops of 1848 were harvested that the specter of starvation was laid. Although the "Saints" were not wholly immune to the alluring news of gold discoveries in California, comparatively few of them were sufficiently attracted to sever the ties that bound them to the struggling colony of the faithful. As a matter of fact, from an economic standpoint, the great majority who remained at home profited at least as fully from the gold excitement as the small minority who rushed off to the diggings. Prosperity came as though by providential decree when the throngs of weary, overburdened forty-niners and gold-seekers of succeeding years found in the Mormon colony a place where they could obtain sorely needed food and other supplies.

Governmental functions were exercised by the Church without any separate organization for that purpose during the first year and a half of the community's existence. After the close of the Mexican War, however, more formal provision for government seemed desirable. Since Congress had not given any attention to the matter, the Mormons took affairs into their own hands. In March a convention assembled at Salt Lake City and drew up a constitution for the State of Deseret. Shortly afterward Brigham Young was elected governor and the other offices were filled by the choice of church officials. Apparently there was some confusion regarding the differences in the status of state and territorial governments, for in July the legislature elected a Delegate to Congress. This representative went to Washington with the constitution and the application of the State of Deseret for admission into the Union. These documents were presented in Congress late in December, 1849, but no action was taken. Instead, one of the compromise measures of 1850 created the Territory of Utah in that part of the Mexican cession north of the Territory of New Mexico and east of California.

Many pages could be filled with a recital of the turbulent events of the ensuing decade. Brigham Young was appointed governor of the Territory, a position which he held until 1858, and even then his power and influence were in no way diminished. The non-Mormons appointed to other territorial offices encountered an opposition that made it impossible for them to perform their duties. The Mormons were determined to manage their own affairs without interference from gentiles, even though backed by the authority of the United States government. Whatever may have been the merits of the controversy, matters had reached such a pass by 1857 that an army of fifteen hundred men under Colonel Albert Sidney Johnston marched across the plains toward Utah. The Mormons, on their part, took up arms, prepared to resist the "invaders," and threatened to lay waste to their settlements and take to the mountains, rather than submit to outside domination. The troops were harassed by small parties of Mormons who captured supplies and ran off stock as they approached their destination, and they were not able to enter Utah until 1858. Soon afterward a compromise was patched up and the so-called "Mormon War" was ended without actual bloodshed.

Meanwhile, in September, 1857, at a place called Mountain Meadows about 350 miles south of Salt Lake City, a party of 140 men, women, and children from Arkansas on their way to California, was entirely annihilated in a brutal massacre perpetrated by white men and Indians. While official complicity in their terrible affair was never definitely brought home to the leaders of the Church, there was sufficient evidence that the white men guilty of the crime were Mormons, and one of them later paid the penalty. The entire nation was incensed at news of this massacre. It is true that many of the stories and reports regarding the Mormons and their polygamous practices that were widely circulated and believed, were greatly exaggerated. But these stories, together with the events just mentioned, explain why it was that Utah was long regarded with aversion by the rest of the nation.

The area of the Territory of Utah was whittled down to its present boundaries by successive acts of Congress during the decade of the sixties, when new territorial governments were erected to the east, north, and west. As will be seen later, it was not until 1896 that statehood was achieved.

STATEHOOD FOR CALIFORNIA

Most disturbing of all the questions pressing for settlement in 1850 was that presented by the request of the people of California for admission into the the Union as a free State. Not only did California lie across the extension of the Missouri Compromise line, but the granting of its request would upset the balance between the sections in the United States Senate, which had been maintained since the historic struggle over the admission of Missouri. There was no slave State to be paired with California. It is probable that few southerners really believed that slavery would thrive in the newly acquired Pacific Coast region, but they were unwilling to yield the principle of balance between North and South, and in the end did so only in return for compensating concessions on the part of the northerners. Thus arose the most crucial issue in the great forensic battle of 1850.

For three years during and after the American conquest, California was under the rule of a series of naval and military commanders: Commodore John D. Sloat, Commodore Robert F. Stockton, Major John C. Frémont, General Stephen W. Kearny, Colonel R. B. Mason and General Bennett Riley, the latter of whom was appointed as civil governor. There was much uncertainty regarding the political status of the newly acquired region, especially after the signing of the Treaty of Guadalupe Hidalgo. Rigid adherence to the law of nations would have meant the continuance of Mexican rules and institutions of government until superseded by Congress, but any such plan was unacceptable to most of the people of California. The military governors left local government largely in the hands of *alcaldes,* appointed by them. But the power of the *alcalde* was comprehensive and arbitrary, and soon gave rise to complaint and resentment, particularly in communities where

Americans predominated. Early in 1849 the people of San Francisco took matters into their own hands and elected a legislative assembly of fifteen members and three justices of the peace. This action was declared illegal by both General Persifor F. Smith, the military commandant, and by General Riley, the new governor.

Dissatisfaction with military rule became even more widespread as Americans began to pour into the mining regions late in 1848 and early in 1849. It was confidently expected that Congress would speedily establish territorial government, but this hope faded when the federal legislature adjourned in March, 1849, without taking action. An impetus was now given to a movement already under way in various communities to elect delegates to a convention to form a provisional government. Governor Riley, however, regarded it to be his prerogative to take the lead in such matters. On June 3rd he issued a proclamation calling for the election on August 1st of delegates to a constitutional convention. The people were inclined to question Riley's right to dictate to them; but since the end to be achieved would be the same in either case, they yielded and proceeded to select delegates. Although Riley's proclamation called for thirty-seven delegates, forty-eight were chosen and seated in the convention, all but ten of whom were from northern California.

The constitutional convention met at Monterey on September 1, 1849, in the schoolhouse, known as Colton Hall in honor of its builder. The personnel of the convention included eight Californians of Spanish or Mexican descent, two foreign-born members, and thirty-eight Americans who hailed from twenty-one States and constituted a cross-section of the American population as far as occupations or professions were concerned. William M. Gwin from Tennessee early gained a position of leadership; and the recently adopted constitution of Iowa was the model most closely followed, although the fundamental laws of various other commonwealths, especially that of New York, were freely used. Although fifteen members came from southern States, the convention unanimously adopted a section of the bill of rights declaring that "Neither slavery nor involuntary servitude, unless for the punishment of crimes, shall ever be tolerated in this state." Various resolutions designed to prohibit the entrance of free negroes into California were debated and finally rejected. The location of the eastern boundary of the new State was the only question which provoked angry discussion. The boundary as it now exists was adopted as a compromise between those who proposed the Sierra Nevadas as the eastern limit, and those who wished California to extend much farther east—some even advocating the Rocky Mountains as the boundary.

The constitution was completed and signed on October 13th, while outside the convention hall the event was celebrated by the booming of a salute of thirty-one guns and the hoisting of flags on government buildings and on ships in the harbor. November 13th was the date set for a popular vote on the constitution and for the election of state officers and members of Congress. The vote was light, for various reasons, but the constitution was ratified by the overwhelming vote of 12,061 to 811. Peter H. Burnett, a former pioneer of Oregon, was elected governor and G. W. Wright and Edward Gilbert were chosen to represent California in the lower house of Congress. The first state legislature assembled at San José on December 15th, and two days later selected John C. Frémont and William M. Gwin as United States Senators.

Thus the people of California proceeded with great unanimity and despatch to set up and organize a state government for themselves. But the more difficult goal of admission into the Union was still to be achieved. For months the nation anxiously awaited a solution of the many troublesome questions which seemed so inextricably involved in each other in the perilous year 1850. Before that solution was found there were angry threats of secession and all lovers of the Union were filled with alarm. Clay's "omnibus bill" proposing to settle the problems of California, New Mexico, Utah, and Texas in one measure went down to failure. Only by submitting each of the main proposals of the Great Compromise to a separate vote was success attained. Not until August 13th did the bill admitting California into the Union pass the Senate. On September 7th it was adopted with less difficulty by the House of Representatives. On September 9, 1850, President Fillmore attached his signature and California achieved statehood. Curiously enough, although admitted as a free State, the new commonwealth was represented for a time after the expiration of Frémont's term in 1851, by two pro-slavery Senators.

THE KANSAS-NEBRASKA BILL

The sectional struggle had been so bitter and the danger of disunion so great that a large majority of the American people accepted the Compromise of 1850 with satisfaction and relief. Both major political parties pledged themselves to its support, and on all sides efforts were made to quiet any further discussion of the slavery controversy. But in retrospect we can see how insecure were these hopes. Even in 1850 forces and ambitions and motives were at work that in four years were not only to upset the truce of that year, but were to destroy long-established Indian policy, secure the repeal of the well-nigh sacred Missouri Compromise, precipitate political re-alignments, and add increased bitterness to the relations between the sections. The center of interest of these forces, motives and ambitions was the Great Plains, and especially the country west of Missouri and Iowa.

As early as 1844 the Secretary of War suggested the establishment of a Territory to be known as Nebraska in the Great Plains region, in order to strengthen our claims to the Oregon country and facilitate emigration thither. In December of that year Stephen A. Douglas introduced a bill for that purpose in the lower house of Congress. Two more unsuccessful bills for the creation of the proposed Territory were introduced in March and December, 1848, by Douglas, who was now in the United States Senate. Then the problems connected with the Mexican cession claimed attention to the exclusion of all other topics. In 1852, however, in western Missouri and among the Wyandot Indians there began a movement for the creation of a Territory west of Missouri. From this time, not only in Missouri and Iowa but in Congress as well, the subject was agitated until Douglas's Kansas-Nebraska Bill was enacted in 1854.

The true nature of the forces and motives behind this cata-

clysmic measure are not even now fully known. It is not difficult to understand why the bill as finally passed declared the
Missouri Compromise inoperative and void. As long as the
parallel 36°30′ continued to be regarded as an unalterable dividing line between free and slave soil, the South would not consent to the establishment of a new Territory north of this line.
Southern statesmen were hesitant at first to advocate the overthrow of an agreement that had become so firmly fixed in
American thought. But they found in the compromise measure
of 1850 a principle that seemed to offer a solution of their
difficulties—namely, the principle of Congressional non-inter-
ference with slavery in the Territories. New Mexico and Utah
had been established with the understanding that their people
should decide the slavery question at the time of seeking admission into the Union. California had been admitted as a free
State because her people so desired. This principle should be
applied in all the remaining regions of the Far West, and the
Missouri Compromise line should be abandoned. Senator
Douglas agreed with this reasoning. At any rate he was willing
to pay the price of embodying the definite repeal provision in
his bill in order to secure its adoption.

The reasons for the rather sudden insistence upon the creation of a new Territory west of Missouri and Iowa have been
somewhat clarified by recent studies. There was no real
pressure of population to account for the demand. Much good
land still lay open for settlement behind the frontier line. To
be sure the myth of a great American desert had been dispelled,
and the idea of permanent Indian occupancy of the Great
Plains was becoming increasingly irksome. It seems reasonable to believe, however, that the principal cause of the appearance of the Kansas-Nebraska issue to be found in the rivalry
of sections and cities and the ambitions of individuals in connection with the location of a railroad to the Pacific coast.

For several years, as will be seen in a later chapter, there
had been a growing interest in a Pacific railroad. In 1853
Congress made an appropriation and authorized the Secretary
of War to direct surveys of the proposed routes. Not only were
the two great sections of the nation desirous of securing the
benefits of such a railroad for themselves, but cities such as

New Orleans, Vicksburg, Memphis, St. Louis, Chicago, and Milwaukee had their favorite routes. Until after the Mexican war the only possible route to the Pacific through country belonging to the United States lay in the north. The Mexican cession altered the situation materially. After the creation of the Territory of New Mexico, the admission of California, and the Gadsden Purchase, negotiated largely for the purpose of facilitating railroad building, a far southern route had many advantages. It could run through organized States and Territories all the way from the Mississippi to the Pacific, construction over the mountains would be easier, and it could count on the support of a pro-southern administration in Washington. In fact, when Congress assembled in December, 1853, the southern route seemed all but assured.

This was the situation confronting the people of Missouri, Iowa, and Illinois, who were clamoring for the selection of a central route to the Pacific. Two great obstacles blocked the way. From Texas to Canada stretched the Indian country which had been given to its inhabitants under a solemn pledge that they would never again be molested. In the second place, an organized government in this region was clearly necessary before a railroad could be built or expected to succeed. A later chapter will reveal how the pledges to the Indians were violated in 1853, when Commissioner G. W. Manypenny, much against his will, negotiated treaties with the tribesmen which made way for railroad building and territorial government. The Kansas-Nebraska Bill provided the essential governmental organization. Thus the demand for a railroad to the Pacific by a central route was at least one of the important factors that produced Douglas's ill-fated measure.

It is no doubt true, as some recent writers have asserted, that Stephen A. Douglas was given too much credit or blame for the Kansas-Nebraska Bill. Nevertheless, his name has been more closely identified with the measure than that of any other person, and his motives have ever since been the subject of speculation and interpretation. For many years it was generally believed that he was motivated by the hope of winning southern support to further his ambitions for the presidency. He probably was not indifferent to this possibility.

Other writers have asserted that Douglas was sincere in his adherence to the fundamental principle of popular sovereignty, and in his belief that its application would remove the vexed question of slavery extension from the national arena. It is certain that he remained true to this principle during the stormy struggle over the fraudulent Lecompton constitution. A more satisfactory explanation of Douglas's motives, however, is that advanced by Professor Frank H. Hodder, who has pointed out the Illinois Senator's deep interest in the same subject of a railroad to the Pacific that animated many of the other leaders working for the passage of the bill.

Douglas had been an enthusiastic advocate of railroad-building in Illinois since as early as 1836. In 1850 he was instrumental in securing the first Congressional land grant for a railroad—the Illinois Central. Amid the rivalries over the route of the proposed railroad to the Pacific he was determined that the interests of his own city of Chicago should be protected. Hence his championship of the Kansas-Nebraska Bill, designed to open a central route. To gain this end he favored the creation of two Territories instead of one, as the original bill had contemplated; and he even accepted Senator Archibald Dixon's startling amendment specifically repealing the Missouri Compromise.

THE STRUGGLE FOR KANSAS

Whether Douglas was actuated mainly by one of these motives or whether they all contributed to his action, he was destined to experience dismay and disappointment. The passage of the bill virtually destroyed any possibility that he might attain the presidency. Far from removing the question of slavery from the national arena the application of the doctrine of squatters' sovereignty gave rise to sectional conflict so violent that civil war was the result. Because of this conflict no railroad to the Pacific was even chartered until after Stephen A. Douglas was in his grave.

It is possible for us now to view the situation dispassionately and to realize the tragedy of two sections building up hate against each other over a question that was determined by an "ordinance of nature," to use the phrase of Webster's famous Seventh of March Speech. It is now conceded, as Professor C. H. Ramsdell has pointed out, that the natural limits of slavery extension had already been reached. The economic system with which negro slavery was inseparably linked could not possibly have prospered in the region of the new Territories. But in neither section was there recognition of this simple fact. Instead, politicians and agitators in North and South played upon the passions of their followers in the struggle for sectional advantage. It is not too much to say that a calm and enlightened disposition throughout the nation to allow the physical environment to determine the status of slavery in the Territories would have averted the Civil War.

Calmness and sanity were sadly lacking, however. The passage of the Kansas-Nebraska Bill was followed by the struggle for Kansas which was only the prelude to conflict on a larger stage. That the creation of the new Territories was not necessitated by the normal progress of the westward movement is evidenced by the fact that the earliest movement of settlers to Kansas from North and South was stimulated by sectional enthusiasts, bent on winning the Territory for freedom or slavery. Americans are familiar with the events of the turbulent years that followed: the rival legislatures, the free-state and pro-slavery constitutions, the raids of border ruffians, the murders and savage reprisals, the angry debates in Congress over the Lecompton constitution, Charles Sumner's stinging philippic on "the Crime Against Kansas," the brutal assault upon Sumner by Preston Brooks, and all the other far-reaching effects of the attempt to solve the problems of slavery extension on the basis of squatters' sovereignty in a region in which practically all of the settlers arrived after the establishment of territorial government. Not until January, 1861, when the new Republican party was in control in Congress, was Kansas admitted into the Union as a free State, as it would have been ultimately if neither section had made any effort to determine the result. Meanwhile, six southern States had adopted ordinances of secession partly at least because of the hatreds engendered in the struggle for Kansas.

Kansas received the present boundaries when statehood

was achieved.   The area of the Territory was larger, extending from the western boundary of Missouri to the eastern boundaries of New Mexico and Utah and thus including the central part of what is now Colorado.   The Territory of Nebraska embraced a huge area, stretching from the northern border of Kansas to the Canadian line, and from the Missouri River to the summit of the Rocky Mountains.   It was reduced in area in 1861 when the Territories of Colorado and Dakota were established.   In 1867 Nebraska was admitted into the Union over President Johnson's veto, after the people once voted against statehood and then adopted by a narrow margin a constitution framed by some Omaha lawyers and submitted to a referendum by the territorial legislature.

CHAPTER XXXII

THE STAGE-COACH ERA

"It is doubtful if there was another section of country on the face of the globe over which, in the sixties, passed so much traffic by ox, horse, and mule team." Thus did a veteran of the stage-coach era summarize and characterize the immense service of overland transportation and communication which developed, before the coming of the railroads, to meet the needs of the growing populations of the new States and Territories, whose beginnings have been described in the preceding chapters. One of the most fascinating portions of the history of the Far West is that which deals with the stage lines, the pony express, the slow-moving wagon freighters, and the steamboats on the upper Missouri.

Within the compass of a single chapter it is possible to give attention only to some of the outstanding features of the story covering the two decades between the beginning of the California gold rush and the completion of the Union Pacific Railroad in 1869. It must be remembered that after the latter event Concord stage-coaches and lumbering freight wagons long continued to be the only means of transporting mail, passengers, and merchandise to extensive sections of the Far West.

Ocean Mail Service to California

Twice a month, for several years after 1849, the residents of San Francisco eagerly watched for the signal on Telegraph Hill which announced the approach of the mail steamship. Long before the ship had docked a long line of people formed at the postoffice, waiting with such patience as they possessed for letters from far-distant loved ones, friends, or business associates. Passengers poured down the gang-plank of the mail steamer, as they did from every other vessel of any kind that entered the Golden Gate in 1849 and the years immediately following. In the first year of the gold excitement he was a lucky captain who could find even a crew to take his vessel out of port. For two or three years the outgoing ships were almost entirely without passengers. Thereafter the number of passengers booking passage on vessels leaving San Francisco was not greatly lower than that of those arriving. For many years the ocean route offered the easiest and quickest journey to the Pacific coast.

The regular ocean mail service to California was launched in 1848, and the first vessel, the steamship *California*, operated by the Pacific Mail Steamship Company, reached San Francisco on February 28, 1849. The mail was carried by steamship from Atlantic ports to Chagres, overland across the Isthmus of Panama, to the city of Panama, and thence by steamship to California and Oregon. At first the service was monthly, but it was soon made semi-monthly. After a time a route across Nicaragua was tried with only temporary success, and still later a shorter route by way of the Isthmus of Tehuantepec was employed. The journey from New York to San Francisco occupied from twenty-six to thirty days, although in 1858 it was made in slightly more than twenty-one days. Letter postage to California was forty cents at first, but after 1855 a rate of ten cents was in force for several years. The volume of mail carried by steamship increased year by year until in 1859 it was reported that more than two million letters and nearly four million newspapers reached California by the ocean route. Even after overland stage lines were established much mail continued to go by steamship and in times of severe storms or Indian disturbance the ocean highway was the main reliance.

EARLY STAGE LINES TO CALIFORNIA

Government authorities were satisfied with the steamship service and were slow in yielding to a growing demand for an overland mail, because of the difficulties and hazards of the route. Neither Californians nor residents of the border, however, were dismayed by the prospect, especially after the Oregon and Mormon migrations and the rush to California. As early as 1848 a letter express to Independence, Missouri, was advertised in California and one trip was apparently made. The gold excitement of the following year tempted some residents of St. Louis to undertake a mail and passenger stage line to California. One trip was made and one hundred twenty passengers were taken, after which the enterprise fell through.

On July 1, 1850, two stage lines began operation. One of these was the result of a four-year contract awarded to Samuel H. Woodson to carry the mail once a month from Independence to Salt Lake City. Service on this line for several years was quite irregular, due to insufficient capital and equipment, to difficulties of winter travel in the mountains, and to attacks by Indians. The other line also began at Independence and followed the well-traveled trail to Santa Fé. Wagons drawn by four or six mules carried mail and passengers once a month. There were no stations along the way during the early years. Passengers slept at night in the wagons or on the ground, and the animals were tethered and allowed to graze. The fare was $150, including meals and the transportation of forty pounds of baggage.

Official overland mail service to California was inaugurated in 1851, when George Chorpenning set out from Sacramento on May 1st under a contract which had been awarded to him and Absalom Woodward to carry the mail once a month to and from Salt Lake City, at the compensation of $14,000 a year. The route was extremely difficult and in winter wellnigh impassable, even to men on horseback or on foot. Later the attempt to operate on a direct route was abandoned and for several years the mail was carried between Salt Lake City and Los Angeles, from which point it was taken to San Francisco by boat. Nevertheless, despite all its uncertainties and vicissitudes, the Chorpenning service, taken in conjunction with the Independence-Salt Lake City line, made it possible to send letters overland from the Missouri River to California.

These pioneer ventures were soon followed by more adequate service by stage line to the Pacific coast. To be sure, the route of the line next established seems to have had no discoverable justification, since it ran, to use the words of one writer, "from no place through nothing to nowhere," or from San Antonio to San Diego. Apparently it was a part of the plan of a pro-southern postal administration that the mail to California should be carried by a far southern route, in anticipation of the time when a railroad would connect the South with the west coast. Be that as it may, in June, 1857, a contract to carry the mail twice a month each way in thirty days between San Antonio and San Diego was awarded to James E. Birch, who had already had extensive experience in the stage-coach business in the mining regions in California. On July 1st the first mail left San Antonio on what came to be called the "Jackass Mail," because the coaches were drawn by mules. Birch died soon after the stage service began, and his successors lacked his wide experience. As a consequence, travel over the southern plains, deserts, and mountains was beset by many uncertainties and hardships. Nevertheless, during 1857 and 1858 the mail was carried with a fair degree of regularity, and often in as short a time as twenty-two to twenty-six days.

"Passengers and Express Matter forwarded in new coaches, drawn by six mules over the entire length of our Line, excepting from San Diego to Fort Yuma, a distance of 180 miles, which we cross on mule back," announced an advertisement in a San Francisco newspaper in 1858. The coaches left each end of the line on the ninth and twentieth day of each month at six o'clock in the morning. An armed escort accompanied each string of coaches through the Indian country. The fare for the through trip was $200, including meals, except at public houses, and thirty pounds of baggage, exclusive of arms and blankets.

BUTTERFIELD'S OVERLAND MAIL

Within two years the "Jackass Mail" was superseded over the stretch between El Paso and Fort Yuma by the more famous Overland Mail of which the directing genius was John Butterfield, one of the notable figures in the annals of overland transportation to the Far West. The route followed a gigantic semi-circle nearly 2800 miles in length. The eastern termini were at St. Louis and Memphis. From St. Louis the mail was carried 160 miles by railroad to Tipton. From Tipton the stages traveled southward to Fort Smith on the western border of Arkansas, where connection was made with the line from Memphis. Thence the road led southwestward to El Paso, westward over plains and desert by way of Tucson and Fort Yuma to Los Angeles, and northward by a devious, mountainous course to San Francisco. It is obvious that southern dominance in the federal government determined the selection of this circuitous route, so far south of the more direct and well-worn central track traveled by a vast majority of the emigrants to the Pacific coast. In its support it was argued that $200,-000 had been already appropriated by Congress for a road from the Rio Grande to Fort Yuma, and that it was open to travel even in the winter. The Postmaster General declared it to be "the pioneer route for the first great railroad that may be constructed to the Pacific," a statement which contained the real reason for the choice.

It must be said, however, that Butterfield's Overland Mail furnished the first dependable, well-organized service to the Pacific. The six-year contract, which was let in September, 1857, provided for semi-weekly service in each direction on a twenty-five-day schedule, and at an annual compensation of $600,000. Service was to begin on September 15, 1858. In the interval preparations went forward with energy and on a large scale. Work was begun on more than 160 stations and corrals, constructed of logs, stone, or adobe, depending on available material. Wells and cisterns were dug, bridges built, some road grading done, and repair shops set up. From both ends of the route Concord coaches and stage wagons began to move to designated points, together with large numbers of horses and mules. A personnel of 750 experienced men was recruited to serve as superintendents, agents of divisions, drivers, station-keepers, hostlers, and mechanics.

On the appointed day, September 15, 1858, stages left both ends of the line carrying the mail from San Francisco, St. Louis and Memphis. In both cases the mail reached its destination in less than the twenty-five days demanded by the contract, with more than a day to spare. In San Francisco there was a noisy celebration when the first mail stage, with horn blowing and the driver's whip cracking, dashed along Montgomery

Street. Equal jubilation was shown in St. Louis, where the "Silver Band" met the train that brought the mail from Tipton. The skeptics who had predicted failure were confounded. The achievement was hailed as another triumph of American enterprise.

Those who may have thought that special effort was made to get the first mails through on time were destined to further surprises, for throughout its existence the Butterfield line continued to give regular and dependable service. Almost always the mail in each direction was carried through in less than scheduled time—frequently in as short a time as twenty-one days. The volume of mail increased from month to month. Through passengers were never numerous, although there were often many way passengers. A through trip, bowling ahead day and night in the cramped quarters of a stage-coach for nearly twenty-five days, was an experience to test the endurance of the strongest. Many passengers chose to break the journey by stop-overs at stations along the way. The fare from St. Louis or Memphis to San Francisco was $200, and for the eastward journey it was at first $100, then increased to $200 and afterward reduced again to $150. The fare included forty pounds of baggage, but did not include meals, which cost the passengers from seventy-five cents to one dollar at the stations.

THE PONY EXPRESS

Meanwhile the advocates of a central route were active in their contentions that the Butterfield line, while efficient in its service, was unnecessarily circuitous, and that the familiar California Trail could be used to greater advantage. Some concessions were made in 1858. The service from St. Joseph to Salt Lake City and from Salt Lake City to Placerville, California, was placed upon a weekly basis and more adequate remuneration was given to the contractors. Although without apparent justification, a new line was opened between Kansas City and Stockton, with service monthly on a sixty-day schedule. Then in 1858 gold was discovered in the Pike's Peak region and in 1859 a stage line between Leavenworth, Kansas, and Denver was inaugurated. After several changes the company operating this line also acquired the contract for the Salt Lake mail, and still later secured the contract formerly enjoyed by George Chorpenning for the service between Salt Lake City and California. By this time all these lines had been absorbed by the Central Overland California and Pike's Peak Express Company, operated by the great freighting firm of Russell, Majors and Waddell.

In 1860 this firm determined upon a daring plan to dramatize the feasibility of a central route for a through overland mail service that would be more expeditious than that of the Butterfield line. The hope of securing a lucrative contract was, of course, their motive. This project was nothing less than the establishment of a pony express which would, said the promoters, provide communication each way once a week between San Francisco and New York in nine days. They offered to carry despatches between the termini of the telegraph lines pushing out from San Francisco and Missouri in that time, and letters between the coast and St. Joseph in thirteen days. In general the route was the same as that by which the same firm was operating stage lines to Salt Lake City and California, following the Mormon Trail and the road around the southern end of the Great Salt Lake and across central Nevada to Sacramento, although some short cuts were taken.

The promoters were possessed of ample resources and experience and they set about the enterprise with vigor. Where stage stations did not already exist they built new stations at intervals of about fifteen miles. Fleet, wiry, mustang ponies were secured; and a group of young, courageous, light-weight riders was recruited. When all was in readiness a service was inaugurated on April 3, 1860, that was to continue for more than eighteen months. It was like a giant relay. At the stations riders were given only two minutes in which to transfer the saddle-bags to a fresh mount and be off on the road again. After riding the designated distance, one rider would arrive at a station where another was waiting to receive the mail and carry it on with equal speed to his successor. If, for some reason, the new rider was not on hand, the one who had already performed his part must ride on until he found someone to take the mail, and then with little or no rest hasten back to his regular post to receive the next mail. It is said that "Buffalo Bill" Cody once rode 320 miles continuously in a little less than twenty-two hours. Day and night, in storm and in sunshine ponies and riders galloped on over dusty plains, through mountain snows, down precipitous trails, and sometimes amid the arrows of hostile Indians. It is small wonder that the story of the pony express still fires the imagination and furnishes the theme for spectacular episodes in frontier celebrations.

There is no more vivid description of the pony express rider and his mount than that written by Mark Twain in *Roughing It*. Many had passed him in the night as he traveled by stage-coach to Carson City, but once he had a daylight glimpse. "Here he comes!" exclaimed the driver. "Every neck is stretched further, and every eye strained wider. Away across the endless dead level of the prairie a black speck appears against the sky, and it is plain that it moves. Well, I should think so! In a second or two it becomes a horse and rider, rising and falling,—rising and falling—sweeping toward us nearer and nearer, more and more sharply defined—nearer and still nearer, and the flutter of the hoofs comes faintly to the ear—another instant a whoop and a hurrah from our upper deck, a wave of the rider's hand, but no reply, and a man and horse burst past our excited faces, and go winging away like a belated fragment of a storm!"

The pony express seldom quite lived up to the promises of its promoters in the matter of schedule, but it greatly expedited communication with California. The best time made was in November, 1860, when news of Lincoln's election was carried from Fort Kearney, Nebraska, the end of the eastern telegraph line, to Fort Churchill in Nevada, the end of the western line, in six days. The real test of service came during the winter, when the schedule between telegraph termini was extended to eleven days, and actual performance averaged a little less than thirteen days. This, however, was regarded as a great achievement. Only one trip was missed, even in the midst of winter. Letter rates, at first five dollars, were later reduced to one dollar, and the service became semi-weekly. All this time the telegraph lines were being pushed forward fro mboth ends, and when they were joined in October, 1861, the days of the pony express were over.

Without this heroic exploit the history of the Far West would have been deprived of one of its most entertaining chapters. But as a matter of fact, the pony express not only proved financially ruinous to its operators, but as events transpired, it was unnecessary as a demonstration of the practicability and advantages of a central mail route. After the election of 1860 and the secession of the southern States northern leaders and northern interests were in control at Washington. It was no longer thinkable or feasible that a far southern route should be retained for the principal mail line to the Pacific. In March, 1861, Congress authorized the establishment of a daily mail stage service by a central route and the continuance of a semi-weekly pony express until the completion of the telegraph line, at a combined compensation of $1,000,000 a year. To their grievous disappointment the contract was not awarded to Russell, Majors and Waddell, the operators of the pony express. Instead, the Butterfield Overland Mail Line, whose contract was still in force, was moved to the central route. Russell, Majors and Waddell made an arrangement with this company to operate the pony express and the stage line from the Missouri River to Salt Lake City, while the Overland Mail Company conducted the business west of that place.

BEN HOLLADAY AND THE OVERLAND STAGE LINES

It would be impossible here even to outline the main features of Congressional legislation concerning overland mail service, the exploration of new routes, the establishment and success or failure of stage lines, the rivalries and consolidations that occurred during the Civil War and the years that followed before the completion of the Union Pacific Railroad. In 1862 there appeared upon the scene a man whose name became more widely known than that of any other person ever connected with the overland stage business in the Far West—Ben Holladay. In that year he gained possession of the Central Overland California and Pike's Peak Express Company, of which he was the largest creditor when the operating company failed.

Before he sold out to Wells, Fargo and Company late in 1866, he had for the first time consolidated under one management the central stage lines to California, and operated numerous lines in the intermountain region from Colorado north to Montana, Idaho, and Oregon—a total, it has been said, of nearly five thousand miles of stage lines, for most of which he held mail contracts.

Ben Holladay was a man about whose character and abilities we know very little, except as they are reflected in his extensive enterprises, which included not only stage and wagon freight lines, but railroads and steamship lines as well. That he built up a comfortable fortune is evidenced by his palatial residence in New York City and his mansion in Washington, D. C. The judgment of his contemporaries depends upon whether it was pronounced by one of his many admirers or by one of his equally numerous critics. He was an efficient organizer, but it is doubtful if the standard of service on his lines was as high as that maintained by John Butterfield or James E. Birch or George Chorpenning. It is true, however, that he had great handicaps to contend with—some unusually cold winters with heavier than normal snows in the mountains, floods, and above all, repeated and disastrous attacks by hostile Indians that at times disrupted his service.

Sufficient has now been related to indicate the high points in the development of mail and stage lines to the Pacific coast. If space permitted it would be interesting to trace the history of stage-coaching in California, between California and Oregon, between Fort Bridger and Walla Walla and the Montana mines, between the Minnesota frontier and Helena, and in other regions of the Far West. As late as the beginning of the present century Concord coaches, drawn by dashing six-horse teams were to be met on roads in sections not served by the railroads.

STAGE-COACH TRAVEL IN THE FAR WEST

A mere recital of the establishment and routes, the fortunes and failures of stage lines carries with it little of the life and color of stage-coach days, unless it be in the magnitude and audacity of the enterprises. To gain a conception of what it meant to travel across the plains and deserts and mountains by stage-coach one must go to accounts written by those who actually made the trip. A few quotations will serve to illustrate the vivid, first-hand descriptions to be found in these sources.

General James F. Rusling traveled to California by the Ben Holladay stage line in 1866. "We found his stages to be our well-known Concord coaches," he wrote, "and they quite surpassed our expectations, both as to comfort and to speed. They were intended for nine inside—three seats full—and as many more outside, as could be induced to get on. . . . The animals themselves were our standing wonder; no broken-down nags, or half-starved Rosinantes, like our typical stage-horse east. . . . Wiry, gamey, as if feeling their oats thoroughly, they often went off from the stations at a full gallop; at the end of a mile or two would settle down to a square steady trot; and this they would usually keep up right along until they reached the next station. These 'stations' varied from ten to twelve miles apart, depending on water and grass, and consisted of the rudest kind of shanty or sod-house ordinarily. Here we would find another team, ready harnessed, prancing to be gone, and in fifteen minutes or so would be off on the road again. Halts were made twice a day for meals, forty minutes each, and with this exception we kept bowling ahead night and day." The average distance made per day was from 100 to 125 miles.

Rusling tried to talk to the drivers, but as a rule he found them a "taciturn species" while on duty, although when off the box they were loquacious enough. Many of them had been driving for years. "As bearers of the U. S. Mail, they felt themselves kings of the road, and were seldom loth to show it." While most of the passengers preferred the inside of the coach, Rusling and a companion chose the outside. In daytime it gave them a wider view of the country. At night, with their blankets and a little hay borrowed from a station and with a strap or rope from railing to railing to keep them from rolling off, they "managed to secure not a little of 'tired nature's sweet restorer, balmy sleep,'" while their fellow-passengers "down below (nine inside), packed like sardines in a box, got seldom a wink." On the whole, Rusling seems to have enjoyed the experience.

The same could scarcely be said of the more critical and crotchety Demas Barnes. "It is not a *pleasant*, but it is an *interesting* trip," he wrote shortly after reaching Denver in June, 1865. "The conditions of one man's running stages to make money, while another seeks to ride in them for pleasure, are not in harmony to produce comfort. Coaches will be overloaded, it will rain, the dust will drive, baggage will be left to the storm, passengers will get sick, a gentleman of gallantry will hold the baby, children will cry, nature demands sleep, passengers will get angry, the drivers will swear, the sensitive will shrink, rations will give out, potatoes become worth a gold dollar each, and not to be had at that, the water brackish, the whiskey abominable, and the dirt almost unendurable. I have just finished six days and nights of this thing; and I am free to say, until I forget a great many things now very visible to me, I shall not undertake it again. Stop over nights? No, you wouldn't. To sleep on the sand floor of a one-story sod or adobe hut, without a chance to wash, with miserable food, uncongenial companionship, loss of seat in a coach until one comes empty, etc., won't work. A through-ticket and fifteen inches of seat, with a fat man on one side, a poor widow on the other, a baby in your lap, a bandbox over your head, and three or four persons immediately in front, leaning against your knees, makes the picture, as well as your sleeping place for the trip."

When Horace Greeley crossed the Sierras on his trip to California in 1856 he traveled along a road "eaten into the side of a steep mountain, with a precipice of from five to fifteen hundred feet on one side and as steep an eminence on the other. Yet along this mere shelf, with hardly a place to each mile where two meeting wagons can pass, the mail-stage was driven at the rate of ten miles an hour (in one instance eleven) or just as fast as four wild California horses, whom two men could scarcely harness, could draw it." If the horses had seen fit to run away, Greeley was sure the driver could not have held them, and, he said, "we might have been pitched headlong down a precipice of a thousand feet, where all of the concern that could have been picked up afterward would not have been worth two bits per bushel."

Many of the accounts of trips made during the middle sixties agree that, although mail contracts offered handsome remuneration to the operators, too often the mail was given scant consideration. "The mail is piled up at different places, and I think the bottom of it here will hardly move for a month," wrote Demas Barnes from Denver in 1865. "It is outrageous the way the public are swindled by the proprietors of this stage-route. I speak only what I know, and repeat a remark made by the agents: 'Too much trouble to tear the pile out from the bottom.' . . . I have seen the stages pass through here loaded with passengers, and not carry a pound of mail, while perhaps two weeks' mail, or more, lay heaped up in the office!" Other writers were no less emphatic in their complaints. They even told of mail sacks deliberately thrown off to lighten the load and abandoned or used to fill up bogs in the road. Before the stage-coach era came to an end the mail service in the Far West became involved in the national scandal of the "star-route" frauds during the early eighties.

Wagon Freighting Across the Plains

Important and spectacular as was the service of the stage-coach lines and the pony express in carrying the mails, a service more vital to the existence of the Indian agencies, the military posts, and the settlements in the plains and mountain regions was that rendered by the prosaic, slow-moving freight wagons. There was, of course, comparatively little overland freighting to the Pacific coast before the coming of the railroad. The ocean was a more economic and expeditious highway. But the people of the interior were entirely dependent on the wagon freighters for their groceries, merchandise, and manufactured supplies of all kinds. As a consequence, the freighting business grew to huge proportions as the population of the Rocky Mountain area increased by leaps and bounds.

At Leavenworth, Kansas, in 1859 Horace Greeley had opportunity to observe the headquarters of Russell, Majors and Waddell, the firm that was soon to launch the pony express.

"Such acres of wagons!," he exclaimed, "such pyramids of extra axletrees! such herds of oxen! such regiments of drivers and other employees! No one who does not see can realize how vast a business this is, nor how immense are its outlays as well as its income. I presume this great firm has at this hour two millions of dollars invested in stock, mainly oxen, mules and wagons. (They last year employed six thousand teamsters, and worked forty-five thousand oxen.)" Greeley saw many of these wagon trains as he traveled westward. The heavy, canvass-covered wagons with loads averaging five thousand pounds, were drawn by six teams of mules or six yoke of wild looking oxen, whose drivers were as wild and rough in appearance. Progress, under the best of conditions, was at a snail's pace, and when roads were miry a train might do well to "corral" at night two miles from the place it had left in the morning.

Although volubly impatient with the inconveniences and discomforts of stage-coach travel, Demas Barnes was not immune to the romantic aspects of the scenes he witnessed on his trip in 1865. "The great feature of the Plains," he wrote, "is the transportation trains, usually consisting of thirty to fifty wagons, five yoke each. . . . As they wind their slow course over the serpentine roads and undulating surface in the distance, a mile in extent (I saw one train five miles long), the effect is poetic, grand, beautiful. They select a high position for camping, draw the wagons in a circle, enclosing say a quarter, half, or full acre, the exterior serving as a fort, the inside as a camp, and a place wherein to drive the animals in case of danger, and to yoke or harness them for the next trip. One of these camps, seen at sundown, with night fires kindled, and from five hundred to a thousand head of animals feeding near by, is well worth a long visit to behold."

General Rusling was interested in the teamsters and the lives they led. "Even here on the Plains, about the last place we would suppose," he wrote, "the inherent aristocracy of human nature cropped out distinctly. The lords of the lash *par excellence* were the stage-drivers. The next most important, the horse or mule teamsters; and the lowest, the 'bull-drivers.' The horse or mule teams made from twelve to fifteen miles per day; the ox-trains eight to ten. For real vagabondage, pure and simple, life with one of these trains seemed hard to beat. An Arab of the desert, or a Gaucho of the pampas, could ask for nothing more nomadic."

At Leavenworth, Atchison, St. Joseph, Omaha, and other points along the Missouri a large number of firms and individuals were engaged in the business of overland transportation, until the Union Pacific Railroad began to push its way westward. Out of the maze of figures and statistics which may be collected from public documents, newspapers, and journals of travels a few may be selected to give some impression of the volume of the traffic. At Atchison alone in 1865 it was estimated that six million dollars were invested in the business operated by twenty-seven individuals and firms. That same year the shipments to Colorado were computed at 104,000,000 pounds. It was estimated that in 1866 the sum of $31,000,000 was paid for freight hauled from Missouri River points to the mountain region; and $13,000,000 for freight from California to Nevada and Utah. Merchandising firms in Virginia City, Montana, Salt Lake City, and Denver paid as much as $100,000 a year for freight. It is no wonder that prices for merchandise in Montana and Colorado reached levels commensurate with twenty to thirty dollars for a sack of flour, eighteen to thirty cents a pound for potatoes, thirty-five to fifty cents a pound for onions, and fifty to seventy-five cents for a box of matches. The cost of living was necessarily high when prices had to include the expense of transportation that occupied fully five weeks from the Missouri River to Denver and twice that length of time to Salt Lake City.

THE CAMEL EXPERIMENT

Before leaving the subject of overland transportation, mention should be made of an episode which adds an exotic touch to the story. Prospectors and other wanderers during the Civil War and the following years frequently told camp-fire companions of having seen camels in the southwest. Often these tales were accepted as the products of brains befuddled by liquor or hallucinations. As a matter of fact the stories were doubtless true.

In the spring of 1856 a herd of camels was brought to Texas, as the result of encouragement by Jefferson Davis, Secretary of War, and a Congressional appropriation. Another herd was added a little later. It was hoped that camels might solve some of the problems of transportation, especially across the desert areas, where water was scarce or absent, and where horses and mules suffered severely. Experimentation under the command of Lieutenant Edward F. Beale showed that the camels would carry heavy loads long distances without water and reach their destination in good condition. Beale took a camel brigade across the southern trails to California and paraded his animals in Los Angeles in January, 1858. The promoters were enthusiastic. Various factors, however, prevented the experiment from being carried further. Horse and mule teams along the trails were badly frightened by the camels and became unmanageable, and the opposition of the teamsters was aroused. The outbreak of the Civil War caused a suspension of interest; and the improvement of stage-coach and wagon freight service made a revival of experimentation with camels improbable, even before the coming of the railroads.

Year by year the number of camels in the Texas herd, as well as at Beale's ranch in California, increased; many of the animals wandered away; and later in one manner and another the herds were dispersed. For years they or their descendants were seen and sometimes used in isolated sections of California, Nevada, and Arizona. Camels were at one time introduced in British Columbia and were seen in the Cariboo region and in northern Idaho during the mining period. As late as 1907 a prospector reported that he had seen two camels in Nevada.

Steamboating on the Upper Missouri

A previous chapter was devoted largely to the role of rivers as highways of transportation and communication to the middle western frontier. Relatively little space need be given to river transportation in the story of the development of the Far

West, for the reason that most of the region is inaccessible to navigable rivers. Local and regional histories of the Pacific coast properly give considerable attention to traffic on the Sacramento and the Columbia in the early years, and even to-day the latter stream is a great avenue of commerce which gives the city of Portland the status of a world port. Steam-boat transportation on the Red and Arkansas rivers played an important part in serving the needs of the military posts, In-dian agencies, and early settlements along their lower courses.

The Missouri was the only river navigable for a sufficient distance to make it usable for continuous water transportation from the Mississippi to the Rocky Mountain area. On that stream steamboating had a notable history—one worthy of a record as imperishable as that given by Mark Twain to his early days on the Mississippi. Fortunately Hiram M. Chit-tendon has furnished us an account of steamboat navigation on the Missouri River, centered about the career of Joseph La Barge, whose services as steamboat pilot and captain spanned almost the entire period of steamboat traffic on the upper river.

As has already been related, in 1830 the American Fur Company decided to renew the experiment of steamboating on the upper Missouri which had been abandoned after the fail-ure of Stephen H. Long's attempt with the *Western Engineer* in 1819-20. The *Yellowstone* reached Fort Tecumseh (later called Fort Pierre) in the present South Dakota in 1831, and in the following year pushed on as far as Fort Union at the mouth of the Yellowstone River. In 1834 the *Assiniboine* went one hundred miles further, to a point near the mouth of the Poplar River, which for nearly two decades remained the most distant point reached by steamboats. In the meantime steam-boating on the lower river developed steadily and performed valuable services in supplying the needs of such frontier out-posts and "jumping-off places" as Independence, Leavenworth, and Council Bluffs, as well as those of Indian agencies and mili-tary posts. By 1857 a considerable number of boats were making regular trips as far north as the newly established vil-lage of Sioux City in northwestern Iowa, with a tonnage valued as a million and a quarter dollars. Many of these were fast, side-wheel boats with handsome accommodations for travelers;

and the thrilling though dangerous sport of racing was not un-known.

The navigation of the upper Missouri was extended some distance further in 1853, and in 1859 the *Chippewa* reached a point fifteen miles from Fort Benton in western Montana. The next year the same boat and the *Key West* reached the fort. This achievement has rightly been called "one of the celebrated feats of steamboat navigation," for as Chittenden points out, Fort Benton was "a point further from the sea by a continuous water route than any boat had ever been." According to his figures it was 3,575 miles from the Gulf of Mexico to Fort Benton. This place was thereafter known as the head of navigation of the Missouri River, although in favorable seasons it was possible for steamboats to reach the Great Falls, thirty miles further, as was proven in at least one instance.

As chance would have it, the arrival of the first steamboats at Fort Benton was almost coincidental with the discovery of gold in Montana and the precipitation of a mining rush to that region. "Stores and other buildings began to appear," says Chittenden, "and in 1865 a town site was laid off. The young city grew with astonishing rapidity and became a place of very great importance. Strange indeed must it have seemed to the Indians and to the old trappers to behold upon this spot, where for so many years there had been only a single palisade—sole habitation of white men within five hundred miles—buildings of metropolitan style and quality, trains of wagons coming and going, and lines of noble steamboats lying at the bank along the entire front of the town."

The number of steamboat arrivals at Fort Benton increased rapidly until the peak was reached in 1867 when the number was thirty-nine. It is said in that year these boats brought more than eight thousand tons of merchandise and about ten thousand passengers. On the return journeys the steamboats often carried rich treasures of gold. This was the golden age for the owners of the steamboats. Profits were reported as high as $40,000 for a single trip. For a few years the traffic remained large, but it declined rapidly after the Union Pacific brought rail transportation within competing distance. Later in the seventies, the coming of the Northern Pacific spelled approaching doom to steamboat transportation on the upper Missouri. The year 1878 is said to have marked the close of commercial steamboating between St. Louis and Fort Benton.

CHAPTER XXXIII

THE MINERAL EMPIRE

THE transportation and communication service by stage-coach, pony express, wagon train and Missouri River steamboat, described in the preceding chapter would never have attained its great proportions if the vast region between the border settlements and California and Oregon had remained unpopulated. Between the eastern foothills of the Rocky Mountains and the Sierra and Cascade ranges stretched a region nearly one thousand miles in width that appeared forbidding—a land that God had forgotten—to typical American pioneers seeking new land for farms. For the trappers and fur traders, however, as has been seen, this region was a paradise. In the exploitation of the rich resources of pelts they ranged far and wide over the entire region, interested in little else but furs and the high adventure of their occupation, and changing the aspect of the country scarcely at all.

Then, at a time when the best days of the fur trade had passed, hidden treasures of gold and silver were discovered. Within a decade no section where the precious minerals might possibly be found was left unvisited by the hordes of eager prospectors. When the feverish excitement of the gold rushes subsided the region was no longer a wilderness. Extensive grazing and farming areas were discovered and occupied. Towns had sprung up as if by magic. Some of them dwindled and disappeared when the lodes and placers were exhausted; while others remained as trading centers or grew to be thriving cities. A network of roads and transportation facilities remained as permanent assets. By 1870 not a foot of soil in the United States lay outside the bounds of some State or organized Territory. Thus mining was the basis of settled life in a region that, except for the Mormon settlements, had hitherto been only the haunt of wild animals, warlike Indian tribes, and roving fur traders, with here and there an isolated military post.

THE STAMPEDES TO PIKE'S PEAK

Ten years after the memorable rush of the forty-niners to the gold fields of California the plains were again thronged by thousands of searches for the glittering metal in a new mining region in which Pike's Peak was the dominating landmark. It was a gold rush in which, according to some estimates, 100,000 persons participated. The time was propitious, because throughout the country people were still suffering from the effects of the Panic of 1857 and ready to seize any opportunity to retrieve their losses. But there was lacking much of the glamor which is associated with the first mad rush to California. The distance from the Missouri River was scarcely more than one-third as great; and there were no lofty mountain ranges or thirsty deserts to cross.

Although pieces of quartz rock flecked with gold had frequently been found in the Rocky Mountains by Indians, trappers, and wandering prospectors, their discoveries created little interest in the possible wealth of the region until 1858. In the spring of that year a party of Georgians, Cherokee Indians, and men from the border towns, led by William Green Russell of Georgia, traveled into the Colorado mountains and began prospecting along Cherry Creek. About the same time another party from Lawrence, Kansas, arrived. Gold was found, but in such small quantities that many of the prospectors returned disheartened to their homes. Nevertheless, exaggerated reports of the gold finds reached the settlements along the Missouri and were relayed to the States further east. Before fall, therefore, a considerable number of gold-seekers rushed across the plains and a much larger number were busy with preparations to make the journey early in the spring. The towns of Denver and Auraria, later to be united under the name of the former, came into existence. Here those who had not yielded completely to disillusionment spent a dreary winter in the unfloored, leaky cabins which they had hastily erected.

Very early in the spring of 1859 a much larger number of excited gold-seekers set out across the plains, their imaginations stimulated by grossly exaggerated stories of the discoveries thus far made and by glowing publicity on the part

of the towns along the Missouri, which hoped to profit by outfitting the emigrants. "It is doubtful whether such scenes of
human misery, as were enacted on the Plains last spring, were
witnessed even at the height of the California excitement,"
wrote Henry Villard, who, as the representative of a Cincinnati newspaper, traveled to Denver on the second stage-coach
of the Leavenworth and Pike's Peak Express Company.
"None of those, that were about crossing the Plains the first
time, should have started previous to the first of May, and
even then not without being well provided with wagons,
draught animals, food and clothing. . . . Many set out as
early as the first of March, and were daily followed by others
that were equally impatient of delay and anxious to tread the
gold-bearing banks of Cherry Creek. Among these not a few
started out in a manner that could not fail to bring suffering
upon them. For, whoever is at all familiar with the peculiar-
ities of a trip over the Plains, knows that it is suicidal folly to
undertake it, as many did last spring, hitched to hand-carts
loaded with a scanty supply of provisions and clothing, or, a
still greater infatuation, worrying along afoot with their all on
their backs."[1] Others pushed their few belongings in wheel-
barrows. Needless to say, there were numerous instances of
extreme suffering, amounting in some cases to death by starvation.

Hardships would soon have been forgotten if hopes had
found fulfillment. But bitter disappointment was the only
reward of the vast majority of those who participated in this
early spring rush. In Denver, Auraria, and along Cherry
Creek they encountered gloom and stagnation. The stories of
abundant gold, which they had so willingly and uncritically
believed, proved to be without foundation. Within a few
weeks came a reaction, as unreasoning and unwarranted as the
impulse that had sent these thousands across the plains. Without attempting to investigate other regions, a few disillusioned
men set out for their homes, and soon the return movement
assumed the proportions of a mad stampede. Wagons that had

[1] Henry Villard, *The Past and Present of the Pike's Peak Gold Region*
(reprint, 1932, edited by LeRoy R. Hafen), pp. 22-23. By permission of the
Princeton University Press, publishers.

come west bearing gay banners reading "Pike's Peak or Bust" toiled over the back track with signs altered to read "Busted, by gosh!"

Then, before these resentful stampeders had reached the settlements with their reports that the Colorado gold mines were a great humbug, as though by a prank of fate there came a discovery that disproved their doleful stories. Early in May a miner entered the express office in Denver where Henry Villard and two companions were discussing the discouraging aspect of affairs. The stranger appeared confident of the mineral wealth of the region. When asked for his reason, he reported that he had been a member of a party headed by John H. Gregory, which within the last few days had discovered "pay dirt" on the North Fork of Clear Creek. He guaranteed that as many men as would follow him to the region in question could make a dollar to the pan of dirt. Two days later unimpeachable confirmation of this report was received, and the news spread like wildfire along Cherry Creek.

"On the following day an universal exodus took place in the direction of North Clear Creek," wrote Villard. "Whoever could raise enough provisions for a protracted stay in the mountains, sallied out without delay. Traders locked up their stores; bar-keepers disappeared with their bottles of whiskey, the few mechanics that were busy building houses, abandoned their work, the county judge and sheriff, lawyers and doctors, and even the editor of the *Rocky Mountain News,* joined in the general rush." [2]

The news sped back along the trails to the settlements, and there came another and greater rush of gold-seekers. By the middle of June observers estimated that as many as ten thousand men were delving into the quartz rock of the Gregory Diggings, seeking the crevices or "pockets" where "pay dirt" yielded such rich returns. Mountain City, later renamed Central City, came into existence almost over night—a city with hotels, stores, express offices, a newspaper, lawyers, doctors, saloons, and gambling houses. Newspaper men did not fail

[2] Henry Villard, *The Past and Present of the Pike's Peak Gold Region* (reprint, 1932, edited by LeRoy R. Hafen), p. 37. By permission of the Princeton University Press, publishers.

to warn their readers that only a small proportion of those who came to the region were lucky enough to make even the equivalent of poor wages. Those who struck it rich were few indeed. "One man may possibly acquire wealth faster in this gold-lottery than in New England or Kansas," wrote Horace Greeley, "but let one thousand poor men come hither to mine, while the same number resolve to win a competence by eminent industry and frugality in the east, and the latter will assuredly have more wealth at five years' end than the former—and will have acquired it with far less sacrifice of comfort, health and life."

Except for those fortunate individuals who discovered the rich "pockets" in the Gregory Diggings, the prospect soon proved discouraging. Most of the gold was imbedded in quartz rock and could be extracted only by the use of expensive machinery. By the mid-summer of 1859 there was a second homeward stampede of weary, disheartened men. Others left to join the throngs rushing to other sections of the Colorado region, where rich strikes were reported. The Jackson Diggings on South Clear Creek, where placer mining was remunerative, attracted a great number. Before the year was over prospectors crossed the continental divide to South Park and the Blue River Diggings. Every stream and ravine and gulch was examined and mining camps of varying size and duration appeared wherever traces of gold were found.

In general it may be said that the year 1859 marked the end of the Colorado gold rush. Although it had been established that the region held immense wealth in the precious metal, it was equally well demonstrated that it was no country for thousands of poor, independent miners. After 1859 mining companies and individuals with capital entered the field, brought in the necessary machinery, and developed gold-mining as an industry. This does not mean, of course, that there was no further excitement when new lodes or placer mines were discovered. "It is almost impossible not to partake of the general enthusiasm," wrote Demas Barnes, who visited Denver in 1865, "for you hear gold discussed morning, noon, all night, and far into the next day. It is no myth. You see it . . . you hear the turning of the water-wheels, the puffing of the engines, the pounding of the stamps, the clatter of the pans—you see the steam of the retort and assay—you hold the pure golden nuggets in your hands, your eyes dilate, your mouth waters."

Silver Mining in Nevada

When Horace Greeley was in Placerville, California, in the summer of 1859, he made a speech in the course of which he commented upon his trip across the Nevada desert, then included in the Territory of Utah. He called it "a desolate and terrible country, a land seemingly worthless forever." As he had crossed the "awful region" the thought had come to him that since it was apparently "useless for every other purpose, it may be a land of vast mineral wealth." Greeley could scarcely have guessed that within a few months his remarks would be remembered as prophetic. Late that same year there was discovered in the Washoe region, just east of the California border, the world-famous Comstock lode of rich, silver-laden ore, mixed with gold, which in little more than a decade was to yield returns of more than $145,000,000 to its exploiters.

There had been prospectors in the western Nevada country ever since the days of the California gold rush. A few of the forty-niners had stopped there and others had returned after unsuccessful operations in California. Gold was found in several of the ravines in the vicinity of Mount Davidson, but not in sufficient quantities to attract any considerable number of miners until the years 1858 and 1859. By that time there were several mining camps, such as Johntown and Gold Hill; and Carson City had been established. Thus far, with one exception, there seems to have been no suspicion of the region's hidden riches in silver. As early as 1856 two brothers, Ethan Allen and Hosea B. Grosh, and two companions, had become convinced that there was a rich vein of silver ore in Gold Canyon. This belief was confirmed the following year, and the associates laid plans to secure capital and organize a mining company. Before this could be accomplished, both Grosh brothers died, one from exposure in the high Sierras and the other from infection due to an accident; one of their companions was murdered by desperadoes, and the other abandoned the life of a miner on account of broken health. If the brothers had lived two years longer, their name would doubtless have been given to the great silver lode, which made Nevada famous.

The other miners were interested only in gold. In 1859 exceedingly profitable diggings were found at Gold Hill and in Six-Mile Canyon, yielding the most fortunate from five hundred to a thousand dollars a day. One and all, they were exasperated by the presence of "blue stuff" or "base metal" which made it difficult to extract the gold. They little suspected that they were casting aside ore worth far more than the portion which they gathered with such pains in their sluice boxes. On June 12, 1859, the Comstock Lode was discovered, and was named undeservedly for Henry T. P. Comstock because he claimed the land where the discovery was made. Even then, neither he nor his associates realized the true significance of the event, since what was found was only a huge ledge of the hated blueish ore. It remained for a plain farmer by the name of Harrison to carry a few lumps of this "blue stuff" to an assay office. Here it was learned that a ton of the supposedly useless ore was worth $1,595 in gold and $4,791 in silver!

The news spread rapidly. Two enterprising speculators from Nevada City saddled their horses and started immediately for the Washoe. "They could not have travelled faster," says one writer, "if a score of *vigilantes* had been on their track." Arriving at their destination, they bought out most of the best claims, Comstock's included, at ridiculously small figures from men who were still convinced that the region had seen its best days. From all directions came a crowd of miners and speculators. In California, especially, there was wild excitement. Even though the season was already late, hundreds of prospectors braved the high mountain passes and began staking out claims. By the close of the year 1859 it is estimated that the population of the Washoe mines had leaped to four thousand. The center of the region was the new town of Virginia City. Here, in tents, rude shanties, and dug-outs, the inhabitants shivered and nearly starved during the unusually severe winter of 1859-60, when five or six feet of snow fell and for weeks there was no communication with the outside world.

With the spring of 1860 the rush to the Washoe began in real earnest. From the Pike's Peak region and even from Nebraska, Kansas, and Missouri, came excited searchers for wealth. But it was California that furnished the great majority of the incoming prospectors. Steamers on the Sacramento were laden to capacity with freight and miners bound for the Washoe. Placerville became little more than a way-station on the trail. Stores were closed, offices abandoned, ships deserted and farms left untilled, as the mad rush of twenty thousand people got under way.

J. Ross Browne, who visited Virginia City, has left us a vivid picture of the upstart town as he saw it in the spring of 1860. "Frame shanties pitched together as if by accident; tents of canvas, of blankets, of brush, of potato-sacks, and old shirts, with empty whiskey barrels for chimneys; smoky hovels of mud and stone; coyote holes in the mountain-side forcibly seized and held by men; pits and shafts with smoke issuing from every crevice; piles of goods and rubbish on craggy points, in the hollows, on the rocks, in the mud, in the snow, everywhere, scattered broadcast in pell-mell confusion, as if the clouds had suddenly burst overhead and rained down the dregs of all the flimsy, rickety, filthy little hovels and rubbish of merchandise that had ever undergone the process of evaporation from the earth since the days of Noah." Before the year was over board cabins had replaced many of the huts, there were thirty-eight stores, twenty-five saloons, ten livery stables, eight hotels, nine restaurants, bakeries, lawyers' offices, and other establishments. When Samuel Bowles visited the town in 1865 he described it as "exceedingly well built, in large proportion with solid brick stores and warehouses; and though the fast and fascinating times of 1862-63 are over, when it held from fifteen thousand to twenty thousand people, and Broadway and Wall street were not more crowded than its streets, it . . . contains a population of ten thousand." Gambling was now put "behind an extra door," churches were numerous, and the Sabbath was recognized by the closing of many of the stores.

There is no need for an account of the exploitation of the
marvelously rich Comstock Lode, which sent the stock of the
principal mining companies up to fabulous figures. Silver mining, like gold mining in Colorado, was principally quartz mining and required expensive machinery. The Washoe diggings,
therefore, proved disappointing to a great majority of the
prospectors, except as they could discover and stake out claims
and sell them, at so much a foot, to the mining companies.
Nevertheless, mining fever continued to rage in Nevada for
many years. "Every few days news would come of the discovery of a bran-new mining region; immediately the papers
would teem with accounts of its richness, and away the surplus
population would scamper to take possession." Thus wrote
Mark Twain in *Roughing It*, the immortal story of his sojourn
in Nevada as private secretary to his brother, the Secretary of
the new Territory. "Cartloads of solid, silver bricks, as large
as pigs of lead, were arriving from the mills every day, and
such sights gave substance to the wild talk about me. I succumbed and grew as frenzied as the craziest."

The most important of the new discoveries during the sixties were on Breese River in central Nevada, where the town
of Austin became the principal center, with a population of six
or eight thousand by 1865. "All up the Austin hill-sides,
among the houses, and beyond them," wrote Samuel Bowles,
"are the big ant-hills which denote mines or the hopes of such.
Down in the valley are the mills for crushing and separating
the ore. Back and around the corners, and over the mountains
for many miles, are similar though less frequent signs. . . .
The veins of ore lie thick in the rotten granite of the hills, like
the spread fingers of some mineral giant." The town of Austin, said Bowles, "bears family likeness to Central City and
Black Hawk in Colorado; houses are built anywhere and
everywhere, and streets are then made to reach them, . . .
not a tree nor a flower, nor a grass plot does the whole town
boast,—not one; but it has the best French restaurant I have
met since New York, a daily newspaper, and the boot-blacks
and barbers and baths are luxurious and aristocratic to the
continental degree."

The Mining Advance into the Inland Empire

The years covered by the development of mining in Colorado and Nevada witnessed a similar movement to the northward in the area, sometimes called the Inland Empire, embracing British Columbia, eastern Washington and Oregon, Idaho, and western Montana. A stranger finding himself in the American portion of this region during the fateful years from 1860 to 1865 would have been astonished to learn that a great civil war was in progress to determine the perpetuity of the nation. Draft evaders from both North and South, deserters from both armies, people fleeing from war-devastated sections, along with thousands of other foot-loose and avid gold-seekers poured into the region by every possible road and by Missouri River steamboat. Added to these novices at the game were thousands of representatives of that cosmopolitan class of habitual or professional prospectors, recruited from all parts of the world, which had been so conspicuous in the early mining days in California. Permanently afflicted with mining fever, always hopeful though seldom successful, these men were to be found in every rush to each new section where gold was said to have been found.

As early as 1855 and 1856 a number of prospectors, mainly from the Willamette Valley and Puget Sound, ventured into the country east of the Columbia and between the Spokane and Pend o'Reille Rivers, generally designated as the Colville region. Their presence aroused the active hostility of the Indian tribes and caused grave concern to Governor Stevens and the military authorities. Mining operations, not very profitable at best, were brought to an end by an Indian uprising that developed into warfare over a large area in the Northwest.

Following the suggestions of Angus MacDonald, the Hudson's Bay Company's factor at Fort Colville, a considerable number of the Colville miners went northward into British Columbia. Here, along the upper Fraser River, in 1857 several rich gold-yielding bars were discovered, and with the approach of winter the miners went down to Victoria with the news. By spring there was excitement all up and down the coast. On Puget Sound at Steilacoom, Bellingham, and other places, mills and coal mines lost their laborers. Soldiers deserted their posts and sailors their ships. The floating population of Victoria disappeared. But it was in California that the news of the Fraser River finds had the most startling effect. Mining in the "Golden State" had entered the phase of capitalistic enterprise. The placer mines were practically exhausted. Good claims were hard to find. Thousands of miners were faced with the alternative of very meager returns or of the acceptance of employment at wages from the mining concerns. Hence the good news from the Fraser River seemed providential. It was estimated that twenty-three thousand Californians, including not only miners but merchants, laborers, artisans and gamblers, went by ship from San Francisco to Victoria; and that as many as eight thousand more started overland.

While there were many rich finds in the bars of the Fraser River, as was nearly always the case in such pell-mell rushes, the great majority were disappointed. Besides, as the river rose with the melting of the snow in the mountains, the bars were submerged and gold-digging almost stopped. Soon there was an exodus. Most of the Californians returned home, where they arrived in time to have their hopes raised once more by reports from Pike's Peak and the Washoe. One important effect of the Fraser River rush, however, was the creation of the colony of British Columbia to take over many of the functions hitherto exercised by the Hudson's Bay Company. Furthermore, it is significant that laws and regulations affecting mining and mining communities were adopted and enforced by governmental authorities from the beginning. Consequently, as mining developed on the Canadian side of the boundary in the succeeding years, in the Cariboo and Kootenai regions and along the upper Columbia, there were marked contrasts with the chaotic methods of regulation in vogue on the American side.

Several events and circumstances were now combining to prepare the way for a large movement into the mining sections of the American portion of the Inland Empire. In 1858 the Indians were pacified after a determined campaign under the leadership of Colonel George Wright. Between 1858 and 1862 there was laid out a military road, more than six hundred miles in length, connecting Fort Benton on the upper Missouri and the junction of the Snake and Columbia Rivers. It was known as the Mullan Road in honor of Lieutenant John Mullan who had explored the route. In 1859 the first steamboat appeared on the Columbia River above The Dalles; and it was at this same time, as has already been seen, that a Missouri River steamboat first reached Fort Benton.

During the summer of 1860 Captain E. D. Pierce and a party of prospectors found gold in Canal Gulch near Oro Fino Creek in the Clearwater country of northern Idaho. During the ensuing winter news of these discoveries reached the coast. The spring of 1861 witnessed another mining stampede. The little town of Walla Walla was alive with prospectors, five hundred of whom started for the mines in March. Farms in the Willamette Valley were deserted. There was another large exodus from California. The town of Lewiston came into existence in June at the junction of the Clearwater and Snake rivers, to serve as an outfitting point for miners. Additional steamboats were being built for service on the Columbia. By mid-summer six or seven thousand people were in the region, with Pierce City and Oro Fino as the principal mining towns. New finds on the South Fork of the Clearwater attracted miners to that section, and the town of Elk City appeared.

In September 1861, all but the most successful of the miners and other residents of the Oro Fino diggings rushed to the Salmon River region, from which had come reports of extraordinarily rich discoveries. Their fortitude and endurance were put to a severe test during the severe winter of 1861-62, when snow from seven to ten feet in depth blocked all communication, and food supplies ran low. With the coming of spring, a swarm of prospectors, estimated at thirty thousand, poured into the Salmon River country from all directions— from the mining regions to the south, from the States, from Canada. Nearly four thousand men left San Francisco in May. By June the town of Florence boasted a population of more than four thousand.

Gold fever now prevailed throughout the entire Northwest and no promising region was left unprospected. Late in 1861 placers were discovered on the John Day River in eastern Oregon and in the following year that beautiful area was the mecca of a crowd of miners, including many who had suffered disappointment in the Washoe diggings. Simultaneously, there was a movement to the Powder River country, where by 1862 the town of Auburn had three thousand inhabitants, although in a short time it shared the fate of the village by the same name in Goldsmith's well-known poem. Both of these mining booms in eastern Oregon contributed to the permanent settlement of the region, because of excellent farming and grazing lands in the country contiguous to the mining areas.

The Boise Basin in southern Idaho next attracted attention on account of its placers. By 1864 the region had a population of sixteen thousand, one-half of whom were miners and the other half were engaged in other occupations. It was early noted that the country had assumed an aspect of permanency. Idaho City was for a time the largest town, with Boise City as its nearest competitor. The latter was from the start quite different from the typical mining town, for it was carefully laid out, with wide streets, by its founders who no doubt had prophetic visions of it as the future capital of a Territory and State. To the southwest of Boise City, along the Owyhee River and especially on War Eagle Mountain, high-paying quartz lodes were discovered in 1863, from one of which a party took $250,000 in two weeks.

The greatest of the gold rushes to the Northwest were those to the western part of what is now Montana, around the headwaters of the Missouri. By 1861 there were numerous prospectors in the Deer Lodge valley—a sort of overflow from the Salmon River diggings—but they met with indifferent success. In 1862 the first important Montana discovery was made by John White, who found gold on Grasshopper Creek, a tributary of the Missouri. The town of Bannack City had come into existence before the year was over. From this place and from all the other mining regions, as well as from the States, there was a real stampede the following year when there came news of a marvelous new discovery.

A party of prospectors, of which Henry Edgar was a member, set out from Bannack City in the spring of 1863 with the intention of joining James and Granville Stuart in an exploration of the Yellowstone Park country. They missed connection with the Stuart party, ran afoul of some unfriendly Indians, and were obliged to retreat. As they were camped one evening on a small creek in the Gallatin valley, southwest of the site of the present city of Bozeman, one of the party saw some rim rock that looked auriferous. He chipped off a few pieces, proceeded to pan them, and in a short time had gold worth $2.40. The next day they panned out $150.00 worth of the metal—enough to grubstake them for a thorough examination of the region, which they named Alder Gulch, and which within three years yielded thirty million dollars worth of gold. A new Virginia City grew with rapidity fully equalling the phenomenal rise of its Nevada precursor. By 1864 the place claimed ten thousand inhabitants. To the southward were other mining towns nearly as large—Central City, Nevada, and Junction City. It was in this same year that the last of the important Montana gold discoveries was made in what was called Last Chance Gulch, where there quickly sprang up a busy mining camp, which was first called Crab Town but was soon renamed, more euphoniously, Helena.

Mining in New Mexico and Arizona

A few words will suffice to indicate the main developments in the southern portion of this vast mineral empire during the decade of the sixties. Mining had been carried on in New Mexico ever since the early days of Spanish rule. After the Mexican War numerous prospectors had operated successfully in the region between the Rio Grande and the Colorado. The country acquired by the Gadsden Purchase of 1853 was valued both as a route for a railroad and because of its mineral wealth. Here, near the old Spanish towns of Tubac and Tucson, Sylvester Mowry and Charles D. Poston organized companies which engaged profitably in silver mining. Tucson became a typical mining town, described as "the headquarters of vice, dissipation, and crime."

The outbreak of the Civil War checked mining activities for a time. The Confederates early took possession and were

not driven out until 1862.   In that year placer gold fields were
discovered east of the Colorado River in the vicinity of Bill
Williams Creek, and later in the Lynx Creek and Weaver
Mountain districts to the eastward.   There was an immediate
rush to these sections, not only from Tucson and other parts
of New Mexico, but from California as well.   Important quartz
lodes of gold and silver were discovered, but placer mining was
short lived.   Besides, the bitter hostility of the Apache Indians
for more than a decade discouraged widespread prospecting.
The great episodes in Arizona's mining history came in a later
period.

TERRITORIAL AND STATE GOVERNMENTS IN THE MINERAL EMPIRE

A later chapter will contain some account of the social and
economic aspects of life on the miners' frontier.   Here a few
pages will be devoted to the effect of the mining advance just
described in causing the carving of a vast area into Territories
during the decade of the sixties.   There was more truth than
poetry in the following lines of H. N. Maguire which appeared
in a Montana newspaper in 1866:

> "Away our published maps we'll have to throw—
> The books of yesterday, today are lame."

Congress was kept busy in responding to the requests for territorial and state governments made by the rapidly shifting
populations of the mining regions.   Map-makers found it difficult to keep up with the rapid changes in political boundaries.

On February 28, and March 2, 1861, there were approved
acts of Congress creating three new Territories.   One of these,
to be sure—Dakota Territory, established by an act of March
2nd—was not a result of the mining rushes, but was set up because of the desirability of reducing the huge Nebraska Territory to manageable size.   The new Dakota Territory would
itself have been too large for practical purposes if it had
possessed more than a very small population, for it included
all the region now embraced in North and South Dakota, Montana east of the continental divide, and the northern half of
Wyoming.

The establishment of the Territory of Colorado came after more than two years of urging on the part of the people of the mining regions. As early as the winter of 1858 a small group of Pike's Peak miners on Cherry Creek decided a territorial government was desirable, elected Hiram J. Graham as Delegate, and sent him on a fruitless mission to Washington to present their needs. In the following April, in spite of the great outgoing stampede then in progress, a meeting was held in Auraria, and a call was issued for an election of delegates to a constitutional convention to meet in Denver in June and organize a state government. When June arrived, political matters were receiving scant attention, for everyone was chiefly interested in the recent gold discoveries. A few self-constituted delegates convened and adjourned until August. At that time a much larger body of men came together and after due deliberation adopted both a constitution for the proposed "State of Jefferson," and a memorial to Congress asking for the creation of a Territory of the same name. Both of these measures were submitted to a popular referendum and the latter was adopted by a large majority. There ensued another campaign for the election of a Delegate to Congress, during which, according to Henry Villard, "Returns from imaginary districts were manufactured without stint, ballot-boxes stuffed and emissaries sent in every direction for the purpose of bringing in votes." Beverly D. Williams seems to have been the successful candidate, although his election was contested by Dr. George M. Willing.

Then, without waiting for Congress to act, another convention was held and a provisional government for the Territory of Jefferson was organized. A full set of administrative offices, courts, and a general assembly were provided, and soon a full-fledged government was in operation.

Congress was in no position to satisfy the demands of the Pike's Peak community as long as the sectional deadlock prevailed. After the withdrawal of the southern members, however, action was speedy. A bill introduced on January 30, 1861, became a law with President Buchanan's signature on February 28th, and the Territory of Colorado was established. Neither the name proposed by the petitioners nor the extensive boundaries they desired were adopted. The boundaries of the present State are the same as those prescribed for the Territory.

Fifteen years now elapsed before Colorado gained admission into the Union. In 1864 Congress extended an invitation by passing an enabling act. A constitution was drafted, but when it was submitted to the people they rejected it. The flush years of the gold rush were over and the voters were apparently not eager to assume the added burden of taxation which statehood would entail. In 1865 an irregularly chosen convention drew up another constitution which was ratified by the people. President Johnson declined to issue the necessary proclamation of admission. At succeeding sessions of Congress he twice vetoed bills admitting Colorado; and there was not sufficient support for the measure to pass it over his veto. The census of 1870 credited the Territory with less than forty thousand people. For several years the statehood movement languished. Then in 1875 another enabling act was passed, a constitution was drafted and ratified, and Colorado became a State by proclamation of President Grant on August 1, 1876, just in time to play a significant role in national affairs by choosing three electors favorable to Rutherford B. Hayes.

Nevada was the third Territory created in 1861, its organic act being approved on March 2nd. As early as the autumn of 1859 there had been a spontaneous statehood movement at Carson City, which amounted to a virtual declaration of independence from Utah Territory, in the jurisdiction of which the Washoe mines then lay. The new Nevada Territory as first established included all that portion of Utah Territory west of the thirty-ninth meridian west of Washington. Surprisingly enough, its people were obliged to wait only three years for admission into the Union. The same Congress which, in 1864, invited Colorado into the family of States also passed an enabling act for Nevada. There was no rejection in this case. A constitution that had been adopted in 1863 was brought out and revamped, and on October 31, 1864, statehood was achieved. The fact that the new commonwealth contained only a fraction of the population usually considered necessary for statehood, was not a point to deter the party in power which was looking for loyal votes in the approaching, critical election of 1864. The eastern boundary of Nevada was extended to the thirty-eighth meridian by the enabling act of 1864, and to the thirty-seventh meridian by an act of 1866, when new territory was also added on the south, at the expense of Arizona Territory.

Two new Territories—Arizona and Idaho—were organized in 1863, both as the result of the mining advance. For some time there had been agitation for separate territorial organization in the western part of New Mexico Territory. This movement was accelerated by the gold discoveries of 1862 along the east bank of the Colorado River. On February 24, 1863, the region west of the thirty-second meridian was made into the Territory of Arizona. Its area was reduced in 1866 by the section added to Nevada Territory. On March 3, 1863, the governmental needs of the rapidly filling mining areas of the Northwest were recognized by the creation of the huge Territory of Idaho, embracing not only what is now the State by that name, but Montana and Wyoming as well.

Before the territorial government of Idaho, with these extensive boundaries, could be organized and put into operation, the rush of population into the mining sections around the headwaters of the Missouri led to a division of the jurisdiction and the establishment, on May 26, 1864, of the Territory of Montana with practically the same boundaries as the present State. Finally, on July 25, 1868, Idaho was reduced to its present limits when Congress established the Territory of Wyoming, not so much because of any mining activities in the region as because of the building of the Union Pacific Railroad.

The political organization of the Far West was now complete. Nevada came into the Union on a "fluke" in 1864. Three years later, on March 1, 1867, due to adequate increase in population, Nebraska was admitted. With the exception of Colorado, admitted in 1876, all the Territories whose establishment has just been outlined were obliged to wait much longer before attaining the dignity of statehood.

Mining of the precious metals continued to be the principal industry throughout the inter-mountain region for many years. There were even repetitions of most of the features of the gold rush days, as at Leadville and Cripple Creek in Colorado from 1877 to 1879 and from 1891 to 1893, respectively; at the Great Bonanza mine in Nevada in the early seventies; and at the famous Tombstone mines in Arizona beginning in 1879. The stampede to the Black Hills in Dakota Territory during the late seventies was productive of widespread excitement. The mining town of Deadwood and the Deadwood coach gained world-wide notoriety during succeeding years through their delineation as episodes in Buffalo Bill's Wild West Show.

CHAPTER XXXIV

RAILROADS TO THE PACIFIC

"THE distance between New York and the Oregon is about three thousand miles,—from New York we could pursue the most convenient route to the vicinity of Lake Erie, thence along the south shore of this lake and of Lake Michigan, cross the Mississippi between forty-one and forty-two of north latitude, cross the Missouri about the mouth of the Platte, and thence on by the most convenient route to the Rocky Mountains, near the source of the last named river, thence to the Oregon, by the valley of the south branch of that stream, called the southern branch of Lewis' River."

Thus did a writer in a weekly newspaper called the *Emigrant,* published at Ann Arbor, Michigan, outline in February, 1832, the possibility of a transcontinental railroad from the Atlantic to the Pacific. It was the voice of one crying in the wilderness. Railroads were new in the world. It was only two years since the first steam locomotives had run on the rails of the Charleston and Hamburg and via the Baltimore and Ohio. In all the United States there were not more than 250 miles of railroad in 1832, and everywhere the innovation encountered skepticism and even active opposition. Clearly then, the suggestion of a railroad three thousand miles in length largely through an uninhabited country, crossing mighty rivers, great plains and lofty mountains, was an idea too fanciful to be given serious consideration. And yet the proposal, made years before there was thought of even a stage line to the Pacific, was destined to attain realization thirty-seven years later, when the last spike was driven and the rails of the Union Pacific and the Central Pacific were joined at Promontory Point.

As a matter of fact, the Michigan writer may have been the first publicly to propose a railroad to the Pacific, but he had numerous contemporaries who saw similar visions. Hartwell Carver, a grandson of the famous Jonathan Carver, Samuel B. Barlow, and Lewis Gaylord Clarke all wrote articles on the same subject. In 1836 John Plumbe of Dubuque, Iowa, published a pamphlet advocating a railroad from Lake Michigan to Oregon, and in the succeeding years he was active in keeping the subject before the public. By 1840 the idea of a Pacific railroad was at least not new and strange, even though any prospect of its accomplishment seemed indefinitely remote. Within the next decade, however, the movement passed from the stage of half-timid suggestion to one of vigorous agitation. The events of this decade—the migrations, the acquisitions of territory, the discovery of gold—produced a great surge of interest in the hitherto virtually unknown Far West. By 1850 a great number of people would have agreed that a railroad would some day be built to the western ocean.

Asa Whitney's Plan for a Pacific Railroad

On January 28, 1845, there came before Congress a memorial requesting a charter and a land grant for a railroad to the Pacific. The author of this proposal was Asa Whitney, a man whose persistent, widespread agitation in the press, on the platform and in conference during the next six or seven years earned him the title of "Father of Pacific railroads." Even though his plan was never adopted, he stirred up interest and discussion from one end of the country to the other, and he lived to see the day when trains were running from the Missouri to the Pacific.

Whitney was a merchant in the China trade. In 1842 he made a trip to the orient, returning two years later, just after the signing of Caleb Cushing's commercial treaty with China. The prospects of the development of oriental trade by a route much shorter than the long ocean voyage around the Horn seems to have been the objective of Whitney when he drafted his memorial to Congress. "You will see that it will change the whole world," he assured his readers. Not only would such a railroad bind the nation together, but it would "allow us to traverse the globe in thirty days, civilize and christianize mankind, and place us in the center of the world, compelling Europe on one side and Asia . . . on the other to pass through us." When Thomas Hart Benton became converted to the railroad idea he, like many others, seems to have been most enthusiastic with respect to its connection with the oriental trade. In addressing a convention at St. Louis in 1849, Benton declared that when a railroad was completed there should be a huge granite statue of Columbus at the summit of the mountains, "pointing with outstretched arm to the western horizon, and saying to the flying passenger, 'There is the East! There is India!' "

Whitney's plan as set forth in his memorial was certainly startling. He proposed to build a railroad from Lake Michigan to the mouth of the Columbia River. Congress was asked to grant him a strip of land sixty miles wide extending along the entire route. Laborers, mostly immigrants, would be paid as far as possible in land. They, together with other settlers who would be attracted to the land along the road, would develop the country rapidly and thus make operation profitable. Any surplus over costs would be retained by Congress in a special fund to be used to aid in construction in the western sections where land could not be sold. Whitney later presented other memorials to Congress in which the basic plan remained the same, although various details were altered, such as the suggestion of other termini for the road after the acquisition of Oregon and California.

Fantastic, chimerical and impractical were terms applied to Whitney's proposal. Others charged that he was seeking to deprive the people of a huge portion of their heritage in the public domain for his own private aggrandizement. He denied any selfish motive and offered to relinquish any claim for compensation. "I have undertaken the mighty work," he declared, "because I know that someone's whole life must be sacrificed to it." Undaunted by ridicule, criticism and opposition, for several years Whitney conducted a campaign of agitation that was amazingly vigorous and extensive. He wrote articles for newspapers, interviewed editors and often secured their support, addressed public meetings, sought out and waylaid members of Congress, and visited legislatures, a large number of which were prevailed upon to send resolutions to Washington favoring his project. Altogether, Asa Whitney's activities had the value of bringing a definite proposal before the country and giving widespread publicity to the project of a Pacific railroad. Committees of Congress considered his memorials, bills were introduced, and there were debates. After the failure of a bill introduced in 1850, the "prince of projectors" seems to have given up hope of success. In 1851 he made a trip to England where he sought with little effect to stir up interest in a railroad across Canada. His declining years were spent at Locust Hill, near the national capital, where he died in 1872, probably not in virtual poverty as some writers have asserted.

RIVALRIES OVER THE ROUTE FOR A RAILROAD

Whitney's plan might have been adopted in modified form if its visionary aspects had been the only objections to it, for these could have been removed. When proposed in 1845 and again in 1846 his line running to the mouth of the Columbia gained some half-hearted support even in the South, for at that time the Oregon country was the only American territory bordering on the Pacific. With the close of the Mexican War and the acquisition of New Mexico and California, the situation was very different. Thereafter the rivalry of cities and localities and the jealousy of sections was so pronounced that no route for a Pacific railroad could command sufficient support to win Congressional approval until the southern routes had been eliminated from consideration by the secession of the South.

Every city of any size from the Canadian border to the Gulf—Duluth, Milwaukee, Chicago, Cairo, St. Louis, Memphis, Vicksburg, and New Orleans—was ambitious and determined if not to be the actual eastern terminus of the railroad, at least to have a short and easy connection with it. The States along the Mississippi joined forces with the cities, and the people of commonwealths farther east were only less interested. Railroad conventions in Memphis, St. Louis, Chicago and various other cities worked up high enthusiasm for railroads in general, and railroads to the Pacific in particular.

Even to mention the great number of bills introduced into the two houses of Congress by the proponents of these various interests would require too much space, to say nothing of the committee reports, amendments, substitute motions and lengthy and often impassioned debates. More obstructive to a decision of the question than the rivalries of cities and localities was the all-pervading antagonism between the sections. Neither North nor South would support a route that would give the other section the coveted connection with the Pacific coast. "If any route is reported to this body as the best, those that may be rejected will always go against the one selected," complained Senator Gwin of California in 1853, after the failure of his bill that would have provided a railroad from San Francisco to Fulton, Arkansas, with branch connections to almost every important city from Matagorda, Texas, to Dubuque, Iowa.

In 1853 a measure passed Congress adding the sum of $150,000 to the army appropriation bill for the purpose of surveying feasible routes for a railroad to the Pacific. Under the direction of the Secretary of War, Jefferson Davis, parties were sent into the field and five routes were surveyed. The northernmost route, from St. Paul to the mouth of the Columbia River between the forty-seventh and forty-ninth parallels, was surveyed with great vigor and enthusiasm by Isaac I. Stevens, the newly appointed first governor of Washington Territory, who was assisted by a party under Captain George B. McClellan moving eastward from the Pacific. Lieutenant E. G. Beckwith was in command of the survey of that portion of the now familiar emigrant route to California which had not already been carefully described by Frémont and Stansbury. Between the thirty-eighth and thirty-ninth parallels westward from the mouth of the Kansas River a difficult route was surveyed by Captain J. W. Gunnison, who lost his life in an attack by Paiute Indians. This was the route favored by Thomas Hart Benton of Missouri and was often called the "Buffalo Trail" because he had so referred to it, in order to emphasize its practicability. A fourth survey, conducted by Lieutenant A. W. Whipple, proceeded in general along the thirty-fifth parallel from Fort Smith on the Arkansas to Los Angeles. Finally, a far southern route along the thirty-second parallel was explored in sections by several parties under Captain John Pope, Lieutenant J. G. Parke and others.

These surveys constituted an important chapter in the history of the official exploration of the Far West. The reports, ultimately published in twelve large copiously illustrated volumes, contained a vast amount of valuable information dealing not only with the topography of the regions traversed, but also with the geology, botany, animal life, and Indian tribes of the Far West. They helped not at all in bringing agreement on a route to be selected for the railroad. Despite Stevens' stout championship of the northern route which he surveyed, it received little serious consideration. There were no centers of population at either end to justify such a road. Benton's favorite route was given scant support, because of insuperable difficulties in crossing the mountains and the Colorado River. It had long been known that a railroad could be built by the central route along the California Trail, but the South would not listen to such a selection.

Although northern Senators and Congressmen could not be expected to agree, Jefferson Davis, in transmitting the survey reports recommended the far southern route along the thirty-second parallel. The topography and climate of the route were such, he said, that "the progress of the work will be regulated chiefly by the speed with which cross-ties and rails can be delivered and laid. . . . Not only is this the shortest and least costly route to the Pacific, but it is the shortest and cheapest route to San Francisco, the greatest commercial city on our western coast; while the aggregate length of railroad lines connecting it at its eastern terminus with the Atlantic and Gulf seaports is less than the aggregate connection with any other route." An ardent pro-southerner's advocacy of a southern route did not carry much weight with northern supporters of a central course. But there was one important advantage in favor of a southern line: it could run through three States and one Territory all the way from the Mississippi to the Pacific. Advocates of the central route, however, were confronted by the wide-stretching, unorganized Indian country west of the Missouri River.

The following chapter tells how the nation's solemn pledge

that this Indian country should be the perpetual home of its inhabitants was forgotten and repudiated. In 1853 Commissioner G. W. Manypenny began the unpleasant task of negotiating treaties with the tribes of the Great Plains preparatory to the white advance beyond the Missouri. Then came the Kansas-Nebraska Bill which established organized government in this region. As has already been shown, there is reason to believe that Stephen A. Douglas was motivated in his active support of this measure, at least in part, by his intense desire that the Pacific railroad should run by the central route, thus giving his city and State of Chicago and Illinois coveted advantages in transcontinental trade. Although he did not live to see the fulfillment of his dream, the object he sought was later attained by his constituents. Immediately, however, the prodigious efforts connected with the Kansas-Nebraska struggle had no fruits in railroad-building toward the Pacific. In 1855 the Senate passed a bill, introduced by Douglas, for the building of three transcontinental railroads—one by a northern, a second by a central and a third by a southern route—but the bill met bitter opposition and defeat in the House of Representatives. Thereafter, for seven years, no railroad bill met a better fate.

By this time the people of the entire country were convinced of the practicability and necessity of a Pacific railroad. In 1856 the Democratic platform declared it to be the duty of the federal government "to exercise all its constitutional power to the attainment of that object, thereby binding the Union of these States in indissoluble bonds, and opening to the rich commerce of Asia an overland transit." The new Republican party was even more emphatic and definite. Its platform asserted that "a railroad to the Pacific Ocean by the most central and practicable route, is imperatively demanded by the interests of the whole country, and that the Federal Government ought to render immediate and efficient aid in its construction." The same declarations were repeated in 1860 by the Republicans and by both wings of the divided Democratic party. But inability to agree upon a route, due to growing sectional bitterness, prevented an attainment desired by all. Not until after the obstacle of sectional controversy was removed by the withdrawal of the South from the Union was the way opened for the settlement of the long-debated railroad question.

The Pacific Railroad Bills

All through the long contest to secure agreement on a route for a Pacific railroad the people of California were, of course, deeply interested in the subject. It was in that State that the first definite activity took place after the beginning of the Civil War. On June 28, 1861, the Central Pacific Railroad Company of California was incorporated. Its leading promoters were Leland Stanford, Collis P. Huntington, Mark Hopkins, Charles Crocker, and Theodore D. Judah, the last named being the chief engineer for the company. Judah proceeded immediately to explore routes across the Sierras, and to make estimates of costs. He then hastened to Washington, D. C., to secure Congressional aid and to lend his assistance in the selection of a central route.

A number of railroad bills were already before Congress. With the two southern routes eliminated, the only remaining problem was to reconcile the rivalries of St. Louis, Chicago and St. Paul or to make a selection among the routes favored by these cities and the communities they represented. The northern route was regarded to have little merit, because of the sparse population in the region concerned. Missouri was still a doubtful State with respect to its loyalty to the Union. After a long debate the central route advocated by Chicago and the people of Illinois and Iowa was chosen. On July 1, 1862, President Lincoln attached his signature to "An act to aid in the construction of a Railway and Telegraph line from the Missouri River to the Pacific Ocean." The long struggle over routes was ended.

Several companies were to co-operate in building the road. Of these the most important was the Union Pacific Company, created by the act, which was to build from a point to be selected by the President on the one hundredth meridian in Nebraska to the western boundary of Nevada. Here it would connect with the line to be built to that point from the coast by the Central Pacific Railroad Company. From the designated point on the one hundredth meridian connecting lines were to be constructed by various companies to Kansas City, Atchison, to a place on the western border of Iowa to be selected by the President, and to Sioux City. Since the Union Pacific Railroad Company built the line to the western border of Iowa at Council Bluffs, as was authorized by the act, that connection in reality became an integral part of the Union Pacific line.

The government aid provided by Congress to assist in the construction of the railroad was extremely generous. The policy of land grants had become well established after the success of Stephen A. Douglas in securing such aid in 1850 for his Illinois Central Railroad. The companies constructing the Pacific railroad were granted a right of way four hundred feet in width, with permission to use building materials from the public domain; and ten sections of land for each mile of railroad completed. These sections were arranged checker-board fashion in a ten-mile strip on either side of the line, the alternate sections being retained by the federal government. In addition, a subsidy was given in the form of a loan of United States bonds at the rate of $16,000 a mile of line in the level country, $32,000 a mile in the high plateau region, and $48,000 a mile in the mountains. This loan was secured by a first mortgage.

The passage of this act, however, did not result in immediate activity in railroad-building. Ground was broken for the Central Pacific in February, 1863, and a few miles of line were in operation by the end of the year; but the Union Pacific was more dilatory. A controversy over the gauge of the railroad occupied much time until in March, 1863, an act was passed by Congress and approved by Lincoln establishing the now familiar gauge of four feet, eighth and one-half inches. But a much greater difficulty confronted both companies in securing funds with which to begin operations and complete a sufficient number of miles of railroad to entitle them to receive the first installment of land grants and bond subsidies. The government was drawing heavily upon the resources of the people for funds with which to finance the war. Men of means were hesitant to invest their money in an enterprise on which the government would hold a first mortgage, and in which the prospect of attractive dividends seemed indefinitely remote. It was generally recognized that something had to be done to make the inducements to investment sufficiently alluring to insure the completion of a project launched with such a fervor of national approbration; but, as John P. Davis has said, "the point where the limit of aid to patriotic capitalists should be set was difficult to determine."

At length in July, 1864, an amendatory act was passed, after much debate and after, to use the words of a Congressman, "gilded corridors were filled with lobbyists, who broke through all rules and made their way upon the floor and into the seats of members." The land grant was increased from ten sections for each mile of track to twenty sections. The security for the government loan of bonds was reduced to the status of a second mortgage; and the companies were permitted to issue and market their own first mortgage bonds to an amount equal to the government subsidy. The Central Pacific was authorized to extend its line 150 miles into Nevada.

Although both companies still found it difficult to raise the necessary funds immediately, this amendment provided the needed stimulus to investors. Those interested in the methods by which construction was financed will find adequate treatments in the various histories of the Union Pacific Railroad. As is well known, a number of the promoters, as well as many members of Congress, were later involved in the great Crédit Mobilier scandal.

By the close of the year 1865 the Union Pacific had laid about forty miles of track. Thereafter grading, bridge-building, and track-laying proceeded at a more rapid pace. In 1866 the provision regarding the place of meeting of the two lines was repealed: both companies were permitted to build until their tracks met. An administrative ruling of President Lincoln had classified the relatively level high Nevada plateau as mountainous country. Both companies now raced to lay tracks in this region and thus secure the treble bond subsidy provided in the original act for railroad building in the mountains. There came a time when it became evident Congress must take a hand and determine a meeting-place, for parallel grades were being extended with feverish haste across northwestern Utah and northeastern Nevada. Finally the two companies came to terms in the spring of 1869 and agreed that the rails should meet at Promontory Point, north of the Great Salt Lake; a decision that was in accord with a Congressional resolution.

BUILDING THE FIRST RAILROAD TO THE PACIFIC

Important as are those phases of the history of this first railroad to the Pacific which are concerned with Congressional legislation and the financing of construction, it may safely be said that the general public was most interested in the actual railroad-building—especially after both companies began work in real earnest. The vastness of the enterprise, the nature of the country traversed, and the speed and energy which characterized construction all appealed to the imagination and made the project a part of the romance of the Far West.

All the rails, heavy tools and equipment, and rolling stock used by the Central Pacific had to be shipped into San Francisco by the long ocean route. Since no railroad reached the Missouri on the western border of Iowa until late in 1867, the Union Pacific was obliged to depend upon Missouri River steamboats and slow moving wagon trains for the transportation of its equipment to the eastern terminus of its line. For the Union Pacific grading and track-laying was comparatively simple across the level plains until the mountains were reached. Construction, from the beginning, was more difficult for the Central Pacific because of the high Sierra range to be crossed; but there was a compensating advantage in the abundance of stone and wood for construction which was absent on the treeless plains.

General Grenville M. Dodge, the chief engineer of the Union Pacific, has left us a graphic account of the procedure followed. Parties of surveyors, with armed escorts for protection against the Indians, formed the advance. They made rapid preliminary surveys covering from eight to twelve miles a day, followed by more careful making of plots and profiles of definite locations for the line. "The location party," wrote Dodge, "was followed by the construction corps, grading generally 100 miles at a time. That distance was graded in about thirty days on the plains, as a rule, but in the mountains we sometimes had to open our grading several hundred miles ahead of our track in order to complete the grading by the time the track should reach it. All the supplies for this work had to be hauled from the end of the track, and the wagon transportation was enormous. At one time we were using at least 10,000 animals, and most of the time from 8,000 to 10,000 laborers. The bridge gangs always worked from 5 to 20 miles ahead of the track, and it was seldom that the track waited for a bridge." On the plains "everything, rails, ties, bridging, fastenings, all railway supplies, fuel for locomotives and trains, and supplies for men and animals on the entire work, had to be transported from the Missouri River. Therefore, as we moved westward, every hundred miles added vastly to our transportation."

As the Union Pacific steadily pushed westward many newspaper men and other tourists made the journey to rail's end to observe the process. W. A. Bell, among others, wrote a vivid story of track-laying as he witnessed it. "A light car," he wrote, "drawn by a single horse, gallops up to the front with its load of rails. Two men seize the end of a rail and start forward, the rest of the gang taking hold by twos, until it is clear of the car. They come forward at a run. At the word of command the rail is dropped in its place, right side up with care, while the same process goes on at the other side of the car. Less than thirty seconds to a rail for each gang, and so four rails go down to the minute. . . . The moment the car is empty it is tipped over on the side of the track to let the next loaded car pass it, and then it is tipped back again; and it is a sight to see it go flying back again for another load. . . . Close behind the first gang come the guagers, spikers, and bolters, and a lively time they make of it. It is a grand 'anvil chorus' that those sturdy sledges are playing across the plains. It is in triple time, three strokes to the spike." In level country the Union Pacific had no difficulty in laying from one to three miles of track a day. During the race of the last months records of as high as eight and one-half miles a day were made. The Central Pacific once laid more than ten miles of track in a single day toward the end of the race.

Each company operated from a series of about twelve

temporary bases of operation, or terminal towns, as the work progressed. These places had many characteristics in common with the mining camps and the towns on the border of the cowboy country. To them were attracted the swarm of parasites that usually appear where a large number of men are gathered and where, especially, there are pay checks to be spent. "Hell on Wheels" was the name which, said Samuel Bowles, most aptly described these short-lived aggregations of humanity. Bowles described one of these places, called Benton, as "a village of a few variety stores and shops, and many restaurants and grog-shops; by day disgusting, by night dangerous; almost everybody dirty, many filthy, and with the marks of lowest vice; averaging a murder a day. . . . Like its predecessors, it fairly festered in corruption, disorder and death. . . . But in a few weeks its tents were struck, its shanties razed, and with their dwellers moved on fifty or a hundred miles farther to repeat their life for another brief day. Where these people came from originally; where they went to when the road was finished, and their occupation was over, were both puzzles too intricate for me. Hell would appear to have been raked to furnish them; and to it they must have naturally returned after graduating here, fitted for its highest seats and most diabolical service."

At times some of these terminal towns had populations of as high as ten thousand, including workmen and hangers-on. White laborers, among whom Irish predominated, were employed by the Union Pacific. The Central Pacific, on the other hand, was built chiefly by Chinese laborers. Because of this fact and also because of the strict regulations of the construction company, the terminal towns of the Central Pacific were far more quiet and orderly than those of the Union Pacific. As at one place after another the tents and shanties and false store fronts were taken down, put on trains and moved to the next location, nothing but desolation was left in some cases. Frequently, however, as at Cheyenne, Laramie, Green River, Reno, Winnemucca, and other points, a nucleus of permanent population was left to form towns which soon outgrew the turbulent character of the first months.

"Our Indian troubles commenced in 1864 and lasted until

the tracks joined at Promontory," wrote Grenville M. Dodge in alluding to one of the problems confronting the builders of the Union Pacific. Surveyors and workmen were killed by the Indians, trains were captured and damaged, and livestock was stolen or stampeded. Although the government offered military protection, the laborers themselves were usually able to provide their own defense. Large numbers of them had recently been in the army during the war and many of their bosses had been officers. They stacked their guns along the right of way, where they could be seized in case of attack. It required only a few moments to convert a railroad gang into an effective fighting force.

On May 10, 1869, a motley crowd of officials of both railroad companies and their friends, tourists, laborers, soldiers and Indians gathered at the last of the terminal towns—Promontory Point. Two engines faced each other across a space as wide as the length of two rails. At the designated time a gang of paddies brought forward two Union Pacific rails, while a gang of Chinese coolies placed two Central Pacific rails in position. A prayer was said, brief speeches were made, and then came the ceremony of driving the last golden spike. Telegraph wires were so connected that the taps on the last spike were transmitted to instruments in all the cities from the Atlantic to the Pacific, in many of which enthusiastic celebrations of the completion of the railroad were in progress. When the final stroke had been given, the telegraph signalled "Done!" Thereupon the two engines moved up until they were touching, each engineer broke a bottle of champagne over the pilot of the opposite locomotive; and thus, to use the words of Grenville M. Dodge, "the two roads were wedded into one great trunk line from the Atlantic to the Pacific."

The Other Land Grant Railroads to the Pacific

"There will speedily be other railroads across our Continent," predicted Samuel Bowles in 1869 in a chapter devoted to the Union Pacific. "The rivalries of sections, the temptations of commerce, the necessities of our political system, will add at least two more through lines within a generation's time.

But this, the first, will forever remain the one of history; the one of romance." His prophecy, considered extravagant by many people when it was made, actually underestimated the amount of railroad building in the Far West during the succeeding two decades. He was entirely correct in his belief that no later transcontinental railroad would attract quite the general public interest given the Union Pacific. Just as the mad rush of the forty-niners to California has a place in history not accorded to the equally large migrations of the years immediately following, so Americans never again were thrilled as they were when the Union Pacific and the Central Pacific were joined at Promontory Point. Nevertheless, other railroads to the Pacific were eagerly awaited and warmly welcomed by the people of the regions they served, and their construction is of less general interest only because the story of the Union Pacific had taken away some of the novelty and romance.

Before the policy of federal land grants to railroads was abandoned three additional transcontinental lines were the recipients of such aid. The Northern Pacific was chartered in 1864 to run from Lake Superior to Puget Sound along the route favored by Asa Whitney and surveyed by Isaac I. Stevens. Two years later, in 1866, a charter was given the Atlantic and Pacific Railroad to build a line from Springfield, Missouri, to the Colorado River at Needles, by way of the Indian Territory, northern Texas, and Albuquerque, New Mexico. The California promoters who had built the Central Pacific were authorized to build a road in California to join the Atlantic and Pacific at Needles. In 1871 the Texas Pacific Railroad was given permission to construct a line from Marshall, Texas, across the central part of that State and on to San Diego by way of Fort Yuma. A generous right of way was given each of these roads. Congress had repented of its liberality in the matter of the bond subsidy given the Union Pacific, and none of these later railroads received any bonds. By way of compensation, however, each company was given twenty sections of public land for each mile of line in the States traversed and forty sections in the Territories. In Texas, where the federal government had no public lands, the two southern railroads were given assistance by the State.

The history of the financing and construction of these railroads is a complicated one. Not until 1882 and 1883 were through trains running on these lines between the Pacific terminals and the Mississippi River. The Northern Pacific was organized immediately after the granting of the charter in 1864, but six years passed before real progress was made, aside from the making of surveys. There was almost no market for the bonds and stock of the road. Congress was asked for assistance in the form of the payment of interest on the company's bonds in return for the relinquishment of a portion of the land grant, but without result. In 1869, however, a new and brighter day dawned for the discouraged company, when Jay Cooke, of one of the country's great banking firms, took an interest in the Northern Pacific and became convinced that it had a promising future.

Jay Cooke had gained a reputation as a financial wizard, by his success in marketing government securities during the Civil War. He originated and carried into effect many of the features of the modern "drive" for funds. By investing liberally in printer's ink in newspaper articles, advertisements, pamphlets, handbills and posters he succeeded remarkably in inducing a great number of people to invest their hoards and savings in government bonds of small denominations. The Northern Pacific Railroad Company, therefore, had cause for elation when Jay Cooke agreed to underwrite the financing of the line, even though the bargain he drove was a hard one. He entered the new enterprise with the same zeal he had displayed, and with the same methods he had employed, in selling government securities during the war. The bonds now sold rapidly, mainly in this country but also in Europe, and money came rolling in by the millions of dollars. Duluth, where Cooke had invested in lands, was chosen for the eastern terminus of the road. Ground was broken in 1870 and for nearly three years construction proceeded steadily. The railroad was completed to Brainerd on the Mississippi the first year, to Fargo on the Red River in 1871, and to the new town of Bismarck on the Missouri River, near the site of the old Mandan village, by 1873. By this time considerable work had already been done west of the Cascade Mountains in the Territory of

Washington. Then railroad-building came to a sudden end, for the whole country was in the throes of a panic.

There were, of course, many causes of the Panic of 1873, but they may be summed up in one word which goes far to explain all episodes of this painful nature in our history—overinvestment. The reaction from the prosperity following the Civil War became felt. The wide sale of railroad securities had absorbed much of the available capital. Farmers had gone into debt to purchase expensive farm machinery. The South was ruined and faced a long struggle toward economic rehabilitation. European markets for American securities declined. The exposé of the Crédit Mobilier and the other scandals of the period lowered public confidence. The Northern Pacific, like all other large enterprises, encountered a sudden cessation of the sale of stock and bonds. Jay Cooke exemplified his confidence in the future of the line by turning from a seller to a buyer of Northern Pacific stock and by buying until his firm was obliged to close its doors and go into bankruptcy. All construction was abandoned.

Bismarck remained the western terminus until 1878, when work was resumed, after the company had passed through a period of reorganization and refinancing. Thereafter there was no serious interruption to the steady progress of the line, which was completed five years later, under the leadership of a man remarkable for his organizing ability. Henry Villard, whose reports from Colorado have already been quoted, was a German immigrant who was active as a newspaper correspondent during the Civil War. After the Panic of 1873 he was employed by a number of German investors in Northern Pacific securities to look after their interests. He took up the task with energy, and soon his activities began to extend beyond the scope of his commission. He realized the importance of eliminating competition in the Columbia River region. With this in mind he secured control of the Oregon Steam Navigation Company and the Oregon Railroad and merged them into the Oregon Railway and Navigation Company. Then in 1881 he went to New York City and persuaded his friends to entrust their funds to him to form a "blind pool," the purpose of which was not announced. He then set about buying Northern

Pacific stock until he had control. Frederick Billings was voted out of the presidency of the road, and Villard took his place—thus controlling virtually all rail and water transportation in the Pacific Northwest. In 1883 the last spike was driven and the "Golden Spike Special" hauled a trainload of noted guests to the western terminus at Tacoma.

No adequate history has been written of the other two transcontinental land grant railroads, the Atlantic and Pacific and the Texas Pacific, possibly for the reason that they eventually became merged into one of the great railway systems of the Southwest. The Atlantic and Pacific had laid tracks to Vinita, Indian Territory, and the Texas Pacific to the vicinity of Fort Worth, when the Panic of 1873 halted operations. The history of these roads after work was resumed, about 1878, is entangled in a maze of reorganizations and rivalries with other railroads building, or planning to build, in the Southwest. Before through trains from the Pacific coast ran to St. Louis and New Orleans in 1882 and 1883 the Atlantic and Pacific and the Texas Pacific had been absorbed by the Atchison, Topeka, and Santa Fé and the Southern Pacific.

The Southern Pacific was organized by the same men who built the Central Pacific. By building lines across California to Needles and Yuma they virtually had the Atlantic and Pacific and the Texas Pacific at their mercy, as far as traffic in California was concerned. The story of how the Southern Pacific gained control of the two roads and of a large part of the transcontinental railway business of the Southwest is an interesting phase of the frenzied manipulations of the late seventies and the eighties.

The Santa Fé and the Denver and Rio Grande

It would be interesting to describe the manner in which the large number of other lines which are included in the extensive railway network of the Far West were financed and built, without the aid of federal land grants. There is much that is colorful in the story of how the Atchison, Topeka, and Santa Fé built up its great system of more than 11,000 miles of railroad. Organized in 1860 under the leadership of Cyrus

K. Holliday, this company later obtained a land grant from Kansas, and by 1872 had its tracks laid across the State and was entering Colorado. While its main objectives lay to the southward, the company became interested in building a branch line to tap the rich mineral region of central Colorado. In furthering this ambition they came into conflict with the Denver and Rio Grande. This company was formed in 1870, with General William J. Palmer at its head, for the purpose of diverting the Santa Fé trade for the merchants of Denver and Colorado Springs. This company, likewise, was attracted by the prospects of profits to be earned by a line to the Leadville district. Since the only route to this region was through the Royal Gorge, where there is room for only one railroad, the two companies engaged in a long contest for the right of way, during the course of which there were bloody fights between the rival construction gangs. After much litigation a settlement was reached and the Denver and Rio Grande was left in possession.

A lengthy chapter could also be written about the developments of railroads in the States of the Pacific coast, and especially about the struggles in Oregon which preceded the acquisition of control by the Southern Pacific. The building of the Great Northern and its completion in 1893, under the directing genius of James J. Hill, was the last great exploit of railroad-building in the Far West before the frontier era came to its close.

CHAPTER XXXV

THE MILITARY-INDIAN FRONTIER

EARLIER in these pages there is a chapter devoted to the outstanding features of the story of how the American Indians were disposessed of their ancient homes and hunting-grounds throughout the middle western frontier. The narrative has now reached a point where it is disagreeably necessary to describe the continuation and completion of that process in the Far West. Innumerable books and articles have been written about various phases of Indian affairs on the Great Plains, in the mountain region, and on the Pacific coast. There is a huge mass of data in government documents, in records of Congressional debates, in newspapers, and in letters and reports of traders, missionaries, and travelers. Unfortunately, however, no adequate general history of our dealings with the Indians has yet been written. It is still impossible, therefore, to view the subject as a whole. At the most, a brief account can present only the main events, policies, and practices connected with the inglorious record.

THE PROBLEM OF ADMINISTERING INDIAN AFFAIRS

That the Indian policy of the federal governments was one of conscious dishonor cannot be maintained. And yet, because of the confusion of attitudes, prerogatives and interests among those who sought to formulate and execute that policy, the results were as disastrous and unjust to the Indians as would have been a deliberate and acknowledged program of conquest and extermination. Two departments of the national government were charged with responsibility for Indian affairs. Under the War Department the army was given garrison and patrol duty in the Indian country and, especially in the period after the Civil War, was called upon to fight the tribesmen in a series of punitive campaigns. Under the Interior Department, after 1849, were the Indian commissioners at Washington, the superintendents in the Territories, and the agents among the various tribes. Too many of the latter were either incompetent or corrupt, or both. Besides, there was conflict of function, authority, and attitude between the army and the civil officials. This conflict was seen in its most extreme form when, as often happened, the Indian agents, in the performance of their duty, issued to their charges guns and ammunition which made them more formidable in battles with the army.

The Indian agency system might have been shorn of its abuses and made to work satisfactorily, and the army might have had little fighting to do, if settlers had not crossed, and later desired to occupy, the lands of the Indians. The hatred of the frontiersmen for the red men, described in previous chapters, was in no degree abated among most of those who moved into the Far West. The great majority of the settlers had little or no regard for the rights of the Indians, whose country they invaded and whose removal they demanded in tones so insistent that the government was forced to give heed. No Indian policy, not even that which solemnly pledged the maintenance of a permanent Indian country, could long stand in the face of the persistent and growing pressure of the settlers.

On the other hand, the Indians of the Far West, like their brethren to the eastward in earlier years, feared, and learned to hate the settlers. Explorers came into the land of the red man and generally aroused curiosity and interest, rather than hostility. With some exceptions, the relations between the Indians and the fur traders were friendly, for in most respects the interests of the two were identical. But the coming of the settlers meant the end of the Indians' world. When streams of emigrants poured across the plains to Oregon and California, when later a horde of white men began digging up the earth throughout the mountain area in search of gold, when stage lines and railroads were pushed westward, and when the farmers' frontier advanced, the Indians reacted in the only manner of which they were capable. They harassed emigrant trains, they disrupted stage service, they attacked railroad gangs, and they carried death and destruction to the settlements. Thereby

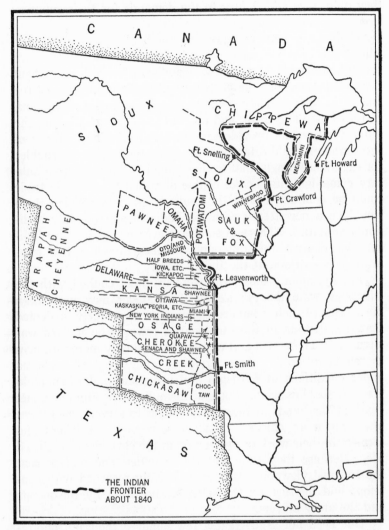

XIII. THE INDIAN FRONTIER ABOUT 1840

Showing the Indian frontier line and the location of the tribes west of the line.
(Based on maps in *American State Papers, Military Affairs*, Vol. VI, p. 177,
Vol. VII, p. 780; and on Kappler, *Indian Affairs, Laws and Treaties*.)

they only gave added fury to the demands for their suppression.

Besides the settlers there was another class of white men whose activities complicated the Indian problem. These were the dealers in whiskey and merchandise, who, with or without licenses, hung about the agencies and along the border of the Indian country. They debauched and cheated the Indians, extended credit to them, and then all too often gobbled up the annuity payments provided for in treaties. The interests of these traders could often be best served by fomenting trouble; for experience taught that trouble would be followed by a military campaign, during the course of which a profitable trade could be conducted with the soldiers, and after which there would be a new treaty with the Indians, and possibly additional annuities. There is sufficient evidence at least to indicate that many of the traders played discreditable, sordid roles in the tragic drama of the Indian wars.

Finally, among those who were in direct contact with the tribesmen were the missionaries. Whatever may have been the success of their religious teaching, it can scarcely be denied that the attitude of the missionaries toward the natives was altruistic. These men and women received only mere pittances as remuneration for their services. They lived and labored under conditions of hardship and privation, and often amid great personal dangers. Some of them, like the Whitmans, met death at the hands of those they sought to serve. They were often far more efficient than the government teachers and farmers in their work of instruction in the elements of civilized life. Because they were inclined to understand and present the Indians' viewpoint, they were usually regarded with contempt and distrust by the settlers, and often by the agents and the army officers.

One need not argue that a few hundred thousand aborigines should have been left in possession of all the vast area of the Far West. He may express the belief, however, that the Indian problems might have been solved with far greater humanity and justice to all concerned.

The "Permanent Indian Country"

During the decade of the thirties the Indian removal policy, inaugurated by President Monroe, was carried into effect, and there was created what was confidently called a permanent Indian country west of Arkansas, Missouri, and an irregular line running through eastern Iowa and northern Wisconsin to Green Bay. "The plan of removing the aboriginal people who yet remain within the settled portions of the United States to the country west of the Mississippi River approaches its consummation," declared President Jackson, with evident satisfaction, in his annual message to Congress in 1835. "The pledge of the United States has been given by Congress that the country destined for the residence of this people shall be forever 'secured and guaranteed to them.'. . . After the further details of this arrangement are completed, with a very general supervision of them, they ought to be left to the progress of events."

By 1840 the Indian frontier was practically complete, especially between the Red River and the Platte west of Arkansas and Missouri. The Indian Intercourse Act of 1834 and other laws of the same year prohibited the entry of any white person into the Indian country without a license; forbade the selling or giving of spirituous liquor to the Indians; and set up superintendencies, agencies, and sub-agencies. Along the border was a line of forts, stretching from Fort Howard and Fort Snelling in the north to Fort Smith and Fort Towson in the south. Each of these forts had a small garrison whose duty it was to prevent encroachments on Indian lands, as well as to protect the farmers' frontier. Teachers, blacksmiths, and other artisans were to be sent among the tribes to assist them along the pathway toward civilization. It must be said that, so far as was in its power, the federal government sincerely endeavored to establish the conditions essential to the fulfillment of the guarantee of permanency for the Indian country on the Great Plains.

The decade of the forties may be summarized briefly, as far as Indian affairs are concerned. In spite of the best efforts of numerous military officers and Indian agents, the intercourse act proved no more effective in protecting the red men from the activities of unprincipled traders and the encroachments of settlers than previous laws of a similar nature. Companies of the First United States Dragoons made extensive expeditions in the Indian country, for the purpose of impressing the Indians with the power of the government, holding councils to promote peace between warring tribes, and protecting caravans to Santa Fé and emigrant trains on the Oregon Trail. In the south the Five Civilized Tribes, especially the Cherokees and the Creeks, made remarkable progress in adapting themselves to their new environment, governing themselves, and providing for their own educational and social welfare. Several treaties were made in which tribes living in Wisconsin and Iowa ceded their lands and agreed to move into what are now Minnesota and Kansas.

The Abandonment of the Indian Frontier Policy

In the meantime, "the progress of events," to which Andrew Jackson had said the Indians should be left, was rapidly dooming the permanent Indian frontier policy to failure. In 1840 government officials and a majority of the American people no doubt still believed that the limits of western expansion had been reached. They may have been satisfied with the thought that the Indians had been removed from the settlements and placed in a region unsuited to the uses of white men. Within a few years, however, all such ideas were abandoned. Already the trade with Santa Fé had begun the destruction of the myth of a great American desert, and had caused modifications of the military frontier. Then came the migrations to Oregon, with no regard for the fact that the trail crossed a region into which white men were forbidden to enter without permission. The Oregon country came into the possession of the United States, to be followed soon by the territory acquired at the close of the Mexican War. The Mexican treaty was still recent when the California gold rush took place. The Indian country, which was referred to as outside the American nation in 1840, was decidedly not outside it in 1850.

It can scarcely be contended that the government should have sought to maintain its policy of a permanent Indian frontier in the face of these unforeseen developments. It was unthinkable that a barrier should be allowed to exist between the States and the new possessions and settlements on the Pacific coast. In spite of its repeated pledge that the Indians on the plains would never again be asked to move, the government might have sent its commissioners to the tribes and frankly explained the altered situation and the revisions of policy which were now necessary. But there was no time or inclination to work out a well considered plan of dealing with the Indian problem. The determination of the American people to occupy their new possessions swept everything before it: pledge or no pledge, justice or no justice, the Indians must get out of the way. Instead of attempting to formulate a broad general revision of Indian policy adapted to the needs of the time, the government returned to old practice of expediency which had characterized the period before Monroe's removal plan was inaugurated.

The first of the new treaties were made in 1851. During the summer of that year Alexander Ramsey negotiated treaties in which the Sioux Indians ceded all of their lands in the State of Iowa and the Territory of Minnesota, except a narrow strip along the upper Minnesota River. The compensation promised the Indians was generous, both as to down payment and annuities. Settlers, however, rushed into the newly ceded area before the treaties were ratified and before appropriations were made to provide the payments. Furthermore, the claims of traders were more than sufficient to absorb all the money due as soon as the Indians had removed from the ceded area. Thus these Siouan tribes were left with grievances which rankled for years in the minds of the more belligerent warriors, and were to find expression later in murderous attacks on the settlements.

In September, 1851, a treaty was concluded at Fort Laramie, largely through the efforts of Agent Thomas Fitzpatrick, with a number of tribes of the northern plains, among which the western Sioux, the Cheyennes, and the Arapahoes were the most important as far as succeeding events are concerned. The main purpose of the negotiation was to secure an arrangement with the Indians that would insure greater safety along the great emigrant route to Oregon and California. The assembled tribes agreed to "recognize the right of the United States Government to establish roads, military and other posts, within their respective territories." The tribes also bound themselves to accept and recognize limits to their tribal hunting-grounds. The Sioux, for instance, were to remain north of the trail along the North Platte River; while the range of the Cheyennes and the Arapahoes was to lie between the North Platte and Arkansas rivers. In return for these concessions the government agreed to pay the Indians $50,000 a year for fifty years in provisions, merchandise, domestic animals, and agricultural implements. The United States Senate saw fit to reduce the period of the annuity payments to ten years, with a provisional extension of five additional years. Since this amendment was never ratified by all the tribes, the treaty did not have real validity, although the government carried out its terms, and the Indians in general remained peaceful in spite of their resentment.

Thomas Fitzpatrick made a similar treaty in 1853 with the Comanche, Kiowa, and Apache tribes at Fort Atkinson. These Indians, living on the southern plains, promised to remain at peace with the United States and with each other. They also acknowledged the right of the government to lay out roads and establish posts within their territories, to make restitution for injuries done to any white persons "lawfully residing in or passing through" their territories, and "to refrain in future from warlike incursions into the Mexican provinces." The last mentioned clause referred to raids which had been causing much trouble along the border. In consideration of these agreements and "of the losses which they may sustain by reason of the travel of the people of the United States through their territories," the tribes were to receive annuity goods to the amount of $18,000 for a period of ten years, and for an additional five years at the discretion of the President.

Then, early in 1854, in order to make way for the organization of Kansas and Nebraska Territories and the opening of a central route for a railroad to the Pacific, there were signed a large number of treaties with tribes, most of whom had been colonized along the eastern border of the Indian country in accordance with the removal policy. To George W. Many-penny, Commissioner of Indian Affairs, fell the thankless and unpleasant task of holding councils in the Indian country during the summer of 1853 and arranging agreements to be embodied in treaties the following spring. There was naturally much hesitation on the part of the Indians, for they had received the promise of their Great Father in Washington that they should never again be disturbed in their homes on the plains. But Manypenny stuck doggedly, if reluctantly, to his assignment. Ranging from north to the south, the Omaha, Oto and Missouri, Sauk and Fox, Iowa, Kickapoo, Delaware, Shawnee, Ottawa, Kaskaskia, Peoria, Piankashaw, Wea, and Miami tribes ceded lands aggregating more than thirteen million acres. Most of the tribes agreed to accept land elsewhere, although many of them held out for small reservations within their former territories. Each and all granted rights of way for roads and railroads. In effect, the old Indian country was now reduced to the southern area, in the present State of Oklahoma, where the Five Civilized Tribes still held their lands.

Certain of the tribes, especially the Delawares, ceded their lands with the stipulation that they should be offered for sale to the highest bidders and not at the minimum price of $1.25 an acre. A land office was set up and a land survey was begun. But before the date of legal entry speculators, squatters, and military officers rushed in to seize the choice locations, without regard either to the rights of the Indians or the laws of their country. The Indians could only nurse their resentment, for these remnants of once powerful tribes were now too weak to make effective resistance.

In the following years some rearrangement of tribal reservations was made by treaties with the Pawnee, Ponca, and Kansa Indians and with several tribes of the Sioux nation. At the end of the decade the Colorado gold rush caused uneasiness among some of the tribes through whose country the gold-seekers passed, but there were no serious disturbances.

The Indian Wars on the Great Plains

Such was the situation in Indian affairs on the Great Plains at the outbreak of the Civil War. During this struggle the positions of the Cherokees, Creeks, Choctaws, Chickasaws, and Seminoles—the Five Civilized Tribes—was especially difficult and pathetic. Situated west of Arkansas, these Indians were easily accessible to the Confederates, who demanded their allegiance. It was a cruel dilemma. If they resisted the Confederates they had reason to fear immediate military subjugation. On the other hand, if they yielded they could look forward to punishment later if the United States reestablished its authority. Chiefs and leaders, like the able, well-educated John Ross of the Cherokees, sought to maintain neutrality, but were obliged to submit to the Confederate forces which overran the territory. Large numbers of the tribesmen, however, remained loyal to the federal government. Thousands of them fled northward and received such protection and care as could be afforded them within the Northern lines. After the war was over these tribes suffered undeserved retribution. They were obliged to cede the western portions of their lands, and into this area were moved other tribes, some of which were indigenous to the plains, while others had previously been moved from east of the Mississippi to the Indian country west of Missouri.

To the northward the wild, powerful tribes displayed increasing uneasiness and by the close of the Civil War the entire plains area was aflame with Indian wars which continued for five years, with frequent outbreaks still later. In the North it was widely, and perhaps naturally, believed that this unrest among the tribes was fomented by agents of the Confederate government. There has never been produced sufficient evidence to substantiate this charge. As a matter of fact, there is ample explanation of the inflamed state of mind among the Indians, without seeking for a cause in Confederate instigation. The grievances which were the results of the treaties of 1851 have already been mentioned. More important to the Indians were the large number of emigrants pouring across their country, the stage lines, the railroad surveys and later the actual beginning of railroad building, and the rush of one hundred thousand gold-seekers to Colorado. In all these the Indians could not fail to see their approaching doom in white occupation. Already the buffalo, upon which their life depended, were being destroyed.

The tribes of the plains like the Sioux, the Cheyennes, and Arapahoes, the Kiowas and Comanches, were warlike and powerful. In one respect they were especially formidable: they possessed horses and rode them with a proficiency that has seldom if ever been excelled anywhere. Although there is no evidence of a general conspiracy or agreement, with one accord the plains tribes seem to have decided that the time had come to resist further encroachments and redress their grievances.

The first blow was struck by the Sioux in 1862 along the exposed frontier in southern Minnesota. After the treaty of 1851, as has been described, these Indians saw the money promised them for their land gobbled up by the traders, and their lands invaded by settlers before the treaty was ratified. Moreover, they were not permitted to enjoy all of their reserve along the Minnesota River. A portion of the tribesmen, known as the "farmer" faction, accepted the inevitable and settled down peacefully. The others, called the "blanket" faction, remained unreconciled and were a constant source of worry to the Indian agents. Small outlaw bands roamed the country and committed depredations on the settlers. One of these bands, led by the villainous Inkpaduta, attacked the little settlement at Spirit Lake in northwestern Iowa in March, 1857, and massacred thirty-two men, women, and children, and carried four women into captivity. Following this outrage there were several scares along the frontier, but no serious disturbance until August, 1862, when the Sioux, farmer and blanket Indians alike, under Little Crow perpetrated one of the bloodiest massacres in frontier history.

On August 7th there was a fracas in Meeker County, Minnesota, in which five white men were killed. Little Crow and other friendly Sioux, realizing that in the retribution that was sure to follow, innocent and guilty Indians would suffer alike at the hands of the frontiersmen, cast in their lot with the more reckless young braves. On the following day there began a reign of terror, which had its center in the settlements around New Ulm, but spread during the ensuing week along two hundred miles of frontier. Fort Ridgely on the Minnesota River was attacked by Little Crow and his warriors, but withstood the siege. Before the week was over the Indians had slaughtered and mutilated several hundred settlers. The number of dead was placed at 737 by contemporary officials. More recent figures have reduced it to 644 or 490, depending upon which authorities are accepted. In addition to those killed, several hundred women and children were carried into captivity. Nearly 270 were later recovered.

The punishment of the Sioux for this massacre was swift, severe, and undiscriminating. Upon receipt of the first report of the outbreak Governor Ramsey of Minnesota and the military authorities rushed aid to the stricken frontier. A small army under command of Henry H. Sibley pursued the Indians and defeated them in a series of battles early in September. Nearly two thousand Sioux, a large portion of whom had previously been friendly, were made prisoners, and a large number of white women and children were released from captivity. Later nearly four hundred of the Indians were placed on trial, and more than three hundred of them were sentenced to death for murder, rape and arson. President Lincoln pardoned all but thirty-eight, who were hanged on a single scaffold at Mankato late in December, 1862.

Although eastern sentiment approved Lincoln's order mitigating the severity of the punishment, the frontier clamored for revenge and for the extermination of the Sioux. General John Pope was transferred to the region. Under his command and that of General Alfred Sully, military operations were continued against the Sioux tribesmen during 1863, without any decisive result. The scene of principal interest now shifted to another region and to another massacre—this one committed by white militiamen.

After the treaties made at Fort Laramie and Fort Atkinson in 1851 and 1853, respectively, there was comparatively little trouble with the Indians of the Great Plains until the rush of gold-seekers to Colorado at the end of the decade. The

Cheyennes and the Arapahoes, whose territory lay between the Platte and Arkansas rivers, now saw their country crossed and invaded by hordes of white men who paid no heed to the rights of the native occupants. Mining operations were begun and towns were laid out in violation of the treaty rights of the Indians. Even more important was the effect of this movement in driving out the wild game upon which the Indians depended. On account of increasing sullenness on the part of the tribes, it was deemed advisable to remove them from the region of greatest friction. Accordingly, the Cheyennes and the Arapahoes were summoned to a council at Fort Wise, on the site of Bent's old fort on the Arkansas River. Here in a treaty dated February 18, 1861, these two tribes relinquished all their former extensive territory except a relatively small reserve in southeastern Colorado along the southwest bank of Sand Creek. Their new agency was located at Fort Lyon at the junction of Sand Creek and the Arkansas.

As a matter of fact, the treaty signed by their chiefs found little favor among the Cheyennes and Arapahoes. The new reserve was dry and desolate and the Indians continued to wander about the plains as they had always done. They viewed with growing alarm and resentment the rapidly increasing traffic by stage-coach and wagon freighters and the number of settlers and gold-seekers pouring westward. There were depredations on both sides, and the situation grew more and more tense. Finally, in the summer of 1864 Ben Holladay's stage line was attacked along almost its entire length, and service was completely disrupted. Freight traffic was harassed, and isolated settlers were murdered or driven away.

The Cheyennes and Arapahoes had already been ordered to gather on their reserve in the vicinity of Fort Lyon. During the summer they paid little attention to this order, or to the warning that those who did not display their friendship by obeying the order would be punished. As winter approached, however, they began to drift into Fort Lyon, with protestations of friendship and a desire for peace. This attitude was not acceptable to the people of Denver and Colorado, who demanded the punishment of the Indians for their depredations of the preceding summer. After some preliminary and inconclusive negotiations, two regiments of Colorado militia, commanded by Colonel J. M. Chivington, marched toward Fort Lyon. Instead of rounding up and chastising the leaders and the hostile warriors, the troops, at daybreak on November 29th, fell without warning upon a camp on Sand Creek occupied mainly by women and children. The massacre that ensued was as brutal and barbarous as any ever perpetrated by the Indians. Except on the frontier Chivington's "victory" was regarded with horror throughout the nation, by civilians and military men alike. In 1865 Congress made an appropriation for reparations to the widows and orphans of those who had been killed.

Nevertheless, the Cheyennes and Arapahoes were crushed temporarily by the massacre. Many of them fled northward to the western Sioux. In 1865 a number of the chiefs signed a treaty relinquishing the Sand Creek reserve, in return for territory further east. This treaty was not ratified by the United States Senate and as a consequence these tribes remained without a home for several years. Between 1865 and 1869 they made numerous attacks on settlers and transportation lines, and in 1868, particularly, they occupied the attention of the army in an arduous campaign. They were eventually placed on lands in the western part of the Indian Territory, ceded by the Five Civilized Tribes.

In the meantime there was war on the northern plains. During the decade following the Fort Laramie treaty of 1851 relations with the western Sioux, or northern Sioux as they were sometimes called, were generally peaceful. In 1855 there was a brief campaign under General Harney, following a disturbance caused by the alleged theft by the Indians of a cow from a Mormon emigrant party. The western Sioux tribes became more restless, however, after the Minnesota uprising and the arrival of refugee Sioux from that region, and especially after the Sand Creek massacre, when numbers of Cheyennes and Arapahoes came north. In 1865 the Sioux were assembled for a council at Fort Sully on the Missouri. A treaty of peace was signed and once more the signatory chiefs agreed to permit the laying out of roads through their country.

The particular purpose of this treaty was to clear the way for the establishment of what was called the Powder River Road or the Bozeman Trail, connecting the Oregon-California road at a point west of Fort Laramie with the mining districts in western Montana. Shortly after the making of the treaty Colonel Henry B. Carrington was ordered to erect and garrison forts for the protection of the new road. A site was selected for Fort Phil Kearney on Piney Creek, a tributary of Powder River; Fort C. F. Smith was located ninety miles further north on the Big Horn; and construction work began.

The Sioux chiefs who signed the treaty of Fort Sully by no means represented the wishes of the great majority of their brother tribesmen. The proposed road ran through some of their best hunting-grounds and its opening and use would drive away the plentiful game. The great leader of these Sioux was Red Cloud. He had not been present at the Fort Sully conference in 1865. In 1866 he broke up another council held at Fort Laramie. Almost immediately, at the head of a formidable body of Indians he began a series of attacks on the partially completed Fort Phil Kearney, which kept the garrison constantly on guard. More than 150 men were killed near the fort during the last five months of 1866.

Then on December 21st of that year occurred the so-called Fetterman massacre. In the morning a wood train, getting out logs for the fort, signalled that it was being attacked. Carrington organized a relief party of eighty-one officers and men under Captain W. J. Fetterman and despatched them to the scene of disturbance, with strict orders not to pursue the Indians after giving protection to the wood train. These orders were disobeyed. The troop disappeared over a ridge and not a member of it was again seen alive. The impetuous Fetterman led his men into an ambush and they were all slain by the Indians who fell upon them in vastly overwhelming numbers.

News of this disaster shocked the nation. Reinforcements were immediately rushed to Fort Phil Kearney. In the summer of 1867 another wagon train was attacked—this time with different results. Barricading themselves behind dismounted wagon boxes, and barrels and bags of supplies, the party consisting of not more than thirty-two men under Captain James Powell successfully withstood the repeated attacks of a large body of Indians, probably not less than one thousand in number, among whom were some of the ablest Sioux warriors, including Red Cloud himself.   Captain Powell estimated that 180 of the redskins were killed or wounded.   This surprising reversal was a great blow to the spirits of the Sioux and to the prestige of Red Cloud.   He persisted in his hostility, however, and in 1868 he had his reward.   In that year there was signed a treaty in which the United States agreed that "the country north of the North Platte River and east of the summits of the Big Horn Mountains shall be held and considered to be unceded Indian territory."   Even more gratifying to the Indians was the agreement that the hated forts and the Bozeman Trail should be abandoned.   In August the garrison of Fort Phil Kearney hauled down the flag and marched away.   Scarcely had they gone when the jubilant Indians applied the torch to the stockade.

For eight years there was peace with the Sioux of the plains and the Cheyennes, many of whom were now living among them.   Before the end of this period, however, the stage was being prepared for another, and the last important, Sioux war.   In 1874 there came authentic news of the discovery of gold in the Black Hills, and in the following year there was a rush to that region.   Once more there was utter disregard of treaties and of the rights of the Indians.   It is true that the troops endeavored to keep the gold-seekers out of the Black Hills, and efforts were made to purchase the region from the Indians, but to no avail.   Furthermore, the Sioux were aroused by well-confirmed mismanagement and dishonesty at the Red Cloud Agency.   Under the leadership of Sitting Bull and Crazy Horse, they became increasingly belligerent—so much so that late in 1875 they were ordered to gather around the agency under penalty of being regarded as hostile and dealt with accordingly.

The Indians were both unable and disinclined to obey these orders.   Three military expeditions were therefore sent against them from different directions during the spring of 1876.   One army under General George Crook fought a desperate and inconclusive battle with them on the banks of the Rosebud. On June 25th occurred the most famous event of the war. On that day General George A. Custer and his entire command of more than two hundred men were totally annihilated in a battle against greatly superior odds on the Little Big Horn. Only a friendly Indian scout escaped to tell the story of the tragedy. Out of the controversy, that has raged ever since, concerning the causes of this disaster there emerges the rather commonly accepted belief that it was due to the fact that Custer, smarting at the time under censure from Washington, yielded to a strain of recklessness in his bravery and rushed into a situation which a more cautious officer would have avoided.

It was a great day for the Sioux, but their rejoicing was short-lived. Within a few months they were completely humbled by the army under General Nelson A. Miles. Crazy Horse was captured, but Sitting Bull and a small band escaped across the Canadian border. Here they remained for several years, a source of annoyance to the Canadian authorities. In 1881 Sitting Bull returned to the United States and surrendered. For two years he was held a prisoner, and then was allowed to return to his old home near the Standing Rock Agency in what is now South Dakota. In 1889 the Sioux became affected by the craze of an Indian Messiah, which spread throughout all the western tribes. The ritualistic Ghost Dance was revived and the religious frenzy of the Indians assumed proportions that aroused fears of an outbreak. The army took charge in 1890 and it was determined that Sitting Bull must be taken prisoner. In the mêlée that accompanied his arrest the noted chief was killed. A few weeks later occurred the so-called battle of Wounded Knee, which was in reality little more than a massacre of more than two hundred Indians, mostly women and children, by a greatly superior force of soldiers armed with rapid-fire guns. The Sioux wars, and the Indian wars of the United States were thus brought to a close.

It was on the Great Plains that the Indians made their most formidable and determined stand against the white race. It is not to be supposed, however, that the tribes living further west yielded their homes and hunting-grounds without a struggle. The Indian wars in the early history of the Pacific northwest have already been mentioned. In the mining regions, both in California and in the Rocky Mountains, there was conflict between the miners and the natives. During the decade of the seventies there were two disturbances that attracted widespread interest.

The first of these was the Modoc War along the boundary between California and Oregon, in the region of Tule Lake and Lower Klamath Lake. The Modocs were long known as troublesome, both by settlers passing through their country and by neighboring Indian tribes. They had been assigned to a reservation, but a portion of the tribe, under Captain Jack, as he was generally called, continued to roam about their old haunts around Tule Lake, occasionally harassing the settlers. In 1872 the Indian agent determined that there would be no peace until Captain Jack and a few other leaders of the small band were arrested and sent to some distant reservation. Troops from Fort Klamath proceeded to the Indian camp, but Captain Jack and his followers resisted arrest. There was a brief skirmish, with casualties on both sides, and the Indians fled to the lava beds where, they boasted, the little band of scarcely more than fifty warriors could withstand a thousand soldiers.

This was no idle boast. General E. R. S. Canby, a veteran of the Mexican War and the Civil War and an experienced Indian fighter, led the small army which entered the lava beds early in 1873. "I have never before encountered an enemy, civilized or savage," he wrote, "occupying a position of such great natural strength as the Modoc stronghold, nor have I ever seen troops engage a better-armed or more skillful foe." After some fighting, the difficulties proved so great that the troops withdrew to await reinforcements, including artillery. Before the campaign was resumed orders came to attempt a peace conference. Captain Jack delayed the meeting for nearly two months, and then, although professing a desire for peace, he and his companions treacherously murdered General Canby and one of the peace commissioners. The war against the Modocs was now prosecuted in deadly earnest. Finally the Indians were rounded up and captured. Captain Jack and three of his associates were hanged, and the remainder of the tribe were removed to the Indian Territory.

Four years after the defeat of the Modocs there occurred the last important Indian war in the Northwest, and one of the most remarkable displays of Indian generalship in the entire history of warfare between the races. Chief Joseph and a party of not more than three hundred Nez Percé warriors, accompanied by their women and children and encumbered by baggage, conducted a masterful flight for more than 1300 miles through an unknown country, with several thousand troops chasing them or facing them, and almost escaped to safety in Canada.

The Nez Percés had their habitat in the valley of the Snake River when the Lewis and Clark expedition came in contact with them. Despite the fact that they were a strong and virile tribe, they maintained friendly relations with the whites, even during the early Indian wars in the Oregon country. In 1855 by treaty they ceded a considerable portion of their lands. The government was lax in providing the annuities promised in this treaty, but still there was no trouble until the gold discoveries were made in northern Idaho and Lewiston was founded. In 1863 a new treaty was signed by some of the chiefs, by which they agreed to accept and live on the Lapwai Reservation in Idaho. A considerable portion of the tribe, of which Chief Joseph, son of an older chieftain by the same name, was the outstanding leader, refused to consider themselves bound by this treaty. In this attitude they were entirely in accord with Indian practice and custom. Even a majority vote among the Indians was not considered as placing any obligations on the minority which they did not choose to observe. Consequently the non-signatory Nez Percés continued to live outside the Lapwai Reservation in their favorite haunts in their ancient hunting-grounds. The region favored by Chief Joseph and his followers was the Wallowa country in northeastern Oregon. Here they spent most of their time, and in 1873 an executive order of President Grant made it a reserve for them. They did not confine themselves entirely to the region, however, and in 1875 the order was revoked.

Finally, in 1877, it was decided that the Nez Percés must remove to the Lapwai Reservation. Troops under General O. O. Howard went to the Wallowa country and the Indians sullenly moved out. Chief Joseph resented the order, but made efforts to preserve peace which were rendered unavailing by the actions of some of his young and impetuous braves. To revenge a recent murder of one of the Indians, a few of the braves killed a number of settlers. War now seemed the only choice. Chief Joseph would have preferred to fight it out in their old home land, but most of the other chiefs decided otherwise. Yielding to their counsel he began a flight, lasting over a period of seventy-five days, that furnished his opponents with valuable lessons in strategy. Desperate battles, with the advantage on the side of the Indians, were fought before the flight began. Then in the succeeding weeks they broke their own trail over the difficult Lolo Pass, up the Bitter Root Valley, across Yellowstone Park, eastward nearly to the Big Horn River, then northward to a point east of the Bear Paw Mountains about thirty miles from the Canadian boundary.

Time after time Chief Joseph tricked his enemies by creating a diversion in their front and getting his main body around their flank. General O. O. Howard was pushing ahead as rapidly as possible in his rear and troops from every fort in Montana were sent against him. Whenever a pitched battle could not be avoided, the Indian leader sent the women and children ahead and stood his ground, directing his steadily dwindling band of warriors with a skill that challenged the admiration of the opposing commanders; and each time getting away undefeated. Even the Montana ranchers bore no ill-will toward these Indians, who obeyed all the rules of civilized warfare, refraining from depredations and even paying for supplies and animals which they secured. Then, early in October, the weakened, weary band reached a point where they could go no further without rest, even though Canada was scarcely more than a day's ride head of them. They might still have eluded their pursuers from the west, but General Nelson A. Miles with a fresh army had come up from the southeast. Fighting till all hope was gone, Chief Joseph surrendered on October 4th. "I am tired of fighting," he said. "Our chiefs are all killed. . . . The little children are freezing to death. My people, some of them, have run away to the hills and have no blankets, no food. No one knows where they are,—perhaps freezing to death. . . . My heart is sick and sad. From where the sun now stands I will fight no more forever."

The remnants of the Nez Percé band were taken to a reservation in Kansas, where they pined for their old homes. It is pleasant to record that they were permitted to return to the northwest in 1885, when they were placed on the Colville Reservation in northeastern Washington. There Chief Joseph lived the remainder of his years, honored by white men and red men alike, until his death in 1904.

Far to the southward Indian wars also raged during the seventies, on the plains of Texas and in New Mexico and Arizona. The most extensive of these conflicts was the Red River Indian War of 1874-5, with the Comanches, Kiowas, Cheyennes, Arapahoes, and other tribes who refused to be confined to their reservations in the Indian Territory. Forty-six companies of cavalry and infantry were sent against the hostiles and many pitched battles were fought before peace was restored. All through this decade and far into the next the Apaches, Navahos, Utes, and other tribes of New Mexico and Arizona, led by Victorio, Geronimo and other chiefs, kept the settlements in turmoil, and taxed the army to the utmost before they were finally subdued.

THE INDIAN AGENCY SYSTEM

Warfare is the phase of Indian affairs which has received the most attention from first to last. One who would understand our relations with the race which we have displaced must also study the efforts made by the government to aid the

Indians along the "white man's road" toward civilization. It
must be said that these efforts were made in all sincerity. If
in their accomplishments they often fell far short of the
intended purposes, the result was due to faulty co-ordination,
mistaken views of the needs of a successful policy, and to the
weaknesses of human nature which caused men in important
positions to use them for private gain rather than Indian
welfare.

The system of Indian superintendencies and agencies was
worked out gradually in the years following the establishment
of the national government. The Indian agents, who lived
among the tribes, were to be the eyes and ears of the government, to keep the government informed regarding the condition and attitudes of their charges. They were also the
advisers and instructors of the tribes to which they were
assigned. In 1832 the office of Commissioner of Indian Affairs
was created by Congress. Down to 1849 all of these officials
were attached to the War Department. In that year the
Indian Office, with all its subordinate superintendents and
agents, was transferred to the newly established Department
of the Interior. By the time this change was made the most
important problems of the Indian administration were confined to the Far West. To this period may be traced the
beginnings of the reservation policy, which resulted in the consolidation and segregation of the tribes on specified tracts of
land around which the settlements flowed.

The tasks of the Indian agents were extremely difficult at
best. Some of the agency districts were very large, like that
of the Upper Platte where Thomas S. Twiss presided over an
area equal to that of the New England States, New York,
and New Jersey combined. As has been indicated, there was
frequent conflict of authority and opinion between the agents
and the military officers. Unscrupulous traders were a constant cause of complaint on the part of agents who had the
best interests of the Indians at heart. The aggressiveness of
settlers passing through, or encroaching on, the Indian country,
made it increasingly difficult for the agents to hold their
charges in check. Even in periods of great unrest, however,
the Indian agents were seldom molested by the tribesmen.

While many of the agents were men of ability and honesty who endeavored faithfully to promote the welfare of the Indians, there were too many others of whom this can not be said. In 1856 Congress appropriated more than $240,000 to cover drafts made by California agents without legal authority, supposedly in return for beef and flour, although there was no satisfactory evidence that the Indians had received these supplies. In the period following the Civil War there were exposures of numerous instances in which agents connived with traders in selling annuity goods, sharing the profits, and covering up the theft by perjured vouchers. There is no way of knowing how much graft and corruption escaped detection. Horace Greeley is said at one time to have asked, pointedly, how it was that an Indian agent on a salary of $1500 a year could save $40,000 in four years. The opportunities for personal gain were too great to be resisted by men whose appointments in many cases, were made solely in accordance with the code of the spoils system. "Lo, the poor Indian agent!" wrote an Indian editor, "Who shall lighten his burdens, who shall make his name honorable, and who shall give him understanding and clear the way that he may work honestly, intelligently, and to good purpose whether he wills it or not?"

Early in Grant's administration the policy of appointing army officers as Indian agents was inaugurated. It was shortly abandoned, and a plan of allowing various religious organizations to nominate agents was adopted. This was the so-called "Quaker policy" which received much ridicule by advocates of stern measures against the Indians. The plan was purely administrative in nature and passed out of use. It was soon discovered that the qualities that made a man a good missionary did not necessarily insure his success as an Indian agent. In general it can be said that government regulations in the later years removed some of the possibilities of abuse, salaries were made more adequate, and the tone of the service was improved.

Indian education is an aspect of the work of the Indian Bureau which might well receive considerable attention if space permitted. Reservation day schools and agency boarding schools, with their respective advantages and disadvantages, were early inaugurated. Their efficiency was conditioned by the general incompetence of the teachers, especially until appointments were removed from the realm of political spoils and placed under civil service regulations. Non-residence boarding schools have provided the best educational facilities for the Indians since their establishment, following the opening in 1879 of the first institution of this nature at Carlisle, Pennsylvania.

In 1871 the practice of making formal treaties with the Indians was abandoned. It does not appear that this change of policy was brought about by a recognition of the absurdity of the long-continued pretense of treating with the tribes as independent nations, or by a realization of the Indians' incapacity to understand the binding nature of treaties. Rather the abandonment of treaty-making seems to have been the result of a determination of the lower house of Congress to have some voice in the making of agreements which entailed large appropriations of money. As a matter of fact, the change made little real difference in Indian relations. After 1871 "agreements" took the place of treaties, and these "agreements" required the approval of both houses of Congress, instead of merely the consent of the Senate as in the case of the treaties previously made.

When the wars were over and the Indians had all been gathered on reservations it at last became possible to adopt a policy more in harmony with the realities of the situation, and better adapted to the needs of a race which must perforce adapt itself to a new type of existence. The Dawes Act of 1887 and the Burke Act of 1906 provided for individual allotment of lands to the Indians, and opened the way to the full enjoyment of citizenship granted by law in 1924. Thus, after three centuries of misunderstanding, hatred and conflict, the remnants of the Indian race were merged with the citizenry of their conquerors.

CHAPTER XXXVI

CATTLE KINGS AND LAND-GRABBERS

AMERICAN settlements were well established on the Pacific coast before the Civil War. By the close of that struggle gold and silver mining in the Rocky Mountains had furnished the basis of permanent occupation of that region. In Kansas and Nebraska settlers had begun their march up the slope of the high plains. But between this fringe of settlements and the Rocky Mountains there still stretched the country once called the great American desert—the Great Plains. Hundreds of thousands of settlers and gold-seekers had crossed this region. Stage lines and later railroads ran through it. Military posts were scattered over it. The desert myth had been disspelled. But still the Great Plains were unoccupied by white men. Here was the last American frontier. At the close of the Civil War it was the land of the Indians, whose valiant resistance to displacement was outlined in the preceding chapter. It was also the grazing-ground of vast herds of buffalo.

THE DESTRUCTION OF THE BUFFALO

Any effort to indicate the number of buffaloes on the plains must, of course, be based upon figures that are only estimates. As late as 1870 the number was placed at seven million, after the slaughter had already begun. The wagon and stage traffic by the central route and the building of the Union Pacific had the effect of dividing the animals into two main herds. Another estimate describes the northern herd as including five million buffaloes, and the southern a somewhat smaller number scattered over a larger territory. This does not mean that the bison all herded together in either case; but they did graze and travel in enormous herds. One sportsman told of traveling for more than one hundred miles through an almost continuous herd.   General Sheridan stated that he rode for three days through a single herd.   Trains were occasionally delayed for hours to allow herds to cross the track.   A traveler described a herd which, according to his estimate, covered an area thirty by seventy miles in extent.

By 1885 these great herds had been almost entirely destroyed by the buffalo-hunters.   Exploring parties, fur traders, soldiers and emigrants killed buffaloes for food and hides, and hunters like "Buffalo Bill" Cody were employed by the railroad construction companies to supply the gangs with meat.   But slaughter of these animals on a large scale seems to have begun early in the seventies.   Buffalo-hunting was considered a great sport, and thousands of the animals were killed just for the fun of it.   The greatest havoc, however, was wrought by regularly organized companies and by individuals who sought hides to sell in a profitable eastern market as buffalo robes.   The southern herd was the first to go.   It is estimated that three railroads carried more than one and one-third million buffalo hides from the southern plains in the three years from 1872 to 1874, inclusive.   The larger northern herd was attacked in the next decade and by 1885 it was practically annihilated.   In ensuing years a profitable activity was found in picking up buffalo bones and shipping them to be used in making phosphates for fertilizer and carbon for sugar refineries.   Trainloads of bones moved eastward. There is mention of one pile of buffalo bones twelve feet high and one-half mile long.

There is a close relationship between the slaughter of the buffaloes and the solution of the Indian problem.   The Indians of the plains were largely dependent upon the buffalo for food, clothing, and other necessities.   The killing of these animals by the whites was one of the causes of fear and hatred on the part of the tribesmen.   The organized slaughter during the seventies brought on warfare, but the destruction continued.   The government not only did nothing to stop this wanton exploitation, but indirectly encouraged it, for it made the Indians easier to control.   As long as there were buffalo herds to be chased over the plains it was next to impossible to keep the Indians on the reservations to which they were

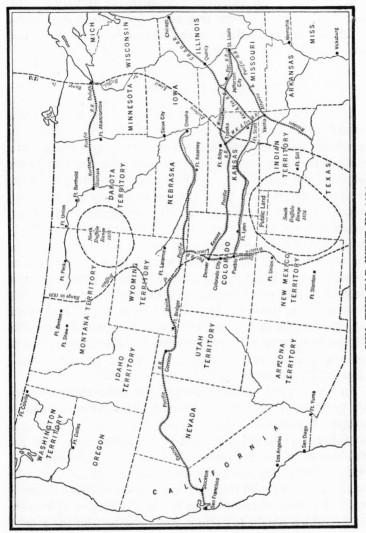

XIV. THE FAR WEST IN 1876

(Based on map in Richard I. Dodge, *The Plains of the Great West*, 1877.)

assigned. When the buffaloes were gone the Indians became more docile, for they were dependent upon the rations issued at the agencies, and were more inclined to settle down and learn the white man's ways.

THE RANGE CATTLE INDUSTRY

Before the destruction of the buffaloes was completed the country which had for so long resounded to the thunder of their hoofs was the scene of the development of a range cattle industry that constitutes one of the romantic chapters in the history of the Far West. The first white men really to utilize the Great Plains were the cattlemen and especially the cow-boys, whose fame and deeds still live in frontier celebrations, motion pictures, and western fiction. The frontier had nearly always had a pastoral fringe as it moved westward. But the cow country of the Great Plains was no mere fringe. It was a huge area in which the range cattle industry grew to gigantic proportions with every intention on the part of its participants of maintaining permanency. Possibly it would have been well, in the light of later experience, if a region so admirably adapted to grazing, and on the whole so imperfectly suited to farming, could have been reserved under proper control, primarily as a cattleman's country.

In addition to its intrinsic interest, the range cattle industry had profound effects in the country at large and even in Europe. It produced a great supply of much better beef than the nation had before known and, in conjunction with the introduction of the refrigerator car and the development of great packing plants, made the Americans a beef-eating people. Eastern farmers found themselves unable to meet the competition. The same situation prevailed in the nations of western Europe, which sought to exclude American beef on the ground that it was diseased. This check to our exports in turn led to the establishment in this country of the Bureau of Animal Husbandry and the machinery for the inspection of beef and other food products.

The Cattle Industry in Texas

The range cattle industry on the high plains had its origin in two widely separated areas—Texas and the Wyoming and western Nebraska country along the overland trail to Oregon and California. Until after the Civil War the cattle business in each section developed independently. Then, as the northern range area was extended into Colorado and Montana and later into Dakota, cattle to stock these ranges were brought from Texas by means of the long drive across the intervening plains. Various factors operated to break this connection after a few years, and eventually the cattlemen of the two regions found that their interests were not identical in all respects.

Cattle-raising in Texas goes back to an early period when the Spanish brought their long-horned cattle into the southern border of the province. When the American settlers came, after the Mexican revolution, they brought some cattle with them. These, running at large on the range, mixed with the Spanish cattle. By the time the Texans won their independence many of them possessed fairly large herds of the distinctive, long-horned Texas cattle. The breed was not especially good for beef, nor did it produce good milk cows, but it was tough and sturdy. "It is the domestic animal run wild," wrote Colonel Richard I. Dodge, "changed in some of his habits and characteristics by many generations of freedom and self-care." The country was admirably suited to the raising of cattle, which could safely run at large the year round.

The greatest problem of the early Texas cattleman was to get his animals to market. In 1842 the first herd was driven to New Orleans, which for several years was the principal market. Many cattle were driven to Shreveport and sent down to New Orleans on steamboats. Shipments were also made from Galveston and other gulf ports to New Orleans, Mobile and Cuba. The first authenticated northern drive of Texas cattle came in 1846 when Edward Piper drove one thousand head to Ohio. In the ensuing years there was a considerable movement of cattle northward, one herd reaching Chicago in 1856. The best overland route to northern markets was through Missouri, and this route was soon closed by irate farmers, who were aroused by the appearance of Texas fever among their cattle after the passage of the southern herds. In the meantime, the number of cattle in Texas increased enormously. It was estimated at more than three and one-half million in 1860. During the Civil War the business languished, although the herds probably did not suffer seriously from lack of attention.

When the Texans returned after the war they were busy for a time rounding up their herds and settling questions arising out of the large number of unbranded animals. Then again they turned their thoughts toward getting to northern markets. At the same time northern buyers arrived seeking Texas cattle. It is estimated that 260,000 head of cattle started north in 1866 toward the upper Mississippi Valley. The experiment resulted so disastrously that it was not repeated on any large scale the following year. The drivers lacked experience in handling cattle on a long trail, and the country was new to many of them. There were rain storms and swollen streams. The Indians caused stampedes and other delays, and cattle-thieves and outlaws were troublesome. To climax the difficulties, armed bands of farmers, remembering the disease spread by the earlier drives, met the herds in Kansas and Missouri and assaulted and even killed some of the drivers. Many turned back, some selling their cattle for what they could get. Others got through by round-about routes. In 1867 and 1868 many cattle were shipped by steamboat down the Red River and up the Mississippi and Ohio. But when these cattle were placed on farms, chiefly in Illinois, they spread Texas fever among the other cattle. There was a great outcry and this movement was practically brought to a close.

In 1867, however, a new day dawned for the Texas cattlemen. In that year Joseph G. McCoy of Illinois, who was much interested in Texas cattle, decided to find a point on one of the railroads pushing westward from the Missouri to which the cattle could be driven and from which they could be transported by rail to eastern markets. After some investigation he chose the little station of Abilene on the Kansas Pacific Railroad—a place which he described as "consisting of about one dozen log huts, low, small, rude affairs, four-fifths of which were covered with dirt for roofing; indeed, but one shingle roof could be seen in the whole city." McCoy invested money, brought in laborers and materials, and soon had yards and loading-chutes for cattle. He then sent a messenger south to intercept and bring the good news to any drovers who might be on the trail with their herds. It was good news, indeed, to the drovers whom the messenger encountered or overtook. Before the end of the year about 35,000 Texas cattle reached Abilene. The first shipment to Chicago early in September, 1867, was made the occasion for a joyous celebration.

Abilene was the first of a series of "cow towns" in Kansas, such as Wichita, Ellsworth, Dodge City, Ellis and Caldwell, and they all were the precursors of similar towns on the northern railroads. In their early years they resembled, for wildness and general disorder, the mining towns and the "hells on wheels" of the railroad builders. At these places buyers waited for the cattle or they rushed down the trails to meet the herds. It is stated that nearly a million and a half head of Texas cattle reached Abilene over the famous Chisholm Trail during the five years after its opening as a "cow town" by Joseph G. McCoy. The number of cattle reaching all the Kansas shipping points between 1867 and 1880 is said to have been nearly four million.

THE CATTLE INDUSTRY ON THE NORTHERN PLAINS

The cattle industry on the northern plains had its beginning in the period of the early migrations to Oregon and California. Men who had been engaged in the fur trade came down to the trail, operated ferries, supplied forage, and sold merchandise to the emigrants. They also found the travelers ready to exchange two of their worn-out, footsore work steers for one fresh animal. The former could be placed on the range, fattened, and traded the next year to other emigrants. In this way herds of considerable size were developed. By moving the cattle about there was an abundance of forage the

year round even during the winter. The freight-hauling companies also discovered that they could winter their oxen on the
plains. It is said that Russell, Majors and Waddell wintered
fifteen thousand oxen in 1857-1858 on the plains south of the
trail.

Markets for cattle were the great need. These were furnished first by the miners in the Rocky Mountains. The
Colorado gold rush opened up a profitable market for the
early "cattle kings" like John W. Iliff, who had a herd that
grazed a large area along the South Platte River. The gold
discoveries in western Montana led to the rapid growth of
cattle-raising in that section. Another stimulus was given by
government contracts to supply beef for the garrisons of newly
established forts. Then the feeding of construction crews of
the Union Pacific Railroad opened an additional outlet. Of
far greater importance, however, was the service of the railroads in providing transportation to eastern markets. By 1870
the range cattle industry on the northern plains was on the
verge of a great expansion that extended over a period of
fifteen years.

A large part of the cattle to stock the northern ranges
were brought up from Texas. As the Union Pacific was completed across the plains many of the Texans found it profitable
to drive their cattle northward to shipping points on this road.
The cattle could be fattened on the grass of the plains as they
moved northward, and arrive in better condition along the
Union Pacific than if they had been shipped from points
further south. Olgallala, Sidney, Schuyler, and other places
in Nebraska became "cow towns." Cheyenne soon forgot its
rail-end origin and became the great center of the cattle industry in Wyoming and there were other shipping points in that
Territory. To these towns, like Olgallala and Schuyler, came
the northern buyers to purchase Texas cattle. More often
they went down the trail to meet the herds and drive them
to their ranges in Colorado, Wyoming, and Montana. Thus
originated the "long drive" which was one of the picturesque
features of the range cattle industry.

It is not possible here to trace the great growth of the
cattle business on the northern plains during the seventies.

The range in Wyoming and eastern Montana was limited by the fact that much of the country still belonged to the Indians. The cattlemen made numerous complaints because the government seemed unable or unwilling to curb the cattle-stealing raids of the Indians.

Boom Days and the Decline in the Range Cattle Industry

The decade of the eighties was the great boom period in the range cattle industry. The earlier connection between the cattleman of the northern plains and those of Texas was by this time considerably modified. In the first place, the long drive became increasingly difficult. The legislature of Kansas forbade the driving of Texas cattle across that State, except in the winter when the drive was impracticable, because of the occurrence of Texas fever after the herds had passed. Farmers, also, were spreading westward in Kansas, thus breaking up the open range. It was necessary, therefore, for the trail of the long drive to bend far to the west and pass through eastern Colorado. Railroads entering Texas made it more and more possible and profitable to fatten cattle on the southern plains and ship them directly to eastern markets. The northern cattlemen began to secure an increasing number of "pilgrims," or young breeding stock, from the States of the upper Mississippi Valley.

The basic interests of the cattlemen on the northern plains and in Texas remained the same. For example, in both sections railroad rates were the subject of much concern and many complaints. But in some respects the objectives of the owners in the two sections diverged. The Texans were not unmindful of the northern market, and they bent their efforts, unsuccessfully, to secure the establishment by Congress of a national quarantined cattle trail through the public domain. The northerners, on the other hand, became advocates of the adoption of a plan, equally fruitless, for the leasing of the public lands for grazing purposes.

In many respects the cattle boom of the eighties was most notable on the northern plains—in Wyoming, Montana, and Dakota. The concentration of the Indians and the opening of

Indian lands greatly extended the range. The Northern Pacific Railroad was built across Montana and the Union Pacific constructed a line northward from Corinne. Miles City and Glendive became great shipping points and centers of the cattle industry of eastern Montana.

Cattle-raising became the great bonanza of the period. Livestock journals, periodicals, and newspapers carried stories and reports describing the great profits to be made in the business. It was shown how a calf worth five dollars could be matured at very little cost on the grass of the public domain, and sold at the end of four years for forty or fifty dollars. An investment of $5,000, it was said, could be made to yield a net gain of $40,000 or $50,000 in four years. There were reports of companies that declared dividends ranging from twenty-five to forty per cent annually. It is small wonder, then, that capital was invested in the industry by the millions. Most of this capital came from the eastern part of this country, but much of it also came from abroad, especially from England and Scotland. In the year 1883 twenty companies, with individual capitalization of from ten thousand up to three million and a total of twelve million dollars, were incorporated in Wyoming alone. The Union Cattle Company and the Swan Land and Cattle Company each had an initial capitalization of three million dollars. The latter was formed by the merger of three smaller companies, with a total of more than 100,000 head of cattle and control of a range extending over an area one hundred miles by more than fifty miles in extent. These are only examples of what was transpiring throughout the northern cattle country.

Until the region became crowded with cattle the process of gaining control of a range was very simple. It was only necessary to secure title to the available water supply of a given section in order to render the adjacent public land, for many miles around, as available for exclusive grazing as if it had been actually owned. This could be done under the homestead, preemption and other land laws, either legitimately or fraudulently, by having cowboys and other employees take out claims. At the location of the main water supply were to be found the headquarters of the companies, the ranch homes, corrals, hay-land and pastures for the horses. The larger companies owned many water sites scattered over a large area.

In Texas and the adjacent region the development of the cattle industry paralleled that on the northern range during the boom period. Capital rushed in, and huge ranches were established. One of these was the famous X I T ranch, said for a time to be the largest enterprise of its kind in the world. The proprietors leased from the State of Texas more than three million acres in the panhandle, and at one time owned as many as 160,000 head of cattle. The Matador Land and Cattle Company, Limited, drew its original capital of $2,500,000 from Scotland. In addition to large holdings in Texas, this company later opened great ranches in Montana and Dakota. In the Indian Territory the cattlemen raised large herds on lands leased from the Indians until this practice was forbidden in 1885 by executive order of President Cleveland.

The middle of the decade of the eighties may be said to mark the high point of cattle-raising, both in the north and in the south, as an industry based primarily upon the use of the open range. Gradually the cattle companies began to acquire and extend the area of private ranches. Several causes contributed to this movement. The ranges became overstocked and as a result not only did grass become exhausted, but the control of grazing areas became increasingly difficult. Many cattlemen found it more economical and productive of better cattle to raise hay and feed the stock through the winter. In many sections the entry of farmers broke up the ranges and forced the stockmen to acquire title in self-defense, as did also the widespread opposition to the monopolization of the public domain by a relatively few owners of cattle. The process of transformation in the nature of the cattle business, already under way for these and other reasons, was hastened by a series of disasters.

On the southern plains the winter of 1885-1886 was unusually severe and a great number of cattle died. The presidential order forbidding leasing of Indian lands was a severe blow. It was soon followed by another, perhaps even more disrupting, directing that all fences on the public domain should be removed. It was on the northern plains, however, that the greatest catastrophe occurred. The winter of 1886-1887 was one long series of terrific blizzards, with intense cold and deep snow. For weeks at a time the cattlemen were confined to the ranch houses, wholly unable to do anything for their starving, freezing cattle. When warmer weather came at last and the snow melted, the full extent of the disaster was learned. Coulees were filled with the carcasses of cattle, streams were choked by them, and the pitiful remnants of large herds wandered about gaunt and emaciated. Losses of as high as eighty per cent were not uncommon. Even some of the largest cattle companies, like the Swan Land and Cattle Company, were ruined.

For a time it was feared that the cattle business could not recover from this blow. The disaster certainly furnished an effective lesson as to the great risks run in wintering cattle on the open plains. The industry did recover, but privately-owned ranches rapidly supplanted the open range. The story of the later developments deals with a period beyond the scope of this volume.

ORGANIZATIONS OF CATTLEMEN

Wherever the range cattle industry developed, organizations of cattlemen soon became a necessity. In many respects it was in the northern plains area that these organizations became most active and powerful. There were numerous cattlemen's associations in Nebraska, Colorado, Montana, and Dakota. In these Territories, however, other interests, such as mining in Colorado and Montana and farming in Nebraska and Dakota, offered effective competition to the cattlemen. Wyoming, on the other hand, was preeminently a cattle empire. The Wyoming Stock Growers' Association, organized in 1873, soon became, and long continued to be, the dominating influence in that Territory and State.

The causes leading to the establishment of these associations are to be found in the need of mutual protection on the part of the owners of cattle. As soon as a given region became crowded with cattle, the problem of the control of the range became acute. There was necessity for agreements and rules governing the alternation of summer and winter grazing areas.

Newcomers must be discouraged from entering ranges that were already filled. The cattlemen were thrown upon their own resources to provide such protection, since they were occupants of the public domain by suffrance only, and could expect no legal protection, unless, as in Wyoming, they could control the legislature.

The protection of ownership of herds and cattle was another matter in which co-operation was essential. When out on the range the cattle of various owners grazed together. Identification was made possible only by branding. Each owner was required to adopt a distinctive brand for his cattle, to which he was given the exclusive use after it had been recorded in the brand book of the association. The problem of the "maverick," or calf whose mother could not be identified, was solved by the Wyoming Stock Growers' Association by the requirement that all mavericks must be sold to the highest bidders. The proceeds of these sales went into the treasury of the association. In most cases the round-up became a community affair, under the direction of persons appointed by the association. This procedure was not only economical of time and effort, but it was conducive to the welfare of the cattle, which suffered considerably if the herds were worked over many times in succession by individual owners.

The activities of the cattle-raisers associations which attracted the most public attention were those arising out of the need for protection against Indians and cattle thieves. As long as there were still buffalo to be found on the plains and the Indians left their reservations to hunt them, depredations were a constant occurrence in the cattle country. The cattlemen were openly resentful of a government that seemed more concerned with the welfare of the Indians than with the protection of those whose cattle were being wantonly slaughtered. Of course these men overlooked the fact that they themselves were interlopers on the public domain, with little valid claim to special consideration on the part of the government. In Montana, particularly, the association organized patrols, which frequently broke up camps and drove the Indians back to the reservations.

The danger from Indians diminished with the passage of

the years, but the cattle thief was a constant menace. Under the existing governmental organization in the plains region the need of mutual protection against cattle rustlers would have brought the cattlemen's associations into existence if there had been no other problems. Cattle-stealing was necessarily mainly the work of men who had had experience in handling cattle. Cowboys often had small herds of their own. These might be augmented by the process of altering brands or by branding mavericks before the round-up. Against these, their most hated enemies, the larger associations, like the one in Wyoming, employed a large force of detectives and inspectors. The work of the detectives was done in the cattle country itself, where the movements of every newcomer and of every cowboy whose record was not unimpeachable were watched with suspicious vigilance. The inspectors performed their functions at the shipping towns on the railroads, at Indian agencies where many cattle were sold, and at the principal market points, like Omaha, St. Paul, and Chicago. They became expert in detecting altered brands and recovered large numbers of cattle for members of the associations. Punishment was usually swift and severe for those convicted of cattle-stealing.

Still another menace to the welfare of the cattlemen were the sheep herders who began to pasture their flocks on the open range during the seventies, and came in such large numbers during the eighties that nearly one-half of the sheep in the United States at the end of the decade were in the Far West. The coming of the sheep raisers led to a competition for ranges in which the cattlemen were at a distinct disadvantage. Cattle would not graze on land where sheep had previously fed. Friction soon developed wherever the owners of cattle and sheep sought to pasture their animals in adjacent areas. To the economic basis of their animosity there was added personal dislike between the cowboys and the sheep herders. As a result, especially during the nineties, there occurred numerous miniature wars, in which cattle and sheep, though more of the latter than of the former, were killed, and cowboys and herders met in bloody encounters.

There were numerous other functions performed by these associations of cattlemen, which properly belong in the group of frontier organizations and tribunals, of which the claim clubs of the farmers' frontier and the organizations of miners are other representatives. Like the regulations of the miners, many of the rules adopted by the stock growers' associations ultimately became embodied in law, especially where cattle-raising on a large scale continued to be a dominant industry.

The Round-Up and the Drive

The two great spectacles of the range cattle industry were the round-up and the drive, in which that colorful figure, the cowboy, played his most important roles. As has been indicated the round-up early became a community affair, conducted under the direction of men chosen by the association or group of owners in a given region. There were two round-ups each year, one in the spring and one in the fall. The main purpose of the spring round-up was the branding of the calves. Summer calves were branded at the fall round-up. In Texas the cattle to be driven north to the shipping points along the railroads or to the northern ranges were cut out of the herd at the spring round-up and started on the drive. Despite the long hours and the hard work, the cowboys eagerly looked forward to these occasions, when all was life and activity, and when men from a considerable number of outfits were brought together.

The drive, and especially the long drive to Wyoming and Montana, was a task that called for experience and skill. The most capable and dependable cowboys were selected for this duty, and placed under the direction of a drover thoroughly acquainted with the technique and problems of taking cattle over the trails. Experience proved that from 2,500 to 3,000 cattle constituted the size of herd most satisfactory for the drive. With them went from sixteen to eighteen cowboys. Accompanying them were the cook with the chuck wagon and the wrangler with the "remuda" or string of cow ponies.

The herds destined for the northern ranges left Texas early in the spring, after being branded, at least in many cases, with a trail brand to distinguish them from the herds of the country through which they might pass. Great care in the early stages of the drive was taken to "trail-break" the cattle and to prevent stampedes. Herds that stampeded a few times became very difficult to manage. In times of storm the danger was especially great, but any unusual sound or sight might precipitate a mad, headlong break on the part of the herd from which it could be diverted only by great determination and ingenuity. When on the trail the cattle were strung out in a long, thin line, with the stronger animals in the lead. On opposite sides of the herd the cowboys rode in pairs. At the head rode the "pointers," who were the most experienced and capable. Then came those riding the "swing" and the "flanks," and at the rear the "dragmen," who not only suffered the full effect of the dust raised by the herd but also had the irksome duty of keeping the stragglers on the move. At night two men were usually sufficient to keep the cattle quiet. It was then, as they patrolled the herd, as well as in periods of relaxation, that they sang the characteristic cowboy songs that have become perhaps almost too familiar in recent years through constant use in radio programs.

All in all, the true service and character of the old-time cowboys should be judged, not by their behavior while in the cow towns seeking recreation, but by their honest, loyal work when with their cattle. Eighteen hours was not an unusual day when on the drive, which might extend over a period of sixty, ninety, or more days. When the cattle industry passed into the ranch stage many a cowboy felt that his life had lost some of its savor. Riding fence and putting up hay were drab occupations for men who had participated in round-ups on the open range or in the long drive.

Fencing the Public Domain

The range cattle industry, as the term implies, was based upon the utilization of the public domain for grazing purposes. As long as the range was left open and as long as the country was not wanted by homesteaders, there was no valid ground for objection and no serious public complaint occasioned by the use of a national resource by the cattlemen. The invention of barbed wire during the seventies, however, ushered in a new day on the plains, where the problem of fencing had hitherto been a difficult one, because of the lack of materials. The introduction of barbed wire fences into the cattle country was productive of violent fence-cutters' wars. Fences broke up the open range, and, besides, many cattle were mutilated by the barbed wire until they became accustomed to it.

Fencing commended itself to many of the larger land companies, since it provided means of securing exclusive control of huge ranges and facilitated the care of the cattle. The manufacture of barbed wire increased rapidly, and no small part of the demand came from the cattle country. Soon there were enormous enclosures of public land, made for the most part without a shadow of right or legality. Complaints poured in to the Commissioner of the General Land Office in Washington and he began a series of investigations which revealed a startling situation. In his report of 1884, this official called attention to thirty-two cases of illegal fencing averaging more than 138,000 acres per enclosure. One enclosure was said to contain fully 600,000 acres, or an area two-thirds the size of the State of Rhode Island. In Colorado forty townships were within a single fence. One cattleman in the Red River region was listed as having 250 miles of fence.

Mail carriers frequently found their way blocked by fences; and homesteaders were prevented from access to land which they desired to enter. In 1883 the Secretary of the Interior advised the latter to cut fences which illegally barred their way. This advice was encouraging, but in many cases it was scarcely necessary, for growing hostility toward the "cattle barons" inclined the settlers to aggressiveness in defense of their rights. There were numerous instances of armed encounters between fence-cutting settlers and employees of the cattle companies. Of course the advantage rested with the former, for they had right and numbers on their side and the government behind them. The cattlemen, like the Indians and the fur traders, were obliged to yield to the resistless pressure of land-hungry settlers. In 1885 Congress enacted a law which permitted vigorous prosecution of persons guilty of illegal fencing. In the succeeding years most of the fences were removed, but some public domain was still enclosed in the early years of the present century.

Many of the fences would have come down, even without governmental action, since they were the cause of frequent disasters. In the winter cattle drifted before the blizzards and survived if they could keep moving. But when they came up against a fence they were lost: the passing of the storm left a huddle of frozen carcasses. Costly experience, therefore, led many cattlemen to take down their long fences of their own accord. Barbed wire, however, together with the windmill to pump water from deep wells, played an important role when the cattle industry on the plains passed into the private ranch and cattle-farming stages.

Land Legislation for the Far West

Although illegal, the fencing of the public domain, especially when it was done on a relatively small scale, was a natural reaction both to the needs of the cattle industry and to the nature of the plains country. As has already been said, the cattlemen endeavored unsuccessfully to secure the adoption of a plan for leasing the public lands for grazing purposes. Public opinion and governmental policy were opposed to this proposal, as well as to any measure making it possible for cattlemen to acquire title to any considerable amount of land. There was a growing antagonism to the granting of privileges to an industry that was regarded as monopolistic. Furthermore, there was no general recognition of the differences between the country west of the one hundredth meridian and that east of it. The ideal of a quarter-section farm for the poor man had become fixed in the thinking of the American people. To be sure some modifications were made in the land laws, as will be seen, but they were far from being adequate. Much evasion and fraud on the part of cattlemen and speculators, and many failures among bitter, impoverished farmers might have been avoided if a frank realization of the character of the semi-arid plains had led to the early adoption of a homestead unit large enough to serve the needs of the industry best adapted to the region.

In 1873 there was passed the first of the "timber culture laws." Its purpose was expressed in the title: "An act to encourage the growth of timber on western prairies." Although there were several amendments to this law within the next few years, the basic provisions remained the same. Any person having the prescribed qualifications, who would plant forty acres of timber and keep the trees in a healthy, growing condition for ten years, could obtain title to the quarter-section in which the forty acres were located. A law passed in 1878 reduced the number of acres which must be planted to ten, and also reduced the number of trees which must be in a thriving condition when the patent was issued.

Although beneficent in purpose, these timber culture acts were ill-conceived and gave rise to a great amount of fraud in actual operation. Under their provisions cattlemen made choice locations where water was available and held them by making a show of meeting the minimum requirements of the law from year to year. Cattle companies had their employees take out timber culture claims and thus acquired the use of many quarter-sections strategically distributed over their ranges. Speculators also engaged in the fraudulent enterprise on a large scale, selling their claims to others at the first opportunity, at a good profit on the meager investment. The Commissioner of the General Land Office reported his belief in 1887 that not "one timber-culture filing in a hundred is actually made in good faith for the purpose of cultivating it to trees." Even those who attempted to observe the law in many cases found that timber would not grow. In 1891 the timber culture laws were repealed, but not before nearly ten million acres of public land had passed into private hands, chiefly in Kansas, Nebraska, and Dakota.

The first recognition, within the period covered by this volume, of the unsuitability of the homestead law to the semi-arid and arid regions, as well of the possibilities of irrigation, is to be found in the so-called Desert Land Act passed by Congress in 1877, and made applicable to eleven States and Territories. This law made it possible for a person to buy an entire section, or 640 acres, at $1.25 an acre, provided he would irrigate it within three years after filing his claim. Twenty-five cents an acre was to be paid at the time of filing, and the remainder at the end of the three years, at which time proof of compliance with the requirements of the law must be made.

Scarcely had this law been enacted when a considerable amount of land was entered under its provisions, and in each succeeding year many persons availed themselves of the opportunities presented. Soon, however, there accumulated evidence that here again the real purpose of the law was being evaded. Stockmen and speculators were filing on land and having their friends and employees do likewise, for the purpose of gaining control of choice sections of hay land or land along streams, with no intention of irrigating it. For twenty-five cents an acre they could obtain the exclusive use of the land for a period of three years, thus indirectly gaining some of the advantages of a system of leasing which they had failed to obtain directly. Toward the close of the three-year period they could either sell their claims or hope to secure title through the favor of local land officials, on the basis of plow-furrows or shallow ditches run without reference to water supply or the contour of the land. Fraudulent entries became so notorious by 1891 that Congress amended the law, reducing the area that might be obtained to 320 acres, and making the requirements much more stringent. This law and its effects, and the interesting history of later reclamation legislation and projects belong to a period not embraced in the scope of this volume.

In this connection mention should be made of the efforts of public land officials and of Congress to solve the problem of the disposal of the valuable timber lands of the Far West, although of course the laws passed on this subject have no reference to the region of the Great Plains. Before 1878 valuable timber land could be readily acquired under the homestead and preemption laws; and timber could be cut without much restriction. In the hope of correcting abuses that had become evident, two laws were enacted in 1878. One of these was the Timber Cutting Act designed to permit miners and actual settlers to cut timber on the public domain for their own needs without charge, but to prevent illegal exploitation. The law had little effect, for as early as 1882 the Commissioner of the General Land Office was reporting alarming depredations on the publicly-owned timber "by powerful corporations, wealthy mill owners, lumber companies and unscrupulous monopolists."

The other law passed in 1878 is known as the Timber and Stone Act. It provided for the sale, at not less than $2.50 an acre, of lands chiefly valuable for timber and stone, in tracts of not exceeding 160 acres to a person. The buyer must make an affidavit that the timber or stone was desired for personal use and not for purposes of speculation or for the benefit of others. This affidavit did not prevent perjury or fraudulent entries. Not many years passed before the Commissioners of the General Land Office reported gigantic swindles, in which large lumber companies and speculators gained title to great tracts of timber by the device of dummy entrants, or by hiring people to file claims under false and perjured affidavits. One of the most glaring instances was that of a corporation which thus gained title to 100,000 acres of immensely valuable redwood timber in northern California.

There were numerous modifications of these laws before the close of the century in the effort to remove their defects. In 1891 the fifty-year-old general preemption law was repealed. Other laws sought to protect the dwindling mineral resources of the nation from exploitation, with results that fell far short of success. Unfortunately, the movement for conservation did not gain headway or support until after the frontier had disappeared and the rich heritage of the whole nation in natural resources had been almost entirely alienated and had passed under private ownership. The process by which this alienation was accomplished constitutes one of the unpleasant chapters of American history.

CHAPTER XXXVII

THE PASSING OF THE FRONTIER

THE story of the rise and fall of the range cattle industry is the last chapter in the series of romantic episodes which make the history of the Far West a tale of romance and adventure. Explorers, fur traders, gold miners, stage-coach drivers, railroad builders, cowboys, desperadoes and banditti—these are the best known actors in a drama that was not only fascinating to its contemporaries, but has never lost its power to thrill readers of frontier fiction, film addicts, and audiences at rodeos and round-up pageants. To be sure, the real character of many of these actors and of the life in which they participated has been obscured by imaginative and fictional treatment. Nevertheless, there is an abundant literature, written by those who had personal knowledge or have made a careful study of each of these various episodes, which present a truer picture. What is lacking is a synthesis, and it is possible that none can be written, because of the divergence in the types of regional beginnings in the vast area between the eastern border of the plains and the Pacific coast.

DIVERSITIES IN THE DEVELOPMENT OF THE FAR WEST

In earlier pages of this volume an attempt was made to outline the social and economic beginnings and to describe the frontier society of the Middle West. Although it was pointed out that even here there was sufficient variety to make generalization dangerous, it was shown that the development of the frontier of the Ohio and upper Mississippi valleys was marked by a high degree of homogeneity. Each frontier area witnessed a fairly regular procession of hunters and trappers, backwoodsmen, pioneer farmers, intensive farmers, and town-builders. A general similarity of physical environment and common purposes of needs on the part of the settlers made the middle western frontier a unit which may be, and has been, studied as a unit with respect both to its development and its effects in shaping American ideas and institutions.

The early phases of the American occupation of the Far West, on the other hand, exhibit no such homegeneity. The plains, the mountain region, and the Pacific slope each had its own peculiar type of early activity. There were distinct differences in physical environment and natural resources. Furthermore, in each of these principal geographical divisions there was regional variation in development from north to south. The Great Plains were the scene of the range cattle industry, but, as has been seen, there were differences between the development on the northern plains and in the south. In the middle section, first in Kansas and later in Nebraska, the typical farmers' frontier early made its appearance and rapidly pushed westward. The continued existence of the Indian Territory, the last remnant of the old Indian country, until nearly the close of the frontier era, caused special problems in the region that was to become Oklahoma.

The mountain region was first a fur traders' frontier. The fur trade, however, here as elsewhere was a temporary activity, destined to dwindle and disappear as soon as the country in which it was conducted became attractive to other elements of the population. Thus, as far as effective American occupation was concerned, the mountain region was a miners' frontier. Mining fever produced communities that were much alike wherever they were found. The history of Arizona and New Mexico, however, is markedly different in many respects from that of Montana and Idaho, partly because of different geographical determinants and partly perhaps because of the Spanish and Mexican background. Then, in the mid-mountain area was the Mormon community in Utah, with its particular purposes and characteristics.

Diversity also existed in the origin and early development of American life on the Pacific coast and helps to explain differences that still exist. In fact, not only did California differ from the Pacific Northwest, but in each of the Pacific coast States themselves there were regional dissimilarities. From

the beginning, northern and southern California had distinguishing characteristics. The Willamette valley in Oregon and
the Puget Sound country in Washington were outposts of the
farmers' frontier; but the eastern portions of both of these
States were on the border of the miners' frontier, they witnessed the rise of cattle and sheep grazing on the open range,
and they became great centers of wheat production.

It is obvious, therefore, that the early history of the Far
West must continue to be written largely on a sectional or
regional basis. Geographic and economic influences worked
toward diversity rather than uniformity. The data thus far at
hand indicates only a few characteristics or practices that were
shared in common by those who advanced the frontier to the
Pacific.

GENERAL SIMILARITIES IN THE LIFE OF THE FAR WEST

In general it may be said that everywhere in the Far West
during frontier days life was lived dangerously. Doubtless it
is for this reason that we still look back to those days with a
sort of nostalgia for a period when, at least as we imagine, men
were free and adventure was to be encountered at every turn.
It may well be that life and limb are as much or more in
jeopardy today, because in some respects we have become the
helpless victims of our mechanical civilization. But the dangers
encountered by the fur trader, the pony express rider, the
miner, the migrating settler, or the cowboy were dangers
against which a man could pit his courage, endurance, strength
and ingenuity. Starvation or thirst, summer or winter storms,
stampeding buffalo herds, hostile Indians, swollen streams,
perilous mountain passes, bandits and highwaymen—these
were the perils to be encountered. If a man lost in the struggle
he could at least go down fighting. If he won his was the satisfaction of overcoming in a contest in which wit and valor and
fortitude counted.

The migrations to Oregon and the early gold rushes to various regions were made up of representative cross-sections of
the American people. In the main, however, the Far West in
its early days called mostly to the rougher, more restless and

venturesome elements of the male population. On no other frontier was the "he-man" so glorified or, conversely, the "tenderfoot" at such a disadvantage. Desire for adventure, hope of making a fortune, were motives impelling many to seek the mining camp or the cattle range. Failure or maladjustment sent others west. There is evidence, also, that the Far West had its full share of men who were glad to escape to a region where their past careers would not be a subject of interest or question.

Mention has already been made of the swarms of parasites—the gamblers, whiskey-sellers, and dissolute women—who settled down in the mining towns, the rail-end camps, and the cow towns. At the best they furnished dubious and demoralizing relaxation for men whose lives held far more of drudgery and boredom than our romantic frontier fiction would lead us to believe. Too often these gamblers and grog-shop keepers were in league with the bandits and desperadoes who infested the country. Many a dime novel and frontier thriller has found its theme in the exploits of the highwaymen who held up and robbed stage coaches, the desperadoes who terrorized the mining regions, and the cattle thieves who were a constant menace in the days of the open range. Billy the Kid and the James boys, for all their crimes, have attained almost the status of American Robin Hoods.

The mining regions and the cattle country were alike in that they were both occupied before there were local or federal laws governing the industries concerned. Both the miners and the cattlemen drew up regulations for their own protection and observance. In California and in the Rocky Mountains associations or groups of miners drafted rules governing the size and location of claims, the use of water, the methods of settling disputes, and many other matters. So well were these rules drawn up, and so admirably were they adapted to needs of the mining business, that they became the basis of all future legislation on the subject. We have already seen that a similar development took place in the cattle country, where the stockgrowers' associations were the first legislative bodies for the industry, and adopted regulations that later became embodied in the laws of western Territories and States.

The miners and the cattlemen often found themselves in situations where they were either beyond the jurisdiction of regularly established forces of law and order, or where the local officials were inefficient or in league with the lawless elements of the region. In both cases the participants in the industry took matters into their own hands and administered justice according to codes and by methods of their own adoption. In settled communities actions such as those often performed by these men would properly be called lynching. Under the existing conditions in the regions where this procedure prevailed it may be more fairly termed extra-legal law enforcement. On the plains it was the cattlemen's associations which in many cases provided their own protection against cattle rustlers. There is reason to believe that many of these "public enemies" met their death at the end of a rope, without the aid of courts or sheriffs. The difficulties of these organizations were increased when homesteaders and small ranchers became numerous, and an antagonism against the great cattle companies developed which made it almost impossible to secure the conviction of cattle thieves.

The "lawless reign of law" in the mining regions was the work of vigilance committees whose activities may be said to have been best organized and most effective in California and Montana. Some writers have pointed out that in the mining communities there were three general classes of people. In the first place, there were the professional or habitual miners, who might be a rough, heterogeneous lot, but who were intent on their main occupation and seldom troublesome. The second group was made up of the "novices at the game" and those who came into the community to engage in business, professional practice, or agriculture. Finally, there were the hangers-on who sought to obtain the miners' gold at the gaming table or in the dance hall or by the more direct methods of murder and robbery. The second group, as a rule, had not lived in a place where crime was rampant and unchecked, and they had no desire to do so.

When the regularly constituted officers proved either unable to deal with the situation or were unwilling, because secretly in collusion with the criminals, the vigilantes took charge of matters. It took time to perfect an organization, and much courage and absolute secrecy on the part of those who began the movement, for their lives would certainly have been in grave danger in case of premature discovery. But when thoroughly organized the vigilance committee were effective. In bringing desperadoes to punishment they observed the forms of law and even-handed justice, but they usually had evidence of guilt that was beyond dispute. The lessons they administered seldom had to be repeated. In many a town which had its origin as a mining camp, the old hangman's tree or hangman's beam long remained objects of approving interest. In the little cemetery outside Virginia City, Montana, there can be seen, or could be a few years ago, several headstones with inscriptions like "Club Foot George Lane, Hanged January 14th, 1864," as grim reminders of the work of the vigilantes in that once thriving mining town.

ADVANCE OF THE FARMER'S FRONTIER

When the nineteenth century entered its last decade the Far West of the Indian, the miner, the cowboy, and the transcontinental railroad builder had largely disappeared. The farmers' frontier had advanced into some part of almost every section and region. Each region still bore many of the imprints of its distinctive origin, as it must long continue to do, but the old days of the "Wild West" were gone, never to return.

The history of the settlement of the Far West as a whole has never been written, and it cannot be written until in each of the States, or at least for each of the regions, adequate accounts have been prepared. The sources are too scattered and the task too great for any one person to undertake such a history without unlimited time at his disposal. A general summary is therefore impossible.

Some idea of the volume and direction of the movement which peopled this great region can be gained from the federal census reports. In 1860 there were about 1,364,000 people living in the country west of the first row of States west of the Mississippi. Thirty years later the population of the same area was more than 8,686,000. A study of the following table will show more satisfactorily than any brief analysis could do, which Territories and States received the greatest accessions of population during each of the three decades from 1860 to 1890:

	1860	1870	1880	1890
Kansas	107,206	364,399	996,096	1,428,108
Nebraska	28,841	122,993	452,402	1,062,656
Dakota	4,837	14,181	135,177	539,583*
Oklahoma	......	......	......	258,657
Texas	604,215	818,579	1,591,749	2,235,527
New Mexico ..	93,516	91,874	119,565	160,282
Arizona	......	9,658	40,440	88,248
Nevada	6,857	42,491	62,266	47,355
Utah	40,273	86,786	143,963	210,779
Colorada	34,277	39,864	194,327	413,249
Montana	......	20,595	39,159	142,924
Wyoming	......	9,118	20,789	62,555
Idaho	......	14,999	32,610	88,548
Washington ...	11,594	23,955	75,116	357,232
Oregon	52,465	90,923	174,768	317,704
California	379,994	560,247	864,694	1,213,398

* North Dakota, 190,983; South Dakota, 348,600.

It is not difficult to imagine the long lines of covered wagons and the crowded passenger and freight trains which carried homeseekers westward, especially during the decade of the eighties when the population of the Far West increased by nearly four million. Newspapers contain jubilant accounts of the coming of crowds of settlers. Letters and journals of travelers tell of the transformation that was being wrought in the aspect of various sections. That a large proportion of the newcomers sought homes on farms or in small villages and towns is indicated by the fact that a region which had only one city with more than ten thousand inhabitants in 1860 (San Francisco with a population of 56,902), contained only two cities with more than one hundred thousand even in 1890—San Francisco and Denver. Los Angeles was a city of scarcely more than fifty thousand people in 1890. The movement which led to the rapid growth of cities came in a later period, after the frontier days were gone.

The Far West, between the one hundredth meridian and

the Pacific Coast is, as a whole a semi-arid or arid region; although there are some fairly large areas to which this description does not apply. Agricultural development, therefore, was conditioned by a general insufficiency of rainfall and characterized by a persistent conservation of soil moisture and a desperate search for water. The Great Plains, with their immense stretches of level or gently rolling, treeless country were inviting to thousands of farmers, beginning in general during the decade of the eighties. If these settlers realized the semi-arid nature of the land on which they settled, many of them comforted themselves with the belief that settlement and cultivation would result in increased rainfall. All too soon they learned the fallacy of this expectation. It was in this region that the most fantastic efforts at rain-making by the use of explosions were made.

Only a small percentage of those who took up farms on the Great Plains placed confidence on the production of rain by such bizarre expedients. Most of them soon settled down to their work in the grim hope that crops could be raised in spite of insufficient rainfall. They learned the technique of dry-farming, which meant deep plowing and the frequent cultivation or pulverizing of the surface, in order that surface moisture might be conserved. Drilled wells and home-made or manufactured windmills made possible a fairly dependable supply of water for man and beast and the irrigation of vegetable and flower gardens. In fact, the possession or lack of windmills very frequently determined whether farm families could hold on and maintain life in years of drouth, or whether they must give up in utter despair. But even a deep well and a windmill, or several of them, could not begin to solve the problem of bringing water to thirsty fields.

The only other possible method of counteracting the deficiency in rainfall was by irrigation, and this method could of course be applied only to lands located along streams. Despite the hopes and the agitation of a few enthusiasts, irrigation proved impracticable throughout the greater part of the Great Plains area. Along the western border of the plains and in the inter-mountain region, however, the reclamation of arid lands by irrigation eventually became an activity which claimed the interest and participation of individuals, associations, irrigation companies, and the government, both state and national. The main features of the story of this development deal with a period beyond the scope of this volume. A brief statement will suffice to indicate some aspects of the experimentation in irrigation which preceded the Carey Act of 1894, the Newlands Act of 1902, and the launching of the federal government upon an extensive reclamation program.

Irrigation had been practiced in a few regions by the American Indians. The Spanish in the Southwest set precedents that were followed after American occupation. From the beginning of their settlement in Utah the Mormons dug ditches and irrigated their fields. There were other projects in Colorado and California during the seventies. Then came the Desert Land Act of 1877, passed in the expectation that it would promote agricultural development in regions of scanty rainfall. We have already seen how the cattlemen took advantage of this law and gained control of extensive ranges, by locating claims along the rivers and thus monopolizing all the available water, with no intention of engaging in farming or of actually irrigating the land. When the range cattle industry began to decline, after about 1885, however, irrigation entered a phase more in conformity to the purposes for which the Desert Land Act had been passed.

Farmers in increasing numbers began to enter lands under the terms of the law in the Territories of the inter-mountain region, from Arizona and New Mexico to Montana and Idaho. They paid down the twenty-five cents an acre required by the law and then sought to bring water to the 640 acres to which they were entitled. By the end of three years they must show land under irrigation and pay the remainder of the total price of $1.25 an acre in order to gain title to the land. The incongruity of charging for arid land when good homesteads were being given away free in other parts of the country did not pass without comment from western officials and farmers.

Irrigation as an individual enterprise was possible in the case of the few who had claims along the banks of streams. In the main it was at first a co-operative venture on the part of joint-stock associations or companies of farmers, who pooled their funds and their labor and were entitled to stipulated amounts of water when the ditches were completed. Unfortunately the prospects of wealth to be made through the control of water in regions where water was precious soon attracted the attention of speculators and men with money to invest in business enterprises. In many localities irrigation soon ceased to be an individual or communal affair and passed into the hands of corporations or irrigation companies controlled largely by non-residents. Speculators, in one way or another, gained title to the land along streams and organized companies for the purpose of selling water to farmers in the adjacent area.

The census report indicates that more than 3,600,000 acres of land were under irrigation by 1889, as compared with about one million acres at the beginning of that decade. There is no way of knowing how truly these figures represent successful accomplishment. At any rate many irrigation problems had arisen, not the least of which were the complicated questions concerned with water rights. Moreover, there had emerged the more fundamental question of whether the use of a vital natural resource should be controlled by private corporations or regulated in the public interest by the government. These were questions for future discussion and solution.

THE PUSH TO OKLAHOMA

Just as the frontier was about to disappear, however, there occurred an episode which recalled scenes that had been witnessed many a time in the Middle West when new lands were opened to settlement, although no previous occurrence of the kind ever had quite such a dramatic quality. A previous chapter has shown how the Indian country, set aside during the days of Calhoun, Monroe, and Jackson was finally reduced to the region long known as the Indian Territory west of Arkansas and lying between Kansas and Texas. The story of the government's dealings with the numerous Indian tribes crowded into this tract during the years after the Civil War would fill many pages of unpleasant reading. The main point of interest in this connection is the fact that even this last remnant of the old Indian country did not long escape the covetousness of settlers. An area in the center of this tract early acquired the name Oklahoma, and at least after the early seventies there was constant pressure and activity on the part of aggressive "boomers," aided by the railroad interests, to have this region opened to white settlers. The cattlemen, who desired to retain their use of much of the land under leasing arrangements, opposed this movement, but here as elsewhere the settlers eventually had their way. Between 1879 and 1885 troops were kept busy driving well organized parties of "boomers" off the Indian lands.

In 1885 Congress partially yielded to the demand and authorized negotiations with the Indians looking toward the purchase of a portion of their lands. Four years ensued during which there was constant lobbying to secure the opening of the region to settlement. At length President Harrison issued a proclamation setting the hour of noon on April 22, 1889, as the time when settlers might legally enter the area they had coveted so long.

The scenes which ensued have appropriately furnished the background of many a work of fiction and motion picture. For weeks before the appointed day thousands of people gathered along the northern and southern borders of the tract. They came from all parts of the nation, but especially from the nearby States. Along the southern boundary of Kansas temporary towns sprang up, some of them with as many as 1,500 inhabitants. On April 22nd the borders were thronged with men and women on foot, on horseback, in wagons, buggies and hacks. Long railroad trains, jammed with men and women who filled the aisles and platforms and even clung to the outside of the cars, awaited with steam up for the signal. The cordon of soldiers held the excited crowd in check until the hour of twelve arrived. When pistols cracked out the signal there was a mad pell-mell rush and the wildest confusion. In an incredibly short time sixty thousand people had entered the tract and either staked out claims or founded thriving towns. By November the city of Guthrie was reported to contain eight thousand inhabitants. All too often those who had obeyed the law found the choicest locations occupied by "sooners" who had eluded the troops and entered the country before the time set by the President.

The Territory of Oklahoma was created by an act of Congress signed on May 2, 1890. From time to time new tracts of Indian land were opened to settlement and there was a repetition, on a smaller and less disorderly scale, of the scenes attending the first opening. In 1907 Oklahoma was admitted into the Union with its present boundaries, and the Indian Territory was entirely gone.

FRONTIER DISCONTENT

One of the arguments used in support of homestead legislation was that it would establish conditions productive of a contented, prosperous population. This prediction can scarcely be said to have been fulfilled, especially in what has sometimes been called the homestead area—Kansas, Nebraska, and the Dakotas. The fault, of course, did not lie in the original homestead law, but in the failure of public opinion to endorse an adaptation of public land policy to the realities of the situation on the Great Plains. The operation of the timber culture acts and the desert land laws, as has been seen, was characterized chiefly by fraud and corruption. The large number of settlers living on quarter-sections on the semi-arid plains were foredoomed to a precarious existence. In the happy intervals between successions of dry seasons and drouths the farmers not infrequently saw their fields devastated by swarms of grasshoppers or "Rocky Mountain locusts," as they were sometimes called. Real experience is reflected in the poem entitled "Starving to Death on my Government Claim," by Edwin Ford Piper.

It is not surprising, therefore, that the homestead area of the Great Plains, from the time of its settlement, was a region in which the population was characterized by discontent and a readiness to espouse any panacea which promised relief from their troubles. The agricultural frontier here, as everywhere, was a debtor section. Its people naturally supported the greenback movement, first known as the "Ohio Idea," although they could not in any large numbers bring themselves to vote the Greenback ticket in national politics during the late seventies and early eighties. Almost from the beginning of settlement the prospect and actual building of railroads made this region seem especially attractive. But in the minds of the distressed farmers the railroads soon turned to monsters, voraciously eating up all the profits of agriculture by the high freight rates charged for hauling grain and cattle to markets. The people entered enthusiastically into the granger movement. In this fight they had the satisfaction in helping to win some measure of success. State laws regulating railroad rates were upheld by the Supreme Court, and later the Interstate Commerce Commission was established.

Then came the Populist movement which had its adherents principally in the South and the Far West, including the silver-producing States and Territories. But in no region more than in Kansas and Nebraska did the new People's Party have a infatuated following. "It was a fanaticism like the Crusades," wrote William Allen White. "Indeed the delusion that was working on the people took the form of religious frenzy. Sacred hymns were torn from their pious tunes to give place to words that deified the cause and made gold—and all its symbols, capital, wealth, plutocracy—diabolical. At night, from ten thousand little white schoolhouse windows, lights twinkled back vain hope to the stars. For the thousands who assembled under the schoolhouse lamps believed that when their Legislature met and their Governor was elected, the millennium would come by proclamation." It was this same William Allen White, who wrote an editorial entitled, "What's the Matter with Kansas" for his *Emporia Gazette,* which has become famous in the history of American journalism.

Staid easterners were deeply shocked. Men like Senator Hoar of Massachusetts expressed their alarmed astonishment that the people of Kansas, many of whom were descendants of New Englanders, a people well supplied with schools and churches, could yield themselves to such a campaign of repudiation and disaster.

It is altogether fitting that the long history of the frontier in the United States should close on a high note of protest and discontent, much as it had begun a century earlier in the days of Shay's Rebellion. The failure of this last characteristic frontier uprising to attain its major objectives is also indicative of the fact that a new era in American history had begun. For the first time business and industrial forces were able to withstand a determined agrarian revolt.

THE COMPLETION OF THE ROLL OF STATES

After the admission of Colorado in 1876 thirteen years elapsed before another star was added to the national flag. Throughout this period the people of the Territories chafed under their inferior status and their subjection to officials not of their own selection. As in the earlier Territories, in addition to those genuinely desirous of attaining the benefits of self-government, there were groups and factions selfishly hopeful of securing control of the elective offices which statehood would create. Constitutions were drafted and adopted in all the Territories, and memorials presented to Congress. Bills providing for the admission of various States occasionally passed the Senate, but all to no avail.

Instead of the sectionalism between North and South which had delayed and prevented the admission of States before the Civil War, it was now the comparative equilibrium in Congress between the two major political parties which precluded action. The Senate was usually Republican, but during the eighties when the statehood advocates were most insistent, the Democrats were in control of the House of Representatives. The Democrats were of no mind to admit States which would in all probability return Republicans to Congress, and they had some support from Republicans who for various reasons objected to the creation of new States.

The barrier was removed by the elections of 1888 when the Democratic majority in the lower house of Congress was broken. The demand of Dakota was most urgent at this time. The Democrats in Congress, knowing that their opponents would control the next session, seem to have decided to yield and gain whatever credit or benefit their action would bring the party. In fact, they were almost precipitate in their eagerness. Not only was Dakota to be admitted, but an "omnibus bill" enabled three other Territories—Montana, Washington, and

New Mexico—to adopt constitutions and become States by presidential proclamation. The Republican Senate amended the bill by dividing Dakota and striking out New Mexico, which was expected to be Democratic. After a struggle in the conference committee the bill as amended became a law in February, 1889.

The year 1889 was a great year of constitution-making. In South Dakota a fundamental law drafted in 1885 was revamped. New constitutions were framed in North Dakota, Montana, and Washington. Similar action was taken in Idaho, Wyoming and New Mexico, although no enabling act had been passed for these Territories. Congress had laid down a number of conditions which must be observed by the "omnibus" States in drafting their constitutions. Among the most interesting of these provisions were those which required that any claim to public or tribal lands should be renounced; that there should be no discrimination in taxation between residents and non-residents; and that public school systems, free from sectarian influence, should be maintained. All these conditions were easily met. These new constitutions were far from being mere frameworks of government. In their greater length than the earlier documents of a similar nature they reflect not only the dislike of their framers for corporations, banks, and railroads, but also their distrust of their own legislative bodies. By November, 1889, the four constitutions were in the hands of President Harrison, and in a series of proclamations he declared North Dakota, South Dakota, Montana, and Washington full-fledged members of the Union. In July of the following year Idaho and Wyoming were admitted.

A few words will suffice to state the bare facts regarding the completion of the roll of States. The Mormons in Utah, long denied admission into the Union because of their adherence to the sanctity of plural marriages, formerly renounced that doctrine in 1890, after having been governed by a federal commission since the passage of the Edmunds Act in 1882. In 1894 Congress passed an enabling act and early in January, 1896, Utah was given statehood. The events leading to the admission of Oklahoma in 1907 have already been outlined. Its constitution set a new record for length and for the variety of subjects which it sought to remove from legislative determination. In New Mexico there was a continued movement for statehood following the refusal of Congress to grant admission along with the "omnibus" States in 1889. A proposal that New Mexico and Arizona should be united was rejected by the latter. Finally, in 1910 enabling acts were passed for the last two States, and both were admitted in 1912. New Mexico came in a few weeks earlier than its neighbor, for the reason that President Taft refused to recognize Arizona under a constitution providing for the recall of judges. The objectionable provision was removed and Arizona was admitted on February 14, 1912. Shortly afterward the recall feature was restored to the constitution by amendment.

The long process of carving our national territory into States was thus completed, unless or until statehood is at some future time granted Alaska or one or more of our island possessions. The history of this unique process, with all its variations in individual cases, is worthy of more careful study than has thus far been made of it.

The Disappearance of the Frontier

A matter-of-fact statement in a bulletin of the United States Census for 1890 gave official recognition of the ending of what may well be called the first great epoch in American history. "Up to and including 1880," said the Superintendent of the Census, "the country had a frontier of settlement, but at present the unsettled area has been so broken into by isolated bodies of settlement that there can hardly be said to be a frontier line." The facts are so in accord with this official announcement that the closing decade of the nineteenth century is properly regarded as the period when the frontier ceased to be a vital, contemporary force in the life of the nation. Here and there, to be sure, in isolated areas of the Far West frontier conditions long continued to prevail. But, as a whole, the the pioneer phase of the occupation of the land within the boundaries of the United States was finished, and the influences of that process upon the people and the nation could be studied as something that was completed.

The first definitely to evaluate and point out these influences was Frederick Jackson Turner. In 1893, before the American Historical Association, he read a paper on "The Significance of the Frontier in American History," which deservedly ranks among the great works of historical interpretation. "Up to our own day," he declared, "American history has been in a large degree the history of the colonization of the Great West. The existence of an area of free land, its continuous recession, and the advance of American settlement westward, explain American development."

Turner's elaboration of this thesis may be briefly divided into four main concepts. In the first place, the frontier was the region of the most effective Americanization and produced a composite American people differing from the various elements which entered into the fusion. In the second place, the substantial equality of frontier life was a vital factor in the promotion of democracy. Thirdly, the frontier was a laboratory for the testing of social, economic and political ideas and institutions. Finally, the growth of American nationality was in large degree the result of influences originating on the frontier.

In the years since Professor Turner read his paper a great amount of research and writing has been done in the field of frontier history. And yet, as Frederic L. Paxson has said, "The Turner hypothesis stands today as easily to be accepted as it was when launched." A few individuals have read implications into the thesis which the author never intended to convey. Others have romanticized the story of the frontier, and thus helped to obscure its reality and meaning. The simple, penetrating interpretation of Frederick J. Turner has become without important modification, a part of the general currency of American historical thought. It has even attained to the unenviable position of being quoted in support of widely divergent causes or policies, none of which was in the mind of the originator of the hypothesis.

There is no lack of realization that the frontier has disappeared. There is general appreciation of the role played by the frontier in shaping American ideas and institutions during the long period when cheap or free land was luring people westward. It is not so clear that, as a people, we have begun to recognize how largely we continue to view our problems in a new and different age with the attitudes and philosophy of the frontier era. What is to take the place of the frontier as a haven for the maladjusted or under-privileged, or as a safety-valve for discontent? On the frontier equality and personal liberty might and did exist to a high degree without serious conflict between the two ideals or their realization. If both cannot continue to exist in full measure, which shall be regarded as the more essential to human welfare? Where shall we look for a promoter and preservative of democracy now that the frontier is gone? What we need now is a careful study of the influences, originating in the frontier era, which still color our life to-day, and an evaluation of their serviceableness in a changed world.

If the effects of the three-century-long process of settling the wilderness of America were ephemeral, and we are destined to become merely an extension or subdivision of the western world, then the story of the frontier will still merit study. At the least, the frontier may continue to be a land of romance, whose "happy ghosts," as Professor Paxson has said, "will endure forever, a happy heritage for the American mind." On the other hand, if the long frontier experience permanently impressed upon our character as a people some of the distinguishing traits developed or encouraged by life on the frontier, then we may face our future and its problems with something of the resourcefulness, co-operative goodwill, and hope that characterized the pioneers.

BIBLIOGRAPHICAL NOTES

BIBLIOGRAPHICAL NOTES

THE sources and secondary works mentioned in these bibliographical notes have been selected for the following reasons. In the first place, they are those which have been most useful in the preparation of the various chapters in the book, and in the case of the source materials they indicate where many of the quotations in the text were obtained. Secondly, they will provide the reader with useful, and in the main authoritative, reference lists for further reading. Thirdly, most of them should be accessible in the better college and public libraries.

CHAPTER I

Ellen Churchill Semple, *American History and its Geographic Conditions* (1903, revised edition 1933) is the best and most readable work in this field. Others are Albert P. Brigham, *Geographic Influences in American History* (1904); N. S. Shaler, *Nature and Man in America* (1891); N. S. Shaler, *The United States of America,* Vol. I; Livingston Farrand, *Basis of American History* (1904), Chs. I-IV; and Ellsworth Huntington, *The Red Man's Continent* (1921), Chs. III and IV, dealing in an interesting manner with the geographic provinces of North America and the garment of vegetation.

Works dealing with the American Indians are legion. Ellsworth Huntington, *The Red Man's Continent* (1921), Ch. V; and Livingston Farrand, *Basis of American History* (1904), Chs. V-XVIII, contain general accounts, and the latter has an excellent bibliography. Clark Wissler, *The American Indians* (1922) is a study of Indian life and culture; and William C. Macleod, *The American Indian Frontier* (1928) deals with the relations between the Indians and the whites. The books by Semple and Shaler mentioned above also contain much material regarding the Indians.

CHAPTER II

Contemporary narratives of the early Spanish explorations which are readily available are: Ad. F. and Fanny Bandelier, *The Journey of Nuñez Cabeza de Vaca* (Trail-Makers Series, 1905); Edward G. Bourne, *Narratives of the Career of Hernando de Soto* (Trail-Makers Series, 1904); and George Parker Winship, *The Coronado Expedition, 1540-1542* (Fourteenth Annual Report of the Bureau of American Ethnology, 1896).

Among the numerous works dealing with Spain in America the following will be found helpful: Herbert E. Bolton, *The Spanish Borderlands* (1921); Edward G. Bourne, *Spain in America* (1904); Woodbury Lowery, *The Spanish Settlements within the Present Limits of the United States* (1901); Frank W. Blackmar, *Spanish Institutions of the Southwest* (Johns Hopkins University Studies in Historical and Political Science, 1891); Charles E. Chapman, *History of California: The Spanish Period* (1921); Herbert E. Bolton, *Outpost of Empire: The Story of the Founding of San Francisco* (1931); Alfred B. Thomas, *Forgotten Frontiers: A Study of the Spanish Indian Policy of Don Juan Bautista de Anza, Governor of New Mexico, 1777-1787* (1932); and Irving B. Richman, *California Under Spain and Mexico, 1535-1847* (1911).

The volumes of Hubert Howe Bancroft's *Works* dealing with the Southwest contain a wealth of material, together with citations to sources. A brief, but useful bibliography is found in Bolton, *The Spanish Borderlands.*

CHAPTER III

Published source materials relating to the explorations, early fur trade, and missionary activities of the French in the West are abundant. Two collections which are widely accessible are: Reuben Gold Thwaites, *The Jesuit Relations and Allied Documents* in 73 volumes, published both in French and in English translation (1896-1903); Louise Phelps Kellogg, *Early Narratives of the Northwest, 1634-1699* (1917). See Isaac J. Cox, *Journeys of La Salle* (1923).

Among the numerous works dealing with this period the two volumes by Francis Parkman, *Pioneers of France in the New World* and *La Salle and the Discovery of the Great West* (several editions), still lead, because of their charm of literary style and their substantial accuracy. In briefer compass and covering a narrower scope, but in a very readable style is John Carl Parish, *The Man with the Iron Hand* (1913). Justin Winsor *Cartier to Frontenac* (1894), is comprehensive and contains many reproductions of early maps. Other accounts are: Reuben Gold Thwaites, *France in America* (1905), Ch. I-IV; and Louise Phelps Kellogg, *The French Régime in Wisconsin and the Northwest* (1925).

CHAPTER IV

An excellent statement of the early development and importance of the fur trade in the English colonies with a special chapter on New York is presented in Charles H. McIlwain's introduction to a reprint of Peter Wraxall, *An Abridgment of the Indian Affairs, 1678 to 1751*, (1915). This volume contains valuable source material on the Anglo-Iroquois alliance and the place of Albany in the fur trade and in the contest with the French. Cadwallader Colden, *The History of the Five Indian Nations* (first published in 1727) is a classic in this field. The largest published collection of source materials on these subjects is in the fifteen volumes of *Documents Relative to the Colonial History of the State of New York* (1853-1887).

Clarence W. Alvord and Lee Bidgood, *The First Explorations of the Trans-Allegheny Region by the Virginians, 1650-1674* (1912), contains a lengthy introduction, and journals and other contemporaneous materials dealing with these explorations, and a memorial written by Dr. Daniel Coxe.

Verner W. Crane, *The Southern Frontier, 1670-1732*, (1928) is a thorough and scholarly study of the western expansion of South Carolina, the first three chapters covering the period down to 1700. Peter J. Hamilton, *Colonial Mobile* (Revised edition, 1910), Chs. V-VI, gives an excellent account of Iberville's settlement on the Gulf.

Among the other writings which have been helpful in the preparation of this chapter are Francis Parkman, *Count Frontenac and New France under Louis XIV;* Justin Winsor, *Cartier to Frontenac* (1894), Chs. XV-XVI; Justin Winsor, *The Mississippi Basin* (1898), Ch. II; Louise Phelps Kellogg, *The French Régime in Wisconsin and the Northwest* (1925), Chs. XI-XII; Herbert L. Osgood, *The American Colonies in the Seventeenth Century* (3 vols. 1904-1907); Helen Broshar, "The First Push Westward of the Albany Traders," in *The Mississippi Valley Historical Review*, December, 1920; Arthur H. Buffington, "The Policy of Albany and English Westward Expansion," in the same publication, March, 1922; Herbert E. Bolton, "Spanish Resistance to the Carolina Traders in Western Georgia, 1680-1704," in the *Georgia Historical Quarterly*, Vol. IX, No. 2; and George A. Cribbs, *The Frontier Policy of Pennsylvania* (1919).

CHAPTER V

Most of the works cited in the bibliographical notes for Chapter VI also deal with all or a part of the period and events covered in this chapter.   Verner W. Crane, *The Southern Frontier, 1670-1732* (1928) is especially valuable for its comprehensive account of the conflict between South Carolina and Louisiana.   Louise Phelps Kellogg, *The French Régime in Wisconsin and the Northwest* (1925) contains a full account, not only of the events in that region mentioned in this chapter, but also of many other phases of French life and activity in the West.   Justin Winsor, *The Mississippi Basin* (1898) still serves as one of the best surveys of this whole period.

Other works which should be consulted include the following: Herbert L. Osgood, *The American Colonies in the Eighteenth Century* (four volumes, 1924-5); Francis Parkman, *A Half-Century of Conflict;* Newton D. Mereness, *Travels in the American Colonies, 1690-1783* (1916), which contains several journals which illustrate the trade rivalry of South Carolina and Louisiana and the relations of these two colonies with the Indian tribes; Herbert E. Bolton and Thomas M. Marshall, *The Colonization of North America* (1924), Chs. XIV-XV; and Reuben Gold Thwaites, *France in America* (1905).

CHAPTER VI

It is fitting that reference should be made at this point to Frederick J. Turner's momentous paper on *The Significance of the Frontier in American History* (1893).   Two other papers by him have a special bearing on the period covered by this chapter namely: *The First Official Frontier of the Massachusetts Bay* (1914), and *The Old West* (1908).   All three of these papers are included along with others, in a volume entitled *The Frontier in American History,* published in 1921.

Among the other writings which have been useful in the preparation of this chapter are: Justin Winsor, *The Mississippi Basin* (1898), Chs. VI and VIII; Lois Kimball Mathews, *The Expansion of New England* (1909); Herbert L. Osgood, *The American Colonies in the Eighteenth Century* (four volumes, 1924-5); C. A. Hanna, *The Wilderness Trail* (1911); Ellen C. Semple, *American History and its Geographic Conditions* (1903); Henry Jones Ford, *The Scotch-Irish in America* (1915); Albert B. Faust, *The German Element in the United States* (1909); G. D. Bernheim, *History of the German Settlements in North and South Carolina* (1872); C. E. Kemper, "The Settlement of the Valley" in the *Virginia Magazine of History and Biography,* Vol. XXX, pp. 169-182; and Ann Maury, *Memoirs of a Huguenot Family* (1853) which contains John Fontaine's journal of Spottswood's expedition of 1716.

CHAPTER VII

The activities of English fur traders and especially of George Croghan are well described in Albert T. Volwiler, *George Croghan and the Westward Movement* (1926). Reuben G. Thwaites, *Early Western Travels*, Vol. I (1904), contains the journals of Conrad Weiser and George Croghan. William M. Darlington, *Christopher Gist's Journals* (1893) contains also much additional material dealing with this period. General works of special value are Francis Parkman, *Montcalm and Wolfe;* Justin Winsor, *The Mississippi Basin* (1898), Chs. XI-XXI; Reuben G. Thwaites, *France in America* (1905), Chs. IX-XVII; Herbert L. Osgood, *The American Colonies in the Eighteenth Century* (1924-5), Vol. IV, Chs. XIV-XVII. Louis K. Koontz, *The Virginia Frontier, 1704-1763,* (Johns Hopkins University Studies, Series XLIII, No. 2), is an excellent study of Virginia's part in the struggle. Rupert Hughes, *George Washington* (1926), Vol. I, furnishes the best account of Washington's part in the war. An English treatment of the French and Indian War is found in A. G. Bradley, *The Fight with France for North America* (1900).

CHAPTER VIII

Clarence Walworth Alvord, *The Mississippi Valley in British Politics* (2 vols. 1917), is the best and most comprehensive account of British policy regarding the West from 1763 to 1774. Francis Parkman, *The Conspiracy of Pontiac* is the classic account of this Indian uprising. Other works of special value are Albert T. Volwiler, *George Croghan and the Westward Movement* (1926); Clarence E. Carter, *Great Britain and the Illinois Country, 1763-1774* (1910); George H. Alden, *New Governments West of the Allegheny Mountains before 1780* (Bulletin of University of Wisconsin, Series in Econ., Pol. Science and History, Vol. II); Clarence E. Carter, "The Beginnings of British West Florida" in *The Mississippi Valley Historical Review*, December, 1917; W. E. Stevens, "The Organization of the British Fur Trade 1760-1800," in *The Mississippi Valley Historical Review*, September, 1916; and Justin Winsor, *The Westward Movement* (1897), Chs. I-VII.

CHAPTER IX

As is indicated in the text much of the material used in this chapter was drawn from the various published collections of letters and papers from the archives of Pennsylvania, Virginia, and North Carolina. *The Papers of Sir William Johnson* (edited by Alexander C. Flick, 1925-28) are of great value. The published writings of George Washington, both the Ford and the Sparks editions, were used, as well as Stanislaus M. Hamilton, *Letters to George Washington and Accompanying Papers, 1752-1775* (five volumes, 1898), and Consul W. Butterfield, *The Washington-Crawford Letters, 1767-1781, Concerning Western Lands* (1877). Colonial newspapers were searched for information regarding frontier expansion.

James Veech, *The Monongahela of Old* (1858); and Joseph Doddridge, *Notes on the Settlement and Indian Wars of the Western Parts of Virginia for the years 1763 until 1783* (1824), contain much illustrative material. John W. Monette, *History of the Discovery and Settlement of the Valley of the Mississippi* (1846), contains a brief but helpful sketch of the westward movement during this period. Among the more recent writings dealing with various aspects of the movement are: Albert T. Volwiler, *George Croghan and the Westward Movement, 1741-1782* (1926); John S. Bassett, "The Regulators of North Carolina" in the *Annual Report of the American Historical Association,* 1894, pp. 141-212; Archibald Henderson, *The Conquest of the Old Southwest* (1920), Chapters I-XIII; and Frederic L. Paxson, *History of the American Frontier* (1924), Chs. II and III. Reuben Gold Thwaites and Louise Phelps Kellogg, *Documentary History of Dunmore's War* (1905) contains a good introduction, as well as a great mass of documentary material relating to this conflict. See also Cecil Johnson, "Expansion in West Florida" in *The Mississippi Valley Historical Review,* March, 1934.

CHAPTER X

Readily available materials dealing with the subjects covered in this chapter are not numerous. Justin Winsor, *The Westward Movement* (1897), Ch. VI, contains a useful sketch of the events south of the Ohio from 1769 to 1776. Frederick J. Turner, "Western State-Making in the Revolutionary Era" in *The American Historical Review,* Vol. I, is a careful study. Among the works dealing with the early settlement of Kentucky are: John Filson, *Discovery and Settlement of Kentucky* (1793); Thomas Speed, *The Wilderness Road* (1886); G. W. Ranck, *Boonesborough* (1901); Archer B. Hulbert, *Boone's Wilderness Road* (Historic Highways, Vol. VI, 1903); and Archibald Henderson, *The Conquest of the Old Southwest* (1920), Chs. XII-XV. H. Addington Bruce, *Daniel Boone and the Wilderness Road* (1922) is a readable and satisfactory biography. A favorable view of Richard Henderson is presented by Archibald Henderson, "Richard Henderson and the Occupation of Kentucky, 1775" in *The Mississippi Valley Historical Review*, December, 1914.

CHAPTER XI

For an excellent bibliography of source materials and secondary works dealing with the events of the Revolution in the West the student is referred to James A. James, *The Life of George Rogers Clark* (1928). This biography is the best account of Clark's activities, and also gives some attention to other phases of the war west of the mountains. Temple Bodley, *George Rogers Clark: His Life and Public Services* (1926), contains extended excerpts from Clark's memoir and other source materials. Clarence W. Alvord, "Virginia and the West: An Interpretation" in *The Mississippi Valley Historical Review*, June, 1916, gives a somewhat different view of the significance of Clark's services. Paul C. Phillips, *The West in the Diplomacy of the American Revolution*, (University of Illinois, 1913); and Samuel F. Bemis, *The Diplomacy of the American Revolution* (1935), should be consulted.

CHAPTER XII

As is indicated in the text, this chapter was written almost entirely from source materials, such as journals and descriptions of travel, newspapers and early histories which are not widely available. Any library which possesses a set of *Niles' Weekly Register*, edited by Hezekiah Niles and published in Baltimore, has a valuable source for the study of all phases of American history from 1811 to 1849. Among the many early histories and contemporary descriptions of travel for this period the following are especially useful: Timothy Flint, *Recollections of the Last Ten Years* (1826), and *History and Geography of the Mississippi Valley* (2 vols. 1832); John W. Monette, *History of the Discovery and Settlement of the Valley of the Mississippi* (1846); James Veech, *The Monongahela of Old* (Reprint, 1892); Morris Birkbeck, *Notes on a Journey in America, from the Coast of Virginia to the Territory of Illinois* (1818); Gilbert Imlay, *Description of the Western Territory of North America* (1797); Henry O'Reilly, *Settlement in the West: Sketches of Rochester and Western New York* (1838); Francis Baily, *Journal of a Tour in Unsettled Parts of North America in 1796 and 1797* (1856); and

James H. Perkins, *Annals of the West* (1846). The early volumes of Reuben G. Thwaites *Early Western Travels* contain several journals describing travel in the West during this period. The reader is also referred to Seymour Dunbar, *A History of Travel in America* (4 vols. 1915); and Archer B. Hulbert *Historic Highways* (16 vols. 1902-1905).

CHAPTER XIII

The illustrative quotations in this chapter were taken from *Niles' Weekly Register* and selected from a mass of materials collected from western newspapers. Most of the sources and secondary works with dates later than 1820 cited at the close of the preceding chapter are also useful for part or all of the period covered in this chapter. State histories and the publications of the various state historical societies should be consulted for accounts of the settlement of particular states.

CHAPTER XIV

Vivid glimpses of the conditions and methods of emigrant travel as sketched in this chapter may be obtained in contemporary writings such as Morris Birkbeck, *Notes on a Journey in America* (1818); James Hall, *Letters from the West* (1828); Timothy Flint, *Recollections of the Last Ten Years* (1826); and the first six or eight volumes of Reuben Gold Thwaites, *Early Western Travels.* For secondary accounts one need go no further than Archer B. Hulbert *Historic Highways of America* (16 vols. 1902-1905); and Seymour Dunbar, *A History of Travel in America* (4 vols. 1915).

CHAPTER XV

Two excellent accounts of the events leading up to Pinckney's Treaty are Arthur P. Whitaker, *The Spanish-American Frontier: 1783-1795* (1927); and Samuel F. Bemis, *Pinckney's Treaty: A Study of America's Advantage from Europe's Distress, 1783-1800* (1926). John C. Parish, "The Intrigues of Doctor James O'Fallon" in *The Mississippi Valley Historical Review,* September, 1930; and James Alton James, *The Life of George Rogers Clark* (1928), Chs. XVI-XIX, also throw interesting light on the intrigues in the West during this period.

Samuel F. Bemis, *Jay's Treaty: A Study in Commerce and Diplomacy* (1923), gives an adequate account of the western background of this negotiation. Besides the standard histories, James K. Hosmer, *The History of the Louisiana Purchase* (1915) contains some interesting side-lights on the preliminaries to the Louisiana Purchase Treaty. Walter F. McCaleb, *The Aaron Burr Conspiracy* (1903) is the most satisfactory general treatment of this episode. Isaac J. Cox, "The Louisiana-Texas Frontier During the Burr Conspiracy" in *The Mississippi Valley Historical Review*, December, 1923, is helpful. See also James Wilkinson, *Wilkinson, Soldier and Pioneer* (1935).

The general histories, such as those of Adams, McMaster and others deal at considerable length with the War of 1812 as a whole. Julius W. Pratt, *Expansionists of 1812* (1925), is excellent. For helpful articles on the western origin of the war see the following in *The Mississippi Valley Historical Review* for the issues indicated: Christopher B. Coleman, "The Ohio Valley in the Preliminaries of the War of 1812" (June, 1920); Louis M. Hacker, "Western Land Hunger and the War of 1812; A Conjecture" (March, 1924); and Julius W. Pratt, "Western Aims in the War of 1812" (June, 1925). Milo M. Quaife, *Chicago and the Old Northwest* (1913) is also valuable.

Isaac J. Cox, *The West Florida Controversy, 1793-1813* (1918); and Herbert B. Fuller, *The Purchase of Florida: Its History and Diplomacy* (1906), cover this field thoroughly.

CHAPTER XVI

There is no satisfactory, comprehensive work dealing with Indian affairs in the United States. The sources for such a work are voluminous, although of course there is very little which adequately presents the viewpoint of the Indians. Charles J. Kappler's compilation of *Indian Affairs: Laws and Treaties* in four volumes is in most libraries. *American State Papers—Indian Affairs* in two volumes covering the period from 1789 to 1827 are quite generally accessible, as are also the annual reports of the Commissioner of Indian Affairs. Jedidiah Morse, *Report on Indian Affairs* (1822) presents a sympathetic review of the situation in the Indian country in 1820.

William C. Macleod, *The American Indian Frontier* (1928) is a useful book. Kenneth W. Colgrove, "The Attitude of Congress Toward the Pioneers of the West," in *The Iowa Journal of History and Politics,* January, 1910, pp. 89-114, and April, 1911, pp. 196-302, discusses Congressional attitude toward Indian affairs down to 1850. Other helpful articles in the same periodical are: Ruth A. Gallaher, "The Indian Agent in the United States before 1850," (January, 1916); and Ruth A. Gallaher "The Military-Indian

Frontier 1830-1835," (July, 1917). Annie Heloise Abel, "The History of Events Resulting in Indian Consolidation West of the Mississippi" in the *Annual Report of the American Historical Association*, 1906, is a thorough and scholarly study, and contains a lengthy bibliography of source materials and secondary works dealing with Indian affairs down to about 1840. Grant Foreman, *Indian Removal: The Emigration of the Five Civilized Tribes of Indians* (1932) is a recent work in the same field.

CHAPTER XVII

Among the general works dealing with the history of public land policy and administration the following are especially good: Thomas Donaldson, *The Public Domain: Its History with Statistics* (1884); Shosuke Sato, *History of the Land Question in the United States* (Johns Hopkins University Studies, Fourth Series, Nos. 6, 7 and 8, 1886); and Benjamin H. Hibbard, *A History of the Public Land Policies* (1924).

Herbert B. Adams, *Maryland's Influence upon Land Cessions to the United States* (Johns Hopkins University Studies, Third Series, No. 1, 1885) is an illuminating study of the origin of the public domain. See also Merrill Jensen, "The Cession of the Old Northwest," in *The Mississippi Valley Historical Review*, June, 1936. The following are useful treatments of land policy and legislation down to 1820; Payson J. Treat, *The National Land System, 1785-1820* (1910); Frederic L. Paxson, *History of the American Frontier* (1924), Chs. V-VII, XIII; Kenneth W. Colegrove, "The Attitude of Congress toward the Pioneers of the West from 1789 to 1820" in *The Iowa Journal of History and Politics*, January, 1910; and C. F. Emerick, *The Credit System and the Public Domain* (1899). Bibliographies in the general works mentioned above will serve as guides to source materials and additional secondary treatments of various aspects of the land question.

CHAPTER XVIII

In addition to the general works listed in connection with the previous chapter, the following are helpful for the period from 1820 to 1862: Frederic L. Paxson, *History of the American Frontier* (1924), Chs. XXV, XLII, and L; Raynor G. Wellington, *The Political and Sectional Influence of the Public Lands, 1828-1842* (1914); John B. Sanborn, "Political Aspects of Homestead Legislation" in *The American Historical Review,* Vol. VI; and George M. Stephenson, *The Political History of the Public Lands from 1840 to 1862* (1917). Benjamin F. Shambaugh, "Frontier Land Clubs or Claims Associations" in the *Annual Report of the American Historical Association,* 1900; and *Constitution and Records of the Claim Association of Johnson County, Iowa* (1894), contain illustrative material concerning these extra-legal organizations.

CHAPTER XIX

The most recent work on water transportation in the West is Charles H. Ambler, *A History of Transportation in the Ohio Valley with Special Reference to Waterways, Trade, and Commerce* (1932). Seymour Dunbar, *A History of Travel in America* (4 vols., 1915), is interesting and valuable. Archer B. Hulbert, *Waterways of Westward Expansion (Historic Highways of America,* Vol. IX, 1903), is devoted to the history of traffic on the Ohio. A briefer account is W. Wallace Carson, "Transportation and Traffic on the Ohio and Mississippi before the Steamboat," in *The Mississippi Valley Historical Review,* June, 1920, pp. 26-38. For transportation on other western rivers, especially the Arkansas and the Red, see Grant Foreman, "River Navigation in the Early Southwest" in *The Mississippi Valley Historical Review,* June, 1928, pp. 34-55. Archer B. Hulbert, *The Great American Canals (Historic Highways of America,* Vols. XIII and XIV, 1904), deals with early canal building in the East and with the Chesapeake and Ohio, the Pennsylvania, and Erie canals. Frederic L. Paxson, *History of the American Frontier* (1924), Chs. XXIX and XXX, contains an excellent brief treatment of the canals, including those in the Old Northwest. See also Leland D. Baldwin, "Shipbuilding on the Western Waters, 1793-1817," in *The Mississippi Valley Historical Review,* June, 1933.

As is indicated in the text, the writer drew on contemporary newspapers and journals of travelers for illustrative materials in preparing this chapter.

CHAPTER XX

No real synthesis of the history of roads and highways in America has yet appeared. For the region and period covered in this chapter the best general works are: Seymour Dunbar, *History of Travel in America* (1915), especially Vols. I and II; and Archer B. Hulbert, *Historic Highways of America* (16 vols., 1902-1905), one volume of which is devoted entirely to the Cumberland Road. Other valuable works dealing with this important highway are: Thomas B. Seanright, *The Old Pike: A History of the National Road* (1894); and Jeremiah S. Young, *A Political and Constitutional Study of the Cumberland Road* (1902). Julian P. Bretz, "Early Land Communication with the Lower Mississippi Valley," in *The Mississippi Valley Historical Review*, June, 1926, is a brief but illuminating account of the early roads in the Old Southwest. U. B. Phillips, *History of Transportation in the Eastern Cotton Belt to 1860* (1908) contains some pertinent information. See also Louis Pelzer "Pioneer Stage-Coach Travel," in *The Mississippi Valley Historical Review*, June, 1936. The publications of the various state historical societies contain a large amount of illustrative material.

As is the case with roads, there is no satisfactory general account of railroad building east of the Mississippi. Lewis H. Haney, *A Congressional History of Railways in the United States to 1850* (1908) and his companion monograph for the period from 1850 to 1887 contain much information concerning railway construction in addition to the legislative history. Seymour Dunbar's third volume is helpful. Charles F. Carter, *When Railroads were New* (1909) is a semi-popular work. Shorter articles dealing with the railroad history of the region are: Frederic L. Paxson, "The Railroads of the 'Old Northwest' before the Civil War" in *The Transactions of the Wisconsin Academy of Science, Arts, and Letters*, Vol. XVII, and the same author's *History of the American Frontier* (1924), Chs. XLIV and XLV; and Robert S. Cotterill "Southwestern Railroads and Western Trade" in *The Mississippi Valley Historical Review*, March, 1917. There are excellent histories of the principal railways.

CHAPTER XXI

Much of the material used in writing this chapter was taken from contemporary newspapers, journals of travel and books of description, as is indicated in the text. Beverley W. Bond, Jr., *The Civilization of the Old Northwest* (1934), Chs. XI and XIII, is excellent. The following articles in *The Mississippi Valley Historical Review* are especially helpful: Arthur C. Cole, "The Passing of the Frontier" (December, 1918); Theodore G. Gronert, "Trade in the Blue Grass Region, 1810-1820" (December, 1918); Randolph C. Downes, "Trade in Frontier Ohio" (March, 1930); and Beverley W. Bond, "American Civilization Comes to the Ohio Valley" (June, 1932). Harold U. Faulkner, *American Economic History* (1924), Chs. X and XII, devotes considerable space to the economic development of the West.

CHAPTER XXII

As is indicated in the text, the writer has drawn upon contemporary newspapers and journals and writings of travelers for illustrative materials in preparing this chapter. John Bach McMaster, *A History of the People of the United States from the Revolution to the Civil War,* 8 volumes (1883-1913) is the most satisfactory general work. It presents the setting of the various panics with a wealth of detail. The same author's *Wildcat Banking in the Teens* (1893) is illuminating. Much useful material is to be found in Earl S. Sparks, *History and Theory of Agricultural Credit in the United States* (1932). Reginald C. McGrane, *The Panic of 1837* (1924) is not entirely satisfactory, but it contains much material quoted from contemporary sources.

Most of the histories of the western States give attention to banking and financial crises, and should be consulted as should also the publications of the state historical societies. R. C. H. Catterall, *The Second Bank of the United States* (1903); D. R. Dewey, *State Banking Before the Civil War* (1910) and *Financial History of the United States* (1924); E. G. Bourne, *The History of the Surplus Revenue of 1837* (1885); and R. B. Way "The Mississippi Valley and Internal Improvements" in the *Proceedings of the Mississippi Valley Historical Association,* Vol. IV, are selections from a long list of writings throwing light upon various aspects of frontier finance.

CHAPTER XXIII

Early attempts to establish States west of the Alleghanies are described in Frederick J. Turner, "Western State-Making in the Revolutionary Era," an article which first appeared in *The American Historical Review* in 1895 and 1896, but can now be found in the same author's *The Significance of Sections in American History* (1932). S. C. Williams, *History of the Lost State of Franklin* is the best treatment of that subject.

For the origins and adoption of the Ordinance of 1787 see B. A. Hinsdale, *The Old Northwest* (1888); J. A. Barrett, *Evolution of the Ordinance of 1787* (1891); and the published writings of Manasseh Cutler, Samuel H. Parsons, and Arthur St. Clair. Useful references on the general history of territorial governments are: Clarence E. Carter (editor) *The Territorial Papers of the United States* (4 volumes, 1934-35); Dwight G. McCarty, *The Territorial Governors of the Old Northwest* (1910); and William L. Jenks "Territorial Legislation by Governor and Judges" in *The Mississippi Valley Historical Review,* June, 1918. Beverley W. Bond, Jr., *The Civilization of the Old Northwest* (1934), Chs. III-VIII, is an excellent study of territorial government and movements for statehood in the five States covered. The reader is referred to the histories of the various States for more comprehensive treatments.

A general reference of especial value for this and the following chapter is Henry Gannett, *Boundaries of the United States and the Several States and Territories,* Second Edition (Bulletin of the United States Geological Survey, No. 171, 1900).

CHAPTER XXIV

The histories of the various States should be consulted by readers desirous of more extended treatments of the movements described in this chapter. Most of the general histories of the United States contain adequate discussions of the Missouri Compromise. Floyd C. Shoemaker, *Missouri's Struggle for Statehood* (1916) is excellent. Good material on the boundary difficulties in Ohio, Michigan, Iowa and Missouri is to be found in John C. Parish, *Robert Lucas* (1907); and Benjamin F. Shambaugh, *History of the Constitutions of Iowa* (1902). See also Beverley W. Bond, Jr., *The Civilization of the Old Northwest* (1934). Articles of special interest are Frederic L. Paxson, "A Constitution of Democracy—Wisconsin, 1847," in *The Mississippi Valley Historical Review,* June, 1915; and Homer C. Hockett, "The Influence of the West on the Rise and Fall of Political Parties" in the same periodical for March, 1918. Numerous other articles dealing with early western politics are to be found in the pages of this important historical quarterly, and also in the publications of the various state historical societies.

CHAPTER XXV

The descriptions of frontier society contained in this chapter were drawn from, or based upon, contemporary writings. In addition to those definitely cited in the text, the following were of special value: Francis Baily, *Journal of a Tour in Unsettled Parts of North America in 1796 and 1797* (1856); Joseph Doddridge, *Notes on the Settlement and Indian Wars of the Western Part of Virginia and Pennsylvania, from 1763 to 1783* (1912); Henry O'Reilly, *Settle-*

ment in the West, Sketches of Rochester and Western New York (1838); Morris Birkbeck, *Notes on a Journey in America* (1818); Timothy Flint, *Recollections of the Last Ten Years* (1826), and *The History and Geography of the Mississippi Valley*, Vol. I (1832); James Hall, *Sketches of the History, Life and Manners of the West*, (2 vols., 1835); Lyman Beecher, *A Plea for the West* (1835); Charles Fenno Hoffman, *A Winter in the West* (1835); J. M. Peck, *A New Guide for Emigrants to the West* (1837); Michael Chevalier, *Society, Manners and Politics in the United States* (1839); and William D. Gallagher, *Facts, and Conditions of Progress in the North-West* (1850).

Among the great mass of secondary writings, material of special value is to be found in the histories of the various States and in the publications of the state historical societies. On the subject of health and vital statistics see R. Carlyle Buley, "Pioneer Health and Medical Practices in the Old Northwest Prior to 1840" in *The Mississippi Valley Historical Review*, March, 1934.

CHAPTER XXVI

The writer was especially aided in the preparation of this chapter on cultural beginnings by the use of Ralph L. Rusk, *The Literature of the Middle Western Frontier* (2 vols. 1925). Dorothy A. Dondore, *The Prairie and the Making of Middle America*, Chs. IV-VI, (1926); and Beverley W. Bond, Jr., *The Civilization of the Old Northwest* are also valuable general references on this subject.

Catherine C. Cleveland, *The Great Revival in the West, 1797-1805* (1916) is the best treatment of this topic. Among the many writings dealing with religious development on the frontier the following are of special value: William W. Sweet, *Methodism in American History* (1933), Chs. VIII-XI; William W. Sweet, *The Rise of Methodism in the West* (1920); and A. H. Newman, *A History of the Baptist Churches in the United States* (1894), Pt. II, Ch. V. Louis K. Mathews, *The Expansion of New England* (1909) is also valuable in this connection.

Ellwood P. Cubberley, *Public Education in the United States* (1919), Chs. III-V, VIII, contains much material concerning educational development in the West. Donald G. Tewksbury, *The Founding of American Colleges and Universities before the Civil War* (1932) is an excellent study. Arthur R. Mead, *The Development of Free Schools in the United States* (1918) is devoted to the movement in Connecticut and Michigan. The most extensive work on educational history in a single State is Clarence R. Aurner, *The History of Education in Iowa* (5 vols. 1914-1918).

Although not included in this volume, interesting variations from the general cultural development of the frontier were found in the numerous religious and social experimental colonies established in the West between 1820 and 1860. Charles Nordhoff, *The Communistic Societies of the United States* (1875) is an excellent general treatment. Bertha M. H. Shambaugh, *Amana: The Community of True Inspiration* (1908) possesses high merit, both as history and as literature.

CHAPTER XXVII

A bibliography of the reports and journals of the official explorations described in this chapter would run to considerable length, and the list would be greatly augmented by including other expeditions entirely omitted. The reader is referred to H. R. Wagner, *The Plains and the Rockies, A Bibliography of Original Narratives of Travels and Adventure, 1800-1865* (1921). Most libraries of any size contain the following well-edited editions of journals which may be consulted by readers interested in studying the original accounts of the respective explorations: Reuben G. Thwaites, *The Original Journals of the Lewis and Clark Expedition, 1804-1806* (8 vols. 1904-5); Elliott Coues, *History of the Expedition under the Command of Lewis and Clark* (4 vols. 1893), and *The Expeditions of Zebulon Montgomery Pike* (3 vols. 1895); and Reuben G. Thwaites, *Early Western Travels, 1748-1846* (32 vols. 1904-6), which contains along with numerous others the journals of the expeditions of Stephen H. Long, John Bradbury, Henry M. Brackenridge, and Thomas Nuttall. The most accessible original account of Frémont's expedition is contained in his *Memoirs of My Life* (1887).

The most recent and most satisfactory secondary account of exploration of the Far West is E. W. Gilbert, *The Exploration of Western America, 1800-1850* (1933). Reuben G. Thwaites, *A Brief History of Rocky Mountain Exploration* (1914) is a popular, readable account devoted largely to the Lewis and Clark expedition. Cardinal Goodwin, *The Trans-Mississippi West, 1803-1853* (1922), and W. J. Ghent, *The Early Far West* (1931), devote considerable space to exploration. The exploration of California is described in Robert G. Cleland, *Pathfinders* (1929). There have been numerous biographies of John C. Frémont, and of these the following are the best: Cardinal Goodwin, *John Charles Frémont: An Explanation of His Career* (1930); Allan Nevins, *Frémont, the West's Greatest Adven-*

turer (2 vols. 1928); and Frederick S. Dellenbaugh, *Frémont and '49* (1914). Isaac J. Cox, "The Exploration of the Louisiana Frontier, 1803-1806" in *The Annual Report of the American Historical Association,* 1904, pp. 151-174, describes the expeditions of William Dunbar, George Hunter, and Thomas Freeman.

CHAPTER XXVIII

The standard history of the American fur trade is Hiram M. Chittenden, *The American Fur Trade of the Far West* (3 vols. 1902, revised edition 1935). Clarence A. Vandiveer, *The Fur-Trade and Early Western Exploration* (1929); Katherine Coman, *Economic Beginnings of the Far West* (1912), Vol. I, pp. 289-375; and Isaac Lippincott, *A Century and a Half of Fur Trade at St. Louis* (1916), are shorter general accounts.

Printed source material for the history of the fur trade are abundant. The following are illustrative and quite generally available: Reuben G. Thwaites, *Early Western Travels,* Vols. V-VII, XVIII-XX, XXII-XXV and XXVIII-XXIX, which contain the journals of John Bradbury, Henry M. Brackenridge, Gabriel Franchere, Alexander Ross, James O. Pattie, Prince Maximilian of Wied, and Thomas J. Farnham; Harrison C. Dale, *The Ashley-Smith Explorations* (1918); Maurice S. Sullivan, *The Travels of Jedediah Smith* (1934); Elliott Coues, *New Light on the History of the Greater Northwest* (3 vols. 1895), containing the journals of Alexander Henry and David Thompson; Elliott Coues, *The Journal of Jacob Fowler* (1898); Elliott Coues, *Forty Years a Fur Trader: The Personal Narrative of C. Larpenteur, 1833-1872* (2 vols., 1899); W. F. Wagner, *Adventures of Zenas Leonard, Fur Trader and Trapper* (1904); and Frederick Merk, *Fur Trade and Empire; George Simpson's Journal* (1931).

Washington Irving, *The Adventures of Captain Bonneville, U.S.A. in the Rocky Mountains* (1837), and *Astoria: or, Enterprise Beyond the Rocky Mountains* (1839), are classics. Among the biographies of leaders in the fur trade are: Kenneth W. Porter, *John Jacob Astor, Business Man* (2 vols., 1931); LeRoy R. Hafen and W. J. Ghent, *Broken Hand: The Life Story of Thomas Fitzpatrick, Chief of the Mountain Men* (1931); Edwin L. Sabin, *Kit Carson Days* (1914); J. Cecil Alter, *James Bridger, Trapper, Frontiersman, Scout and Guide* (1925); and Richard G. Montgomery, *The White-Headed Eagle: John McLoughlin, Builder of an Empire* (1934).

CHAPTER XXIX

For general surveys of the history of territorial expansion described in this chapter the reader is referred to George P. Garrison, *Westward Extension* (1906); Frederic L. Paxson, *History of the American Frontier* (1924); Cardinal Goodwin, *The Trans-Mississippi West* (1922); W. J. Ghent, *The Early Far West* (1931); E. Douglas Branch, *Westward* (1930), Pt. V; Robert M. McElroy, *The Winning of the Far West* (1914); and Charles A. and Mary R. Beard, *The Rise of American Civilization* (1927), Vol. I, Ch. XIII. Rupert N. Richardson and Carl C. Rister, *The Greater Southwest* (1934), Chs. III-VI, contains a good general account of American expansion in that region. See also Dan E. Clark, "Manifest Destiny and the Pacific" in *The Pacific Historical Review,* March, 1932.

The classic work on the Santa Fé trade is Josiah Gregg, *Commerce of the Prairies* (reprinted in R. G. Thwaites, *Early Western Travels,* Vols. XIX and XX, 1905). Other excellent accounts are: Hiram M. Chittenden, *The American Fur Trade of the Far West* (1902), Vol. II; Henry Inman, *The Old Santa Fé Trail* (1898); and R. L. Duffus, *The Santa Fé Trail* (1930). Archer B. Hulbert, *Southwest on the Turquoise Trail* (1933) is a very useful collection of source materials, as is also James Josiah Webb, *Adventures in the Santa Fé Trade, 1844-1847,* edited by Ralph P. Bieber (1931).

The literature regarding American activities in Texas and the Mexican War is extensive. For reference purposes the following will be sufficient: G. L. Rives, *The United States and Mexico, 1821-1848* (2 vols. 1913); Eugene C. Barker, *Readings in Texas History* (1929); H. H. Bancroft, *The North Mexican States and Texas* (Vol. II, 1889); Eugene C. Barker, *The Life of Stephen F. Austin, Founder of Texas, 1793-1836* (1925); Nathaniel W. Stephenson, *Texas and the Mexican War* (1921); Justin H. Smith, *The Annexation of Texas* (1911) and *The War with Mexico* (2 vols. 1919); and E. D. Adams, *British Interests and Activities in Texas, 1838-1846* (1910), containing also some reference to British interests in California. *The Quarterly of the Texas State Historical Association* and its successor, *The Southwestern Historical Quarterly,* are filled with articles and source materials.

A similar repository of valuable materials on the acquisition of Oregon is the *Quarterly of the Oregon Historical Society.* The following books are especially useful: Robert C. Clark, *History of the Willamette Valley* (1927); Joseph Schafer, *A History of the Pacific Northwest* (1918); Charles H. Carey, *A General History of Oregon*

(1935-6); H. H. Bancroft, *History of Oregon* (2 vols. 1886-8); William J. Marshall, *Acquisition of Oregon* (2 vols. 1905); Cornelius J. Brosnan, *Jason Lee, Prophet of the New Oregon* (1932); Fred W. Powell (editor), *Hall J. Kelley on Oregon* (1932); and Archer B. Hulbert, *Where Rolls the Oregon: Prophet and Pessimist Look Northwest* (1933).

The most satisfactory general reference on the American conquest of California is Robert G. Cleland, *A History of California: The American Period* (1922). Irving B. Richman, *California under Spain and Mexico, 1535-1847* (1911), is also useful. H. H. Bancroft, *History of California* (7 vols. 1884-1890), contains a more detailed account.

CHAPTER XXX

J. M. Shively, *Route and Distances to Oregon and California* (1846); and Lansford W. Hastings, *The Emigrants' Guide to Oregon and California* (1845), reprinted in 1932 by the Princeton University Press, are illustrations of the early emigrant guide books to the Pacific Coast. Katherine Coman, *Economic Beginnings of the Far West* (1912), Vol. II, Pt. IV; and Seymour Dunbar, *A History of Travel in America* (1915), Vol. IV, are useful for the general history of the migration described in this chapter.

Jesse Applegate, "A Day with the Cow Column in 1843," from which quotations are made in the text, may be found in the *Quarterly of the Oregon Historical Society*, December, 1900. Francis Parkman, *The Oregon Trail* (various editions) is a classic, but pays very little attention to the migration to Oregon. W. J. Ghent, *The Road to Oregon* (1929) is an adequate account. Joseph Schafer, *A History of the Pacific Northwest* (1921), Chs. X, XI, is useful; and Eva Emery Dye, *The Soul of America: An Oregon Iliad* (1934), gives an impressionistic, although somewhat highly-colored, view of the early migration to Oregon. See also Archer B. Hulbert, *The Call of the Columbia* (1934); and *The Oregon Crusade* (1935).

For the history of the Mormons and of their hegira to Utah the reader is referred to William Alexander Linn, *The Story of the Mormons* (1902); Cardinal Goodwin, *The Trans-Mississippi West*, (1922), Ch. XII; Robert F. Riegel, *America Moves West* (1930), Ch. XXIV; and Jacob Van der Zee, "The Mormon Trails in Iowa" in *The Iowa Journal of History and Politics*, January, 1914.

Walter Colton, *Three Years in California* (1859), contains a contemporaneous account of events and conditions in California during the gold rush. Among the numerous diaries and journals of gold-seekers may be cited the following: J. Abbey, *California: A Trip Across the Plains* (1850); E. G. Buffum, *Six Months in the Gold Mines* (1850); Franklin Langworthy, *Scenery of the Plains, Mountains and Mines* (1855); O. T. Howe, *Argonauts of '49* (1923); and Charles E. Pancoast, *A Quaker Forty-Niner* (1930). Among the secondary works the following will serve the needs of those wishing extended accounts: Archer B. Hulbert, *Forty-Niners: The Chronicle of the California Trail* (1932); Stewart Edward White, *The Forty-Niners* (1920); Hubert H. Bancroft, *History of California* (1888), Vol. VI; Robert G. Cleland, *A History of California: The American Period* (1922), Chs. XVII-XX; and Owen C. Coy, *The Great Trek* (1931).

CHAPTER XXXI

Valuable general references in connection with this chapter are Henry Gannett, *Boundaries of the United States and the Several States and Territories,* Second Edition (Bulletin of the United States Geological Survey, No. 171, 1900); and Ruth L. Higgins, "The Development of Trans-Mississippi Political Geography" in *The Iowa Journal of History and Politics,* July, 1923. See also Frederic L. Paxson, *History of the American Frontier* (1924), Chs. XLI and XLVI.

For fuller accounts of the movements leading up to the establishment of territorial and state governments in Oregon see Robert C. Clark, *History of the Williamette Valley, Oregon* (1927), Chs. X and XIV; George W. Fuller, *A History of the Pacific Northwest* (1931), Chs. XII and XVII; and Joseph Schafer, *A History of the Pacific Northwest* (1921), Chs. XI and XIII.

The problems of territorial organization in New Mexico and the Texas boundary question receive treatment in Rupert N. Richardson and Carl C. Rister, *The Greater Southwest* (1934), Ch. IX; H. H. Bancroft, *History of Arizona and New Mexico* (1889), Ch. XVII; and W. C. Bankley, *The Expansionist Movement in Texas* (University of California *Publications in History,* Vol. XIII).

Sufficient reference material on the problems of government in Utah will be found in William A. Linn, *The Story of the Mormons* (1902) Book VI, Chs. V, X-XVII.

The events leading up to the admission of California are well discussed in Cardinal Goodwin, *The Establishment of State Government in California* (1914); Robert G. Cleland, *A History of California: The American Period* (1922), Ch. XVIII; and H. H. Bancroft, *History of California,* Vol. VI (1888). Readers interested in the activities of the vigilance committees in California will find treatments in Cleland, Chs. XXI and XXII; and in Stewart Edward White, *The Forty-Niners* (1920), Chs. XI-XVI.

The facts regarding the Kansas-Nebraska Bill and the ensuing struggle may be found in any standard American history. For interpretations of the background of the measure see Frank H. Hodder, "Genesis of the Kansas-Nebraska Act" in *Proceedings of the Wisconsin Historical Society*, 1912; Hodder, "The Railroad Background of the Kansas-Nebraska Act" in *The Mississippi Valley Historical Review*, June, 1925; and P. Orman Ray, *The Repeal of the Missouri Compromise: Its Origin and Authorship* (1909). See also Chas. W. Ramsdell, "The Natural Limits of Slavery Expansion" in *The Mississippi Valley Historical Review*, September, 1929.

CHAPTER XXXII

Vivid first-hand accounts of stage-coach travel to the Far West, as well as descriptions of the wagon freight trains are found in the following: Horace Greeley, *An Overland Journey* (1860); Demas Barnes, *From the Atlantic to the Pacific, Overland* (1866); James F. Rusling, *Across America* (1875); Samuel Bowles, *Across the Continent* (1866); A. K. McClure, *Three Thousand Miles Through the Rocky Mountains* (1869); and Mark Twain, *Roughing It* (any edition).

Three excellent secondary accounts of the mail stage lines and the pony express are: LeRoy Hafen, *The Overland Mail, 1849-1869* (1926); Frank A. Root and William E. Connelley, *The Overland Stage to California* (1901); and William and George H. Banning, *Six Horses* (1930). For a more detailed account of the pony express see Glenn D. Bradley, *The Story of the Pony Express* (1913). Alexander Majors, *Seventy Years on the Frontier* (1893) contains an account of the freighting business by one of the leading participants. See also Alvin F. Harlow, *Old Waybills: The Romance of the Express Companies* (1934).

Lewis B. Lesley, *Uncle Sam's Camels* (1929); and Chris Emmet, *Texas Camel Tales* (1932), deal with the camel experiment.

The best account of steamboating on the Missouri is Hiram M. Chittenden, *History of Early Steamboat Navigation on the Missouri River*, (2 vols. 1903). For a briefer account see Seymour Dunbar, *A History of Travel in America*, (1915), Vol. IV, pp. 1133-1160.

CHAPTER XXXIII

For the general history of the mining advance covered in this chapter see H. H. Bancroft, *History of Nevada, Colorado, and Wyoming* (1890), *History of Washington, Idaho, and Montana* (1890), and *History of Arizona and New Mexico* (1889). Samuel Bowles described his visits to various mining regions in *Across the Continent* (1866) and in *Our New West* (1869). Curtis H. Lindley, *A Treatise on the American Law Relating to Mines and Mineral Lands*, (3 vols. 1914); and Charles H. Shinn, *Mining Camps, A Study in American Frontier Government* (1885) and *Land Laws of Mining Districts* (Johns Hopkins University Studies, Second Series, 1884), are valuable studies.

Contemporary accounts of mining in Colorado are found in Henry Villard, *The Past and Present of the Pike's Peak Gold Region* (1860) which has been edited by LeRoy R. Hafen and published by the Princeton University Press (1932); Horace Greeley, *An Overland Journey* (1860); William Gilpin, *The Central Gold Region* (1860); and Demas Barnes, *From the Atlantic to the Pacific* (1866). T. M. Marshall, *Early Records of Gilpin County, Colorado, 1859-1861* (University of Colorado Historical Collections, 1920, Vol. II), is an important contribution. An excellent secondary account is James F. Willard, "The Gold Rush and After" in *Colorado: Short Studies of its Past and Present* (1927).

For mining in Nevada see J. Ross Browne, "A Peep at Washoe," a series of three articles in *Harper's New Monthly Magazine*, Vol. XXII (1860-61); Mark Twain, *Roughing It* (any edition); Charles H. Shinn, *The Story of the Mine* (1914); and C. B. Glasscock, *The Big Bonanza* (1931).

For the account of mining in the Northwest the writer has depended chiefly upon William J. Trimble, *The Mining Advance into the Inland Empire* (1914). See also J. Douglas Branch, *Westward* (1930), Ch. XXVIII; L. F. Crawford, *Rekindling Camp Fires* (1926); and the *Contributions to the Historical Society of Montana*, especially Vol. III (1900).

Accounts of the organization and history of the various Territories will be found in the state histories by Bancroft and others. See also Henry Gannett, *Boundaries of the United States and of the Several States and Territories* (Bulletin of the United States Geological Survey, No. 171, 1900); and Frederic L. Paxson, "The Territory of Colorado" in *The American Historical Review*, Vol. XII.

CHAPTER XXXIV

Three general works dealing with the history of railroads in the Far West are: Robert E. Riegel, *The Story of the Western Railroads* (1926); Lewis H. Haney, *A Congressional History of Railways in the United States, 1850-1887* (1910); and Glenn C. Quiett, *They Built the West: An Epic of Rails and Cities* (1934).

For early agitation for railroads to the Pacific see Robert S. Cotterill, "Early Agitation for a Pacific Railroad, 1845-1850" in *The Mississippi Valley Historical Review*, March, 1919; Margaret L. Brown, "Asa Whitney and his Pacific Railroad Publicity Campaign" ibid, September, 1933; and the histories of the Union Pacific listed below. A summary of the official surveys is found in George L. Albright, *Official Explorations for a Pacific Railroad* (1921).

In many respects the most satisfactory history of the Union Pacific is John P. Davis, *The Union Pacific Railroad* (1894). Other treatments are Nelson Trottman, *History of the Union Pacific* (1923); Henry K. White, *History of the Union Pacific Railway* (1895); and Edwin L. Sabin, *Building the Pacific Railway* (1919). The last is a popular account, but is reliable and devotes considerable space to the Central Pacific. Grenville M. Dodge, *How We Built the Union Pacific Railway* (Senate Document 447, 2nd Sess. 61st Cong. 1910) is a valuable source of information. Among the many contemporary accounts written by newspaper men and others Samuel Bowles, *Our Great West* (1869) is illustrative and useful.

Among the great number of writings regarding western railroads the following are generally available: Eugene V. Smalley, *History of the Northern Pacific Railroad* (1883); James B. Hedges, *Henry Villard and the Railways of the Northwest* (1930); Stuart Daggett, *Chapters on the History of the Southern Pacific* (1922), containing also some material on the Central Pacific; Glenn D. Bradley, *The Story of the Santa Fé* (1920); and Frederic L. Paxson, "The Pacific Railroads and the Disappearance of the Frontier" in the *Annual Report of the American Historical Association*, 1907, Vol. I.

CHAPTER XXXV

There is a huge mass of source material relating to Indian affairs in government documents, such as reports of the Commissioner of Indian Affairs, reports of the Secretary of War, and reports of Congressional committees. The following government publications are generally accessible and are especially valuable: Charles S. Kappler,

Indian Affairs: Laws and Treaties, (4 Vols. 1904-1920); C. C. Royce, *Indian Land Cessions in the United States* (1899); and *Executive Orders Relating to Indian Reservations from May 14, 1855, to July 1, 1912* (1912).

The following are selections from the large number of writings by contemporaries, including army officers who served in the Indian wars: Richard Irving Dodge, *Our Wild Indians* (1882); Randolph B. Marcy, *Thirty Years of Army Life on the Border* (1866); O. O. Howard, *Nez Perce Joseph* (1881); Nelson A. Miles, *Serving the Republic* (1911); J. P. Dunn, *Massacres of the Mountains, a History of the Indian Wars of the Far West* (1886); and George W. Manypenny, *Our Indian Wards* (1880).

For material on the operations of the Indian Bureau and the duties and activities of the Indian agents see Laurence F. Schmeckebier, *The Office of Indian Affairs: Its History, Activities and Organization* (1927); Lewis Meriam, *The Problem of Indian Administration* (1928); Ruth A. Gallaher, "The Indian Agent in the United States" in *The Iowa Journal of History and Politics,* January and April, 1916; Alban W. Hoopes, *Indian Affairs and their Administration, with Special Reference to the Far West, 1849-1860* (1932); LeRoy R. Hafen and W. J. Ghent, *Broken Hand: The Life Story of Thomas Fitzpatrick* (1931), pp. 192-282; Edwin L. Sabin, *Kit Carson Days* (1914); and Alban W. Hoopes, "Thomas S. Twiss, Indian Agent on the Upper Platte, 1855-1861" in *The Mississippi Valley Historical Review,* December, 1933.

Other references on various aspects of the history of Indian affairs west of the Mississippi are: Paul J. Wellman, *Death on the Prairie: The Thirty Years' Struggle for the Western Plains* (1934); Walter P. Webb, *The Great Plains* (1931), Ch. III; Rupert N. Richardson and Carl C. Rister, *The Greater Southwest* (1934), Chs. XII-XIV; Frederic L. Paxson, *The Last American Frontier* (1924); Louis Pelzer, *Marches of the Dragoons in the Mississippi Valley* (1917); Marcus L. Hansen, *Old Fort Snelling* (1918); Grant Foreman, *Advancing the Frontier* (1933) and *The Five Civilized Tribes* (1934); George Bird Grinnell, *The Fighting Cheyennes* (1915); James C. Malin, *Indian Policy and Westward Expansion* (Bulletin of the University of Kansas, Humanistic-Studies, 1921); Annie Heloise Abel, "Proposals for an Indian State, 1778-1878" in *Annual Report of the American Historical Association,* 1907, Vol. I; Grace R. Hebard and E. A. Brininstool, *The Bozeman Trail,* 2 Vols. (1922); Stanley Vestal, *Sitting Bull, Champion of the Sioux* (1932); Rupert N. Richardson, *The Comanche Barrier to South Plains*

Settlement (1933), and Frederic F. Van de Water, *Glory-Hunter: A Life of General Custer* (1934).

CHAPTER XXXVI

The author has relied very largely on the following recent works in the writing of this chapter: Ernest S. Osgood, *The Day of the Cattleman* (1929); Edward E. Dale, *The Range Cattle Industry* (1930); Louis Pelzer, *The Cattlemen's Frontier* (1935); Walter P. Webb, *The Great Plains* (1931), Chs. V-VII, and C. C. Rister, *The South-western Frontier* (1928). Useful brief accounts are: Frederic L. Paxson, "The Cow Country" in *The American Historical Review*, October, 1926; and Louis Pelzer, "A Cattleman's Commonwealth on the Western Range" in *The Mississippi Valley Historical Review*, June, 1926.

Among the numerous accounts written by participants in, or observers of, the range cattle industry the following are helpful: John Clay, *My Life on the Range* (1924); Joseph G. McCoy, *Historic Sketches of the Cattle Trade of the West and Southwest* (1874); Joseph Nimmo, *The Range and Ranch Cattle Business of the United States* (1885); Granville Stuart, *Forty Years on the Frontier*, 2 Vols. Paul C. Phillips, ed. (1925); and Baron Walter von Richtofen, *Cattle Raising on the Plains of North America* (1885).

For the cowboys and the cattle drives see Will James, *Cowboys, North and South* (1924); Douglas Branch, *The Cowboy and his Interpreters* (1926); Philip A. Rollins, *The Cowboy* (1922); Emerson Hough, *The Story of the Cowboy* (1897); J. Marvin Hunter, *The Trail Drivers of Texas* (1925); Charles M. Harger, "Cattle Trails of the Prairies" in *Scribner's Magazine*, June, 1892; and J. B. Kendrick, "The Texas Trail" in *Wyoming Historical Society Miscellanies*, 1919.

Benjamin H. Hibbard, *A History of the Public Land Policies* (1924), contains discussions of the various land laws mentioned in this chapter.

CHAPTER XXXVII

The most extensive treatment of the activities of the vigilance committees in the mining regions, with special attention to California, is Hubert H. Bancroft, *Popular Tribunals,* 2 vols. (1897). T. J. Dimsdale, *The Vigilantes of Montana* (1882); Nathaniel P. Langford, *Vigilante Days and Ways* (1927); and William J. Trimble, *The Mining Advance into the Inland Empire* (1914), Chs. IX-XII deal with the mining communities of the Northwest. See also Stewart Edward White, *The Forty-Niners* (1920); Emerson Hough, *The Passing of the Frontier* (1920); and C. C. Rister "Outlaws and Vigilantes of the Southern Plains, 1865-1885," in *The Mississippi Valley Historical Review*, March, 1933.

Roy Gittinger, *The Formation of the State of Oklahoma* (1924); James B. Buchanan and E. E. Dale, *A History of Oklahoma;* and Luther B. Hill, *A History of the State of Oklahoma* (1910) are among numerous works dealing with the beginnings of that State. For material on the settlement of the Far West after the Civil War the student is referred to state histories and the publications of the various local historical societies. The best history of the Great Plains region is Walter P. Webb, *The Great Plains* (1931).

S. J. Buck, *The Granger Movement* (1913), and *The Agrarian Crusade* (1921); F. E. Haynes, *Social Politics in the United States* (1924); and J. D. Hicks, *The Populist Revolt* (1931), contain excellent treatments of the discontent in the so-called homestead area. Frederic L. Paxson, *History of the American Frontier* (1924), gives in the last two chapters, a brief but satisfactory discussion of the completion of the process of state-making, together with some conclusions.

Frederick J. Turner's epoch-making paper is now to be found in most convenient form in a book containing a number of his other historical essays and entitled *The Frontier in American History* (1921). Among the many commentaries upon the frontier hypothesis the following will be sufficient to show the general trend: Frederic L. Paxson, "A Generation of the Frontier Hypothesis, 1893-1932" in *The Pacific Historical Review*, March, 1933; Joseph Schafer "Turner's Frontier Philosophy" in *Wisconsin Magazine of History*, June, 1933; and Benjamin F. Wright, Jr., "American Democracy and the Frontier" in *The Yale Review*, December, 1930. Frederic L. Paxson, *When the West is Gone* (1930) is a stimulating discussion of the influence of the frontier in the past, and a thought-provoking glance at the present and into the future.

INDEX

655